Still, the Small Voice

Still, the Small Voice

Narrative, Personal Revelation,
and the
Mormon Folk Tradition

TOM MOULD

UTAH STATE UNIVERSITY PRESS
LOGAN, UTAH
2011

ISBN: 978-0-87421-817-6 (cloth)
ISBN: 978-0-87421-818-3 (paper)
ISBN: 978-0-87421-819-0 (e-book)

Manufactured in the United States of America
Printed on acid-free, recycled paper

Library of Congress Cataloging-in-Publication Data

Mould, Tom, 1969- author.
  Still, the small voice : narrative, personal revelation, and the Mormon folk tradition / Tom Mould.
    pages cm
  Includes bibliographical references and index.
  ISBN 978-0-87421-817-6 (cloth) -- ISBN 978-0-87421-818-3 (pbk.) -- ISBN 978-0-87421-819-0 (e-book)
  1. Revelation--Mormon Church. 2.   Mormons--Folklore. I. Title.
  BX8643.R4.M68 2011
  306.6'4829--dc23
                              2011028245

For Brooke

Contents

Acknowledgments

Pᴇʀsᴏɴᴀʟ ʀᴇᴠᴇʟᴀᴛɪᴏɴ ɪs ᴀ sᴀᴄʀᴇᴅ ᴀɴᴅ ᴅᴇᴇᴘʟʏ ᴇᴍʙᴇᴅᴅᴇᴅ tradition in the theology, religious practice, and daily life of Latter-day Saints. As a spiritual experience, personal revelation can be as subtle as a nagging thought or vague feeling, or as dramatic as a booming voice or vision. While some personal revelations are too sacred or personal to be shared, many are not, and this pervasive experience of guidance from God is regularly shared in a narrative genre distinct and widely recognizable within the LDS community. Stories of personal revelation record some of the most sacred, personal, meaningful experiences of a person's spiritual and temporal life. Written down, they serve as personal scripture. Shared aloud among peers, they can educate and edify in ways parallel to canonical scripture.

The importance of personal revelation among Latter-day Saints cannot be overestimated. Nor can the reverence with which people regard it. Personal revelation is not shared lightly. I have taken to heart the faith and trust people have placed in me to maintain the sacred nature of their experiences. This is a heavy responsibility, one that I hope I have managed to achieve in the pages that follow.

As with any project involving ethnographic fieldwork, I am indebted to scores of people. There are, most importantly, the people I came to know in the course of my fieldwork in North Carolina, first at church, then through their stories, and ultimately in friendship. First and foremost, there was Shawn Tucker, my colleague at Elon University, who introduced me to his faith, his ward, his friends, and his family. It was Shawn who suggested that if I really wanted to understand prophecy and prophetic narratives within the LDS Church, it was the deep tradition of personal revelation, not the spectacular predictions of World War III and the signs of the Second Coming, that should be my focus. Two weeks of fieldwork convinced me he was right. Five years of fieldwork later, I am all the more convinced, and I remain humbly indebted to him for his guidance. I owe similar appreciation to all the people who sat down and talked to me about their faith, many but not all of whom also shared with me their stories of receiving personal revelation: Steve Anderson; Craig, Josette, Jarrett, and Jordan Bailey; Wayne and Jean Chandler; Paul, Pauline, Justin, Carlee, and Cameron Clayson; Michael Doyle; Jackie Foss; Dave and Serena Gammon; Ken, Sarah, Kimberly, and Lauren Jarvis; Mike McCann; Dana, Shasta, Manti, and Layla Mitchell; Ken, Lee, Kenny Jr., Christina, and Phil Mullen; Scott Skogen; Elijah, Katrina, Ashley, Emma, and Alyssa Smith; Keith Stanley; Rich, Tami, Wes, and Taylor Tenney; and Nicole, Justine, Ashley, Bryce, and Gavin Tucker. There were also the missionaries who patiently worked with me, even though they knew my interest was academic rather than personally spiritual. These were young men who had devoted two years of their lives in service to their religion, substituting Elder in place of their first names for the duration of their service: Elder Bailey, Elder Kyle Ballantyne, Elder Spencer Bourgeous, Elder Buckley, Elder Aaron Chavez, Elder Kenny Cox, Elder Joshua Hoffman, Elder Beau Parkinson, Elder Richard Rowe, Elder Staley, and Elder Adam Wicker. There were also those church members who went out of their way to extend a warm welcome, no matter how many Sundays I had missed. Their names are too many to list here, though I would be remiss not to mention Dori Anderson, Vernon Baity, and Terry Holmes.

My debts extend beyond the field as well. In the depths of library archives in Utah, Randy Williams at Utah State University and Kristi Young at Brigham Young University were invaluable in helping me find relevant materials, whether I was hunkered down in the library with them, or calling from North Carolina with requests for one more manuscript or with one more question. I am also indebted to Irene Adams and her student staff, especially Lauren Hardcastle, in the L. Tom Perry Special Collections at BYU for their indefatigable energy, warmth, and willingness to keep digging until we found whatever obscure manuscript I was looking for. I have also grown increasingly dependent on and appreciative of the circle of folklorists who have generously served as sounding boards, intellectual resources, and most importantly, friends. Within LDS studies, Bert Wilson, Eric Eliason, Jill Terry Rudy, Barbara Lloyd, and John Alley either read portions of this manuscript or suffered through my public talks and gave me excellent feedback about the finer points of LDS theology and practice. In the study of religious folkore, both Kerry Noonan and Leonard Primiano have been particularly helpful, with Leonard adding a perspective and sense of humor that I have treasured deeply. In all things folklore, I have regularly relied on the advice and friendship of Michael Evans, Lisa Gilman, Jason Jackson, John Laudun, Greg Kelley and Jennifer Schacker, Ray and Lorraine Cashman, and Pravina Shukla and Henry Glassie. Ray Cashman has gone above and beyond the call of duty, providing feedback on written drafts and serving as my most reliable sounding board. Closer to home, there is my family, a constant source of love and encouragement: Bill and Norma Barnett; Bill Mould and Rob Kleinsteuber; Lucille Mould; and Rob, Laura, Caroline, and Charlie Mould. A particular thank-you to my parents who created a home where thoughtful engagement with the world was the norm, and to Norma, who has exceeded every expectation one could have for a mother-in-law, not least by faithfully reading each of my books. And finally, to Brooke, Lily, and Jack—for everything.

Introduction

Mormonism sprang forth in upstate New York into a world of religious upheaval and rebirth. It was the period of the Second Great Awakening, when men and women voiced dissatisfaction with the impersonal churches that kept God at bay, sequestered behind rigid hierarchies of the clergy. Many disaffected Christians searched for a religion that would reflect the new freedoms and powerful potential of individuals in a new country of seemingly endless opportunity and possibility. Between 1790 and 1840, the Second Great Awakening swept through New England and the Eastern Seaboard, promising a more personal connection to God, as well as a restoration of the gospel. When Joseph Smith emerged in 1830 with the Book of Mormon, he was met with an audience primed for his message of a restored gospel and the promise of personal revelation for every faithful member of the church.[1]

From the beginning of the church, personal revelation has been a cornerstone of the Mormon faith. LDS scripture confirms its central role. The first chapter of the Doctrine and Covenants avows: "The voice of the Lord is unto all men" (D&C 1:2). The Doctrine and Covenants is LDS scripture consisting entirely of revelation, the bulk of which came to Joseph Smith to help him organize the new religion. Because Joseph Smith was prophet of the church, most of his revelations were not personal but rather derived from his calling as prophet and leader and were relevant to all followers of the faith. Yet like his faithful peers, he received revelation specific to his own life as well, personal guidance in spiritual and temporal matters. While his First Vision of God and Jesus is foundational to the church and serves as canonical scripture, it came in answer to humble prayer, a divine answer to a man in search of spiritual truth. This revelatory vision was an example of personal revelation and serves as an Ur-form for conversion narratives of personal revelation of modern-day Saints; it is an experience rarely copied but often referenced (Eliason 1999).

Personal revelation also appears in sacred church history, lying just outside scripture but verging on canonical. Church leaders and publications regularly retell the story of President Wilford Woodruff's prompting by the Holy Ghost to move his wagon just before lightning brought an oak tree down in the exact spot where it stood moments before. There is also the story of the voice that warned a youthful President Harold B. Lee not to climb through a fence to explore some sheds that were falling down. And most well known of all is the story of Joseph Smith's fateful words while returning to Carthage, where he was murdered— "I am going as a lamb to the slaughter"—interpreted widely as reference to personal revelation.

These examples of personal revelation of past presidents of the church are valued primarily because of their protagonists. Yet the stories of church leaders stand as the tip of an iceberg. Readily viewed and easily recognized, they provide a shared heritage for church members around the globe. But these stories of great leaders belie a much deeper tradition that lies below the surface. The bulk of personal revelation narratives exist not as scripture or sacred history but as the stories of lay members, shared by faithful men and women among family, friends, and fellow church members throughout the extensive Mormon communities of the American West and in smaller Mormon enclaves throughout the world. This book, then, is a record of the iceberg below the surface, paying long overdue attention to the thriving oral tradition that puts a contemporary face to scripture.

Literary Tradition

The literature on Mormon revelation, not surprisingly, runs deep. There are hundreds of articles, essays, and books written by the General Authorities— leaders of the church with the authority to interpret Mormon doctrine for the rest of the church. This task is vital for a church founded less than two hundred years ago. While Joseph Smith received literally hundreds of revelations interpreting Mormon doctrine, there remain many areas of doctrine, history, and prophecy that are not fully explained or have not yet been revealed.[2] Article 9 of the Articles of Faith declares: "We believe all that God has revealed, all that He does now reveal, and we believe that He will yet reveal many great and important things pertaining to the Kingdom of God." This statement is more than a vague tip of the hat to a God who is still speaking. There are specific manuscripts named and identified but as yet not held by the church on Earth today. Neal A. Maxwell of the Quorum of the Twelve Apostles explained:

> Lost books are among the treasures yet to come forth. Over twenty of these are mentioned in the existing scriptures. Perhaps most startling and voluminous will be the records of the lost tribes of Israel (see 2 Ne. 29:13). We would not even know of the impending third witness for Christ except through the precious Book of Mormon, the second witness for Christ! This third set of sacred records will thus complete a triad of

truth. . . . Thus, just as there will be many more Church members, families, wards, stakes, and temples—later on, there will also be many more nourishing and inspiring scriptures. (1986)

Essays, articles, and books by church leaders clarifying doctrine are also important for a church so dependent on lay members for the bulk of its teaching. Despite a clear hierarchy within the church at the top ranks of church administration, the LDS Church is a lay church. Members serve as teachers and leaders on the local level, called to serve by the act of revelation. With no trained clergy, lay members are responsible for the bulk of religious discussion and instruction during church services, meetings, and Sunday school. These tasks can be daunting for those called. A massive library of church publications, however, serves as an invaluable resource. For members with personal computers, church resources are easily searched online for material for church talks.[3]

The most recent and relevant of the books published by the General Authorities is Gerald N. Lund's book *Hearing the Voice of the Lord: Principles and Patterns of Personal Revelation* (2007). Lund's goal mirrors that of other books and articles published by the church and its leaders: to clarify and interpret doctrine and promote faith in the church. Directed to church members, the book is meant as practical advice rather than philosophical musings, providing how-to information that will help resolve the ambiguity that can plague revelatory experiences. Such religious instruction presumes to strengthen faith as a vital by-product. Other books take faith promotion as their primary goal. Some of these books are written by church authorities (e.g., B. Hinckley 1956, Lund 2007) and some are edited compilations of modern church authorities and scripture (e.g., Faith Promoting Series 1879–1915, *Wisdom of the Prophets: Personal Revelation* 2005). Others are written by scholars of varying authority who are members of the church (e.g., D. Crowther 1962, 1983; J. McConkie 1988; Marsh 2000; P. Nibley 1943; P. Smith 1996). And still others are written by passionate church members who want to share their experiences and love of the LDS Church and God with a broader public (e.g., Banfield 1983, Hamilton 1998). Many of these books highlight the sacred experiences of church leaders and early pioneers as a way to promote faith today by tying it to a deep historical tradition of both laity and leader.[4]

Approach

This book claims a different heritage. I profess no religious authority and attempt no clarification of religious doctrine. My goal is neither to guide members in receiving, recognizing, or interpreting personal revelation nor to promote faith in the Mormon religion. However, neither does it stand in opposition to these pursuits. For some, this book may help clarify doctrine inasmuch as it explores the belief system as articulated by church leaders and lay members alike. And for some, faith may be promoted by reading the stories of personal revelation within these pages.

My goal in this book lies in exploration, description, and analysis. My approach is academic. The tradition I follow is one not unfamiliar to Mormon studies, Mormon culture, or Mormon readers. In fact, the bulk of the scholarly analysis of Mormon folklore has come from within the Mormon community from Mormon scholars themselves. Austin and Alta Fife, Wayland Hand, Hector Lee, William A. Wilson, and more recently Eric Eliason, Jill Terry Rudy, George Schoemaker, and David Allred have driven the rigorous study of Mormon folklore forward. Non-Mormons have added to this body of research as well. Richard Dorson, Jan Harold Brunvand, Margaret Brady, Barre Toelken, and Elaine Lawless have explored Mormon folklore generally and, in some cases, aspects of personal revelation specifically (see Brady 1987, Lawless 1984, and Toelken 1991).

Within the broad academic tradition, this book is a study within the specific discipline of folklore. The term has plagued the field since its inception thanks to concurrent competing definitions in popular culture and in academia. For many English speakers, folklore encompasses the false, untrue, unscientific notions of uneducated people. It also conjures images of nursery rhymes, fairy tales, and the quaint traditions of people long ago. The academic definition, on the other hand, defines folklore as those expressions of culture that reveal not only the artistry and aesthetics of communal traditions but the shared beliefs and values of a community. As such, folklore is not confined to a finite set of genres but rather describes an approach to the study of culture that recognizes the expressive nature of everyday life, including religious life.

As in all academic disciplines, folklore scholars approach their work with a set of assumptions. These assumptions are many, varied, and dynamic—changing and changed by shifts in the intellectual landscape. New theories result in new assumptions. Not all assumptions of the field of folklore are held by all folklorists, though some are more foundational, pervasive, and tenacious than others. In defining the term *folklore*, I have articulated some of the most fundamental assumptions already. For one, folklore is true. Using narrative folklore as an example, stories may be told as fact, fiction, or faith, or any blurry, contested position between. Stories told as fact may be supported by historical evidence; they may also run counter to it, providing an alternative history. Other stories may be told as expressions of faith, where fact and fiction are removed in the face of a more personal test of authenticity. Many stories do not claim fact, faith, or fiction, as narrators negotiate reality and wrestle with belief for themselves. Even those stories told as outright fictions carry with them elements of truth that are neither historical nor factual but are emotional, affective, psychological, social, or cultural truths that reveal the values of the people who share them.

From these alternate truths follows a second assumption, that the study of folklore provides an avenue for asking questions about the values and beliefs of a community. Folklore is assumed to be an expression of these values. Rarely are those expressions direct reflections; folklore can distort them through accentuation and omission. But they are revealing all the same.

Mining expressive culture for what it can tell us about the beliefs, worldviews, and identities of groups and individuals is not the only task of folklorists. A third assumption is that the folklore itself—the stories, jokes, rites, rituals, objects, and customs that make up the verbal, material, and customary lore of a community—has value as an artistic performance. A well-told story and well-turned pot can be appreciated as performances of great skill and artistry, valuable in their own right. The aesthetic side of vernacular culture has often been ignored, demoted as craft rather than heralded as art. This demotion is the result of the idea of Culture with a capital *C*. Certain genres, forms, and objects are deemed high culture—ballet, opera, violins, oil painting, and sculpture— while others are deemed low culture—step dancing, balladry, fiddles, ceramics, and textiles. The same is true for the criteria by which we judge art. In Western art particularly, originality trumps conservatism, the individual trumps the collective, the formally taught trumps the informally learned. The fourth assumption, then, is that folklorists value the folk—the large numbers of people in any culture who create the world in ways both useful and beautiful in the course of their everyday lives. Their traditions, our traditions, are folklore.

Finally, folklorists assume that genre matters. Ideas can be shaped by the vehicles that drive them. Part of attending to the aesthetic side of culture is paying attention to generic form. An idea explored through a joke may not emerge in the same way when conveyed in a deeply personal memorate.

In addition to the broad disciplinary assumptions of the field of folklore come the assumptions bound up in one's theoretical approach. For the past three decades, performance theory has dominated the field. The idea of performance shifts the focus from product to process. Folklorists explore the social and cultural contexts of specific performances—storytelling events, ritual acts, throwing pots on a wheel—and the processes by which performers create and present their work and express themselves. Of particular importance is how people communicate within a particular genre—negotiating the expectations for the genre, making references to past performances, and responding to current audiences. Further, performance is viewed as a social act, capable of serving multiple functions simultaneously, including the construction of particular social identities.

Both in folklore and in anthropology, focus has shifted from etic analyses developed for cross-cultural analysis to emic interpretations that derive from and resonate with the communities themselves. In the study of memorates—personal experience narratives of encounters with the supernatural—this shift is mirrored by the development of an experience-centered approach that honors, rather than dismisses, the belief systems under study (see, for example, Eliason 1999 and Hufford 1982, 1995).

Applying these assumptions to Mormon personal revelation reveals the approach and goals of this book. I assume that these stories of personal revelation are true in multiple ways. While personal stories are told as factually true, legends vary—some are believed by their narrators; others are not. Most negotiate the ambiguity and gray areas of truth. In all, however, I assume that these narratives reveal beliefs and values held by individual narrators and shared to varying degrees more broadly throughout the LDS community. Further, I attempt to construct an emic analysis to understand how people within the community frame and interpret their experiences with the divine through the narratives they share.

I also assume these stories are more than mere records of past experience: they are aesthetic creations that, while denying artifice, might still be called artistic. Shifts in genre—from memorate to legend, for example—matter, as do cultural and situational contexts of storytelling performances.

Finally, I assume great value and merit in attending to the stories shared by the people sitting in the pews. It is here, among the congregations, that religions are sustained. By no means am I suggesting that the revelations of the General Authorities of the church are not important, only that they already receive the lion's share of attention. Their platform is broad, and their voices reverberate quite literally around the world through satellite transmissions during general conferences. Turning the spotlight from the formal pronouncements of a few prominent leaders to the stories of the many faithful members of the church should not be interpreted as the acceptance of facile divisions between leader and laity or the exclusion of prominent leaders from the folk tradition. In fact, many church leaders narrate their own stories of personal revelation during church talks and in essays published in church magazines. Their stories are as much a part of the folk tradition as the stories shared by lay members to their fellow ward members, families, and friends. Yet by sheer numbers alone, the bulk of the narrative tradition can be found in the pews. This fact, coupled with the entrenched approach of folklore summarized eloquently by Warren Roberts as a mandate to attend to the 95 percent of the overlooked rather than the 5 percent of the elite who garner the bulk of historical analysis and contemporary attention (1988:xiii, 6), explains why this book, too, is rooted in the pews.

Many of the questions I ask in this book about personal revelation derive from these disciplinary and theoretical assumptions, but not all of them. As with any study grounded in fieldwork and emic in its intent, new questions emerge during fieldwork demanding new foci, and challenging old paradigms. Issues and factors I assumed to be relevant were not, and issues I had never considered emerged to dominate my study. In fact, this book began as a study not of personal revelation but of prophetic narratives, particularly those that folklorist Glenn Ostlund has termed "apocalore"—prophecies about the Apocalypse and the Second Coming of Jesus Christ. That study remains on my table, waiting for the time to write it. As I talked with the men and women in the Burlington First Ward just down the road from where I teach and live, however, I began to realize—first with the help of my colleague Shawn Tucker and later, more and more of my consultants—that far more relevant to the people I was meeting, far more interesting to them personally, socially, and culturally, were the personal revelations they received regularly, guiding them in their daily lives. My focus shifted, and with it, the questions that I asked. Further, as I learned about the concept of stewardship, the importance of agency, and the centrality of the family, my questions shifted to address the specific cultural matrix of the Mormon community in which I was working.

The content of this book reflects the themes, concepts, and issues that emerged during fieldwork and in the process of analysis. Its structure, however, derives primarily from the questions posed by performance theory and the discipline of folklore more generally. Chapter 1 explores the boundaries of the oral tradition of personal revelation, locating it first within the Mormon oral tradition broadly, then defining personal revelation as a distinct emic genre of narrative recognized within the community. Chapter 2 tackles the issue of performance, where process trumps product. In this chapter, I explore the social and cultural contexts for performance, including expectations and informal rules within the community for how and when personal revelation narratives should be shared and criteria for how performances are evaluated. Also addressed are the social identities referenced, negotiated, and created in the course of performance. The chapter ends with a series of case studies that examine how situational context affects performance, including how the stories function and how they are interpreted. Chapter 3 shifts to the formal qualities of personal experience narratives, examining how narrative structure reveals an emic yet unarticulated typology of personal revelation experiences translated into narrative. Further, this chapter examines how narrative demands affect not only performance but also the interpretation of the experience. Chapter 4 continues the exploration of structure and narrative as aesthetic performance, moving from large typological structures to smaller narrative structures and formulas. In this chapter, the utility of recognizable patterns as a resource for narrators suggests the impact generic expectations and norms can have on stories as they are shared among family and friends. Chapter 5 takes a more traditional, text-based approach to the narrative tradition, analyzing the content of the stories and highlighting recurring themes and motifs. In this process, the shared values, concerns, and worldview of contemporary Latter-day Saints rise to the fore. Chapter 6 tackles the interplay between oral and written traditions as stories move back and forth across these particularly permeable media boundaries.

Following each of these chapters is a discussion of the theoretical issues at play that hold significance for, but more importantly, *beyond* the Mormon case study. This book is first and foremost a case study of a narrative genre shared widely among Latter-day Saints. While I have accessed relevant scholarship necessary to elucidate the LDS tradition, I have for the most part avoided extended treatises on the theoretical and methodological implications of this study. However, the case study, powerful and valuable in its own right, also has great potential to contribute to discussions that cut across cultures, relevant both to the field of folklore and to related academic fields, including anthropology, religious studies, linguistics, and narrative studies. In these sections, labeled Synthesis, I revisit the theoretical and methodological issues raised in the previous chapter (except in the case of chapters 4 and 5, which are addressed together following chapter 5), both to situate them within the context of current scholarship as well as to suggest new directions for the study of revelation, religious memorates, and narrative more broadly.

Methods

This study relies on three methods of data collection. The most important source of data was from ethnographic fieldwork. In 2005, I began attending church services and functions at the Burlington First Ward in Burlington, North Carolina. Soon after, I began my fieldwork in earnest, employing the methods central to ethnography: participant observation and interviewing. I attended weekly services, went on father/son campouts, attended Wednesday night meetings, went on splits with the missionaries, and attended baptisms, plays, and parties hosted by the ward. While a textbook might say I used convenience and snowball sampling in order to identify people to interview, I would simply say that I found people the way folklorists have always found people to talk to: by having informal conversations, getting introductions from other members, and asking around. Folklore's attention to aesthetics and tradition bearers demands such an approach to identify those people who regularly perform within a tradition. In the case of LDS personal revelation, however, that was virtually everyone. I therefore sought out a range of people of different genders, ages, and socioeconomic classes. Ethnicity was less relevant in the Burlington First Ward, since the Hispanic branch meets separately and, except for a few African American families, the ward is white. Ethnicity is not irrelevant across the spectrum of Mormonism, however, although current research has only begun to address these factors (see afterword).

My participation and observations were not confined to the Burlington First Ward. When I found myself in another city on a Sunday morning, I sought out local LDS churches. I attended services in St. Petersburg, Florida; Provo, Utah; and London, England. These brief forays into other wards were hardly systematic, but they have helped me avoid the trap of assigning regional or ward-specific characteristics to LDS traditions more generally.

This is not to say there are not important regional differences in LDS culture, particularly outside the Intermountain West. As William A. Wilson warns, Mormon culture is not monolithic and can be expected to vary according to rural versus urban, educated versus uneducated, male versus female, and born in the church versus converted members. At the least, he argues, there is a rough distinction between the Intermountain West of Utah, Idaho, and the borders of surrounding states, and "the mission field," which is everywhere else (1983:159–60). Despite this warning, studies of Mormon folklore, including those by Wilson, have rarely addressed variations other than gender. The present study suffers from similar shortcomings. My only excuse is that such comparative studies are difficult to produce until the broad outlines of the tradition have been explored.

The second source of data came from three archives in Utah: the Fife Folklore Archives at Utah State University in Logan, the William A. Wilson Folklore Archives at Brigham Young University in Provo, and the Utah Humanities Research Foundation Records at the University of Utah in Salt Lake City. The archives at USU and BYU were both established by folklorist William A. Wilson and share some of the same material.[5] These archives include undergraduate and graduate student papers and individual "items" of folklore such as discrete narratives collected as part of student projects in English and folklore classes. The Fife Folklore Archive also contains fieldwork collections of a number of folklorists, including Alta and Austin Fife (with the Fife Mormon Collection), Wayland Hand, Don Yoder, Barre Toelken, and William A. Wilson. Fieldwork data housed in the Utah Humanities Research Foundation Records were amassed between 1944 and 1954 and also include interviews that the Fifes drew upon for their book *Saints of Sage and Saddle* (1956).

The final source of data comes from the published record. A wealth of personal revelation narratives can be found in nonacademic books published by the church and by faithful church members, books that fit the substantial genre of faith-promoting books mentioned earlier. The *Saints at War* book series was particularly helpful as it drew upon over three thousand interviews with Latter-day Saint veterans and presented the dramatic, traumatic, and deeply moving war stories of Mormons, some of which included accounts of personal revelation (see Freeman and Wright 2001, 2003). The interviews are part of the archive at BYU. The other major source of published data comes from church magazines such as *Ensign*, *New Era*, *Liahona*, and *The Friend*, magazines that provide the basis for the content analysis of part of the written tradition examined in chapter 6.

Of these three data sources, my own fieldwork is the primary source in this book, providing ethnographic detail, contextual data, in-depth interviews, and ninety-four narratives for analysis. The archives were the next most useful resource, providing a depth to the oral tradition I could never have hoped to develop alone. The archives provided over three hundred narratives directly relevant to my study and hundreds more of related interest. This book focuses particularly on the contemporary oral tradition. I have interpreted *contemporary* loosely, moving as far back as the 1960s for the bulk of my analysis, and farther back only when specifically relevant. And while my focus is on the oral tradition, I also explore the written tradition, as the two are intimately intertwined (see chapter 6).

In all, this book is based on the analysis of well over six hundred narratives. The sheer breadth of this data has allowed me to ask—and more importantly, attempt to answer—questions not always possible with smaller sample sizes. My attempt to corral such a large set of narratives from such disparate sources demands some explanation. I began my initial analysis using ATLAS.ti qualitative software to conduct open coding on the data. My initial survey was broad, examining the range of spiritual memorates, of which personal revelation was one. The benefit of an initially broad approach is that it provides a picture of the forest before the analysis of the tree. In beginning so broadly, I strove to avoid the problem so aptly portrayed in the folktale about the three blind men describing an elephant, each of whom comes to a dramatically different conclusion about elephants based on his narrowly defined data set: for one, the trunk; another, the legs; and the last, the tail.[6] Once my work shifted conclusively to personal revelation, I switched from ATLAS.ti to a more basic spreadsheet in order to systematically catalog and code not only the narratives I recorded in my own fieldwork but the hundreds more from the archives and published sources.[7] By organizing my data in a spreadsheet, I have been able to look for patterns and correlations between factors that might otherwise go unnoticed or be unverifiable, a process particularly useful for the analysis of structural formulas and themes in chapters 4, 5, and 6. For the bulk of this more quantitative analysis, I narrowed my data to 441 narratives by focusing specifically on the oral tradition, specifically stories shared orally and then written down. Of these 441 narratives, 94 were from my fieldwork, 303 from archives, and 44 from published sources. Some of the archival data were incomplete, submitted without situational context such as dates or names of either narrator or collector. Further, some of the narrative elements categorized in the spreadsheet were ambiguous or unknown for a particular story. For example, it was not always clear in the archival data whether a story was recorded verbatim or from memory, casting into question the specific language and terms used throughout the story. These gaps mean that numbers may not always add up to 441 in my charts, requiring an "unknown" category in the results (see the appendix). This "unknown" category, however, is typically small, and has not significantly undermined the ability to identify trends and patterns that run throughout the oral tradition.

Names and Pseudonyms

While ethical standards of fieldwork in folklore and anthropology often run parallel today, they diverge significantly over the issue of confidentiality. There is no single standard for either field, but generally speaking, anthropologists tend to use pseudonyms for their consultants, while folklorists use real names. The reasons are hardly mysterious. Folklorists place great value on the skill and creativity of individuals, treating expressive culture as art as well as artifact. Imagine a book-length study of an unnamed Spanish painter who pioneered cubism. A folklorist would no sooner disguise the identity of a master potter or storyteller than an art historian would disguise the identity of Picasso.

However, the benefit of providing confidentiality and public anonymity to performers of folk traditions becomes clear when one considers that many folk traditions are laden with personal and sensitive information—including a host of isms (sexism, racism, classism)—that could prove embarrassing and harmful. This risk explains one of the reasons anthropologists frequently disguise the identity of the people in their studies; another is the assumption that confidentiality breeds honesty in both the consultant and the researcher.

As a folklorist, it has been my practice to always use the names of the people with whom I have worked, something I make clear from my first steps into the field. People can always opt out any at point in our work together, a rare but occasional occurrence. A few Choctaw men and women told me things that they asked I not attribute to them, but none asked for complete anonymity in the final published record. The same has been true of the potters, collectors, steppers, quilters, mushroom hunters, ginseng hunters, powwow dancers, broom makers, horseshoe pitchers, chainsaw carvers, blacksmiths, glassblowers, stone carvers, herbalists, and storytellers that I have worked with over the years. Virtually all of the Latter-day Saints I have worked with appear in these pages under their own names as well. A few, however, do not, and some explanation is warranted.

The stories of personal revelation shared most frequently by Latter-day Saints are accounts of their own experiences with the divine. As with any overt declaration of a belief system that may not be shared widely, there is a fear of ridicule. There is also a fear of the reverse. In a conversation with his friend and neighbor, "Robert Foster" explained the work we were doing together and his decision to use a pseudonym:

> I told him that I was going to be using a fake name in the book and he said, "Well, why don't you just use your regular name?" And I was like, "Well, you know people, we're humans." And a lot of times we're searching. Even if some of us don't want to accept it, or even realize it, we are searching for something. "Who are we? Why are we here?" Something. "What's the point?"
>
> And it's . . . I don't want to be the guy people cling to thinking that he's some kind of spiritual advisor. Because I'm not. And I don't want to be clung to or depended on or disappoint anybody because I am a human being and I make mistakes. And if someone were to have a vision or a dream and have it come true, people have a tendency to lean in and say, "Tell us more! You're amazing and wonderful!" And it's for nothing other than God granted me this for a purpose. Whether it's for my protection or for someone else's protection.

"Robert Foster" is, of course, a pseudonym. I have indicated each use of a pseudonym the first time a person is mentioned. In some cases, a person appears under two names: their own and a pseudonym. This allows the person to be identifiable for those stories they share more publicly but to maintain privacy for those stories they share only in more intimate contexts.

While my use of pseudonyms is rare for the men and women I have worked with directly, it has been standard practice for the archival data. Only recently have the collections consistently indicated whether people have given permission to have their names used with the stories they shared. Some of even the oldest interviews occasionally indicate that a pseudonym has been used, but it is rare for a collector to be explicit about the use of the names of their consultants. It has not been an easy choice, but I have chosen to err on the side of protecting personal identities at the risk of stripping credit from the men and women who have so generously and skillfully shared their stories. For the archival stories, then, the storytellers and the people they mention in their stories are pseudonyms. The collectors' names, however, are accurate. Further, I have modified the Chicago fifteenth edition style of citations to ensure that complete records are included in the bibliography to facilitate the interests of anyone wanting to return to the original documents.

Texts and Transcriptions

My goal in reproducing those texts here on the page is twofold: accuracy and comprehensibility. The bulk of my analysis is based on the narratives that I recorded in the field. Most of these I recorded using a digital voice recorder, and the texts that follow are verbatim transcriptions. While accurate in word, they are only partially accurate in performance. The quality of oral performance depends on the ear, the written text on the eye. Folklorists have struggled with how to translate the spoken word to the page (for a summary of this struggle, see E. Fine 1984). Although storytelling can be more akin to poetry than to prose, the complex notations and styles often employed in ethnopoetics to convey orality can appear artificial, oblique, and alienating to the reader, creating a chasm between a storyteller and her audience that would never have been present in oral performance. I have decided on a more basic presentation.

To accommodate the shift in medium, I have employed punctuation, paragraph breaks, and bracketed notations to indicate laughter, gestures, and an occasional note of clarification. I have added no words, changed no tenses, nor made any corrections in syntax. Ellipses indicate pauses rather than missing words. The result is a collection of narratives that are textually faithful to performance.

Yet while accurate transcriptions are vital, *exact* transcriptions can hinder rather than aid understanding. When we speak, we omit words, repeat ourselves, make false starts, and reference knowledge that extends beyond the boundaries of the specific narrative, understandable to the audience at the moment of performance but not necessarily to the detached audience of this book. These characteristics of speaking often go unrecognized in oral performance and, if anything, can enhance rather than detract from the story by emphasizing the most important or dramatic points. Yet what rolls past the ear in conversation can glare blindingly from the page.

In order to facilitate understanding, I have occasionally eliminated repetitive verbal ticks such as "you know" when they risk confusion, not just distraction. Further, during a performance by real people in real places, interruptions disrupt storytelling; phones ring, visitors drop by, babies cry. I have omitted these interruptions in the text but have documented them in the endnotes. In doing all this, my hope is first that the storyteller will be allowed to communicate with this new audience of readers; second that the reader will be allowed to understand; and third that the scholar will be offered accurate translations.

Not all of the stories I recorded are transcriptions from audio recordings. For stories I recorded in church where an audio recorder would have been inappropriate, I took quick but careful notes during the service and then transcribed the story as soon as I returned home. These stories are not verbatim—they could not hope to be—but they are accurate in content, terminology, and structure. Often, I recorded whole sentences verbatim, capturing style and specific turns of phrase. I also noted gestures, emotional responses such as tears and laughter, and significant changes in volume and tone. They are useful if not ideal transcriptions.

For the archival material, different collectors with different standards and different modes of recording narratives have resulted in different types of texts. Some are verbatim transcriptions from audiotape. Others were written down as the person told the story. Still others were written by the storytellers themselves, bypassing oral performance altogether. Because of this variation, I have provided information on how each narrative came to be written to the best of my ability, since not all stories include this information. Some of the archival narratives are plagued with typos and misspelled words. I have corrected these mistakes rather than perpetuate them. I have also used the same guidelines for punctuation and line breaks as in my own recorded narratives, providing at least some degree of uniformity in presentation despite the varied sources.

CHAPTER 1

THE BROAD STROKES
OF TRADITION

The Mormon Folk Tradition

From one perspective, the idea of a single Mormon folk tradition is absurd. As in any culture or community, there are hundreds of folk traditions. These traditions can be explored according to patterns in form, function, or group. A single umbrella for both the tradition of ballads sung primarily by Mormons in the Intermountain West that memorialize the trek of Mormon pioneers and the tradition of the customary lore of Mexican Mormon converts in the process of building new churches in a predominantly Catholic land would be unbearably large. While shared patterns might be found, they would no doubt pale next to the rich complexity of each tradition interpreted through more relevant contexts than a single unifying folk tradition. No single set of themes, patterns, or ideas could possibly hope to encompass all of the varied performances of expressive culture by Mormons the world over.

However, it is possible to talk about Mormon folklore as a cultural tradition contrasted with other types of cultural production. A simple dyad between formal and informal culture, for example, positions folklore in contrast with institutionalized and formal aspects of culture. Barre Toelken has argued that folklore's distinguishing characteristic "is that its ingredients seem to come directly from dynamic interactions among human beings in vernacular performance contexts rather than through the more rigid channels and fossilized structures of technical instruction or bureaucratized education, or through the relatively stable channels of the formally taught classic traditions" (1996:32). The prevailing view of folklore as an approach to analysis rather than as a set of inherent objects makes it clear that the folk tradition is neither static nor absent in institutional culture. Nonetheless, the assumptions of the field lead folklor-ists to feed from a well-worn trough.

Broadly speaking, the Mormon folk tradition is that constellation of infor-mal traditions—verbal, material, and customary—shared among people who identify religiously or culturally as Mormon. In religion, the dyad between for-mal and informal culture contrasts doctrine and religious prescription set forth by scripture with the interpretation and practice of beliefs and behaviors of laity and leadership alike. Because Mormon folklore is defined according to group membership in a particular faith, canonical religious doctrine and the institu-tion of the LDS Church serve as the primary formal structures from which the Mormon folk tradition is distinguished.[1]

Some LDS traditions engage only loosely with the religion that bounds them. Hay derricks, Jell-O salad, and father/son campouts do not directly pur-port to express doctrinal belief, even if general values of thrift, hard work, and gender roles can be abstracted and connected to religious belief and church hierarchies. Other traditions, however, are intentionally tied to the practice of religion and can cause religious crisis or anxiety when defined in contrast to formal church beliefs and structures. The serving of the sacrament, the concept of stewardship, the rules laid out for missionaries—all have important prescrip-tions that guide their interpretation and enactment.

The divide between informal and formal traditions is not exclusive; tradi-tions learned and practiced informally draw heavily upon institutional struc-tures and teaching, just as formal instruction relies heavily on folk traditions and personal experiences. Further, because the Church of Jesus Christ of Latter-day Saints is a lay church, the development of informal religious folk tradi-tions is great; all members are expected to engage actively in the running of the church without specific formal training. The folk are the church. Weekly Sunday worship services are led by members from both the pews and the local leadership, none of whom are formally trained theologians. Local leaders in the church—at the level of wards and stakes—are drawn from the lay membership and, after serving in leadership roles, often return to the general membership. This process blurs the lines between the leadership and the laity, between formal and informal religious boundaries. This blurring and blending is most easily seen in how often church members will be talking about a particular topic, shar-ing a personal story, and then open their scriptures and begin quoting a relevant passage to underscore or clarify a point. It is a process well practiced among missionaries but used almost as heavily by adult members, whether former missionaries or not. Rather than downplay this practice to artificially preserve a more coherent divide between official and folk, I have highlighted it to reveal a common, indigenous hermeneutic that reveals the intersection between formal scriptures and the construction of religious belief in daily life.

This intersection nonetheless belies division. While blurred, the lines are hardly erased, existing ideologically as well as practically. A person serving in a presiding leadership position is granted keys—specific powers and duties for the execution of their position—that they maintain only as long as they serve their role. Once a leader returns to the pews, those keys are revoked. Power is contingent on the role, not the person. Former leaders often carry the respect of their peers back to the pews with them but not the prophetic power they once had.

This formal, hierarchical distinction between church leadership and laity creates the space for variation and divergence. Divergences are often subtle and serve to clarify doctrine for an individual, filling in gaps where understanding of LDS theology runs thin. In other cases, those divergences may run counter to the church leadership. Such contradictory interpretations may be unintentional. In his study of LDS folk belief, Richley Crapo found substantial variation between official doctrine as espoused by the General Authorities and the beliefs held by the general membership, attributing this variation to the structure of the church (1987). Divergence, however, is rarely intentional. All of the participants in Crapo's study either thought their beliefs were in sync with the church leadership or were not aware that the church took a formal stance on the particular issue.

Variation between the beliefs espoused by the General Authorities and the general membership is compounded by the fact that the church is founded on the concept of a living prophet and continuous revelations which, despite being disseminated in church literature and general conferences, are rarely codified in a single stable scripture (see Buerger 1982, Crapo 1987, McMurrin 1974). The Doctrine and Covenants is the most likely scriptural home for continued revelation, but of its 138 chapters, 134 record the revelations of Joseph Smith between 1823 and 1846. Only four other chapters have been added since, and only two of those are revelations.[2] Two official declarations have also been added, the first in 1890 by President Wilford W. Woodruff to outlaw polygamy; the second by President Spencer W. Kimball in 1978 to allow all worthy men, regardless of color, to be ordained in the Aaronic and Melchizedek priesthoods.

Church leaders have hardly been idle, however. They have worked to clarify doctrine and disseminate their interpretations through official church publications and general conference—a biannual event that allows all Mormons to gather and listen to the General Authorities provide religious instruction. These talks and publications can be found online on the church's website. Despite

these avenues and resources, maintaining a clear division between those revelations and interpretations of doctrine sanctioned by the church and those
developed at the local level is a perennial problem. While the hierarchy allows
for clear, systematic transmission from the prophet to each and every ward and
branch, and manuals and teaching resources from Salt Lake City guide weekly
services and meetings, the translation and practice of religious beliefs is carried
out among peers at the local level. Fellow Mormons from the general membership command the stage most of the time, everyone taking turns preparing
lessons and teaching doctrine. Combined with a church open to continuous
revelation, discerning doctrine from speculation, revelation from rumor, can
be difficult. Gaps between official church doctrine and the beliefs and stories
shared widely among the general membership are particularly noticeable in
cases when the church has actively sought to refute a particularly widespread
rumor. An example is illustrative.

In the 1960s as fears of civil unrest swept through the nation, a prophecy
was circulating that claimed, among other things, that militant blacks would
march on Temple Square, rioting, ravaging, and terrorizing church members.
The prophecy was said to have been given by President John Taylor in 1885,
but it was not written down until 1951, by Edward Lunt. Lunt claimed his
mother heard Taylor make the prophecy at the hotel in Cedar City, Utah,
where she worked. Writer and columnist Norman C. Pierce claims to have
been the first to publish the prophecy in his book *The 3½ Years* (1963). Pierce
maintains there was no mention of blacks in the prophecy. Yet soon after publication, the prophecy had spread widely, with the prophesied ruin coming
at the hands of black men. William A. Wilson collected two versions of the
prophecy, each with violence perpetrated by blacks (1976a:131–2), and the
church historian's office noted that one of the five versions of the prophecy
they had on file also included violence perpetrated by blacks, though not the
"original" Lunt version.

The prophecy spread so vigorously that the First Presidency issued a formal
statement renouncing the prophecy as false. On March 30, 1970, the statement
was mailed to stake presidents, mission presidents, and bishops to announce in
formal church meetings. A few days later, on April 4, the statement was published in the *Church News* (Turley 1970, Fife Archives; Wilson 1976a:147). The
statement provided eight points of refutation of the prophecy and closed with
a plea to local leaders:

> We would urge you to caution our people against accepting these pur-
> ported statements of the presiding brethren, past or present, without

verification. You may be sure if there is anything of substance in regard to the safety and welfare of our people, we will see that the leaders of the Church are immediately advised so that we might act wisely and unitedly in order to not overreact to present situations.

The real danger lies in our people becoming confused and frustrated and looking elsewhere than to their Church leaders or to civil authorities in matters pertaining to their welfare. (*Church News*; cited in Turley 1970:19–20, Fife Archives)

Not surprisingly, such statements may serve as bandages for specific rumors and legends but seem to have had little effect on the larger tradition. In 2008, a rumor that had been circulating for at least a decade gained new traction among Mormon youth following the death of President Gordon B. Hinckley. During family home evening at Ken and Lee Mullen's home with three of their four children—Kenny, Christina, and Phil—conversation turned to the announcement the bishop had read in church the day before.[3] Kenny recalled when he first heard the story from his sister Nicole:

Kenny: I remember being . . . I don't remember how old I was. I was in Primary, so I was probably under ten years old.

    And I was right out here in the driveway with my older sister.

    And I don't remember what we were talking about, what was going on, all I remembered was that she said, "Well," like she knew.

Ken: Of course. She always knew everything [*laughter*].

Kenny: She said . . . I think she said something along the lines of "After the judgment, when we walk into Heaven, we will be asked, 'In what time did we live?' And we say, 'In the last days' or 'In the times of President Hinckley,' 'and that "the hosts of Heaven will bow out of respect for us for living in these last and perilous times.'"

    And I remember going, "Wow, that's cool" [*laughter*]. I mean, I was a little kid.

    And my whole life up until last Sunday, I have remembered. I never dwelled on it, like, "I can't wait for that moment." Or, I never was a total believer in that. I just remember that being stated. Don't know where it came from, never really cared. And then when he read the statement, I was like, "Aw" [*laughter*].

Ken: Dang [*laughter*].

Kenny: Even as deep as the Primary, those false statements get. It shocked me.

Kenny believes the story was circulated in Primary when he was younger, perhaps even by Primary teachers. His sister had heard it and reinforced it in retelling. Ten years later, with President Hinckley's death, the story had spread widely enough to give church leadership pause. Once again, the First Presidency responded with a letter to church leaders, including the General Authorities; Area Seventies; stake, mission, district, and temple presidents; and bishops and branch presidents. On Sunday, March 9, Bishop Michael Doyle read the announcement during sacrament meeting of the Burlington First Ward:

> A statement has been circulated that asserts in part that the youth of the Church today "were generals in the war in heaven . . . and [someone will] ask you, "Which of the prophet's time did you live in?" and when you say "Gordon B. Hinckley" a hush will fall, . . . and all in attendance will bow at your presence."
>   This is a false statement. It is not Church doctrine. At various times, this statement has been attributed erroneously to President Thomas S. Monson, President Henry B. Eyring, President Boyd K. Packer, and others. None of these Brethren made this statement.

The letter went on to advise: "Stake presidents and bishops should see that it is not used in Church talks, classes, bulletins, or newsletters. Priesthood leaders should correct anyone who attempts to perpetuate its use by any means, in accordance with 'Statements Attributed to Church Leaders,' Church Handbook of Instructions, Book 1 (2006), 173" (Office of the First Presidency 2008).

Local church leaders have also spoken out against widespread legends, prophecies, and rumors, such as stories of the current church president warning a ward or an individual on an elevator that the end is near and they had better put up their food storage (Smurthwaite 1977:9, Fife Archives). Yet despite the modern power of satellites to beam general conference talks around the world and the highly ordered hierarchy for the transmission of information through stakes and wards, such official declarations can rarely compete with a vibrant, informal, and ever-changing legend tradition shared among church members that continues to circulate long after official declarations have been read and forgotten.[4]

So while it would be misguided to define the Mormon folk tradition in opposition to scripture or church officials, the cultural expressions enacted daily and in rich variety by people who share a common religion are not identical to formal scripture. And the declarations of the few General Authorities who have the weight of the entire church behind them stand separate from the declarations of church members during fast and testimony and sacrament meetings in wards across the country and around the world.

The Mormon Oral Tradition

Within the Mormon folk tradition lies a vibrant oral tradition that includes ballads, songs, myths, prophecies, legends, memorates, personal anecdotes, and jokes. Proverbs and other conversational genres clearly exist as well, although the scholarly literature has remained fairly quiet on these genres. At the very heart of the oral tradition lie stories of personal revelation. But not to hear scholars tell it. Instead, the Mormon oral tradition has been studied primarily according to character and theme that cut across, rather than along, the concept of personal revelation. In the first book-length study of Mormon folklore, Hector Lee examined Three Nephite legends, a topic narrow in scope but broad in significance and prevalence in Mormon narrative folklore.[5] Yet legend is not a particularly apt term, as Lee acknowledges in the conclusion of his book: "It is no simple matter to classify the Nephite stories. They are not wholly myth, legend, tale or historical narrative; yet they partake of characteristics of all these types" (1949:116). Lee's classification problem is actually simpler than he believed; by organizing his corpus according to character, he was not dealing with a single form but rather multiple types of stories. It was not that Nephite stories exhibited elements of all these different genres but rather that different narrative genres were being used to recount encounters with the Three Nephites.

One of those genres was the spiritual memorate: stories of personal encounters with the divine. Couched within his study are examples of revelation interpreted broadly, something Lee recognized when he concluded: "Revelation, therefore, is as possible now as it was in ancient times" (1949:103).

Although Lee's book was published first, Alta and Austin Fife were already contributing to the body of folklore study through journal articles. By 1956, they had published *Saints of Sage and Saddle: Folklore among the Mormons*, the book that became the seminal study of Mormon folklore in its time and continues to be used as a valuable reference. The Fifes took an eclectic approach to Mormon folklore, organizing their book initially by chronology and then by theme. Stories of personal revelation occur throughout, mixed primarily among other stories of supernatural intervention, whether legend or personal narrative. Like Lee, the Fifes adhere to natural narrative corpuses based on the protagonist—the Three Nephites, past presidents, angels, J. Golden Kimball, Indians—as well as on theme—conversion, healing, divine protection and aid, treasure hunting, and polygamy. The Fifes do not use the term "personal revelation" but do speak of the pervasive belief in the ability to commune with the otherworldly that underlies many of the stories in their book.[6]

Working at approximately the same time, a number of scholars were exploring the recurring motifs and emic genres of Mormon narrative. They identified
a broad range of types of narratives: Three Nephite stories, pioneer stories, faith-
promoting stories, prophecies, stories of dreams, stories of the still small voice,
stories of healing, anti-Mormon legends, and stories of divination (see Adamson
1959, Bailey 1951, Dorson 1959 and 1964, Hand 1938). Narratives of personal
revelation continued to cross generic lines, appearing primarily under the rubric
of faith-promoting stories, stories of dreams, and stories of the still small voice.

Since then, studies of Mormon folk narrative have continued to subsume
personal revelation within genres defined according to function, experience,
group, and character, including: women's visionary narratives of unborn children (Brady 1987); conversion narratives (Eliason 1999); testimony narratives
(Gilkey 1979, Lawless 1984); missionary narratives (Wilson 1981); temple
stories (Wilson 1995c); urban legends (Brunvand 1970); unofficial prophecies
(Peterson 1976); premonitions (Van Orden 1971); tales of supernatural instruction and caution (Cronin 1984); near-death experience narratives (Canning
1965, Lundahl 1979, Morse 1983); and the ever-popular Three Nephite stories
(see Eliason 2002 and Wilson 1988 in addition to those cited earlier). The genres
are predominantly emic, developed from a corpus of frequently told experiences.

While the concept of personal revelation underlies many of the experiences
recounted by Latter-day Saints, it is rarely brought to the fore as an organizing
principle in categorization or analysis by scholars. Nor does personal revelation
appear as a distinct category in either the Fife Folklore Archives at Utah State
University or the William A. Wilson Archives at Brigham Young University.
Both archives were developed by William A. Wilson, who based them on a
taxonomy he developed from Finnish archives.[7]

As with all systems of categorization, there are multiple traits that can
determine generic identity, both emic and etic. Emic systems are notoriously
inconsistent, where defining characteristics jump from one system to another.
A major fault line in narrative may be tone; another, function; yet another, the
identity of the speaker. Narratives, therefore, might fall into multiple categories
at once, making a single coherent system of categorization difficult. Etic systems
can be neater but may violate emic systems and hence emic interpretations by
lumping dissimilar stories together and separating similar ones.

Wilson's system is a combination of the etic and the emic. He uses etic
genres as the initial organizing principle, dividing the collections into customs,
belief, speech, tales and jokes, songs, games and pranks, legends, material culture, e-lore, and riddles. He then employs emic subgenres to dictate subdivisions, primarily according to theme. The result is a system that is initially

recognizable to the scholar but honors thematic divisions made by the people within the culture. Under the category of legends, for example, Wilson includes the following subtypes: character, contemporary, etiological, human condition, supernatural nonreligious, and supernatural religious. The categories are not mutually exclusive: a contemporary legend, for example, could theoretically be religious, describe the human condition, and apply to a particular character such as the current prophet, placing the story in four of the six areas. The widespread legend of a president (often David O. McKay) forewarning a church member to make sure she has her food supply ready might be cataloged simultaneously as a contemporary legend, a religious legend, and a character legend.

While personal revelation is not identified explicitly as a genre of narrative in and of itself, it appears primarily under "Supernatural Religious Legends." Within this larger subset, personal revelation is scattered among other types of narratives, grouped according to valence (curses, blessings), medium (speaking in tongues, dreams, visions, patriarchal blessings), temporal orientation (forecasts and prophecies), human agency (solicited or unsolicited divine intervention), character (Holy Ghost, saints), and function (e.g., comforts, protects or aids, causes or urges change in behavior, etc.). As in Hector Lee's work, legend is used as a catchall term, including first-person accounts that are more accurately termed personal experience narratives.[8]

The archives also include complete student projects rather than individually cataloged items, indexed by primary and secondary terms that duplicate many of the categories in the genre collection but include many others specific to theme. Again, personal revelation is not used as a category of its own but is found dispersed among memorates, supernatural legends, and personal experience narratives.

LDS scholarly literature and archival material provide clear evidence of the prevalence of stories of personal revelation, even if they do not distinguish them as a distinct genre of their own. Ethnographic and doctrinal evidence, however, indicates not only the prevalence of these stories but also their importance as a distinct, emic category of experience and narrative that should be addressed as a coherent system in addition to being carved up and dispersed among thematic subgenres.

Personal Revelation Narratives

Within the larger generic system of the Mormon oral tradition, stories of personal revelation are spiritual stories of communication with the divine. As such, they fit within the larger etic category of memorates: stories of personal encounters with the supernatural. Spiritual experiences with the divine form a fundamental dimension of many religions, since religion regularly draws the human and the divine together in direct and indirect, as well as literal and figurative, communication. Narratives of those experiences are highlighted in both formal religious ceremonies and informal discourse among members.[9]

Personal revelation stories also fall within a larger *emic* category within LDS culture of faith-promoting stories. It is unclear when the term "faith-promoting stories" was first used to describe a type of LDS narrative, but widespread use of the term can be traced to the popular Faith Promoting Series developed by the church's Juvenile Instructor Office. Its mission was clear, laid out in the introduction to the first of what would grow to include seventeen volumes: "We hope that this little volume will prove of great value to those who read it, by inspiring them with faith, and furnishing them a foundation upon which to build and obtain knowledge from the Lord" (Cannon 1882:iii). While the focus of the series was on young people who had not lived long enough to have sufficient spiritual experiences of their own, they also hoped these stories would encourage adults to record their own experiences for posterity as part of a tradition of record keeping deeply embedded in Mormon culture. The William A. Wilson Archives at Brigham Young University and the Fife Folklore Archives at Utah State University are filled with faith-promoting stories, many of which derive directly from family journals, diaries, and oral traditions (e.g., Brown 1990, Miles 1980, Fletcher 1972; all in the Wilson Archives). Kristy Miles, for example, titled her collection "Faith-Promoting Stories of the Franklin W. Miles and George P. Stock Families," explaining that the stories "can be seen as a testimony of the benefits of faith and righteous living. Through the telling and retelling of these stories and many more like them, I believe that we as a family can increase our love for each other and for the Gospel of Jesus Christ in which we believe" (1980:iii–iv). The sentiment is a common one. Many people have interpreted the informal religious dictum to keep a journal as a request to record their faith-promoting experiences for their posterity (see chapter 6).

The category of faith-promoting stories is broad. Defined as they are by function, faith-promoting stories include a fairly wide range of experience. The collections in the Wilson and Fife archives suggest the range through the specific subheadings used by collectors: affirmations of life after death, visits from heavenly personages, promptings by the spirit, the power of prayer and the priesthood, healing, dreams, miracles, spirit world stories, sacrifices people make that are rewarded by God, missionary work, and the value of honesty. While some stories are mundane, promoting the importance of values such as honesty, economy, and generosity, the vast majority describe spiritual experiences that prove the presence and power of God.

The scholarly published record also recognizes faith-promoting stories as a distinct genre of LDS narrative, though definitions tend to be more restrictive. J. H. Adamson defines the genre as "stories of those who were punished or rewarded through supernatural agency for their loyalty or opposition to the Church, its practices, or its duly constituted authorities" (1959:85), highlighting the function of promoting the faith in the face of great adversity and discrimination to members of the early church. Jan Harold Brunvand also highlights the supernatural element of faith-promoting stories, arguing that they are "accounts of miracles and providences" (1970:58). Wilfrid Bailey suggests that faith-promoting stories "are usually told as personal experiences that show how faith in the powers of Mormonism has carried the individual through many difficulties" (1951:222). Eschewing spurious legends, Bailey recognizes that faith-promoting stories are more powerful when shared by the individuals themselves.

The original Faith Promoting Series, published by the Juvenile Instructor Office, continues to serve as a source for teaching in the LDS Church. Further, the series spawned a number of similar books, such as Preston S. Nibley's *Faith Promoting Stories* (1943) and Bryant S. Hinckley's *The Faith of Our Pioneer Fathers*. The term continues to be used today by church leaders in their talks and writings. However, while all members are familiar with the genre, some members avoid the term. Jan Brunvand argues that young people equate faith-promoting stories with the musty pioneer stories of the early church and dismiss them as irrelevant today. Others fear the term is too aggressively proselytizing. Eric Eliason groups faith-promoting stories and rumors together (1999:138), suggesting the term may have become too closely associated with spurious legends to be useful. Yet despite old-fashioned or coercive connotations, the term remains well known and well used.

Understanding Revelation

Like Russian nesting dolls, personal revelation narratives fit comfortably within the broad category of faith-promoting stories. Yet the image of a neat, tidy system of categorization falls apart quickly. Personal revelation is at one and the same time a concept, an experience, *and* a narrative genre. Definitions among these forms are not identical. Variation also exists between formal definitions and vernacular usage, as well as among members of the LDS community. Nonetheless, there are major points of intersection that not only provide a useful working definition for personal revelation but also highlight those areas of divergence that distinguish personal revelation as *conceived and experienced* from personal revelation as *narrated*.

Revelation writ large describes all divine communication. Committed to the page, it is scripture. When that revelation comes to the leaders and prophets of the church, that scripture is canonical. When it comes to individuals, that scripture is personal. In both cases, revelation is a message from God. One's own revelations taken together are like personalized Bibles, individualized Books of Mormon.

Such a definition paints revelation with a broad brush, asserting its significance if not its character. While any understanding of Mormon revelation must begin with a clear declaration of how sacred and vital it is to laity and leadership alike, its centrality to Mormon culture and theology also necessitates more nuanced definitions in order to be useful to its members.

Of primary interest in this study, a study focused on the experiences of the general membership of the church, are vernacular definitions of personal revelation that underlie the vernacular oral tradition. Lay members draw from multiple sources in establishing their understanding of personal revelation. They quote scripture, the General Authorities, church magazines, and church literature, including the dictionary from the Joseph Smith translation of the Bible. They share their own experiences receiving revelation, and occasionally those of their family and friends and, in doing so, collaboratively construct an understanding from each other. Most personally and importantly, they draw from their own experiences receiving personal revelation, synthesizing the personal with the communal, the informal with the formal, the lay with the leadership.

Scripturally, the most frequently quoted descriptions of revelation in sacrament meeting talks, Sunday school, and formal interviews, come from the Doctrine and Covenants, and the most frequently quoted passage is D&C 8:2–3: "Yea, behold, I will tell you in your mind and in your heart, by the Holy Ghost, which shall come upon you and which shall dwell in your heart. Now, behold, this is the spirit of revelation."[10]

Chatting together one evening in his home, Paul Clayson and I turn to talk of personal revelation, as we often do when we get together. After sharing a story of being prompted by the Holy Ghost, Paul pulls out his scripture and flips to the beginning of the Doctrine and Covenants. The process is familiar, the conversation similar to those I have had with young missionaries who only slightly less seamlessly weave together personal experience and scripture in the act of teaching.

"You've probably been through all these, Section Eight, Section Nine, Doctrine and Covenants?"

I nod. "Absolutely."

"You know it says in Section Eight of the Doctrine and Covenants . . . I believe the process of revelation is right there. It's starting in Verse Two.

"And first of all I should point out in Verse One, there's prerequisites to personal revelation. It says, in Verse One: 'Surely shall you receive a knowledge of whatsoever thing ye shall ask in faith, with an honest heart, believing ye shall receive a knowledge.' That I believe is a prerequisite. It has to be an *honest* heart. We don't go before the Lord and say, 'Prove to me. Come down and slap me.'

"But then the process. Verse Two: 'Behold I will tell you in your mind.'

"I believe that's part of personal revelation. Ninety percent of the revelation I receive is a thought to my mind. It is something that comes to my mind, many times when I'm not expecting it. Is that just the process of how our mind works? Perhaps. Could it be it's the process for how our Heavenly Father guides us daily? Most assuredly.

"'I will tell you in your mind and in your heart.'

"Well, scriptures are replete with the reference to our spirit, our spiritual nature, that inner spirit within us, as our soul or our heart. It says that the still small voice can enter our heart.

"Well, it's not that beating muscle in our chest. It is that inner soul that we have, our heart.

"So revelation comes to our mind and our heart, and then it says, 'by the Holy Ghost which shall come upon you, and which shall dwell in your heart.'

"It is those aching feelings, it is that continuing urge that this is right, you should do this, or follow this path. And those are the feelings.

"And then he says in Verse Three: 'Now this is the spirit of revelation.' And that's key. That's what it is, the spirit of revelation. In our mind and in our heart. And then he goes in Verse Four, which I believe is the key to what happens here, or to the fulfillment of this. He says, 'Therefore, this is thy gift; apply unto it.'

"That is every bit as much a part of revelation as receiving it, is having the courage to *follow* it and *do* it. Sometimes we don't know why, but it happens and we go forward with it. That's my belief about personal revelation. That's what it is. It's that still small voice that we have to learn to listen to and have the courage to follow what we just heard."

Paul's explanation is rich, highlighting many key aspects of revelation, including the process and medium for revelation. It often begins in humble prayer. In response, Heavenly Father sends the Holy Ghost to speak to the mind and stir the heart and soul. It is then up to the individual to listen and have the courage to follow.

Paul Clayson chose to quote the Doctrine and Covenants. Others quote the Bible Dictionary that comes as an appendix to the Joseph Smith translation of the Bible:

> Revelation: . . . . Continuous revelation from God to his saints, through the Holy Ghost or by other means, such as vision, dreams, or visitations, makes possible daily guidance along true paths and leads the faithful soul to complete and eternal salvation in the celestial kingdom. The principle of gaining knowledge by revelation is the principle of salvation. It is the making known of divine truth by communication with the heavens, and consists not only of revelation of the plan of salvation to the Lord's prophets, but also a confirmation in the hearts of the believers that the revelation to the prophets is true. It also consists of individual guidance for every person who seeks for it and follows the prescribed course of faith, repentance, and obedience to the gospel of Jesus Christ . . . In the Lord's Church the First Presidency, the Council of the Twelve, and the Patriarch are prophets, seers, and revelators to the Church and to the world. In addition, every person may receive personal revelation for his own benefit.

The dictionary entry, with its summary of scriptural references and current theological interpretation, is particularly appealing to church members charged with delivering a talk on religious doctrine without extensive training or experience.[11] The definition addresses the origin of revelation, the media through which it is conveyed, its functions, who can receive it, and its basic content. Ethnographic fieldwork confirms these categories as critical in defining revelation. However, fieldwork also reveals fault lines, nuance, contested areas, and shades of gray not present in such a general definition. A more accurate and complete definition depends on attention to the differences between revelation and personal revelation and the specific characteristics of personal revelation implicated by issues of stewardship, origin, the power of the Holy Ghost versus the gift of the Holy Ghost, righteousness, spiritual versus temporal revelation, medium, and the personalization of revelation.

Revelation versus Personal Revelation

There is no strict, formal distinction made between revelation and personal revelation in scripture. Vernacular usage by both church leaders and the general membership, however, suggests that the term "revelation" has two distinct usages. First, it refers to the umbrella concept of communication from God. Second, it refers to revelation received by the General Authorities. It is the second definition that is most relevant here. "Revelation" is what Joseph Smith received for the development of the church, which was then recorded in the

Doctrine and Covenants. Conveyed by a recognized church prophet, "revelation" has the authority and weight of prophecy that "personal revelation" does not. The revelations the General Authorities receive to guide the church are not "personal revelation." They pertain to the church at large and not to the specific individual. This distinction is evident in the Bible Dictionary definition. In fact, the only time the term "personal revelation" appears in the definition of revelation is in contrast to the revelations received by the General Authorities.

Personal revelation is more humble, more restricted in its scope. As the name indicates, it is personal. Like any member of the church, the General Authorities receive personal revelation to guide them in their personal lives, but divine guidance that aids them in their role in the church is revelation exalted above personal revelation. The distinction between revelation and personal revelation reflects not only a hierarchy within the church between the General Authorities and the general membership but also a more basic distinction between one's church calling and one's personal life. All worthy members of the church receive callings to help run the church. Wards and stakes are run entirely by unpaid members. In order to successfully fulfill the obligations of their calling, Latter-day Saints rely on revelation to guide them.

The narrative tradition of personal revelation excludes most revelations related to church callings when they refer to official church business. At the ward and stake level, this would include frequent revelations about who should be called for a particular position in the church. Such revelations are distinct from personal revelation and have a much stricter protocol for sharing.[12]

Church leaders can receive revelation related to their church calling on a more intimate level, however, suggestive of personal revelation. Paul Clayson, for example, occasionally shares the story of being prompted by the Holy Ghost while counseling a member in his stake (for the complete narrative, see chapter 5). The General Authorities may also share relevant stories from their lives serving the church, a practice so common that a talk without a personal story can seem incomplete. During the priesthood session of the Fall 2006 general conference, First Counselor in the First Presidency Thomas S. Monson gave a talk titled "True to Our Priesthood Trust," during which he shared a story about a prompting he received to visit a particular ward member at the hospital, a person he did not even know was sick.[13] The story served as a reminder to his audience of the importance of staying righteous in order to receive revelation to help neighbors and friends. These humble revelations to aid fellow church members fall within their calling but are personal rather than institutional. As such, they are shared as models of the kind of revelation available to all members, not just church leaders.

Characteristics

Stewardship

All revelation, whether personal or not, is subject to the hierarchy of steward-ship. Repeated by all who address the topic even in passing is the well-worn explanation that while every worthy member is entitled to personal revelation, one can receive revelation only within one's stewardship.[14]

Hunkered down in an overstuffed sofa one evening, Craig and Josette Bailey explain the parameters of stewardship in personal revelation. "Here's some lan-guage right out of the *Gospel Principles*," explains Craig, pointing to the passage in the reference book he uses to teach Sunday school to investigators—people interested in knowing more about the church. "'We may receive revelations from God for ourselves and our own callings but never for the Church or its leaders,' or anybody who's not a part of your calling. 'It is contrary to the order of heaven for a person to receive revelation for someone higher in authority. If we truly have the gift of prophecy, we will not receive any revelation that does not agree with what the Lord has said in the scriptures.'

"So again, I have stewardship over certain things, which is myself, my fam-ily, and my job and my church job. So I can receive revelation in those things. I'm not ever going to receive a revelation that's going to cause me to go to the bishop and say, 'Bishop, I know how to fix your home teaching' [*laughter*]. Great. You know? That's not my revelation to get, that's his."

For the individual member, stewardship includes oneself and one's immedi-ate family. It also includes the stewardship a person is granted through a church calling. A bishop has stewardship over his ward, a stake president over his stake, and so on, with the president of the church having stewardship over the entire church and its members. The concept of stewardship applies to all revelation and contributes to the hierarchical distinction between revelation afforded church leaders and personal revelation afforded everyone. The reason for this mandate is not trivial, as a brief historical glance at the development of the concept of stewardship reveals.

That history begins with an experience shared often in conversations about the role stewardship plays in receiving personal revelation. In September 1830, Hiram Page, once a close follower of Joseph Smith but eventually excommu-nicated from the church, began to claim that he was receiving revelations for the church with the aid of a seer stone. Many faithful members were influenced by these revelations, including Oliver Cowdery, second in command of the church after Joseph Smith and the primary scribe for the translation of the Book of Mormon. Joseph Smith saw at once the problem of revelation without hierarchical order and prayed for revelation to resolve the issue. The result is Doctrine and Covenants 28, a revelation that establishes the principle of stewardship: "But behold, verily, verily, I say unto thee, no one shall be appointed to receive commandments and revelations in this church excepting my servant Joseph Smith, Jun., for he receiveth them even as Moses." Challenges to this principle have led to over one hundred splinter groups, beginning with the Church of Christ (Whitmerite), which Hiram Page joined, and the Reorganized Church of Jesus Christ of Latter-day Saints, founded soon after Joseph Smith's death, and continuing today with the formation of multiple polygamous sects that have garnered periodic media coverage in recent years. Considering this history and the continued anguish and confusion caused by self-appointed prophets, it is not surprising that the concept of stewardship is one repeated again and again, both informally by church members and formally by church leaders in general conference talks for the entire congregation, supplemental talks for the youth (firesides), and Sunday school.

Despite what appear to be clear demarcations of the boundaries of stewardship, however, the concept is tinged with gray areas. For one, it is unclear how far church hierarchy extends into personal revelation. In a comprehensive hierarchical system, parents would have stewardship over their children; a bishop over the parents and children; the stake president over the bishop, the parents, and the children, and so forth. This strict hierarchy applies to church governance, but as one indignant woman points out, stewardship may not extend to all areas of one's personal life.

> It was right after I'd had my eighth child, Rachel. She was only three days old and I was feeling a little overwhelmed and wondering what Heavenly Father still had in store for me. Our stake president came over to visit and I asked him, "President, how much more do I need to go through?"
>
> He replied that I had served the Lord well by bearing eight children and said, "Your sacrifice is acceptable."
>
> After he left, I got to thinking about it and it kind of upset me. Through my tears I said, "Whoa, wait a minute. He can't know that for me. I have to have my own revelation [to know] if our family was complete or not." (Vigil 2002, Wilson Archives)

For every story like this one, there are fifty more of bishops and stake presidents who have been prompted to help in personal issues, much to the relief and gratitude of the church member in need. Yet even in clearly spiritual matters, issues of a bishop's stewardship can be questioned. During fast and testimony meeting one Sunday morning in the St. Petersburg ward in Florida, the first man up shared his story of joining the church. He was what many in the church call a "dry Mormon"—someone who had become a member in all but baptism. He sang during services and helped with the Boy Scout troop. Many people thought he was a member, he explained with a laugh, but he wasn't.

At some point, his bishop told him that he had a dream that he was going to be baptized.

This surprised him, he said. He wondered why he had not received this message himself. He was more than a little taken aback.

But sure enough, he did get baptized. "So I guess he was right," he laughed.

While he does not elaborate, the reasons he was taken aback could be multiple. He may have been concerned that he had lost his agency to choose his religion. He might also have felt coerced by the bishop, considering the latter's authority in the church. Or he might simply have been made uneasy by the idea of personal revelation, a concept he presumably now holds as a Latter-day Saint but that he may have questioned when he was still investigating the church. The man ends his narrative noting that he did in fact get baptized and that he knows the church is true. Yet while this resolves the question of the accuracy of the bishop's dream, and the man's laughter dispels fears of any lingering uneasiness about the revelation, the narrative performance does not resolve the question of stewardship and the appropriate boundaries of revelation for church authorities. Nor does scripture. If one assumes that bishops receive revelation on behalf of their ward, then no area of life should be exempt. To limit this revelation is to limit one's blessings. Yet if one assumes the bishops' stewardship is confined to church organization and their spiritual lives only, some areas may be off limits.

While possible violations of stewardship by church leaders is fairly rare in the narrative tradition, violations among peers—where no hierarchy exists to explain why one person might receive revelation to aid another—is less so.

After a sturdy dinner of salad, beef stew over rice, and ice water, Serena Gammon shares a story of how expressions of personal concern can be misinterpreted as revelation outside one's stewardship. "I have a friend who was a convert to the church," Serena explains:

> Serena: She and I went to church actively most of our time in college, but then the final year, we had both been abroad, and we both came back, and she had different experiences, and she wasn't sure about going to church anymore.
>
> And I said . . . I remember feeling just . . . . I knew she wasn't reading her scriptures and she wasn't, and I was worried about her, not staying close to what she had loved so much before. And so, I said something that I guess I regret a little bit

now because I think she might have taken it the wrong way, but, I said something like, "You know what?"

I think we were talking about the future, and she was talking about, I forget what we were talking about, but she was saying . . . we were talking something about our future.

And I said, "Pam, we've talked a lot about how we want to have families in the future, and whatever choice you make now, like whoever you decide to become, your kids are going to follow you or they're going to be similar to whoever you choose to become."

And she looked at me point blank and she just said, "Are you receiving revelation for me?"

And I just sort of paused, and I sort of stopped, because I . . . it was such a straightforward question.

Dave: You didn't think that you were, right?

Serena: No, I thought . . . well, no, I didn't.

I said, and what I think I should have said at that point was, "I'm . . . you know that's not my . . . I'm just thinking about things, and I'm worried about you."

But ultimately the only person who can receive . . . . We believe the only person who can receive revelation for you, besides yourself, and in prayer, would be, like a bishop if you sit down and counsel with him. Or someone who really was called to, you know, I'm sure you use this word, preside over you. And I was sort of, frustrated that I had come across in that way. Because I think to feel that somebody else is telling you what they think God thinks that you should do is offensive.[15]

Serena's friend does not leap to this conclusion without precedent. As Lee Mullen explains, revelation "doesn't just come for those things that we have stewardship over, but to help other people as well." In fact, the narrative tradition is rife with stories of being prompted to help others (see chapter 5). Most of these revelations follow the rules of stewardship, in particular guiding parents to protect their children. But not all.

Lee: I think sometimes that that revelation comes because we are being used to bless other people. And an example I can give . . .

When we lived in Dearborn, there was this single mother who had some emotional problems and she really couldn't hold down a job. And their young daughter babysat for me from a young age.

Ken: She was eleven . . .

Lee: She was eleven.

Ken: . . . when she was babysitting. I know who you're talking about.

Lee: And so we had her watch our kids. And we would hire them because they needed the money, they genuinely needed the money. And they were very sweet people.

But one thing I distinctly remember was, I was out shopping and she was watching my kids and the daughter, who was . . . she had just turned fourteen and it was her birthday. And I thought, "Well, while I'm out I'll just pick her up a gift."

And so I went into the store, and I'm looking at little trinkets or little lipstick or little purse or something and I just really felt to get her a dress.

And I thought, "Get her a dress? Why would I buy her a dress? I don't know her size, I don't know what she likes."

You know, being a woman, everyone's very particular about style and all that.

Ken: [laugh] I never buy her clothes.

Lee: Yeah. Very good. And I thank you for that, dear [laughter].

Ken: Even if I get revelation, I'm not buying you clothes [laughter].

Lee: And so I go over and I'm still looking and just this feeling, this inspiration, whatever, came: "Buy a dress."

And so, I'm thinking, "Buy her a dress?" I'm looking for something five dollars, you know? The dresses start at twenty. We were young marrieds and so it was a lot of money.

Again, I walked away from it and didn't pay any attention and I'm looking for something that I think she'll like. And I finally got it. And I'm like, "OK, I'll get the dress."

And I remember walking over and pulling the rack, it was stuff off the rack, and trying to think what would she like or whatever. And took it home, wrapped it up.

And when I was taking her home I pulled it out and gave it to her and she opened it up and she went in and showed it to her mom. And I'm pulling out of the driveway and her mom comes running out of the house, and tears are just streaming down her face. And I said, "What, what's the matter? You don't like the dress?"

And it was interesting because she said to me, and she couldn't even talk, but she said, "I have been fasting for a way to buy Karen a dress."

They didn't have the money for it and Karen was turning fourteen and going to her first dance, and that was an answer to prayer. [Lee begins to get choked up, as do the rest of us.]

And it made me realize that this doesn't only just come for those things that we have stewardship over, but to help other people as well.

And it's not just members, it's anybody. Someone who's sad or needs something. As you live right, and as you keep that conduit clean, that's when those revelations can come, in their purest form.

Through the Holy Ghost, God prompts people to do his bidding. Lee is in a position to answer the prayers of her young babysitter, both personally and financially, and so she is called upon by God to help. Such acts of kindness explode the strict hierarchical concept of stewardship by extending stewardship to all of humanity. Acting charitably, we are all our brother's and sister's keeper.

Reactions to these acts of kindness and charity are typically embraced in relief and tears when help comes in answer to prayer. When help comes out of the blue, however, responses vary. Josette Bailey remembers a visit from a fellow ward member that caught her off guard:

> Back in Utah, I was struggling. There were some instances that . . . I did not want to go to church. I did not. I quit going. Altogether. I didn't want to see the people there; I didn't want to be around people there. So I quite going.
> There was a sister in the ward.
> Craig had moved out here.[16] The ward knew we were leaving. Craig was out here, I was at home.
> There was a sister in the ward that came and knocked on my door one day. We weren't friends. I mean, we knew each other but we weren't close. And she had just told me that she had just had the strongest feeling to come see me and that she had something to share with me.
> She shared with me the story of the woman at the well. She says, "I don't know why I'm here. I don't know what you're going through. I don't know anything. But I know I'm supposed to be here, and I know I need to tell you this, and I need to give you this."
> And that was that.
> And after that, I started going back to sacrament meeting. I let my kids go to Primary but I still wouldn't go into Relief Society or Sunday school but at least I . . . .
> So she shared that with me, that she had had . . . even though part of her . . . she had felt strongly that she needed to talk to me.
> And the Lord . . . . I wasn't going to church, I wasn't getting the Spirit whatsoever, but he found a way to get somebody to get it to me and say, "Wake up. You know, you're not going to church for these people, you're going to church for yourself."
> And I still struggled for a while, but then once we got here, I was definitely ready to go back to church and be involved.

Josette Bailey is thankful for this experience and to the sister from her ward who took the time to follow the Spirit and deliver the message she needed to hear. Yet others may take offense, not only because their stewardship has been compromised, but because of the implicit suggestion that they are not able to hear the Holy Ghost themselves. The woman who visits Josette reiterates that she does not know why she is supposed to come and share that particular story. In other words, she is not presuming to know what Josette needs to hear; she is merely the messenger.

While these stories suggest that personal revelation can cross the lines of strict stewardship, they do not contradict the initial reason for establishing stewardship for revelation: to avoid undermining church authority. Further, they uphold the primary goal of revelation: to provide guidance and blessings.

Origin

The issue of the origin of personal revelation is similarly straightforward in its basic articulation. Scratch the surface, however, and the blurry boundaries of personal revelation emerge.

The straightforward answer is that personal revelation comes from God through the Holy Ghost. "We have a Father who uses an intermediary to watch over us for our own specific cares and needs," explains Terry Holmes during Sunday school one morning. In narratives, people often identify the source of their revelation, specifically naming the Holy Ghost or the Spirit.[17] Church members, leaders, and scripture consistently point to the Holy Ghost as the proximate origin for personal revelation. "God shall give unto you knowledge by his Holy Spirit, yea, by the unspeakable gift of the Holy Ghost" (D&C 121:26 and cited by Lund 2007:11). The ultimate origin of all revelation is God. But the messenger for revelation is the Holy Ghost.

There are, however, exceptions. Personal revelation can come directly from God or Jesus, but this is rare in experience and even rarer in a narrative tradition restricted by taboos against sharing experiences that might be considered too sacred (see chapter 2). The other exception is somewhat more complex. In addition to God, Jesus, and the Holy Ghost, there are a number of other spiritual beings in the Mormon universe. The plan of salvation—the unifying story of the Mormon faith that explains God's plan for people on Earth as well as their spiritual history and future—explains that in heaven there are spiritual beings with corporeal bodies, and spiritual beings without them. The goal in life is to work toward perfection, something possible only by coming to Earth to gain a corporeal body, and then returning to God with that body. In heaven, therefore, there is God, Jesus, and a host of spirits with no bodies, waiting to be born. There are also angels who have been to Earth and proven so righteous and faithful that God has resurrected them immediately to heaven. They have corporeal bodies. The majority of the people who have died, however, are in the spirit world, continuing to work toward perfecting themselves until the Second Coming, when they will enter one of three heavenly kingdoms based on their spiritual progression.[18]

Angels in heaven and in the spirit world can provide guidance, help, and comfort similar to that of the Holy Ghost, and these experiences form a substantial corpus of stories in the LDS narrative tradition.[19] Children in the premortal existence waiting to be born may also communicate with people on Earth. These experiences, too, appear to be widespread in the LDS community, though the degree to which they are shared is debated.[20]

Many of the visits from unborn children and deceased relatives fall clearly within the purview of revelation generally. Paul Clayson explains that some revelations "are direct personal visits by angelic messengers, by family members who have received specific assignments from our Heavenly Father to help guide and direct us in this life." The revelation may be specific to the deceased person. "I believe there are times when someone may have had a personal visit from a family member who needed to deliver a direct message from our Heavenly Father about the eternal nature of something relating to a family member, perhaps to help someone receive the peace and contentment that that person is truly alive, that there is life after this life."

Angels appear throughout Mormon folk narrative as well as in scripture (see Eliason 2002). Although spirit children and deceased relatives can also serve as God's messengers, people typically distinguish between experiences that come through the Holy Ghost and those that come from angels and deceased family members. Some consider these experiences part of personal revelation; others consider them as revelation or spiritual experiences more generally. They exist on the blurry boundaries of personal revelation but are distinct experiences that occur with a frequency that demands its own study. Because of the sheer breadth of material, this study will focus on the center of the tradition—where vernacular definitions of revelation agree—and address the peripheries where relevant (see figure 1-5).

Even when personal revelation is confined to communication through the Holy Ghost, there is variation depending on whether revelation comes as part of the *power* of the Holy Ghost, or the *gift* of the Holy Ghost. The Holy Ghost can convey revelation to both Mormons and non-Mormons. Non-Mormons have access to the *power* of the Holy Ghost, while Latter-day Saints have increased access through both the *power* and the *gift* of the Holy Ghost. The distinction is one regularly discussed in church, as well as among committed members at home. "Personal revelation is promised to us through the gift of the Holy Ghost when we're baptized," explains Jean Chandler, identifying not only the central role of the Holy Ghost but the unique privilege of baptized members. "We are confirmed a member and we are given the gift of the Holy Ghost. And it's our belief and my personal knowledge that through that gift—through that third member of the Godhead, who is not a person but a spirit—reveals to us things that we pray about, things that might help us, cautions us. And basically his main purpose is a truth sayer to reveal truths."

Her husband, Wayne, continues: "I think that anybody can receive revelation for themselves. And I truly believe that when I was baptized that I received what is called 'the gift of the Holy Ghost.'

"But before I was baptized, I also received promptings and guidance. So I think that you can be led by the Spirit and you don't have to be baptized. I think the gift of the Holy Ghost is a continual thing, it's a constant companionship that people call it."

There is revelation available to all, and revelation restricted to members of the church. One is extended as an act of God's generosity; the other is granted as fulfillment of God's promise to those who live by his covenants as laid out in LDS doctrine. One is occasional and fleeting, the other sustained and dependable.[21]

Despite this distinction, there is no fundamental difference in the *kind* of aid the Holy Ghost provides. The difference is one of expectation. For the non-Mormon or wayward member, personal revelation can be a surprise and may not be understood or fully appreciated. For righteous members, however, the blessing of the gift of the Holy Ghost ensures that personal revelation remains a central part of their spiritual lives. The closer one lives to God, the more dependable the presence of the Holy Ghost. It is a reciprocal relationship that culminates in the constant companionship of the Holy Ghost, a goal that, when reached, must be actively maintained.[22] Many returned missionaries reflect nostalgically on their missions as the only time they have had the constant companionship of the Holy Ghost, and perhaps the only time in their earthly lives that they ever will. During a Burlington First Ward Sunday school lesson titled "Seek Promptings from the Holy Ghost," a young mother remembered her mission as a particularly spiritual time in her life. "When I was on my mission, every thought and action and thing I did was guided by the Holy Spirit." She then added, "It would be nice if it were still true of my daily life today."

Righteousness

The process of attaining constant companionship of the Holy Ghost is simple in description, difficult in execution: simply live a righteous life.

Living righteously is inherently understood by church members, even if the specifics can be extensive and nuanced. At its most basic, living righteously is keeping one's covenants to God and abiding by the values and rules laid out in scripture. *Gospel Principles* suggests that righteousness is a prerequisite for promptings from the Holy Spirit: "As members of the Church of Jesus Christ of Latter-day Saints, we should make ourselves worthy to receive this special messenger and witness of our Heavenly Father and Jesus Christ" (38). The Bible Dictionary entry for "Holy Ghost" notes: "The gift of the Holy Ghost is the right to have, whenever one is worthy, the companionship of the Holy Ghost" (704). This belief is widespread throughout the church and is captured in the well-worn image of a radio. Shawn Tucker explains:

> The Mormon phrase for this is being "in tune with the spirit." In tune with the spirit. And the idea is almost like a radio station that's properly tuned in.
>
> And so for Mormons—to the degree that your life is clean, that you're doing what you should be doing, that your heart is pure, that your intentions are in the right way—that helps you to remove the static. That gets you right on the right station. And when you do that, then you start to be able to hear these [revelations].
>
> But, it is not automatic; it takes practice, it takes learning, it takes experience. You have to grow into it. And you should be patient with yourself. But, one of the things that can help you . . . .
>
> We used to have two radios, one in our bathroom and one in the bedroom. Well, the one in the bathroom was analog and the one in the bedroom was digital. We could set the digital right off because you could get the right numbers, but the analog was harder to get. So one of the things you could do was you could set the digital one and then you could get it on the station you wanted and get it nice and loud. And then play with the analog until they matched up.
>
> So, I use that as a way to say if I read my scriptures every day, if I pray every day, which are important Mormon principles, then that's my digital. I'm sure about that. I'm sure that the Holy Ghost, the influence of the Holy Ghost that I feel as I do those things, is right. And then, in my day, when the other things match up with that Spirit, then I know that it's correct. Or at least I get the best bet that it's correct. Not that it's, you know, beyond question or doubt. Nothing's like that. You always have to be able to look at it carefully, but you've got your best bet of those things happening."[23]

The radio is a beautifully efficient metaphor. As people dial their lives closer in tune with the Spirit, they concurrently increase the volume of communication both in quantity and amperage (see figure 1-1). In other words, living righteously means that personal revelation from the Holy Ghost gets clearer, louder, *and* more frequent. The converse is equally true—not only will the unrighteous rarely receive revelation; they will not be able to hear it through the static.

Theologically, the connection between righteousness and revelation is clear and unproblematic. Socially, however, this connection poses problems. There are two norms in the church impacted by the demand for righteousness. One

Figure 1-1. Tuning in to the Spirit

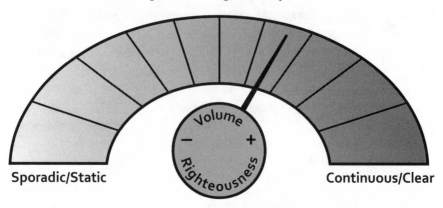

Sporadic/Static   Volume   Continuous/Clear

norm is to be humble. The other is to share your spiritual experiences in order to edify others and give testimony of the truth of the church. Because of the assumption of righteousness for those receiving personal revelation, sharing stories of one's personal revelation upholds the latter norm but risks violating the former. Narrators must negotiate these competing norms carefully in performance, a process addressed in depth in chapter 2.

Spiritual versus Temporal Revelation

Church members and leaders alike describe revelation as functioning in two ways: to confirm the teachings of the church, and to guide individuals in their daily lives. "Personal revelation can have a spiritual side, but it can also have a temporal side," explains Keith Stanley. Revelations can help us in day-to-day life. "Tough situation at work? How to deal with a coworker, or a situation?" Personal revelation can provide guidance.

Church leaders have been explicit about this division. In an article written from the First Presidency, James E. Faust avers: "Personal revelation comes as a testimony of truth and as guidance in spiritual and temporal matters. Latter-day Saints know that the promptings of the Spirit may be received upon all facets of life, including daily, ongoing decisions. Without seeking the inspiration of the Almighty God, how could anyone think of making an important decision such as 'Who is to be my companion?' 'What is my work to be?' 'Where will I live?' 'How will I live?'" (2002).

Theologically, personal revelation encompasses both spiritual and temporal revelations. In the folk narrative tradition of personal revelation, however, temporal revelations dominate. Ask people for their testimony, and they will respond with spiritual revelations. Ask people about personal revelation, however, and they will typically respond with temporal revelations about the guidance they received in conducting their daily lives on Earth. The primary reason for this distinction is that spiritual revelations tend to be shared as part of a person's testimony, a distinct emic genre within Mormon religion and culture. Another reason is that spiritual revelations often lack the dramatic climax that narrative demands.

Spiritual revelations are most commonly shared through the bearing of testimonies: a predominantly nonnarrative oral genre common to many evangelical and Pentecostal Christian faiths and a fundamental part of Mormon church services and religious life. A person's testimony is his or her declaration of faith in the church, its leadership, and its principles and derives from personal revelation. Paul Clayson explains:

> Personal revelatory experience is the root of the testimony that we all have.
> I truly believe with all my soul that when a member of our church says they have a testimony of the Book of Mormon, they have a testimony of the church organization, they have a testimony of the prophet—what they're really saying is that all of those experiences are rooted in the personal revelatory experience that they have. That they've had personal communication from God that says this is true, it is valid, and they now have that personal revelation that they don't deny. They move forward on their actions from that. If not for that personal revelatory experience, it is all meaningless.

Church members have the opportunity to bear their testimonies on the first Sunday of every month, at a service aptly named "fast and testimony," since members fast that morning before church. Not everyone bears his or her testimony at every meeting. In fact, in the hour allotted, there is typically time for only fifteen to twenty testimonies. However, all members are encouraged to bear their testimonies regularly.[24] The benefits of such public declarations of faith are varied. One morning during Sunday school in the Burlington First Ward, the teacher put the exact question of identifying the benefits of bearing one's testimony to the congregation. The two explanations given most often were "to confirm our own experiences" and "to learn from others' experiences." Others included helping us feel that we are not alone, vocalizing our beliefs so we can know them and interpret them, and avowing faith in God as a way to fight Satan.

Testimonies are typically shared as declarative statements rather than narratives. The end product—the truth of a particular doctrine—is far more frequently voiced than the process of gaining the testimony.[25] Non-narrative testimonies are the norm but not the rule. Some people do share specific stories that illustrate how they came to know the truth of a particular gospel principle, though those stories are as likely to be shared during Sunday school, priesthood, or Relief Society as during fast and testimony. Rather than telling full-blown narratives, people may speak generally of their experiences. During a Sunday school lesson that addressed Psalms 19:7–8, which avers God's law to be perfect, the teacher mentioned tithing as an example of a perfect law, a sure thing. If you tithe, you will be blessed. Jackie Foss spoke up. "I *know* this is true," she said. With the amount of money she makes, she says, she should not be able to pay her bills. "And yet we squeak by." Because she tithes, she cannot afford to go to the doctor. But, she says, she has been blessed with good health.

The most fundamental of these testimony-building experiences, and one shared more than any other spiritual experience, is the conversion experience. While church members may still be striving for a testimony of tithing, the Word of Wisdom, or some other gospel principle, *every* member has a testimony of the truth of the church. It is this testimony that leads to conversion.

Like other spiritual revelations, conversion experiences can be dramatic moments well suited to narrative performance. One young woman heard her teacher Cora Bennett recount her grandmother's story of conversion multiple times—while teaching her Laurels class, at a mother-daughter Relief Society program, and several times in informal groups at church.[26] The story stuck with her:

> Cora's maternal family was from the South, in an area where Mormonism was looked on with both skepticism and hatred.
>   One night Cora's grandmother dreamed she was sitting on the porch shelling peas and two young men came over the hill. She felt that they had something of importance for her and her family.
>   Within a week after the dream, she was sitting on the porch shelling peas, and she looked up and saw two young men coming over the hill. Remembering her dream, she invited them in and listened to their message. She was converted, and so were most of the children, but her husband was not.[27]

The narrative tradition favors dramatic stories of conversion for their clear and compelling evidence of God's presence. Experientially, however, conversions are rarely so dramatic. Far more common are experiences that describe a slow conversion to the church. Kendra Wagstaff's testimony is typical of many new converts. Kendra was asked to share her testimony on a Missionary Sunday, a sacrament meeting that occurs a few times a year, whenever there is a fifth Sunday within a single month. On such Sundays, members are asked to speak on various topics and experiences dealing with the missionary work of the church. Kendra begins by averring that her experience was likely similar to that of other converts who were members of another church when they first encountered Mormonism. She was Baptist, she explained, and lived at home with her mother. When she heard a knock at the door, Kendra assumed it was a salesman and went back to her bedroom to avoid him. Her mother answered the door and found two missionaries on the front porch. Being a kind Christian woman, she let them in, and Kendra, astounded that a church "made house calls," came out to meet them.

The next part of her story is painfully familiar to Latter-day Saints. Kendra agreed to take a few discussions with the missionaries despite her mother's quiet disapproval. Eventually, Kendra went to church and "really liked it." It was so different from her past church experiences. "People were so warm and friendly. They really helped each other out." She describes "feeling something" at church, but she was not sure what. However, her mother's disapproval became more pronounced. She forbade Kendra to go back to the Mormon church, and Kendra obeyed.

Soon, Kendra became pregnant, and by her own admission, "things weren't going so well." She decided to go back to the church, and again, she felt a sense of love. Despite her mother's opinion, she decided to join the church.

Kendra then leaps into the present with a remarkably positive update. Her mother now approves of her choice and may even join Kendra in church someday soon. And Kendra is bringing her best friend to church now, a young woman sitting in the pews that very morning, caring for Kendra's baby.

She ends her talk as most church members do, by asserting that she knows Joseph Smith was a prophet and that the church is true.

Kendra's conversion experience is typical of new converts, as is the lack of a dramatic "aha" moment. The subtle shift toward belief in the church for converts is even more common among people born into the church. Shawn Tucker points out that in his family, "none of us are converts, so all of our stories tend to be slowly accruing." "Conversion" is not confined to people who convert from one faith to another. People must also convert from following the faith of their parents to knowing for themselves that the church is true. Even people born into the church by Mormon parents must receive a testimony of the truth of the church and convert to the faith.

The existence of testimonies as a recognizable genre provides only part of the reason the oral tradition of personal revelation favors temporal revelations. The other explanation is that internal spiritual understanding can be difficult to narrate. Conversion experiences are often drawn out for months, even years. Some members born into the church may not even be able to identify the exact moment when they finally gained a true testimony of the church (Eliason 1999:141). With no clear climax, narrative structure falls apart.

Experiences that are effective as narratives identify a specific moment of conversion, when the truth of the church overtakes someone unexpectedly or all at once. People may be so overcome by the Spirit that they break down in tears (Eliason 1999:140). Even with a clear moment of understanding, however, such experiences do not lend themselves to narrative performance. Knowing in one's heart that Joseph Smith was a prophet or that the Church of Jesus Christ of Latter-day Saints is true can be an intense, powerful moment for an individual, but that experience can be hard to describe.

In most spiritual revelations, evidence of the Holy Ghost remains internally felt rather than externally observed. People may experience a sense of peace or of knowing, but clear confirmation of the presence of the Holy Ghost may be elusive.[28] When spiritual experiences *do* include climactic moments and external "proof" of the presence of the divine, they are more likely to be narrated when people talk about personal revelation. Stories of tithing where budgets should not balance but do suggest external proof of God's blessings. So do conversion experiences that describe prophetic dreams fulfilled. These experiences are far more likely to be shared as personal revelation than experiences with no observable climax.

Even more likely to be shared, however, are temporal revelations. Stories abound of protection from accidents; guidance in choosing a spouse, career, or home; and comfort at the death of a loved one. While spiritual testimonies allow people to express their spiritual maturation and knowledge that will ultimately be rewarded in the afterlife, temporal revelation narratives provide an avenue to express and explore the guidance they receive in this world *for* this world. All religious people strive to maintain a view of the larger mission, of the goal of attaining eternal life, but the temporal world dominates daily life.

Recognizing the difference between spiritual and temporal revelation, some members acknowledge the tendency to value one over the other. Craig Bailey describes a revelation his wife received about not going to a wedding as one of the "quote unquote 'less important' ones." By placing quotes around the idea of important or not important revelation, Craig acknowledges but questions any hierarchy that would place spiritual revelations above temporal ones.

It is true that without spiritual revelation, one can never gain a testimony of the truth of the church. Spiritual revelation is necessary. Temporal revelation, on the other hand, is not. One can lead a faithful life and attain the highest kingdom of heaven without receiving personal revelation of the temporal world. However, scripture, leaders' talks, and the beliefs and actions of LDS members make it clear that faithful members can and do expect both types of revelation in their lives.

Despite the distinction between spiritual and temporal revelation, all revelation, temporal included, is sacred. Guidance from the Holy Ghost in temporal matters is understood to be a cherished blessing. As such, even temporal revelations lead to spiritual growth and contribute to a person's testimony in the truth of the church. This fact reveals the fault line between temporal and spiritual revelation to be a matter of directness. Spiritual revelation is a direct revelation of the truth of a specific principle of church doctrine. Temporal revelation, on the other hand, is a direct revelation about earthly living that *indirectly* proves God's love, the power of the Holy Ghost, and the blessings that follow righteous living. In this way, both spiritual and temporal revelations can build one's testimony in the truth of the church.

The relationship between these two types of revelation can be seen clearly when stories of personal revelation are told in church. Stories are typically shared to illustrate a specific doctrine (see chapter 2). In this way, the personal experience is transformed into evidence of a general tenet of religious faith, a belief shared throughout the church. Whether implicit or explicit, specific or general, the questions of God's nature and power that frame narratives of personal revelation transform the personal into the shared, making these narratives generally relevant and theologically meaningful to all other church members.

While the narrative tradition of personal revelation is dominated by temporal revelation that provides guidance in daily life, it cannot be divorced from its broader religious context. Temporal revelation confirms the truth of the church and its doctrine just as a strong testimony in the church begets temporal revelation. The cycle is internally logical, economical, and self-sustaining.

Medium

While personal revelation may come primarily through the Holy Ghost, the medium of that communication is hugely variable. "Some people, through the burning in your bosom, you hear very well," explains Shasta Mitchell. "Some people have heard just soft voices. I've never had that experience before but some people have. At the temple, a lot of people have seen people and received things there. So between, just, hearing things, feeling things, seeing things in other ways. Sometimes I've even had dreams that I'd go to sleep just worried about something, just worried, worried, worried. And then I'd wake up and, 'Oh, OK,' you know, 'That's what I need to do,' or 'I'm at peace with things.'"

Shasta points out that people receive revelation in both waking and sleeping states through feeling, hearing, and seeing. People are also prompted through thoughts to the mind; Paul Clayson estimates that 90 percent of the revelations he receives come as thoughts.

Within each of these media are degrees of intensity. Feelings range from subtle stirrings to the burning of the bosom. Hearing can include soft whisperings internal to the mind as well as booming voices external to the ear. Thinking has a smaller range, although ideas can enter one's mind both subtly and strongly. And seeing can occur when asleep through dreams as well as when awake through visions and visitations, both of which typically have important aural dimensions (see figure 1-2).[29]

The most common term used to describe the way the Holy Ghost comes to people is the "still small voice." The term comes from the Bible, when the Lord speaks to Elijah not loudly through the power of wind, earthquakes, or fire but in a "still small voice" (1 Kings 19:12). The term and concept are echoed by church members and appear throughout the Book of Mormon.[30] "There's a scripture," explains Pauline Clayson, "that says it won't come in the wind and it won't come in the storm but it will come in the still small voice. That is profound. Because it's not usually a big visitation. It is not usually an earthquake, the shaking of a soul. What it is, it's the stillness that moves you with incredible force."

This is a voice heard inside the mind rather than by the ear. It closely parallels the thoughts and feelings that the Holy Ghost can also evoke but typically is felt more viscerally than the more abstract, indirect thoughts and feelings people also frequently receive. While "the still small voice" is used most often in conversation, both the narrative tradition and experience within the community favor the more ambiguous media of thoughts and feelings. "You hear people say 'the still small voice,' which I'm sure you've heard," explains Dana Mitchell, Shasta's husband. "I think that a lot of times more than actually hearing a voice, it's just the thoughts you have. You know, you have a thought; all of a sudden it pops into your head. You can't really discern it; it's almost as if someone just whispered that statement in your ear. And all of a sudden you've got the answer to whatever you were looking for."

The overlap between thoughts, feelings, and the still small voice is evident even when people attempt to distinguish among them. Searching for a coherent

Figure 1-2. Medium for Receiving Personal Revelation

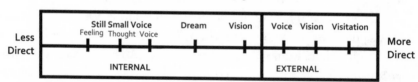

media to describe their experiences, people translate thoughts and feelings into specific words that can be quoted (see chapter 4 for a more complete discussion of this phenomenon).

Despite this quoting, speakers clearly distinguish feelings, thoughts, and the still small voice from actual voices and visions, experiences far more rare. Not confined to one's mind, heart, or internal ear, these revelations are given in sound, image, and body. In a religious community where God, Jesus, and the saints in heaven are believed to have corporeal bodies, the distinction between external senses and internal ones is significant.

For most church members, such dramatic voices, visions, and visitations are rare. Visitations implicate the corporeal and therefore could not derive from the Holy Ghost, the only figure in the Godhead without a corporeal body. External voices and visions also presume an origin distinct from the Holy Ghost and are also rare, both experientially and in the narrative tradition. If they do occur, members expect them to come to people high in the church hierarchy.

"It's not very common that a vision will take place," explains Justin Clayson, the son of Paul and Pauline Clayson, who recently returned from serving a mission in Italy. "Even in the scripture where it's a lot more condensed and you see a lot more visions than you would ever hear about in today's world.

"Even in the scriptures, visions are really kind of few and far between and only certain people in positions of authority have received a vision from God or from Christ who have visited them and told them something important that needed to happen."

The General Authorities may receive visions, but the assumption is that lay members typically do not. This is a cultural norm rather than doctrine, reflecting a widespread belief that the higher people rise in the church hierarchy, the greater their connection to the divine, both in terms of the frequency as well as the directness of their revelation.[31]

The impact of these social and cultural norms is that the narrative tradition of personal revelation diverges from general discourse about the phenomenon of personal revelation. The narrative tradition favors the compelling but not overly dramatic experience. The experience must have some degree of dramatic impact, some degree of the unusual, to be a viable narrative, but if it is too dramatic, it becomes inappropriate for sharing. "There are some kinds of faith-promoting things that maybe are faith-promoting to you, but don't seem spectacular enough to affect anyone else," explains one church member. A fellow ward member concurred, adding, "You want something flashier" (Gilkey 1979:54). Yet sharing too intense an experience risks violating social, cultural, and religious norms, because a person may seem to be claiming an authority that belies their calling and status in the church.[32] Church members therefore self-censor *both* their most dramatic *and* their more subtle promptings.

These norms help explain why revelatory dreams may be experienced rarely but are narrated frequently. Dreams, common to all humans, allow for dramatic and elaborate scenes of the future without violating social and cultural norms for acceptable sensory experiences. Dreams are conveyed internally through the mind rather than externally through the senses. Aural, visual, or visceral encounters with God or angels, however, challenge social norms, both outside and within LDS culture. The narrative tradition reflects both the infrequency of physical manifestations of the divine and the taboo against sharing such experiences (see figure 1-3).[33]

Personalized

Many church members point out that personal revelation is not just personal, but personalized. The distinction is between content and media. Personal revelation is specific to an individual's concerns in life, but it is also personalized in how a person receives revelation. Where one person needs only a quiet nudge, someone else may need a colossal shove. "That's a pretty consistent pattern across Mormons that I've known," explains Dave Gammon. "We all believe in personal revelation but we also believe in *personalized* revelation. That God will speak to you perhaps differently than the way he speaks to me."

Matt Larson receives revelation though subtle feelings and promptings and is ill prepared for anything more dramatic.[34] "I myself, if I had a vision while I slept . . . it would never happen for me. I don't dream. If I do dream, I remember it for two seconds, and [*snap*] it's forgotten. I would know it if it's a vision because it'd probably scare me, because I just don't dream, I can't remember them.

"So, I rely heavily on the promptings, feelings, other stuff.

"Other members of the church? It's hard for me to say what they feel. Because that's their own personal way they feel. Everyone feels the Spirit differently; everyone receives revelation differently."

Figure 1-3. Medium for Receiving Personal Revelation in the Oral Tradition

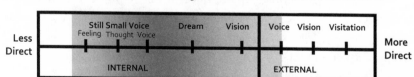

The nature of the question for which revelation is sought can also affect how revelation is experienced. Elder Chavez, a missionary from Mexico serving in the Spanish branch in Burlington, believes that a bigger push from the Holy Ghost may be needed for some particularly difficult decisions.

"In Mexico, getting away from the Catholic Church and belonging to another church is a lot harder than here, just more like free. You know, like when the son is eighteen years old, he's free to do anything he wants to.

"In Mexico, there's always that, 'I'm your father. You have to respect me in my house.' That's kind of how it is. So, definitely I think that person would need a stronger . . . when he has a revelation, the Spirit will go a lot stronger to give him the strength that he needs to overcome his obstacles."

Lee Mullen faced such a dilemma when her husband interviewed for a job in New York. The prospect of moving from a home and ward she loved, where she was surrounded by friends and family, to New York, where she knew no one and everything was more expensive, was troubling and challenged her understanding of the revelatory experience. "I actually thought I had the whole revelation thing down," Lee explains. "Because things came to me in a certain way." That "certain way" was a general feeling of happiness and peace. But not this time. What she was asked to do was too great a change.

"And I realized that the normal, good feeling probably would not have worked in that situation. And I had received revelation in a totally different way. And I've never received it that way since. But I would not have moved had that not occurred" (for complete narrative see chapter 5).

Personalized revelation is not without its paradoxes, however. Many members narrate instances when they ignored the promptings of the Holy Ghost, whether intentionally or because they confused a subtle prompt with their own fears or desires. The question arises: Would a harder push have been more effective? Further, church members are warned by their leaders not to expect burning bushes. After all, God comes not in hurricanes and fire but in the whisperings of the still small voice. And finally, the metaphor of the radio repeated so often among members reminds Latter-day Saints that they have to learn to hear the Holy Ghost. Stubbornness does not earn one dramatic revelation, nor does it alleviate the mandate to listen carefully to spiritual promptings.

Ultimately, these are superficial paradoxes rather than contradictions. Personalized revelation does not ensure a person will hear, much less respond to, a divine prompt; rather, it hedges against alienating that person before he or she can evaluate the experience. As Serena Gammon points out, the goal of the Holy Ghost is to guide, warn, and comfort, not to scare, upset, or confuse. "I think I would be scared out of my mind if I saw a vision. That might be partly why I *don't* see a vision, you know?" Her husband, Dave, concurs: "If they really are boom, bam, revelations from God . . . . Like Serena was saying, she'd be terrified if she got a vision from God, some flame of fire coming out. I probably would too; I'd be freaked out and like, 'This is not normal,' you know, for me. It's personalized."

Expectations for how the Holy Ghost will communicate revelation may be cultural as well as personal. Many middle-class white church members suggest that it is culturally normal to view voices and visions as unusual, and that were they to receive a vision as opposed to the still small voice that they are accustomed to, they would be shaken and disconcerted, responses antithetical to the comfort that revelation should bring. Further, those members familiar with Spanish-speaking wards or who have done their missionary work in Latin America have suggested that more dramatic experiences such as dreams, voices, and visions are more common among Latinos because of what is culturally accepted and normalized within these communities.

"In general, the white American middle class in the States, it's the still small voice," explains Shawn Tucker, echoing many others in the ward. "Now, there in the Spanish branch, there would not be the same level of skepticism. Maybe it's cultural, maybe it's whatever, but it's just different. I don't know why that is.

"And I think that if I had a dream or a vision or something like that, you know, having a dream . . . really, it would be much easier for me to tell it in the Spanish branch than to tell it in Elder's Quorum. Just because of those certain cultural expectations for how those things are received. So . . . and maybe that's what holds us whiteys back from having them [*laughter*]. Because we don't expect them and we have a hard time when they come."

Justin Clayson suggests a similar cultural norm for the Italian Mormons he met on his mission. Within the LDS Church in North America where this study is focused, however, and where 86 percent of the church identifies as ethnically white, the more subtle promptings of the Holy Ghost dominate more visceral, external encounters.[35]

Conclusion

At its most inclusive, personal revelation encompasses any communication with the sacred, a definition that would include phenomena as disparate as a sense of knowing that the Book of Mormon is true, a prompting from the Holy Spirit about the future, and a visit from a dead relative asking to have his or her temple work done.

The specific criteria that help define the boundaries of personal revelation can appear straightforward at first glance but reveal far more complex and blurry boundaries for the genre on closer examination. The standard dictum that revelation should be received only within one's stewardship runs counter to the ethic of charity deeply embedded in LDS doctrine. The Holy Ghost is the primary messenger for revelation, but God, Jesus, and a panoply of angels can also communicate with people on Earth. The more righteous the members, the more likely they are to both hear and receive revelation. Yet personal revelation can also come to help guide members back to the narrow path of righteous living or bring new members to the fold. Further, while revelation can be either spiritual or temporal, the two types blur in practice, since all temporal revelation is sacred and can support specific doctrine.

Ethnographic analysis of the narrative tradition of personal revelation, however, provides insight into how church members negotiate these issues. The result is a working definition for personal revelation and a list of criteria that help define its boundaries. Two figures clarify these parameters. The flowchart (figure 1-4) depicts the broad linear structure for receiving personal revelation compared with other types of revelation. The circle (figure 1-5) depicts the core of personal revelation—those experiences widely agreed upon and representative of the most common experiences and narratives—in relation to other spiritual experiences that some, but not all, members regularly refer to as personal revelation.

These parameters are not rigid, although they do reflect a general consensus derived from fieldwork and textual analysis about the center of the narrative tradition of personal revelation. The discussion that follows in this book draws upon this definition as a useful heuristic model to aid analysis. The alternate

Figure 1-4. Process for Receiving Personal Revelation

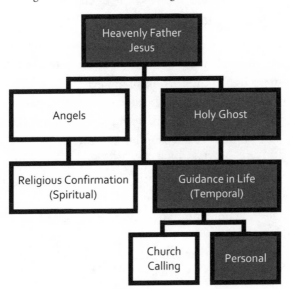

Figure 1-5. The Core of Personal Revelation

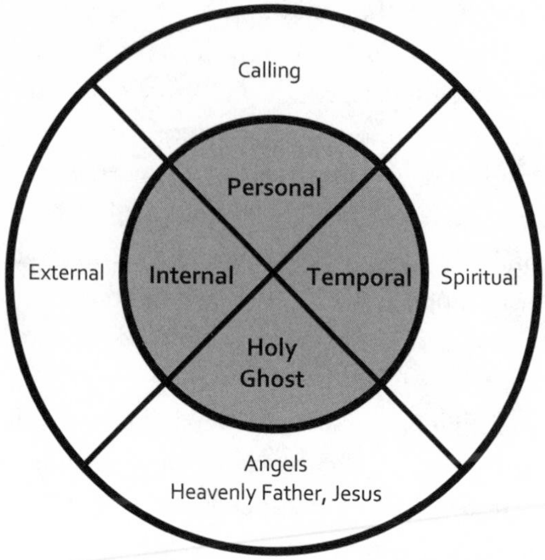

routes to revelation and the rich traditions on the periphery are nonetheless relevant both as texts and contexts in the study of personal revelation. Therefore, while not the focus of the study, they too emerge in this analysis, awaiting the more extensive attention they deserve.

Synthesis: The Boundaries of Genre

The Slippery Nature of Genre

Scholars often approach genres as agreed-upon categories that are quickly recognizable within a community, greasing the wheels of discourse. For literary scholars, stories can be divided into fiction and nonfiction, short story and novel, poetry and prose. For the art historian, genres are often divided according to medium—painting, drawing, sculpture, textile, ceramic, printmaking, photography, video, mixed media, performance—with subdivisions in each, such as oil, acrylic, and water for painting. For the folklorist, genres are regularly divided according to the verbal, customary, and material, with extensive subgenres within each. The divisions provide useful heuristic models for analysis, but they are hardly a priori or Platonic pure forms. Things fall apart. The dichotomy between fiction and nonfiction is challenged by creative memoirs, historical fiction, and films "based on a true story." Ethnopoetic studies of American Indian oral narrative challenge the poetry/prose divide. The novella maps the space between short story and novel, but other stops along the way could be marked as well. The genres recognized by art historians and folklorists similarly dissolve, particularly when examined outside academic categories and within the semantic systems employed by performers and audiences.

Focusing on emic rather than etic genres has provided one of the most compelling and oft employed solutions to folklorists challenged by the variation in generic forms across cultures. Yet just as etic categories such as legend, myth, and folktale erode in application to specific traditions, emic genres can be contested as well. What one person in a community calls a legend, another calls a myth. What one person views as sacred anecdote, another questions as spurious legend. The parameters of a genre can also be contested. Some Latter-day Saints see encounters with angels as part of scripturally defined personal revelation; others view them as related and important, but outside this category, linked only more broadly as sacred experiences.

German philosopher Ludwig Wittgenstein introduced the idea of family resemblance as a means for exploring systems of categorization that are not predicated upon a finite set of essential elements, a phenomenon common in social and cultural worlds. For an animal to be a mammal, it must be warm-blooded, have hair or fur on its body, breathe air through lungs, have vertebrae, and drink milk from its mother. These are essential characteristics that serve as taxonomic watersheds. But cultural genres rarely have such hard-and-fast rules. Wittgenstein used games as an example, challenging his readers to find the single essential element that links all of the activities subsumed under this term (1958:31–2). The same dilemma arises in trying to define a genre such as personal revelation. Are there characteristics that all personal revelation must have, essential elements without which it cannot be called personal revelation? Or is there simply a constellation of commonly occurring characteristics that approximate a genre, where only as a system is its nature defined and recognizable? One might be tempted, for example, to say that all revelation must come from God. But when the message, prompt, or visitation comes from a deceased family member, is it revelation? Those who believe that the family member is serving as God's messenger on par with the Holy Ghost may answer yes. But for those who see their deceased grandparents or parents acting out of their own personal love for their offspring, the experience is certainly sacred, but may not be revelation.

There is no single formula for generic categorization; essential characteristics may serve well for some genres, family resemblance for others. Even the most strictly defined genre will have room for variation, requiring scholars of expressive culture to continue to pay close attention to the emic construction of genres within communities, even when the local term is etic and the category familiar. Nor should we expect that generic definitions are agreed upon within a particular community, no matter how homogeneous it may appear. Marie-Laure Ryan argues in her study of genre and linguistic competency: "There is no such thing as *the* native taxonomy" (1981:114; italics in the original). Nor is there such as thing as *the* native genre. While genre clearly remains useful at the level of the group, an assumption this study has depended upon, it is also useful to consider genres as individualized systems. For the Clayson family, angels move from the periphery of personal revelation to its center. This inclusion is not insignificant. For the Claysons, personal revelation is even more personal than for most people, with relatives in the spirit world working on their behalf. The family, already central to the concept of personal revelation thanks to the rules of stewardship and, as discussed in chapter 5, theme, takes an even greater role; God and family become linked in shared mission together.

While the lens of the folklorist is trained firmly on shared norms, beliefs, and traditions, there has been a growing appreciation for the role of the individual at the center of those traditions. Until recently, attention on the individual has focused on the performer. However, scholars are increasingly addressing the role of audience members not just in shaping the performance but in interpreting it for themselves (see, for example, DuBois 2006). Thinking about individualized generic systems can help to highlight how meaning is constructed in multiple, disparate ways, with the potential for great chasms between the intended meaning of the performer and the constructed meaning of individual audience members. Future studies of personal revelation narratives specifically, and generic systems broadly, could benefit from such an individualized approach.

Religious Memorates

Despite the complexities of the concept of genre, or rather because of them, identifying generic categories as a means toward interpretation is a vital and necessary process. Individual systems build toward an emic understanding of the genre in context. From there, etic systems provide the means to draw the case study into dialogue with human experiences similar if not identical around the world.

Personal revelation narratives fall within the etic genre of the memorate—stories of personal experiences with the supernatural.[36] Memorates have been studied with sustained interest since the second half of the twentieth century, as scholars began to examine firsthand stories as well as legends further removed from their initial sources. With the acceptance of personal experience narratives more generally within the canon of folklore scholarship in the 1970s and '80s, memorates continued to earn academic attention.

The bulk of this scholarship has focused on the supernatural that exists apart from formal religious beliefs. The affiliation between the memorate and the supernatural has been so pervasive that Patrick Mullen questioned whether the term memorate could even be applied to sacred narratives that describe religious rather than superstitious belief (1983:17). Encounters with the numinous found cross-culturally, such as ghosts, spirits, and the Old Hag—as well as culturally specific beings such as banshees among the Irish, jiang shi among the Chinese, and jinns among Muslims—dominate the literature. Demons and the devil appear frequently as well, but rarely within a religious context.

Folklorists have too frequently focused on the fantastical, monstrous, and superstitious, rather than the far more common, though sometimes less spectacular, encounters with the divine. Of course the divide between the supernatural world of ghosts and the supernatural world of the divine is rarely entirely distinct and may not be useful even as a heuristic model in some cultures. For many American Indian cultures, for example, even the divide between the natural and supernatural worlds can be a blurry, indistinguishable one, where Western binaries cannot explicate local belief systems.

It remains both possible and useful, however, to examine the stories people tell of encounters with their God, gods, goddesses, and divine beings, stories specifically framed and interpreted as religious experiences, interpreted through coherent doctrine outlined in scriptural texts. As with all personal experience narratives, memorates are assumed to index experience. Religious memorates in particular are assumed to index religious experience with the divine, including revelation, prophecy, healing, church callings, dreams, visions, and visitations with divine beings.

While the experience can be utterly transformative, it is also transitory. People may seek repeated encounters with the divine and receive them, but the specific experience, located in time and space, occurs but once. Narratives, on the other hand, are transferable and repeatable, allowing a person to remember, revisit, and share the experience again and again.

Religious memorates can also operate as more than an index of past experience, constituting spiritual experiences of their own. In his study of the Primitive Baptist Church in Appalachia, Brett Sutton argues that while religious conversion experiences typically occur in private, "they are cast ultimately into verbal form, since no personal experience is really complete until it has been shared and, to an extent, validated through public testimony" (1977:99). Narration is part of the spiritual experience, making it meaningful as a public rather than purely private event, situating conversion within a religious community, arguing, just as public baptisms do, that conversion is a communal, not just personal, act.

The narration of religious memorates can also do more than complete the experience; it can replicate them. Latter-day Saints who receive personal revelation and are filled with the Holy Ghost often share their stories with the hope of edifying their listeners, literally drawing them to God and filling them with the Holy Ghost. In doing so, the narrator strives for mutual edification, where both speaker and audience are filled with the Spirit. The initial spiritual encounter is not duplicated; rather, the narrative invites a new religious experience, mirroring the feeling, if not the specific knowledge, of the encounter with the divine. The same effort at mutual edification occurs in Christian churches throughout the world, as preachers and ministers share their stories and experiences in an effort to draw their congregations closer to God. In Pentecostal churches, that effort may be focused on receiving the Holy Spirit in visceral ways, evinced by joyous dancing, spontaneous tears, or speaking in tongues. In this way, narrative and experience work symbiotically in the practice of religious belief.

The religious experiences indexed, interpreted, and constituted in narrative are broad; the scholarly study of these narratives, however, has been less so. In the United States, the bulk of the scholarship on religious memorates has emerged out of Pentecostal and other evangelical and charismatic churches (Clements 1980, Lawless 1984 and 1988, Orsi 1996, Titon and George 1978, Titon 1988). This is true in no small part because of the centrality of bearing one's testimony during the religious service, also a central part of LDS religious worship both at the end of each sacrament meeting talk and on the first of every month during fast and testimony meetings. As both an etic and emic term, a testimony can have multiple, nuanced meanings across cultures. Common to most definitions, however, is the idea that a testimony is a personal account of the presence of the divine in one's life and an affirmation of religious belief and the principles that shape a person's religious practice. Testimonies are envisioned as an abstract body of knowledge and experience people carry with them at all times, as well as a coherent performance shared orally—and often kinesthetically—in front of a congregation. In performance, testimonies are not inherently narrative in form, though they regularly include narratives, most notably religious memorates. As personal experiences that provide proof of God's presence in the world today, religious memorates are particularly effective in achieving the goal of the testimony.

Theoretically, any personal spiritual experience is appropriate as part of one's testimony, since a testimony is both an abstract compilation of one's personal spiritual knowledge and experience as well as a publicly performed genre. However, as people translate their knowledge and experience into the public sphere, social and religious norms may encourage some experiences to be shared regularly, others less so. In their analysis of evangelist fundamentalist Baptists and Pentecostals, Jeff Todd Titon and Ken George note that relatively mundane stories of answered prayers to find lost objects may be shared only a few times, while more personally significant or viscerally dramatic stories such as conversion narratives, visions, and miracles can become fundamental aspects of a person's narrated testimony (1978:69; see also Dégh 1994).

Religious memorates are hardly confined to testimonies in church. They are regularly performed as part of more formal sermons—both first- and third-person accounts—as well as outside the religious service itself, among family and close friends in semiprivate settings. Tracking the shifts in performance from one framed context to another, one narrator to another, is crucial in understanding the multiple functions and meanings of religious memorates. Shared in testimony, religious memorates are personal expressions of belief that can call forth the Holy Ghost, both to the individual and to the congregation, and aid in the evangelical mission of the church. Shared in sermons, they have a more didactic function, serving as exempla to the congregation. Chapter 2 examines these functions in their specific performance contexts among Latter-day Saints, examining specific shifts in form, style, rhetoric, and content as people shape their narratives for different audiences and to different ends. With no division between preacher and congregation (as a lay church, "sermons" are given by lay members), the divide between testimony and sermon is less pronounced, though not irrelevant, for Latter-day Saints.

As didactic exempla, religious memorates also serve as more intimate and contemporary examples of the same kinds of experiences codified in Christian scripture. As Linda Dégh points out, "*exemplum mirabilis* [miracle legend] in the traditional practice of the Christian church since Biblical times was always regarded as a powerful educational tool. Christ's disciples, the Apostles, spread their miracle experiences, and following their example, preachers throughout the Christian world enriched their sermons with didactic narratives taken from existing collections or collected directly from contemporary oral tradition." She continues, explaining the codification of biblical stories in some, but not all, churches: "While the majority of these stories concern the lives and miracles of accredited saints of the past, the exempla of fundamentalist sects are contemporaneous, treating wonders that happen to average people in everyday situations, to people they know, to the preacher himself" (1994:138–9). In mainline Protestant faiths, hagiography dominates, with a general scriptural focus on stories of biblical figures, prophets, and saints. In Pentecostal churches, memorates of contemporary members rise to the fore in worship. In

Mormon churches, the parallel is even more explicit: members are themselves called Saints. Austin E. Fife draws exactly this parallel when he argues that "one cannot become familiar with these popular legends without observing in their candor, in their religious zeal, and in their unrestrained credulity a spiritual feeling similar to that which is frequently observed in the lives of medieval saints" (1942:105). Boundaries erode between past and present, scriptural and vernacular, arguing implicitly for a consistent and still-speaking God.

Because religious memorates are both intimately personal and publicly shared, both part of the construction of a religious self and part of the act of instruction and evangelizing to others, they demand analysis that attends to functions directed and reflected inward as well as outward. The outward, didactic function is perhaps the easiest to access. Used in sermons, the message of God's power is rarely left to be assumed and is often highlighted throughout the story rather than confined to a coda as in "The moral of the story is . . ." in fables. Less easy to address is the personal dimension of how religious memorates function for their narrators. The experience itself is of primary importance, but after frequent retellings, the narrative can come to embody that experience, replacing the fully felt experience with the boiled-down narrative. Further, like all memorates shared among others, religious memorates require the construction and presentation of the self. Erving Goffman's work in this area remains foundational (1959) and has been employed widely in folklore studies. In the research of religious memorates specifically, the presentation of self is complicated by the conversion experience, challenging what Goffman refers to as "coherence" and Walter Fisher in his theory of narrative more specifically calls "characterological coherence" (1984:8). Citing Fisher, Charles J. G. Griffin avers: "An authentic conversion experience necessarily threatens characterological coherence because it disturbs the basic patterns of motive and behavior that have characterized the writer's life up to that point" (1990:160). Reinhold Hill applies Griffin's argument and his concept of a "mythic self" to Mormon conversion narratives in Louisiana, exploring how narrative both requires and provides the forum for the construction of a distinct religious identity (1996).

That religious identity is central to the performance of religious memorates. William Clements recognized not only the importance of the construction of the self in Christian conversion narratives but the appearance of a consistent persona, that of the redeemed sinner. He argues that this persona is authentic, despite being shared widely. "I naturally do not mean that the storytellers are consciously putting on masks or assuming roles that do not correspond to their perceptions of reality. Instead, I suggest that they are employing narrative patterns—probably unconsciously—which have traditionally been deemed appropriate for relating this kind of experience" (1982:107). Clements focuses on a religious persona constructed to conform to community expectations and norms, with a focus on the active role of the speaker. Diane Goldstein, on the other hand, focuses on the unique identities of speakers, with a focus on audience perception and evaluation. Goldstein argues that the narration of spiritual experiences during church services at an independent, ecumenical, mystical church was evaluated in the pews primarily according to the social identities and motives of the speakers and the spiritual effects felt by the congregation: "Though structural norms and rules for genre performance were significant among these variables, they were secondary to the determination of competence based on the congregation's knowledge of the individual speaker, the speaker's past and potential performances, indications of the Grace of God in emergent performance, and perceived motives of narration" (1995:32). Goldstein refers to these as "spiritual rules and norms," (30) but the degree to which they implicate the social identities and reputations of the speakers is notable. Performed religious expression is inherently both social and religious, and its ability to transform the mundane into sacred space is powerfully impacted by the identities of individual participants.

The criteria for evaluation Goldstein identifies are remarkably similar to criteria used within the LDS community, suggesting patterns that may extend to the performance of spiritual narratives more widely. Such evaluative systems that foreground individual identity and related stylistic elements such as "sincerity" over formal, structural, and artistic competence are common in religious expression. However, the two need not be at odds. It is common for artistic competence to be required for religious efficacy. Unappealing, asymmetrical, poorly constructed Navajo sandpaintings, for example, will not invite habitation by the Holy Ones—without whom the ritual healing process will not work (see Parezo 1983). Sustained attention to the impact of individual identity and artistry on the development of religious belief and the efficacy of religious ritual will help to move us beyond simple dyads that do not capture the deeply personal, social, and cultural dimensions of religious thought and expression.

CHAPTER 2

SHARING THE SACRED

Defining Performance

"Performance" is an ambiguous term. Like "folklore" and "myth," it has a connotative meaning in vernacular usage that runs counter to its academic definition. In the United States, "performance" often evokes images of formal, pre-arranged theatrical displays laden with artifice. Trained actors, clearly set apart from their audiences, give performances. Like the false dichotomy between fine art and folk art, performances are marked as elite and esoteric, the actions of a small cadre of trained specialists. However, beginning in the 1970s, performance theory emerged as the dominant paradigm for folklore analysis, and with it came a discipline-specific definition that exploded both denotative and connotative meanings of performance, expanding the scope of the term a thousandfold. At its most basic and inclusive, performance is "aesthetic action in social life" (Feintuch 2003:5). Storytelling, joking, dancing, healing, worshipping, woodworking, and painting can all be understood as performance. While the discipline-specific definition includes formal moments of high artifice, it is not confined to them. In fact, because the field of folklore focuses on the often ignored traditions of "the folk," "performances" for folklorists are more often informal, deeply contextualized acts of creation widely shared throughout a community.

Because of these conflicting definitions, most folk performances would never be called "performances" by the people who give them. Some people may even take offense at having the account of their deeply spiritual experience called a performance. Competing connotations of artifice versus heartfelt experience do not mesh comfortably. Nonetheless, I use the term "performance" throughout this book, partly because it is the accepted term in the field of folklore studies, but mostly because I have found no better term that satisfactorily evokes issues of context, skill, aesthetics, and active engagement so relevant to the sharing of one's traditional culture with others.

This study relies not only on the term "performance" but on the theory that gave rise to its use. In 1972, Richard Bauman provided one of the first and most enduring definitions for this new approach in folklore scholarship by defining performance as "an organizing principle that comprehends within a single conceptual framework artistic act, expressive form, and esthetic response, and that does so in terms of locally defined, culture-specific categories and contexts" (in Paredes and Bauman 1972:xi). In subsequent publications over the next few decades, Bauman identified four key characteristics of performance: (1) artful, as aesthetic acts of social living; (2) reflexive, as symbolic representations of society and culture; (3) performative, as the effective accomplishment of social action; and (4) traditional and emergent, as the drawing together of past into present for meaning that simultaneously transcends the moment while being firmly situated within it (summarized in Bauman and Ritch 1994:255). Performance theory provides the means for understanding how people effectively and aesthetically communicate with one another and what social action is accomplished in doing so. At the heart of performance theory, then, lies the interplay among the aesthetic, the cultural, and the social. Form and function are negotiated through broad cultural contexts and specific situational ones. Because folklore is traditional, norms for performance are established and shared throughout the community. Yet because folklore is also emergent, those norms vary from context to context, guiding rather than dictating.

The entry point for analysis can be any one of these areas—aesthetic, cultural, or social—since each leads quickly to the next, exploding a restrictive focus that attempts to isolate one element from another. Rather than randomly favoring one area over another, I begin with the question that narrators themselves begin with: Should I tell my story?

Norms for Performance

People face a confounding and perennial dilemma in the narrative tradition of personal revelation: whether to share their sacred experience or contemplate it in isolation. There are great benefits in sharing, but also great hazards. It is a dilemma both social and sacred in nature, at the heart of which lies a paradox between competing social and cultural norms.

Benefits

The benefits of sharing one's personal revelation can be charted along two axes: one, according to who benefits—oneself, others, or both—and two, according

Figure 2-1. Benefits of Sharing Personal Revelation

	Temporal	Spiritual
Self	• Membership • Social Standing	• 2nd Witness • Strengthen Testimony
Others	• Religious Instruction • Life Instruction	• Religious Instruction • Encourage Testimony • Recognize Revelation
Both	• Entertainment • Triangulate & Interpret • Social Bonding	• Triangulate & Interpret • Mutual Edification

to the type of benefit—whether primarily temporal and social or spiritual and sacred (see figure 2-1). Social benefits to the individual involve a clear articulation of membership within the group. All LDS members are expected to receive personal revelation. Sharing one's experiences helps to confirm this membership. Further, receiving regular or continuous personal revelation can establish some degree of authority for the individual as a worthy member in the church. While anyone can receive personal revelation, only righteous members can expect to receive it regularly. Being a member in good standing is particularly useful in teaching situations where experience is valued. This benefit is double-edged, however. With prestige can come accusations of a lack of humility, a serious violation of social and sacred norms.

While temporal benefits are rarely discussed, spiritual benefits to the individual are commonly enumerated by church members. By sharing one's sacred experience, a person can gain a second witness from the Spirit, a feeling that confirms the initial revelation. While such confirmation can also be achieved through writing, narrating the experience to any audience more clearly translates the Spirit from the realm of the abstract and supernatural into the social space of lived experience. In turn, by cementing the experience in the temporal world through social interaction, one can further cement one's testimony in the doctrine underlying the experience. Ken Jarvis echoes the fundamental belief behind fast and testimony meetings, averring that "sharing testimony helps it grow." Repetition of one's beliefs not only confirms those beliefs but can magnify them.[1] The result is a spiritual feedback loop (see figure 2-2). With each revelation, people have the opportunity to build their testimonies and move closer to God, thus encouraging more revelation.[2] This process can be compared to the metaphor of tuning in to the Spirit, where increased righteousness leads to the increased ability to hear the Spirit, which leads to increased opportunities to hear the Spirit (see chapter 1).

Figure 2-2. Magnification of the Spirit

**Holy Ghost
Brings Revelation**

**Strengthen
Testimony**

**Narrate
Experience**

The benefits to sharing one's personal revelation are not only self-serving. One of the most frequent contexts for sharing personal revelation is during religious instruction. Such instruction can focus on either the temporal or the spiritual world. Opportunities abound for such instruction within the church: sacrament meetings, Sunday school, youth seminary classes, fireside meetings, priesthood and Relief Society meetings, and stake and general conferences, as well as a host of church-sponsored summer camps and classes.

People also share their experiences with friends and family in attempts to provide counsel or support. As Elder's Quorum president in Fort Collins, Colorado, Dave Gammon struggled with how to help the men in his ward. In answer to prayer, he was led to a particular scripture that helped him immeasurably. Not long after, a good friend of his was called to be the Relief Society president, the equivalent calling for women in the church. Dave explains:

> She was quite young, about twenty years old. Just really felt over her head in a lot of ways. And she . . . I could see, and I could . . . more than I could see, I could *sense* from her that she was struggling with the same thing. And I don't think many people saw it. But I was in a religious class with her, it's called Institute program with a bunch of other single adults.[3] And I could hear as she prayed that she was struggling with the same thing that I was. It was so clear to me.
>
> And so afterwards I went to her and said, "Hey, Robin. I have a scripture that I want to share with you." And when I shared it to her, it was like this veil or this darkness over her mind or this mist suddenly cleared and she's like [*Dave opens his eyes wide and forms an O with his mouth suggestive of a sudden understanding*], you know? She just had this intake of breath and she's like, "Thank you so much."

And she referred back to it a few times after that, that that particular scripture gave her exactly what she needed at that time.

Revelation that one person received while having trouble with a church calling, a stubborn child, or a fractious marriage can help another facing similar problems. Guidance in temporal matters is often the focus of such discourse. But a by-product of such conversations can be to encourage listeners to gain their own revelations in a particular matter and their own testimony on a particular issue. In this way, more sacred benefits emerge. Further, hearing one person's revelation can help others recognize revelation in their own lives. A person may dismiss an event as coincidence until hearing a similar incident narrated as personal revelation.

Finally, there are benefits equally shared by both performer and audience. Relegated to little consequence, but nonetheless relevant, is entertainment. Sharing stories, even sacred stories, can be enjoyable. More readily acknowledged, however, are the benefits of social bonding. "As far as when to share and how to share, that goes to like you were saying, the question: Who's going to get anything out of this and why?" explains Ken Jarvis. "You know, is somebody sharing this to bolster themselves up? Or is someone sharing this to build a bond? To create a bond? And those times are needed; that's when it's needed, when that bond needs to be built, constructed."

This bonding can be social or spiritual. Sharing personal revelation can lead to mutual edification, when both narrator and listener feel the power of the Spirit lift them closer to God. This is an intensely powerful experience. In sharing their personal revelation, people can evoke the Spirit and reexperience the Holy Ghost again and again, not only for themselves but jointly with their audiences. While edification bonds people spiritually rather than socially, the two often go hand in hand. Missionaries regularly talk about the importance of sharing stories of personal revelation in the mission field as a means of socializing with their companions and peers as well as receiving spiritual edification. Further, what might begin as a mentoring relationship where one person shares an experience to help another can turn into temporal and spiritual group therapy. Members share their experiences in an effort, as Shawn Tucker describes it, to "triangulate their experience" and make sense of it within and outside their own personal lives. Again, these shared performances have both social and sacred dimensions.

Hazards

The hazards of sharing personal revelation can be charted according to the same two axes—in this case, who may be harmed and the type of harm faced,

Figure 2-3. Hazards of Sharing Personal Revelation

	Temporal	Spiritual
Self	• Ridicule • Labeled Immodest • Priestcraft	• Demean the Sacred • Lose Access to the Sacred
Others	• Inappropriate • Hurt Feelings	• Inappropriate • False Expectations
Church	• Ridicule	• Attract Spiritualists

whether temporal or spiritual (see figure 2-3). In the temporal world, a person risks ridicule for sharing an experience that lies outside the spectrum of everyday experience. Many people, LDS and non-LDS alike, get feelings and premonitions about what they should or should not do. Some call it intuition, some revelation. Some see mundane explanations grounded in human mental capacities; others see the hand of God. In cultures where the supernatural lies far outside the realm of widely accepted norms, people may be hesitant to share their spiritual experiences beyond the walls of their religious communities. In the United States, a recent national poll suggests that 52 percent of all adults have been filled with the Spirit, 41 percent have felt called by God to do something, 23 percent have had a dream of religious significance, 22 percent have witnessed or experienced a miraculous, physical healing, 15 percent have heard the voice of God speaking to them, and 21 percent attend a church that either encourages or allows its members to claim new revelations from God.[4] Yet people are hesitant to share supernatural visions, voices, or spiritual promptings, fearing they will be viewed with suspicion at best, or labeled fanatical or crazy at worst. As Keith Stanley explains, "Sometimes I tend not to know how the other person is taking it. If they think, 'This guy is way out there,' you know? So that's sometimes the hesitancy of talking about it. Sometimes you're not sure."

The fear is not unfounded. Mormons have been branded with many derogatory slurs over the years, some due to their belief in personal revelation. Those slurs have become tamer today and focus more clearly on theological issues, as opposed to the panoply of personal, political, and economic attacks of the past, but Mormons are still accused of being overly superstitious, mystical people with secret ceremonies.[5] Many LDS members are understandably hesitant around nonmembers.

"If they're open to it, it makes a difference," Shasta Mitchell explains. "If you're telling somebody something that they don't really even remotely care about, it can not only make you feel bad because they're going to bash what you believe in, what's in your heart.

"If they're open to it," she continues, "it can edify both of you. But if they're not, then it's not going to."

Shasta was born in the church; her husband, Dana, joined after they began dating. Both are open to sharing their spiritual experiences with close friends of all faiths but believe that the odds are better of finding an interested and respectful ear among members of their own church.

"You wouldn't even share an experience with them," Dana adds. "If it's somebody who doesn't care for religion and they're going to make a mockery of it, you just wouldn't share it with them.

"Not to say that we don't all have, as members of the church, have friends or acquaintances who would make a mockery of it. You can go on and have a relationship with the person, you just know that you wouldn't share any of your spiritual experiences with them," Dana says.

"The Spirit to us, as Latter-day Saints, the spiritual experiences are what matters the most to us. So if it's someone that you can't share those experiences with if you want to, or if the conversation you're having leads to it, then that kind of hinders how close of a relationship you can have with them.

"I think that's why you see a lot of times most Latter-day Saints, most of their friends are Latter-day Saints, just because you want to share those things that mean the most to you and you want to share them with somebody who is going to understand them and care to hear them."

Despite the fact that personal revelation is a cornerstone of the LDS religion, even Saints can be skeptical of the stories their peers share. After a long evening of sharing spiritual experiences, many of them involving voices and encounters with spirits as well as subtle promptings and the still small voice, Carl and Patty Miller turn to the subject of belief within the church and the frosty reception they have received when they mention some of their more dramatic experiences. One recent experience involved hearing a voice while they prayed, an experience one of their LDS brethren dismissed.

"There's a lot of disbelief," Carl states simply.

"Everybody takes it differently," Patty responds diplomatically.

"Why?" I ask.

"I don't know," Carl replies. "But there's a lot of . . . like seeing spirits or heavenly beings, if you tell somebody about it, like that incident that we had.[6]

I was at the church. I needed to talk to one of the church leaders and that was the day after we had prayed and heard the voice say, 'Hi.' And so I went to the church leader and I asked him what I needed to ask him.

"And out of the blue, he says, 'Carl, have you ever seen spirits?'

"And I'm like, 'All right [*laugh*]. Is he asking me for a reason?' You know, 'What's going on here?'

"And so I was like, 'Yeah I see them. Quite often actually.' And I said, 'In fact, we heard one last night.'

"Because here I'm thinking that maybe he was prompted to ask me for a reason.

"Well, he didn't believe me; he thought I was making it up. So."

"And he said that?" I ask, surprised.

"Well, he didn't say it outright. But he said, 'I don't believe in spirits.'"

Skepticism may be about spirits generally—as the church leader suggests when pressed—or about a particular encounter by a particular person. Either way, such skepticism is not new. In 1892, church apostle Marriner Wood Merrill tells of a miraculous experience of answered prayer for the *Juvenile Instructor* church magazine. He ends his narrative saying, "I have hesitated to narrate this incident because of the skepticism which is so common at the present day, even among some who profess to be Saints, concerning things somewhat supernatural."[7]

Even when audience members have no trouble believing in divine discourse, listeners may accuse the speaker of a lack of humility, of sharing an experience for the gains in social and religious prestige personal revelation can bring.

"I think a lot of the people that have stories like this or like that are people that are living their life kind of like you said, in a good way, that they're kind of worthy to have them," explains Elder Cox, a young missionary to the Burlington First Ward. "You don't see too many inactive members of the church that are not living their good life, that are on drugs, or whatever it might be. You don't see too many of them having stories like this. Well, they may have maybe a prompting that changes their life but I think a lot of this depends on people's righteousness. The better, more righteous person that you are, the more open to revelation and things they are going to be."

For Jean Chandler, receiving revelation is a comforting sign that she is living close to the gospel. "My sister gets upset with me," she laughs. "'How come you get to see these things and I don't? I've been a member longer than you' [*laugh*].

"'I don't know' [*laugh*]. But that's a comfort to me. It reminds me that I'm still worthy in my Heavenly Father's eyes of what he knows I'm capable of doing, and that I'm still on that right path."

Jean's sister is joking, but her reaction mirrors feelings of jealousy perceived to exist among fellow church members. Frequent revelation signals a righteous person; frequent *narration* of revelation signals a *self-righteous* person. Many people are wary of sharing personal revelation for fear that they will be judged as immodest, for claiming social or moral status that they do not have or deserve.

"I think a lot of times with personal revelation people tend to not want to share it because they don't want other people to think that you think you're better than other people or other people will think that you're so righteous and you're so good," explains Lee Mullen. "So you kind of tend to think, 'Well, I don't want to share a lot.'"

Few listeners go so far as to accuse a person of inventing revelation solely for the social prestige it could bring, though some do, both now and in the past. A particularly forthright journal entry from Martha Hancock describing events in 1878 makes it clear that these fears were realized from the very beginning of the religion:

> I was shown in what seemed a very striking way, that Mosiah Hancock was the one for me. Next morning I told Grandpa Hancock my dream, and he said, "Yes, that's from the Lord; do not get discouraged."
>
> The main reason that I thought in the weeks following that my prompting had been from the Lord was that it seemed as though the Devil was doing all he could to discourage me. I had considerable trouble with members of my family at home, especially my sister Elizabeth. She said, "You pretend to have dreams and think you're worthy of a son of Grandpa Hancock. You married Johnson against father's consent [she was previously married and had a daughter but her husband ran afoul of the law and they divorced], and you aren't worthy to have dreams from the Lord. Your dream must be from the Devil." I said to her, "Your actions, and the actions of some others, are proof to me that the Devil is working against me in this very thing. And Grandpa Levi thinks I'm worthy to have the right dreams."
>
> But Rachel Ann Brimhall, another sister of mine, remarked, "Martha, don't get discouraged yet. If your dream is from the Lord, it will surely come true."[8]

Jean Chandler's sister jokes about sibling jealousy. Martha Hancock's sister is decidedly more begrudging.

Less common than the fear of being labeled immodest, but even greater in implication, is the fear that the listener will move in the opposite direction, granting prestige far beyond the narrator's stewardship. Humility is not only a social norm but a sacred one, and having others grant you sacred power you do not possess is troubling. Shawn Tucker echoes many in the community when he worries: "What you're afraid of is that you get through this story and people are edified, but then they stop looking at the story and they're looking at you." Well meaning but spiritually disastrous, this tendency to find prophets in one's midst can lead to accusations by others of priestcraft, the willful act of falsely claiming spiritual power for oneself rather than for God (see 2 Nephi 26:29). Frank Nielson continues to be haunted by an experience where others viewed him as a prophet because of a miracle he witnessed. "I can see how very, just detrimental that is," he says. "Not just to one's own self but to those around him who put faith in a man, or a woman, who's been involved in a miracle that God performed." Frank Nielson's experience is rare, but the fear remains widespread, no doubt partially because occasionally people *are* claiming spiritual power beyond their stewardship, as attested by the numerous LDS splinter groups that exist today (see chapter 1).

The perils of false accusations of priestcraft are primarily temporal, since truth will be borne out in the spirit world and celestial kingdom. Yet while temporal hazards to an individual are distressing, spiritual hazards can be devastating. Closely related to the fear of personal ridicule is the fear of demeaning the sacred. Fear of ridicule hurts emotionally; fear of demeaning the sacred hurts spiritually. Ken Jarvis explains his fear of speaking in church not as a fear of public speaking but as a fear of both personal exposure and of demeaning the sacred:

> Somebody asked me why I was so nervous because I was in the military and I've gotten up in front of some high-ranking officials and our troops, and I'm not nervous in front of them. So why am I nervous in church talking to people?
> And I had to analyze it to figure out I'm baring my soul, you know? I'm standing up in front of a bunch of strangers and I'm telling them stuff that means something to me, that is important to me, that I really believe. I'm not standing up there saying, 'Sir, if we follow this plan of action, we'll be at serious risk you know? 'Am I throwing pearls before swine?' is the worry.[9]

By sharing the sacred with those who do not appreciate its spiritual value and power, people risk devaluing that which they hold so dear. Such devaluing is important for its implications both to the nature of the sacred and to the individual. The sacred is defined in contrast to the profane. It transcends the everyday. Some definitions equate the sacred with the supernatural. Others focus on the ability of the sacred to inspire awe and reverence. Within a particular faith, the divine is inherently sacred. But the sacred is a cultural construct, a value conferred by the faithful. Crassly put, one person's sacred cow is another person's hamburger.

Sharing the sacred with someone who does not bestow equal reverence risks undermining the system that defines what is sacred. Further, sharing personal revelation among church members who doubt one's spiritual experience can risk a personal attack on one's testimony. The former is theologically damaging, the latter personally so, and far more common.

People also fear that sharing sacred experiences inappropriately will deny them access to the Spirit in the future. Some further fear that they may actually lose the blessings they have already received. Revelations of promised blessings flaunted for social effect, rather than reverently shared for edification or counsel, risk being revoked.

The dangers of ridicule and loss of the sacred are felt not only by individuals but by the church as a whole. The General Authorities have been all too aware of the negative stereotypes and slurs heaped upon Latter-day Saints and have occasionally sought to protect the church and its members by encouraging people to keep supernatural experiences to themselves. In 1949, responding to folklorist and LDS member Hector Lee's query about personal encounters with the Three Nephites, President George Albert Smith wrote the following words of caution: "These stories are regarded as sacred by those who have them, and while they may on occasion repeat them, generally speaking . . . they are for the individual who receives them" (Lee 1949:22). In 1983, as a member of the Quorum of the Twelve Apostles, Boyd K. Packer avowed, "I have come to believe also that it is not wise to continually talk of unusual spiritual experiences. They are to be guarded with care and shared only when the Spirit itself prompts you to use them to the blessing of others" (1983:54). Packer's statement has been repeated in missionary handbooks and other teaching materials since then. More recently, during a fireside address on November 7, 2004, member of the Presidency of the Seventy D. Todd Christofferson echoed these sentiments: "Sacred things should not be disclosed or discussed with those who are not prepared to appreciate their value and who may even attack rather than appreciate them."[10] Further, online resources for preparing lessons for church talks include the following interdiction, drawn from the Doctrine and Covenants: "Do not speak of sacred things unless you are prompted by the Spirit. The Lord said, 'Remember that that which cometh from above is sacred, and must be spoken with care, and by constraint of the Spirit'" (D&C 63:64).

These formal interdictions join many other interdictions and warnings from the General Authorities to preserve the sacred.[11] When singled out, these warnings may appear to have a chilling effect on the narrative tradition of all spiritual memorates, including personal revelation. However, these warnings exist within the context of thousands of talks by church leaders in which they stress the importance of revelation and share their own spiritual experiences to anyone listening to general conference, reading church magazines, or visiting the church website. Spiritual memorates should not be broadcast without thought, but in religious contexts, among an audience dominated by fellow Mormons. One must be careful but not close lipped.

In addition to these general statements against sharing the supernatural and sacred experiences of one's life too freely, the General Authorities have issued statements against specific revelations that have circulated among church members (see chapter 1). Such statements serve a public relations purpose, but they also function within the LDS community by helping ensure the concept of stewardship is enforced. As President George Albert Smith suggests, personal revelation is personal, and what is intended for one person may not be intended for others. While most of the hazards of sharing personal revelation are directed at the person sharing the story, there are also hazards to the audience. Revelation provided to a bishop to be shared with his ward may not be appropriate for members of other wards. Revelation provided to parents of one child may not be appropriate for parents of another. This confusion can be temporal or sacred in nature. The first may misdirect someone in the choice of a job or house or school; the second may misdirect someone in tithing or the Word of Wisdom.

Hearing accounts of another's personal revelation may also prompt listeners to either reflect back and wonder why they did not receive similar revelation, or project forward and expect similar revelation for themselves. Matt Larson explains with an example that continues to resonate in the minds of many:

Well, when 9/11 happened . . . I think you have to be really careful with some of the stories that you listen to, some of the experiences that you listen to.

9/11 was a tragedy, and sometimes we hear stories of faith. You hear stories, "Oh, well this person didn't do this act, that's why he was saved." But that's not necessarily . . . I don't know if that's necessarily true or not, because, still, almost four thousand people died.

And so, I think, yes, some people have wonderful experiences, but sometimes that's why they're sacred, you keep them to yourself. It may not necessarily help other people.

I mean, it's hard to tell sometimes, yeah, they may have a wonderful experience, but those other four thousand families, didn't necessarily . . . . Yes, they're in that tragedy, but was God against them? No, of course not. I mean that was a terrible tragedy.

Some people may have been warned by God, but most were not. Hearing stories from those who were warned can be terribly painful to the families who lost loved ones.

"I think we have to sometimes be very careful because it could hurt other people," Matt continues. "I'm sure there were members of the church who were probably in the buildings at the time or who were on the plane, and I'm sure there were many other wonderful, wonderful, good people who may not have even been in the church."

Another tragedy far smaller in scale but certainly devastating to the families affected highlights how painful such stories can be if narrated widely. Camilla Allen recorded the following story of personal revelation from a fellow student at BYU:

All of the stakes in the Provo area were attending camp at now the Timp Lodge, at Timpanogos, up above what is now currently Sundance. That year, the owner of the then Timp Haven had installed for the first time a double chair lift. And they had offered the girls at camp the opportunity to go just take a ride on the chair lift. There were 300 girls on the mountain, maybe 250.

As a junior camp counselor, those girls my age had each been assigned a different ward to work with. And I had talked with the girls in that ward and everyone seemed excited to go. And as a skier myself, I was excited to see the new lift.

I visited with one of my friends who was a junior camp counselor of another ward, and she was not a skier, and I said, "Would you like to go do this with your group later this afternoon?" And she said, "Yeah, that sounds fun."

Well, during the morning, we saw each other a couple of times and in both of those visits, we mentioned the afternoon ski lift ride, and both of us said, "Well, you know, we're kind of busy. How are you feeling about it?" And both of us were just not really as excited as we had originally been.

When it came time for us to go, we saw each other and both of us said, "You know, I don't really think that we're going to be able to make it. I just feel that we have other things that we need to do."

Well, looking back on that experience, I realize that this prompting to both of us was more in the nature of a stupor of thought. It was not a direct, "Do not go," but just a confusion and a kind of taking away the desire to do this.

Well, during that experience that afternoon, there was something wrong with the ski lift and four of the people were thrown off of the lift before it was able to be stopped. And two of those four lost their lives.

They came for help and it was called down the canyon and somehow in the call word got to the radio station and pretty soon everybody in the valley knew that the girls at Girl's Camp were involved in a pretty serious accident. (1996, Wilson Archives)

In her notes introducing the story, Camilla Allen adds that the two girls' mothers also received promptings that day, revelations that their daughters were all right. For the families of the LDS girls who died, such a story would be difficult to hear.

For most people, however, the fear of causing emotional distress does not restrict them from sharing their experiences, since their audiences are not likely to be people also affected by the same tragedy. Yet the perennially thorny religious questions—why me and not them? or why them and not me?—remain relevant in many stories of personal revelation. Keith Stanley is saved from a fatal car accident that claims the life of someone else. A neighbor warns a young woman to ride with one sister back to Salt Lake City, but not the other. She listens, and while she is spared, her sister is decapitated in a gruesome car accident (Paakanen 1966, Wilson Archives). LDS members who have served in war have returned home with story after story of being warned out of harm's way, while many of their fellow soldiers have been lost (see, for example, the *Saints at War* book series, Freeman and Wright 2001, 2003). Was one person more righteous than the other, more deserving of personal revelation? Because the frequency and "volume" of revelation is contingent on righteousness, this is a very real concern. There is of course a standard refrain in many religions, including Mormonism, that frames death not as unfair punishment but rather as part of God's will and his desire to have them back home with him. Such comforting explanations do not always resolve the concerns that linger in people's hearts and minds.

Another more common fear of sharing one's personal revelation is that others will expect similar revelations in their own lives. One woman notes that she enjoys hearing other people's stories of revelation "because it makes me believe that I could have one, too" (Allen 1996:21, Wilson Archives). There is a paradox. One of the benefits of sharing is encouraging others to seek their own revelation and build their own testimonies. But the downside is that people may expect to receive revelation in similarly dramatic ways. Elder Richard Rowe, a missionary serving in the Burlington First Ward explains:

A lot of missionaries, when we first talk to people, we share the Joseph Smith story where he saw God the Father and Jesus Christ, the Son, known as the First Vision. Well, when we tell that to people, a lot of times they're thinking they're going to get a vision as well, telling them that it's true. You know, we tell them to read it, to read about it and pray about it.

And so you got to help them, you know, "No, he may give you a vision, you know, it's up to him. But he may just tell you through your thoughts, through your feelings."

A lot of people think they're going to get a vision, they're like, "So I'm going to get a vision for this?" You're like, "Maybe [*small laugh*]. Who knows?"

For members of the church, the danger is just as real. With so many stories of men and women meeting someone and being impressed that the person would become their spouse, many young singles expect to be guided directly, divinely, and dramatically to their intended husband or wife. One should seek revelation but not expect it for every question in the same way that others have received it.

Another danger in sharing revelation is that the storyteller will inadvertently coerce the listener. "You don't want to show off," explains Shawn Tucker. "There's a certain modesty factor about it that's appropriate. I think people in the church are aware of this. I'm conscientious with the youth that I tell stories, like my story where the trailer hit my car.[12] If I'm teaching a lesson and it's a natural fit, I will actually sort of like internally check with myself if it's right for me to tell that, if it's appropriate. Because those stories are powerful, and they can be manipulative."

I ask Shawn how.

"They can be forced upon people. 'I had this great thing and it must be true so you must believe,' you know what I mean? They're powerful and that power can be abused and it can be used wrong. It can be used in a way that doesn't respect the agency of your audience. It almost bullies them into believing this. You've got to believe this because this happened to me. And instead of being like a free gift that you give them, it's a push. So, you have to be careful about that."

Stories are powerful, particularly as social agents for the creation and negotiation of belief. When people share stories of their personal experiences, they implicitly ask their audience to accept the events of their experiences as true, even if the meaning of the events is up for discussion. Ideally, a speaker provides space in performance for audiences to come to their own conclusions. However, when stories are used in teaching, they are often didactic examples expressly meant to confirm a particular religious tenet. In these cases, room for interpretation narrows considerably. Narrators must balance their goal of teaching with the worry that too didactic a performance risks stripping the audience of their agency to decide for themselves.

"Because you're always aware of your audience, of course," Shawn continues. "If I'm working with the youth, I want to persuade these youth that living the gospel is the right choice for them. But I also have to respect the fact that they have to choose. And I fundamentally betray my faith if I'm coercive or manipulative in any way. And if I use these stories or these narratives in ways that can be that, the Holy Ghost won't be there. It will be the opposite of it. Because then I'm not trusting the Holy Ghost, I'm not trusting these things to speak for themselves, I'm using them to shoo cattle, you know, to force them to reach conclusions, to kind of compel them to come to answers like this."

Sharing stories of personal revelation is both a sacred and a social act. Ideally, audience and narrator come together, each extending the other an initial degree of trust and friendship. However, that trust is social, not ideological. To demand more is inhospitable at best, coercive at worst. If a story provides support for a particular theological tenet, then to question the story risks questioning the tenet. Likewise, accepting the story can suggest compliance with the tenet. Neither scenario is desirable. Further, the danger in sharing stories of one's spiritual experiences puts both narrator and audience at risk. The audience is at risk of being bullied, the narrator of driving away the Spirit.

One final danger of sharing personal revelation too freely, especially dramatic experiences such as visions, voices, and visitations, is that it may attract people to the church who are interested in the supernatural rather than the spiritual. In sacrament meeting one morning, a church member shared a particularly dramatic personal revelation. A number of members were somewhat taken aback. "Now, I'm not saying that didn't happen or saying it's crazy, no way," explains one young member present that morning. "But this was going on from the pulpit, in sacrament. And I remember going, 'If that is true, that's a very sacred and private experience and isn't something that should be shared publicly.'"

His father adds, "It wouldn't be understood well publicly."

The young man continues: "If you think about an investigator in there, going, 'What?!' I mean I could picture that. I mean, 'I'm a brand new person, my first Sunday at this church, and this guy's talking about dreams? And who's Joseph Smith?' I mean, 'What's going on here? And what's the spirit world?'"

"And that sort of thing can attract a certain type of person, too," the young man's father explains. "We believe in spirituality but not spiritualism. You know what I'm saying? And there's a very distinct difference between that.

"Stories like that, if they're told too publicly and too often, could attract people into the church that don't really belong in the church. They wouldn't really accept the doctrines that we have; they're into spiritualism and things that we don't espouse, fortune telling. And you start to get into mysticism. And we're very much on the other end of the spectrum on that; but you can see where the two can get confused. And so you have to be careful about that."

With all of these dangers in sharing personal revelation, it is a wonder that anyone narrates them at all. However, the list is misleading. The complexity of the dangers requires space on the page that the benefits do not. While there is much to be said about the risks in sharing, the fundamental benefit of increasing one's own access to the Spirit and moving both oneself and one's peers closer to God is too powerful an experience, too beneficial a process, not to share. To always remain quiet risks squandering God's gifts.

Strategies to Negotiate the Paradox

To resolve this tension between the benefits and hazards of sharing personal revelation, members have developed a series of strategies to guide them, some based on *when* to share their stories, others based on *how*.

Situational Context: *When* to Share

Ideally, the decision to share personal revelation is explicitly sanctioned by God. At best, a person may actually be prompted to share past promptings, whether as a clear and explicit prompting or a more subtle sense of peace or comfort confirming one's choice, a process employed daily as a means of resolving life's decisions. "You certainly want to have the Spirit with you at all times," Matt Larson says, describing how he decides whether or not to share his spiritual experiences. By having the Spirit with you, you create sacred space, no matter the location, whether in church or at work.

That said, most people acknowledge that some contexts are better than others. Craig Bailey describes a hierarchy of appropriate settings for sharing personal revelation:

> Certainly as the level of reverence goes up the more apt you would be. I mean, you're not going to find two people sitting at a UNC basketball game chatting about personal revelation they got that week [*laugh*].
>
> But then you move to a family home evening thing, maybe more so. Church maybe more so. Going to the temple, more so. So there's certainly a correlation between the environment that you're in and what you're willing to talk about. You're talking to a room full of people who don't understand the first thing about the church and have negative opinions about Mormonism and they hear you talking about that, there may be a negative reaction [*laughter*].
>
> So there's certainly some level of sensitivity as well to who understands, who doesn't, who you want to know, who you're comfortable talking with.

A thorough analysis of the situational contexts for sharing personal revelations follows later in the chapter. Relevant here is simply the recognition that choosing an appropriately sedate, sacred setting and an appropriate audience allows people to mitigate the dangers of sharing personal revelation. Church membership is not a guarantee that a person is prepared to hear personal spiritual experiences, but all things being equal, it helps. A respectful, knowledgeable nonmember, however, is a far more appealing audience than an unfamiliar, skeptical church member.

Narrative Strategies: *How* to Share

Because so many of the hazards in sharing personal revelation revolve around the issue of ridicule and humility, strategies for appropriate narration involve downplaying the supernatural elements of the experience and humbling the self.

Coded Language

While church members regularly use explicit scriptural terms when *discussing* personal revelation, they typically avoid them when *narrating* their experiences. Instead, a host of culturally defined synonyms are substituted. In the 441 stories I analyzed, only 10 narrators used the term "revelation" in their stories, and of those, 7 were responding to my question where I used this term. Further, in virtually all cases, speakers used the term only at the end of their performance, as a coda bringing us back to my question and repeating the term I had used as a bookend. Other scriptural terms—burning of the bosom, miracles, and the still small voice—were also used only 10 times. In other words, while explicitly religious terms were used 20 times, ambiguous terms were used 438 times (see chart 3 in the appendix; the total does not equal 441 because some narrators used multiple terms).

Craig Bailey explains the powerful connotative meaning of using the term "personal revelation": "It could be personal revelation to me, but if I'm then reintroducing that to a larger audience, at fast and testimony meeting or something, it may be a story, it may be an experience, but I'm not going to say 'personal revelation' because there may be that air that, you know, now I'm preaching to you, which I don't have the right and/or authority to do.

"So, to me it's revelation, to you it's just the story I'm telling you."

To call one's own experiences revelation too closely echoes scripture and can suggest an authority one does not have, a decidedly immodest presentation of oneself to one's peers. Further, by not being explicit in terminology, one deflects possible ridicule incurred by forthright claims of powerful supernatural experiences. Instead, people employ words with wider usage outside of religion and with connotations that extend into secular matters, words such as "thought," "feeling," "impression," "inspiration," and "prompting."

"A lot of times I think people, they won't say, 'I received a personal revelation,'" explains Kenny Mullen Jr. "Sometimes they'll say, 'I received a prompting from the Holy Ghost,' or they'll say, 'Something came to my mind,' even I'll hear that phrase a lot. And they're really saying, 'I was prompted,' or 'I was inspired to do something.' Lot of times you hear terms like that."

People *describe* the experience rather than name it.

Outside the LDS community, these terms can easily be interpreted as secular in nature, something that deflects ridicule but can also veil meaning. "People think that it just happened that way," explains Mike McCann.

"If I tell nonmembers," he says, they would typically respond, "'That's cool. It worked out that way for you.'

"And I'm like, 'Yeah, well, I know the cool part.'

"Tell it to people that are members of the church, and they're like, 'Well, you were guided that day.'

"It's just a different view of it, I think, and how things come about."

Within the LDS community, however, these terms are widely understood to signify revelation. "People always say, 'Yeah, I got this feeling,'" Mike continues. "Well, that's what we call 'having the Spirit.'" Modifiers such as "strong" and "distinct" are regularly added, signaling even more clearly that the person is describing a spiritual experience (see chart 3 in the appendix).

By using nonscriptural terms that are nonetheless clearly recognized within the community, narrators can have their cake and eat it too. Terms such as "thought," "feeling," "impression," "inspiration," and "prompting" are not explicit claims of supernatural experience.[13] Eschewing explicit terms for implicit ones is socially and culturally powerful. In fact, the tendency to avoid explicit language in sharing revelation is true as well of contemporary leaders in the church, people who *do* have the authority to claim revelation and evoke scripture.

"I was listening to a conference talk given by Elder Bednar," volunteered Paul Clayson during a Sunday school lesson on personal revelation, "and he told us, when you hear a bishop or president or church authority say, 'I'd like to speak to you about something that has been pressing upon my mind lately,' you'd better listen. You'd better take notes. Because that's revelation."

Ken Mullen reflects back on church talks over the course of his lifetime and is hard pressed to remember a time when a prophet introduced his talk by declaring, "I had a revelation."

Revelation in the church, as you I'm sure have come to learn, often deals with prophets, seers, and revelators—in our case today, the fifteen brethren who run the church globally. And it's a very sacred thing and very important, and we never would want to put ourselves in a situation where we seem to put ourselves on that spiritual plane. And I think that may be the hesitance with the word "revelation." You'll hear members say "inspiration" or "prompting" a lot. They're all three the same thing. But getting the linguistics of it, I think that's partly what that is.

And you never hear the prophets say it: "I had a revelation." Study President Hinckley's writings. I don't remember one time he said that.

"*Other* people will call it a revelation, that he received a revelation," Ken's wife, Lee, adds. "But very rarely."[14]

The cultural norm for humility extends beyond the church membership to *all* Latter-day Saints, even the president of the church. So, too, does the strategy for avoiding explicit scriptural language to establish humility. Paul Clayson and Ken and Lee Mullen all point out that church leaders tend to avoid calling their own revelations "revelations" even when they apply to the whole church. Not surprisingly, they are equally circumspect when it comes to their own *personal* revelations. A story shared by President Thomas S. Monson is representative of the way many church leaders incorporate and narrate their spiritual experiences. Well known for his storytelling, President Monson draws frequently on his own life to illustrate the points of faith he propounds during general conference talks. In a talk titled "True to Our Priesthood Trust" during the priesthood session of the general conference on September 30, 2006, he shared a story to illustrate the power of the priesthood:[15]

I conclude with an example from my own life. I once had a treasured friend who seemed to experience more of life's troubles and frustrations than he could bear. Finally he lay in the hospital terminally ill. I knew not that he was there.

Sister Monson and I had gone to that same hospital to visit another person who was very ill. As we exited the hospital and proceeded to where our car was parked, I felt the distinct impression to return and make inquiry concerning whether my friend Hyrum might still be a patient there. A check with the clerk at the desk confirmed that Hyrum was indeed a patient there after many weeks.

We proceeded to his room, knocked on the door, and opened it. We were not prepared for the sight that awaited us. Balloon bouquets were everywhere. Prominently displayed on the wall was a poster with the words "Happy Birthday, Daddy" written on it. Hyrum was sitting up in his hospital bed, his family members by his side. When he saw us, he said,

"Brother Monson, how in the world did you know that today is my birthday?" [*laughter*] I smiled, but I left the question unanswered [*laughter*].

President Monson refers to a "distinct impression" rather than personal revelation and avoids the term "revelation" anywhere in his speech. He does, however, playfully insinuate the divine origin of his experience when he leaves Brother Hyrum's question unanswered, a joke where the humor lies in knowing not only that Brother Monson did not in fact know it was his birthday but also that Brother Monson's "distinct impression" was revelation.[16]

The only consistent context in which church members use explicit language is when teaching specifically about personal revelation. Avoiding explicit terms during such teaching contexts risks confusion at the least and at the worst suggests that people should be embarrassed about receiving divine communication.

Passive Voice and Ambiguous Identification

People also deflect accusations of a lack of humility by using the passive voice: "I was prompted," "I was guided," "I was impressed," and "A thought came into my mind." Passive voice is inherently humble. Further, it alleviates the need to identify the source of their experience. By avoiding explicit identification, people mitigate both the lack of humility and the possibility of ridicule for claiming a divine encounter. The same benefits are drawn when people avoid naming the source or nature of their experience in active voice sentences, as in "Something told me . . ." and "I had this experience . . ." Some narrators are even more explicit in their bids to create ambiguity or uncertainty in their performance, saying: "It's kind of silly to think about it [as revelation]," "So I don't know what that was," and "It was just kind of weird to me."

In addition to the goal of deflecting ridicule and establishing humility, these strategies make the narrative performance dialogic. The audience is expected to join the narrator in interpreting the experience, often by supplying the scriptural terminology that transforms an ambiguous experience into an undoubtedly spiritual one. Mike McCann points out that while non-Mormons hear his story of returning home at the exact moment his house was being robbed and interpret it as luck or coincidence, LDS audiences typically aver that he had been prompted by the Spirit that day. When Keith Stanley told his story in priesthood meeting of inexplicably altering his work routine and then running into a former investigator of the church, he ended humbly by saying it might have just been a coincidence. Immediately, the bishop of the ward declared that it was certainly not a coincidence, and that we have to listen to God's voice, as he is constantly directing us in this world.

During a Gospel Principles class, Paul Clayson, a senior member in the church who has been both bishop and stake president in wards out West, provided a similar interpretation for a story shared by Elder Kyle Ballantyne, a missionary in the Burlington ward. "When I first started my mission, I was pretty nervous," explained Elder Ballantyne. "I didn't feel I knew as much as I should know before sitting down with people. When I spoke to people, I taught for five minutes. I didn't know how to expand the discussion.

"So we found this guy, really great guy, and met him at Burger King. And we started talking to him. And I just talked and talked. It felt like about fifteen minutes but we looked at our watches and it had been two hours.

"But when we left, I asked my companion, 'What did I say?'"

After the appreciative laughter died down, Paul Clayson replied: "This is meant as no disrespect to your knowledge, but you probably didn't have the wisdom to say those things. The Spirit allowed you to say the right things to him." Paul went on to quote Doctrine and Covenants 46:17–18: "And again, verily I say unto you, to some is given, by the Spirit of God, the word of wisdom. To another is given the word of knowledge, that all may be taught to be wise and to have knowledge."[17]

"You had the words," Paul concluded, "even if you didn't fully understand them."

In the cases of Brother Stanley's and Elder Ballantyne's stories, a listener with greater authority in the church supplied the interpretation, confirming the divine provenance of the experience. One's peers can also provide the interpretation. Because the avoidance of explicitly naming an experience is typically a rhetorical move, the meaning supplied by the listener is one of confirmation rather than contradiction. As such, an audience's interpretation affirms both social cohesion and shared theology.

Persona: Doubt, Weakness, or Dependence

Choices in specific terminology, syntax, and metadiscourse are strategies easily transferred from one performance to the next. However, narrators also mine the experience itself, highlighting elements that deflect self-aggrandizement. For example, personal revelation that comes out of the blue can catch people off guard and challenge them to have faith both in God and in their abilities to interpret the voice of the Holy Ghost. This can be difficult, and many people pause in confusion, indecision, or lack of faith. While narrating these experiences, people often highlight rather than subsume such spiritual weakness, pointing out that they ignored a prompting once or even multiple times.

Another strategy is to highlight the humble nature of their encounter. A young mother prefaces her story of being impressed not to begin birth control after the birth of her first child by downplaying the experience: "An angel didn't appear to me, or anything. It was just a small experience" (Vigil 2002:16, Wilson Archives). Serena Gammon concludes with a similar caveat:

> But I felt like those small ways, I felt like those were so small but some of the most powerful ways where I really felt like I got it. The Spirit really . . . you know, this wasn't confusing. I really did feel like going to DC and being stuck there was a blessing. I was helped there. I was guided there. I felt peaceful about it. I felt peaceful about the temple.
>
> I didn't get some big specific direction, like, "You must go to Washington DC and start a career" [*said in a deep voice*]. It was like, "Believe me when I say I'm going to bless you and be happy about it and don't worry and be still and know that I am God," or whatever the scripture is.[18]
>
> But those are the ones I love to share because they are so small but to me it felt like those were the "aha" moments, you know? "Oh, I got it for once." It made sense and it worked. And kind of led me through.[19]

While such caveats about the humility of one's experience may denotatively suggest a lack of importance, this would be a gross misinterpretation of the rhetorical move the narrator is making. To dismiss any spiritual experience as insignificant is to demean the sacred. Serena Gammon notes that she loves to share more subtle and "small" revelatory experiences because they often have the greatest impact on her life.

By highlighting aspects of their experiences that suggest humility through their doubt, weakness, or dependence on God, or through the unassuming character of the experience, narrators key their performances in a humble tone. In doing so, they help deflect unvoiced accusations of self-righteousness by their audiences. Such strategies shape the experience rather than create it. They are not fabrications. Confusion and doubt over the sacred nature of an experience is a very real dilemma. In subsequent narrations, that doubt may be mitigated in the minds of the tellers, but the social work accomplished by highlighting these humble elements of the experience is so powerful, necessary, and efficacious that such elements often remain with each retelling.

Evaluating Performance

Implicated by the process of deciding whether to share one's personal revelation with others is the parallel process of evaluation undertaken by the audience.

Narrative performances are evaluated according to criteria intimately tied to the benefits and risks that a speaker negotiates in deciding whether or not to share a story. This is not surprising, both because many of the benefits and all of the risks in sharing one's story are negotiated in the act of performance, and because one moment's speaker is often the next moment's listener. While related, the pros and cons for sharing personal revelation are not identical to the system for evaluating performance. Evaluation is based on criteria that include whether or not the story edifies, the reputation and perceived motive of the speaker, and whether the story is a memorate or a legend, all of which contribute to whether or not the story is believed.

Edification

Above all else, the sharing of personal revelation is effective, successful, and deemed "good" if it brings the Spirit and edifies the listener. No greater function can be achieved. No matter how much a person stumbles through their story or how tainted their reputation in church, if the story edifies the listener and evokes the Spirit, the performance is good. Such criteria place heavy emphasis on the participation of the audience, not just the performance of the narrator. A well-told, compelling, true story told by a well-respected church member can still fall on deaf ears if a listener is not prepared to hear the Spirit.

"The good ones are the ones where I feel the spirit," explains Lee Mullen. "And sometimes it's me, it's not them, meaning that I'm not living or doing whatever, or I'm just not in the place . . ."

"Had a bad morning," suggests her husband, Ken.

"Had a bad morning, yelled at the kids and I'm not at that place. So it doesn't mean that their story isn't true. But the ones that really touch me are the ones where I'm listening and I understand it on a spiritual level, where I feel it.

"And we call it when the Spirit kind of bears witness of the truth of the words. And I think in one of the scriptures it talks about 'to some it is given to know.' And it talks about gifts of the spirit. And then it says, 'and to some it's to believe on the words of those, of others.'

"And so, sometimes I think that's what it is, that there's a gift of the spirit that comes with being able to hear someone, to understand that the spirit is communicating between what they're saying and what you're receiving."

In this way, interpretation and evaluation have as much to do with the competency of the audience as the speaker.

Believability

The presence of the Spirit ensures believability, confirming the truth of the experience shared. Audience members testify to the truth of the experience when they mention feeling the Spirit while listening to someone share a story of personal revelation. BYU student Heidi Lietz provides the rationale for why the audience believed the story of a revelatory dream by noting, "The young women were all sitting in a circle and the Spirit was very strong when she was telling them this experience" (Lietz 2000:12, Wilson Archives; see chapter 5 for complete narrative). Another BYU student recalls hearing a story told in the Missionary Training Center in Provo and "remembers feeling the Spirit during the meeting" (Long 1995:18, Wilson Archives). Merrill Long, who recorded the story, adds that the student narrator "believes that mission presidents can receive this kind of revelation about the missionaries they preside over," explicitly tying edification to belief.

The issue of believability is crucial to the performance of personal revelation. If the story is not believed, or if sufficient doubt is raised as to its authenticity, the story may be dismissed. Of course, belief is rarely static or an either/or proposition. In between believing so deeply that one "knows" something is true and the equal conviction that something is false are many shades of gray. Joanne Kandare recorded a story about John Koyle's infamous "dream mine" from a fellow BYU student, summarizing his beliefs by noting he "isn't a firm believer in the Dream mine but thinks there may be some truth in it" (Kandare 1985, Wilson Archives).

Performances that do not bring the Spirit may still be judged good stories, effective in meeting intellectual, doctrinal, or temporal expectations. Without edification, however, belief must be established in other ways. The most prominent and pervasive is the evaluation of the speaker's social and spiritual reputation. Even before a person begins a narrative, audience members have begun their evaluation. Revelation comes to the righteous. Whether the audience believes the performance or not is often contingent on a speaker's reputation. Keith Stanley suggests:

> It all depends on, I think, that perception people have of that individual. If it's somebody that they really look up to, that they consider a spiritual person that they go to for advice—you know what I'm saying?—then they tend not to doubt it. But if it was just the common Joe, the guy that sits on the back row, started talking about it?
>
> And I think that's true in any society. They would look at them [*he tilts his head and narrows his eyes suspiciously*] and say, "What have you been

drinking?" Or "What have you been . . ." You know? Versus if it's somebody that they consider of caliber or a spiritual person, they wouldn't tend to doubt it.

Cora Bennett narrates her grandmother's prophetic dream about conversion, a story that fits a pattern of well-worn conversion stories that might strain her credibility (for complete narrative, see chapter 1). However, as the fellow ward member who recorded her story noted, "The people in the ward really respect Cora, which may cause them to give more than normal credence and heed to her stories" (Williams 1976, Wilson Archives).

While a good reputation can instill faith in what might otherwise be a dubious story, a poor reputation can create doubt in an otherwise believable one. Many church members express skepticism about talks given by particular members of the church.

"I'd be less than honest to say that I—I know that Susan has too—to sit in a sacrament meeting or a testimony meeting sometimes and be skeptical. You know, a person will be sharing something and I'll be going, 'Hm. Hm' [*laugh*]. You know?"

Susan agreed. "It sounds a little way out for me."

"Yeah. And so, I have to say that, too.

"And that doesn't happen a lot but we've had a couple members of the ward, and you may have picked up on that, where you're hearing that and you're going, every month, they have this huge revelation, you know a vision or something. And you're going 'Huh?' You know, I've been a leader in the church, and I've never had anything like that. I'm just being honest with you. I just kind of don't believe it. I'm sorry."[20]

The loss of credibility typically occurs after repeated performances of dramatic revelations by lay members. Such performances risk violating three related cultural assumptions: that dramatic revelations (1) are rare, (2) should not be shared widely, and (3) come primarily to church leaders (see chapter 1). Carl Miller was met with open disbelief when he admitted to having heard voices and received visions, and many members admit to being skeptical of such dramatic revelations generally. Ignoring social norms and narrating such experiences signals to many church members that a person is too eager for attention and may be likely to embellish, misinterpret, or fabricate their revelatory experience. The reputation of a person is so important, in fact, that it can make people question a performance even when they feel the Spirit. One BYU professor described hearing a story shared by a fellow ward member during a fast and testimony meeting. Despite feeling a sense of awe upon hearing the story, the professor "didn't strongly believe it" because the speaker was "off the edge a little," someone who tended toward hysteria (Nielson 1990:10, Wilson Archives). His dilemma raises a troubling possibility: that a poor reputation can become an insurmountable obstacle not only to belief but to edification. In this way, social reputation may be the most important temporal factor of all in the process of evaluation, interpretation, and edification.

Motive

Tied to but not synonymous with social reputation is the perceived motive for sharing one's personal revelation experiences with others. Volunteers during fast and testimony meetings may be met with greater skepticism than people who have been asked by church leaders to speak. The same is true for members who volunteer their stories during church meetings with only tangential connection to the topic at hand. Paul Clayson quotes scripture when he points out that you must declare "whatsoever thing ye declare in My name with solemnity of heart and the spirit of meekness in all things" (D&C 100:7). The Holy Ghost will come only if the Lord is recognized and credited for his power. Paul continues: "If you're attempting to use that feeling of the Spirit for your own self-aggrandizement or to show how smart you are or to prove a point or to show a sign, more often than not, he that receiveth will not be blessed with the Spirit because your motive is incorrect."

Motive can also be questioned if an experience fits the situation a bit too neatly or corresponds too closely with personal desires. Cheryl Nielson recorded a story from an acquaintance about feeling manipulated by an overeager boyfriend. The couple was engaged, but the young woman was getting cold feet. So her boyfriend went to the temple to pray to find out whether she was the one he was supposed to marry. He received a dream that night that his wife would be wearing a red dress. "He was completely convinced that it was an answer to his prayer in the temple," she remembers. The woman believed that her fiancé was misinterpreting the dream, both in its meaning and its divine origin. Further, she felt the story was coercive and called off the engagement (Nielson 1990, Wilson Archives). William A. Wilson recalls his own experience with such coercive tactics. "A young man who was dating my daughter off and on told her one day, 'I'm going to be a son of perdition and it's your fault.' When my daughter asked him what he was talking about, he replied, 'I received a witness from the Holy Ghost that I was to marry you, and by your refusing me, you are causing me to deny the Holy Ghost.' I think she suggested that he might like to visit a doctor."[21]

In many cases, the motive is selfish. Craig Bailey is only half joking when he laughs that "at least in Utah LDS culture, you can buy off a lot of excuses because 'I had a premonition,' you know? 'Oh, I didn't come because I felt this or I felt that,' kind of thing." However, the charitable impulse may also evoke suspicion. A stake president was about to speak at a funeral where an entire family except for one girl was killed in a car crash:

> Mom was saying that at the funeral, that the stake president—as he was preparing to say something to the daughter at the funeral—prayed and saw in a vision the pre-existence. And Heavenly Father was there, and this family was there. And he said, you know, good news, bad news type thing. And he's like, "The whole family's going to come up together, but one of you has to stay behind to pass on the family line and to do some important work in the family."
> And the daughter's like, "I'll do it."
> And the mom was like, "No. We can't let you do that."
> And she's like, "No. I'll do it."
> And the mom said, "As long as she can find her fiancé, the man she's supposed to live with for the rest of her life, before you take us."
> And two weeks before they were killed she was engaged.
> (Long 1995:14, Wilson Archives)

The student collector went on to ask his sister, the narrator, whether she believed the stake president really had the vision: "You never want to say he lied, and I don't think he did, but it was like comforting to the teenage daughter, it must have been."

Personal Connection to Experience: Memorate versus Legend

Believability and the ability to edify are also impacted by whether the narrative describes the experience of the speaker—a memorate—or that of someone else—a legend. The divide between memorates and legends is initially wide. Delbert Tenney is clear in his distinction between the two after narrating a story of his miraculous ability to free his father from a twisted yoke: "That's another miracle that happened. It's not some story somebody else told, it happened to me" (Hendrix and Hendrix 1994:185). Legends are inherently suspect. In her study of narratives involving angels, Sherami Jara was told by many of the people she interviewed that they would never use a legend to teach with because they could not have a strong personal witness that the story was true (2000:8, Wilson Archives).

Much of the power of edification is contingent upon a story being first person. Sharing a personal experience allows a person to invoke the Spirit and reexperience the Holy Ghost, something far more difficult with a secondhand story. "I think if something comes second person it loses a lot of the strength," explains Ken Jarvis. "If I'm telling you a story that happened to me, my spirit, witnessing to your spirit, this happened. This is real, this is true, there's a confirmation of the truth. There's not a doubt in my mind that it happened, and that same power, that same presence, is able to transmit to the next person.

"Second person? 'Yeah, friend of mine, Joey, had this thing happen to him' [*laughter*]. OK, well, you know, good for your friend Joey."

The restricted utility of legends is grounded in LDS doctrine and culture. Church members are expected to gain testimonies for themselves, to feel the Spirit that confirms doctrine. Other people's stories can be instructive and edifying, but they cannot and should not replace one's own testimony. "The problem arises," suggests William A. Wilson, "when we ground our testimonies on these [apocryphal] narratives." He goes on to explain: "If we base our faith on one of these stories and the story later proves to be inaccurate, what will happen to our faith?" Further, "If we pay too much attention to stories of other people's spiritual experiences, the stories can, even if true, divert our attention from our obligation to seek our own spiritual experiences" (1995a:52). Rich Tenney concurs: "People may worship the creation rather than the creator. Like an airplane pilot who gets off one degree, they are quickly far off course. They'll lose that connection. If that faith is based on that story, it's just fluff. It's a great story, but it's the message behind it that's important."

Despite the fundamental divide between a memorate and a story told second, third, or fourthhand in terms of edification and the ability to invoke the Spirit, legends and memorates are not bifurcated into isolated poles. There are stories told by people present during the experience but not by the protagonists themselves. There are secondhand stories from close family members and friends who are trusted implicitly. There are third and fourthhand stories where names are still known, even though the people themselves may not be. And there are unattributed legends where the basic plot may be all that remains. Stories have distinct genealogies that affect the extent to which they are believed.

As a story moves further from the person who received the revelation, it typically becomes less believable. When people share their own experience, they have the ability to invoke the Spirit and edify those listening. Edification is not impossible with legends, but the distance between the speaker and the Spirit is greater. Further, because the social reputation of the person receiving revelation is so important, knowing the person purporting to have had the revelation is vital. Unattributed legends, therefore, are easily dismissed, with too many people of unknown reputations separating the experience from the current performance. They are also perceived to be more susceptible to embellishment. In one unattributed legend shared among some BYU students, a mother is prompted to turn down her older son's heavy metal music, an act that results in the ability of her recently deceased younger son to finally make contact from the spirit world. While the listeners were initially "touched" by the story, one became skeptical after the narrator said she did not know if the story was true or not. "It could have been a story invented by some mother who was trying to deter her kids from listening to heavy metal music," the skeptical roommate suggests (Condie 1994:9, Wilson Archives).

Despite the room for exaggeration, embellishment, and outright invention in unattributed narratives of personal revelation, legends continue to be shared. One reason is that not all legends are created equal. Examining where a legend falls on a continuum of attribution and authority is critical in understanding how legends can be evaluated positively and why they continue to be told. In fact, experiences told by people other than oneself may even be preferable to memorates, since secondhand stories allow for more dramatic experiences to be shared without the dictum for humility. In Sunday school in the Burlington First Ward one morning, for example, the teacher begins with the idea of the right hand of God being about love, the left hand about justice and damnation. After identifying the topic, she introduces stories that she wants to serve as focal points for the lesson that morning. The first she informally titles "Tested and Found Wanting:"

I have a good friend, Jim Kaplan. He grew up poor. The only option open to him was to join the Marines. He was a tough, strong guy. After the Marines, he becomes an entrepreneur and makes a *lot* of money; very successful in ways the world judges to be successful. He lived in a neighborhood where the average cost of a home was six hundred thousand dollars.

He doesn't tell this story to very many people.

After a long day, he decided to return to the office to do some more work. At the elevator, he hears a voice, "Help me." He turns and sees a sofa but no one around. So he turns back but hears it again, "Please, help me." He turns again, and sees nothing and no one. Finally, the doors to the elevator open and he's about to get on when he hears the voice for the third time, "Why won't you help me."

Now his calling as First Counselor in the bishopric is to help LDS members who have been in jail get reacclimated into society.

He turns this time and sees a homeless man on the sofa. He lets the elevator doors close and goes and talks to the man, saying he won't give him money but offering to buy him dinner. The man says that would be great.

Jim picks up food at the drive-through and comes back but feels a nagging at his conscience. He gives the man the food and asks where he'll sleep that night. He's homeless, so Jim calls all the shelters in the area until he finds one with a space open. He drives the man to the shelter and registers him, giving the people his own name since he doesn't know the man's name. He then drives home, feeling smug.

But he can't sleep, and in the morning he goes back to the shelter to inquire about the man. When he gets there, the doors to the shelter are still locked; it's so early in the morning. He knocks on the door and when he finally gets in to talk to someone, they tell him the man is not there and that no one came last night and dropped anyone off. There was no record, no record at all.

Jim said he felt that he had been tested, and had been found wanting. It was very sobering. A month later, his business tanked.

He's built it all back up, but the story still haunts him.

The Sunday school teacher then introduces the second story, which she titles "He Bore the Countenance of Jesus Christ":

I first met Burt Carlton at a funeral, where people were packed along the walls and in the overflow area. We were standing beside each other and he turns to me and says how nice it would be to live a life where one is so appreciated in death. We continue talking and eventually we become friends.

At the time, Burt is a chemist and flavors food. But he has MS and his health is deteriorating and he falls a lot at work. Finally, he is fired. His employer tells him that a wrongful termination lawsuit will be less expensive than paying the insurance companies.

He goes home and finds that his wife has left him, taking half the furniture and half the kids—she takes the girl and leaves the boy. [*teary*]

He moves from California back to Utah, and moves back in with his parents in the ground level basement where he can avoid stairs. He gets another job and is appointed First Counselor to the bishopric to keep him busy, and tries to forgive his wife.

Finally one night, he has a dream where he sees Jesus who tells him that he bears Christ's countenance. [*long pause*]

Burt finally knew he had forgiven his wife.

Not long afterwards, his body finally gave out and he died. At his funeral, it was so crowded, the walls were packed as was the overflow area.[22]

The teacher pauses again, waiting for the story to sink in as well as to compose herself after sharing such emotionally charged stories. When she speaks again, she returns to the theme of the lesson and makes connections to the stories, the first about providing aid to those in need and truly loving thy neighbor, the second about forgiveness and redemption, a synthesis of love and justice.

These two narratives fall far outside the realm of the kinds of revelatory experiences typically shared in such large groups. Dramatic experiences such as visions, voices, and visitations are rare and are almost exclusively shared in small groups of intimate friends and family, particularly when God or Jesus is part of that revelation. Yet what may be inappropriate for the individual can be acceptable for the close friend as long as some degree of confidentiality is maintained (no one in the ward except the narrator knew these two men). Jim Kaplan tells only a few close friends; the Sunday school teacher tells the entire ward. The result is the inclusion of stories into the narrative tradition that extend the boundaries of experience into the more visceral and extraordinary. Such stories are memorable and can be particularly effective in teaching about the power of the Spirit (see figures 1-3, 6-5, and 6-6).

Because the Sunday school teacher is the narrator, her reputation is also a factor in evaluating the narrative. The visibility, status, and nature of her calling suggest her reputation is good. Because the stories are not personal, however, there is also the question of the reputation of the two men who received these revelations. The Sunday school teacher goes to great lengths to provide biographies for both men. In particular, she highlights Jim's role as First Counselor in the bishopric. He is also a prominent businessman outside the church, a fact less relevant than his spiritual reputation but helpful in establishing his credibility. In many ways, Burt is the polar opposite. We see him lose his job, his health, his wife, his child, and eventually his life. Yet he, too, is deemed worthy to hold a position in the bishopric, and his ability to forgive in the face of such cruelty is awe inspiring. His spiritual reputation is confirmed with the overflowing attendance at his funeral.

Not only can secondhand stories allow more dramatic experiences to be shared without drawing accusations of immodesty, but they can be more effective than memorates in highlighting the particular theological issue being taught. People worry in sharing their own revelations that their audiences will focus on them rather than the doctrine that underlies their experience. This is one of the fears of priestcraft—that human personality will overshadow the divine message. With secondhand stories, the person is effectively removed from the picture; the story is able to operate much like a parable, but with the power of specific human experience and the credibility of a specific source. Further, because the gap between the narrator and the person in the story is so small, people worry less about embellishment and error. For this reason, secondhand stories tend to be evaluated exponentially more favorably than third and fourthhand stories and unattributed legends that fall toward the other end of the continuum of attribution.

This is not to say that unattributed legends are never told, or that they can never be evaluated favorably. With sufficient authority propping them up, even unattributed legends can carry powerful spiritual weight. Such authority is achieved almost exclusively through the backing of the church. While secondhand legends are used frequently by the General Authorities during general conference, as leaders share stories from the people they have counseled over the years, unattributed legends are common as well. James E. Faust, Second Counselor of the First Presidency, recounted the following story during general conference on September 30, 2006:

> A few years ago, a young man who was starting his senior year in high school resolved to nourish himself by studying the scriptures for half an hour each day. As he began reading the New Testament, he hit a stumbling block. He didn't feel the anticipated spiritual high, and he wasn't getting any insight. So he asked himself, "What am I doing wrong?" Then an episode at school came into his mind. He and some friends had been sharing jokes—some of which were not so funny, and downright shameful. He not only had joined in but had even added some off-color comments of his own. Just as he thought this, his eye fell on these words in Matthew: "But I say unto you, That every idle word that men shall speak, they shall give account thereof in the day of judgment" (Matthew 12:36). He knew that the Spirit had directed him to these words at this time. He turned from his Bible and offered up a prayer of repentance.
> The answer to his question "What am I doing wrong?" was simple. He was reading the scriptures, marking the scriptures, and even enjoying the scriptures, but he was not living the counsel given in the scriptures. As he renewed his scripture reading and tried to live by Christ's example, he soon noticed how different areas of his life began to blossom. By incorporating the scriptures into his life, he had added an important spiritual nutrient. (2006:53–4)

James E. Faust does not attribute the story in his talk, although the story *is* attributed in the transcript of his talk available online and published in the *Ensign* magazine the following month. The story comes from Carl Houghton, who sent in his memorate to *New Era*, a magazine for young adults in the church (Houghton 1987). While some listeners that morning might assume the story is from someone James E. Faust knows, many will hear an unattributed legend. With only the weight of his authoritative role in the church, the story rises from the least believable category of narrative to one of the most.

James E. Faust's decision not to include the young man's name in his talk is standard practice. Leaders reference devout young women, confused young men, faithful church members, dying ward members, excited newlyweds, and humble widows but protect individual names. Names distract, drawing attention to the person rather than the principle. Without names, the stories can be drawn out of their specific contexts, interpreted as parables with the weight of truth, and reapplied in the lives of all those listening.

While many members are wary of teaching with legends, legends that bear the weight of approval from the church are acceptable, even desirable. Teaching manuals regularly include stories of personal revelation, sometimes attributed, sometimes not, with the expectation that teachers will share them during their lessons. Such vetting by the church allays fears of spreading false rumors that may detract from church doctrine. Stories published in official church magazines such as the *Ensign*, *New Era*, *The Friend*, and *Liahona* carry similar weight. While many of these stories are attributed in the magazines, church members follow the precedent set by church leaders and rarely mention names when they quote these stories during church talks.

Legends shared informally among peers are among the least valued in terms of spiritual edification and believability. They are, however, valued as entertainment, particularly among young adults. The archives at USU and BYU are rife with legends shared among college students. Dorm rooms serve as particularly fertile settings for legends, as they do on campuses across the country.

Yet despite their entertainment value, dramatic legends can also be useful tools for exploring doctrine. While most of the unattributed legends shared among peers are not believed outright, they may not be fully discounted, either. Those church members who do share legends have often commented after a particularly incredible account that while they did not know if they believed a particular experience actually happened, they maintained that the doctrine underlying the experience was true. Cynthia Sollis, for example, records a story her father told about a woman driving through the desert with her young son without enough gas to get to the next gas station. "She felt prompted to say a prayer for their safety," he narrates, "and as she prayed, she heard a voice tell her that if she wouldn't look at her gas gauge until they reached the next service station, all would be well." She upholds her end of the bargain and God upholds his. Cynthia notes that "my dad doesn't know the person to whom it happened, and he is unsure of whether or not it is a true story" yet adds that her father "loves to hear and tell stories that illustrate the power of faith" (1997, Wilson Archives). For Cynthia's father, even a legend that may not be true can nonetheless confirm church doctrine and promote faith in the church.

Because of their dubious origins, such stories are typically shared socially rather than during church instruction. Accordingly, stories may not edify or be believed but may nonetheless succeed in encouraging members to evaluate church doctrine and search for a more complete testimony of the truth of their church.

Form and Aesthetics

Audience members are not immune to the power of good storytelling. While the bulk of evaluation is centered on spiritual and social dimensions, members also allude to formal, stylistic, and aesthetic qualities that make a good performance. In an article titled "To Be Edified and Rejoice Together," Sunday school general president A. Roger Merrill recounts a story attributed to past LDS president Spencer W. Kimball:

> Consider the response of President Spencer W. Kimball when someone once asked him, "What do you do if you find yourself caught in a boring sacrament meeting?" President Kimball thought a moment, then replied, "I don't know; I've never been in one."
>
> With his long years of Church experience, President Kimball had undoubtedly been to many meetings where people had read their talks, spoken in a monotone, or given travelogues instead of teaching doctrine. But most likely, President Kimball was teaching that he did not go to sacrament meeting to be entertained; he went to worship the Lord, renew his covenants, and be taught from on high.[23]

Both President Kimball and A. Roger Merrill affirm the importance of edification and religious instruction over any other criteria for evaluating church meetings. Yet in doing so, Merrill points out that church members, even President Kimball himself, recognize poor oratory in church. Church talks should be orated, not read; animated, not monotone; spiritual, not secular or self-serving. Similar norms apply to the narration of personal revelation.

People laughingly complain about stories that meander all over the place, muddying the message and driving away the Spirit. Stories should have a clear narrative structure that leads a person from beginning to middle to end. Further, in order to be useful for teaching, there should be a climax of action and a conclusion that provides clear evidence of the hand of God (see chapter 3).

In formal settings like testimony meetings, stories should be short and to the point. In many wards, fast and testimony meetings begin with a member of the bishopric reminding the congregation: "Keep your testimonies brief and gospel centered." The connection to church doctrine should be unambiguous. In casual settings, stories can be longer, developed with detail and personal significance, though the connection to doctrine should remain evident.[24]

Good, effective stories support church doctrine. Those that violate stewardship or seem to contradict a particular theological tenet are rarely shared (see chapter 4). The performance should also be sincere. A person should not overdramatize their narrative, as it renders the experience less believable and the speaker less reliable (see Eliason 1999:145). Paralinguistic elements, such as tears, are common to performances but are complex in how they are evaluated. Judged sincere, they bolster a performance considerably. Judged insincere, they undermine credibility. That judgment has as much to do with the individual audience member as with the performer and the performance.

Conversations about formal qualities of the performance of memorates are rarely explicit among church members. Despite the central and vital role of storytelling in LDS culture, the term can smack of the secular and risk demeaning the sacred. "For most members of the church, nuances of intellectual concepts are not edifying," explains Shawn Tucker. "As brilliant as people might think that they are, it's in the storytelling that we really connect with our experiences and connect with God. I think it's a lot more important. I think that in the church, we don't want to call it storytelling because it can seem like it trivializes it."

There are, however, members in the church known as good storytellers. The current president of the church, Thomas S. Monson, is one. Yet the criteria people use to assess good storytellers center on the secular elements of their stories, not the sacred (see Mould 2011). Verbal genres cast primarily as secular—such as jokes—or that can accommodate the secular—such as fast and testimony meetings, which often blend temporal trials and achievements with spiritual ones—are more likely to be assessed for their formal, aesthetic qualities. For testimony meetings, for example, many members comment on the lack of sincerity, the rote delivery, and the subsequent boredom that ensues during some testimonies: "I see people who, I mean when they get up and bear their testimony, I see people who I'm excited about, because of certain things. I see people who I'm like, 'Can we just turn on the tape recorder from the other five thousand times you've done this?' Which is fine, you know? But for me as an audience, is maybe not as interesting, you know?" Others point out the tendency to ramble on and on, jokingly referring to the meeting as "slow and testimony" or "open mic Sunday," when anyone can get up and say anything, suggesting an amateurish quality to the testimonies and their delivery.

While such formal assessment is common with testimonies that typically involve the temporal trials of life as well as the confirmations of spiritual truth, it is rare for memorates, which are inherently and exclusively spiritual. Recognition, much less critique, of formal elements of the sharing of spiritual experiences can be uncomfortable, pointing out the secular, temporal, even artificial dimensions of the generic form. Such discussion forces attention to the gap between experience and narrative.

That gap and the formal, structural, and aesthetic qualities of narratives of personal revelation are explored in depth in chapters 3 and 4. While such analysis risks violating emic analysis of the tradition, asking questions of the narrative tradition generally eschewed by the people who share these stories, there is equal risk in ignoring the creative dimension of expressive culture or the power of generic form to shape interpretation. Further, LDS men and women constantly struggle to distinguish truth from embellishment. The vast, culturally constructed divide between memorates and unattributed legends makes it clear that people are very much concerned with the role of the individual, the process of transmission, and the nature of generic style and form in the narrative tradition of personal revelation.

Variation in Performance

The majority of the factors that contribute to the evaluation of a narrative performance are dynamic, shifting as people negotiate and renegotiate their social identities, narrate new experiences and borrow from others, and encounter audiences who may be more or less open to revelation than others. Of all these variables, the situational context of performance is one of the most dynamic. Different situations demand different norms for performance. Stories appropriate in small groups, for example, may be less appropriate in large ones. Evaluation of a narrative performance is at least partially contingent on setting, participants, and function, all factors that can shift from one context to the next. In fact, one of the most effective strategies in negotiating the risks of sharing personal revelation is to carefully choose the situation for sharing.

Oral traditions are particularly vibrant because they are re-created anew each time they are shared, except in rare instances when verbatim repetition is demanded (such as in rituals where particular phrases or formulas must be repeated exactly or they will not be effective). Narrators assess their setting, audience, and goals for sharing their story and proceed accordingly. This dynamism ensures that a story told in one setting may not be interpreted in exactly the same way as in another.

Setting

The most common public setting for sharing stories of personal revelation is the church; the most common private setting, the home. In the church, there are ample opportunities for sharing stories in the three formal parts of a church service: (1) sacrament meeting (and once a month, fast and testimony meeting), (2) Sunday school, and (3) priesthood or Relief Society, depending one one's gender. There are also a multitude of church-sponsored activities that may prompt the sharing of personal revelation, including fireside meetings and summer camps for the youth, father/son campouts, activity days, missionary splits, baptisms, missionary farewells and homecomings, and temple trips. Outside of the church, Latter-day Saints may have "missionary moments" virtually anywhere, engaging with nonmembers at work, in shopping malls, in their neighborhoods, and on vacation, occasionally sharing their revelatory experiences. Dorm rooms are particularly significant for BYU students, as is the classroom. At home, stories may be shared during family home evenings or more casually and spontaneously around the kitchen table or over dinner with friends. The norms for performance in these settings can be plotted roughly according to in church versus outside of church, public versus private, and formal versus informal. Each binary represents a continuum rather than isolated poles, with norms for performance shifting accordingly.

Participants

The binary of in church versus outside of church can be applied to participants as well. Experiences are shared most often among LDS members, but they may also be shared during missionary moments and casual conversations with non-LDS friends and acquaintances. Participants can also be identified according to social role, whether in binary contrast to another group—leader versus general member, teacher versus student, member versus investigator, parent versus child—or simply by the nature of the relationship—friends, family, coworkers, missionaries. Many of these roles are clearly hierarchical, others not, but each role has its own expectations for how and when to share personal revelation. Specific demographic characteristics can also be mapped, such as gender, age, and ethnicity. Distinguishing between a Relief Society meeting of adult women versus a priesthood meeting of adult men for example can be important in understanding how meaning is constructed through performance.

Function

The enumeration of participants reveals some of the basic functions of sharing personal revelation. Teaching is the largest, subsuming a variety of very different kinds of teaching situations. There are, for example, fairly formal teaching settings in classrooms with an authoritative teacher, as with Primary and youth Sunday school, seminary, training at the Missionary Training Center, temple preparation classes, and some BYU classes. Slightly less formal and hierarchical are adult Sunday school classes, where the teacher leading the group is viewed more as a peer; teachers provide structure and topics but much of the discussion comes from the congregation. Less formal teaching situations can occur in the home during family home evenings. Missionary work typically occurs in the home of the investigator, but more casual missionary work can occur anywhere. In addition to basic instruction, missionary work further functions to move people toward conversion.

Sharing stories of personal revelation can also function to edify speaker and listener. Where teaching can be thought of as focusing on the intellectual, content-driven elements of theology, edification focuses on the affective, spiritual dimension of religion. The distinction between teaching and edification, mind and spirit, is hardly firm or exclusive. Good teaching leads to edification and edification can lead to intellectual understanding. Both can lead to testimony building and confirmation of the Spirit.

As a social act, stories of personal revelation can function to establish bonds between people as well as create and negotiate social identities. By sharing their own experiences and revelations, people can extend a hand of support and guidance to others.

Synthesis and Emergence

Setting, participants, and function all intersect to shape performance and explain how and why stories are shared. Some stories are carefully incorporated into planned talks. Missionaries have stories they use to illustrate specific tenets of the church and may use them again and again as an illustrative tool. Members asked to speak during sacrament meeting often draft their remarks, making sure to include stories to capture attention and cement abstract concepts in daily life. Often, however, stories of personal revelation are shared more spontaneously. In counseling a friend, a relevant revelatory experience is recalled and shared. A casual conversation among friends about an upcoming baptism inspires a story about the personal revelation a woman received before her own son's baptism. Physical as well as discursive settings can prompt stories, such as the icy roads that inspire one woman to share a dream she had that saved her from a wreck on a similar icy road years earlier (Van Orden 1971:4, Wilson Archives). In many cases, the topic of conversation that inspires the story retains the focus. In such cases, a story serves as an example to further discussion rather than divert it. In other cases, however, the story may reorient discussion altogether. One memorate inspires another as people take turns contributing their own stories. Generic form rises to the fore and provides the coherence for conversation.

The sharing of personal revelation can function in both sacred and secular contexts, with both sacred and secular goals. Some functions primarily serve the speaker, others the audience, but most serve both. While some performances invite multiple interpretations, negotiation, and discussion, others are presentational, even authoritative. Formal teaching tends toward the monologic, informal teaching and casual conversation toward the dialogic.

The situational contexts for the sharing of personal revelation narratives are vast. Despite the virtually infinite combinations of factors that can contribute to the creation of a performance, there are some fairly typical performance contexts. By describing and analyzing typical contexts, it is possible to discern the rules—best understood as shared expectations and norms—that govern these performances.[25]

Church

Both the formal structure and informal norms of LDS church services and activities encourage the sharing of personal revelation at church. Going to church typically involves spending three hours at the meeting hall. Just over an hour is spent in a worship service, another hour in Sunday school, and the third hour in priesthood or Relief Society meetings, depending on gender. The youth have their own groups, initially divided only by age, but by age twelve they are divided by gender as well. On Wednesday nights, groups such as Boy Scouts and Activity Day Girls meet at the church. On weekends, wards or stakes may sponsor special events, firesides, campouts, and dances. Church members also gather to help each other in service—help a member move, do yard work for an elderly member, or clean a part of the highway the group has adopted.

In areas where buildings are in short supply, multiple wards may share a single church building. In these cases, the order of the service and the chosen day for extracurricular events vary. In Provo, Utah, for example, where the Mormon population is regularly estimated at 90 percent, a single building may house three, four, even five separate wards.[26] In Burlington, North Carolina, the percentage of Mormons in the area is fairly small, though because of the sizable Hispanic population, the church building houses both the Burlington First Ward and the Hispanic Second Branch. In the fall of 2009, the LDS population grew sufficiently for the First Ward to split into two separate wards, both of which still use the same church building. Until the split, the Burlington ward began with sacrament meeting, followed by Sunday school, then priesthood and Relief Society. Now that the ward has split, the Burlington First Ward continues to follow this schedule, while the Burlington Third Ward operates in reverse order.

Worship Service

Sacrament Meetings

On all but the first Sunday of the month, the worship service is a sacrament meeting. After prayers, hymns, and the passing of the sacrament, the three members who have been asked to speak that Sunday give their talks. In many wards, a teenager gives the first talk, followed by two adults, often a woman followed by a man. The final speaker is afforded more time than the others to speak, though he may end up with less time if the first two speakers are particularly long winded. The speakers are generally given three weeks to prepare their talks. Some begin by pondering the topic in their hearts, searching their own experiences and testimonies. Others begin with formal dictionary definitions or Bible indices to find scriptural references to guide them. Others move directly to the many online and print resources provided by the church to aid in exactly this task.[27] Most members will use a combination of these resources. Further, most members realize the importance of the personal anecdote, not only to capture and keep the attention of the audience (as suggested in the "Ten Tips for Terrific Talks" entry on the church website), but to make theology understandable.

"When I was writing my talk, one of the things that was lacking in that talk and that Nicole even picked up on, too, was that there weren't very many stories," Shawn Tucker explains, describing a recent sacrament meeting talk he was preparing that he shared first with his wife. "And that's what, as audiences, that's what we latch on to. That's what makes these abstract principles concrete. That's what really gives them the credibility of lived experience."

Stories are crucial to a good talk, but they should never displace the spiritual theme of the talk. Nor should the individual. Because the LDS church is a layperson's church, members must teach members. Sacrament meeting provides the equivalent of a sermon for religious direction. Doctrine must claim center stage. When stories of personal revelation are shared, they are framed by the assigned topic, serving as an example rather than a focus.

Because of this focus and because of the process for constructing a talk, speakers may draw upon stories from their own lives as well as from church publications and church leaders. While memorates dominate, legends from church sources carry the weight of church sanction and are therefore appropriate for formal instruction.

Fast and Testimony Meetings

The first Sunday of the month is a fast and testimony meeting. Members fast before going to church and then spend the worship part of the service bearing their testimonies before the rest of the ward. While the emotional power of spiritual edification and experience can emerge in the sacrament meeting talks that occur on the remaining Sundays of the month, it is during fast and testimony meetings that emotions more quickly and commonly bubble to the surface. Despite the common introductory warning from the bishopric to keep testimonies "brief and gospel centered," fast and testimony is a time for lay members to come forward as individuals, where their lives and their stories take the foreground. People's testimonies are formed on their knowledge of the truth of church doctrine, so a person's testimony is presumably gospel centered. Yet testimonies are also deeply personal and grounded in the events and experiences of a person's life. In addition to using fast and testimony meetings to espouse the truth of the church, people use them to express gratitude to Heavenly Father for the blessings they have received, as well as to family, friends, and church members for their support. The result is that fast and testimony meetings are as much about individual members and their experiences as they are about LDS doctrine.[28]

While personal stories take a subservient role in sacrament meeting, they are often the driving force of fast and testimony meetings. Not only are the stories provided more prominence, they are often less polished and more emotionally raw than in sacrament meetings, for a number of reasons. For one, people prepare their sacrament meeting talks over several weeks. With the luxury of time, they are able to ponder the topic and their lives and experiences, searching for stories that can be used to illustrate their talk. Old, well-worn, oft repeated stories are as useful as new ones. And for those new ones, time allows practice in sharing, getting used to the idea of reliving a particularly sacred experience. Much of this preparation is codified, as most people write out their sacrament meeting talks to alleviate nerves and ensure smooth performance.

For fast and testimony meetings, on the other hand, such preparation is rare. There are people who have specific times they bear their testimony, such as on the anniversary of their baptism or at regular intervals, but rarely is participation more premeditated than waking up that morning with a feeling that they should bear their testimony. More often, people are prompted while sitting in the pews moments before rising to speak. Further, people often use fast and testimony meetings to share their most recent experiences, ones they are continuing to interpret. In fact, fast and testimony may be their first time narrating the experience at all, much less to a large crowd. The result is a narrative that may lack polish but can be invigorating for being so fresh and emotionally charged. Lack of definitive interpretation or full appreciation of the significance of the experience before speaking can result in epiphanies in the act of speaking.

Further, because people are temporally closer to the actual experience, they may be more apt to experience the same heightened emotions as when they initially received the revelation. In the sacred space of fast and testimony meetings, crying is acceptable, even desirable, for both genders.[29] In fact, tears are so common that a box of tissues perennially sits on the podium.

Because fast and testimony meetings are personal expressions of faith, legends are rarely if ever shared. The personal dominates. Stories shared during fast and testimony meetings also differ from those in sacrament meeting due to the structure of the event. In sacrament meeting, three speakers are selected in advance and prepare their talks regardless of the others. While the quick-thinking speaker may make reference to previous speakers, the talks and the stories shared within those talks are monologic. Fast and testimony is marginally more dialogic. While members do not engage in back and forth dialogue, it is common for one member to be inspired by the testimony of another. Speakers make explicit reference to previous talks and share their own experience in order to add support, suggest an additional dimension, or (rarely) to contradict a point made earlier. The result is that testimonies may derive not only from the internal impulse to share one's personal testimony but also from the external prompt of another person's story. While fast and testimony meetings *can* be a series of self-contained monologues, they as often lead to an emergent dialogue among members.[30]

Finally, a major difference between sacrament meetings and fast and testimony meetings is the assumed motive of the speaker. Talks given in sacrament meetings are invited. The request comes from the bishopric and carries with it the weight of authority. The assumption is that speakers are there out of duty, not personal interest. Many people begin their talks noting how uncomfortable they are speaking in front of crowds. Speakers in fast and testimony meetings, however, are entirely self-selected. Ideally, the motive for speaking derives either directly from the Holy Ghost or from the religious expectation that all members should regularly bear their testimony as a means of strengthening their own faith and that of their fellow members. However, if a member wants attention, fast and testimony meeting provides an open forum to claim center stage. This explains why so many members admit to doubting some of the stories of personal revelation shared during fast and testimony meetings. Consequently, the strategies for establishing humility are employed heavily during fast and testimony meetings. People avoid specific, scriptural terms for revelation and express doubt or ambiguity about the divine nature of the experience. For others, the risk of being misunderstood is too great. People regularly bear testimony that they *know* that God answers prayers, and they *know* that the Holy Ghost provides guidance in life, making it clear that they have received such answers and guidance but without providing specific narratives that exemplify this testimony. Instead, many save dramatic stories of personal revelation for other settings, even other parts of the church service, such as Sunday School or priesthood or Relief Society meetings, when spiritual memorates may be explicitly invited and more clearly relevant to a particular theological claim.

Sunday School

Sunday school is typically the second part of the three-hour block of Sunday services. Children aged three to twelve go to Primary, while the adult men and women gather for a lesson taught by one of their peers who has been called to serve in this position. Different wards and different teachers will have different norms for how class is run. In the Burlington First Ward, there have been some teachers who have maintained fairly tight control of the lesson plan, while others have encouraged more collaborative discussion. In all, however, teachers ask for some degree of participation from the other members, such as questions, comments, and stories from their lives to clarify the topic at hand. One Sunday in the Burlington First Ward, the topic of the lesson was miracles. Having heard these stories shared before, and asking permission to call on them before class began, the Sunday school teacher specifically asked two women to share their experiences with miracles. The stories were dramatic and involved clear divine intervention. Shared during fast and testimony, they may have been viewed with skepticism. Shared by invitation, they were well received.

The Sunday school setting is also more spatially conducive to humble sharing. Rather than standing on a raised platform at a podium with a microphone in front of a captive audience as during sacrament and fast and testimony meetings, people share their stories from their seats among their peers. Many people will hear a story without clearly seeing the person sharing it.

Finally, Sunday school is smaller than the worship service. The youth are in Primary with their adult teachers, investigators and their teachers are in a separate Gospel Principles class, while some members leave after the worship service. In the Burlington First Ward, Sunday school is less than half the size of the worship service. With a smaller audience and less formal structure, people are more likely to share their sacred experiences.

Priesthood and Relief Society Meetings

The benefits of Sunday school are multiplied for priesthood and Relief Society meetings. The adult men and women divide for their respective groups: men to priesthood, women to Relief Society, again, halving the number of people in the group. Further, after a hymn and announcements, the priesthood splits again into High Priests and Elder's Quorum. The result is an atmosphere of even greater intimacy and collegiality, with similarly democratic seating arrangements for performance. Further, because less active members of the church have gone home by this point, people can be more assured that their peers share their degree of spirituality.

Priesthood and Relief Society meetings are even more dialogic than Sunday school. Leaders regularly ask members to share their experiences with the group during that day's discussion. In addition, the missionary president in the Burlington First Ward typically begins priesthood meetings by asking members if any of them have had a "missionary moment" they would like to share. Often these "moments" include a prompting from the Holy Ghost that brings them in contact with someone open to hearing the gospel.

The division of genders and the more dialogic nature of these meetings also make them more conducive to the sharing of the personal and the sacred, particularly in supporting each other, offering advice, and working through personal problems together. Josette Bailey explains: "We share those stories quite a bit to help each other and to build each other's testimonies. So there's a lot of sharing that goes along in Relief Society. In fact, those I think are my most favorite lessons. When people . . . not so much the right-out-of-the-book. The stories, experiences, where you can really go, 'Yeah. I've been there. They've survived it, I can survive it. That was a prompting. I should have noticed that was a prompting.'"

Josette may not always receive a specific solution to a specific problem, but the experiences shared by the other women give her hope in facing her own trials. This sharing can be very emotional, far more so than among the priesthood. "Women are more teary," Josette continues. "We cry. It's a tear fest most of the time [*laugh*]. Everybody's passing around the tissue. That's probably the main difference. I don't think the guys are in there crying the whole time. But yeah, emotions I think are definitely there when it comes to Relief Society." Her husband, Craig, laughs, adding that the Relief Society probably has better stories. "They don't couch their stories in football analogies and racing analogies."

The topics and themes of the stories each group shares also reflect traditional gender roles. Of the archived stories told in Relief Society meetings or all-women homemaking clubs at the church, two themes dominate: marriage and children. Other themes that appear regularly are genealogy work and the deaths of relatives. Men, on the other hand, share personal revelations related to their jobs and missionary work, though they, too, share stories about raising their children. Family, particularly children, is a consistent theme for both (see chapter 5 for a more complete discussion).

While tears are not as socially acceptable in priesthood meetings as they are in fast and testimony meeting, men often share problems they are facing. Like the women in Relief Society, men respond with stories of personal revelation they have received in their own lives. In priesthood meetings, the focus is perceived to be more heavily weighted on solving problems than on providing emotional support through shared trials. Shawn Tucker points out that rarely are revelations allowed to remain ambiguous, or worse yet, wrong, in a priesthood meeting. Explanations are sought and suggested. After struggling to interpret a particularly ambiguous dream, Robert Foster asked the priesthood for help. He did not narrate the full dream; it was too personal, too confusing, too raw. But he asked about particular images and whether any of them were familiar. His brethren tried to help, offering various interpretations, but the dream remains ambiguous to this day.

Gender also plays a role in who tells legends. While legends are taboo in fast and testimony meetings, they are occasionally shared during Sunday school, priesthood, and Relief Society. Like sacrament meeting with its focus on instruction, these meetings are framed as classes as much as meetings. Personal stories typically carry more weight, but legends can be usefully shared to further the goal of learning and edification. Legends shared are often drawn directly from lesson guides provided to the leaders and tend to be heavily didactic, though church settings across the board encourage clear, faith-promoting stories with morals that can be easily extracted. One young woman growing up in Provo, Utah, heard the following story in Sunday school, at a Young Women's Camp gathering, and at a baptism:

> Little Billy loved to play baseball and he played everyday with his friends. He even slept with his mitt under his pillow.
>
> One day, when he came home from a day of playing baseball, he had a strange look on his face. So his mother asked him, "How was the game today?"
>
> And little Billy replied, "Today, I was playing center field and something told me to take off my glasses. I didn't want to at first, but then it told me again. So I took off my glasses. When the ball was hit, it came my way and it bounced up and hit me in the face."
>
> If Billy had been wearing his glasses, he could have had a serious eye injury.
>
> Moral: We are supposed to listen to that still small voice. It is the Holy Ghost and the Holy Ghost is there to help us. We just need to listen.[31]

It is not insignificant that two of the three settings for this story were restricted to groups of young women. While men will share legends drawn from church leaders and magazines in the act of teaching, they are less likely to share unattributed legends socially than women. A study devoted to the collection and analysis of legends is necessary to explain why this is the case.[32]

Church Classes, Meetings, and Activities

In addition to Sunday church services, there are a host of other church classes, meetings, and activities where stories of personal revelation may be shared. These activities can be sorted according to one of two models: the monologic teacher-to-pupil model or the dialogic peer-to-peer model. In the teacher-to-pupil model, teachers share stories as authorities on a subject to illustrate a particular point with the primary goal of education. In the peer-to-peer model, stories are shared in dialogue, resulting in a broader range of functions that include but are not restricted to education, edification, and support. Both models may be employed in a single setting, as in Sunday school, priesthood, and Relief Society meetings. Classes and meetings such as seminary and temple preparation tend to foster the teacher-to-pupil model and occur as part of a planned program. Other activities are a mix between the monologic and dialogic. Youth conferences, firesides, and campouts have programmed elements where stories may be shared as part of instruction, as well as social time where peers may share stories as much for entertainment as for spiritual edification and instruction. Home teaching, where active church members make house calls to other members in the church to teach and encourage continued faith in the church, also employs both monologic and dialogic discourse. Memorates and legends may be shared in both models of discourse, but as discussed earlier, their reception will vary dramatically.

Missionary Work

Missionary work also combines monologic and dialogic models of narrative performance, varying according to audience. The opportunities for sharing stories as part of the missionary effort are vast because of the pervasive missionary element to LDS religious life, the structure for training, and the nature of the work. Missionary work can extend throughout one's life, since "missionary moments" can occur at any time, anywhere. Latter-day Saints are expected to always be prepared to discuss their church with others with the hopes that they may eventually join the church. Active members often go on "splits" with full-time missionaries, accompanying them to the homes of investigators. Upon retirement, some older couples serve missions together. The most common mission experience, however, is the mission that young men between the ages of eighteen and twenty-one undertake for two years, though it is increasingly common for young women between the ages of twenty-one and twenty-five to also go on missions for a year and a half. For men, having served a mission is a clear marker of identity, a rite of passage that confers social and religious status.

Before heading out into the mission field, all missionaries from the United States and many from abroad spend time at the Missionary Training Center (MTC) in Provo, Utah.[33] For up to three months, soon-to-be missionaries follow a grueling schedule of classes on doctrine, teaching the gospel, effective communication strategies, and language if they are going abroad. As in all religious instruction in the church, stories are used as illustrative examples. MTC trainers share personal experiences as well as legends. Not surprisingly, many of these stories involve promptings and revelations that missionaries have received to aid them in their work. As such, the stories serve to inspire the soon-to-be missionaries and encourage them to seek their own personal revelations in the field. The parents and wards of young people about to leave for their missions often throw going-away parties at which people, particularly older men who went on missions when they were younger, share stories of their own missionary experiences, including stories of personal revelation received while in the field.

Once the young missionaries hit the mission field, they begin a strict regimen of tracting, religious study, and prayer. Much of their daily work is spent teaching people about the church. In the course of these "discussions," missionaries share their own memorates as well as legends they learned during training at the MTC in a teacher-to-pupil model. Missionaries are also encouraged to share their experiences during monthly zone conferences that bring together all the missionaries in a particular area for instruction and fellowship. As in priesthood meetings, there is a mix of instruction and peer-to-peer sharing.

As important to the narrative tradition are those moments when elders can relax and socialize with one another. Elders are always paired, though rarely for more than three to six months, after which they are moved to a new area with a new companion. In addition, missionaries may go on elder splits, where two pairs of nearby missionaries trade companions for a day. The result is a constant revolving door of companions and mission fields. With each new companion comes a period of acquaintance. Sharing common missionary experiences dominates these introductory periods and carries into future social interaction. The result is a snowballing of stories, as missionaries share not only their own stories but those of past companions. In short order, memorates become legends. Despite their intense focus on spiritual growth, some of these stories are shared more for entertainment and social cohesion than edification. Most of the stories express the concerns of the missionaries themselves, both spiritual and tempo-ral. Stories about spiritual tracting dominate: a missionary prays to be guided to a person receptive to their message, the Holy Ghost guides them accordingly, and the person ends up baptized. Other stories include revelations about the girl back home. While most stories depict the missionary as the receiver of the revelation, occasionally they are the fulfillment of revelation, as in the common story of an investigator having a prophetic dream about the arrival of two men in black pants and white shirts with an important message (see chapter 5 for a discussion of these themes).

When missionaries return from the field, they are expected to speak to their wards in multiple venues—sacrament meeting on any regular Sunday as well as on Missionary Sundays (the rare fifth Sunday of the month), fast and testimony meetings, Sunday school, and priesthood meetings. While the first months upon return are the most concentrated for sharing their experiences, they will continue to narrate these stories for the rest of their lives.

Despite the common denominator of the missionary narrator, context matters. As returned missionary James Oliveros explained: "I have found that missionary stories vary widely depending on the context and environment. When missionaries tell stories during church services and in front of parents and family, we share faith-promoting experiences. These stories are told to edify members of the church, helping to increase their belief in God and His work. However, the purpose of these stories and the stories themselves change when missionaries share entertaining stories with the purpose to scare, excite, and humor our audience" (Oliveros, 2001:3, Wilson Archives).

Outside Church

The divide that separates church from nonchurch settings can be mislead-ing. The distinction is easily demarcated if "church" includes only a building. However, churches typically extend far beyond their walls, hosting conferences, meetings, summer camps, club groups, sports teams, and excursions to places near and far. Church *sponsorship* is a far more useful criterion for division by identifying those activities structured, organized, and led by the church body. Gray areas persist, however. Men and women who have received an official church calling as a missionary may share stories within the exercise of their official duties. However, informal conversations among active missionaries may be shared outside of this official frame, allowing for greater freedom in narra-tion. Such informal conversations also can occur at church-sponsored camps and meetings in those spaces between official programming where individuals chat to pass the time, connect with their peers, and explore their faith. Family home evenings pose a similar categorical dilemma. Encouraged and structured by the church, family home evenings are clearly church sponsored in concept and intent. Families may use guides and materials produced by the church in order to lead these evenings of worship and spiritual growth at home. However, the home setting and the informal nature of these evenings for many families suggest a context perceived as outside of church.

The distinction is not irrelevant. While many of the social settings outside church may continue to encourage faith-promoting stories, there is greater latitude in storytelling than in church-sponsored events. Stories may be shared for entertainment and social bonding. Informal settings outside the church also provide an avenue for the kinds of sharing that are typically absent in church meetings: stories that are messy, unresolved, or ambiguous. They may not clearly confirm the truth of one of the principles of the church but instead focus on personal issues in people's lives.

Appropriate contexts for sharing personal revelation outside the church cannot be identified in a static list. Any place can be appropriate if it can be transformed into sacred space. A dorm room can be the setting for a loud party or an intimate gathering of close friends. The same is true of one's home, a place that regularly fosters both the social and the sacred among family and friends. While the church is generally assumed to be sacred space, it can also host secular events such as basketball games and Boy Scout meetings. Even at church, sacred space is consciously created. Formal dress and opening and closing prayers help to frame religious activities within the church as sacred activities. Prayer is the most common and powerful agent in transforming the secular into the sacred, both in church and outside of it. Family home evenings always begin and end with prayer. Many of the interviews I conducted in the homes of LDS members began and ended the same way, preparing the participants to explore the sacred experiences in their lives.

Without formal prayer, sacred space can still be created in informal settings. Conversation can find its way to sacred topics. As it does, laughter becomes more rare, the tone more reverent and circumspect. Narrators pause significantly before sharing a sacred story and often begin with an implicit entreaty to the audience to respect what follows by noting how sacred and special the experience is to them.

This is especially true of stories shared among young members of the church, in dorm rooms at BYU or at church camps and youth meetings during the summer. Legends may be told more often during contexts that remain fairly secular, where the primary goal is to entertain, and often shock, one's peers. However, legends can be told as sacred narrative, even if they are not decisively believed, and these stories may help create sacred space sufficient for sharing personal experiences and more deeply felt stories heard from one's family and friends. In BYU dorm rooms, common themes address the tragic deaths of young people (particularly in car accidents), dating, marriage, and missionary experiences. These reflect the visceral, practical, and religious concerns and experiences of those sharing the stories. Typically missing, at least from the stories collected in archives at BYU and USU, are revelations dealing with schoolwork, exams, and the mundane activities of student life. Personal revelation stories have also been shared and recorded on bus trips and at beauty salons, football games, and dinner parties. In these more public and secular venues, the stories shared are predominantly legends rather than personal experiences, the actions fantastic and dramatic rather than humble.

More than any other setting—in or out of church, formal or informal, public or private—the home dominates as the primary place for sharing personal revelation. The home provides intimate space for conversations among friends and family, where concerns about social perception diminish. People are wary of sharing personal revelations with anyone who might misconstrue their motive, humility, honesty, or sanity. So, deeply personal stories that would never be shared publicly at church may be shared in private settings at home.

Family home evenings, family councils, and more informal conversations around the dinner table can all provide the setting for sharing personal revelation. During family home evenings, the setting can be fairly formal, with a clear topic for discussion and a goal of religious instruction as the primary function. Less formal conversations are no less powerful, though they may be less didactic. Further, among family members, personal revelation can function in more immediately relevant ways. Many revelations directly impact the family. In these cases, revelations are shared for the joint benefit of the family. Revelations about buying a new home, taking a new job, deciding to have children, and raising those children are all extremely common (see chapter 5). Less immediately relevant, but no less important, is the goal of creating and maintaining family histories through the sharing of personal revelation narratives. The experiences of grandparents, great-grandparents, and even older pioneer ancestors are important parts of a family's history. Stories of their personal revelations serve not only as faith-promoting stories but as character portraits of loved relatives. For a culture that so highly values family and record keeping, and for a people who expect to be reunited with their ancestors in the celestial kingdom for all eternity, such stories serve important cultural, social, and personal functions. These smaller, private settings provide an atmosphere where stories no longer need to be so clearly didactic or faith promoting. The personal can dominate the theological without negative evaluation.

Case Studies in Context

Describing the various settings for the performance of personal revelation narratives is a useful but incomplete step in understanding and appreciating the narrative tradition of personal revelation. While space does not allow for all of the narratives in this book to be resituated in their performance contexts and analyzed accordingly, a few narratives can serve to illustrate how these stories emerge in specific contexts. The result is not only a descriptive glimpse of the performance but also a better understanding of the norms for the performance of personal revelation narratives. Those norms emerge in the study of a single performance as well as in the comparison of performances. As Richard Bauman argues, tracking a particular genre across different settings can be a particularly fruitful way to explore it.[34] Tracking a specific narrative across multiple contexts can be equally fruitful, helping to isolate the elements of a narrative that remain relatively constant from those that change. It is also possible to identify the multiple meanings that emerge in separate performances.

In my fieldwork in North Carolina, I recorded narratives in two distinct contexts in two distinct ways. The first was in church. While many Christian churches in the United States video record their services to air on public-access television, share with homebound members, or archive for posterity, LDS churches typically do not. General conferences led by church leaders in Utah are recorded and broadcast around the world, but Sunday services in wards are more humble affairs, led by lay membership. No one I spoke to thought tape recording church services was appropriate. Taking notes and recording services by hand, quietly and unobtrusively in my pew, however, was fine. And that is what I did. The narratives from church services are re-created here from thorough notes taken during the service and transcribed directly afterwards. The results are transcripts that cannot be entirely verbatim but are fairly complete in terms of content, phrasing, and word choice. I paid particular attention to the use of specific terms and turns of phrase. I also recorded gestures, tone of voice if it varied during the performance, and instances of emotional display such as tears and laughter. While nuanced questions about style and diction cannot always be asked of such transcripts, questions about theme, content, phrasing, gestures, and voice quality can.

The second context was outside of church in informal settings among family and friends. Sometimes stories were shared after I specifically asked about their revelatory experiences; other times stories emerged more naturally according to the topic we were discussing. Once one story was shared, others often followed. Further, as first interviews turned into second ones, and then into third and fourth, formal interviews became conversations among friends. Accordingly, while it might be tempting to categorize only those stories shared in church as occurring in a "natural" context, the fact is that our conversations at home often mirrored the same casual conversations held among friends and family. Most often, these conversations are held among other Latter-day Saints, but not always. Time and time again, people recounted stories they had shared with coworkers and neighbors—friends all, Mormons none. More important than religious affiliation was a shared value placed on the sacred. I was not a Mormon, but I was sincere and respectful.

Often I heard a story in church that I heard again informally in a person's home. Sometimes this was because I actively sought out the storyteller, but as often, it was because I already knew the person and simply asked about the story at our next meeting. The result is that most of the stories I recorded by hand during church I recorded again with an audio recorder in informal settings among family and friends. Comparison of the two performances reveals subtle rather than dramatic variation, yet descriptions of each provide a more complete appreciation of the narrative tradition of personal revelation.

Case Study 1: Sacrament Meeting versus Home Among Family and Friends

Sacrament meeting the morning of April 13, 2008, had begun with a hiccup. There was no bread for sacrament. Announcements had been made, the opening hymn sung, the invocation given, and ward business addressed, but still no bread. Craig Bailey leaned over and whispered that he had never been this far into a service before bread arrived. But it did, and after quiet, relieved laughter, the service began.

As usual, three members were tapped to speak that Sunday. The order was familiar: first a youth, then a woman, and then a man. The first was Jeremy Harper, a high school student asked to speak on the topic "How to Be in the World, But Not of It." He spoke from experience, discussing the temptations of premarital sex and illegal drugs that he sees threatening his peers daily. Echoing a worldview common, though not universal, among Latter-day Saints, Jeremy cast the temporal world as a place of struggle and temptation, where Satan worked to lead the righteous astray. The solution was to set one's sights on the spiritual world and resist worldly influence.

Next to speak was Pauline Clayson. She had been given the topic "The Despair We Feel in Our Lives." Within the first few sentences, Pauline framed her talk around the idea of hope, the antidote to despair. She quoted scripture to show how hope, coupled with faith, can lead us through despair. Again quoting scripture, she pointed out how hope and faith lead to charity. Then, from behind the podium, she pulled out an uninflated yellow balloon. She likened despair to the balloon. "When we are full with joy, we float in the wind. But despair is a balloon without air, deflated and useless." She paused:

May I share with you an example? And let me say that I do not have this principle, so this was not something I expected to happen.

I was lucky enough to care for my mother in the last years of her life. She came to live with us. She was very spry, very alert. She always moved around well. One day, she was different. She wasn't herself. She wasn't sharp.

She told me she had met with people, relatives, who had died years earlier. She was watching TV and a cow came on the TV and she mooed at it. This was not my mother.

She had had a little bit of dementia, but you could always carry on a normal conversation with her. I knew something was wrong, but I'm not a nurse and I didn't know what to do. So I prayed. And the Lord said, "Take her to the hospital."

So I did. And when they took some tests, they found out she had a very bad infection. They hooked her up to tubes and gave her medicine.

The next day, she was just laying there in the bed like a vegetable. And the nurse came in and had forms she wanted me to sign to discharge her. And I was incredulous. How could they discharge her? She could barely move. The nurse said she had the medicine and that's all they could do for her. The forms were for her to be discharged to a convalescent home where they would take care of her. The nurse said her dementia would never get better.

I started praying.

I just couldn't believe it and asked her what would happen if I didn't sign it. She said they would take over custodial rights from me. I was feeling despair. I asked if I could take her back home. She said I could but I would have to sign a form that said I was doing this against the doctor's recommendations. All I knew was that the Lord was saying, "Take her home."

So I told her to go get the forms and I would sign them. I felt like a fugitive, like I was robbing a bank. I had to find a wheelchair to get her out to the car. We were racing around. My daughter asked if I knew what I was doing. I got the Suburban but it took ten minutes to get her up into the seat. She only weighed a hundred pounds and I knew I couldn't lift her, but somehow the strength came and I was able to get her into the car and home.

Might I suggest this is hope?

I had no idea where I was going with her or what I was going to do. But I got her home and as I was leading her down the hallway, an incredible peace came over me that I had done the right thing. The next morning, she woke up back to her normal self. She lived fourteen months longer of a comfortable and good life. I had faith I didn't know I had. I listened to what the Lord wanted me to do.

Pauline returned to her talk, picking up on the despair she felt before applying her faith and hope in an act of charity thanks to the guidance provided her by God. Her talk was moving, no doubt edifying for many in the congregation, some of whom came up afterwards and told Pauline so. I, too, lingered to compliment her on a powerful talk, adding that I looked forward to talking to her more the following evening, when I was set to sit down with her and her husband Paul for another conversation.

The following night, Paul greeted me at the door of his home. His son Justin was just back from his mission in Italy and was home for a few months. Younger siblings Carlee and Cameron, both in high school, were also there, along with a friend of Cameron's, a young woman who was Christian but not Mormon. Pauline fixed root beer floats and we all sat down to talk, with Cameron and his friend coming and going during the evening. After about an hour, we came around to Pauline's talk in church and I asked if she would mind sharing it on tape:

> Pauline: We as a family had the opportunity for caring for my mother during the last couple of years of her life. It was kind of unexpected. She had come out for Justin's graduation from high school. And she had just come for a visit. And it ended up happening that she took ill while she was visiting and it seemed right that she would just stay with us for a little bit longer. And a little bit longer grew into a little bit longer, and during that period of time, we had a number of instances that happened that to me were a marvel. But this particular instance seemed to clarify what I was speaking on, on Sunday. So I chose to use it.
>
> She had been feeling quite well. She had been making bread the night before. Carlee was being home schooled at the time, and so we were together, the three of us were together twenty-four/seven. And the next morning my mom woke up and she just didn't seem quite right. She kind of had been babbling, she was talking about uncles that had come to this house in Salt Lake who had never been there,

and actually were dead. And she said they had come and
were talking to her and telling her things. And so we thought
maybe it was . . .

Paul: Maybe they were.

Pauline: Yeah. We've gone back and said maybe they were.

But, then when she started talking to the television, and
having these conversations . . . Cameron's closest friend . . .
his fondest memory of my mother is when she turned to the
television and a cow came on and she . . .

Cameron: There was a cow on the screen. And she looks at me and
goes, "Mooooo" [*laughter*]. So I did it back at her. That
used to be our, how we talked to each other. It was awesome
[*laughter*].

Pauline: Anyway, she was just acting strange. And then when she'd
get up to leave the dining room, the dining room area to
her bedroom, it kind of seemed like she didn't have quite
the balance she should have, and I thought, "Oh no. Maybe
she's had a stroke or something."

So, the impression was very clear: "This isn't something
you can deal with. Get her to the hospital."

So I didn't even take the time to call the doctor. Carlee
and I got her in the car, I mean she was able to walk there
with our help on either arm, and got her into the Suburban
and drove her to the hospital and took her into the emergency room and they quickly identified the fact that she
had a very severe urinary tract infection. Which in elderly
individuals can manifest itself in severe dementia.

And we were learning a lot about this as our time went on.

So they put her into the hospital, started giving her
IVs and antibiotics, and they said within a day or two,
this should clear. And we stayed, Carlee and I would stay
twenty-four/seven. We found chairs that we could sleep on
and that way we knew every doctor, every nurse that came
through, every pill that they gave her, every time they took
a blood test and every time she was ever in the hospital; we
lived there.

And this particular time, we got to about the third
morning, and we were expecting her to wake up brighter,
more clear headed. But instead she seemed worse, worse
than ever. She was very much like a vegetable, laying in
that bed and when the nurse came in, I was anticipating
being able to talk to her about what the doctor had said
and diagnosis and all. Her only intention was to come in
and talk to me about signing papers to have her released.
And I was appalled at the thought that she would want to

release her. And I said, "You don't understand. This woman is in this state, but this is not something that has been coming on. She was fine; just three days ago, she was making bread, talking to us as a family, walking around on her own. Something has happened."

And she said, "Well, from all of our testing, there's nothing more that we can do . . ."

And this is a large hospital in Utah.

". . . there's nothing more that we can do for her and we need to transfer her to a convalescent center."

And I said, "She does not belong in a convalescent center. We need to identify what's wrong with her and make sure that the diagnosis is correct."

And they turned to me and said, "What you need to realize is that your mother has severe dementia, and dementia can come on at any time, and with any strength," and that "she will never recover out of this, she will not pull out of this. And the best place for her is at a convalescent center."

And I said, "What if I refuse to sign these papers?"

And their reaction to me was, "We will take custodianship away from you, and we will admit her to the convalescent center anyway."

And I started having these fears of someone taking my mother's responsibility out of my hands. And it just frightened me. And I started praying like crazy. Just in my heart. And I had no idea what I was going to do. There seemed to be no options.

And what kept coming back to me was, "Take her home."

But that seemed really dumb, so I dismissed the idea. And as I continued to talk to this nurse, the thought came again, "Take her home."

So I asked the nurse, "Well, what happens if I want to take her home?"

"Well," she laughed at me and said, "you're welcome to take her home, you just have to sign a form that says that, going against the better judgment of the personnel at the hospital, you are choosing to take her home."

And I said, "All right. Give me that piece of paper and I will sign it."

So she left the room. Carlee and I looked at each other. She thought I was absolutely insane. I mean, she'll do whatever I ask her to do, but, "Hey Mom, you're nuts" [laughter].

As I looked at my mom, and she was just lifeless, and hooked up to IVs, and the nurse came back with the papers, I signed them, they removed the IV from her arm, and walked away. Walked away.

And I just remember thinking, "Now what?"

So I said, "Carlee, go find a wheelchair." So Carlee went, found a wheelchair. Between the two of us, we maneuvered my mom to the edge of the bed, changed her clothes, got her into the wheelchair, gathered up her goods, and headed down the hallway.

And like I said on Sunday, I felt like I was robbing a bank. It was like I had to get out of there as fast as I could before somebody took my mother away from me.

And we got to the elevator, and we went down the elevator and headed to the front door, and I still thought, "Somebody's going to catch us. Somebody's going to stop us; I'm doing something wrong."

And we took her to the front curb. Carlee stood at the front curb with my mom in the wheelchair. I ran to get the car like it was this mass emergency. Drove around and pulled up in front of the hospital. And between us, it was nearly impossible to get this little hundred-pound woman up high enough to get her into a Suburban seat. Had it been a normal car, it would not have been a problem. But I had to literally lift her up. And after trying everything possible, I just put one arm under her back and one under her legs, and with all the strength I could gather, I just lifted her up and sat her in that seat and we buckled her in and we took off, feeling guilty. And I called my sister along the way and gave her the word that I was traveling with mom in the car and she said, "What are you doing?"

I said, "I don't know. But all I know is that I'm supposed to take her home."

So we get her to the house, and we don't have a wheelchair at the house; we've never needed one. So, we went into the office and, like the chairs that are in there, that are on wheels. We brought that chair out to the car, slid her down out of the Suburban and got her situated onto that chair and Carlee held her in place while I pushed her up the walkway. And then we had to go up a couple of steps and got her into the house, wheeled her down the hallway and into her bedroom. Got her into bed and there was almost a peace that came upon her. She was irritated when we were traveling, but there was almost this peace when we laid her down in the bed. We covered her up. And I remember walking down the hall thinking, "I don't know what I'm doing, but I do feel relief. I feel at peace. This is all right. I don't know why, but this is OK."

And then we spent the next day or so spoon-feeding her. Chicken soup, pastina that she would eat very easily. Anything that we felt . . . yogurt . . . anything that we felt we could get in her because she no longer had the IV to keep her alive.

And it took a day, and she was communicating with us, and moving around more normally in bed, but her legs were still weak.

By the second day, she was up and moving with a walker. And from then on, she just gained strength to the point where she didn't need the walker any more.

Now months went by, probably another year went by and we did really well with her until she fell and broke her hip. And then it was another series of going downhill.

But even with those, we had amazing experiences with hospitals. All of our experiences were with doctors and hospitals where we became . . . we were the caregivers. Not the hospitals, not the doctors. It was through listening to the Spirit, encouraging us what to do, and our doing it, that changed the outcome of her stay in the hospital.

The two narratives are noticeably similar. Both provide the basic plot: her mother took ill suddenly, the Lord directed her to the hospital, the doctors and nurses were misguided in their diagnosis, the Lord directed her once again this time to return home, and her mother recovered. In both, Pauline expresses fear, doubt, and confusion. And in both, she ends her story with confirmation that if we listen to the Spirit, we will be guided and blessed. The ultimate meaning of the story remains consistent.

The differences are minor but not insignificant. In sacrament meetings, a person is given ten to fifteen minutes to speak. Stories must be concise if they are to be incorporated into a talk. At home, Pauline has the luxury of time; her story takes about eleven minutes to narrate. With this freedom, she provides a far more detailed and personal account of her experience. She provides background to her mother's condition. She explains the mooing at the television, a detail that may have stuck out as particularly odd during sacrament meeting but becomes understandable as a significant bonding moment between her mother and her son.

The two performances also vary according to how they are framed. The story in church is told to illustrate a talk on despair and is framed accordingly, with the hope that can be achieved through faith in God. She uses the term "despair" explicitly. Her second performance the following night follows an hour of conversation about personal revelation. While the specter of sacrament meeting lingers in the performance at home, carrying with it the theme of hope and despair, she pays more attention to the general concept of revelation.

The anxiety she felt is visceral in both accounts. What becomes clear in her narration at home, however, is that her decision to follow the promptings of the Spirit was not an easy one. At home, she recounts how she struggled to distinguish the voice of the Holy Ghost from other interferences—whether her own desire to get her mother to a place more hospitable than the hospital, or darker influences trying to lead her into making a bad decision. This struggle to interpret the source of a prompting is central to the experience of personal revelation.

Finally, there is the issue of humility. In both performances, Pauline expresses humility, yet she does so at different points in the narrative and in different ways, allowing her to meet the norms specific to each setting. In sacrament meeting, she humbles herself by stripping away the authority thrust upon her by the very nature of the event. She has been chosen by the bishopric to speak to the entire congregation. She stands at a podium set apart and above the rest of her ward. She has a microphone and the expected attention of everyone in the room. Yet twice, she asks permission of her peers to indulge in a personal experience and her own interpretation of that experience. She introduces her story by asking rhetorically, "May I share with you an example?" As she nears the end of her story, she suggests an interpretation of the events by asking, "Might I suggest this is hope?" Despite the authority granted her by the bishopric and the setting, she conforms to social expectations for humility. She also conforms to religious norms for humility by addressing the limitations of her testimony and her knowledge. She does this within the narrative performance but outside the specific narrated event: "And let me say that I do not have this principle, so this was not something I expected to happen." By "this principle," she is referring to not having a clear testimony about personal revelation. Again, she helps to ensure that her fellow church members view her as a peer, someone struggling to gain testimonies in the doctrine of the church.

By establishing her humility as a framing device for the narrative that follows, she frees herself to narrate her story according to the norms of a faith-promoting story: I prayed, I listened, I acted, I was blessed. In keeping to the model of personal revelation as faith-promoting story, the narrative places the focus not on Pauline as an atypical member with an atypical experience but on her message: God can replace despair with hope if you have faith.

In the second narration a day later, Pauline has no need to strip away the trappings of authority. There is no bishopric, podium, microphone, or captive audience. Instead she is at home surrounded by family. Further, there is no expectation for her to narrate the model of a faith-promoting story, or to confirm the power of hope to drive away despair through faith in God. There remains, however, a religious expectation for humility. Rather than separate her bid for humility from the narrated event, Pauline highlights her human frailty in the experience itself as she hesitates to act.

Pauline's experience is confirmation of the caveat she gave in sacrament meeting: that she does not "have this principle." In action, rather than as introduction, she admits to not always discerning the voice of the Spirit. By incorporating her shortcomings into the narrative, she makes the performance more personal than doctrinal.

Case Study 2: Sunday School versus Home and Restaurant

On the morning of September 10, 2006, members of the Burlington First Ward found themselves without a Sunday school teacher. Steve Anderson had been called as the missionary president, but no one had yet been called to fill his previous position as Sunday school teacher. Shawn Tucker had been asked to step in. Whether leading Sunday school, Elder's Quorum in priesthood, or the Young Men, Shawn's teaching style is often humorous but always participatory. On this morning, Shawn opened with a question: "Why is the Bible important?" Members of the congregation were quick to provide answers: it is a road map for life, a rule book, a set of expectations for the faithful, a history book of what the Lord has done, and a description of our human tendencies. The lesson continued, with members contributing the bulk of the content. Discussion moved to apostasy, the Second Coming, gratitude, and then to promptings. To ignore a prompting is to spurn God's gifts. To ignore a prompting is to suggest we know better. This is pride, and therefore exhibits a lack of humility and gratitude, Shawn reasoned, tying the loose threads of discussion together. He then quoted Amos, who prophesied a famine of God's voice (8:11–12). Shawn interpreted the passage to mean that if you stop listening, God will stop talking to you. Many in the congregation echoed their agreement, but not all. One woman said she believed that God will keep after you, keep hounding you and will not give up on you. Shawn agreed but pointed out that you have to listen carefully: "It's quiet, it's small, you have to listen for it." "It speaks to the heart and the mind," clarified another member.

And then Shawn did what many church teachers and leaders in Sunday school, priesthood, and Relief Society do: he asked if anyone had any stories of when they had been prompted that they would like to share. Shawn's question was open ended, but the larger frame established by the connection between gratitude and revelation guided the speakers. Shawn's father-in-law, visiting the ward that Sunday, volunteered that promptings had saved his life twice, but he chose not to elaborate. Keith Stanley picked up on this idea of being saved and shared a story of being prompted to take a different route home one night:

> I was driving along Highway 87. That's the road I always took to go back and forth to Sherrie's house.
>
> One night, I thought to take a different road. I shrugged it off but it came again, really strong. So I did.
>
> Well, I read in the paper the next day about an accident on 87 that was at the same time I would have been driving. It would have been me in that accident.

Keith quietly sat back down to the affirming nods of his peers. Paul Clayson then stood, moved by Keith's story:

> I was visiting California for work and I had a few hours before I had to be at the airport. My in-laws lived in town so I thought I would drive over and visit them.
>
> As I was driving, I drove right past the house of my former brother-in-law and I felt I should stop in and see him. I ignored this prompting and kept driving. But the prompting came back again. "Go see Skip."
>
> But again I ignored it and I went on to visit my in-laws.
>
> Three days later, after flying back home, I was in church and someone came up and handed me a piece of paper. It said my brother-in-law had died.
>
> I had not followed that prompting.
>
> Promptings can be teaching experiences. I've tried to listen every time now.

Just as Shawn attempted to tie disparate parts of conversation together by linking humility, gratitude, and revelation through logical argument, Keith and Paul responded through story to the remarks of the speakers who preceded them. Keith chose a narrative about having his life saved, just as the previous speaker had. He also referenced the issue of gratitude, if implicitly: "It would have been me in that accident." And finally, Keith picked up on the theme of taking God's gifts for granted when he described how he initially ignored the voice of the Spirit. The dialogic nature of his narrative—referencing the topics and themes of previous speakers—is repeated by Paul Clayson, who also ignored a prompting from the Holy Ghost.

Both Keith and Paul shared these stories for me again, in more private settings. Six months after he shared the story in church, I met Keith Stanley for an early supper at a local restaurant in town. We chatted casually for a while before I turned on the tape recorder. Keith knew the focus of my research and once the recorder was on, we focused right away on personal revelation. I asked him about the difference between revelation that comes as a response to prayer and revelation that comes out of the blue, and which, if either, was more common to him:

> Well, lots of times, I have found for me, in my personal life, it kind of comes when things happen. There's times it comes where when you're praying for it that, you know, you do get those promptings to do certain things.
>
> I always talk about, to me, something that was a personal revelation was . . . and it goes back to when I was seventeen. I lived about twenty miles away from where my wife now lived down here in Burlington.
>
> I was headed home one evening from a date, and it's a straight shot to my house down 87. And something kept telling me to go a different way. You know, and I kind of like brushed it off. Came again, that strong prompting, to go a different way, and I did.
>
> Didn't know why . . . until the next morning. There had been an extremely bad wreck at an intersection that night during that time that I would have been coming through.
>
> So to me, that's kind of been a firm belief that I, you know, to follow the promptings. To me that was a personal revelation that came to me.
>
> And I share that with my kids, and I've shared that with the young men. Many times, you know, we brush those promptings off. And sometimes we don't do the things we should, you know, that we're prompted to do, and we find out, you know, results, that's not the same.
>
> And so, that's one that I remember when you talk about something that just kind of happens. It's not something that you prayed for, but it was a prompting that came, that to me, is probably the reason I'm here now.

Keith narrated the story assuming I had not heard it before. Just as when he shared the story in church, Keith interpreted his experience as an example of how important it is to listen to the promptings of the Spirit. Rather than tailor his narrative to a particular issue, Keith chooses a narrative that fit the situation. The situations, however, varied. In Sunday school, following the prompt of the teacher, his narrative served as an example of how important it is to listen to the Spirit. In the restaurant following my prompt, his narrative served an example of how personal revelation can come out of the blue.

There are other subtle differences. His narrative is longer, but not dramatically so. He explained when he typically shares this story and why. More importantly, however, he used the terms "personal revelation" and "prompting" throughout his narration. Both the performance in Sunday school and that in the restaurant came after unequivocal framing of the discourse as being about personal revelation. Yet only in the more informal setting, among a small, familiar audience of one, does Keith label his experience explicitly. In Sunday school, he refers only to a thought, but in the restaurant, he uses explicitly religious terms. The obligation for public humility in church among many is mitigated in informal settings among few.

Paul Clayson's narrative is also similar to his public performance in church. When he shared this story at home with his family and me, it was a year and a half after he shared it in church. He does so the same evening Pauline shared her story about her mother and the hospital. Pauline not only prompted him to share this story but provided the frame for its interpretation.

> Pauline: Have you told him the story about Skip?
>   Paul: I don't know, I may have. I think I did. My brother-in-law who I was . . .
>   I was in California one time and I was . . .
> Pauline: This is an example of hearing the Spirit and not adhering to it.
>   Paul: I can tell you far more stories about when I haven't paid attention [*laughter*].
> Pauline: That's right.
>   Paul: But I was driving along, I was there on business . . .
> Pauline: This would be in California.
>   Paul: . . . and her parents live in California and her sister and brother-in-law had been divorced and her brother-in-law lived on a street going to her parents.
>   And I was going over after a business appointment and I was going over to see her parents. And I thought I needed to try to stay in good graces with these guys [*laughter*].
> Pauline: They love him.
>   Paul: And as I was going down the road, I looked over to where his house was coming up, where he now lived, and I thought, "You need to go see"—his name's Skip—"you need to go see Skip."

I thought, "Yeah, but I really want to go see her parents."

So I kept driving and as I passed his house, I thought, again, it was just a very strong . . . prompting, "You need to go see Skip."

And I kept going. Turned the corner, headed down the street, and a couple more times going down that street, I just thought, "You need to turn around and go see Skip."

And I didn't, and I didn't.

And I didn't. I went to her parents, had a great time, visited with them, got done, had to rush to the airport, got on the plane, went back, this was on a Friday. Got off the plane. Saturday went by.

And on Sunday, I was in my church meetings. I was sitting up on the stand because I was the stake president at the time. I was sitting on the stand and I happened to just notice the door in the back of the chapel open, and somebody walk in.

And the instant that door opened I knew they were coming to talk to me. I mean, I just . . .

So I watched them walk right up, walked up, handed me a note, across the dais there. And it just said "President Clayson" on top. And I picked up that note and I opened it up and it said, "Your wife called. She wanted you to know that her sister called and said that Skip passed away in his sleep last night."

And wow, did that hit me with a ton of bricks.

I don't know what I would have said to him. I don't know what benefit it would have had. I just know that I was prompted to go visit him for some reason and I didn't do it.

And those kinds of things sometimes can have as dire a consequence as following revelation can have positive consequences.

And I've never forgotten that. It's been a real governing thing to me. And I try, when I feel strongly about something, to follow what I'm bidden to do.

Pauline: But again, that's part of that practice; it's part of reviewing your life and saying, "I heard it, I knew it, I chose not to. Next time I will listen more closely, next time I will be more obedient." It's just all part of the learning process.

The interpretive frames for the two performances—one in Sunday school, one at home—are identical: shared as an example of the perils of ignoring the Spirit. In both performances, Paul uses the term "prompting" explicitly. He humbles himself in the eyes of his audience not through linguistic choices but from details specific to his experience: ignoring the Spirit.

As with Keith Stanley's story in the restaurant, however, the setting encouraged adjustments in performance; in this case, that led to a longer, more detailed narrative wrought with emotion. Paul repeats his failings to heed the Spirit: "And I didn't, and I didn't. And I didn't." Unanswered questions linger in his mind: "I don't know what I would have said to him. I don't know what benefit it would have had. I just know that I was prompted to go visit him for some reason and I didn't do it." Plagued by what he should have done, he is reminded by the experience to listen next time. In church, Paul's story is primarily doctrinal, a reminder of appropriate action; at home, it is far more personal, a record of a very real experience that continues to affect him emotionally as well as intellectually and spiritually.

Both Keith and Paul share their stories regularly. Their experiences have become touchstone narratives: stories they return to again and again to remind themselves and others of the importance of listening to the Spirit. Their meaning and use is so well established that Keith regularly tells the story when teaching, and Paul's wife is so familiar with the story and its interpretation that she instigates and frames the story for Paul. This familiarity leads to a performance that is shared between husband and wife, dialogic both in how it emerges in conversation as well as how it is performed.

Case Study 3: Gospel Principles Class versus Home

When people refer to Sunday school, they generally mean Gospel Doctrine, the class intended for members of the church. During that same hour, however, many wards have a Gospel Principles class for investigators of the church, although anyone is welcome to attend. In the Burlington First Ward, a few senior church members come to help ensure discussions are robust and engaging, since investigators may not be able to contribute much to the discussion of doctrine. The class serves the function of missionary work, and the full-time missionaries assigned to the ward typically attend.

On the morning of March 2, 2008, three investigators, the two ward missionaries, and six church members had come to class. The topic that Sunday was "The Gift of the Holy Ghost." Craig Bailey was leading the class that week and had wrapped small boxes, each with a different gift of the Holy Ghost written on a slip of paper inside. Discussion and the sharing of personal experience narratives followed the opening of each box. "The Gift of Tongues" inspired Steve Anderson to share his experience as a missionary in Guadalajara hearing General Authority Russell M. Nelson shift from English into "the most beautiful Spanish I have ever heard," prophesying that if people in attendance there that day continued to live righteously, the LDS Church would build a temple there, a prophecy that has been fulfilled. "The Gift of Healing and Miracles" led Craig to recount the famous miracle of the gulls and crickets along with his own experiences with "Mormon crickets." "Of course, miracles don't have to be so big or dramatic," Craig concluded. Paul Clayson picked up on the topic of small miracles to share his story of what he called the "simple miracle" of an answered prayer that brought a snowstorm to the Mojave Desert, keeping an investigator home long enough for the missionaries to finish their discussions and have him baptized.

The next box was "The Gift of Knowledge of Wisdom." One of the missionaries, Elder Ballantyne, offered his story of being prompted by the Spirit to know what to say to an investigator they met at a Burger King (the complete narrative appears earlier in this chapter). Elder Ballantyne's companion, Elder Bailey, followed with his story of listening to a speaker at the Missionary Training Center who abruptly stopped his talk and began talking about doubts the neophyte missionaries might have about spending two years in the field. Elder Bailey believed the teacher had been prompted to change his topic to address what they needed to hear at that moment. It was this context of knowing what to say at the right moment that led Craig Bailey to share the following story:

That's like what happened to me at work.
A woman I work with asked me where I was from. I told her Utah and immediately she asked me if I was a member of the church. Well, I was "Hssssss" [imitates a cat baring its claws, hissing].
I was in the South and I wasn't ready to show my colors yet, you know?
But I said, "Yes," and we talked about the church for a while.
I didn't know what to say to her, and I don't remember exactly what I did say to her, but I know that it was what she needed to hear.
And she's been talking to me a lot more about the church, especially now that her parents aren't doing so well.

A few days later, I was sitting with Craig, his wife, Josette, and their two children, Jarrett and Jordan, in their home. We were talking about anti-Mormon sentiment in the area, something that initially surprised Craig and Josette, having moved from Utah, where "everyone was Mormon." They shared the experiences they had had with skeptical, unfriendly, and downright rude neighbors, PTA members, and coworkers. "So I understand what it's like, a little bit, to be discriminated," Craig explained. "One of my great friends at work is African American and he's very timid about what he does. He always has this polarized view of the world that he doesn't get stuff because he's black or whatever. And until I moved here, I never would have even understood what that was like. And I can't say, I've been . . . I mean, obviously my plight is not the plight of the black man in the United States, especially in the South, but I understand that 'I'm not going to tell you everything about me' kind of thing, because I'm worried about what you're going to think." Craig goes on to explain:

> Like I said on Sunday, Jan—that's the other manager I work with that's been coming to me more and more talking about the church as her parents get ill. I probably had worked at Blue Cross a matter of weeks and she's like really open, she wants to know everything about everybody. "You're from Utah. Are you a Mormon?"
>
> And I wanted to keep my mouth shut and say, "No," OK?
>
> But I had that little experience where I was overtaken by the Spirit and I said, "Yes I am." And "blah blah blah blah blah." In some sense of the word, I did that against my will.
>
> Like I said, I was not ready to show my colors yet, and here I'd just been asked point blank the question I did not want to be asked. But obviously I think that happened for a reason.
>
> Because like I said at church, she's been coming back and more and more dealing with end of life issues with her parents and "What does your religion think about that?"
>
> I mean, she grew up Catholic, too,[35] and her parents are Catholic. And I wish I understood more about any religion beside my own but I don't. Because I'm a Utah Mormon and that's all there is there [*laughter*].
>
> But she comes and talks to me about different things, with the humanitarian work that the church does. She started giving me money on her behalf to donate to the church because it all goes to the cause; none of it is taken in administration fees."

Craig wraps up his story with the recognition that "if I had not told her who I was, if I had not shown her my colors, we probably wouldn't be having any of these conversations."

As with the stories told by Keith Stanley, Paul Clayson, and Pauline Clayson, the two versions are similar in content and plot. However, at home, Craig is far more explicit in his references to the prompting and the role of the Holy Ghost. In the version told at church, Craig glosses over any actual prompting or divine experience. The conversation is about gifts of the Holy

Ghost, so he can be fairly confident that his audience will understand that he felt divinely directed to open up to his coworker. However, his hesitancy in being explicit also reflects the more public setting of class and the greater need for humility.

The two stories are also framed differently according to the discursive context. In class, conversation about knowing the right thing to say prompts Craig's story and provides a dominant interpretation centered on this theme. At home, however, conversation about discrimination prompts his story, and the interpretation centers instead on this topic and the fear of revealing one's Mormon identity in the US South. In class, the story serves as an example of saying what needed to be said; at home, it serves as an example of receiving the guidance and courage to share his religious identity and the personal and missionary benefits of doing so. Both meanings are present in each performance, but Craig highlights different aspects according to the discursive situation.

Conclusion

Tracking the same story through different contexts makes it clear that narratives of personal revelation are fundamentally stable in terms of basic content and structure but vary substantially in length, interpretive focus, level of personal information and emotional attachment, strategies for establishing humility, and the degree to which one must negotiate a humble persona. In formal church settings, for example, narratives are typically subservient to the doctrinal theme of the speech event. Personal details disappear or are heavily abbreviated, making personal experiences more easily adaptable as parables to be used by audience members in their own lives. In more intimate and casual settings, narratives are richly embroidered, conveying not only religious doctrine but also family histories, personal views, and insights about both sacred and secular life. Among family and friends, shared familiarity substitutes for reliance on public reputation. While humility is always desirable, it is not as necessary as it is in public performance, where people avoid explicit terms for personal revelation, employ passive voice, and highlight doubt both external and internal to the experience. The public/private divide is less relevant for the degree of discursive engagement, however. The monologic nature of sacrament meeting talks contrasts with the far more dialogic nature of stories shared in other church meetings such as Sunday school, priesthood meetings, and Relief Society meetings, not only in how they emerge—with peers sharing stories back and forth—but also in terms of joint storytelling by family members and increased interjections, commentary, and questions between narrator and audience.

Tracking the larger narrative tradition reveals additional conclusions. For one, the level of formality of a particular setting—a criterion that implicates the location, participants, and goals of a particular performance—can dictate not only how a story is shared but what stories are shared at all. Typically, people do not share their most dramatic and sacred experiences in formal, public settings; the risk of ridicule and of accusations of immodesty are too strong. More intimate groups of close friends and family, however, encourage many people to share even these experiences. Secondhand stories provide a compromise by alleviating these fears, thereby drawing dramatic experiences into public performance.

Synthesis: The Paradox of Performance

The exploration of the social landscape of performance in the narratives of personal revelation among Latter-day Saints implicates a range of issues that extend to other cultures and other narrative traditions. One of the most significant is the paradox of performance, where social and cultural norms run counter to narrative and performance demands. The humility required for the presentation of a public self, coupled with the importance of socioreligious reputations and identities for the performance and interpretation of personal experience narratives, poses a paradox for performers that must be carefully negotiated for successful communication and edifying experience. Three interrelated issues emerge from this "paradox of performance"—humility, communitas, and the secondhand memorate—all of which implicate past and future scholarship in performance generally and religious folklore specifically.

Humility and the Performance of the Sacred

Permeating the performance of personal revelation among Latter-day Saints are efforts to remain humble while narrating an experience imbued with great spiritual and social power. The potential for stories of divine communication to confer social prestige and authority on their tellers, particularly in a religious community, is not uncommon. Hector Lee addresses this issue directly in terms of Three Nephite narratives: "It [telling Three Nephite legends] enabled any individual to identify himself with the functioning of his theology in a manner that would bring him attention and prestige. . . . That a Nephite experience is a means of securing social approval may never have occurred to most of our narrators. However, like nodding assent to a preacher's remarks, it can become an unconscious bid for attention" (1949:90–1). Crucial to the performance of personal revelation is the construction of an identity that is sufficiently humble to meet religious and cultural norms and sufficiently sincere to be believed, but also sufficiently righteous to make receiving revelation plausible. Negotiating the paradox between humility and prestige is hardly confined to personal revelation, Latter-day Saints, or religious memorates. Efforts to distance oneself from the power and responsibility implied by public performance have been recognized by scholars of performance theory from the start.

In his seminal and still eminently useful book *Verbal Art as Performance*, Richard Bauman provides a partial list of common strategies for keying performance, an act that provides clues about what will follow and how that expression should be interpreted (see also Goffman 1974 and Hymes 1974). That list includes special codes, figurative language, parallelism, special paralinguistic features, special formulas, appeals to tradition, and, most relevant here: disclaimers to performance (1977:16). It is not uncommon for people to begin a story by distancing themselves from it, claiming, "I'm just repeating what I heard" or "I'm not sure if this is true or not." Bauman describes these disclaimers as "a surface denial of any real competence at all," suggesting that the denial is primarily rhetorical. He goes on to explain: "Such disclaimers are not, of course, incompatible with taking responsibility for a display of competence, but are, rather, concessions to standards of etiquette and decorum, where self-assertiveness is disvalued. In such situations, a disclaimer of performance serves both as a moral gesture, to counterbalance the power of performance to focus heightened attention on the performer, and a key to performance itself" (1977:22).

Scholars have continued to explore disclaimers of performance as framing devices, noting how they can signal performance, rather than deny it (see, for example, Edwards 1984). Disclaimers and other rhetorical moves to mitigate "the power of performance" are not confined to introductory formula, however, and may move far beyond surface denials. Rather, deference and humility may be enacted throughout performance, in multiple contexts—a goal rather than a framing device.

Those contexts can be broadly cultural, though they may also vary according to social role or genre. In some communities, for example, youth may be expected to exhibit more humility than elders, women more than men, students more than teachers, confessors more than priests. In other communities, deference, distance, and humility may vary according to genre. Henry

Glassie's ethnography of the storytellers, singers, and musicians of Balleymenone in Northern Ireland reveals the surface denial of competence as a cultural norm: "Nothing brings censure more swiftly than an effort to make oneself seem 'bright'" (2006:67). For the wealth of verbal genres of wit and humor in Balleymenone known locally as bids, pants, and exploits, these denials quickly give way to star performances where men and women claim responsibility for their performances and deliver them with great skill, competence, and artistry. Other genres, however, demand more than introductory disclaimers and denials; heavy attribution and repeated evaluative comments that reflect back upon the story are needed, such as with stories of fairies where belief is both aggressively and ambiguously negotiated. The same is true among the Mississippi Band of Choctaw Indians. People readily share *shukha anumpa*—humorous personal anecdotes, tall tales, and animals stories—fully claiming responsibility for their stories and embellishing them to great comic effect. Stories about the origins of the world and the tribe, the sacred Nanih Waiya mound, and the prophecies that predict major, often cataclysmic change, however, are typically narrated more tentatively by narrators sensitive to the communal nature and power of these stories (see Mould 2003, 2004).

Perhaps not surprisingly, expectations of humility, coupled inextricably with sincerity, are particularly common in religious contexts. In his study of African American sanctified Christian communities, Glenn Hinson explores how church members evaluate their fellow members in the act of worship as they express themselves orally, visually, and kinesthetically. This evaluation is efficiently captured by the phrase "form and fashion," as in Brother Stevens's declaration: "We didn't come for no form or fashion. We didn't come for outside show" (2000:232). Form and fashion refer to the style of expression and the consciously manufactured persona that the insincere adopt to draw attention to themselves, *feigning* rather than *feeling* the Holy Spirit. This impulse displays a profound lack of humility and is criticized heavily by church members. Yet for even the devout, the paradox of performance remains. Members of the choir rehearse rigorously, investing themselves deeply in their musical performances. "Singers are quick to point out that their artistry is not theirs to claim," however. "'It's really the Lord's,' they say. 'We're just its vessels.' By denying their role as 'performers,'" explains Hinson, "singers thus deflect any acclaim their singing might garner, tacitly giving the credit to God" (238). These verbal disclaimers are general and easily employed in multiple social contexts. But the system of decrying the "form and fashion" performances of the insincere speaks to a far more pervasive culture of humility and sincerity.

Expectations for humility may also explain the common pattern of the redeemed sinner in Christian conversion narratives. William Clements argues that the persona that evangelical Christians construct in narrating their conversion experiences operates not only to emphasize God's power but also to persuade listeners to convert (1982:108–9). Such an interpretation assumes an audience of nonbelievers. Conversion stories are shared at least as often among fellow Christians, however, and in most churches far more often. In these cases, redeemed sinners are working less to identify with nonbelievers and more to establish their humility before God and their peers. The crisis conversion experience in particular, where conversion happens suddenly and dramatically, tends to focus on the humbling nature of the conversion experience, as in the Ur-form of the Christian conversion story of Saul being brought to his knees on his way to Damascus, a physical humbling repeated in conversion narratives in the past and today (Clements 1982:108). Brought low, the redeemed sinners are no longer a lost soul, but neither are they proud; their obedience and humility to God is expected to remain. Sharing these stories, however, no matter how humbling the spiritual experience, positions the speaker as saved, even righteous, and therefore endows some degree of prestige. Accordingly, analysis of the performance of personal revelation narratives by Latter-day Saints and of religious expression more generally suggests the merit of paying greater attention to the paradoxes raised by performance, where the social power of being "on stage" runs counter to the humility often demanded in social and religious contexts.

Communitas and Socioreligious Hierarchies

The power and importance of the construction of individual religious identities not only poses a paradox for performance; it also risks undermining the construction of communitas in religious expression. Communitas—as introduced into folklore and cultural anthropology by Victor Turner in his study of ritual—describes a state of human interrelatedness where a sense of togetherness and community spirit dominates and shared experience trumps social hierarchies. Of the different types of communitas that can exist in society, religious worship is most likely to strive toward and achieve existential or spontaneous communitas (Turner 1969:132). In the decades that followed Turner's work, folklorists picked up on the idea, applying it to the study of religious expression in both narrative and ecstatic performance. William Clements explored this intersection among the Baptists and Pentecostals with whom he conducted fieldwork in northeastern Arkansas in the 1970s, finding the concept of communitas useful in describing crisis conversions, glossolalia, and other encounters with the Holy Ghost that remove the individual from the social structure of human interaction and replace it with the unstructured experience of the divine (1976). Sharing stories of these experiences during worship services, particularly in the act of testifying, has the potential to reestablish communitas by foregrounding experiences shared throughout the congregation (42). Patrick Mullen found the concept useful as well in his study of Primitive Baptists in the Blue Ridge Mountains of North Carolina, arguing that the divine experience can erase social hierarchies of the world beyond the church: "Each member of the church exists within a political-economic-social structure with its own hierarchies and status positions; they may be farmers, doctors, or laborers in the outside world, but within the church they share in undifferentiated communitas as equals. Thus the rituals and formulas of the church service function symbolically to bring them together" (1983:35). And Elaine Lawless observed that during testimony meetings in an all-white, Pentecostal church in southern Indiana, "the performer and the members of her community become one, in sentiment and in purpose" (1983:457).

There is, however, a tension between the ideal of communitas and the process of actually achieving it, a tension suggested implicitly in the work of both Clements and Mullen. In his exploration of why people testify, Clements recognizes the "ego satisfaction which public performance can bring" (1980:27), a motivation that risks undermining a sense of communitas in the individual and, if perceived by an audience, among the congregation. "Communitas," Clements points out, "is an ideal state and always becomes corrupted by structural intrusions" (1976:44). Mullen, too, recognizes that while communitas is an ideal, it is not easily enacted. Further, while members raised in the church may be particularly primed for the liminal experience that would induce communitas, the worldly can nonetheless intrude on religious experience generally, and the narration of conversion specifically (1983:21, 23). These concerns are made manifest by the doubts expressed by the men and women in the African American charismatic churches observed by Glenn Hinson, who believed it not uncommon for people to manufacture experience with the Holy Ghost for self-aggrandizement. Frank Korom's analysis of a Hindu ritual in West Bengal echoes the skepticism of how frequently hierarchies are dissolved and communitas achieved in religious experience, arguing that social hierarchies are never abandoned during the Hindu ritual he examined, despite its explicit reversal of caste status. However, perception and interpretation vary according to the social identities of the participants. While Brahmins felt the ritual enforced social hierarchies, low-caste devotees felt that it did in fact reverse these orders and that they did become Brahmins during the liminal space of the ritual (2002).

The socioreligious identities members construct for themselves and that their peers construct about them can have a significant impact on the potential to achieve communitas at all. Latter-day Saints skeptical of a particular person's motivations, discernment, and honesty may in effect close themselves off from feeling the Holy Ghost and sharing in the divine experience being recounted and reevoked. One BYU professor refused to believe a story told by an unreliable narrator despite feeling awed (as discussed earlier in this chapter). Competent in all other ways, a story told by an "unreliable" narrator may be dismissed out of hand. Diane Goldstein found similar weight placed on individual identity, based not only on assumptions of someone's righteousness but on that person's history of performance. Comparing the testimonies of two women, Goldstein notes that "Mary, who rarely speaks in the church service, is noted as really sharing when she publicly reads a quote from the Bible selected for her by the Pastor. Ingrid, who performs at virtually every service and who generally shares moving mystical experiences, will be judged uninspired if she tells a personal narrative that does not reveal some aspect of her true self or does not provide insight into her experiences. This same narrative, if told by other members, would be evaluated more positively. Each is judged based on her perceived capabilities" (1995:34). Evaluative criteria are applied unevenly, depending on the individual.

While Mullen is surely right that in some congregations, the hierarchies outside of church may carry little if any weight inside it—something my field-work with the Burlington First Ward supports—it is certainly also true that church members establish social hierarchies and socioreligious identities within the church. These identities can dictate whether a performance is deemed sincere and authentic and therefore capable of inspiring communitas among the congregation.

Secondhand Stories

The tension between the prestige of performance and the humility demanded in many cultures, among many peoples, and for many genres, finds some relief in the secondhand tale. The secondhand tale is liminal in many ways: it is not a first-person experience in the strictest sense, nor is it a legend. It is betwixt and between the two, narrated with an eye both to the accuracy of the original experience and to the needs of a performer and audience separated, if only ever so slightly, from the experience itself.

In their attempt to define the memorate, Linda Dégh and Andrew Vázsonyi consider the role of the secondhand narrative as one part of a process of transmission that can lead to the transformation of generic form altogether. They trace the eventual expansion of the genre of the memorate from Carl Wilhelm von Sydow, who restricted the genre to first-person narratives (1948), to Riedar Christiansen (1958) and Gunnar Granberg (1969), who allow for secondhand accounts, to Juha Pentikäinen (1970), who expands the memorate as far as fourthhand accounts but no further (cited by Dégh and Vázsonyi 1974:225–7). At this point, argue Dégh and Vázsonyi, the experience is either narrated as a fabulate or legend, or the genealogy of the tale is amended—whether consciously or not—to maintain the degree of personal connection deemed necessary to engender trust, truth, or belief (1974:225–31).

While the secondhand tale does not cease being a viable narrative—in fact, its continued transmission is testament to exactly the opposite—it is qualitatively different from a story in the first person. Elliott Oring picks up the term "distancing" from Georgina Smith to describe "the degrees of separation between a narrator and the presumed source of the narrator" (2008:133). Distancing is of central importance in evaluating legends and, by extension, first-person memorates. Oring argues, as have scholars before him, that "the first person memorate is likely to be the most suasive type of account, for the narrator claims to report something he or she has experienced" (133). The further from the source, the less credible the account. Among Latter-day Saints, there is great suspicion of the secondhand story, and many members put little faith in such stories when heard and altogether refuse to narrate them themselves. The issue is not merely one of trust and fear of embellishment. The chance of invoking the Holy Ghost may be diminished without the person who received the revelation present.

Despite these strikes against it, however, the secondhand narrative has found a place of distinct utility within the LDS community, negotiating the paradox of prestige versus humility. The dramatic revelatory experience that would draw an unseemly amount of attention to the first-person narrator is shared to great effect by the close friend, acquaintance, or fellow ward member. For the narrator of treasure-hunting tales in Mexican culture, the secondhand memorate plays a similar role in deflecting the prestige that comes with performance, redeeming personal experience narratives that could not be told firsthand but find voice when shared by others. Manuel José Cordero recounts two stories about acquaintances of his from Acuitlapilco who found treasure. "Both of these stories are memorates only in the broader sense of pertaining to known, specifically named individuals," points out author Shirley Arora, who then adds as an afterthought: "They could not, incidentally, exist as first-person narratives because a successful treasure-hunter would not risk the dangers of *envidia*, envy, by telling of his own stories" (1987:85).

The relatively low level of distancing in the secondhand tale, coupled with the benefits of alleviating the prestige of the experience, if not the narration, makes the secondhand tale a powerful solution to the paradox of performance, particularly in a culture that invests so much value in the personal experience narrative for religious instruction. In this way, it would be difficult to chart the characteristics of the transmitted legend in a uniformly incremental path from one end of a continuum to another as scholars have tended to do, assuming that each step further from the source results in uniform shifts in assumptions about truth, embellishment, persuasiveness, and efficacy.

Chapter 3

TRANSFORMING LIFE INTO STORY

Genre

Genres are powerful. Whether as a system of classification or an emergent form of discourse, genres provide the means for creating and interpreting performance.[1] The shared structures, themes, styles, and contexts link past performances with present ones, setting up a series of expectations for both performer and audience. The "knock-knock" joke provides a useful example.

A knock-knock joke told among six-year-olds in the present does not emerge fully formed in the moment of performance. Themes change, contexts change, but basic structures are fairly conservative. Children learn very quickly, for example, that a knock-knock joke must begin with "knock, knock." And they learn the required response: "Who's there?" and will prompt a young listener if this is his or her first knock-knock joke. They also learn that the joke comes in two parts, where the second part transforms the first into something that will ideally elicit a laugh. These "rules" can be understood as expectations of the genre. Those expectations carry over from one performance to the next. Accordingly, a knock-knock joke told in the present can be understood within a broad context of other knock-knock jokes linking one text to another. These textual connections describe a process of intertextuality and have been useful in highlighting how present performances are affected by past ones.

Yet audiences construct different "histories" for any given genre. Some children may have heard knock-knock jokes from their parents and grandparents and interpret the joke told by their peer on the playground within this generational history. Others will have heard the jokes only from other children on the playground and may narrate them only in similar contexts. Their intertextual connections will be more restricted. In both cases, however, the child will typically learn to tell knock-knock jokes from hearing other people perform them.[2] When they hear a knock-knock joke, they will expect it to follow these basic rules. Further, if they innovate and create their own knock-knock joke, they will draw heavily upon the structures and formula and rules for the genre in order to be effective and make their audience laugh. Genres are therefore self-reifying—performance reinforces generic expectations, which in turn shape performance. More prescriptive, heavily regulated genres are more conservative than genres with fewer, less formalized rules. Personal anecdotes, for example, provide far greater leeway for innovation in performance than knock-knock jokes. Yet for both, and for all genres, there are expectations that must be met for effective performance. Those expectations guide the audience in evaluating performance (as discussed in chapter 2).

Personal revelation narratives are no different. By narrating personal revelation within a narrative genre recognized throughout the community, heard again and again in church and in the home, speakers are confronted with a series of expectations that they must negotiate in the context of their specific experience. Those expectations are formal, functional, stylistic, interpretive, *and* ideological. For example, as a narrative genre, there is an expectation for dramatic tension and resolution. Such narrative requirements, coupled with social constraints on narrative performance, can translate into constraints on the interpretation of personal revelation as shared in performance. The result is that genre is an agent, not just a vehicle, for interpretation.

Index versus Interpretation

Personal experience narratives purport to report. They reference a set of experiences and translate them into verbal form to share with others. In the absence of formal recording—video footage, audio recording, stenographer's notes— the oral narrative often becomes the primary record of the event, an index of the past, told in the present. That act of translation from experience to story is also an act of interpretation. At the most basic, we choose what to include and exclude. However, transforming experience into story is far more nuanced than the choice of content; our perceptions and perspectives of the event, our reasons for narrating, and the images of ourselves and others all reflect important interpretive decisions that shape our stories.

Beyond our own specific motivations, social and cultural beliefs and norms also shape what we see and how we interpret it. A cow asleep in a field may evoke the sacred for a group of Hindu teenagers in India, while the same image may prompt a prank by teens out cow-tipping in the United States. A statue falling off a mantle may be attributed to the effect of passing traffic for a young white folklorist, but may be evidence of a visiting spirit to a Choctaw police officer.[3] The tendency to see the sacred or supernatural in what others may see

as mundane is gently parodied in a story shared informally among LDS magazine editors and staff:

> Back in the days when David O. McKay was president of the Church,
> it was Bruce R. McConkie's habit to dash down the stairs of the G. A.
> building (South Temple Street) and, when he came to the last several
> stairs, to leap to the landing below, often by hoisting himself over the ban-
> ister with his hands.
>
> One particular day, Bruce R. McConkie came running down the steps
> and dove over the banister, landing directly in front of President McKay,
> who was being wheeled down the hall. The two looked at each other in
> amazement for several seconds.
>
> "Oh, it's just you, Bruce," President McKay said at last. "For a minute
> there, I thought I was having a vision."[4]

Even the ability to perceive an event is shaped by our past experiences and
beliefs. A person living near a railroad track does not hear the roaring train that
shocks her visitor awake. We become accustomed to specific experiences and
interpret them (if we do not dismiss them altogether) according to past experience and contemporary cultural norms in addition to our observations during
the experience.[5]

One must be careful not to extend this thesis too far, however. Some past
studies have explained away the supernatural according to cultural, social, and
psychological factors, and David Hufford has rightly criticized them for dismissing the unfamiliar experiences of others as subjective creations of the cultural mind. Such an approach, he argues, further dismisses as delusional the
people who purport to have encountered the supernatural. Hufford's remedy
is to reverse the tables, assuming truth and rationality grounded in experience,
rather than psychosis and irrationality.[6]

These two theoretical approaches to interpreting supernatural experiences—cultural source theory versus experiential source theory—need not be
polarized, however. Few would doubt the presence of the cow, whether they see
a sacred life or the chance for a prank. Variation in cultural perception remains
even when we agree on the reality of the object before us. The same should be
true of the supernatural. If we accept the possibility of the supernatural, it does
not mean we cannot also accept that culture can shape the interpretation of the
supernatural experience.[7]

The Demand for Interpretation

The process of interpretation is fundamental to all experience, both mundane
and supernatural. However, by being less common and less familiar than the

mundane by virtue of sheer frequency of exposure, supernatural experiences typically demand more consistent, conscious, and often explicit interpretation. Further, within a particular experience, some elements are more familiar and straightforward than others. The unfamiliar and ambiguous elements of a particular experience will demand greater attention. To manage interpretation, people often break down the experience into discrete questions: What exactly did I see? Where did that voice come from? Why should I pull over? Often these questions are voiced aloud; other times they are implicit in performance. However, paying close attention to the questions that structure narrative performance can reveal how people interpret their experiences, both in terms of process and meaning.

Analysis of personal revelation narratives shows that not all revelation poses the same questions. Rather, there are two major types of revelation–prescriptive and descriptive–distinguished both by the type of information provided and by the subsequent questions raised. Prescriptive revelation prescribes a course of action, providing information on what should be done, but not why. Human action is prescribed. The present is outlined, but the future is ambiguous. Descriptive revelation, on the other hand, provides a picture of what will or could happen, but not how it will happen, or what if anything should be done about it. The future is outlined, but the present is ambiguous.

Ethnographic data and textual analysis reveal another binary: solicited versus unsolicited revelation. George Johnson explains a revelation he received earlier that week in answer to his prayers. "I had a lot of anxiety over it and I was asking Heavenly Father what I should do," he explains. "And so, I think that's what spurred it is because we had had a question or a concern. And that's what spurs a lot of revelation. And then there's the other type where you're in danger, and you receive revelation to either get yourself out of it or protect yourself."

Like prescriptive and descriptive revelation, these two types of revelation are not distinguished with native terms, yet people clearly distinguish between the two both in discussion and in narrative performance. Further, narrators have clearly internalized a distinction between both sets of binaries, approaching each type with a distinct set of expectations for how to interpret the initial experience and then narrate that experience within specific social settings.

Prescriptive Revelation

Solicited Revelation through Prayer

Some of the most common revelations are prescriptive: revelations that provide people with a specific prompt for what they should do. And the most common way people receive this type of revelation is through prayer. As in many religious faiths, LDS members are taught as children to turn to God for help in all things, a process modeled for LDS members by their founding prophet.[8] As the introduction to the Doctrine and Covenants explains, Joseph Smith turned to God again and again for guidance through prayer: "These sacred revelations were received in answer to prayer, in times of need, and came out of real-life situations involving real people." The model is clear: when a problem or question arises, humble prayer to God will provide an answer. This is the model that politician George Romney followed when he announced his intention to run for public office by "alluding to his meditating over the question and listening for the still, small voice to advise him."[9]

In the narrative tradition of personal revelation, prayers offered during moments of crisis are particularly common. A woman loses directions to the house where she needs to pick up her son. She prays and is prompted on a route that leads directly to the house (Layland 2001, Wilson Archives). A woman is only four and a half months pregnant when her water breaks. The doctor tells her to come to the hospital but she prays and is prompted to stay home instead, a choice that likely saves her baby's life (Layland 2001, Wilson Archives). A girl goes missing. A man in the ward prays for guidance and receives revelation that guides the search party directly to the girl (Fischio 1970, Wilson Archives). "Another instance that I can think of was when we had Julie," explains Sandy Johnson. "She was maybe six months old." Her husband George nods, "Oh yeah."

Sandy: We lived in Phoenix, and we lived there about three months.
But while we were there, she was about six months old and she was learning how to crawl. And I had cleaned the house from top to bottom. And somehow she had picked up something and swallowed it. Don't have a clue. Well, I know what it was now, but at the time I could not figure out what she had swallowed because my house was spotless. But yet kids can find the craziest things.
And I thought, "Well, it was probably a penny," because the girls had dumped out pennies. And I was like, "I must have missed one." So I thought she had swallowed a penny.
And she started choking for a little bit and we did the little . . . not Heimlich . . .
George: Heimlich, yeah, it's Heimlich for a kid.
Sandy: Yeah, for an infant. You know, on the back.
And she stopped choking, and we thought, OK, well, she's OK now.
But she was breathing funny to me.
George: It sounded like it was rattling.

Sandy: Yeah. It just didn't sound like normal breathing. But she wasn't choking, and I was like, I couldn't figure out what was wrong. I just thought . . . I didn't know what to do. I wasn't sure, "Is she fine, or is she not?"

So we said a prayer.

And we both got the feeling that we needed to take her to the hospital.

Well, we took her to an emergency . . . one of those emergency walk-in clinic type things. And they told us that because she wasn't choking, they weren't going to look at her. For two hours, they didn't have a pediatrician. We both looked at each other and thought, "Nah." And we got the feeling that "No, we need to do something about it now."

So we drove to the hospital. And while we're at the hospital, we went to the emergency room, we told them what was going on, and they said she's not choking.

And I said, "But she's breathing funny. Trust me on this. She's breathing funny."

So they decided to go ahead and take a look and give her an X-ray and all that stuff, and I was praying real hard, because I was like, "Come on, I know there's something funny," because I just felt that there was something wrong, it just wasn't right.

And when we were in the X-ray . . . they took the X-rays, and the doctors weren't believing me, they were like, "She's fine. I don't hear any funny breathing."

And I'm like, "She's got something in her throat."

And I said this to them over and over again. And they finally took the X-rays out, and they found a little white line on the X-ray.

And so they're like, "OK, well, there's something there, you're right. But it's not a penny"—because I told them I thought she had swallowed a penny—and they said, "Well, if it's a penny, it will show up on the X-ray, because it's metal."

But it was just a little white line, that just showed up on her X-ray, and they said, "It's not a penny. I don't know what it is but there's something in her throat so we're going to go down and get it."

So they took her into the emergency room and basically got it out of her throat. And what they pulled out was a little piece of plastic, this big [an inch long].

Plastic does not show up on X-rays. [*long pause*]

George: At all.

Sandy: Plastic does not. It will only show up metal. [*pause*]

And the doctors looked at me and they're like, "What's this?"

It turns out it was a little white . . . you know those little samples of lotion that you get sometimes at the store? They have those little rip off plastic tops. She had found the top of one of those. Don't know where she found it, but she had found it and swallowed it. And it showed up on that X-ray.

And we just felt funny that we needed to take her to the hospital.

Well, the doctor told me later that if that had flipped—it stayed in her throat straight up and down—and if that had flipped to where it was laying flat it would have cut off the oxygen and she would have suffocated pretty bad.

George: Real quickly.
Sandy: Real fast.

You know, obviously that was a pretty traumatic event.

But that's one of the things that I know that that was, I guess prophecy or revelation to me and George that we needed to take her to the hospital and if we hadn't she wouldn't be here because she would have died.

There are ways that prophecies and revelations and promptings from the Spirit do help you out. And on numerous occasions it has I think saved us from a lot of headache and stress and death [*small laugh*]. You know?[10]

Prayers offered in the moment of crisis are often general and open ended—cries of desperation: What should I do? For guidance in less immediate matters, prayers are often more specific: Should I take this job? Should I marry this person? Should I have more children? In such cases, members are expected to contemplate the issue first before turning to God, a process laid out explicitly in church doctrine and quoted frequently by lay members: "But, behold, I say unto you, that you must study it out in your mind; then you must ask me [God] if it be right, and if it is right I will cause that your bosom shall burn within you; therefore, you shall feel that it is right" (D&C 9:8).[11] People are expected to be active in determining their life's path. "One of the biggest things that people don't know about us is that we're encouraged to study it out in our minds first, and think about it, and then pray about it to get confirmation for ourselves," Michele Doyle pointed out during a discussion about personal revelation in Sunday school one morning. "We don't just blindly follow."

Revelations that confirm decisions reasoned out in the mind are an emic category of personal revelation. In her introduction to her class fieldwork project, one BYU student explained: "One of my friends told me to do stories where thoughts, feelings, or actions were confirmed by some abnormal means. She called these stories 'confirmation stories'" (Allen 1996:1, Wilson Archives).

Revelations of affirmation are a similar emic category of revelation. Instead of confirming a decision suggested by an individual, revelations of affirmation confirm previous revelation from God. Revelation of affirmation is necessary for joint decision making. The most common context for revelations of affirmation is among the church leadership. As leaders decide who should be called for a particular church position, a slate of names is typically prayed over. One member may receive revelation about a name. He or she then shares that revelation with the others and asks whether they can affirm this choice.[12] The other church leaders then offer their own prayers asking for divine affirmation.

Such revelations typically fall outside the realm of *personal* revelation, since they derive from a person's church calling and extend beyond a person's individual stewardship (see chapter 1). However, parents may also seek and receive revelation of affirmation, since they have joint stewardship over their children. Lee Mullen prayed about whether they should send their daughter to private school. She received revelation that they should. She shared this revelation with her husband, Ken, who explained: "I didn't receive the inspiration or the revelation, Lee did. But as a holder of the keys, you affirm it. You receive that revelation that they've received a revelation, if you will."[13]

Narrative Structure and Experience

Considering the importance placed on prayer in the LDS Church, and considering that many members pray multiple times a day, the narrative tradition should be rife with stories of prayers answered through personal revelation. Although the daily guidance people receive from God is treasured absolutely, such experiences are not shared widely and repeatedly. Only 20 percent (90 out of 441) of the personal revelation narratives recorded in the archives and in my fieldwork were revelations solicited through prayer. The vast majority—80 percent (351 out of 441) came unsolicited (see chart 4 in the appendix). One reason is that regular, answered prayers may not be particularly dramatic.

Revelatory experience does not demand dramatic tension, but narrative does. Dramatic tension has been mapped in a number of ways. One of the most enduring is Gustav Freytag's narrative triangle (1863). Stories begin with an incentive moment that creates an unresolved tension. This tension builds until the climax, at which point the dramatic tension is relieved and the story moves toward resolution. Sandra Dolby Stahl has noted the efficacy of this model for understanding the narrative structure of personal experience narratives (1989:16–7). Also working in the genre of the personal narrative, William

Labov and Joshua Waletzky developed a model similar in its basics: orientation, complication, and resolution (1961). Further, although his goal was to identify motifemes in American Indian folktales, Alan Dundes's binary structure of "lack/lack liquidated" reduces narrative to a single pair of opposites (1964). While such a structure has proved less useful for the study of motifemes, it is an efficient articulation of the fundamental narrative core that appears universally in discussions of narrative structure where dramatic tension is introduced and resolved in a series of paired questions and answers. These pairs guide the interpretation of the experience and provide the structure for narration.

Revelations solicited though prayer require some degree of dramatic tension in order to be narrated regularly. Those experiences that do have this tension are narrated according to shared structural patterns. The basic structural elements are fairly uniform across all narratives of personal revelation. However, the subtle differences—particularly in the questions asked by narrators, whether explicitly or implicitly—reveal distinctions among types of revelation that help shape the interpretation of the experience, the meaning of the narrative, and the application to one's life. Using the narrative shared by George and Sandy Johnson as a reference point, stories of solicited revelation can be mapped to reveal their underlying structure and the process of interpretation.

Introduction to Narrative Performance

As a performance shared within specific social contexts, narratives of personal revelation must be framed to provide a rationale for sharing the story. (See figure 3-1. The frame for the narrative event is represented by the large gray rectangle.) When prompted during an interview, the narrative frame may be established by the question asked. When personal revelation narratives emerge more organically, the introductory frame is established by the topic at hand. Having shared a number of stories of personal revelation already, Sandy Johnson, for example, continues with one more about her daughter and their trip to the hospital.

Introduction to the Narrated Experience

Once the narrative performance is introduced and framed, narrators begin their story. (See figure 3-1. The narrated event is represented by the large white rectangle.) Grounding the experience in its relevant situation and cultural contexts, narrators introduce the event, typically including information about the setting, the people involved, and general background information that helps to explain the events to follow.

Complication and Crisis

The reported experience then begins in earnest as narrators describe the complication that poses a particular crisis. A person faces a difficult decision, a crossroads in life, or any of a number of small or large hurdles. That initial complication leads them to God through prayer. They ask the question, what should I do? This question sets in motion a course of action that invites the divine, both into one's life and into the narrative performance. Implied by this question is another, one projected further into the future: Will it be OK?

Revelation

Experientially, there may be a gap between prayer and revelation as people wait for an answer. In narrative, however, the story typically jumps straight to the revelation. For George and Sandy Johnson, their prayer was answered immediately: "Take her to the hospital." The revelation serves to answer the explicit question posed in prayer: What should I do? It does not, however, provide a resolution to the narrative. Still unclear is whether their daughter will be OK. This question haunts them throughout their experience. Further, the revelation itself raises another question: Why? Why, for example, is it necessary for Sandy and George Johnson to take their daughter to the hospital immediately? Something is wrong, but what? And how serious is it?

Revelation provides a turning point in the narrative. Having received guidance from God, George and Sandy move into action. The story tracks the action people take in order to follow the guidance they received. George and Sandy find themselves stymied at the walk-in clinic and continue to heed the Holy Ghost, taking their daughter to the hospital. There too, they are stymied by doctors who cannot find the source of the problem. Thanks to the revelation, Sandy persists, convinced something is wrong or they would not have been prompted to go to the hospital.

Climax

The climax of the narrative comes when the question *why* is answered. For Sandy and George, this is when the doctors find a piece of plastic lodged in their daughter's throat. The rationale for going to the hospital is made clear. The implicit promise of revelation is fulfilled and the divine nature of the prompting is confirmed.

Resolution

The resolution of the experience follows with an answer to the question, will it be OK? For Sandy and George, resolution comes when the plastic top is successfully removed and their daughter avoids suffocating to death.

Coda

Having finished recounting the experience, narrators shift from the *narrated* event to the *narrative* event of the current storytelling performance, a means of tying the story back to the conversation in which it is embedded. This narrative act closes the performance frame, resolving the question that prompted the story in the first place: Why share this story? For Sandy, the answer is to provide a testament to the power of God to prevent everything from the small stresses of life to death. For other stories of personal revelation, the narrative coda can confirm any of a number of key religious tenets. In its most general articulation, that confirmation can be summarized as "how God helps." More specific confirmations include: God answers prayers, God loves his people, God provides comfort, God guides the righteous, God protects the righteous from physical danger, God protects the righteous from spiritual danger. Considering that the most common public performance contexts for sharing stories of personal revelation are in church (see chapter 2), doctrinal confirmation is not surprising.

The narrative structure of solicited, prescribed revelation can be mapped onto a modified narrative triangle to depict visually what narrators do verbally (see figure 3-1). The result is a series of peaks within the triangle. Questions

Figure 3-1. Solicited Prescribed Revelation

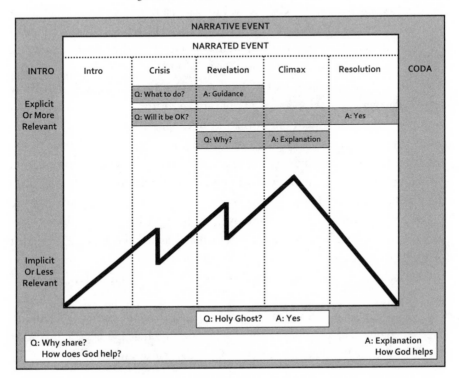

raised by people during their revelatory experience drive the narrative forward, providing the complication and resolution necessary for narration. Each peak in the narrative triangle marks a shift in action. At the moment of crisis, people pray. At the moment of revelation, they act. Dramatic tension climaxes when the revelation is finally understood, when the question *why* is answered.

These narrative moves are not inconsequential. The movement to action after receiving revelation reveals a fundamental aspect of LDS doctrine that distinguishes revelatory experiences from other divine encounters. The climax, centered as it is on resolving the truth of the revelation rather than the ultimate outcome, reveals a fundamental aspect of performance that shapes how these narratives are interpreted and shared.

Agency

One of the most significant structural elements to narratives of personal revelation is the break in narrative action that occurs after receiving revelation. This additional step in the rising action reveals the critical themes of agency and faith that pervade LDS religious thought and distinguish revelation from divine intervention.

While revelation is one way God answers prayers, it is not the only way. People often pray for direct divine intervention: for a loved one to recover, a wife to become pregnant, a child to be protected, a ring to be found, a business deal to go through, a trip to be completed safely. The most dramatic examples of direct divine intervention are viewed as miracles. The story of the seagulls that ate the plague of crickets and saved the early Utah pioneers' crops is a fundamental (if contested) part of Mormon history (see Hartley 1970). More personal experiences exist as well. People are saved from accidents at work and at home, pushed and lifted out of the way of danger by unseen forces.[14] Before joining the church, Jean Chandler struggled with the Word of Wisdom, the LDS doctrine that encourages members to live healthy lives by abstaining from smoking and alcohol, among other things.[15] She prayed for help to kick these habits. The next day, her prayers were answered. The smell of cigarette smoke made her physically sick, as did the smell of the bar where she was joining her coworkers for an after-work drink. "And that was it," she explains. "I didn't smoke again; I didn't drink again. And I know it was an answer to my prayer. Did I receive personal revelation that that was an answer? I didn't need to. I knew."

Culturally, this distinction is important. The issue of agency is central to LDS theology. The plan of salvation—the doctrine that more than any other distinguishes LDS religion from other Christian faiths and to which virtually all other LDS doctrine can be linked—is founded on the issue of agency. "The reason agency is so important is because that's what the war in Heaven was fought over," George Johnson explains. God held a council in heaven and proposed a plan for his spirit children to go to Earth, experience mortality, attain a body of flesh and blood, and strive to follow his teachings in order to return to heaven with a body and attain eternal life. Lucifer, however, offered an alternate plan that would have removed human agency and guaranteed everyone safe passage back to heaven. Lucifer was ultimately cast out of heaven and God's plan was put into action, with human agency a central aspect of mortal life.

Direct intervention is no less faith promoting or powerful than revelation. However, direct intervention does not prompt a moment of crisis when a person is forced to act on faith. Prayers can be launched by the faithful *or* the faithless in times of need. But it is revelation that tests whether the individual has the faith to follow God's advice. The decision to act ultimately leads to the climax, when the promise of revelation is fulfilled.

Experientially and theologically, this decision is critical. Yet rarely is this decision narrated for solicited revelation. One reason stems from the nature of the experience. Solicited revelation introduces the divine with the act of prayer. Having explicitly asked for divine help, people not only are expecting God to answer but are eager to follow the advice provided. The decision to act is often an easy one. Instead, narrators focus their performance elsewhere: on the divine nature of the experience.

Social Demands of Performance

Social performances of divine encounters shared with an audience require narrators to provide evidence to support their story. As discussed in chapter 2, stories that ask an audience to believe not only that God communicates with people today but that God communicated with *them* on *that particular day* demand proof of the divine. This proof is a fundamental part of the narrative performance, serving as both the driving force of the dramatic tension and the climax of the narrative.

The question *why* derives from the revelation itself. The explanation serves as the climax. In Sandy Johnson's story, for example, the *why* is explained by the discovery of the plastic top. At the heart of the question *why* lies another question, also derived from the revelation: Is this the Holy Ghost? This question, too, is answered with the discovery of the plastic top and serves as proof that the revelation Sandy and George received is divine. Confirmation of the divine is made even more explicit when Sandy reveals that the plastic top should not have been visible on the X-ray: "Plastic does not show up . . ." she says, trailing off pointedly. In fact, she pauses so long that her husband can further highlight the climax by reiterating the importance of this fact. Sandy continues to describe what happened, ending once again with the dramatic climax: "And it showed up on that X-ray."

The climax comes not only when the question *why* is answered but when the truth of the divine nature of the revelation is confirmed. The fulfillment of the promise of revelation resolves a question implicit in the social act of narrating: Was this in fact revelation? Was this the Holy Ghost? This question frames the core of the narrative, connecting the promise of the revelation with the climax of its fulfillment. (See figure 3-1, white box. The questions in white boxes that exist outside the white rectangle are questions posed by the narrative event but not necessarily the narrated event.)

The positioning of the climax around the validity of the experience suggests a fundamental departure from the initial experience. At the time of the revelation, George and Sandy are consumed above all else with whether their daughter will be all right. In sharing the story of the experience, however, a different focus emerges. George and Sandy now know their daughter will be all right; so, too, do the audience members who know the family. Instead, the story is framed as an example of personal revelation generally, and an example of how God helps more specifically. Further, the story is performed socially, where belief and trust are negotiated. The dominant question, will she be OK? is matched, even overshadowed, by whether this was in fact divine revelation.

Is this the Holy Ghost? is a question that may also be asked by the person at the time of receiving revelation. As with the decision to act, however, the nature of the experience helps to render this question moot. Having introduced the supernatural through prayer, a divine response is expected.

The map of solicited prescribed revelation can be revised to accommodate interpretive questions that can emerge during the experience but may not be narrated explicitly (see figure 3-2). As questions that underlie the experience, they are located underneath the narrative triangle. The decision to act, however, demands an additional column. Whether easy or difficult, the decision to act must nonetheless be made. The lines of the triangle itself indicate the narrative arc. Because most narrators do not address the decision they made to act, the line does not dip again after the revelation until the climax.

Expectations

The nature of the revelation—solicited and prescriptive—sets forth a series of expectations for *both* the experience *and* the narrative performance. Because solicited revelation introduces the divine *before* the revelation, the divine is assumed. Because help is actively sought, the decision to act is assumed. The expectations for narrative performance repeat the expectations for experience. Even in cases where people admit to questioning the origin of their revelation and struggling with their decision to act, they rarely narrate them as part of the experience, reserving them for discussions that follow or mentioning them only in abstract conversations about personal revelations. In figure 3-2, the additional questions—Should I act? and, Is this the Holy Ghost?—can be part of the *experience* of revelation without appearing in the narrative performance. Further, because narratives are created in social contexts with specific goals, meaning can shift, so that elements crucial in experience fade to the background in narrative. Expectations for one type of revelation, however, do not extend uniformly to other types. In *unsolicited* prescriptive revelation, questions of human agency and divine origin emerge as two of the most important questions that structure narrative performance.

Unsolicited Revelation

Unsolicited revelation catches people unaware. Out of the blue, people are prompted to take a different route home, go visit a person they do not know,

Figure 3-2. Solicited Prescribed Revelation: Narrative and Experience

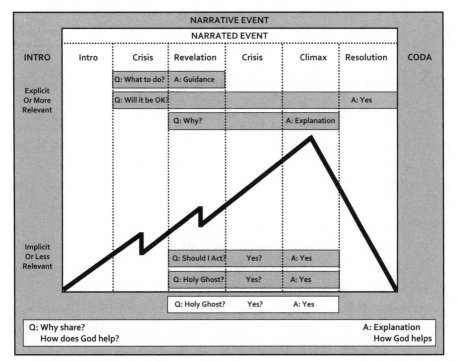

search a particular place for a lost item or child. They have had no time to study this out in their minds. They have not struggled to make a choice and then prayed for God's advice. Rather, God has come to them.

While *solicited* revelation dominates revelatory *experiences* among Latter-day Saints, it is *unsolicited* revelation that dominates the *narrative* tradition of those experiences. One explanation is the significance of God's role as initiator in unsolicited revelations. This is a proactive God who gets involved, not simply a God who responds. Susan Swetnam argues that stories of unsolicited divine aid and guidance are particularly attractive to writers and storytellers "at least in part because the heavenly guidance given through such manifestations is an even more impressive sign of God's care than his reaction to prayers" (1991:75). At least as compelling a reason can be traced to the increased dramatic tension in unsolicited revelation. While the question *why* drives *solicited* revelation forward, its answer is rarely inconceivable. Sandy and George may not know exactly why they need to take their daughter to the hospital, but they can conceive of a logical if somewhat vague answer. Solicited revelation therefore requires clear evidence of divine provenance in order to compel an audience to see revelation rather than just logical thinking. Such evidence is elusive in most answered prayers. *Unsolicited* promptings, on the other hand, provide a seemingly random prompt that typically defies easy assessment or logic. Unsolicited revelation thereby poses a more compelling "question" that can translate to a more compelling narrative when revelation is fulfilled. Mike McCann begins:

> A couple of years ago, another little story that we had, that I received inspiration was . . .
> I was in downtown Burlington, driving back from an appointment and it was midmorning, like ten, ten thirty in the morning. And I had this feeling I needed to go home.
> Didn't know why.
> And I questioned, "Why do I need to go home?"
> But I went home anyway.
> Walked in, looked around, everything was fine, didn't see anything out of the ordinary and decided to just leave and go back to the office. And as I was leaving, there was a deputy sheriff car had pulled up to our neighbor that's up the hill. And I noticed that they were up there when I went to get back into the car.
> Backed out of the driveway, and I didn't really think anything of it. We've never really spoken to that neighbor. He's a fairly new neighbor anyway, and so I didn't really think anything of it. He works an odd shift and so we very rarely even see each other. We wave and are friendly, but we've never really spoken.

And as I'm pulling down the street, they're walking down through his yard to my yard. And I thought that was odd. kept watching as I drove. and I turned the corner and drove, and they actually jumped the creek onto my property, and I thought, now this is strange.

So I turned around and came back, and when I did, they were down on our . . . we own an acre lot and they were on the lower portion of the lot. I come back down, and I got out of the car and said, "Uh, guys, can I help you with something?"

And that's when the officer said, "Well, your neighbor here saw somebody down here with this bag. And we're trying to find out what this bag is."

And it was kind of hidden. And I stepped around and said, "Oh, that's my son's duffel bag." He had a large duffel bag that he kept, actually, hockey equipment in.

And he said, "Do you know what's in the bag?"

I said, "Well, I would assume his hockey equipment."

And they tried to lift it, and it was quite heavy. And so they were very cautious about opening the bag or anything like that.

Well, come to find out, there was a guy that was standing with the bag and the neighbor saw him, and he took off running. Come to find out he had broken into our house, found the duffel bag and just loaded it with video games and movies and all kinds of stuff. And it was so heavy you couldn't lift it.

And something that day told me to go to the house.

And now I know why.

And you know, it's not, I mean it's kind of a big thing but it's not a big deal, I mean, nobody got hurt. We got all the stuff back, or most of the stuff back anyway. We did learn later that after our sons got home that . . . it was right after Christmas and we had gotten our sons both leather jackets for Christmas. And one of the leather jackets was missing. And so he had walked away and put the leather jacket on and walked away with it.

And I had a bowl of dimes—I separate my change and this bowl of dimes was on my dresser and he had taken that. Left the bowl but took the cash. It was about sixty dollars in dimes.

But, you know, most everything else was safe in the bag.

And of course then they brought the detectives out and they did their thing, but, never did, as far as I know, never did catch the guy.

You know, if I wouldn't have come home, or if the neighbor wouldn't have been home . . . you know?

All that stuff . . . and it's just stuff, which, that doesn't bother me, especially PS 2 [Play Station 2]. I mean if they took that, that would be OK [*laughter*]. Consume some time. Not my own, obviously.

And actually, what's interesting, that got broken. It was on the bottom. When he set it down, I guess it broke it, which is good [*laughter*]. They didn't like it that much, but . . . [*laughter*]

In unsolicited revelation, the question *why* continues to drive the narrative. Reviewing the situational context of the moment, however, rarely provides a logical answer. Nothing about Mike McCann's circumstances at the time provides any rationale for why he would need to return home. Mike must act on faith that the prompting is divine.

The dramatic tension in unsolicited revelation is heightened as people act *before* having even a remote guess as to why they should act, trusting that the result will be positive if they do. The assumption of a positive result is an expectation church members bring to revelation from an LDS worldview where God is benevolent and actively works to help and guide his faithful servants. There is no question that God helps. The question is whether or not this is God speaking.

Interpretive Question: Is this the Holy Ghost?

While the question of the origin of a prompting is relevant for all types of revelation, it is exponentially more relevant for unsolicited revelation, where the divine is not already a part of the experience. A person driving down a road or sleeping peacefully is not specifically expecting or prepared for revelation. Latter-day Saints recognize that the feelings and promptings they receive may come from many sources, some divine, some mundane, and some evil. Accordingly, the need to evaluate unsolicited promptings weighs heavily. The question—is this the Holy Ghost?—not only underlies the narrative performance, it reflects a fundamental interpretive crisis during the initial experience of receiving revelation, a crisis often repeated explicitly in the narrative performance.

"You know, it's a common Mormon question," explains Shawn Tucker. "Is this a burning in the bosom from God or is this the bean burrito I had for lunch." He laughs, but the sentiment is real and the question an important one.[16]

The struggle to distinguish the Holy Ghost from a range of physical, mental, and external sources is difficult, particularly when the prompting is subtle, which most promptings are—felt rather than heard or seen. Many members point out that a person must learn to recognize the Spirit. Discerning the Holy Ghost from the cacophony of other voices—one's own thoughts, fears, and desires; those of one's peers and society; and even those whisperings of Satan and his followers—is difficult and can take a lifetime of practice. This struggle is highlighted in narrative performance by how often people dismiss a prompting initially, only to be prompted a second or even a third time, often with each successive prompting getting louder and more forceful. Such delay is a dramatic departure from how people typically respond to solicited revelation—instantly, without pause or second thought.

Accordingly, people employ a range of strategies for evaluating whether a prompting is in fact revelation from the Holy Ghost. The most common process involves comparison to one's own past revelations.[17] Is this feeling similar to what I have felt in the past that turned out to be revelation? Feelings can range from a subtle sense of comfort and peace to a burning in the bosom. They can also be physical. Jackie Foss gets chill bumps on her arms. Keith Stanley and Wayne Chandler feel a shiver run along their spines. For all members except the very youngest, past experience helps determine what is and is not the Spirit.

The presence of the Spirit can also be evaluated by relying on what one feels is right. "It wasn't just it made sense, but I also . . . I could back it up in my own heart, you know?" explains missionary Adam Wicker, describing the revelation he received encouraging him to go on a mission. "Because sometimes my mind doubts, but I could back that one up with my heart. Like I could convince my own doubting mind with my heart because I felt it."

"One's heart" in this case is the repository not of personal desires but rather of one's spiritual conscience rooted in the light of Christ that Latter-day Saints believe exists for all people.[18] Guidance from "one's heart" therefore derives not from specific revelation from the Holy Ghost but from a lifetime of living close to God.

Elder Adam Wicker mentions the importance of backing up his revelation with a feeling. In his case, his revelation supported what he already felt, but did not necessarily think, was the right path. But for many, revelation runs counter not only to their own thoughts but to their desires and fears as well. It may even be illogical. In fact, it is *because* the thought is illogical or unexpected that some people are convinced that it is revelation. When Paul Clayson was prompted to ask a member of his ward whether he had thanked God for his beautiful family, he is struck by the incongruity of his own question. "That was a powerful experience. Because, in my mind, that was an illogical thing for me to just ask him out of the blue, given what he had just told me. Why would I ask him if he's prayed about his family?" (see chapter 5 for complete narrative). Erika Layland's mother was similarly struck when she was searching for a cure for her daughter's colic: "For several mornings when I was quietly feeding Erika a bottle, a thought completely foreign to rational thinking kept pushing its way to center-stage of my mind: Why don't I go to our local library and look for a book by Adele Davis? Immediately I questioned inwardly, *'Who is Adele Davis, and what could any book written by her have to do with Erika's well-being?'*" (italics in original letter written by Erika's mother; for complete narrative, see chapter 4). Joanna Gibb's mother received advice that was not only "completely foreign to rational thinking" but contradictory to what she had been taught about child safety:

I was downstairs while Joanna, who was about two or three, was upstairs playing quietly in her room alone with her toys.

I was getting ready to go somewhere when I was literally commanded to go to Joanna's room. I immediately did so and found her on the floor, bluish grey in color and unable to breathe. She was obviously choking on something.

I immediately went through the steps to perform the Heimlich maneuver, and when that did not work, I held her upside down to try and dislodge 'it.'

I knew that there wasn't time to get help. I had been taught in first aid classes to not stick a finger in someone's throat because it would lodge the object further down. However, again I was commanded to [do] just that.

I did and popped out a marble.

Joanna began breathing, and her color returned. (1999:10, Wilson Archives)

While illogical prompts may convince people that they are receiving revelation, backing that revelation up with their heart may convince them to actually act.

Yet another strategy is to compare the prompting with church teachings. This strategy is irrelevant in many cases, since the church has no stance on whether you should sit at a green light, look in a particular place for a lost earring, or visit a particular relative. But in cases where revelation suggests action relevant to church doctrine, the assumption is that only promptings that support the church could have originated with the Holy Ghost.[19] The missionary teaching manual addresses this concern by quoting a talk given by President Gordon B. Hinckley: In answer to the question, "How do we recognize the promptings of the Spirit?" President Gordon B. Hinckley read Moroni 7:13, 16–17 and then said: "That's the test, when all is said and done. Does it persuade one to do good, to rise, to stand tall, to do the right thing, to be kind, to be generous? Then it is of the Spirit of God. . . . If it invites to do good, it is of God. If it inviteth to do evil, it is of the devil."[20]

The strategy of comparing revelation to church teachings risks being circular: anything that fits church doctrine is revelation, anything that runs counter to it is not. While logically problematic, such a strategy can be rationalized spiritually: revelation is given by the Holy Ghost. The Holy Ghost is defined and understood through religious doctrine specific to the LDS Church. Therefore, to accept revelation is to accept the teachings of the church that explain that revelation.[21]

Interpretive Question: Should I Act?

Because the origin of unsolicited promptings is unknown, the decision to act is more difficult than with solicited revelation. The solution for many people is to put the spiritual question of origin on hold and consider the matter from a practical standpoint: Will following the prompting cause me undue trouble? If the answer is yes, people are often tempted to dismiss the prompting as mundane. If the answer is no, many, like Shawn Tucker, follow the prompting, believing "better safe than sorry":

So when I was in high school, I was coaching soccer, and I was taking kids home from soccer practice. They were my boss's kids; I was coaching his soccer team.

So, we had left soccer practice, and we were driving back to the house, and I saw someone that I knew from the congregation, from our ward. And she was walking with her baby in the stroller, and they were walking up the street.

And I saw them and my first thought was, "Well, I should stop and say, 'Hi' to them."

I was like, "Nah, it's too late."

And then I kept going down the street and that thought came to me again: "I should stop and say, 'Hi' to them."

And I was like, "No, no, no."

And at the time I'd been thinking a lot about what's my own feelings, what's really an inspiration, what's really coming from the Lord, what's not.

And so, a third time, and I felt really strongly, "I should stop and go say, 'Hi' to them." And I did.

Now I have no idea why, but I thought I might as well go with it. You know, it's not going to take a bunch of time and I may be wrong, even if it's wrong, it's not doing something bad.

So, I turn around, and I go back, and I pull the car up nearby, and we're talking for just a minute.

She was actually sort of a ways back, so she kind of had to come up with the stroller, up to where I was at.

And not long after we'd started talking, *wham!* This strong *wa-wom* knocks into the car.

And what had happened was a trailer, a truck pulling a trailer, had come down the street, and the trailer carrying lawnmowers had become detached from the truck, skidded across the street and hit my car, and slammed in the back of the car.

And, you know, it was a little town, so like they call the fire department and the paratroopers come in, you know, it's the whole fireworks thing.

So then I'm on the way home and I'm like, "You know, that really stinks [*laughter*]. I'm not listening to that again [*laughter*]. Look what it's done to my car."

And then I put it together, that had I not gone back, that trailer would have come across and hit them. It was just the way that it was all lined up. That's what would have happened. And so that was just, you know, very powerful thing to me.

Speaking on the topic of personal revelation during Sunday school one morning, Paul Clayson admitted: "There are times in my life where I don't listen to revelation, inspiration, because I can pass it off as my own thoughts. But I've learned I need to listen." He learned to listen from experiences such as the time he was prompted to take a different route to work, ignored the prompting, and got stuck in a traffic jam. Or when he was prompted to visit his ex-brother-in-law, ignored it, and found out his brother-in-law died a few days later (see chapter 2 for complete narrative). In the narrative tradition, ignoring revelation is met with consistently disastrous results.[22]

Narrative Structure

The major structural elements of unsolicited revelation are similar to solicited revelation (see figure 3-3), with two major differences. The narrative crisis shifts to *follow* the revelation rather than precede it, and questions *implicit* in solicited revelation—Should I act? and, Is this the Holy Ghost?—become explicit.

These shifts can be traced to differences in expectations for this type of revelation as well as in the narrative demand for complication. In *solicited* revelation, the crisis emerges from life, revelation provides guidance,

Figure 3-3. Unsolicited Prescribed Revelation

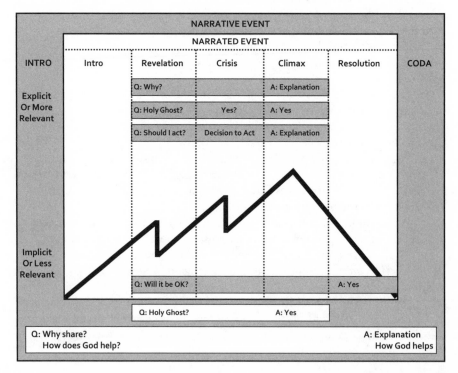

and faithful action is rewarded. In *unsolicited* revelation, there is no initial crisis. Only with the revelation does the potential for crisis emerge, when a person must determine the origin of the prompting and decide whether or not to act.

The decision to act emerges as a crisis rather than a more modest shift in narrative action following revelation. Further, the question of the divine origin of the revelation arises not only as part of the frame of narrative performance but as a central element of both the revelatory experience and the narrative, demanding a distinct step in the narrative triangle. The process of evaluation is extensive, the decision to act, difficult.

Descriptive Revelation

Prescriptive revelation provides guidance for what should be done in the present in order to benefit in the future. People are guided to take actions—take a different route home, approach a neighbor about the LDS Church, marry a particular person—with the expectation that good will follow and harm will be averted. Prescriptive revelation reveals what to do now, but not what is going to happen in the future. The present is provided; the future is implied. The question, why should I do this? drives the narrative action. Additional questions, including whether the prompting is divine or not, shape the interpretation of the experience and the narrative performance.

Descriptive revelation, on the other hand, reveals what will or could happen in the future as a means of deciding how to act in the present. People receive dreams and visions of the future with the expectation that they will need to act now. Descriptive revelation reveals what is going to happen but not what to do about it. The future is provided; the present is implied. The question, how and when could it happen? drives the narrative action. Additional questions, including the evaluative question, is it good or bad? and the philosophical but deeply practical question, is the future tractable? shape the interpretation of the experience and the narrative performance.[23]

Less relevant is whether the revelation was solicited or not. The vast majority of descriptive revelations appear as unsolicited dreams. As such, one might expect narratives to be dominated by questions about the origin of the dream. However, the expectation within the LDS community is that dreams are a common media for communication with the divine, even if most dreams are just the strange meanderings of a sleeping mind. While this expectation may not completely alleviate the question of divine origin experientially, it does preclude explicit mention in narrative performance.

Interpretive Question: How and When?

In descriptive revelation, images of the future are revealed in the present. These images are rarely complete or unambiguous. As with prescriptive revelation, descriptive revelation raises as many questions as it answers. People wonder how exactly this future will appear in real life and when. The revelatory image of the future lurks in the mind until the real world of lived experience catches up.

That temporal gap between revelation and experience can be long, where revelation may be forgotten until fulfillment. "I had a dream somewhere around, I think I was a teenager," remembers Sandy Johnson, "and I dreamed about the guy I would marry. Well, actually, I dreamed I was getting married.

"And the funny thing is, I don't remember the face of the person but I knew he had spiky hair. And you look at my husband now, he's got the spiky hair. And he's had it since I met him."

It was only after meeting George years later, however, that she remembered her dream. The revelation provided an image of her husband, but details were sparse, the image incomplete. Sandy knew he would have spiky hair, but little else. Further, she did not know when this was supposed to happen. When she met George, however, she remembered her dream and saw him as fulfillment of her revelation.

In other cases, the gap between revelation and fulfillment is short, where the revelatory scene appears in life almost immediately. For a young girl traveling with her family to California, her troubling dream was fulfilled the following day:

> When I was about twelve years old, my family took a trip to California. We traveled by car from Utah to California. We stayed one night in Las Vegas and then traveled on to California, staying in a different motel each night. Part of the trip was a day in Disneyland.
>
> One night on the trip I had a dream that I still remember parts of. My sister Pam and I were sitting in a café eating and talking. There was a man that kept looking at us. Later we returned to our motel and there was something really wrong. We were chased and hiding. It was a nightmare.
>
> Well, the next day we had traveled and were looking for a motel to stay in. Dad drove in to a parking lot and suggested to Mom that we stay in that motel.
>
> Well, there it was. The exact motel I had seen in my dream.
>
> I told my Dad that I didn't think we should stay there.
>
> He asked me why.
>
> I told him that I had had a bad dream about that place.
>
> He respected my opinion and drove on.
>
> I've always thought that my family had been watched over and protected from a bad experience on that trip.[24]

Again, the dream is ambiguous, not least because it is unclear whether it is merely a nightmare emerging from her fears of traveling and sleeping in strange places, or whether it is a revelation of the future sent to warn, protect, and prepare her. The moment she sees the motel from her dream, however, she recognizes the dream as a revelation of warning. She listens and acts, and the family completes their journey unmolested.

Ambiguity

One reason descriptive revelation is structured according to how the revelation will be enacted is due to its ambiguity. Ambiguity is particularly prevalent in descriptive prophecy partly because of the dominant media through which it is conveyed: dreams. Feelings, inspiration, and the still small voice all engage the mind as well as the senses; people often directly quote the Holy Ghost even when they identify the prompting as a feeling (see chapter 4). These various media convey thoughts and ideas, understandable in content if not in purpose. Dreams, on the other hand, provide images and scenes that demand translation into idea. Further, dreams can often be interpreted literally or metaphorically, while ideas are specific and literal. Finally, revelations may provide only a glimpse of the future or a partial view, raising questions about the larger context. The gap between the narrow view of revelation and the fully contextual experience in the future provides ample leeway for questioning how the revelation will be enacted and when.

Metaphorical dreams are particularly compelling for their tantalizing but ambiguous images of the future. In 1838, a man has a dream about being bitten by snakes all around his legs but knows he must keep running to survive. A week later, the man finds himself in the middle of the massacre at Haun's Mill. As he runs to escape, his legs are peppered with gunshot but, remembering his dream, he keeps running and escapes.[25] Another man dreams of a hen and two chicks stuck in a muddy stream. He saves the hen and one of the chicks but not the other. Soon, one of his sons dies. He joins the LDS Church, and just before his second son is about to die of the same illness, he receives a priesthood blessing and is healed.[26] Yet another man dreams of riding a bus with his girlfriend. When the bus stops, he gets off to take a short break and it drives on without him, taking his girlfriend with it. He races after it and encounters major obstacles, including falling off a cliff, before he finally catches it. Later, he realizes this dream was about his arduous, challenging courtship but eventual marriage to his girlfriend.[27]

Dreams with incomplete information also pose major interpretive challenges. A man forced to emigrate from Poland during World War II has a recurring dream twenty years later about a particular house with typical Polish architecture. In the dream he sees the specific street address for the house. He finally writes to the address and is reunited with lost family members.[28] A woman has a dream of a house in Salt Lake City. With no other information, she tracks it down and finds the current tenants about to burn some old things they found in the house. Those things include a box of records of her ancestors that allow her to continue her genealogical research.[29] A woman dreams of four-leaf clovers. A series of events lead her to an antique store where she finds a Bible with four-leaf clovers pressed between the pages. She buys it and then realizes the Bible was owned by her great-great-grandfather and contains her family genealogy.[30]

The interpretive demands for descriptive revelation are rigorous, and it is not uncommon to misinterpret revelation. Flipping back through his missionary journal, Robert Foster partly narrates, partly reads a particularly confusing dream where he sees a rooster that seems to signify death, a monkey that seems to signify joy and happiness, and a pregnant woman whose fetus is kicking to get out. A few days later, he finds himself at a hospital, laying hands on a young girl who looks like a rooster who is about to undergo surgery, a young boy who had been in the hospital for three years, surrounded by toy monkeys, and a woman whose newborn baby was hooked up to tubes and fighting for its life.

"So, here I am having a dream about a monkey and a rooster and a woman with a child in her womb," Rob explains, "but that's really not what was happening. That was just how my mind was receiving the information, how it made sense of the direction it was being given."

Rob points out that he was confused, having focused too heavily on the specific images rather than the meaning associated with them. Accordingly, he initially misinterpreted the meaning of two of the three images, wondering in his missionary journal: "Now I sit here amazed at all that happened, and I don't know what to do or think of it. The question is, why don't I understand it until it has happened?"

Provocatively, he suggests that the metaphoric images may have been created not by the divine but rather by his own mind. Translating the divine is difficult. Numerous scriptural passages in the Bible and in other LDS scriptures reinforce the idea that the human mind cannot fathom pure divine knowledge or view, much less comprehend, "the face of God."[31]

One possible interpretation of the unknowable nature of the divine is that God himself provides the metaphor. Another is that the human mind does the translating, substituting mundane, comprehensible images for incomprehensible ones. Rob had another dream where he saw a terrible man, a leader of a group, with glowing red eyes. He is convinced that the man did not actually have glowing eyes but that he provided that image in order to approximate the feeling of evil he sensed from his dream.

"There's a spiritual transmission, you know? This is what's happening. But then the mind has to take and interpret it.

"OK, scary being. Leader of something bad. Let's make this guy *really* bad. So of course it's not a guy with physical eyes glowing red, but somebody that's . . . pretty bad."

Rob is supposed to understand that the person is evil. For Rob, religious and cultural images readily supply him with one: a dark image with glowing red eyes who cracks a whip.

Therefore it may be wrong to assume that descriptive revelation is always delivered as an image. Instead, God may be sending value-laden ideas as well as images of future events. Interpretations of revelation can get distorted if people focus on an image they created in an act of interpretation rather than the idea or feeling that the Holy Ghost initially conveyed.

Interpretive Questions: Positive or Negative? and Is the Future Tractable?

The questions *how* and *when* launch the narrative performance. Yet underlying these questions is a more basic query that determines the expectations people bring to their interpretation of revelation: Is the future positive or negative? This question poses no crisis in interpretation itself; the answer is typically obvious, despite the ambiguity of revelation. However, the valence dictates the questions and actions that follow. If the future is positive, people assume a predominantly intractable future where action may be required only upon fulfillment. If it is negative, however, people pray for a tractable future and struggle to determine what action is needed in the present to avoid the predicted fate.

Positive Future

If the future is positive, the revelation is interpreted as a blessing, requiring little else beyond remaining faithful to God, since blessings are divine promises contingent on righteous behavior. Yet revelation also demands, or rather allows, the exercise of agency. Therefore, "righteous behavior" includes following not only God's general covenants as laid out in LDS doctrine but also his specific suggestions, either implied or explicit in revelation. The future, therefore, is at least partially tractable.

Camille Brennan recorded a story from her aunt that had been told across multiple generations in her family. It serves as a family origin story, explaining how they became Mormon:

> This is about my grandpa's great-great-grandmother that was in the *Ensign* about ten years ago. And this . . . Appelina, Appolinia Cabot, is that her name? It's something like that. Anyway, it's something like that.
>
> She went to bed and had a dream that she was reading a book. And she was reading the book all night long. In fact, the morning she woke up and she was really tired. She felt like she had actually been reading. Not only that night, but several nights in a row she was reading that book.
>
> And she didn't know what the name of the book was. And I don't think she knew what she was reading but was very impressive to her when she woke up.
>
> She knew what the book looked like, and she would ask her friends and family to be on the look out for that book, and they were but they never saw it.
>
> One day her aunt asked her if she could stay there while she went on a trip and take care of her house. She said she had a big chest full of books, and she was welcome to look through the books and read any of them you would like.
>
> So after she finished doing her work and chores around the house, she decided she would go to that chest and open it up and look at some of the books. After she took a few books and looked at them, she saw laying before her eyes the book of her dreams. And saw the book was the Book of Mormon. And she took it out and read it from cover to cover. And was really impressed.
>
> And later on, she had the missionaries come visit her, and she was converted to the Church. And she was baptized and moved to Ogden, Utah, and raised a big family. And lived until she was about eighty-three years old.[32]

In another family story, Mrs. John Patterson recounts how her father found their home after receiving a revelatory dream:

> We lived in Sterling and we didn't have a home there, we just rented. We wanted to buy a home with what money we had to buy with.
>
> One night Dad dreamed that he left Sterling and came north to Manti by foot. He went through Manti and he couldn't see anything that he could afford. He came on to Ephraim and came a little ways north, then he went east, and then he came north again. There he seen this home. It had trees around to the back and there was trees in the front and a corral out to the side. Just a little home.
>
> We came into Ephraim to look around to find this home. We went to President Otto Nielsen and he said if you go out to Brother Frost's, maybe he could help you out, maybe he's got just what you're looking for.

We went out to Brother Jim Frost's and he said, "Why, I believe I got just what you're looking for."

He was going to hand us the key to come and see it, and then he said, "I'm going to go with you."

He kept the key and put his coat on. We came north along Main Street, then 'cross the school grounds, and up to this corner, and we come across this bridge. When we was on that foot bridge, my husband says, "Why, this is the place!"

Brother Frost says, "How do you know it's the place? I didn't tell you."

Dad said, "No, but I seen it in a dream. And this is the place."

So you see, this place means a lot to me.[33]

Like prescriptive revelation, the climax in descriptive revelation comes when the truth of the revelation is confirmed. For Sandy, the climax comes when she meets George and remembers the revelation, not when she actually marries. For Mrs. Patterson's father, the climax occurs when he sees the house from his dreams, not when he buys it, officially making it his own. For Appolinia Cabot, the climax occurs when she sees the book that inspired her, not when she actually converts. The narrative performance focuses on proof that the dream was revelation, deriving its dramatic tension from whether the dream was prophetic and if so, how it will be fulfilled.

As with all personal revelation, people must exercise their agency. Having seen the image from revelation appear in life, the person must then act to attain the blessing. In most positive revelation, the action required is obvious. If the man you meet is supposed to be your husband, your actions require marrying him. If the book you dream about turns out to be religious scripture, you should convert. If the house you see is supposed to be your home, you should buy it. Descriptive revelation therefore serves to prime the pump, to prepare people for action when the time comes. When Mrs. Patterson's father finally sees the house literally of his dreams, he has been primed to act, but he must still exert his agency and choose to do so.

Because of the demand for the exercise of agency, descriptive revelation includes a prescriptive element. For positive revelation, the prescription typically follows the climax of the revelation. As with solicited prescriptive revelation, however, the decision to act is assumed. Having seen the revelation fulfilled, one has no doubt about the divine nature of the experience. More than any other type of revelation, positive descriptive revelation erases any spiritual crisis over whether or not to act.

Practical crises may remain, however. Having found his dream house in Ephraim, Mrs. Patterson's father must face practical realities: the price may be high, the location less than ideal, the neighbors noisy. He must place faith in God that the choice is a good one. Such dilemmas common in life are rare in the narrative tradition, however. Explicitly ignoring the revelation of God transgresses against cultural and religious norms, norms reflected in the narrative tradition.

Action *upon* fulfillment is assumed. Action *before* fulfillment, however, is not. The expectation for positive descriptive revelation is that one need only wait for fulfillment to act. Sandy Johnson does not actively seek out spiky-haired men to date; but when she realizes she is dating a man with spiky hair, she remembers the revelation and proceeds accordingly.

There are exceptions. Some descriptive revelations are more clearly prescriptive than others. When Mrs. Patterson's father sees his dream house in Ephraim, he realizes that he needs to act now and go to Ephraim, in addition to acting later to buy the house once the revelation is fulfilled and he finds it. The prescribed action is clear. However, determining the degree of prescription for primarily descriptive revelation can be a challenge. People may be so anxious to ensure fulfillment of the promise of a positive future that they do not wait for the image of revelation to appear in their lives. Such preemptive action is typically harmless but rarely helpful. When Appolinia Cabot sees an important book, she actively searches for it. This action ultimately appears unwarranted. The future was intractable; she would find the book, and when she did, only then was it necessary for her to act and seek out missionaries in order to convert.

The same is true when Monty Jenkins receives a dream about his future home in Utah, a dream that he is so eager to see fulfilled that excitement overrules his better judgment.[34]

> Monty: So another dream that I've had that's prophetic is . . . and again, at the time I didn't know it . . .
> We were in Kansas and we were trying to sell our house.
> And of course I was stressed out about it big time, praying a lot, asking what was going on, you know, what I should do, what was going to happen to us once we got up here.
> Nancy: Because we went through a big ordeal trying to sell the house.
> Monty: Yeah. It was just, ugh. I was asking if we should stay in that area, or what was going on.
> Gertie: Even me.
> Monty: So I had this dream. And in the dream I was a realtor. And I was walking up some stairs. And I walked up the stairs and there was a bathroom in front of me, and I turned to the left, and I walked into this kind of odd-shaped room. The ceiling was really low and it went up and then the ceiling was flat.

And so, I, in the dream, what I perceived as me, I walked into the room.

Meanwhile I'm seeing the back of me; I have a bald head, or what I perceive as myself, because I think bald head, me.

So I walk into the room, and I turn around, and as I turn around, I can see the face a little bit. I'm a lot older and I have a mustache. And I'm like, "Hm. Interesting."

Well, so, in my dream I stop at the door and watch myself walk into the room and talking and pointing out stuff. In the room, there's these doors that are . . . you've got the ceiling, it's like this, and you've got a part that's straight, here, and then the ceiling up here is straight. And you've got little lines that come down here [Monty draws a picture of the room with the doors and angled ceiling as he speaks].

So there's doors on here. There's one on this side and two on this side. And they're open, and you can see the attic.

And so, I get done talking, and I come out of the room, and it's kind of weird because I'm two people at once. And so I'm still standing by the door, I step back and let myself out, or what I perceive as myself. And I walk over and I adjust the thermostat on the wall, which is, you've got the stairs that come up into the room and you turn left and the door's here and then there's a wall here. And so the thermostat is on the wall, here [Monty continues to draw]. You can't get this on the tape, but . . .

So anyways, I adjust that, and that's when I woke up.

Well, you know, afterwards, I thought, you know, man, should I grow a mustache?

Nancy: Yeah, and he was asking me, and for the first few days, he actually tried, and then like, "You got to stop doing that."

Monty: I hate facial hair.

Nancy: I don't like him with facial hair either.

Monty: I hate facial hair. I've got to be clean shaven. And so I tried that for a week. I tried growing a mustache and I just, and I'm like, "I don't know what you [God] want me to do, but mustaches are out" [*laughter*].

Well, we get up here, and we [had] contacted Brother Heller in Utah.

Tom: Ohhhhhh . . . [*drawn out, in realization*]

Monty: And the funny thing is . . .

Tom: . . . bald head and mustache.

Monty: . . . we didn't know he was LDS.

Nancy: No we didn't.

Monty: We had tried five different realtors, and nobody would give us the time of day, because . . .

Nancy: And he was the only one that would actually return my calls and took us seriously. We told him we're looking for a house, we'll be up there we think around this time, we're supposed to close this day but I don't know if that's certain, and he's like "OK. Well, call me when you get up here and I'll be looking for your criteria."

Monty: The reason they didn't want to touch us is because we said we want a house that's under seventy thousand. And they're like, that's not even worth our time.

But anyway, we get down here and we're staying in a hotel, we met Brother Heller the first time. Didn't occur to me that I had seen him in a dream.[35]

Well, because we were church members, he was very concerned about us and didn't want us staying in the hotel, because we were staying kind of in a bad part of the town, too.

Nancy: We didn't know it, it was just a cheap motel and we found it.

Monty: It was cheap, it was what we could afford because we were saving our money so we could purchase our home.

So he finds a house for us that we can rent while we're getting into this house. And, uh, we get into the house, and we're walking through the downstairs, and we walk up the stairs, and I'm like, "I have seen this before."

We walk up the stairs, there's the bathroom. We turn left, and there's that funky room.

He walks into the room, walks around. I stay at the door, and he walks back out, adjusts the heat for us so we can stay there that night.

Tom: Wow.

Monty: And you know, Brother Heller looks quite a bit like me. You know, he's got a bald head like that.

Nancy: Bald head and everything [*laugh*].

Gertie: I sometimes think he's my dad, too. Because when he turned around, I even run to him sometimes like, "Dad, I've been looking for you forever." And then he turns around and he's like, "What?" And I'm like, "Oh shoot, you're not Dad" [*laugh*].

Nancy: And it was pretty funny because he didn't tell me the dream right off the bat, he just started growing the mustache. So I came home, right, and he's growing out his little mustache thing and I'm like, "New phase? You want to explain this to me?" [*laughter*] And then he tells me about this dream, and I'm like, "Honey, you are not growing a mustache. No, that's out."

Monty is so anxious to find a house to move his family into, so anxious to move decisively forward at this crossroad in his life that he flirts with growing a mustache to help conform to his revelatory dream. As he finds out later, such an attempt was futile, his interpretation of the dream mislaid. The revelation was, in fact, intractable insofar as he continued to maintain his covenants with God. He needed only to relax and wait for the virtual world of the revelation to match the actual world of lived experience.

In figure 3-4, the narrative triangle depicts how positive descriptive revelations are typically narrated. Again, the basic structural elements are consistent with other types of revelatory experiences, but the order shifts and the interpretive questions change. The dilemma over whether action is required before the revelation appears is typically slight, though as the examples mentioned above suggest, it can emerge as relevant in some cases, both experientially and in performance. The same is true for the dilemma over whether to act upon fulfillment. Experientially, agency must be exercised and a decision made. In narrative performance, that decision is rarely mentioned

Negative Future

For descriptive revelation that brings an ominous image of the future, the questions remain the same but shift in significance, orientation, and response. Instead of wondering what must be done to fulfill the future, people ask what if

Figure 3-4. Positive Descriptive Revelation

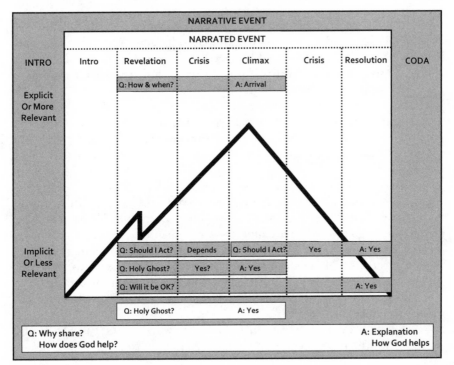

anything can be done to avoid it. Further, the expectation, as well as the hope, is that negative futures are tractable, that actions can be taken to avoid them. These expectations derive from the belief that God works on the behalf of those who are keeping their covenants with him. Through personal revelation, the Holy Ghost helps to protect the faithful, providing them with revelation to guide them through life. Revelation of future adversity is therefore generally viewed as a warning demanding action.

The primary challenge comes in knowing what to do in order to avoid the future. Since action is expected *before* the revelation appears on the horizon, negative revelations are particularly troubling. When the young girl dreams of a man stalking her family at a motel, she is provided no path of action. What is she supposed to do? One response would be to avoid motels altogether. Had she done this, she may have altered the future so entirely that no part of her revelation would be fulfilled (see chapter 4). However, in the space of uncertainty, she delays. At first sight of the motel from her dreams the following day, however, a plan of action becomes clear. She advises her father to keep driving. In doing so, they avoid the horrors revealed in her dream. This pattern is typical of negative descriptive revelations. "I had a 19 . . . I guess it doesn't matter what year it was," begins Robert Foster. "But it was a really nice little Subaru, four-wheel drive Subaru. It was my only means of transportation at the time.

> And I had a disturbing dream that I was driving the car, and while I was driving—it was dark—and I went over a bridge and I saw a blue sign, and I was headed somewhere, and I remember it saying C-4 on the sign. C-4, which struck a nerve because C-4 is also an explosive device for the military. So that's why I remembered it right then.
>
> And, while I was driving over the bridge, the car stalled.
>
> And the next thing in the dream that I remembered was seeing the car on the side of the road and the windows were knocked out and that the car . . . the hood was up and just the insides were all ripped out of it.
>
> So this got me a little concerned, worried about my car.
>
> And, about, I guess a week or so later, two weeks later, we had a youth activity . . . a young single adult activity, not youth thing. And I was invited to go to this activity, and it was at Jordan Lake. And the grounds, the campground that we were going to meet at was C-4. So, immediately I panicked. And I'm like, "I gotta, ugh. I want to go, I definitely want to go, but what am I going to do because this dream, about my car? And I've had dreams like this before, so, I gotta be extra careful. Maybe that's what it's about, be extra careful."
>
> So, I went to the gas station, and filled up with the best gas that I could get, the little ninety octane or whatever. And, I got some gas treatment,

and checked my spark plugs and just did everything. Checked the oil levels and everything. My car's going to run fine. I don't have any worries.

So while I was driving to this event, I got over the lake, Jordan, Jordan Lake, and right on the bridge, the car stopped. All the electronics went dead. And I panicked [*small laugh*].

I was able to coast off the bridge onto the side of the road, and there it was, sitting in the grass, just like the dream.

And a deputy pulled up and said, "Can I take you somewhere?"

And I was like, "No, I got to stay with my car, got to stay with my car."

He was like, "You can't have your car, or you, sitting here on the side of the road. So you're going to have to go."

And he took me to a, like a gas station, and I called my brother. And immediately rushed back. I had the police officer drop me back off over at the car. I said I'd meet my brother at the car, is what I told the police officer.

So he took me back over there, said he'd stop back by in about twenty minutes if I needed any more help.

So my brother shows up, and he's like, "Well, we're going to have to leave you here over night, because we can't do anything about it right now."

And I just, "No, you don't understand. I had this dream. The car is going to get all messed up somehow. Somebody's going to do something to it."

And he's like, "Man, this old piece of junk; nobody's going to do anything to your car" [*laughter*].

So we drove back home and I made him promise we were going to get up first thing in the morning and go out there and fix the car. And he's like, "Sure, sure. We'll worry about that tomorrow."

So we got up early, went back out to Jordan Lake, and pulled up, and the car was just, you know. And my heart's just beating through my chest as we're coming up over the bridge, looking to see the car. And I see the back of it, and I'm like OK, there's the back of the car, how's it looking? And there it was; it was still all in one piece. So I was like, "Whew. We're good."

So my brother lifts the hood up on the car and he's looking around, different parts, and he says, "What, what did you say you did to this?"

I said, "Man, I did everything. I put in good gas, I put in gas treatment, checked the oil, filters, everything."

He said, "Yeah. I think you were running such a high octane here, you busted your distributor cap" [*laughter*].

I said, "That's impossible. That's a brand new distributor cap from like a month before."

And he pulled it out and it had a crack in it. And he said, "I know there's a car place here close by, it's about ten minutes away, we can go there and get one."

I was like, "I'll stay with the car."

And he said, "No, no, no. C'mon let's go, let's go, it'll be fun. It's not that far."

So against my better judgment, I went with him. We went, we got the distributor, and the same feelings that I had pulling up there the very first time, the same feelings I had the night before when the car actually died, all returned.

And as we came up over the bridge, we saw another Subaru parked in front of it, and it was a tan Subaru. And the guy was out of the car, looking at my car, and lifting up on the door handle and looking inside.

And so, of course my brother, being the aggressor that he is, immediately pulled off on the median. Well, first, he slowed down, he was like, "Let's see what this guy's going to do." And watched him, and that's when we watched him jiggling the handle and peering into the car. So he sped up real fast, pulled over to the side of the road, got out, was like, "Can I help you?"

The guy said, "Oh no. I just saw this car here and was wondering if maybe you guys needed some help."

My brother, being the stalwart aggressor, bunched his shoulders up, "No. We're fine."

But the thing I didn't mention before all this was the night that I actually left to go, I was praying like crazy that nothing would happen to this car. I know it sounds kind of silly, it's just a car, but you know, that was . . . I think as a teenager, the car was a symbol of freedom. This is where I can declare my independence. I can go and do whatever I want, whenever I need to. And as an adult, it's more of a necessity. And it was how I got to where I needed to be to make a living.

And it was with that earnestness, that anxiousness, that I prayed.

So. Got to have my car. Safe.

And, I don't know. It was just a witness that that particular time, when I needed it, my Heavenly Father was watching out for me, and letting me know about some things that were going to possibly happen. And even though I was hard headed, went ahead and did exactly what I was warned not to do, there's still a little bit of saving grace in there.

Robert Foster clearly believes that the future is tractable, that he can avoid having his car vandalized if he takes precautions. But, since the revelation was descriptive rather than prescriptive, Robert is not guided in what he should do to avoid this future. In retrospect, when he realized the C-4 of the campsite was the C-4 from his dream, he should have cancelled his camping trip. His compromise, along with sincere prayer, ends up altering the future but not wholly avoiding the negative consequences. Further, in an ironic twist, he believes he actually may have caused the car to malfunction in his misguided attempt to interpret the revelation to avert disaster. Determining what action should be taken to avoid a negative future is difficult and poses one of the greatest challenges to a person who receives revelation of a negative future.

While the expectation for revelation of a negative future is that it is tractable and can be avoided, the narrative tradition reveals that this is not always the case. People hope they can avoid future suffering, but they recognize that even a loving God does not protect people from all adversity. Bad things happen. Sometimes God's love is displayed by preparing a person to face adversity, by providing comfort in times of hardship.

Frank Nielson recounts three separate occasions where he received revelation that tragic events were on the horizon. The revelations were descriptive but came as feelings of dread rather than specific images. Not knowing what would happen, but knowing it was bad, he pleaded with God to alter the future. Eventually, he accepted that the event would occur, finally realizing that God was preparing him for the tragedy so that he could serve as support for his family to help them through the hard times.[36] "It's kind of a burden sometimes," he explains, "to think you know or to have that feeling that something bad is going to happen to a family member and drag that around. It's not fun. But, if that's the preparation that I need . . .

"If it blindsided me I don't know how I'd react because that hasn't really happened yet, where somebody just died without having that kind of prompting, that nudge, to get me ready. So I'm going to be grateful for it."

Adhering to cultural expectations, Frank approached the revelations with the expectation that they were tractable. They were not. No action on his part could alter these futures. However, he was not stripped of his agency. Rather, the cultural and religious expectations that God helps his children made it clear that these revelations were provided for a reason. The revelations provided the time needed to actively prepare for these events for the benefit of himself and his family.

Structurally, negative descriptive revelation mirrors positive. However, the crises are more pronounced, emerging as explicit elements in the narrative. People struggle with what to do in the face of impending tragedy or hardship. Often, a plan of action emerges only once the images from the revelation begin to appear in real life. For this reason, explicit crises over what to do appear both before and after the climax when the truth of the revelation is confirmed (see figure 3-5).

Experience and the Narrative Tradition

Parallels and Divergences

Analysis of personal revelation both as experience and as narrative reveals differences that suggest distinct types of personal revelation. These types are based on the interpretive questions posed during the experience, during the

Figure 3-5. Negative Descriptive Revelation

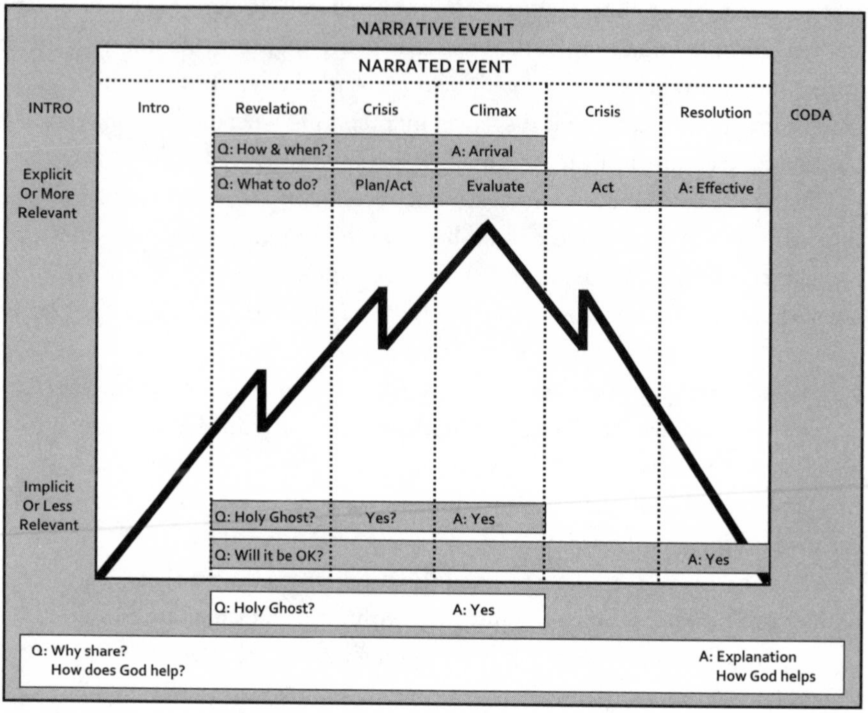

NARRATIVE EVENT

NARRATED EVENT

INTRO	Intro	Revelation	Crisis	Climax	Crisis	Resolution	CODA
		Q: How & when?		A: Arrival			
Explicit Or More Relevant		Q: What to do?	Plan/Act	Evaluate	Act	A: Effective	
Implicit Or Less Relevant		Q: Holy Ghost?	Yes?	A: Yes			
		Q: Will it be OK?				A: Yes	
		Q: Holy Ghost?		A: Yes			
	Q: Why share? How does God help?					A: Explanation How God helps	

narration, or both. Analysis also reveals areas where experience and narrative can diverge, where people highlight or subsume specific aspects of the experience, particularly in deciding whether or not to act and in assessing the origin of the revelation.

Divergence between experience and narrative can also occur on a more fundamental level in the kinds of experiences narrated. Despite their pervasiveness in LDS experience, stories of revelation that come in answer to prayer make up only a small fraction of the narrative tradition. Answered prayers are rarely remarkable enough to meet the narrative demand for drama or the social demand for proof of the divine.

Similarly, narrative demands for a climax and resolution preclude revelation without confirmed fulfillment. People may receive promptings but never see the effects of their actions. This is particularly true of warnings. When dangers are witnessed, stories are shared. The woman who is prompted to pull over, does so, and moments later sees a truck careening out of control on the wrong side of the road. But the person who is prompted to stay home, does so, and encounters no harm lacks a clear climax, resolution, or proof of revelation. Without these critical narrative elements, such experiences are rarely narrated.[37]

The same is true for descriptive revelation of the future where the gap between revelation and fulfillment is wide. Until fulfillment, there is no climax or resolution, making revelation difficult to narrate. Only in fulfillment is the revelation confirmed as divine. Revelatory experiences may be held in limbo until fulfillment, thought about but not shared. In fact, until fulfillment, the experience may not be considered revelation at all.

Experientially, however, revelations without evidence of fulfillment are the norm, not the exception. During a Sunday school discussion about personal revelation, Terry Holmes warned the congregation that they need to follow the promptings of the Holy Ghost even though they may not know why. "Sometimes we find out why we were prompted," he says, "but probably most of the time we don't." Paul Clayson concurred, adding, "Maybe this life, maybe in the next life, maybe never." Again, the narrative tradition is selective in its reflection of experience.

Cultural norms also affect which experiences are narrated and which ones are not. The narrative tradition is dominated by narratives where a person receives revelation, the person ultimately acts on the prompting, the promise of the prompting is fulfilled, rationale for the action is explained in the course of events, the person is guided in beneficial ways, and the presence and power of God is confirmed. In a smaller but substantial number of narratives, however, the person does not act or accept the promise of the revelation, the revelation is borne out to be true, and the person realizes their mistake and vows not to ignore the Holy Ghost again. The experience is narrated and shared, since the promise of the prompting is fulfilled, the rationale for the action is explained, and the power of the Holy Ghost is confirmed. These stories remind the teller and the audience of the importance of listening to the Holy Ghost. The narrative tradition favors these two types of experience (see figure 3-6).

The narrative tradition accommodates a fairly narrow body of experiences. Charting the possible options for personal revelation reveals two types of experience rarely narrated. In one type, a person chooses not to act and finds the promise of the prompting unfulfilled. The experience is interpreted correctly, the action taken was appropriate, and religious norms are upheld. Yet such experiences are forgotten quickly, ignored, or actively excluded.[38] One explanation derives from the fact that generic categories are by nature self-reifying. As Virginia L. Brereton points out in her discussion of one type of spiritual narrative: "Conversion narratives themselves can hardly provide a full picture of the experience since ipso facto they all end happily—they are invariably success stories" (1991:xiii). The result is that once again, experience and narrative

Figure 3-6. Experience and the Narrative Tradition

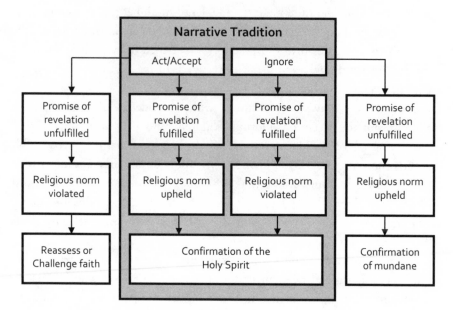

diverge. Ambiguous promptings do not always turn out to be divine revelation in real life, but they do in the narrative tradition.

The other type of experience missing from the narrative tradition describes those times when a person interprets a prompting as divine and responds accordingly only to find the promise unfulfilled. Such a violation of expectations can be spiritually troubling. For less devout members, these experiences can challenge their faith. More devout members, however, may continue to search for answers, looking inward for an explanation rather than blaming God. For them, such experiences can be useful as a way to reassess how they distinguish the Holy Ghost from other stimuli. Shawn Tucker was convinced he had received a prompting that his first child would be a boy. When his wife gave birth to a girl, he was shaken:

> When Nicole got pregnant with Justine, she was having sort of a tough time. And so she asked me to give her a blessing. So, because I have the priesthood, I put my hands on her head and I gave her the blessing.
> When I gave her this blessing, I felt very impressed that she would have a boy. And all this stuff about this boy.
> At least on a conscious level, I didn't care if we had a boy or a girl. And so this didn't seem to be coming from me. But I was convinced that we were going to have a boy.

When Justine was born, C-section, she was a girl. And this was hard for me, because I had felt like this was going to be a boy.

The other thing was, I wasn't invested in it for myself, but then I was like, why did this go this way?

And, I'm really grateful for that experience because it reminds me that I can be wrong. That things that I can take as the Spirit can be inaccurate. And that, you know, you always have to be listening.

Because I'm convinced now that had I listened better, I would have understood that voice differently than what actually happened. But part of it is learning to listen.

Shawn Tucker remains convinced that the prompting was divine. Accordingly, he finds fault not with God's ability to make good on his promise but with himself for his inability to correctly interpret the Spirit. He continues to narrate this story because it is useful to remind him—and others who may be struggling with similar questions—that interpreting the Spirit is a difficult enterprise. Shawn's interpretation transforms an experience that lies outside the realm of the narrative tradition of revelation into an experience that can be comfortably accommodated within it, by confirming the power and presence of the Holy Ghost.[39]

In his study of marriage confirmation narratives, George H. Schoemaker presents a story shared by a woman who received personal revelation that told her: "If he asks you to marry him, it will be the right thing to do, but it will be very difficult" (1989:44). The marriage ultimately ends in divorce. The woman explains: "There are a couple of ways that I have tried to rationalize it. One way is that you can't make a person's mind up for him, he had changed during the marriage, and of course I had changed too." She continues to provide reasons for what they might have done to salvage the marriage. She concludes: "I can't deny that there was a confirmation, and I don't regret it."

The woman has clearly reconciled the revelation and her divorce. She does so using two distinct strategies. If this story suggests failed revelation, there is precedent for how it can be rationalized by blaming behavior outside one's control. She points out "you can't make a person's mind up for him." A similar rationale is often provided for Joseph Smith's revelation that Independence, Missouri, would be built up as Zion (see D&C 84:3–5, 97:18–20, and 101:16–21). Independence may prove to serve as Zion yet in the latter days, but the prophecy that "a temple shall be reared in this generation" (D&C 84:3–5) clearly did not come to pass. Shawn Tucker explains: "Joseph Smith was told that they would settle in Zion, that they would build a temple there, that the world would congregate there. Then it was like, "Nah, we're not going to do that [*laugh*]. It didn't happen." I ask him how people reconcile this turn of events.

"There's a verse in the Doctrine and Covenants that comes later on that says that 'when I give you a commandment to do something and you do all that you can to do it, but you're prevented from doing it because of evil people, then I rescind the order, the command for you to do that.' And so, that's how that's sort of answered.[40]

The woman blames both her husband and herself, noting that he did not do what he needed to make the marriage work, and both of them had moved too quickly without sufficiently getting to know each other.

The woman also rationalizes her divorce by implicitly questioning whether this was failed revelation at all. The revelation itself seems to hint at the possibility of failure, noting that "it will be very difficult." Divine confirmation of the marriage does not alleviate the hard work that the couple must undertake to make the marriage work. Without this work, failure is not only rationalized, it is expected. In this way, divorce does not undermine the truth of the revelation, it supports it. From this perspective, this woman's experience is not an example of failed revelation at all.

What might appear initially as "failed" revelation can also be attributed to faulty assumptions. When Marcia Nesbitt's sister dreams of seven blond children but then has only non-blond children, Marcia reassesses both her initial interpretation and the nature of heaven:

> Before my sister Susan was married, she kept having these . . . dreams. And in these dreams, she dreamed that she had seven little blond children. And she knew what they looked like and everything. I forgot what order they were in, something like . . . boy, boy, girl . . . and I forget the rest, but it was something like that.
>   But she never had them.
>   But you know what? She's had so many miscarriages that they could be them. Because she had like four miscarriages before she had her first kid. And she had a couple in between her second and third kids. But none of her kids have blond hair. But, you know, don't know what color of hair the miscarried babies had. It could be them.[41]

Marcia Nesbitt initially interprets the dream according to the extensive subgenre of spirit children revelations and assumes the children her sister sees are destined to be her children on Earth. As such, the revelation would appear to be unfulfilled. However, Marcia reassesses this assumption. The babies in the dream could have been the babies her sister miscarried. Such an interpretation demands a refiguring of the premortal existence so that even miscarried babies are sealed to their parents, a principle with no scriptural basis but that resonates with the widespread belief that parents and children know each other in heaven before coming to Earth (see chapter 5). Convinced that her interpretation of the dream was correct, Marcia finds an interpretation that accommodates her belief and her lived reality. The contextual comments that collector Camille Brennan provides to introduce Marcia's story explain: "Marcia was hesitant to share this story with us because it never happened. However, she believes that her sister did have the children she dreamt of through her miscarriages." In other words, she decides to narrate the experience because her interpretation transforms what appears to be failed revelation into fulfilled revelation, confirming the presence and power of the Holy Ghost.

In most cases, however, people reassess "failed" revelation and find fault with their assumption of a divine origin. The dream is just a dream, the prompting an expression of personal desire or random thought. Relegated to the mundane, these experiences are not personal revelation and cannot be narrated as such. And only rarely, when they can function to highlight the difficulty of distinguishing the Holy Ghost, are they narrated at all.

The Power of Genre

Divergences between the narrative tradition and revelatory experience highlight the primary function of personal revelation narratives: to confirm God's love, his hand in all things, and his power and inclination to answer the prayers of the obedient, faithful, and righteous. Stories of personal revelation are regularly referred to as "faith-promoting stories," partly for this confirmation of God and the Holy Ghost, and partly in consideration of their dominant performance contexts: in the act of religious instruction and edification. The performance context encourages and reaffirms a specific function and ideology for the genre of personal revelation narratives. These generic expectations are powerful, encouraging a spirit-driven, internally supported interpretation of personal revelation.

The ideology interwoven into the genre of personal revelation narratives is so powerful that it can shape not only the narrative tradition—by what is and is not included—but also the meaning of the experience itself, by suggesting interpretations that would otherwise appear tenuous in light of experiential evidence. In Mike McCann's story about returning home to find his house broken into, for example, he concludes that God was watching out for him. Yet there is no particular evidence that his early return resulted in a more favorable outcome than had he continued on to work. While his interpretation that God was watching over him seems initially unfounded from the description of the event, it conforms perfectly to the expectations of the genre, and to one expectation in particular: the Holy Ghost does not prompt without a reason. Receiving a prompting to return home, then discovering that one's house has been broken into is not coincidence but evidence of the divine. Mike tentatively suggests a logical interpretation: that his neighbor was also prompted by the Holy Ghost: "You know, if I wouldn't have come home, or if the neighbor wouldn't have been home . . . you know?" Mike points out throughout his narrative that his neighbor's presence scared the robber away before he could escape with the bulk of the stolen goods. This action was a blessing for McCann, suggesting God's hand not only in prompting him to go home but in prompting his neighbor to go outside.

God's protective power is an expectation—both in life and for personal revelation narratives—strong enough to *direct* interpretation rather than merely *facilitate* it. Ideological expectations for the genre, and cultural norms for revelation more generally, serve as important resources for the interpretation and narration of personal revelation. As Mike McCann's story suggests, experience interpreted through a particular LDS worldview can suggest interpretations that might strike non-Mormon as tenuous but be perfectly consonant within the LDS community.[42] Further, the specific ideological orientation embedded in the genre of narratives of personal revelation repositions individual experience within a shared religious tradition. The result is a narrative tradition that confirms both religious doctrine and the narrator's identity within the religious group.

Conclusion

Personal revelation demands a great deal of interpretation. The divine is mysterious. The Holy Ghost prompts with subtle feelings, thoughts, and voices, and with metaphoric, incomplete, or ambiguous images. Personal revelation challenges people to answer a series of practical and spiritual questions in order to benefit from the guidance and blessings revelation provides. Tracking the interpretive challenges and questions posed by personal revelation reveals that different types of revelation pose different questions. Further, while the type of personal revelation a person receives dramatically affects the kinds of interpretive questions confronted at the time of the experience and posed in the narrative performance, narratives are not identical indices for experience. Some elements get highlighted, others subsumed. Further, some experiences get narrated while others do not. These choices reveal narrative and cultural norms embedded in the generic expectations for personal revelation narratives.

As part of social discourse, successful performance requires transforming experience into narrative for an audience. Narrators recognize that their audiences may doubt the supernatural nature of their experience, even when narrator and audience share the same religion. The result is that the focus of the narrative is often directed to the fulfillment of the revelation that provides proof of the divinity of the experience as much as on the resolution of the particular problem or the religious tenet that frames the performance.

Cultural and social norms also shape narrative performance. The heavily didactic use of narratives of personal revelation in various church and teaching settings have shaped a narrative tradition that favors experiences that confirm the role and power of the Holy Ghost in caring for God's children. Experiences assumed to be revelation but that go unfulfilled are ignored unless they can be reinterpreted to confirm this role.

The types of revelation, interpretive questions, and shared norms for narration that emerge in this analysis favor broad patterns that define generic performance. However, it is important to remember that narrators exercise great autonomy in what they include in their narratives, how they frame them, and what meanings they ultimately draw. Each performance provides another opportunity for narrators to interpret their experience. Specific situational contexts will demand specific narrative choices. As discussed in chapter 2, variations in interpersonal relationships between narrator and audience, variations in explicit and implicit motivations for narrating and the ensuing functions of performance, and time constraints of the performance setting all affect the structure and content of narrative performance. The patterns identified here in structural analysis remain an accurate reflection of the expectations for the genre, but such patterns should be understood as loose prescriptions for narrators rather than strict rules. Even more flexible are the smaller structural patterns and formulas that appear across different types of personal revelation (explored in chapter 4). In these patterns one can more clearly glimpse the aesthetic elements of personal revelation narratives that synthesize experience and art.

Synthesis: The Interpretive Challenge of Religious Memorates

Interpretation and Evidence as Narrative Imperatives

Religious memorates enter the world as narratives of persuasion: arguments for belief. At their heart is an experience that challenges the norms for rational thinking and that, despite the widespread belief in the divine and divine communication, remains a question mark for audience members, even for narrators. The result is that interpretation is often constructed as an evidentiary argument cast into narrative, performed in social context.

Analysis of Latter-day Saint narratives of personal revelation reveals the degree to which the interpretive moves of narrators at the time of their spiritual experiences structure narrative performance. The narrator transfers the search for evidence and support for the validity of the spiritual encounter from the experience to the narrative performance. In doing so, narrators position themselves alongside rather than apart from their audiences, encouraging a sympathetic connection that avows, "Just like you, I wasn't sure if this was divine or not. Just like you, I found it hard to believe."

In her phenomenological case study of the religious memorate of a Pentecostal woman's experience with the Holy Spirit, Christine Cartwright recognizes this rhetorical move as a significant element in religious memorates, particularly those that challenge the rational beliefs widely accepted as the norm in the United States. Cartwright argues that the structure of religious memorates may be evidential rather than dramatic (1982:64). The woman's narrative is structured according to a series of moments when she questioned the validity of what was happening, and it provides repeated evidence for why she came to believe her experience with the Holy Spirit was real. Cartwright imagines the dangers of ignoring this structure and the ongoing interpretation and evaluation of the experience: the narrator "might have been described as a woman who believes that people can have spiritual snakes coming out of their heads. She could have been introduced as an emotionally damaged individual, and her religious participation and experience described as symptomatic of her emotional needs. The study could have focused upon her conviction that she received the equivalent of ten years of psychotherapy in about three minutes, and made the argument that charismatic religion caters to the desire for quick and easy solutions to problems of personal growth" (65). In other words, analysis could cast the narrator of religious memorates as delusional, the same critique David Hufford levels against positivist approaches to the study of supernatural experience (1995).

Cartwright's analysis is based on a single narrative performance. However, published texts of testimonies, conversion narratives, and other religious memorates suggest that evaluative and interpretative moves are common in religious memorates (see, for example, narratives published in Lawless 1988, Stromberg 1993, Sutton 1977, Titon and Geroge 1978, Titon 1988, Woodward 2000). Diane Goldstein suggests that religious memorates may not have significant referential elements of action but instead may be "largely analytical, interpretive and emotional in content" (1989:44). "Our error" she argues, "is not to be found in including such accounts as narrative, but rather in our notion of narrative action as somehow dichotomous with interpretation" (45). The personal revelation narratives of Latter-day Saints suggest an even stronger argument: that evaluative and interpretive elements can in fact be dramatic and that the questions people ask in the moments during and following a spiritual experience can in fact provide the primary structure for narrative performance.

In this way, the performance of religious memorates can provide a map of the process of both receiving and, importantly, *interpreting* religious experience. Religious memorates are therefore valuable to audience members not only for instruction and edification but also as models of processes and strategies that can be abstracted and applied in their own lives, to their own spiritual experiences. By encoding the "instructions" for interpretation in their very texts, religious memorates provide both question and answer, code and codex. In a revision to the adage "Give a man a fish, he eats for a day; teach a man to fish, he eats for a lifetime," the religious memorate does both at once, providing people a single concrete experience as spiritual sustenance for the moment as well as providing the process for interpreting their own experiences for the rest of their lives.

The Ambiguity of Divine Communication

Even with a redefined concept of narrative structure, drama, and "action," spiritual experiences often remain largely internal and difficult to describe. In stories of receiving the Holy Ghost, the Pentecostal church members Elaine Lawless worked with often leaped over the actual spiritual experience, an act she interprets as a move to allow "for the necessarily 'ineffable' quality of the actual moment of union with the supernatural" (1988:17). A survey of divine communication bears out this pattern not merely of the "ineffable" but also of the ambiguous.

The ambiguity of divine communication, revelation, and prophecy in particular, is widespread throughout folk literature as well as the Western literary canon. In versions of *Oedipus* by Aeschylus, Euripides, and Sophocles, prophecies abound. While the predictions themselves are typically clear, the identities of those involved are obscured, creating the dramatic tension of the story. One exception appears in Sophocles's version of the play, in which the old prophet Tiresias inverts this model, making the identity of the protagonist clear but the meaning obscure, declaring to Oedipus: "This day shall give thee birth and give thee death" (1966:26). The Delphic Oracle also figures heavily in the Oedipus story and was also known to produce enigmatic prophecies. The same is true of the trio of witches in Shakespeare's *Macbeth*, who prophesy in riddles that Macbeth interprets literally as firm impossibilities. The Delphic Oracle and the three witches all exemplify Stith Thompson's motif M305, Ambiguous Oracle, and their utterances represent M306, Enigmatical Prophecy—both of which are common in folk narrative (1966:49–50). I have argued elsewhere that these enigmatic prophecies are often constructed as riddles, citing examples from the first- or second-century Second Epistle from Peter in the New Testament, the fifteenth-century Mayan prophet Aj Tomojchi', the sixteenth-century French seer Michel de Nostredame (better known as Nostradamus), traditional Hopi prophecy repeated in 1955 by Julius Doopkema, and a deep tradition of Choctaw prophecies that continue to be shared today (Mould 2002). To this list of enigmatic prophecies could be added those attributed to individuals such as Mother Shipton—who is believed to have lived in England in the sixteenth century, had her first prophecies published in the seventeenth century, and had prophecies fabricated on her behalf in the seventeenth and nineteenth centuries—as well as prophecies and predictions shared widely throughout a particular region, nation, or culture in locales that span the globe.[43] What is clear is that prophecy and revelation are often ambiguous and vague, characteristics recognized so widely that historian Keith Thomas has argued that the surest sign of fabricated prophecy is too much detail (1971:422).

Explanations for Ambiguity in the Divine

Why mantic discourse should be ambiguous is a much thornier issue, one that I tackled only in broad strokes in my study of Choctaw prophetic narratives (Mould 2002:398). Skeptics argue that the ambiguity of divine discourse is actually constructed to provide wiggle room for the false prophet to shape prophecy to fit emerging events (see Friedrich 1997:175 and Thomas 1971:394). Assuming that divine discourse is possible, however, allows for a more robust list of explanations, including the semiotic problem of translating thoughts and images into words, the linguistic problem of interpreting metaphoric language, and the cognitive and communicative problem of providing complete textual and contextual knowledge in typically brief bursts of communication.

A more comprehensive argument can be found in Robert McKim's book *Religious Ambiguity and Religious Diversity*, in which he tackles the question of the "hiddenness of God." Although McKim approaches this question as it relates to the existence of God, he recognizes that this fundamental question applies to religious ambiguity more broadly, and in fact, his approach can be mapped directly onto the question of why revelation is often vague and ambiguous. Structurally, McKim identifies two types of theories to explain God's hiddenness as: (1) a consequence of God's nature, and (2) "goods of mystery," an intentional act to provide some particular benefit that clarity would undermine.

One explanation emerging from the consequence of God's nature is the problem of divine transcendence. For Christians, the Bible describes a God who cannot be fully known or seen. In 1 Timothy 6:16, Jesus Christ is described as "dwelling in the light which no man can approach unto; whom no man hath seen, nor can see." Even more explicit is God's response to Moses after he beseeches God to "show me thy glory" (Exodus 33:18): "I will make all my goodness pass before thee, and I will proclaim the name of the Lord before thee; and will be gracious to whom I will be gracious, and will show mercy on whom I will show mercy. And he said, Thou canst not see my face: for there shall no man see me, and live" (33:19–20). He does, however, allow a glimpse: "And the Lord said, Behold, there is a place by me, and thou shalt stand upon a rock: And it shall come to pass, while my glory passeth by, that I will put thee in a clift of the rock, and will cover thee with my hand while I pass by: And I will take away mine hand, and thou shalt see my back parts: but my face shall not be seen" (33:21–23). The image of God provided is partial, incomplete, intentionally obscured. So, too, may be his messages.

For Latter-day Saints, this pattern of limited knowledge is echoed in the belief that God apportions knowledge incrementally over time. In particular, there are scriptures that have been sealed up, hidden from view until the time God deems appropriate. The Book of Mormon was one such set of scriptures, sealed until the latter days, when they were revealed to Joseph Smith.[44]

Coupled with the notion of divine transcendence, the limits of divine knowledge can be either inherent or temporal. They may also be individualized based on spiritual development. Religious leaders are typically assumed to have greater knowledge and greater access to the divine then the laity—whether the Dalai Lama, leading Islamic imams, the pope, or the president of the LDS Church. Rhetorically, church members of evangelical Christian faiths often avow the democratization of spiritual access, while nonetheless supporting, promoting, or at least perceiving their leaders as standing above the congregation as more spiritual, with more powerful and sustained contact with the divine. Among Latter-day Saints, the memorates of the General Authorities and discussions by lay members clearly support a view that spiritual knowledge and divine communication are intensified for church leaders, those men and women who have proved themselves particularly righteous and worthy (see chapters 1 and 2). The one instance in LDS scripture of God showing himself to a human is explained by God as a blessing received for showing the utmost faith, obedience, and devotion: "And never have I showed myself unto man whom I have created, for never has man believed in me as thou hast" (Ether 3:15).

The incomprehensibility of God can also be cast as an aspect of human deficiency, a problem to be remedied or overcome (McKim 2001:4, 16–8). These deficiencies may be inherent and shared by all humans, or they may be specific to those who have sinned, are ignorant, or have willfully shunned God. In terms of revelation, the ambiguous dream or vague prompt can result from a lack of experience receiving and interpreting revelation or from the inability to hear the divine thanks to the distractions of worldly matters, benign and harmful alike. Both of these causes derive from human fallibility. Latter-days Saints speak regularly of these deficiencies, through their metaphor of tuning in to the Holy Spirit and the lifelong process of learning to hear and heed the Holy Ghost (see chapter 1). Shawn Tucker, for example, is convinced that if he had been more attentive, more attuned to the Spirit, more practiced in interpreting revelation, he would have understood the revelation about the gender of his first child (discussed earlier in this chapter). What is vague and ambiguous to one person, therefore, may not be for the next.

These human "deficiencies" can be understood as a more widely shared semiotic problem as well. As discussed earlier in the chapter, divine discourse may come as images, thoughts, or feelings; not words, mandates, or clear and complete scenes. Complicating matters is the need to determine whether a revelation is literal or metaphoric, and to what extent the individual is unconsciously translating the divine in order to make sense of the message. The layers of translation are multiplied outside of personal revelation when divine messages are shared through the collaborative efforts of multiple people. The oracle at Delphi needed priests to translate her murmurs and mumblings into intelligible prophecies. In Pentecostal churches, one person may receive the gift of tongues, while the gift of translation allows another to make sense of the otherwise unintelligible vocables. Multiple voices and steps in translation risk confusing a message that may have been ambiguous, incomplete, or vague in the first place.

Returning to McKim's structure, there are also theories to explain the ambiguity of the divine rooted in the concept of "goods of mystery." McKim explains: "The implication in all such cases is that God would be harming us by revealing God's existence or character to us in a clear and unmistakable way. Thus it is argued, for example, that God's hiddenness makes possible human autonomy or a measure of control over whether to believe that God exists, or that it makes possible a choice of whether or not to have faith and trust in God" (18). Both of these explanations—the importance of agency and faith—are central to Latter-day Saints' rationale for the ambiguity of revelation. "I think that ambiguity is so important," explains Shawn Tucker. "Because, one, it helped me connect with other people," he says, referring to a recent prompt to call a fellow ward member he barely knew, for reasons he did not know but that became apparent later. "Two, it's empowering because if it were just, 'You're going to do all these steps,' it would almost just make us little children, you know, who are just 'Do this, do that.'"

George Johnson explains the centrality of agency to the war in heaven and the plan of salvation (see chapter 1). He further explains the flaw in Satan's plan to mandate belief in God and return every person to heaven. "But what that did is that took away our agency. Because we had agency in the premortal world where we were able to choose whether or not we wanted to follow Heavenly Father or follow Satan.

"Now that is *the* best gift he could give us. And if he went with Satan's plan, that would frustrate his whole plan and we wouldn't be able to become like him.

"Now here on Earth it's the same way. If there was a burning bush in everybody's front yard, nobody would have faith and be able to choose or have that agency and say, you know, I know there's not concrete evidence, I don't have the burning bush in my front yard, but I know that this is true. I choose to follow this."

As George suggests, closely tied to the need for agency is the need for faith. All religions demand some degree of faith, an extension of belief that cannot be defended through rational argument. While Latter-day Saints speak of "knowing" the church is true, they recognize that faith remains a necessary and fundamental aspect of the church. With complete and clear revelation, the worry is that faith could become devalued, viewed as a crutch rather than a fundamental and important aspect of religious practice that confirms humility and commitment. Further, revelation typically operates according to faith that God will make good on his promise if we remain righteous. In this way, revelation demands the constant reification of a reciprocal relationship. Express your faith in God and you open yourself to revelation and blessing.

Regardless of the reason for the ambiguity of the divine, in virtually all cases such ambiguity is assumed to be unavoidable. Clarity is God's to give. Yet in some traditions, ambiguity may result not with God or with the inability of humans to comprehend the divine but with humans themselves, acting rationally in a politicized world. The infamous Nostradamus, for example, claimed a political rationale for his vague, ambiguous, figurative prophecies, saying he feared persecution as a sorcerer. James P. Kiernan found similar fears of social and political repercussions in his study of Zulu Zionist revelation. While some revelation was inherently ambiguous, very powerful prophets could receive direct revelation. Rather than receive a message symbolically—I see hail, I see a coffin, I see a car crash—such prophets receive revelation directly, with full understanding (1985:308–9). However, direct revelation is so powerful and definitive, the prophet must detach himself and any connections to living social relations, adding a degree of ambiguity if not to the message, then to the source: "The general principle can thus be stated: the more explicit and uncompromising the revelation, the more necessary it is to wrap the source in mystery and obscurity; the more flexible and indeterminate the revelation, the more likely is the source to be fully identified and accountable" (312). Here, ambiguity is affected rather than inherent. This distinction is important for the prophet, less so for the adherent struggling to interpret the ambiguous message. Universal, therefore, is the need for strategies to interpret prophecy and revelation.

Interpretive Strategies for Dealing with Ambiguity

In his book *Biblical Ambiguities*, David Aaron argues that two questions emerge with divine discourse. First, is this revelation to be interpreted literally or figuratively? Then, if figurative, what does it represent? (2002:1–2). The first question is hardly an easy one. The General Authorities in the LDS Church, for example, have disagreed over this issue, with at least one side assuming that the question is an all-or-nothing proposition. Between 1835 and 1847, both Parley Pratt and Heber C. Kimball served as members of the Quorum of the Twelve Apostles. Parley Pratt argued for literal interpretation, Heber C. Kimball for metaphoric. In his introduction to his book *Late Persecution of the Church of Jesus Christ of Latter Day Saints*, Pratt avows: "We also believe that the scriptures of the Old and New Testament are true; and that they are designed for our profit and learning, and that all mistical [*sic*] or private interpretation of them ought to be done away; that the prophecies, and doctrine, the covenants and promises contained in them have a literal application, according to the most plain, easy, and simple meaning of the language in which they are written" (1840:vi–vii).

Pratt is even more polemical in his 1837 book *A Voice of Warning*, arguing that a vague prophecy is worse than no prophecy at all: "No prophesy or promise will profit the reader, or produce patience, comfort, or hope in his mind, until clearly understood, that he may know precisely what to hope for. Now the predictions of the Prophets can be clearly understood, as much so as the almanac, when it foretells an eclipse; or else the Bible of all books is of most doubtful usefulness. Far better would it have been for mankind, if the great Author of our existence should have revealed nothing to his fallen creatures, than to have revealed a book which would leave them in doubt and uncertainty, to contend with one another, from age to age, respecting the meaning of its contents" (13–4). As proof of the folly of metaphoric prophecy, Pratt imagines the fate of Noah had he not interpreted his revelation literally: "It was well for Noah that he was not well versed in the spiritualizing systems of modern divinity; for, under its benighted influence, he would never have believed that so marvelous a prophesy would have had a literal meaning and accomplishment. No, he would have been told that the flood meant a Spiritual flood, and the Ark, a Spiritual Ark, and the moment he thought otherwise, he would have been set down for a fanatic, knave, or fool; but it was so, that he was just simple enough to believe the prophesy literally; here then is a fair sample of foreknowledge; while all the world who did not possess it, perished by the flood literally" (19).

Writing at the same time, however, Heber C. Kimball described receiving multiple revelatory dreams that he interprets as figurative, not literal. Two of those experiences revolve around dreams he had while conducting missionary work in England:

Soon after my arrival in England, having been invited to preach about fifteen miles from Preston by a minister, of whom mention has been made in the former part of this Journal; while there, I dreamed one night that an elderly gentleman came to me and rented me a lot of ground which I was anxious to cultivate.

I immediately went to work to break it up, and observing some young timber on the lot, I cut it down; there was also an old building at one corner of the lot which appeared ready to fall. I took a lever and endeavored to place it in a proper position, but all my attempts were futile, and it became worse. I then resolved to pull it down. I did so, and with the new timber built a good house on a good foundation. While thus engaged the gentleman of whom I had rented the place, came to me, and found great fault with me for destroying his young timber, &c.

This dream was fulfilled at that place, in the following manner. After Mr. Richards had let me preach in his chapel, I baptized all his young members, among whom was his daughter, and most of the members of his church. He then reflected upon himself for letting me have the privilege of his chapel, and told me that I had ruined his church, and had taken away all his young members.

I could not but feel for the old gentleman, but I had a duty to perform, which outweighed every other consideration, and I was assured, that if I sought to please man I should not be the servant of Christ.

One night, while at the village of Ribchester, I dreamed that I, in company with another person, were walking out, and we saw a very extensive field of wheat, more so than the eye could reach, such a sight I never witnessed. The wheat appeared to be perfectly ripe and ready for harvest. I was very much rejoiced at the glorious sight, which presented itself; but judge of my surprise for when on taking some of the ears and rubbing them in my hands, I found nothing but smut, not any sound grain could I find. I marveled exceedingly, and felt very sorrowful; and exclaimed what will the people do for grain, here is a great appearance of plenty, but there is no wheat.

While contemplating the subject, I looked in another direction, and saw a small field in the form of the letter L, which had the appearance of something growing in it. I immediately directed my steps to it, and found that it had been sown with wheat, some of which had got up about six inches high, other parts of the field not quite so high, and some had only just sprouted; this gave me some encouragement to expect, that at the harvest, there would be some good grain. While thus engaged, a large bull looking very fierce and angry, leaped over the fence, ran through the field, and stamped down a large quantity of that which was just sprouted, and after doing considerable injury he leaped over the fence and ran away.

I felt very much grieved, that so much wheat should be destroyed, when there was such a prospect of scarcity. When I awoke next morning, the interpretation was given me. The large field with the great appearance of grain, so beautiful to look upon, represented the nation in which I then resided; which had a very pleasing appearance and a great show of religion, and who made great pretensions to piety and godliness, but who denied the power thereof; destitute of the principles of truth, and consequently of the gifts of the spirit.

The small field I saw clearly represented, the region of country where I was laboring, and where the word of truth had taken root, and was growing in the hearts of those who had the gospel, some places having grown a little more than others. The village I was in, was that part of the field where the bull did so much injury, for during my short visit there, most of the inhabitants were believing, but as soon as I departed, a clergyman belonging to the church of England, came out and violently attacked the truth, and made a considerable noise, crying false prophet! delusion! and after trampling on truth, and doing all the mischief he could, before I returned, he took shelter in his pulpit. However he did not destroy all the seed for after my return I was instrumental in building up a church in that place. (1840:51–3)

Heber C. Kimball is hardly the only Latter-day Saint to interpret revelatory dreams as metaphorical, as the discussion earlier in this chapter attests. Conversely, interpreting dreams as metaphorical hardly rules out the possibility for literal revelation within the same tradition. Dreams may be particularly ambiguous because of the medium, while voices heard when awake may be less so. It is perhaps not insignificant that the revelation Pratt uses as an example—the story of Noah's ark—appears to come as direct speech to Noah while awake, rather than in a dream, though the scripture is not conclusive, saying only: "And God said unto Noah . . . " (Genesis 6:13). It may also be worth pointing out that Parley Pratt's fears of having even the Noah story reinterpreted as figurative rather than literal have been borne out (see, for example, Browne 1983 and Young 1995).

Kimball's dreams and the extensive oral tradition make it clear that revelation among Latter-day Saints can be either literal or figurative, that distinguishing between the two can be difficult, and that figurative meaning can be addressed at multiple levels, including the linguistic, visual, and semiotic. Analysis of LDS narratives of personal revelation further suggests that the ambiguity of revelation poses many more than the two questions posed by David Aaron, including, first and foremost, is this revelation? If the answer is yes, a series of questions quickly follow: Is the prophesied event positive or negative? Is it tractable or intractable? and most important of all these secondary questions, what should be done about it? Depending on the information provided and the primary areas left open and ambiguous, other questions emerge such as, how will this happen? when will it happen? and who else will it impact?

Answering these questions and resolving the ambiguity of revelation is far more difficult than identifying the relevant questions to ask. Nor are the strategies for answering these questions universal. For Latter-day Saints, strategies include a combination of rational thought, assessment of spiritual feeling and intuition, past precedent, continued prayer, consultation with peers and spiritual leaders, and the most effective and most common but least timely of strategies: waiting until signs of fulfillment appear.

The current scholarship on religious memorates provides little clue about the actual strategies people employ to resolve the questions and ambiguities of divine discourse. But the primary texts published in that scholarship do. People who have encountered and communicated with the divine often include their doubt, their struggle, *and* their process for resolving these ambiguities in their narratives. Accordingly, analysis of religious memorates provides a fruitful method for understanding both experience and the narrative tradition as long as one is mindful of those areas where the two are most likely to diverge.

CHAPTER 4

THE BUILDING BLOCKS OF
A NARRATIVE TRADITION

Pattern in performance begins with pattern in experience. The similarities in stories of people who have shared experiences such as natural disasters, biological processes, and holiday airline travel all begin with similar circumstances. The same is true of personal revelation. While different types of revelatory experience lead people to ask different questions and construct distinct narrative performances, there remain broad commonalities across types.

Of course narratives are not only descriptions of events, they are interpretations of those events, and interpretation begins with the senses. We see, hear, feel, smell, and taste. Through our senses, we attempt to assess experience. Concurrently, we process those stimuli according to cultural patterns and norms. We tend to focus on those images, sounds, and smells that fit a particular pattern, searching to fit this new experience within existing paradigms and past experiences.[1] Narration introduces additional guidelines for interpretation. Cultural and social norms coupled with narrative demands for performance favor some experiences over others and shape how personal revelation is shared (see chapter 3).

Further, once stories move beyond personal experience and begin to be narrated by family, friends, distant acquaintances, and perhaps even unknown strangers, narrative patterns can become a heavily relied upon resource for the performer. Personal beliefs, gaps in memory, or the desire to inspire a particular reaction in an audience can encourage storytellers to employ these patterns in the act of performance. In any case, the aesthetic and rhetorical power of common patterns is never the sole explanation for their use. The nature of divine communication, human fallibility, cultural norms, and accurate reporting all help explain the existence, power, and appeal of these patterns.

Narrative Patterns

Personal revelation narratives exhibit a number of recurring patterns that can be usefully called motifs. A motif is a distinct, recognizable, and recurring element found in artistic works. Motifs can be identified according to specific objects, characters, phenomena, actions, behaviors, or relationships.[2] Many are tied to theme and will be addressed in the following chapter. Others, however, are primarily structural, helping to provide part of the skeletal framework for narration.

Discussions about motifs occur most often in the analysis of fictional stories, where storytellers have full license to imaginatively create new stories. The master storyteller is often one able to not only perform stories learned from others but create new stories, drawing upon the resources of motifs and other formulas and structures from other stories.

Applying this process to the narration of nonfiction is understandably problematic. To suggest that people recounting their own sacred experiences are borrowing motifs and formulas from other stories can be offensive. People sharing their revelatory experiences are *reporting*, not *creating*. Nonetheless, as experience is interpreted and translated into narrative, generic norms prove valuable tools for narrators. Patterns in experience become patterns in narrative. The use of these patterns in sharing memorates does not undermine their truth; it merely suggests that people have worked out a way of communicating effectively, efficiently, and expressively with their peers. As stories move from memorate to legend, however, there is a greater chance that these patterns are relied upon for more than reporting, by filling gaps in narrative or memory.

In narratives of personal revelation shared among Latter-day Saints, a number of motifs and patterns appear, evidence of shared experience as well as shared aesthetics. They include quoting the Holy Ghost, ignoring initial promptings, repeating the number three, and proving fulfillment.[3]

Quoting the Holy Ghost

The promptings of the Holy Ghost are most often discussed as the still small voice. This voice is quiet, subtle, whispering. Some people talk about physically hearing a voice, but for most, the voice is inside the mind or heart, arriving as thoughts or feelings, abstracted from direct speech. Despite this, it is common for people to talk about receiving a feeling or a thought and in the course of describing their experience, quote the Spirit directly. Elder Spencer Bourgeous recalls a prompting that "wasn't like an audible voice," yet he quotes the voice repeatedly throughout his narrative (see chapter 5 for complete narrative). Pauline Clayson receives revelation about her ailing mother and describes receiving an impression and a thought but quotes a voice (see chapter 2 for complete narrative). Her husband Paul mentions a "distinct thought" but quotes the Holy Ghost directly: "Do not get on that freeway." While serving a mission in Guadalajara, Steve Anderson received an inspiration while preparing for a baptism. He, too, quotes the Holy Ghost.

> Steve: We had a baptism, and one little miracle I can think of . . .
>
> There was this one baptism that we were getting ready for, and the fonts down there, I'd say ninety-five percent of the time you can't just turn on the water and it works. The water sits in these big giant tubs, either up above the church or there's like this well thing under the ground.
>
> So, anyway, so I went to this baptism. And we couldn't baptize him because there was no water, you know? Turn it on and it's like this murky brown stuff coming out. Like, "OK. Can't do that." And I just, it was just like, and this won't seem like anything, but it was just like, "Go to the well and grab buckets, and fill it up."
>
> Well, it was like, it would be like from that tree to the middle of your house [about 35 yards]. It was like, "OK." And so, you know I just had that inspiration, "Do that."
>
> And we go there, and there's a lock on it. And that thing was locked. I looked at it; it was locked. And I just felt the inspiration, "Pull on it." And so I did. I pulled on it, and it came open, you know.
>
> And this probably seems really weird to you, but—
>
> Tom: No.
>
> Steve: I mean, this kind of stuff happened a lot as a missionary.
>
> So I pulled on it, and it comes open. I was like, "Oh. Get buckets." So we make this line, we're passing the water out, and we fill the font, you know? It's like hot out and we're all sweaty and everything, and we had the baptism.
>
> And then some time after that, I can't remember, it must have been a couple hours later, the janitor comes up. I don't know where he had been. He's like, he was like really angry with me. He was like, "How did you get that open?" And I said, "I pulled on the lock and it came open." He said, "No. I made sure it was locked." He goes, "That stays locked all the time." He was probably worried about kids falling in, or whatever, but . . . .
>
> Anyway, that was just one, personal little prophetic thing, and it wasn't prophetic, but just how inspiration can kind of work in my life.

One explanation for these linguistic moves may derive from the taboo against using explicit or scriptural terms for revelation during performance of the narrated event (as opposed to the intro and coda of the narrative event, as discussed in chapter 2). If "inspiration" is used instead of "the still small voice," direct quotes that seem anomalous are easily explained. Another explanation is that divine discourse, above and beyond human language, must be translated into terms and language that can be understood. Thoughts to the mind may arrive as commands, but even ideas may be translated into direct speech. When that discourse is particularly vivid, it can be quoted, not just described, in the act of translation. This is not evidence of corruption or invention. Rather, it is an approximation of an experience that defies simple repetition. Shawn Tucker highlights this interpretive process, translating a vague feeling of peace into a clear message from God:

Shawn: Perhaps one of the most significant experiences that happened to me was when I was sixteen, I was a sophomore, I was between my sophomore and junior year in high school and I went to pick pineapple in Hawaii.
　　　　Did I tell you about this?

Tom: I don't think so.

Shawn: [*laugh*] If you die and you find yourself in Hawaii picking pineapple, it's because you did something seriously wrong in your life [*laughter*].

Tom: You're in spirit prison?

Shawn: Yeah, you're in spirit prison and it doesn't look good [*laughter*].
　　　　So, I was there and I had this friend, I had this friend back in Virginia who'd gone to college. Gone to college for a semester and he was getting money together to go on his mission.
　　　　This is Greg. I think I told you something about Greg.
　　　　Well, I found out from a letter—it wasn't even for me it was for someone else—that Greg had contracted bone cancer. And the letter indicated that it was really bad and that I might not ever see him again. That it was progressing really fast and it was a terrible thing. And this was just a, this is a horrible shock. This is very ironic and all these other sorts of things.
　　　　So, so I went back to this room where we stayed. And there wasn't anybody there, luckily. And I knelt down and prayed about this.
　　　　And I was really concerned and really upset.
　　　　And I remember that as I prayed about it, I suddenly had . . . I felt the influence of the Holy Ghost very strong, felt the Spirit. And I felt this amazing sense of calm and peace come over me. And that peace seemed to communicate to me that God was saying, "I know you. I know your friend Greg. I love you and I will take care of you." And that was it.

And I felt distinctly, this is not an answer. This is an answer but this is all you get for an answer [laugh]. This isn't "This is what's going to happen" or "That's what's going to happen," or the other. It's just . . . it's on a need to know basis. And that was all I needed to know and that was all I got.

And so, what happened was, I got home, he was still alive but he was in bad shape. He sort of got better but then nine months later he died from the cancer.

But the whole time while this was happening, he got a lot of blessings and a lot of different things happened. And I always felt that I could come back to that; I always knew the Lord knew me, that he loved me, that he would take care of us. But I never felt like, you know, he's going to be healed, or any of these other sorts of things. That never sort of came through for me.

And it was a tough time because you're like, "Do I just not have enough faith to make him . . . you know, to get him healed. Is it this? Is it that?" But I was seventeen.[4] I was just doing my best, you know? [laugh] So I didn't really let it bug me too much.

Whether felt, thought, or heard, the Holy Ghost is succinct and declarative when speaking directly to people. "Pull over to the side of the road," "Don't throw that log," "Go check on him," "Don't let them take you to that hospital," "That is what you are to do," "Return to the girl, tell her she will live," "Just stay on your feet and you'll be fine." Often the Holy Ghost directly addresses a person: "Robert, we're ready for you," "Art, get away from this tree," "Morgan, come home," "Mosiah, remember the fate of George A. Smith," "Look out, Elizabeth," "Amos, camp here, go no further," "Glen, let your heart be at ease and watch." All of the statements are simple declarative statements. Many of them are direct commands, words to prompt action. Others are words of comfort or general guidance: "I know you. I love you and I will take care of you," "This is the way," "There are two more," "She's the one," "Everything in the book is true."[5]

Further, direct speech of the Holy Ghost may reflect the idioms and vernacular speech of the individual receiving revelation. Frustrated in her current job, a woman hears a voice telling her, "Go to ZCMI," an acronym for the Zion's Cooperative Mercantile Institution that is widely used and recognizable in the LDS community in Utah (Bonnett 1980, Wilson Archives). Even in cases where people hear the voice of the Spirit as clearly as they would the voice of a neighbor, there appears to be some degree of translation from the divine, including into the vernacular of the person receiving it. While it is possible that the Holy Ghost is personalizing revelation even to the extent of diction, it is as likely that people are translating divine promptings into their own vernacular speech (see chapter 3 for discussions of the ambiguity of revelation and the translation of the divine).

There is both a practical and aesthetic benefit to directly quoting the divine. Direct quotes make the experience more vivid, as well as more clear, a double benefit for an audience, particularly considering how vague personal revelation can be. Such performance qualities not only heighten the dramatic aspects of performance but they clearly delineate the sacred from the mundane.

While people regularly quote the Holy Ghost when sharing their *own* experiences, they use direct quotes less often the further from the source they move. In secondhand stories, quoting the Holy Ghost continues to appear regularly (12 percent of the time), though less frequently than in personal experience stories (19 percent of the time). Among legends, that percentage drops again, to 9 percent. The further from the source, the closer to report rather than performance the story becomes. First person shifts to third, direct quotes shift to reported speech, and the struggle to translate the divine dissipates.

Ignoring Initial Promptings

Promptings can be subtle and therefore easily dismissed. They can also be inconvenient to follow and therefore ignored. Stories of ignoring revelation only to realize the harm that followed or the blessing forsaken are common in the narrative tradition. Such stories remind individuals and their audiences of the importance of listening and acting on personal revelation. The experience is common, the message useful, and such stories fit neatly within the narrative tradition (see chapter 3).

Stories where people initially ignore the prompting only to finally listen are also common. This pattern emerges not as a distinct type of experience or story but rather as a motif, a distinct narrative element that recurs frequently. Keith Stanley initially ignores the prompting to take a different route home but finally listens and avoids a car accident (see chapter 2 for complete narrative). Shawn Tucker ignores the Holy Ghost three times before finally pulling over, thereby protecting a mother and child from a runaway trailer (see chapter 3 for complete narrative). Elder Aaron Chavez ignores a prompting to tract in a particular trailer park; when he finally acts on it, he finds a woman eager to learn more about the church. A young mother working on her parents' farm gets a feeling to stop filling the gas tank and check on her father but dismisses it. The feeling persists and she finally goes and discovers her father trapped under the combine.[6] In a more common experience, the roles are reversed and parents are prompted to save their children:

So there was this woman, and she was in her room doing something, and
her little child was having a bath in the other room, and she just heard
this voice that said: "Go check on him. Go check on him."
　　And she thought, "No, no, no."
　　And she heard it again and again.
　　And so finally she went into the bathroom, and he had gone and
plugged in the hair dryer and he was just about to climb back into the tub
and she grabbed it from him and saved his life.[7]

The choice to include an aspect of the revelatory experience that shows
human weakness is not only honest but humble, and humility is vitally important in sharing personal revelation (see chapter 2). The result of being both
common to experience and socially useful in performance is that hesitating
before acting has become a recognizable motif in personal revelation narratives.

As a motif, such hesitation can shift from a simple element of one's
experience to a narrative feature common to a particular genre. While narrators would not include hesitation where there was none in sharing stories of
their *own* experience, they may do so when narrating other people's stories.
Without personal memory to fall back on, motifs can emerge as useful narrative resources.

One of the most well-known stories of an unsolicited prompting by the
Holy Ghost is the story of Wilford Woodruff, who is prompted to move his
wagon just before lightning strikes. Woodruff, president of the church from
1889 to 1898, shared this story often. He published it in the *Millennial Star*
newspaper twice, the *Deseret Weekly* newspaper, and in the Faith Promoting
Series published by the Juvenile Instructor Office. In 1898, he shared the story
orally during general conference. Since then, the story has appeared in church
magazines, newspapers, and teaching manuals. LDS authors from both the
General Authorities and the lay membership have also picked up the story,
publishing it in books intended for faith promotion, historical survey, religious
instruction, and scholarly analysis.[8]

Versions of Woodruff's story are similar but not identical. The most frequently cited version is the one from the *Millennial Star* on October 12, 1891:

After I came to these valleys and returned to Winter Quarters, I was sent
to Boston by President Young. He wanted me to take my family there
and gather all the Saints of God in New England, in Canada, and in the
surrounding regions, and stay there until I gathered them all. I was there
about two years.
　　While on the road there, I drove my carriage one evening into the yard
of Brother Williams. Brother Orson Hyde drove a wagon by the side of

mine.[9] I had my wife and children in the carriage. After I turned out my team and had my supper, I went to bed in the carriage. I had not been there but a few minutes when the Spirit said to me, "Get up and move that carriage." I told my wife I had to get up and move the carriage.

She said, "What for?" I said, "I don't know."

That is all she asked me on such occasions; when I told her I did not know, that was enough. I got up and moved my carriage four or five rods, and put the off fore wheel against the corner of the house. I then looked around me and went to bed. The same Spirit said, "Go and move your animals from that oak tree." They were two hundred yards from where my carriage was. I went and moved my horses and put them in a little hickory grove. I again went to bed.

In thirty minutes a whirlwind came up and broke that oak tree off within two feet from the ground. It swept over three or four fences and fell square in that dooryard, near Brother Orson Hyde's wagon, and right where mine had stood. What would have been the consequences if I had not listened to that Spirit? Why, myself and wife and children doubtless would have been killed. That was the still, small voice to me—no earthquake, no thunder, no lightning; but the still, small voice of the Spirit of God. It saved my life. It was the spirit of revelation to me.

The second most common version comes straight from Woodruff's journals, published in *Leaves from My Journal*. In this version, only his wife and one child are with him in the wagon; the other children are in Brother Williams's house. Also, he mentions mules rather than horses. The major plot elements and much of the language, however, are the same.

The third version is less common but is the one example of an oral rather than written narrative. Woodruff told this story during general conference and it is recorded in the conference report. Again, the story is virtually identical. However, one addition is noteworthy. After tying up his animals and getting ready for bed, Woodruff says: "As I laid down, the Spirit of the Lord told me to get up and move my carriage. I did not ask the Lord what He meant. I did as I was told."

In none of these versions does Woodruff hesitate, and in his one existing oral account, he explicitly points this out. Nor does Woodruff hesitate in the comic strip version of this experience printed in the August 2006 editions of both the *Liahona* (F6–F7) and *The Friend* magazines (28–9) of the church. The version is adapted from the most common one in the *Millennial Star*.

Wilford: I think we should sleep here tonight. I know of some brethren
         who will let us stay with them.
         *Wilford, his wife, and one of their children decided to sleep in
         the carriage.*

Wife: It looks like all of the other children are settled down in the house for the night. Good night, Wilford.

Wilford: Good night.

Not long after getting in bed, Wilford heard a voice tell him to move his carriage.

Wilford: I have to move the carriage.

Wife: What for?

Wilford: I do not know. But I do recognize the voice of the Spirit, and it's telling me to move.

Wilford moved the carriage forward. About 30 minutes later a sudden whirlwind blew a nearby oak tree over. The huge tree was snapped into pieces and crushed two fences.

When the Woodruffs' hosts and children came out to look at the damage, they noticed that the tree had landed right where Wilford's carriage was parked before he moved it.

In the morning the Woodruffs were able to safely continue their journey, and they went on their way rejoicing.

Wilford: By obeying the revelation of the Spirit of God to me, I saved my life as well as the lives of my wife and child.

This version had been rewritten to accompany cartoon pictures for the youth but remains faithful to the original in all plot *elements*. As in all the versions, Woodruff tells his wife what he is doing, but he does not delay or wait for further promptings. It was this comic version that Sandy Johnson had read just days before she retold the story around her kitchen table. She and her husband had been sharing stories of their own personal revelation when we began to talk about the different types of revelation: those that come in answer to prayer and those that come to protect yourself or other people.

Sandy: And there are numerous stories of the protection ones. I mean, I've heard multiple, multiple stories. There was one instance in particular, this lady was driving and she was driving in this one lane of the road, and she got the feeling that she needed to move over. It was a two-lane road, and she needed to move over. And there was a curve coming up. And she didn't know why, because there was nobody there, but she moved over.

Well, a few minutes later, this truck comes barreling around the curve and had actually come over into that lane and if she'd have been there, she would have been toast. But because she was over a lane, she was OK.

And there's a story about Wilford Woodruff . . . yeah, it was Wilford Woodruff. He had driven his carriage and parked it under this tree, and he was staying with—I'm not sure if it was

family or friends, I don't remember that part—but he
had parked the wagon carriage under this tree.
And in the middle of the night, this voice comes out in the
middle of the night and says, "Get up and move your
carriage to the other side of the field."
And he's like, "Unh. It's the middle of the night." And he's
just kind of ignoring it, saying, "Unh."
And then it comes again [*thumping the table*]: "Get up and move
your carriage to the other side of the field." So he's like, "I guess
I'd better go do it" [*laugh*]. So he gets up, moves his carriage to the
other side of the field, and then goes back to bed, not knowing why.
Well, some time early in the morning they got a thunder-
storm and this lightning bolt comes out of the sky, hit the tree,
and knocked it over, right where the carriage had been [*laugh*].
So you *know*, there's another story.
And actually, I think they were sleeping in the wagon.

George: Yeah, they were sleeping in the wagon.
Sandy: Yeah, they stopped at this house, they were staying with friends,
but they were sleeping in the wagon, because there wasn't room
in the house. And so he got the feeling that he needed to
move the wagon. Saved his whole family because of it.
But there's all kinds of stories of things like that.[10]

Sandy is not consciously altering the story. Rather, in an effort to recall a story she read a few days earlier, she narrates using patterns common to the genre. The result is that genres self-replicate. Common motifs can be used as a resource for the narration of other people's stories, filling in gaps in memory and ensuring a degree of familiarity, even conformity, to genre norms.

The adoption of patterns common to the *experience* of personal revelation may also reveal ways in which narrators personalize a story by imagining themselves in place of the protagonist. In many of her own experiences, Sandy mentions the dif-ficulty of heeding the Spirit when it runs counter to her own thoughts or desires. For one prompting, she admits that she continues to resist for personal reasons. Recounting the story of Wilford Woodruff's revelation, she places herself in his shoes. She imagines being woken up in the middle of the night to go through the arduous task of moving a wagon and team of horses. The result is a dramatization of a bleary, begrudging, but eventual acquiescence to the voice of the Spirit, a scene reflective more of Sandy's humble character than of Wilford Woodruff's.

The Number Three

Common patterns expressed as in narrative can derive from a specific phenome-non, group, or widely shared cultural tradition. In the case of the number three,

the pattern is relevant for all three areas: LDS personal revelation, LDS culture, and Western culture more broadly. Western or Indo-European storytelling
traditions often favor the number three. This "magic number" is most easily visible in fairy tales and nursery rhymes: "Goldilocks and the Three Bears," "The
Three Little Pigs," "Three Blind Mice." Hero quests often begin with three
sons, with the smallest and youngest of them besting the others (e.g., "Puss and
Boots"). In the Grimms' version of "Cinderella," there are three sisters, three
visits to the ball, and three attempts to ride off into the sunset with the right
bride. Stith Thompson catalogs the number three as a recurring motif throughout the Indo-European folk narrative tradition in 113 distinct motifs (1966,
vol. 6:791–3). The number is so pervasive that Axel Olrik identified "The Law
of Three" as one of the universal patterns of oral narrative (Olrik 1992:52). This
pattern is hardly universal; other cultures favor four or five. Once embedded in
a culture, however, a number can become ever more pervasive and self-reifying.

In his article "The Number Three in American Culture," Alan Dundes
briefly surveys the literature on trichotomy in Western culture (1968:402–3),
citing studies that leave little doubt as to the prevalence of the number three in
Greco-Roman culture (Usener 1903), classic literature, law and medicine (Göbel
1935, Goudy 1910, Tavenner 1916), and more broadly across all of Western
civilization (Deonna 1954, Dumézil 1958, and Lease 1919). Three is particularly prevalent in the folklore of these cultures (see also Lehmann 1914 and
Müller 1903). He also cites the prevalence of the number three in Christianity,
most dramatically portrayed in the Holy Trinity (e.g., Strand 1958).[11] He even
mentions an LDS example: the Three Nephites, which have provided frequent
grist for early LDS folklore studies (see Fife 1940, Hand 1938, Lee 1949, Utter
1892, and Wilson 1969).

Dundes quickly turns his focus to the United States, arguing that this
country ranks beside other predominantly Indo-European cultures as a place
rife with the number three. He provides page after page of examples of the prevalence of the number three in all aspects of American life, not just in folklore.

The recurrence of the number three in American culture is without question; its origin and significance, however, is another matter. Dundes himself
is rightfully wary of any of the explanations he posits. However, even without
understanding the origin for the pattern, significance can be explored, particularly on a case by case basis. As in Christianity generally, the number three is a
significant number in LDS theology.

Precedence for the power and importance of the number three as a sign of
God's presence can be found in scripture, a fact not lost upon many LDS members. In Sunday school one morning, Terry Holmes was teaching a lesson on

revelation and the power of the Holy Ghost. He had the congregation read 1 Kings 19:11–12 and then asked them what they noticed. One man raised his hand and said they all come in threes. First comes a strong wind, then a powerful earthquake, and then a fire. Only then does God appear as a still small voice.[12] The man continues: "In the Book of Mormon, it took three times," he said, referring to the three visions Joseph Smith received before being given the golden plates. "Yes," responded Terry Holmes, not looking for that answer but recognizing its accuracy. "That's right. Anything else?" As the lesson continued, Terry picked up on the man's observation and continued to point out the occurrence of the number three in two subsequent passages—Helaman 5:30–33 and 3 Nephi 11:5—both of which describe God communicating with people in threes, as when he brings news of Jesus's death: "And again the third time they did hear the voice, and did open their ears to hear it; and their eyes were towards the sound thereof; and they did look steadfastly towards heaven, from whence the sound came. And behold, the third time they did understand the voice which they heard" (3 Nephi 11:5–6).

LDS scripture in particular suggests that the divine regularly appears in threes. The corollary may also be true: that the number three serves as a sign of the divine. Such a conclusion is tentative at best, though it gains weight when focused specifically on dreams.

In LDS revelation, dreams are a common medium for revelation, and dreams in threes signify particular importance. Joseph Smith's dream about the golden plates came three times. According to accounts recorded at the turn of the nineteenth century in Vermont and New Hampshire, dreams repeated three times were a part of American treasure-hunting lore (Quinn 1998:139). When a group of non-Mormons attempted to trick Joseph Smith with some fake bronze plates, they began by circulating a story that a man in town had received a dream of buried treasure three times (Fife and Fife 1956:116–7).

The oral tradition of personal revelation also reveals a pattern of dreams that come in threes. A woman dreams three times about the death of a relative soon before her nephew dies (Frank 1961, Wilson Archives). A woman dreams three times of the area where she will move. She then dreams three times about the specific house she should buy (Rollins 1977, Fife Archives; for complete narrative, see chapter 5). A young woman dreams three nights in a row about her friends in a car near a railroad. On the third night, she sees the car get hit by the train. She calls to warn her friends but misses them and they all die in the accident.[13]

The significance of the number three extends beyond dreams to other media of revelation. Dreams and promptings are part of the same revelatory phenomenon. A thrice-repeated revelatory dream is equal to a thrice-repeated prompt.

In his diary, Mosiah Hancock tells of a revelation he received not to camp where he was. After ignoring the voice twice, he heard it a third time, commenting, "I now was aware that I had been warned the third time, and I was thoroughly aroused to the responsibilities in which I was under."[14] Hancock writes "*the* third time," not "*a* third time," suggestive of an awareness of the significance of the number three.

Hancock is not alone in ignoring a prompting twice, only to finally act after the third prompt. During a stake conference, the stake president shared a story to illustrate the importance of staying in tune with the Spirit:

> It was a Wednesday morning and Sister Hawkins was busy taking care of her three small children. There were piles of laundry to do and she still had to finish the stuff for the YW [Young Women] activity that night.
>
> All of the sudden she got a prompting to make a chocolate pie and take it over to Sister Jones, a sister in the ward.
>
> She pushed the thought out of her mind and continued about her business.
>
> Two more times the prompting came and two more times she pushed it aside.
>
> Finally, it stopped coming and she got on with her busy life.
>
> The next Sunday was fast Sunday. In Relief Society, Sister Jones got up and bore her testimony. In it she said that on Wednesday she was diagnosed with cancer. She came home from the doctors and just cried. All she could think about was how she wished that she had a piece of chocolate pie. Sister Hawkins related to the stake president how horrible she felt as she listened to Sister Jones' testimony, and how never again would she ever push a prompting aside.[15]

For many, the appearance of the number three in dreams and promptings suggests supernatural origin, in these cases, divine. This is particularly true of narratives told during the nineteenth and first half of the twentieth centuries. Its continued existence, however, may derive more heavily from narrative tradition than a coherent belief system. Narratives told throughout the United States employ the number three to structure the story. As Alan Dundes points out, the number three is a native category that can "unconsciously affect the formation of supposedly objective analytical categories. This is really the insidious part of cultural patterning. No individual can escape his culture and its built-in cultural cognitive categories" (1968:418).

This cultural patterning appears in other aspects of personal revelation narratives as well. A young girl tries to remove a stone in her dream three times (Fife and Fife 1956:216). In another dream, a young girl approaches, showing her deformed ear three times (Fife and Fife 1956:224). A woman who dreams of burned meat loses her daughter in a fire three days after the dream (Fife and Fife 1956:218). Three unborn children appear to a high school girl to encourage her to reform (Allen 1996, Wilson Archives). It takes a young man three minutes to get to the laundromat after a prompting to help his wife (Allen 1996, Wilson Archives). A man dreams of three paths and is directed to take the third path (Avant 1968, Wilson Archives). Two missionary companions are guided to a woman who has been investigating the church for three years; three weeks later, she is baptized (Condie 1994, Wilson Archives). A young missionary knocks on two doors without success but behind the third finds a willing investigator (Chavez 2008 interview; for complete narrative see chapter 5). No other number appears as consistently in these narratives as the number three.

Proof of Fulfillment

Other patterns that appear in personal revelation narratives coalesce around the climax of the narrative, when the revelation is fulfilled and the promise of God's protection and love becomes evident in one's life. Dramatically, this is the moment of greatest impact. Aesthetically, it may also be. Narratives with particularly impressive confirmations of their divine nature make for more compelling stories.

Additional and Impressive Confirmation

Deborah Morris recorded a story from a woman she describes as a "woman of sincere faith and one who lives to hear and relate the faith promoting stories of her relatives." The story is powerful and sacred to her, a story she refers to as faith promoting, one that "helps her to believe that God will also help her and her family in times of trouble":

> One of the miraculous things that happened in Grandma Winsor's life I heard from her own lips. During their married life her husband had many accidents but this was the most miraculous.
> Her husband was out and she was feeding the baby . . . nursing the baby and her husband was out moving or jacking up a sort of house trailer.
> This was in Enterprise, Utah.
> When the house trailer slipped off of the jack and fell on him and he was, you know, literally being crushed to death.
> And it was a miracle because she knew.
> She didn't hear anything, but a voice inside told her she must go out. Her husband was in distress.
> I guess the voice told her that he was being crushed to death.

So she put the baby down and ran out there and she said, "I was praying as I've never prayed before for strength."

And as she went out, and as she grabbed hold of the trailer, she said
she could feel a legion of angels helping her to lift the trailer off of her
husband.

Later, men came, at least a dozen or so, and they couldn't budge it.
(1984, Wilson Archives)

Confirmation of the prompting is clear when she finds her husband pinned under
a trailer. Continued divine help from angels strengthens the spiritual claim, a
claim that receives its own support when a team of men arrive who are unable to
budge what a woman lifted by herself.

Multiple confirmations also appear in two stories of being helped, only to
have the materials disappear once they have served their purpose. The first story
was recorded by Virginia Skaggs from a friend of her daughter's, who heard the
story in her Sunday school genealogy class:

A woman had been working for some years on her genealogy and couldn't
find a particular name that she needed. She prayed that she would be
able to find the name and continue the work. She continued to pray and
search for several years.

One afternoon she was watering her lawn when she noticed an old
newspaper blowing around the yard. She tried to ignore it but was
impressed to look at it.

Upon reading it, she found one side to be the death notices of several
people, one of which gave birth, marriage, death and other information
concerning a woman whose name was identical to the one she was looking for. She took the newspaper into the house, copied the information
on her own notebook and returned to the yard to turn off the sprinkler.

She could not find the newspaper when she returned to the house but
upon checking the information that she had copied from it, was able to
verify that this was the person that she had been looking for for so long.
(1975, Wilson Archives)

The next story was collected by Erika Layland after asking her mother to write
down and mail her any spiritual experiences in her life. Her mother obliged
with a number of stories, including this one:

The recipe that follows is central to one of the most spiritual experiences
of my life.

When Erika—my fifth and youngest child—was born, I was unable
to nurse. She developed severe colic when she was two weeks old, which
lasted every evening from midnight until about 4 a.m., and continued like
clockwork for the next several months. She began with a painful scream,

arching her back, stiff and rigid, nearly losing her breath. Then, beet-red and gasping for air, she would start all over again. During the day she was fretful whenever she was awake. Although I had four older children ages 8 to 16 to care for, I slept when she slept.

Our pediatrician recommended every potentially helpful medication, every milk- and soy-based formula available. She was very constipated and bled rectally. Nothing seemed to make a difference. Finally, he recommended a meat-based formula, but inside I didn't feel that this would be the answer to her problems.

For several mornings when I was quietly feeding Erika a bottle, a thought completely foreign to rational thinking kept pushing its way to center-stage of my mind:
"Why don't I go to our local library and look for a book by Adele Davis?"

Immediately I questioned inwardly, "*Who is Adele Davis, and what could any book written by her have to do with Erika's well-being?*"

It vaguely came back to me that I had seen a woman by that name for a brief moment on the Art Linkletter television show—*but that had been 17 years ago*! I pushed the idea out of my mind as a bizarre aberration of a desperate mother.

But [the] voice inside of me—and Erika's colic and rectal bleeding—persisted, day after day, until there was nothing to do but go to the library and look for such a book. Without telling anyone, I became convinced that the Spirit must be guiding me to a solution. When she was four months old, I went to the library. I walked immediately to a shelf as if I knew where I was going, and there was a book by Adele Davis. I looked in the index and found a goat's milk formula for use with infant colic.

After checking out the book, I went to [the] General Nutrition Center in the Meadows Mall and bought all of the ingredients called for in the recipe. There happened to be a goat farm nearby, I was told at the store. It was easy to find, and I mixed up the formula, four bottles at a time. Within a few hours, Erika changed before our eyes, much to the wonder of all of our family. She had been a frantic, irritable, and fretful baby; suddenly she laughed, smiled, gurgled, and cooed. She certainly *looked* more adorable to her family, and she responded to us with gusto and happiness!

I returned the book; when I went to check it out again, the librarian said they did not have this book in the county library collection. Bookstores said it was out of print. Much later, I was able to locate and purchase a copy at a used-book store.

I gave Erika nothing but this formula (no solids!) as the book recommended; she grew rapidly and was very content. When she was 14 months old, she bit the end off of the nipple, and that was the end of her "formula days"! Once she tasted "real" food, she wouldn't touch the formula. But she was "over the hump." From then until she was fully grown, she was in the 110th percentile in height and weight compared to other girls her age, according to doctors' growth charts.

I know that she and I owe her health and growth to the Spirit leading me to follow true (but unorthodox) dietary principles that were essential to her health at a very early age. But I had to *listen* first, and then *act*. This has been a powerful testimony to me of the Spirit helping us in our need if we will listen to the still, small voice. (Layland 2001, Wilson Archives)

In each of these stories, confirmation of the divine nature of the experience is established twice. When the nursing mother is prompted to go outside, fulfillment is achieved simply by seeing her husband in need of help. When the woman finds her ancestor in the newspaper, the revelation is fulfilled. Revelation is also fulfilled when the woman finds a cure for her daughter's colic. However, each experience has additional proof of its divine origin, proof that makes the story all the more compelling. The men who cannot do what the woman did with the help of angels, and the newspaper and book that disappear when they are no longer needed are elements of the narrative that are powerful experientially as well as compelling aesthetically.

Such awe-inspiring confirmations may be double-edged swords, however. Their added confirmation should provide even greater proof of divine presence. However, if they seem too impressive, too perfect, they may tip the scales of believability. In most performance contexts, where religious belief is the focus, such endings can pose a hindrance rather than prove an added aesthetic boon. However, in primarily social contexts—when people share stories for enjoyment and as tools for thinking, not solely for spiritual edification or education—such endings heighten the aesthetic appreciation of the narrative.

In other cases, the compelling aspect of fulfillment lies not in the nature of the event but in the fact that fulfillment is known at all. Many promptings of the Holy Ghost warn people from harm. However, prompts to take a different route home, avoid a particular place, or break off an engagement often end without a clear indication of the harm averted. A person prompted not to drive to the store stays home. She remains safe. But is the fact that nothing happened sufficient confirmation of divine revelation? Structural analysis makes it clear that for unsolicited prescriptive revelation—promptings out of the blue—the climax of the experience and the narrative is the moment when the question *why* is answered (see chapter 3). This answer fulfills the promise of revelation: that one's actions in the present will bring blessings in the future. Safety at home is hardly a blessing unless it can be contrasted to a clear harm waiting outside. When it can, when the harm avoided becomes apparent, the experience is more likely to be shared.[16]

Keith Stanley is prompted to take a different route home one night. He does and arrives safely. The nature of the experience is ambiguous until he reads in the newspaper the next morning about a car accident that occurred on his regular route home at the exact time of night he was traveling (see chapter 2 for the complete narrative). It is also a newspaper that provides proof of revelation in a tragedy on the Mississippi River back in the late 1800s:

> I was never more desirous of pursuing my journey than I was on this occasion, yet soon after going aboard, a feeling of aversion to going on that steamer took possession of me. Instead of a sensation of joy, an undefinable dread, or foreboding of coming evil was exercising an influence over me, that increased in its power every moment, until I could resist no longer, and snatching up my trunk, I fled with it to shore, just as the deck hands stopped to haul in the gangway, and the boat moved off.
>
> I put my trunk down on the bank of the river, and sat down on it, too weak to stand on my feet longer.
>
> This was a new experience to me, then. What did it mean? One thing was certain, I felt as if I had escaped from some great calamity to a place of safety.
>
> Two days after this I took passage on another steamer for St. Louis, where in due time I arrived in safety. As I walked ashore I met a newsboy crying his morning paper, and among the items of news it contained, the most prominent was an account of the ill-fated steamer that I had made my escape from at Evansville, on the Ohio River. I purchased the paper and found the boat had been snagged in the Mississippi River below St. Louis, in the night, and sank, with a loss of nearly all that were on board.
>
> The mysterious feeling that impelled me to leave that boat was cleared up to my satisfaction. There remained not the shadow of a doubt that Providence had interposed between me and the great danger.[17]

Evidence of averted danger also appears in two stories depicting Indian attacks on early Mormon settlers in the West. In one, a family is prompted to leave the cabin where they have bedded down for the night. Evidence of divine prompting is confirmed by the dead body of an Apache Indian in the cabin the next morning, presumably left there by his fellow tribesmen after being injured. "Had Brother Rogers remained there, he and his family would have been killed by these Indians" (Morgan and Pearce 1941:340).

In another story of encounters with Indians, the evidence of fulfillment is less lurid but more involved. In this story, James C. Snow is warned not to camp near a particular spring, and then not to make a fire. In both cases, he heeds the voice.

"When he arrived home, he found his family were well. No Indians had passed their place, and nothing had disturbed them. Shortly after he arrived home, a horseman came and said that there had been a company stop at these springs the evening before, and the Indians had come and killed every one of them.

"They were asking for help to go see if they could find the Indians and take care of these people that had been murdered."[18]

Kent M. Young recorded a story from a Utah State University employee whose uncle told him about his early pioneer days in Mendon, Utah:

> On an earlier summer morning around the turn of the century, Jim Blake hitched a team of horses to his wagon for a trip into Mendon. On the way, he encountered a friend with another wagon. The high spirits of youth prevailed, and soon the two were racing toward Mendon.
>
> Jim's team came unhitched and the wagon turned over, pinning Jim underneath. The racing companion went for help and soon returned with Jim's father. After rescuing Jim out from under the wagon, they were preparing to rush him to the hospital. Jim clearly heard a voice sternly proclaim, "Don't let them take you to the hospital."
>
> Jim convinced his father not to do so, and he was taken home instead.
>
> For days, Jim remained motionless and could only speak. After a month, his family delightfully discovered that he could wiggle his fingers. Gradually, over a period of weeks, Jim recovered completely from the accident.
>
> Years later, Jim's brother Maurice Blake who had become a famous osteopath in Chicago was visiting Jim, and they reminisced about that accident that happened so long ago. Maurice took Jim into Logan where he made X-rays of his neck. The renowned osteopath discovered a ring completely around the vertebrae. Obviously it had been completely severed! Had Jim been taken to the hospital on that fateful morning, the attending physician probably would have attempted to straighten the twisted neck. This action would have left Jim paralyzed for life, if he had survived at all.
>
> Jim could thank that unknown saving voice. (1984, Wilson Archives)

The fact that Jim survives the accident could be seen as proof that the revelation was divine, though it is unclear that staying home rather than going to the hospital was necessary until the climactic X-rays years later.

Double Revelation

While some experiences have multiple confirmations of the divine origin of prompting—finding one's husband pinned under a tractor *and* being helped by angels, or receiving the exact advice needed *and* having the source of that information mysteriously disappear—other experiences have no conclusive evidence at all. As Terry Holmes points out, "Sometimes we find out why we were prompted, but probably most of the time we don't" (see chapter 3). Without fulfillment, there is no climax, no resolution, no clear confirmation of revelation and God's love and therefore no story. However, some experiences may have elements that add weight to their divine provenance, providing, if not a climax, enough proof of the divine to warrant narration. Double revelation often provides such proof.

"One of her sisters was getting married," Craig Bailey begins, gesturing to his wife, "and we were going to go to the reception. And this, that, and the other, and the day we're supposed to go to the reception, which is a hundred and twenty-five miles away from where we live, she gets up, and she just says, "I don't feel like we should go. And I don't know why . . .'"

> Josette: I was just sick [about not going].
> Craig: ". . . I just don't feel like we should go."
>   And, you know, "That's a big deal. It's your sister's wedding."
> Josette: Yeah. And we didn't go. We had no idea why.
> Craig: She called her mom and said I just don't think we should come. And her mom said, "I don't feel like you should come."
>   Now, who's to say if it meant anything, I mean, you know? It's one of those things where you can't really prove if it was prophecy or not because by not going you avoided whatever was going to happen to you. So it's like indirect proof because you didn't go and nothing bad happened and so therefore it is. Whereas if you ignored it and went, maybe you get hit by a garbage truck and you die or maybe nothing at all happens.
>   But, you know, those are all personal judgments you have to make when you feel like you're getting those kind of things to you where you have to decide, "Is this the Spirit talking to me?" "Am I paranoid?" "Have I just not slept well for a few days, and I don't really want to go up there, and this is an excuse?"

Craig points out that the results of many of the promptings people receive protecting them from harm may never be known. Craig and Josette continue to share this story because of the added conviction rendered by the second revelation: that of Josette's mother. Fearing she will be scolded for even suggesting that she miss her sister's wedding, Josette calls her mother with dread. But her mother immediately responds: "I don't feel like you should come." In the coded language of narratives of revelation, such "feelings" imply revelation (see chapter 2). Separately, neither feeling—Josette's nor her mother's—might be enough to keep Josette from going to the wedding. Together, they are sufficient to convince Josette and Craig that these vague feelings may in fact be revelation. The Baileys still do not know what they were protected from, if anything. But the double revelation provides sufficient narrative tension and proof of the divine to be consistently shared.

Additional confirmation through double revelation occurs most often in revelations of affirmation. Members may be guided through revelation to make a particular decision that impacts more than just themselves. In these cases, people who share the same stewardship may actively seek revelation to affirm the initial prompting. This is common among parents as they regularly seek guidance in how to raise their children. Such revelations of affirmation are equally common among church leaders as they seek revelation in their church callings, although these experiences typically extend beyond *personal* revelation and because of issues of privacy are not often shared (see chapter 3).

Revelatory experiences that include double revelation or affirmation provide evidence needed not only by individuals in order to act but by audience members in order to believe. It is perhaps not surprising that out of the fifty-six legends analyzed, not one described events that were unfulfilled. Only first or secondhand stories depended on double confirmation to provide sufficient support for the experience. With greater narrative distance between experience and narrator, greater evidence is needed to provide credibility. Another reason unfulfilled prompts are more likely to be shared by the people who experienced them is that they may know in their heart that their experience was divine. Their motivation for sharing their story may therefore be indistinguishable from their motivation to share experiences more easily proved. To the person receiving revelation, both spiritual experiences are valid, valuable, and worthy of sharing. To an audience hearing the story, however, the lack of personal connection and of "knowing" the experience was divine without explicit proof can pose too great a challenge in establishing belief to make continued narration viable.

Superlative Endings

Impressive confirmation and double revelation both serve as recurring motifs for the climax of the narrative. One final motif that emerges frequently in narration *follows* the climax, providing a formulaic close for the narrative. Marianne Reamey was sitting in her philosophy class at BYU when her teacher asked, "Now, what was that story about Hugh Nibley meeting his wife . . ." One of her fellow students offered the following story: "One day Hugh Nibley walked into an office on campus and saw a girl typing. She didn't speak to him or notice him, but as soon as he saw her, he was inspired by the Spirit and knew that this was the girl that he should marry. He was already engaged to someone else at the time. He broke his engagement, married the girl that had been typing, and they have lived happily ever since."[19]

The formulaic "happily ever after" ending is most familiar in fairy tales shared throughout Europe and the United States but functions similarly in other genres as a way of not only wrapping up the story but postulating that the events that unfolded were all for the best, possibly even foreordained. In LDS personal revelation, the "happily ever after" ending suggests a degree of contentment and accomplishment above and beyond what the average lay member might expect. Remarkable spiritual experiences are expected to result in remarkable future lives. Further, superlative endings suggest proof of the divine: only a higher power could be responsible for such an impressive outcome.

The "happily ever after" of LDS revelation is specific to LDS culture. Marriage, children, and leadership in the church are the three most common happy endings used to conclude LDS personal revelation. Specifically, people end up happily married for the rest of their lives, have many children, and rise in the ranks of the church hierarchy above expectation and above their peers. Often the ending matches the story, so that revelations about future spouses end with happy marriages and numerous children (see chapter 5). But some stories employ these endings indiscriminately. In one story, a man dreams three or four times in a row of impending disaster. Unable to avoid the accident, the man is seriously injured and three nights later lies on his deathbed. However, the bishop administers to him, praying that the man "be left upon the earth that he may finish his mission upon the earth." After being dead for a few hours, the man returns to life. "Roy surprised the doctors at the rate he healed. He married a young girl and had five boys. All of his boys were very active within the church, most of which went on missions."[20] Exceptional experiences are expected to provide exceptional results:

> An elderly German fellow who had been receiving lessons from the missionaries was clearing a field of tree stumps. The man, exerting himself perhaps beyond his capacity, fell into a faint.
> While dazed, he had a dream. In this dream he saw a room, completely bare except for a table on which lay a copy of the Book of Mormon. The man heard a voice, which said, "Everything in the book is true."
> The voice continued: it was up to the man to be baptized and bring his family into the church.
> The elderly gentleman was later baptized and he and his family became the most stalwart members in the area. (White n.d., Wilson Archives)

The most common type of experience that concludes with these superlatives are religious conversions, particularly when they result from missionary work, which may help explain why men were three times as likely as women to have had an experience that ended with such an overwhelming abundance of blessings. Missionaries pray for, and often receive, revelation to guide them in their work. Fulfillment of such revelation is typically a successful conversion. Such endings provide confirmation to the person that their choice to join the church was a good one, and confirmation to the audience of the truth of the LDS Church.[21] In these legends and memorates, nonmembers who range from reluctant to aggressively anti-Mormon not only join the church but become some of its most upstanding members. In a legend shared by an MTC trainer with her coworker, a man is converted after some particularly dramatic events:

> I heard about two missionaries that are tracting—the senior companion and a junior companion. And the junior companion is kind of like a scaredy-cat. He's kind of afraid.
>
> And they're out knocking doors in this one area, and this really burly, gruffy man comes out and says, you know, "Get off my property. I don't want anything to do with you," and closes the door in their faces.
>
> And the scaredy-cat's like, "Let's go, Elder. He doesn't want to talk to us. Let's leave."
>
> And the senior comp's like, "No, I really feel like this man needs to talk to us, like he's going to talk to us."
>
> So they knock on the door again. The man comes out and he says, you know, "What? This is private property and I've warned you. If you knock on my door again, I'm going to shoot you. I'll kill you."
>
> And then the scaredy-cat's like halfway down the road; he's like totally afraid. He's like, "Elder, this man's going to kill us if we don't leave."
>
> And he's like, "Well, we'll just try one more time. One more time and if he threatens us again, we're going to leave."
>
> And so they knocked on the door one more time and the man said, "You know what? I warned you." And he went back and he got his gun, cocks the gun and shoots the senior companion in the chest.
>
> And the . . . it threw him back into the bushes.
>
> And then, like five seconds later, the senior companion stands up, the missionary that has just been shot, and walks toward the man and says, "You know, we have a message and you're going to listen and you're going to let us into your home."
>
> And the man, I mean, he just shot him, thought he was dead. He obviously lets them into his home and I guess that he was baptized and he became like a bishop and a stake president or something like that.
>
> And later on after transfers, the senior companion sent the junior companion his garment top and there was a hole through the front and a hole through the back, but nothing had happened to him.[22]

"I've got another story," Ken Mullen begins, having already shared a number of spiritual experiences with his family and me during family home evening one night:

> I was on my mission; I was in Argentina. I had been there a week. I mean literally, Tom, when I got . . . we're on the plane heading there and we

think we know Spanish. [*laughter*]. We've been studying it ten hours a day for two months.

And we land in Buenos Aires, and I get off the plane, and we walk into the airport and I'm thinking, are we in Japan? Because I don't understand anything. Nothing. "Hola," maybe, if I was lucky.

And I'm out a week in the mission, I've been working for a week now at this point. Still can't understand hardly anything. Can't speak a lick, you know, with a native, forget it.

And we walk by this . . . we're walking down the street, me and my companion, and there's this guy with hair down to his shoulders with his shirt off, working on this house, construction worker. Just basically looked like a rough character, hippie-ish type, redneck, whatever you want to use, all of that combined. And I feel this distinct impression to stop and talk to this guy. Just stop. Say something, is really what I feel inside.

Talk about ignoring. I squashed it. There is no way I'm going to talk to this guy.

And what I really should have done is said something to my companion, and I didn't even do that. And I squashed it and I kept walking.

We're down maybe two houses and we hear, "Señores. Señores." The guy was on the sidewalk, calling to us.

And over the next two years, I baptized ten members of his family while I'm in Argentina.[23]

Shared as part of memorates, superlative endings are icing on the cake, additional confirmation of a deeply felt experience. Shared as part of legends, they risk undermining belief, just as stories with impressive confirmations can. As one BYU student argues, such endings can serve as a skeptical wink to the audience: "A listener or a narrator of a legend may never receive a distinct feeling as to whether the story is true or not. Legends are usually mixed with just enough truth that it is hard to tell just whether or not they did happen. I found it interesting that when the informants shared stories they considered to be more like legends, their body language and tone changed completely. Some, when they reached an ending that seemed all too tidy (i.e. they got baptized and became a general authority), they raised their eyebrows or laughed a little. Nevertheless, some claim to suspect the story to be somewhat true" (Jara 2000:6–7, Wilson Archives).

Personal Revelation as Motif

While patterns such as the number three, hesitation before heeding the Holy Ghost, and the formulaic coda of an LDS-specific happy ending can all be viewed as motifs, so, too, can revelation itself. The Aarne-Thompson Motif Index identifies a number of motifs relevant to revelation: V510, Religious visions, includes V510.1, God speaks in vision to devotee and V511.1.1, Saints; M300–M399, Prophecies, includes M301.11, Spirit as prophet, M306, Enigmatical prophecy, and M340.5, Prediction of danger; D1810, Magic knowledge, includes D1810.5, Magic knowledge from angel, D1810.8.1, Truth given in vision, and D1810.2, Information received through dreams; and D1812, Magic power of prophecy, includes D1812.1.2, Power of prophecy from God and D1812.3.3, Future revealed in dream. Distinguishing between personal revelation narratives and narratives that include personal revelation helps to clarify the range of functions and interpretations of personal revelation in the oral tradition. Further, distinctions between essential motifs and nonessential motifs help explain how meaning shifts when the revelatory experience is omitted in performance.

One among Many

Despite the fact that personal revelation is a distinct spiritual experience, revelation from the Holy Ghost may accompany other sacred experiences. When Grandma Winsor is prompted to go outside to check on her husband, she discovers he is trapped under a car. The prompting she receives is personal revelation alerting her to the danger facing her husband (see earlier in this chapter). Moments later, however, she receives help from angels to lift the car off of her husband, an example of miraculous divine intervention. Both revelation and divine intervention are part of a larger miracle; the two experiences are inseparable.

In another story, it is not an abundance of supernatural encounters that vie for attention but rather a deeply spiritual though mundane experience that transforms the interpretation and the narrative. The story was shared during a fast and testimony meeting in Florida by a man in his sixties, picking up on the topic of conversion begun by the first speaker that morning. He describes finding the church at age eighteen as a senior in high school in California. He had gone to church one Sunday just after the New Year, when they had just switched from the Bible to the Book of Mormon for study. "I went to Sunday School and had a testimony of the church right there," he testifies. "I was baptized after a week and a half."

He did his missionary work in Holland. He and his companion had gone to the home of a woman who had tuberculosis and they had given her the first discussion. She and her family were very receptive, and the two missionaries continued to teach the family every three days.

Eventually, his companion told him of a dream he had about a family in which the woman was sick. The companion wrote it down in a letter that he sent home. Almost as soon as he had mailed it, still long before his parents would receive his own letter, the man's companion received a letter from his father, who had had the same dream and wrote to tell him about it. The dream was so specific it even mentioned that the house the woman lived in was on a corner.

The two missionaries continued to work with the family until they were finally ready to be baptized. The entire family went to the church for their baptism, but the woman asked to speak to the bishop first. She told him that she wanted her husband and sons to be baptized, but she admitted she was once a prostitute and could not possibly be forgiven.

The bishop convinced her that God's love is boundless, as is his capacity to forgive. He told her she had been forgiven. The woman wept and joined her family in baptism.

"This really confirmed for me the power of the atonement," explains the man, using the story to launch into deeper discussion of the importance of atonement and forgiveness and the power of God's love.

While he initially frames the story with the topic of conversion and shares a story compelling for its dramatic double revelation, the focus of the man's testimony that morning lies elsewhere. It is the mundane events that follow—the atonement of a humble and sincere woman—that impact the man most deeply and memorably.

Events with multiple, powerful experiences provide one explanation why revelation may either share the focus or be subsumed within a performance. The perspective of the narrator provides another. In the story above, the narrator is sharing *his companion's* revelatory experience, not his own. One might imagine that the perspective offered by the woman in the story would provide yet a different narrative, where the revelatory dream might not be mentioned at all. The impact of the differences in perspective are clear in the following story:

> We went up to Logan . . . to visit Aunt Mattie. While there, a most marvelous case of healing took place with pneumonia.
>
> We had a very good doctor—an L.D.S.—but Rhea became worse with brain fever of meningitis. The doctor said she could not possibly live, that she was really dying then. We had the Elders several times, but she seemed no better. Because of our loss of her little sister, Viola, before we left Star Valley, I did not have any faith. I knew she would die, too. And your father felt the same way.
>
> We were sitting around the crib, waiting for the end. Her eyes were set, her head drawn back, her whole spine as rigid as could be.
>
> A knock came at the door and Aunt Mattie walked in with a dear, old, white-haired sister by the name of Needum. I remember how it vexed me for a stranger to intrude on us at that hour of sorrow.

In a moment, she told us she had been impressed to come and bless our sick child. She asked if she might pray. Of course, we told her she could, but added that the child was dying, that it was too late. She told us she had been set apart in the temple to bless the sick with her prayers, that if the Lord saw fit, it was never too late.

We knelt about the little bed. I will never forget that marvelous prayer and what it accomplished. I had hold of one of Rhea's little hands and her daddy the other one. Her eyes were glazed in death. The good sister first asked the Lord to give the parents of this little child faith. She said that for some reason she knew not why—we had no faith. She prayed on, and before she finished the prayer, Rhea opened her eyes naturally and gripped our hands and smiled. In less than an hour we had her dressed, and she was playing with her daddy's watch. She ate some milk toast and an egg. She had taken nothing for more than a week. She was healed. Of course, she was too weak to walk, but she tried. (J. Crowther n.d., Wilson Archives)

The story is told as "a marvelous case of healing." Narrated by the parents of a sick daughter, the story focuses on the supernatural recovery of the girl and the sincere prayer they offered to the Lord. Far more attention is paid to this prayer and the miraculous healing than to the old woman who arrives to heal the girl. The prompting that brought the woman to the door is dispatched in a single sentence. The diarist never returns to marvel at this prompting and how Sister Needum knew they needed help. Rather than being a central element of the story, revelation acts as a vehicle that sets the story in motion. A phone call from Aunt Mattie could have served the purpose as well. Of course, for personal experience stories, motifs cannot be substituted at will. Sister Needum's prompt to come to the house is narrated as part of a report of past events, not as one possible motif among many.

The prompting is subsumed in the larger story of healing. The perspective of the narrators at least partially explains why. Not having experienced the prompting themselves, the parents are less likely to choose to focus on an experience for which they were not present than on one for which they were. Of course, sometimes one experience is simply more compelling than another. The miraculous healing of little Rhea may eclipse the prompting even in a story told by Sister Needum.

Analysis of revelation as motif suggests that perspective matters. People focus on the elements of experience most meaningful to them, whether because of the information they are privy to, or because of their particular interests or values. Performance context matters as well, with different situations encouraging not only different foci but different constellations of material altogether.

Missing in Action

The revelatory experience may not just take a back seat in the narrative, it may be omitted altogether. John Foss shared his conversion story with the ward twice within the year. The first time was during fast and testimony meeting on March 25, 2007. John Foss woke that morning realizing that forty-one years ago that week he was baptized. He makes a point of bearing his testimony on the anniversary of important junctures in his religious life. Baptism is one of them.

Just before he spoke, Craig Bailey bore his testimony, commenting that he had been at a crossroads, having felt disconnected from the church until he accompanied the young missionaries in their work one evening. Brother Foss picks up on this imagery when he bears his own testimony:

"Forty-one years ago I, too, was at a crossroads," he begins. He goes on to describe how missionaries regularly visited his home, but he continued to procrastinate about getting baptized. "My wife finally said she was getting baptized with or without me," he said, eliciting a laugh from the congregation. "On April sixth, forty-one years ago, I was baptized." Tears well up in his eyes. "It has been a faith-promoting experience to live the gospel in your midst." John sits back down amid a quiet, appreciative audience.

Eight months later, John shared his story again during fast and testimony meeting on November 4, 2007. Again, the date is significant. He begins, tearing up:

> I woke up this morning realizing that today was November fourth.
> Forty-one years ago, I was living in western New York and there was
> a snowstorm, swirling, snowing, blowing.
>
> I was sitting in the window enjoying the storm when two figures
> appeared and stopped outside my house, and conversed, and then came
> directly to my house.
>
> I thought, here was an opportunity to rescue these two young men
> from the storm. They came with a message of salvation through the
> Church of Jesus Christ of Latter-day Saints. Little did I know that they
> were the ones to rescue me from the storms of life.

He adds that conversion wasn't immediate. It wasn't until April 6 of the following year that he joined the church. He then describes the blessings he has received thanks to the church.

"Blessings are priceless. They must be earned through righteous living. Through these blessings, we can one day walk back into his presence." He soon closes, giving his testimony about the truth of the church and its leaders.

Based on these two accounts, one may never have known that Brother Foss received a dream foretelling the visit of these two missionaries. But a year earlier, on July 30, 2007, his daughter Jackie Foss was one of two women asked by the Sunday school teacher to share examples of miracles in their lives. Jackie told three stories, beginning with her father's conversion. Two months later, I recorded a much longer account of the story at her home:

> My father was a die-hard Catholic. He went to church on Christmas and Easter [*laugh*]. I don't even know how old he was when he joined the Mormon Church, but the way it came about is that these two missionaries . . .
>
> We lived in Buffalo, New York. We were like twenty-five feet from the border on south Buffalo, so you get a lot of snow, the snow off of Lake Erie.
>
> And it was a snowstorm, I mean like waist-deep snowstorm.
>
> And now, in hindsight, we knew these guys were about a mile from home. We were the last house, because they'd have to go through a huge graveyard and it's a big cut, but you know, there's no shelter.
>
> So they took shelter. We had a colonial home and there's like an eight-by-eight room before you go in the house that's never locked, and so they took shelter in there, and you know, just knocked on the door and asked my mom if they could hang out.
>
> And of course my mom is like, "Yeah, whatever." And she wanted to feed them, of course, being a mom. But they wanted to teach her the message and she put up the old hand, you know, no, she's not interested [*Jackie mimes putting up a hand as a gesture to stop*].
>
> And she happened to tell my dad about this, I think it was about two or three days later. And my dad was like, taken back, which . . . he's very subdued, very quiet individual more or less, unless he really has something to say, he just hangs out.
>
> And he told my mom, he kind of took her aside, and I'll never forget, because we were doing something as a family, I forget, and they had to go, a game or something, I forget what we were doing, and he took her into another room and—he relayed this story to us years later—that he had a dream, just that very week.
>
> And look, I get chill bumps [*she shows me her arm*]. That's how you know things are true with me. Other people have different ways, but that's me.
>
> And he said that he knew two men in dark jackets, dark suits, and white shirts, you know, were going to come, and this is what he was supposed to do. He didn't know who they were, if it was a job interview. He wasn't looking for religion. He just knew he was supposed to follow these men.
>
> He had never had like dreams or visions before. And he absolutely just said, you know, "Who are they? How do we get a hold of them?"
>
> My mom didn't know.
>
> And sure enough, my mom saw them walking in front of our walk.

Because we lived, like in a city block you have two houses on each side. At the end, they actually had a park [*she begins to sketch out the street for me*], and my grandmother's house was the first one, she had a full lane and then the park started. And so each house had a littler, I mean just a regular lot or an oversized lot, and the park went in front of the houses. That's how you get in the city.

The two guys, when they came out of the graveyard, would have to go through that lane.

And so she saw them and stopped them one day and said, you know, "My husband would like to see you."

And she wasn't real enthusiastic, not at all if you knew my mom, and invited them to come back at a certain time or the number to where my dad was, or something to that nature. Anyways, they made an appointment, and literally, for the next three years, we had missionaries at our home, for breakfast, for lunch, and for dinner.

And that's not the way it is now. But when you were a missionary back then you got sent to an area, and say if it was Graham or Elon, that's where you stayed, the whole time. This was in, oh gosh, way before my little sister was born, so, I want to say sixty-eight-ish. Somewhere in there. Eons ago, I'm old [*laugh*].

And so literally, it's not like my father jumped into the religion thing, because he wasn't . . . . And they just challenged him to read the Book of Mormon, to read the promise given in there by Nephi, you know, if you pray, if you're earnest in the heart, you really want to know what's true, this is what you do.

And my dad really read the Book of Mormon. I know now when you go to join the church, or investigate it, I mean they ask you the very first time, you know, here's the rules, you do it or you don't, you're gone. Then, it wasn't a pressed issue; I guess that's a sign of the times, earnestly, now.

But he took time. He had questions, he wanted answers. He wanted to know if these boys were true, why they were there. And the missionary that baptized my father, we are very close to, to this day. In fact, he called my mom last night. He did.

That's funny. Because I hadn't . . . because when I lived in Arizona, we'd go up to where my ex-husband lived, in Idaho, and it was like thirty minutes away from where this boy lives, with his family. So we've always been intermixed. I mean my parents went to his kids' weddings, I mean, if there's births. It's just very close, very close.

Now when you see the missionaries, you only see them for a few months. And honest, I think my father would have got lost in that, just knowing who my dad is.

But the bond was there. I mean it's not like they ever came, you know mowed lawns, or hung out laundry or painted houses. None of that.

Now I remember they used to take us kids bike riding, because we were allowed to go on streets that we weren't allowed on with them,

I do remember that. And with the missionaries we were riding double on a bike. I got hit by a car one time and, oh yeah, they thought they were dead when they had to go tell my mom.

But anyways, back to my poppa. That just hopefully ties it in to how he does. I mean he studied the lessons, most earnestly, he knew who these men were.

And he didn't relay this story until years later for us as kids. And now to see him, I mean he hasn't missed church hardly ever. If he's out, you know there's something dead dog wrong, you know?[24]

John Foss chose not to include his dream about the missionaries when he shared his conversion story publicly to the ward, but he did include it when he shared it privately with his daughter at home once she was old enough to hear it. Variation in goal, setting, and audience clearly influenced both John Foss and his daughter Jackie's decisions about how to narrate his conversion experience. Both are also influenced by the framing of the event. Jackie was asked by the Sunday school instructor to share stories about miracles in her life. John, on the other hand, was compelled first to discuss the trials of joining the church and then the blessings of membership, the salvation he attained, and the promise of eternal life. Finally, issues of humility and personal tendencies to share or guard supernatural experiences also influence decisions to include or exclude revelation.[25] While Jackie Foss did get some of the details of the event wrong—something she apologized for publicly when she bore her testimony after hearing her father bear his on March 25—she did not invent the dream. Rather, Brother Foss is reserved about whom he shares this story with and when, wary of drawing too much attention to himself. Jackie, however, finds the dream a powerful faith-promoting experience that cannot be omitted.

While omitting the revelatory part of an experience is clearly intentional when the rest of the experience is shared by the person who received the revelation, it may be unintentional when shared by others, especially as stories are passed along through family and friends. It is during this process, when personal connections become tenuous and stories slowly blur into what may rightly be called legends, that the concept of motif becomes more relevant. Memories fail and the mind compensates. The mundane can become supernatural, the supernatural mundane. Further, people may not agree on whether an event was revelation or not. Personal beliefs of the narrator about the frequency and nature of supernatural encounters can encourage divergent narratives. Such variation is particularly striking in a series of stories collected by a family of ten brothers and sisters and bound together under the title *The Tenney Breadbasket*. In the book, the family patriarch and matriarch—Nathan Orson Tenney and Myrtle Mary Wear—share stories of their lives, as do their ten children and some of their grandchildren. The result is a book with multiple versions of the same event. One event in particular appears five times. It is the story of baby Eudora's narrow escape from a home fire.

Boyd Tenney remembers the fire that destroyed the house that his grandfather had built as "one of the heartbreaks of my life."[26] After describing the fire from his own perspective—walking home from school and seeing smoke billowing up over the hill—he told his mother's story: "Mother told this story about the incident: Eudora was sleeping on the bed. She got a feeling, that she should go in to check her. Two hot coals had dropped down from the ceiling on this bed, right next to her baby. She grabbed the baby and the other children and just barely got out with her life" (Hendrix and Hendrix 1994:277–8).

Boyd's sisters Naydene and Opal both tell the story but do not mention the feeling that prompted their mother to check on the baby. Instead, they mention a sound that prompted her action. Naydene recalls:

Well, Mama was in the kitchen washing dishes and heard something in there, kind of like a hen scratching or something and she just thought, "I'd better go in there and see about that baby. That hen might be in there and she might be trying to lay an egg and she might scratch that baby."

Well, when she got in the room and looked up right over Eudora . . . she's kind of against the wall . . . the two by four right along there was on fire, just burning, and there was a terrible high wind that day. She got Eudora up and got her out. (1994:74)

Opal concurs in her account:

Mother said that she was in the kitchen working and she had Eudora lying on a "pallet" as we called it, in front of the stove. She was keeping her warm.

She heard this scratching noise.

I had an old hen that my cousin, Inez Crawford, had given to me when she moved to New Mexico with her family. It was sort of a pet hen. You could call that hen and she would come a running. You could pick her up and play with her like you would a doll. She would come into the house if the door was open.

Mother said she had go through her mind, "I wonder if Inez is in there, because she scratches anything that is bright."

The baby opened her eyes. Mother used to say, "Don't ever let that hen get around that baby, she might peck at the eyes."

All of this went through her mind, so she went in there to check and it was the crackling of this fire that she was hearing. She could see it right over Eudora's head. She swooped down and swept up everything but the first quilt or whatever she had on the floor, she didn't quite get that, and then she looked back and that beam fell right in front of her. She had to move fast to be sure they didn't get hit. That's how fast it happened, or we would have lost our little sister. (1994:225)

Their sister Nina, however, remembers both a sound and a feeling: "One cold morning, Mother thought she heard our old speckled hen upon the roof, scratching. She was working in the kitchen and suddenly got the feeling that she should slip into the bedroom and check on Eudora. As she stepped into the bedroom, she saw the ceiling on fire just above the baby crib. She swooped up the baby and blanket and rushed from the room just as the burning ceiling fell into the baby bed where Eudora had been seconds before" (1994:326).

The presence and significance of the feeling that Myrtle Tenney received is most explicit, however, in the account told one generation later, by Shawna Romney Jackson, Pearl Tenney Romney's daughter.[27] She frames the story as follows: "One day, I asked Grandma about a prompting or feeling that I had about one of our children, and how I later wondered if I should have listened to that voice. She told me to always listen to that still small voice. Then she proceeded to tell me about two stories that happened to her" (1994:464). The first story her grandmother told her was about a prompting that allowed her to save her daughter Naydene from a rattlesnake. The second story described the fire:

Grandma Tenney was in the kitchen making bread and she had an impression that she should go check the baby. She thought that was rather silly because the baby was just in the other room asleep, and if something was wrong she would hear it.

However, when the feeling persisted, she washed her hand of the sticky bread dough, and went to check on the baby. She was horrified to see that the stove that was next to where her baby was sleeping had caught the curtains on fire. Just as Grandma reached for the baby and picked her up, the curtain on fire fell where the baby was laying.

With gratitude in her heart for the promptings of the Holy Ghost, she thanked her Heavenly Father for helping to save her baby. How grateful she was that she had been obedient to that voice.

These are two examples that Grandma related to me that made her always remember to obey, when that still small voice speaks. This was a great lesson to me in my life. (1994:464)

There are of course other discrepancies among the various accounts. The baby was sleeping on a pallet, in a bed, or in a crib. The fire burned through the ceiling, the wall, or the curtains. These minor differences are inconsequential to the meaning of the story. Inclusion of a divine prompt, however, is transformative. The feeling that Boyd and Nina describe, that Opal and Naydene omit altogether, becomes the clear whispering of the Holy Ghost in Shawna's account. Because the term "feeling" can be as clear an indicator of the Holy Ghost for Latter-day Saints as more explicit terms (see chapter 2), Shawna's version is similar to those of Boyd and Nina, if more explicit. It is fundamentally different, however, from the stories shared by Opal and Naydene, stories that serve primarily as family history. The story Shawna heard from her grandmother and that she tells to others serves to remind her to listen to the promptings of the Holy Ghost. Revelation takes center stage, subsuming its secondary function as family history. Performance context matters. In recounting family history of the time the house burned down, a narrator may feel that the reason Myrtle Tenney checked on Eudora is a nonessential element. Narrating faith-promoting stories of the importance of listening to the still small voice, however, demands its mention.

One other motif appears in Shawna's account, an element not seen in any of the other versions told by the siblings present at the fire: ignoring the initial prompting. Only after the feeling persisted did she finally act. This is true in both stories Grandma Tenney told Shawna—the story of the fire as well as the preceding story about being prompted to go check on her daughter Naydene:

> As Grandma looked out her kitchen window, she could watch Naydene playing with her favorite box that she carried around with her all the time.
>
> For some reason that morning, Grandma was prompted to go check under the wooden box. She thought, "That's silly, because Naydene plays with that same box everyday. Why should there be anything to worry about today?"
>
> But the feeling persisted and came back stronger.
>
> Finally, she went outside quickly and overturned the box. There sat all coiled up was a rattlesnake under the box.
>
> Quickly, Grandma grabbed a shovel and killed the rattlesnakes, thus preventing what could have been a tragedy. (1994:464)

Without an account from Myrtle Tenney herself of either of these two events, it is impossible to know whether she hesitated or not. It is possible that like Sandy Johnson who added the motif of hesitation into the Woodruff story, Shawna also added a motif common to the narrative tradition and resonant with the human reluctance to inconvenience oneself without good reason. As likely, however, the hesitation was real, with variation explained by considering the situational context of performance. Grandma Tenney shared these stories with her granddaughter to impress upon her the importance of listening to the promptings of the still small voice. Shawna remembers her grandmother recounting how she almost didn't, and the tragedies she would have faced had she not finally listened. The performance context provides an explanation for why Grandma Tenney might have highlighted her hesitation in sharing these stories with Shawna, but may not have in other circumstances, in other settings, and to other audiences.

Issues of setting, audience, goal, and humility, as well as the possibility of a faulty memory or doubt about the supernatural nature of the experience, all contribute to whether or not a narrator explicitly includes revelatory experiences when narrating stories compelling in their own right. Tenuous connection to the participants seems the obvious explanation for a series of legends about how well-known LDS scholar, author, and BYU professor Hugh Nibley found his wife, where revelation appears in some versions but not in others.[28] However, faulty memory should be considered the interpretation of last resort in most cases, particularly the closer the narrator is to the source.

For revelation to operate as an element that can be included or omitted in a story, the experience must be able to stand on its own as a narrative. A story of finding one's keys is hardly compelling enough to repeat without the revelatory element of praying for help and being prompted to search in an unlikely place. Escape from a burning house, however, makes for a strong narrative, whether a person was prompted by the Holy Ghost or not. So, too, does a story of how a well-known church leader found a wife. Without the prompting, compelling stories can continue to be told as family history, religious rumor, or personal conversion but not as faith-promoting stories testifying of the hand of God and the gift of the Holy Ghost. With the addition of a revelatory experience, however, the nature and function of the story can change fundamentally.

Retroactive Revelation

The fact that revelation may appear in subordinate positions in narratives or disappear from them altogether does not invalidate the experience. It merely highlights the gap between experience and narrative. While conscious omission of revelation is clearly apparent in the narrative tradition, conscious invention is not. At least not explicitly. The concerns people have about the social and spiritual reputations of some of their fellow members suggest that they fear either explicit invention by people seeking attention or unwitting, benign fabrication by people all too eager to commune with the divine.[29] Some stories simply are not believed.

The invention of revelation, however, need not be viewed solely as an act of falsity and fantasy. Assuming the supernatural is objectively real does not alleviate the fact that some people readily perceive it and some do not. The struggle for Latter-day Saints to determine whether the feeling they received was revelation from the Holy Ghost, personal desire, coincidence, indigestion, or the work of the devil, is not an idle one and cuts to the core of the ambiguity of the supernatural. What one person perceives as revelation, another may perceive as coincidence.

Only the Godhead and angels can provide true revelation to Latter-day Saints. Yet because the supernatural must be perceived by humans, revelation can be "created" in the simple act of naming. Typically, interpretation follows quickly and revelation is affirmed or rejected. However, there are times when the recognition of revelation follows much later, after initial interpretation. This reinterpretation transforms the mundane into the spiritual, the coincidence or strange feeling into revelation, in essence creating revelation after the fact. These "retroactive revelations" further illuminate the process of interpretation and its dependence on cultural norms and the act of performance.[30]

The Construction of Retroactive Revelation

Interpreting divine communication is not easy. Nor is the process necessarily finite; interpretations change based on a person's growing understanding of the world and the Holy Ghost. The result is that experiences originally dismissed as mundane may be reinterpreted in hindsight as revelation.

Francine Carter recalls her decision to become a missionary. Many men and most women have distinct narratives of this choice, since it is such a major life decision. Young men are expected to go on a mission and may simply follow this path without great reflection. But young women have only recently begun serving missions and to do so remains rare. Francine remembers her struggle to decide whether she would serve a mission or not. After a single day in her Sharing the Gospel class at BYU, a class designed for prospective missionaries, she was sure this was not the path for her:

> But then there was something inside me that said, "You know, you really should think about going on a mission."
> And so I asked my bishop, I said, "Do you think I should go on a mission?"
> And I was dating someone I really liked.
> And he said, "Well, I think you should think about . . . really talk to your parents."
> This was in February and I got really excited, like I knew I was going to go on a mission, and I was excited about it.

I went home and my parents were really discouraging about it, it seemed. It made me really frustrated. Not that they didn't think it was a good thing, but they just sort of questioned me, just to make me think about it twice, to make sure that I made the right decision. Like, "Are you sure that you don't just want to finish your school? You're almost finished." And just different things like this.

It made me so frustrated and upset, because I had felt like a good feeling about serving a mission. I know it was the Spirit. I know it was. I didn't realize it until later on. All I knew was, it was something that made me really excited, like going, "Yeah, I'm going to serve a mission." But I didn't really know what it was, and I didn't know where it came from. (Leavitt 1995:12–6, Wilson Archives).

Only as Francine became more familiar with how it felt to be inspired by the Holy Ghost was she able to reflect back on her experience and recognize the revelation she received.

While lack of practice and training is one reason revelation goes unnoticed, another is simple lack of attention. In the act of sharing the experience, the unusual nature of the event can become clear and the possibility of divine revelation apparent, whether to the individual or the audience. When Josette Bailey all of a sudden thought she should visit the park office to reserve a picnic shelter for her son's baptism party, she dismissed it as any other reminder of the errands and tasks she had to accomplish. But when she told her mother about it later that day, her mother pointed out that this was not just luck:

Josette: It's kind of silly if you think about it but it still was to me, like, "Hello."

Just yesterday, was it just yesterday? [*pause*] Was it yesterday? Maybe the day before. A couple of days ago, whenever [*laugh*].

We're planning Jarrett's baptism. He's turning eight, a month from today actually, but we're waiting till June for him to get baptized 'cause all, a lot of our family's coming out and we wanted to give them a chance to be out of school and everything.

And we've been planning it and trying to get things all set aside. And we knew we wanted to rent this building over here at the park, because we're going to have fifty so on people coming for dinner afterwards.

And I've been really busy, I guess we've been so busy. And Craig asked me a couple of days, like last week, have you called and got that reserved yet? And I'm like, "No. I'll put it on my calendar; I'll try to remember to do it."

And I hadn't done it yet.

And then yesterday, I came home, I had just got the kids home, just started unpacking everything and I'm like,

"Guys, we've got to get back in the car, I got to go do that,
I got to get that phone number and get that reserved."
    I mean I was fully involved in stuff that was going on, and I
just stopped and said I have to go do that. And I went over there,
and the lady was in the office, so I go ahead and went and asked
her. I called Craig, I said, "Does this sound OK? The money?
Everything." And he's like, "Yeah, go ahead and do it."
    And I sat down and started filling out the contract, and the
phone rang, and the lady who was on the phone said, "I'm sorry.
That time is already taken. The lady is sitting right here filling
out the contract for that date."
    So if I wouldn't have stopped everything and gone over
there . . . .
    I mean, it's kind of silly because it's a building, who cares? But
it's something we wanted for his baptism and it worked out that
way. And if I would have waited . . .

Craig: Another day.
Josette: . . . two minutes, five minutes, we wouldn't have got it at the day
          we wanted. This day is set in stone because we have family flying
          in from Utah to be here at that time. So . . . . And we definitely
          don't have room for fifty some odd people to eat lunch here
          [*laughter*].
Tom: Even if you did, you wouldn't want them [*laughter*].
Josette: No, because I don't want all those high heels on my hardwood
          floors [*laughter*].
              So, you know, not grand angels, grandiose importance, but
          still something important to us, something important to him.
Tom: And so, in terms of thinking about revelation, is it
          something that . . . like, do you always know it when you . . .
Josette: No.
Craig: Nope.
Josette: No. I would have had no idea. I had no idea until I went
          over there, and I was like . . . . I even came home and was like . . . .
          I called my mom, I said, "Guess what?" She's like, "That's
          cool, that's cool that you listened and knew to go do that."
              And I'm like, you know, I didn't even realize I was doing it at
          the time. I was just like, this was just something . . . I just had
          an urgency that I needed to get this done at the moment. Just a
          sense of urgency.
          So I went and did it.

In some cases, performance is the trigger to reevaluate. In others, new devel-
opments prompt reflection. A young woman shares a story told by her father
about her birth. She was born a twin. When it was time for their blessing,
neither the twins' father nor grandfather wanted to bless Diane, the other twin
girl. The father finally ended up blessing Diane but had a hard time doing it.

"When Diane died, they knew why they had had this impression." Only in hindsight did they understand their reluctance to bless Diane as a revelation from the Holy Ghost.[31] A young missionary prepares a plastic zip-topped bag of starch that he will later combine with water to make a ball in order to illustrate the need to keep strengthening one's testimony. As he does, he realizes it looks like a bag of cocaine. Later that day, he remembers the bag just as he and his companion are about to go through a police checkpoint. "Later that night, my companion and I laughed over the experience. Today, however, I realize that my initial thought that it looked like a bag of cocaine was a warning given to me by the Spirit so that I could avoid the bag check, contact with the police, and almost certain arrest. I realize that this was a fulfillment of the promise for protection given to missionaries" (Cope 2003, Wilson Archives). A young woman shares a cautionary tale with her friend; both of them are engaged to be married. In the story, the girl gets to the temple but becomes sick and wants to call off the wedding. Her mother pressures her to go through with the marriage despite the feeling. She does, but not long after, her husband moves out, having fallen in love with a man. What appeared to be a mundane illness is recognized in hindsight as revelation (Peterson 1974, Wilson Archives).

Mike McCann says, reflecting on times he has been prompted by the Spirit:

> Funny thing happened this morning.Brother Stanley is the teacher's quorum advisor. And I don't know what time you got here today, but the bread . . . [*I nod, confirming that I was there when it was time to pass the Sacrament but there was no bread*] for sacrament. He brings the bread. And when I was in that position, I brought the bread every week, but it's supposed to be a responsibility of the young men.
>
> Yesterday we had an interesting experience when we called . . . . My wife and I were going to the grocery store to get groceries for the week. We called back to the house and asked Jordan, our son, "Need anything at the store?" First thing out of his mouth was "Bread." And he never says bread, he never says we need bread. He doesn't even eat sandwiches. And we thought that was odd. But, we knew we were getting low, so we picked some bread up.
>
> This morning—and I didn't know it[32] until after church—but I had this feeling that I should take the bread with me to church. I'm thinking, "Why? I know Brother Stanley's out of town, but . . ." you know, "something." And I was going to bring it and I forgot.
>
> After church, my wife said, you know, something told me this morning we needed to bring the bread. And she forgot it as well. I mean, it was, like, early. And then when we got here, we had the little thing with the bread.
>
> I think that, in a way, was the Lord trying to tell us, and we didn't heed that warning if you will. And it kind of got at me a little bit. It was, like

plain and simple. Jordan first said it and then both of us had that feeling. And then we get here and we had the problem, so.

President Hinckley definitely gets a different level of prophecy. As Melchizedek priesthood holders, we receive prophecy for guidance, if you will, to lead our families. If you don't listen to it, or take heed to it, you can go without your bread.

Of course, we didn't go without, but it was an interesting situation. I don't know how many others had that feeling or sense or whatever, this morning, but we did and I found that quite interesting.

Of course you don't realize it until after the fact.

Hindsight is provoked by the dramatic event that follows. Without the sudden death of a baby, the dramatic run-in with the police, the unusually brief marriage, or the missing sacrament, unexpected feelings and thoughts would likely be forgotten. Like omens, only in fulfillment is the initial experience remembered.[33] Dramatic outcomes demand reflection on possible causes and previous warnings. The reason for this interpretive move is grounded in the widespread belief in the LDS Church that "there are no coincidences."[34]

When Janece Hoopes watches her brother tumble out of a moving car in the middle of traffic, she is horrified. "I began to scream for the lady to stop, as I grabbed for my own door in the back seat and looked out the back window. She yelled that she couldn't stop in the middle of the street and continued to turn, then pulled over to the side.

"I watched everything as if in slow motion; the people at the crosswalk sign all had their mouths open and terrified expressions on their faces. None of the cars at the now green light had moved—there is no way all of the people in those cars could have seen what happened, and reacted so quickly." At a loss to explain how her brother emerged unharmed save a few scratches and bruises, Janece believes God intervened by alerting the other drivers to stop. She is even more explicit describing her own near miss with a car:

It was just after dark when my mother and I got into the car to go to my dance class. Our driveway was a long gravel road going up a fairly steep hill. My mother had just pulled out onto the top of the drive when she remembered an important phone call she had to stay home and wait for, so she stopped the car and ran into my brother's trailer to see if he would drive me to my class.

She couldn't have been gone more than three or four minutes, but to a five-year-old in a cold, dark car, it seemed like forever.

The front of the car was pointing down the hill, and I had waited long enough. I stepped out of the door and, rather than going down the hill in front of the car as I usually would have—it was shorter to my destination that way, I went around the back. Just as I got to the center of the back of the vehicle, it rolled quickly away down the hill.

I'm not sure whether I screamed or not, but my mother, brother and his girlfriend came running out the door of the box just in time to see the automobile disappear into the darkness.

To this day, I am thankful that I was prompted to walk the long way around that night.[35]

Janece does not mention receiving a feeling or hearing a voice to go a different way around the car. Only in hindsight does she see that she was prompted. Barring coincidence, the divine provides what seems to her the only logical explanation.

Such interpretations are common in stories of answered prayers. When people appear as if by coincidence with money to buy an unexpected harvest of eggs (*Gems of Reminiscence* 1915:33–6; Fife and Fife 1956:200) or to read a story from scripture that provides the answer they were looking for (Bailey 2008 interview), the interpretation among many Latter-day Saints is that those benefactors were prompted by the Holy Ghost. People are regularly pressed into God's service to help a neighbor or a stranger, whether initiated by prayer or not. In some cases, proof of that prompting emerges in the course of events. When Mrs. McClellan prays for healing for herself and her son, she is prompted to go to the temple, a long and expensive trip she cannot afford. However, a few weeks later, a man arrives with the money to make the trip. The money is the answer to her prayers, but it is only years later that she learns the man, too, was prompted by God (McClellan 1931, Fife Archives; edited version in Fife and Fife 1956:200–3). In other cases, however, revelation remains an assumption. In the written diary entry of Albert Edward Hopkinson dated August 6, 1934, Hopkinson writes about being trapped in a mine with a fire closing in on him. He prayed for help before passing out. He then recounts how two men who had been fighting the fire "decided to stop and eat, and then, an unseen power possessed them and urged that they hasten back into the mine . . . I know it was the power of the Lord that moved these men to come to our rescue" (Fletcher 1972, Wilson Archives). Hopkinson never mentions talking to the miners and finding out whether or not they were prompted. But his claim "I know it was the power of the Lord that moved these men to come to our rescue" suggests knowledge apart from anything his rescuers might have conveyed. He is convinced that his rescue was an answer to his prayers.[36]

Less dramatic experiences may also be interpreted as results of revelation. As long as people observe an act or event out of sync with their expectations, the desire to find meaning can lead them to the divine. While Mike McCann hints at the possibility that his neighbor was prompted to go outside, thus scaring away the man robbing his house (see chapter 3), others are more convinced of their interpretation. A young man's sister lost control of her car and went flying through a farmer's fence and into his yard. Only minutes earlier, the farmer's children had been playing in that exact spot, but their mother had called them in to dinner. With no specific evidence of divine prompting, the young man "believes that this was the inspiration of God and His power at work that saved his sister and these children" (Mohler 1980:15, Wilson Archives). Mary Morrison was sitting in the celestial room at the dedication of the San Diego Temple when she noticed a poorly dressed woman sitting on the aisle. She was critical of the woman, believing her clothing was not appropriate for the most sacred room in the temple. Yet as the church authorities filtered out through the crowd to shake a few hands and leave the room, every one of them, separately, stopped and shook that woman's hand. The woman's friend leaned over to the first authority to come by to tell him that she was blind. Mary was touched: "There's no doubt in my mind that all of them were prompted to stop and greet her. She couldn't see them, but she could feel their spirits through their hands."[37]

Inferring the divine from the seemingly mundane is partially a matter of personality. Some people are simply more apt to see the divine than others. Serena Gammon, for example, laughs that where she sees the Holy Spirit, her husband, Dave, sees a natural occurrence. A particularly telling story is the one shared by Sarah Miles about her father:

> One afternoon dad went hunting and got lost in the forest. It was during the deer hunt, and it started to snow. He got cold and was afraid that he would freeze to death if he couldn't get back to his car. He walked for hours and hours but only got himself deeper into the forest.
>
> Then all of a sudden he heard a voice and saw a man coming through the trees toward him.
>
> I can't remember who the man was, but he took dad back to the car and saw that he made it home safely.
>
> It's very unlikely that anyone would have been wandering around in the forest at that time of night unless they had been somehow inspired to do so.

The collector, Kristy Miles, is the daughter of the narrator and the granddaughter of the man rescued in the woods. She observes, "What is interesting about this story is that my mother interprets the event religiously, while I'm sure my grandfather would not have." Kristy clearly believes that the final sentence of the story reflects the beliefs of her mother, not her grandfather. If this is true, then her mother has transformed coincidence into revelation.[38]

The blurriness between human and divine inspiration can also lead to the transformation of the mundane into revelation. Some members credit all human insight to God; to claim credit for oneself can risk taking credit for God's work. Others, however, distinguish between human potential and divine revelation. As stories are shared, different narrators, with different orientations toward human and divine inspiration, will narrate stories differently.

There is great variation among Latter-day Saints in terms of how quickly and often they see God in their lives. Nonetheless, as Austin Fife has argued, "the roots of theology of divine intercession" are "deeply implanted in the Mormon folk mentality" (1948:30) and LDS culture "is permeated with folk-lore concerning the intercession of the heavenly powers in the affairs of man and in the rich rewards that are in store for those who practice the arts of pro-pitiation according to divinely revealed forms (1948:25). These roots may be deeper for Mormons than for other Christians. In her comparative study of Christian autobiographies, Susan Swetnam found that Mormons are far more likely to see the hand of God in their lives than non-Mormons (1991:51, 81).

The Normalization of Retroactive Revelation

Evolving interpretations that recognize the supernatural in what was once con-sidered mundane may appear problematic to the outsider and be seen as acts of invention, even outright falsification. Yet LDS theology and culture are par-ticularly open to evolving interpretation, to a dynamic religion that recognizes human fallibility. One is not born "knowing" that the church is true. Nothing irks some members more than to hear earnest children stand up during fast and testimony meetings and repeat the ritualistic mantra of adult testimonies: I know this church is true, I know Joseph Smith is a prophet. As one member laughingly complains, "When kids get up there and say they *know* this to be true, they don't know this yet. They can't." Similarly, members are not born with the ability to discern the Holy Ghost without a doubt. Countless church lessons, manuals, and articles focus on the challenge of discerning the Holy Ghost (see chapter 3).

This process of trial and error to develop a dependable process for identify-ing the Holy Ghost can last a lifetime. There are experiences too ambiguous for their origin to be certain, where people remain unsure whether they are being prompted by the Holy Ghost or some other force, natural or supernatural. It is not only acceptable to reflect back and recognize revelation where you once saw good luck, it is encouraged. Members are warned in scripture, by church lead-ers, and by peers at the pulpit: take your blessings for granted, fail to give God his due, and those blessings will disappear.

Retroactive revelation is not confined to the folk or narrative traditions. Nor is it confined to personal revelation. The history of the church provides a number of examples of statements that began as mundane claims only to be reinterpreted as revelation. In the Doctrine and Covenants, for example, only the second of the two Official Declarations began clearly and unambiguously as revelation. The first, the 1890 Manifesto, may have been viewed as a political declaration as much as a religiously inspired one. Official Declaration 1 proclaimed an end to plural marriage, or polygamy. The church had been facing intense pressure from the federal government to halt the practice of plural marriage. Legislation upheld in the Supreme Court made it illegal to engage in polygamy, and the threat of withholding statehood from Utah loomed large. At least a year before he issued the manifesto, LDS president Wilford Woodruff had been denying permissions for plural marriages in the church. On September 25, 1890, President Woodruff published the manifesto in the church newspaper, the *Deseret Weekly*, followed by a verbal declaration during general conference a few weeks later. Nowhere in the manifesto does Woodruff mention revelation or inspiration. However, First Counselor Lorenzo Snow moved to accept the manifesto during general conference by recognizing Woodruff as "the only man on the earth at the present time who holds the keys of the sealing ordinances," thereby reminding the general membership of Woodruff's divine authority.

Carmon Hardy argues in his book that there is little evidence to suggest that church leaders viewed the manifesto as revelation at the time, noting how the document entered the world in much the same way as a statement earlier that year condemning rumors about the temple ceremony: "Each involved the hand of Charles W. Penrose. Both carried the title 'Official Declaration.' And both were referred to as a 'Manifesto.' Both were addressed 'To Whom It May Concern' and appeared in the editorial columns of the *Deseret News*. Both followed a similar line of argument, amounting to a rebuttal of charges made in the non-Mormon press" (1992:146). In fact, First Counselor in the First Presidency George Q. Cannon published a pamphlet with the original version of the manifesto written by Woodruff alongside Penrose's edited version that was ultimately published.

Within the year, however, Wilford Woodruff was writing and speaking about the manifesto as revelation from God, statements also canonized as part of the Doctrine and Covenants: "I have had some revelations of late, and very important ones to me, and I will tell you what the Lord said to me. Let me bring your minds to what is termed the manifesto. . . ." (D&C, Excerpts from Three Addresses by President Wilford Woodruff Regarding the Manifesto). In the minds of many, the manifesto needed the authority of revelation in order to overturn the 1843 commandment in favor of plural marriage. The political expediency both within the church and outside it caused many to doubt the new claims of revelation.[39]

Despite these doubts, Woodruff's manifesto is clearly viewed as revelation today. Further, "There is no question that, from a doctrinal standpoint, President Woodruff's Manifesto now has comparable status with the revelations found in the Doctrine and Covenants" (Shipps 1985:114).

Similar claims have been advanced about statements made by Brigham Young. Austin and Alta Fife argue that "seldom did he speak of his visions save after works had brought them to partial fulfillment" (1956:95). They go on to quote Brigham Young's speech at the laying of the cornerstone of the Salt Lake Temple, where he describes a vision he had one year previously that matches perfectly with the planned temple inaugurated that day. In other instances, mundane declarations have been reinterpreted by some Latter-day Saints as prophecy even without explicit claims by Brigham Young himself. In a talk given in Salt Lake City on June 8, 1856, later published under the title "Irrigation—Every Saint Should Labor for the Interest of the Community—It is the Lord that Gives the Increase—Etc.," Brigham Young declares:

> Shall we stop making canals, when the one now in progress is finished? No, for as soon as that is completed from Big Cottonwood to this city, we expect to make a canal on the west side of Jordan, and take its water along the east base of the west mountains, as there is more farming land on the west side of that river than on the east. When that work is accomplished we shall continue our exertions, until the Provo River runs to this city. We intend to bring it around the point of the mountain to Little Cottonwood, from that to Big Cottonwood, and lead its waters upon all the land from Provo Canyon to this city, for there is more water runs in that stream alone than would be needed for that purpose. (*Journal of Discourses*, vol. 3:329)

In this speech, Brigham Young appeals to his fellow Saints to help in the communal efforts to build irrigation systems throughout the area. Almost a century later, those words would sound like revelation. Writing in the 1950s, the Fifes observed: "To many these words were prophetic of the vast Deer Creek project which has recently been completed."[40] In hindsight, optimistic thinking can appear prophetic, particularly when voiced by a church prophet.[41]

Far better known than this story of irrigation, however, are two others, both involving Brigham Young. The first is the story of how Brigham Young came to succeed Joseph Smith as the president of the church. After Joseph Smith's death, the role of prophet and president of the church was left vacant, with no single clear plan for succession. Joseph Smith's counselor Sidney Rigdon initially claimed leadership, contested quickly by Brigham Young, leader of the Quorum of the Twelve Apostles. At a general meeting of church members on August 8, 1844, both men gave speeches, after which the Nauvoo congregation "voted overwhelmingly" to sustain Brigham Young as the new leader (Arrington and Bitton 1980:84). Descriptions of this conference were soon cast as miraculous. In their book *The Mormon Experience*, Leonard J. Arrington and Davis Bitton describe the interpretation that became widespread toward the end of the nineteenth century and carried throughout much of the twentieth:

> Many who were present at the August 8 meeting later remembered seeing in Brigham Young that day a new appearance and hearing from him a new voice—one that was very familiar, that of Joseph Smith. For them the "Mantle of Joseph" was given directly, miraculously, to Young. George Laub later recorded in his journal that that day Young's "voice was the voice of Br. Joseph and his face appeared as Joseph's face." Apostle Wilford Woodruff later remembered, "When Brigham Young arose and commenced speaking . . . if I had not seen him with my own eyes, there is no one that could have convinced me that it was not Joseph Smith." (1980:84–5)

William A. Wilson and Jesse Embry join Arrington and Bitton and many other LDS historians who hesitate to confirm this transfiguration as part of the initial experience of audience members, keeping open the possibility of later reinterpretation. Further, the story of transfiguration so widespread during much of the twentieth century has been replaced with a more general narrative that describes Brigham Young being chosen either by revelation or by Joseph Smith before he died as part of the normal practice of succession.[42]

The second is the story of Brigham Young's famous declaration upon entering the valley of the Great Salt Lake, a phrase memorialized in sacred and secular LDS culture today: "This is the right place," although it is quoted more often as simply "This is the place."[43] The phrase is the culmination of no single story but of a massive epic of pioneer strength and sacrifice. During the 150th anniversary of the arrival of the Mormon pioneers to Salt Lake, the church celebrated the pioneers formally through general conference talks and public events. In those talks, First Counselor Thomas S. Monson attributed Young's "inspired leadership" to God's "watchful care and guidance" (1997:50). After reciting the story of the trek and the famous line "'This is the right place,'"[44] President Gordon B. Hinckley added, "I stand in reverent awe of that statement," a statement he went on to describe as "prophetic" (G. Hinckley 1997:66). Whether or not it was viewed as prophetic at the time, however, is open for debate. Richard C. Poulsen echoes LDS historian Leonard Arrington in arguing that the historical evidence suggests that "the Mormons who fled their Nauvoo homes in February, 1846, fully intended to settle the Valley of the Great Salt Lake" (Poulsen 1977:249, quoting Arrington 1966:39). Further, he argues that "the 'This is the place' of Brigham Young undoubtedly meant (if he said it) that this is the place we have studied on maps and in travelers' reports and have heard of from the mouths of explorers, the place we have finally reached" (249). Again, Wilson and Embry survey the scholarship of the event, much of which questions whether this event occurred and whether or not it was initially viewed as revelation (1998:86–8). What is clear from their survey of contemporary Mormons, however, is that the dominant view today is that it did and it was.

There are other stories as well, part of a widespread folk history shared among Mormons, where the mundane is reinterpreted as divine. Written accounts in 1848, when seagulls helped rid Mormon settlers of the plague of crickets that were decimating their crops, suggest that no one viewed the act as a miracle at the time. However, within a year or two, the story began to take on divine dimensions and was soon transformed into a full-fledged miracle known widely by Mormon and non-Mormon alike and memorialized in the Seagull Monument erected in Temple Square in Salt Lake City in 1913. While men and women at the time did not see the hand of God in the presence of the gulls, subsequent Mormons have.[45]

The historical record makes it clear that Latter-day Saints find it meaningful and appropriate to review past events for evidence of the guidance and protection of God. Accordingly, the diligence with which many historians have asked questions about the chronological development of claims and interpretations may be perplexing to some Saints today, as such questions run counter to fundamental expectations of the workings of the divine generally, and revelation specifically. Richard Poulsen echoes many Latter-day Saints in arguing that the mundane, in the mouths of the General Authorities, is inherently revelation. "To understand the Mormon attitude toward the migration myth and revelation per se, one must understand that to most Mormons, the 'General Authorities' of the Church are literally infallible, and everything they say or do (especially that which relates to the Church) is directly or obliquely a result of revelation, or a softer, more mystical term—inspiration. And this belief provides most members with an answer for difficult questions or questions they are not sure of. So in a very real sense, revelation is history to the orthodox Mormon" (1977:250).

When Wilford Woodruff issued the proclamation against plural marriage, his statement was not clearly framed as revelation. However, because it was issued from the president of the church, in the minds of many Mormons today, it could be nothing but. Historical evidence of political, social, or practical pressures for change, therefore, cannot invalidate or undermine the existence of revelation.

Also, while revelation can come unsolicited and out of the blue, it more often emerges after solicitation through thoughtful prayer. The prophet, as president of the church, is expected to go to God for guidance in the challenges the church faces. Joseph Smith did this repeatedly, as recorded in the Doctrine and Covenants. The dictum against tobacco and strong drink emerged explicitly in this way, as described in the introduction to the scriptural passage that records Joseph Smith's revelation: "As a consequence of the early brethren using tobacco in their meetings, the Prophet was led to ponder upon the matter; consequently he inquired of the Lord concerning it. This revelation, known as the Word of Wisdom, was the result" (D&C 89). These solicitations can be open ended— what should we do?—or more directive—should the Saints stop using tobacco? A tradition of revelations of confirmation makes the latter line of questioning as common and acceptable as the former (see chapter 3). As Wilford Woodruff's diary makes clear, he was in constant prayer over the issue of plural marriage, asking for guidance from God. To assume revelation from the prophet of the church, who has solicited guidance from God through prayer, is both logical and rational from an LDS perspective. The same explanation can be provided to understand Brigham Young's "This is the place" story. Joseph Smith prophesied about a migration to the Rocky Mountains. For months, even years, before the mass exodus to Salt Lake, church leaders had been praying for guidance on what to do and where to go, in addition to consulting travelers' reports and maps. This combination of human agency and divine guidance is exactly the expectation for revelation. Had those early Mormon leaders *not* studied it out in their minds first, they could not have expected to receive divine confirmation. Evidence of the former lends credence to an interpretation of the latter.

In LDS culture, accepting and appreciating solicited revelation, continuous revelation, and the power of hindsight and reflection normalize retroactive revelation. In such an atmosphere, reinterpretations of secular statements and mundane events as divinely inspired are to be expected, not eschewed. Shawn Tucker sees this process happening now, pointing to "The Family: A Proclamation to the World," a declaration issued by the First Presidency and the Council of the Twelve Apostles, delivered by President Gordon B. Hinckley in his speech to the General Relief Society meetings on September 23, 1995, and reproduced regularly in church publications. The document begins: "We, the First Presidency and the Council of the Twelve Apostles of The Church of Jesus

Christ of Latter-day Saints, solemnly proclaim that marriage between a man and a woman is ordained of God and that the family is central to the Creator's plan for the eternal destiny of His children." The proclamation is not called revelation, but in the minds of most members, it is. In Sunday school during a conversation about signs of the Second Coming, one member of the Burlington First Ward volunteered that the proclamation was clearly a prophecy, preparing them for the current debates surrounding the Defense of Marriage Act.[46] Latter-day Saints have been encouraged to paste the proclamation into their scripture, a step that would suggest an eventual formal adoption of the statement as revelation, canonized in the Doctrine and Covenants.

During sacrament meeting one Sunday in the Burlington First Ward, ward member and member of the Stake High Council Hollan Pickard reminded the congregation that scriptures say we will know our prophets by the fruit of their labor.[47] Only in hindsight can prophets be discerned. The same can be true of revelation.

Conclusion

Analysis of the structural patterns and motifs that appear in personal revelation narratives provides a window into the process of how people construct stories out of their personal revelatory experiences. It also reveals the culturally constructed narrative norms of the genre and of LDS narratives more broadly.

Of particular significance is the norm for retroactive revelation that encourages people to examine and reexamine their personal experiences in order to become more aware of the presence of God in their lives. Contingent upon this norm, however, is that reflection and reinterpretation are ideally performed by the person who received the revelation. The further removed a story is from its source, the more skeptical people become (see chapter 2). They fear that the personal is transformed into the social, the real into the ideal, the mundane into the awe inspiring. "Sometimes people will just hear a little bit of a story that's not very close to them, and they tend to embellish or elaborate a little bit," worries Steve Anderson. "I think that sometimes that can draw away from the real, actual, very personal things."

Those fears have led many members to eschew legends in favor of personal experiences. "I prefer, if someone's giving a talk, it's either something you know, or you've read, instead of 'Well, I just kind of heard about somebody . . .'" continues Steve. Others concur. Adam Wicker fears unintentional embellishment. "I think it happens naturally. You forget an idea, or you embellish, you replace." So Adam sticks to personal stories or those of his close family. "Sometimes I will incorporate family because my dad's a convert. And so sometimes I'll do that. But that's like as far as I'll go. Sometimes my immediate family, but I'm never like, 'Oh, my second cousin Benny, you know, he was serving wherever and this happened.'"[48]

Legends may be viewed suspiciously, but repeated patterns and motifs, even multiple stories of similar experiences, may not be. Some students have expressed disappointment at discovering that a story they heard and believed to be true existed in multiple versions. A serviceman claiming to have served in Vietnam with his father told Reynol Bowman that he had been prompted to carry his Book of Mormon with him on his patrol in South Vietnam when he was shot by a sniper. Upon coming to, he found a hole in his shirt and discovered that he had been shot in the chest, but the bullet had been deflected by his Book of Mormon. "I believed the story and told it to several of my friends as the truth until I began hearing it in many different versions during my pre-mission year at Brigham Young University," explains Bowman.[49] Rather than viewing it as a powerful personal experience, some people come to doubt a migratory legend that gets multiplied a hundredfold as it is retold again and again by one person's second cousin, another person's Primary teacher, and yet another's roommate's sister.

Others, however, interpret repeated patterns in a radically different way. BYU student LaRae Parker set out to collect spirit world stories and found it "interesting that the stories tend to be so similar" (1971, Wilson Archives). She points out that three stories involved a dream that forewarned of a tragic event, and two others involved seeing Joseph Smith and Brigham Young. "The stories all have things alike within them," she says, explaining that "this can be accounted for by the fact that the same story has been told and retold to the point that many different versions develop.

"Another reason and the one I choose to believe, is that the Lord works in an orderly way and that the things he shows us are orderly and therefore tend to be similar."

It is an explanation deeply emic. It is also the explanation that David Hufford encourages all scholars studying supernatural experiences to value (1982, 1995). Similarities in narrative must not be discounted solely as the products of cultural expectation. Similar experiences with identical origins provide an equally reasonable interpretation.

Chapter 5

ECHOES OF CULTURE

The issue of truth is central to how personal revelation narratives are evaluated, interpreted, and performed. In the spirit of emic analysis, this book has approached personal experience narratives according to the values of the people who share them. Whether or not a story is true, therefore, has figured heavily in this analysis. Yet folklorists have typically shied away from questions about objective assessments of truth. One reason is that in this postmodern world, the idea of objective truth has been rightly questioned into oblivion. Another, more significant reason is that the question of whether or not a story is historically and factually accurate fails to account for the bulk of what the performance of a story tells us about the people who shared it and the culture in which it is embedded. In his many studies of Mormon folklore, William A. Wilson has frequently argued that folk narratives serve as "a mirror for culture, a reflector of what members of the group consider to be most important. Thus the stories we Latter-day Saints tell provide valuable insights into our hopes, fears, dreams, and anxieties" (1989:97).

That mirror is not exact. Wilson points out that mirrors only reflect what is placed in front of them, and scholarly interest in legends has meant that quotidian stories of the human capacity for love, generosity, charity, and kindness have gone unnoticed (1989:107–9). That mirror can also distort, as Ruth Benedict famously pointed out in her study of Zuni mythology. Polygamy is rife throughout Zuni folktales but nonexistent in daily life. Benedict argues these stories function as compensatory daydreams, "a Zuni fantasy of the same order as raising the dead or travelling with seven-league boots in other bodies of lore" (1935:xvi). Stories can serve as expressions of fear as much as fantasy. Further, distortion can appear in personal experience stories, not just in myths, folktales, and legends. A particular theme or experience may emerge in the narrative

242

tradition in disproportionate frequency to daily life. The hundreds of stories about narrowly avoided car accidents do not mean that Latter-day Saints are worse drivers or more prone to vehicular mishap than any other group; instead, they reveal widespread concerns about driving on US roads today and common fears about dangers that cannot be eradicated solely through one's own actions.

The themes that emerge in the narrative tradition of personal revelation, therefore, reflect lived experience as well as personal interests. Experience dictates the "data" one can draw upon to narrate, while personal choice guides which of those experiences one chooses to share. Both reflect the hand of God as well as of men and women. Revelatory experiences reflect God's concerns for people's well-being as well as people's own concerns in what they choose to pray about. The decision to share a particular experience also reflects the hand of both God and humans, as many people decide to share their spiritual experiences only if they feel prompted by the Spirit to do so. Analyzing the themes in personal revelation narratives, therefore, can reveal both the intent of God in heaven and the concerns of people on Earth. For LDS members, the former is of greater interest. For the more modest scope of this book, it is the latter that takes center stage.

The analysis of themes that follows is based almost entirely on oral narratives of personal revelation. I have, however, considered written versions where appropriate, particularly as the majority of written narratives existed or exist concurrently as part of the oral tradition (the major exception being diary entries; a discussion of the written tradition follows in chapter 6). Central to this analysis are the 441 narratives entered into an Excel spreadsheet and coded according to a list of criteria including themes, motifs, and types (see the introduction for a discussion of this process and the appendix for charts reflecting this data). Accordingly, I have been able to provide a rough but fairly accurate assessment of the most dominant themes and patterns in the shared tradition of personal revelation narratives.

While the focus of this chapter is on themes that dominate personal revelation, there are occasions when a particular set of occurrences appear so frequently, in such a similar pattern, that a recognizable tale type can be identified. Antti Aarne and Stith Thompson helped develop and popularize the concept of the tale type through the publication of the *Tale Type Index*, first by Aarne in 1910 under the title *Catalogue of Folktale Types*, then revised and expanded upon by Thompson in 1928. The reference book defines the various types of stories found throughout Europe, East Asia, and the Middle East, as well as among American Indian and French Canadian communities, according to their basic plots and motifs.[1] Their work has facilitated research such as

Alan Dundes's series of casebooks on Cinderella, Oedipus, Little Red Riding Hood, and the Walled-Up Wife that encourage cross-cultural analysis according to a particular tale type.[2] Identifying the presence of a recognizable tale type *within* a culture can also provide fruitful insight into repeated phenomena and shared values of a specific group.

One final note of explanation is in order. This survey of themes adheres to the more restrictive definition of personal revelation laid out in chapter 1 that distinguishes between temporal and spiritual revelation. Accordingly, the themes that emerge derive from revelations provided for the temporal lives of Latter-day Saints. The rich body of spiritual revelations that lead to testimonies about specific doctrine are not explicitly addressed except as they emerge within these temporal revelations.

Danger

More than any other theme, danger dominates personal revelation narratives. Just over half of the narratives involve some sort of threat, danger, or death.[3] Most often, God protects his people. The Holy Ghost prompts people to take a different route home, avoid a particular person, or race back home to protect a loved one. Because personal revelation focuses on a person's personal life, and because people typically only receive revelation for issues and people within their stewardship (the exception being to help others), virtually all personal revelation given in the face of danger protects either the individual or his or her family.

Danger Away From Home

While people certainly face danger at home, it is the liminal space away from home that poses the greatest dangers in stories of personal revelation.[4] During pioneer days, that liminal space was marked by open country, with the greatest threats coming from natural disasters, resource shortages, loss of direction, and hostile Indians. Susan Embry's mother shared a number of stories about her great-grandfather, describing events that would have taken place sometime around the 1860s. In one of them, the family is faced with the darkly ironic problem of both too much water and not enough:

> My mother told another story about this same great-grandfather who was sent down to colonize Arizona.
> On the trip, they came upon a beautiful wide camping spot by a river one evening, and he wanted to stop but a voice inside of him urged him to go on over the ridge. And so he did so. And that night, they camped up high on a flat rock.

Then during the night, the river flooded and washed away the lovely meadow where they had first thought to camp.

Now that they were up high, though, they had no water and no place to get any as the river was all flooded. But one of the sons in the family had a vision of a lovely spot with a cold spring, and he got up and walked right to it about three miles away. (1962, Wilson Archives)

American Indians were also a worry for early settlers in the West. Travel through the western frontier could be dangerous. So could herding cows away from home. One woman shared a story about her grandfather that also took place around the 1860s:

When Grandfather was ten years old, it was his responsibility to saddle a horse and go out towards the hillside to bring in the cows for the evening milking. This was in the Coalville area, near their family farm.

He had a red bandanna around his neck, and it was a hot summer day. He took the bandana off to wipe the perspiration from his brow, and he heard a voice say, "Get off from the trail."

He did not know what to think, and he hesitated, trying to decide what to do. He used the bandana to wipe his face the second time, and again he heard a voice say, "Get off from the trail."

So he urged the horse to carry him into the trees.

Just then along came a band of Indians on horses. As he was hidden from them in the trees, he watched them steal one of his milk cows.

He drove the remaining cows home and went to his mother and told her what had happened. His mother told him that one milk cow was a small price to pay for his life. (Carlisle 1984, Wilson Archives)

Travel through the open country today would seem to be less perilous. While rock slides and flash floods continue to pose threats, paved highways cut this risk dramatically. Hostile Indians have vanished from the landscape, and resources are consistently available along the road in the form of rest stops and chain restaurants. People still get lost, but the result is hardly as catastrophic as it would have been in the past.

Yet despite the mitigation of these dangers, the narrative tradition has not slackened in stories of people requiring protection to make it to their destinations unharmed. One major reason is the addition of cars. The hardships of traveling by foot, horse, and wagon were dramatic, as the countless stories of LDS pioneers attest. But the automobile—with its potential for excessive speeds—suggests the potential for disastrous crashes. And the trust one must place in the hands of other drivers reveals the lack of control and vulnerability of even the most conscientious driver. People receive prompts to take a different route home, pull over, or shift lanes—all actions that protect them from the dangerous driving of someone else on the road:

> It was late in the evening and Daddy was tired of driving so Mom took over. She was preparing to turn into another lane of traffic and looked behind her to see if there were any cars approaching. Seeing only a pinprick of light in the distance to indicate a vehicle, she began to turn.
>
> Suddenly a man's voice loudly warned her to look out behind her. "Look out, Elizabeth!" were the words "he" used.
>
> Mom stopped the car and the mere pinprick of light just barely missed hitting their car broadside. She thanked Daddy for warning her, and he looked at her with a rather puzzled expression.
>
> "I didn't say anything," he told her.
>
> So Mom repeated what the voice had said. Daddy replied, "But you should know after twenty-four years of marriage, I never call you 'Elizabeth.'"
>
> (This is true; for as long as I can remember, Daddy has called my Mom by the nickname "Lizzie.")
>
> This incident is just as puzzling to them now as it was when it took place almost five years ago.[5]

T. Kathleen Sant's grandfather was similarly warned of dangers on the road:

> My grandfather was traveling along a mountain road. There was a sharp drop-off to his right and the mountain to his left. He was going along when he heard a small voice say, "Pull over to the side of the road."
>
> He thought he was hearing things, and so he paid no attention to the voice. In about thirty seconds he heard the voice again, only louder saying, "Pull over to the side of the road."
>
> Again, he paid no attention to the voice.
>
> Almost immediately the voice shouted at him, "Pull over to the side of the road."
>
> He heeded the voice this time, and just in time. For coming around the bend was a huge truck out of control. Had he not pulled over to the side of the road when the voice shouted at him, he would not have known that the truck was out of control, and he would surely have been killed.[6]

As one would expect, the dangers of the road expressed in personal revelation narratives have kept pace with lived experience. Stripped of face-to-face contact, drivers demonize the slight infractions of fellow drivers, transforming the inappropriate lane change into a personal affront and unforgivable sin. The result is road rage. Such perceived infractions put George Johnson in mortal danger:

> George: So here's another account where I've got, this is actually more of a voice, you know, the Holy Ghost telling me to do something.

So we were down in Florida and I was working at Fed Ex, so I was getting up at two o'clock in the morning and driving to Fed Ex so I could start work at four.

And I got to this intersection, which was a major road, and I pulled this way onto this, this is the median here, it's grass and stuff, and this is a two-lane highway going into town [*George draws a four-lane highway with two lanes on either side of a grassy median*].

And so I pull in here, and I pull onto this side, on the left side of the road. And there's another white car right here.

Well, as I pull into this, we're going . . . the speed limit was forty so I'm going forty-five and he's going the same speed as me. And so we're just even, there's no room between our cars. You know, I'm in front of him, he's just right behind me.

Well, this silver car whips around the corner into this lane behind this white car that was here and he just starts freaking out, honking his horn, flashing his lights, and trying to get this guy to move. Well, the guy was slow, and so he switches into the lane I am. And starts flashing his lights, honking his horn at me.

And so, I don't know what's going on. And this guy is just right, right behind me. So I slow down so I'm behind him so I can get into the other lane.

Well, he's impatient and he jumps back behind this guy and starts flashing his lights, honking his horn. And just sits there behind him. There's enough room that he could get in the other lane and go, but he doesn't, he just sits there, flashes his lights, honks his horn. So I speed back up and I get to where I'm even and right as I get to where I'm even, he jumps back behind me and starts flashing his lights and honking his horn.

So I'm getting annoyed at this point, so I stomp on my brake, which causes him to stomp on his brakes, and then I speed back up. He gets behind me again, does it again, and I stomp on my brakes again trying to get him off of me.

Meanwhile, this guy is still just, he's just, for some reason, kind of keeping up with me, you know, never enough, not a ton of room to get . . . that this guy would go around us, I don't know.

Anyway, so, I'm in this lane, and after the second time, I'm like, "You know there's just something wrong here," so I just punch it and I speed up to about eighty miles an hour. Well this guy finally comes around this white guy [*George is referring to the color of the car, not the man*] and starts to come up beside me.

And the Spirit says, "He's going to shoot you; slam on your brakes."

And so I waited until he was right here, even with my passenger door and I slammed on the brakes, which caused him to slingshot in front of me.

Well, he shot the gun right at the front of the car. [*long pause*]

Of course I was stupid . . .

Sandy: My husband is crazy, now listen to what he does after this.

George: I get on my cell phone, call 9-1-1, like, "Somebody shot at me." And I'm chasing this guy down the freeway [*laughter*].

Sandy: What normal person chases the guy with a gun down the freeway?

George: That shot at me.

Brittany: And he's chasing him! [*laughter*]

Tom: That's crazy.

George: That's what I thought too.

Tom: Where were you? This was Florida?

George: This was Florida.

Tom: And this is not a big highway.

George: No.

Tom: It's a four-lane, I guess.

George: Yeah.

Sandy: What were you on? 82?

George: It was Colonial.

Sandy: Colonial. Oh, OK. Colonial has three lanes on each side. It's a six-lane road.

George: [*pause*] But no, it's got two . . .

Sandy: No, no. [*pause*] Well, OK, actually wait, what part? Because it does narrow down.

George: It was the two-lane part. I was . . .

Sandy: OK, so yeah, it does narrow down into two.

George: Yeah, it does widen into six lanes, but the part I was on was the two lanes.

Sandy: Fed Ex is on the three-lane part but he was on the two-lane part. Yeah, you're right.

George: And then you've got the major freeway, right here. You know this is an intersection, then you've got I-75 [*George begins drawing again*], which is where I chased him, you know, because, this is quite a ways, it's like two miles between this intersection and I-75. And you know, we were right about in front of I-75 when I slammed on the brakes. He jumped onto I-75 and I chased after him.

Tom: And what happened?

George: I called the cops . . .

Tom: They catch him?

George: . . . read the tags to them. They were freaking out. They were like, "You can't chase him! You can't chase him! Get off the highway!" [*laughter*] "What are you doing you crazy person? You're going to get shot."

 And so they told me to come in and file a police report. I went in and filed the police report.

 And I had called the tag in to them. They found the guy. He denied the whole thing. He was like, "I don't know what that guy's talking about. I've been home all the time."

 You know they asked him to search his car, of course, it was long enough that he had hidden the weapon, thrown it into the river, whatever it happened to be.

Sandy: I thought that they found out that the car was stolen from somewhere.

George: I think that was just the guy making up a story . . .

Sandy: Probably telling them his car had been stolen.

George: . . . so that—he was in the wrong—you know, that he could say, "Well, it was stolen, I wasn't in the car." Because he had shot at me. You know? That's attempted murder. So, yeah.

This lack of control—where the poor or aggressive driving of another motorist can result in one's own death—is particularly fertile ground for supplication to the divine. In fact, the supernatural is frequently invoked whenever people feel they lack control—farmers' weather signs to ensure good weather and a good harvest, omens that predict untimely deaths, locker-room rituals to ensure success in a sporting event. Such beliefs are often labeled superstitions, as they exist unconnected to a substantial and coherent system of belief. Within a religious context, however, such beliefs are grounded in theology, rooted in faith. For Catholics, for example, a Saint Christopher medal may be placed on the dashboard to ensure a safe journey. As the patron saint of travelers, Saint Christopher is invoked as part of a cultural and religious tradition of supplication to individual saints as well as to God, Jesus, and the Virgin Mary. This physical act of prayer to Saint Christopher is religious rather than superstitious. The same is true for Mormons, where personal revelation is not merely grounded in theology; it is a fundamental part of it.

Personal revelation narratives clearly express concern and anxiety about the dangers of driving. However, these stories can also provide some degree of comfort, even suggesting a measure of control in the face of such danger. While locker-room rituals are enacted and Saint Christopher medals are invoked *before* the possible challenging event, personal revelation emerges at the moment of crisis. Further, the majority of revelations that protect drivers appear out of the blue, unsolicited. In other words, no specific, ritualistic, premeditated act by the driver helps ensure a positive outcome. These features would seem to strip away any potential for control. However, personal revelation is assumed to come more regularly to those who live righteously. Ultimate control is held by God, but daily choices to live righteously can establish continual revelation from the Holy Ghost. Personal revelation is a gift and cannot be relied upon as readily as a particular ritual that people instigate themselves. Nonetheless, narratives of personal revelation do not merely give voice to the anxiety of driving; they provide example after example of hope in the face of danger, of safety under God's watchful care.

Tale Type: A Warning to Move

Peril emerges as a dominant theme in personal revelation. Often, that peril is avoided with a prompting to move to avoid danger. In addition to all the stories of people prompted to move while driving, there are stories of avoiding disaster at work, at home, in war, and in the course of one's daily routine. A man working in a mine hears a voice say "Move!" Seeing no one, he continues to work only to be prompted again: "Move!" more insistent this time. He does and narrowly avoids a rock fall (Rollins 1977:73–6, Fife Archives). A woman is walking down a snowy street and feels she should move to the other side of the road. She does and narrowly misses a large icicle that would have smashed into her head (Newell 2002, Wilson Archives). A woman is sitting in the doctor's office and is prompted to move. She hesitates but, after the second prompting, gets up just as a heavy piece of metal from the ceiling falls and destroys the chair she was sitting in (Allen 1996, Wilson Archives). A soldier is awoken by the prompting of the Spirit to move off his cot and under the bunker just in time to avoid a rocket explosion (Freeman and Wright 2003:356–8).

From all of these stories, a general pattern emerges, suggesting a coherent tale type pervasive in the LDS narrative tradition of personal revelation:

1. *Unfamiliar / Dangerous Setting*: A person finds himself or herself in unfamiliar or potentially dangerous surroundings.
2. *Prompting to Move*: Without any indication of a specific threat, the person is prompted to move.
3. *Hesitation*: Often, but not always, the person hesitates.
4. *Action to Move*: At the insistence of the Holy Ghost, the person moves.
5. *Threat Realized*: Almost immediately after moving, the threat becomes apparent and the person realizes he or she has narrowly escaped injury or death.

A total of 44 stories roughly adhere to this tale type (33 percent of all narratives involving danger away from home, 26 percent of all narratives involving danger generally, and 10 percent of all the narratives in the collection). Within this substantial corpus of narratives there is also a recognizable subtype. The Wilford Woodruff story of moving his wagon has been reprinted and retold regularly since it first appeared in 1881 (including in this book in chapter 4). In brief, Woodruff is prompted to go out into a terrible storm to move the wagon where he and his family are sleeping away from a particular oak tree. He does so and is soon prompted to move his animals as well. He again follows the prompting. Thirty minutes later, lightning strikes the tree, causing it to crash down in the exact spot where his wagon and animals had stood.

There are a number of family stories that closely mirror Woodruff's experience. Kathy Page recounts a story she heard multiple times from her grandmother, who traveled to Utah with one of the handcart companies, which would date her experience to 1856. She was very young at the time, but one of the fathers in the group with which she was traveling received a prompting again and again as he tried to sleep that he needed to move the company away from the tree under which they were camped. Unable to sleep, he finally relented and woke up the other men in the group. They all moved their wagons. In the morning, they woke to find that lightning had struck the tree and it had crashed down exactly where their wagons had been (Page 1982, Wilson Archives).

Around the turn of the century, the Holy Ghost once again protected a pioneer from a tree felled by lightning. Michael Root recalls a story told regularly in his family about his relative Arthur Horning. He was riding toward home and got caught in the middle of the country by a violent storm. He sheltered under a pine tree but before long, he heard a voice: "Art, get away from this tree!" He looked around but saw no one. Again, the voice spoke, repeating its warning. He hesitated once again but decided to move. "Moments later, the sky lighted up and he heard a sharp crack behind him. He turned to see the tree crashing down, having been struck by lightning" (Root 1971, Wilson Archives).

One woman's uncle received a similar warning. En route to a sheep camp to deliver supplies, her uncle had bedded down for the night when "he received the impression, 'Go move your camp.'

"The feeling was so strong that he immediately went out and hitched up the horses and moved the camp. He had no more than got everything bedded down again and himself retired when lightning struck. It struck a huge tree which fell on the exact spot where the camp had been before" (Louder 1969, Wilson Archives).

Another woman told her daughter of a prompting her brother received one night during a bad storm to move his grandpa's old Model T Ford. He did. "The next morning, we discovered that a big tree had been blown over and lay right in the spot where the car had been" (Strong 1930, Wilson Archives). A man from Heber, Utah, tells the story of a similar near-disaster averted thanks to revelation received by his great-grandfather:

> Once when my grandfather was just a young boy, he went camping with his father and other brother and some friends. They arrived in the afternoon to their camping site and made camp.
>
> By the time night had come they were ready to bed down. Before going to bed, they all knelt together and said their prayers to the Lord as they usually did.
>
> In the middle of the night my grandfather's father woke everyone up and told them he thought they had better move the tent about ten yards from its present position. They did this and about an hour later a rainstorm set in. Thunder cracked and lightning lit the sky.
>
> The next morning they all got up in the fresh rain air and looked out of the tent. They found that during the night a large tree had been stricken by lightning and had fallen in the very place the tent had once been. If they had not moved before the storm started they probably would have been killed. (Sue 1.7.2.3.2, Fife Archives)

Around 1920, Myrtle Tenney was prompted to warn her husband to come in out of a storm. He survived, but the horses did not fare as well. Nathan Boyd Tenney, their son, remembers the incident:

> Another interesting and faith-promoting story is: I remember the best as a small boy, when we were living at High Creek [Arizona]. We had a cornfield out in front and a big oak tree by the house. I remember the creek on the side of the house and the corrals on the side of the house.
>
> One day, and I remember this very well, in the summertime it had started to sprinkle just a little. My Dad brought his horses into the corral. He had a beautiful blue mare with a bay colt. He had decided to shoe his horses, so that he could go to work with them.
>
> Just as he started to shoe this mare, my Mother got the inspiration that he should come in out of the rain. She stepped to the door and suggested that he come in. He said, "No, it is only sprinkling. I'll go ahead and get the horses shod."
>
> She went back to work, but got the inspiration again. She went to the door and called the same message to him. He still refused. The third time, she got the deep inspiration that he should come in immediately, so in a commanding voice, she said to him, "You must come in now."

He responded to her call, although he wasn't very happy about having to take that time out. So, he laid his shoeing tools down and walked away from the horse that was standing tied to this oak tree. He had hardly gotten to the door of the house when the lightning struck the oak tree and killed both the mare and the colt that was standing next to her.

My Mother responded to the whisperings of the spirit and saved the life of my Father. Had he been just a few seconds later, Dad would have been killed and we would only have had five or six kids, instead of ten brothers and sisters.

To me this is an indication of the inspiration Mother has always had and how she has followed her intuitions and her great faith in life, to do the right thing, at the right time. (Hendrix and Hendrix 1994:276–7)

Each of these experiences took place in the Intermountain West or Midwest in the decades before and after the turn of the twentieth century. Dangerous storms were clearly a concern for these men and women. Such stories provide not only evidence of a caring God but comfort in the face of storms literal and metaphorical. While these various family stories no doubt reflect true experiences, the pervasiveness of the Woodruff story in Mormon culture exercises great power in the narrative tradition. Its frequent appearance in publications and church talks virtually ensures that many members would have heard the story at some point during their lives. As family stories are passed along, experiential memory may be replaced with narrative memory, and narrative memory may draw upon other narratives as events are reconstructed. Stories can blend and blur. Elements of one story seep into another. This blending and borrowing helps explain a story shared among the descendents of Benjamin F. Johnson.

Benjamin F. Johnson was the private secretary of Joseph Smith and a member of the Council of Fifty.[7] In his autobiography, he recounts having been blessed by Joseph Smith, who told him "an Angel should go with me and protect me." Johnson continued to think about that blessing, regularly crediting his "angel" for guiding and protecting him. As he set out for Zion in the West, Johnson had two experiences that convinced him of the presence and power of God. He narrates them one after the other. The first is a story of being protected during a terrible storm:

We left Kirtland the first of June 1842 and with the beautiful weather and good roads, we had hopes of a safe and pleasant journey. But our animals were young and spirited and we had need both to watch and pray, for we were often in great danger.

An incident or two I will relate to show that the Angel promised was always near. Soon after our start, our horses still fresh and mettlesome,

descended a long, steep and dangerous dugway,[8] with my wife and sister
in the wagon. Just at the bottom as I drew rein upon the level, the ring
from the neck-yoke with the wagon tongue dropped to the ground. The
thought of the certainty of deaths had it dropped a minute before, almost
dazed me—but the Angel was there.

Another day, on appearance of a storm we put up at a tavern. I drove
the covered wagon in which my wife and self slept, under a large swinging
signboard hung between heavy posts, my father and sisters finding rooms
in the tavern while we occupied the wagon. In the terrible night storm
lightning shattered posts and signboard, piling the debris upon the front
of the wagon. Although for a time we felt ourselves killed, we were out all
right in the morning, with the footprints of the same Angel clearly
in view.[9]

He follows this story with another faith-promoting experience in which
he learned the hard way the importance of keeping the Sabbath holy. Both
events took place in 1842. Over one hundred years later, his great-great-great
granddaughter Gail LeBaron was continuing to share these family stories. As in
Johnson's autobiography, Gail LeBaron tells the two stories together, one after
the other. The story of keeping the Sabbath holy follows Johnson's account
closely. The story of the storm, however, has shifted in significant ways:

One evening, toward sundown, Benjamin set up camp beneath the
branches of a huge tree, which stood alone on the prairie, for a storm
was brewing, and he sought shelter from the rain. During the night, he
awoke with a start, thinking that he had heard a voice telling him to move
his camp from under the tree. Putting it aside as his imagination, he fell
back to sleep but was abruptly awakened once more. This time he heard
a voice—distinct and penetrating—which told him to arise and move his
wagon away from the tree. Hastily he arose. Stepping out into the drench-
ing rain, he groped his way to his horses and hitched them to the wagon.
Seconds after he had led his team and wagon to safety the tree was struck
by lightning and crashed to the ground. The monstrous trunk came to
rest directly on the spot where Benjamin had been sleeping.

The story Gail LeBaron recounts is clearly drawn from the oral tradition
in her family and not the written journal of her ancestor Benjamin Johnson. In
fact, she outlines the pedigree of the narrative in her contextual notes: "These
stories were told by him [Benjamin F. Johnson] to his granddaughter, who in
turn passed them to her grandson, who is my father, Arthur B. LeBaron" (1965,
Wilson Archives). In the course of narrations across six generations, the story
has been transformed from an act of divine providence, where Johnson is a passive player protected by God, to an act of personal revelation, where Johnson is

an active player, prompted to act to receive God's protection. The transformation brings the narrative closely in line with Woodruff's story. The signpost of a tavern becomes a tree. Debris that covered their wagon is gone, Johnson and his family left unharmed. Most significantly, Johnson is prompted by a distinct and penetrating voice to move. Guided into action, Johnson gets up in the rain and moves his wagon. All of these changes parallel Woodruff's story.

The one significant variance is that Johnson must be prompted twice, while Woodruff acts immediately. This is the same addition that Sandy Johnson makes when she retells Woodruff's story soon after reading it in a church magazine. Both Johnson and LeBaron seem to be drawing this motif from the larger tradition of revelation rather than Woodruff's story specifically. However, it is not coincidence that the "waiting to move" tale type includes hesitation before acting. While it is impossible to conclusively trace the changes in Johnson's story to Woodruff's narrative, it is clear that in the Mormon narrative tradition there is a recognizable tale type for which Woodruff's story serves as the prototype.[10]

Children in Peril

The liminal space—both literal and psychological—found in the undifferentiated wilderness, at the far edges of one's property, or on roads that connect but are not of themselves identifiable places is a particular source of danger. In the face of human vulnerability, the Holy Ghost steps in to help. The same is true of the liminality and vulnerability of childhood.

The cultural and theological importance placed on the family is clearly evident in personal revelation narratives. The protection offered by God through the Holy Ghost in personal revelation covers those areas of one's personal stewardship: oneself and one's family. Yet young children are singled out in the narrative tradition as needing particular protection. Thirty-five percent of all the narratives that include danger involve a child in peril.

While small children can experience the promptings of the Holy Ghost, it is rare. Most are simply too young to distinguish the Spirit from their own ideas and desires. Parents and teachers in church regularly talk about the importance of teaching children this skill, spending lesson after lesson in Primary and family home evening on the topic. There is no magical age for mastery; after all, adults spend their lives perfecting this ability. But before baptism (typically at age eight), parents are particularly blessed with promptings from the Holy Ghost to protect their children.

One young mother had a dream where her son burst into the room on fire and burned to death at her feet. Several years later, her son is tending to the wood stove when his shirt catches on fire and he runs to his mother. She immediately remembers the dream and smothers the flames with a blanket, saving her son's life (Embry 1962, Wilson Archives). Another woman is downstairs and is "literally commanded" to go to her daughter's room. She finds her daughter choking and tries the Heimlich maneuver, but it doesn't work. She knows from first aid that you shouldn't put your fingers in someone's throat, but she was "commanded" to do just that. She finally does and out pops a marble, saving her daughter's life (Gibb 1999, Wilson Archives). Erika Layland's mother was prompted to save her son from certain death:

> It was about four p.m. on a hot and busy summer day when Jim was not yet five years old. He was an active and curious child. Once I had found him on top of the refrigerator, unable to get down. Another time I found my wedding band in his pocket, when it had been in my jewelry box on the top shelf of the closet!
>
> I was washing dishes by hand when suddenly I was propelled by a voice that said, "Go now!" With water dripping off my hands, I ran through the open front door out into the front yard. Instantly I perceived the impending collision. A car was coming at a good speed down the hill on the street in front of our house. Hidden from view of the street by a tall row of closely spaced oleander bushes was the steep driveway directly across the street from our house. At the top of that steep driveway and starting downward was Jim on his Hot Wheels!
>
> I ran immediately out into the street, yelling and waving my arms wildly. The car screeched to a stop with the blare of its horn, just as Jim went rolling behind me, intersecting the street and coming to a stop in our driveway near our front door.
>
> I take no credit for quick thinking or extra-sensory perception. What I do know is that I heard a voice, and no one was around. I somehow *knew where to go*. It still takes my breath away when I think about it. How humbling it is to know the power of the Spirit to work through me to save my beloved child's life. There is no doubt whatsoever in my mind that the timing was perfect for impact, and impact was aborted by the intervention of the Spirit in a mother's soul—my soul, my child. I am forever grateful for this humbling experience. (2001, Wilson Archives)

Just under half of the stories about children in danger occurred in or around the home, evidence that the domestic realm is not exempt from danger.[11] In these stories, women are four times as likely to be present and receive revelation as men, reflecting fairly traditional gender roles. Men are expected to be at work outside the home while women remain in the home to care for children. Fears and anxieties inherent in caring for children while balancing the daunting list of household chores can be overwhelming. Personal revelation narratives both reflect this anxiety and provide reassurance that the Holy Ghost can provide help.

The promptings that men receive for their families, on the other hand, typically occur while they are at work outside the home. Sometime around 1878, one of the men working on the Salt Lake Temple received a prompting that something back home was wrong. Almost one hundred years later, his granddaughter shares his story:

> Grandfather was called on a mission to go work in the quarry when they were building the Salt Lake Temple. His job was cutting out stones from the granite there to make blocks for the Salt Lake Temple.
>
> While he was away, his family contracted diphtheria and was very ill. One of the boys especially.
>
> Grandfather had gone to bed one night—his bed consisted of a pallet laid on the brush. He was so restless he could not sleep. And he thought there was something wrong at home so he got up and went out on the brush and prayed to the Heavenly Father that if anything was wrong at home that he would bless them and make everything all right there.
>
> When he got home—they didn't get home only about every six months—for a visit, he found that his son had been very ill with diphtheria and when they compared time for when he had taken a change for the better, it was the same time grandfather had offered up a prayer in his behalf. (Snow 1971, Wilson Archives)

A more recent story was written down by Sharlene Noland.

> A case of a man being inspired to do something is given about a religion teacher here on the BYU campus.
>
> He lived near a canal, which he had told his two small boys never to go near.
>
> One day, while away from his home, something told him to go home, that something was wrong. He hurried home and asked his wife where his two sons were. She said that they were outside playing someplace. He rushed to the canal just in time to see one of them fall in, and he was able to save him. (1961, Wilson Archives)

When children face danger away from home, more men than women who receive revelation to help them, particularly if that revelation is successful in preventing harm. Of the thirty-three stories of this type, seventeen describe men receiving revelation. In all but one of these cases, they are successful in averting disaster. Of the thirteen stories where women receive revelation about children in peril away from home, however, they are successful in averting disaster in only seven of those cases. In the other six cases, they receive revelation alerting them after the fact, much like what many non-LDS members might call a mother's intuition.[12]

Men have also tended to receive revelations to find children when they go missing. Women protect but men rescue. When a child goes missing, "Uncle Ned" is able to find the lost boy in the mountains. He tells the townspeople where to find him and that they should hurry, since a large animal was following him. They follow Uncle Ned's instructions and find the boy, who says he wasn't afraid because a large cat had been with him the whole time (McDaniel 1972, Wilson Archives). According to the collector's grandmother, who told this story, Uncle Ned had been granted both the power of healing and continuous revelation during a near-death experience where he went to "the other side" and was given the choice of staying in the spirit world or going back to Earth to heal and protect. Brother Anderson's reputation for revelation is less clearly outlined than Uncle Ned's, but similar in effect. When a little girl goes missing, her parents enlist Brother Anderson, who prays and receives guidance that directs them straight to the girl. She, too, had been tracked by a mountain lion, though again, she is comforted rather than scared by the animal (Fischio 1970, Wilson Archives).[13] Adults get lost, too, as do keys and rings and money. Stories of lost children, however, not only appear more often, they are more likely to be retold by others, spawning legends as well as personal experience narratives.

More recently, however, as social norms in the United States have shifted and gender roles have become somewhat less rigid, men appear to be receiving more revelations about the care and rearing of their children than in the past. George Johnson is regularly prompted to protect his daughters from harm, whether from an accidental ingestion of a household cleaner, or a child predator roaming the neighborhood. The explanation is simple: George has often been the primary caregiver for his children while his wife works outside the home.

Similarly, women have become more active in rescuing, as well as protecting. The two stories of lost children cited above occurred in the 1920s and 1930s. In the 1970s, however, a young woman went outside to call her daughter in from playing and couldn't find her. She called neighbors and the police to help her search, but it was only after praying for help that she received a "sudden impression" to check a particular part of the woods where they had already looked. Sure enough, she found her daughter (Steed 1984, Wilson Archives). In this story, one she shares regularly in Mutual meetings for young men and women in the church, the woman is both protector and rescuer.

The shift is slow, however. In personal revelation narratives, the role of men in decisions about child rearing continues to be restricted mostly to revelation of confirmation. Most often, women receive initial revelations about the children that men—as priesthood holders—confirm through their own solicited revelations.

Death and the Spirit World

Danger is typically averted in personal revelation narratives. But as the age-old adage avers, bad things can happen to good people. God does not always intervene; good people, LDS or not, get hurt in car accidents, home fires, and muggings. The narrative tradition of personal revelation provides little evidence of such tragic events, however, unless they occur after a person has ignored a prompting. In these cases, the message is clear: if only they had listened, they would have been protected.

Death, however, is different. The narrative tradition is full of stories of people prompted by the Holy Ghost with knowledge about the death of a relative, even of themselves, *without* the promise of protection or avoidance.

Death is inevitable; nonmortal wounds and accidents are not. People do not tell stories of receiving revelation to comfort them in the face of a car accident, a dog bite, or a violent neighbor. Revelation in these cases is typically tractable, intended to *avert* the danger, not make peace with it.[14] The majority of the stories dealing with death, on the other hand, are focused on either preparing someone for the death of a relative or comforting them afterwards:[15]

> One morning in July of 1956 about ten forty-five a.m. I was going from my home in Orem to Provo to buy some goods. I had traveled only about one mile distance from home when I was startled by the promptings of a still small voice in my mind. The voice said, "Your son and his wife are dead."
>
> The voice was pleasant, reassuring, and illustrated no tragedy. I immediately returned home and told my wife of the incident. I then tried to phone my son's home in Lincoln, Nebraska. I received no answer.
>
> About four o'clock that afternoon my wife and I received word that our son and his wife had been killed in an automobile accident about ten thirty a.m. (our time). (Healy n.d., Wilson Archives)

Some stories that foretell death prepare people for practical reasons, such as the woman in charge of funeral arrangements who is warned before each death in the community (Holt 1963, Wilson Archives). In other stories, people mention how important it was to be prepared. Frank Nielson has received revelation before each of the major deaths in his family. While it is hard to bear the burden of such knowledge, he remains grateful for the preparation.

Preparation seems to be the reason a couple grieving at the funeral of their son both receive the same revelation that they are going to lose another child soon (Call 1996, Wilson Archives). Often, however, a clear explanation for the revelation is lacking. A woman receives revelation that her nephew has died before official word is sent (Hall 1969, Wilson Archives). A man dreams of a funeral with his uncle's relatives in attendance. He writes to find out what happened and receives a letter confirming the death of the uncle and describing the funeral exactly as he had dreamed it (Beckstead 1961, Wilson Archives). These revelations seem to exemplify the powerful connection among family members, even distant ones, as much as the power of the Holy Ghost, an interpretation strengthened by the fact that the bulk of these narratives describe revelations delivered by dead relatives in the spirit world rather than by the Holy Ghost.[16]

There are also a small but significant number of narratives of experiences where people receive revelations while on the brink of death. These revelations occur in an altered state of consciousness, either in dreams or visions. Often, the person receives revelation to guide them in their remaining years on Earth, marching orders for an incomplete mission (see Ice n.d. and Holt 1963, both in the Wilson Archives). Many of these experiences involve the spirit world, and glimpses of those who have died before them. While women are more likely to have and narrate revelations of the premortal existence, specifically of unborn children asking to be born, men are the ones who have and narrate experiences of the spirit world, the other side of the veil separating the earthly world from the spiritual world. In fact, all fifteen narratives about visiting the spirit world were experienced by men. In 1988, Gregory K. Tuft collected a particularly telling story from his father about a woman his father met while serving a mission. The woman is having a difficult time committing to the Word of Wisdom until her son dreams about his dead grandfathers in the spirit world, one of whom is waiting for his temple work to be done. The dream convinces the woman of the truth of the church, and she joins (Tuft 1988, Wilson Archives). Even though the logical person to receive revelation is the mother, it is the son, a male, who receives the vision of his relatives in the spirit world. Women may encounter guardian angels and deceased relatives who have come to Earth from the spirit world, but visions of visiting the spirit world itself occur to men.

As with many near-death experiences and "visits to the other side," bright white light is a recurring motif in these narratives. More generally, white as a symbol of the sacred and holy appears throughout personal revelation narratives, most frequently in spirit world revelations and dreams leading to conversion. White robes signify holy men, often angels. White shirts signify missionaries, who come bearing God's true message. White light signifies the divine and often the celestial kingdom. As a symbol, the color white is particularly powerful in the context of ambiguous dreams where the significance of other images—books, strange men, foreign lands—can be alien, confusing, and disconcerting. White immediately signals the sacred. In the story collected by George K. Tuft, the son's dream is particularly ambiguous and is interpreted metaphorically. One of the boy's dead grandfathers is dressed in white, the other stands with black hands. The missionary who interprets the dream for the boy explains that the man in white is waiting for his temple work to be done, while the man with black hands has already rejected the church. Not only is white the color of the sacred and holy but black represents the opposite, symbolizing opposition to the church.

Domestic Life

Mormon theology clearly places the Godhead—God, Jesus, and the Holy Ghost—at the center of the universe, guiding both spiritual and temporal matters in the lives of the Saints. Second is the family. The family is the central structural unit of Mormon life, both on Earth and for all eternity. In his study of marriage confirmation narratives among Mormons, George H. Schoemaker argues that "the institution of marriage in the Mormon culture is the single most important initiation into full fellowship in the culture" (1989:38). The spiritual dimensions of marriage are equally central to Mormon life and theology. According to Russell M. Nelson of the Quorum of the Twelve Apostles, the possibility of a celestial marriage that binds a couple and their children together for all eternity is one of the greatest gifts God has bestowed upon mankind, and one of the most central to eternal happiness. Citing various passages in the Doctrine and Covenants (76:53, 132:7, and 131:1–3), Nelson explains: "While salvation is an individual matter, exaltation is a family matter. Only those who are married in the temple and whose marriage is sealed by the Holy Spirit of Promise will continue as families after death and receive the highest degree of celestial glory, or exaltation. A temple marriage is also called a celestial marriage. Within the celestial glory are three levels. To obtain the highest, a husband and wife must be sealed for time and all eternity and keep their covenants made in a holy temple" (2008:92).

This message is repeated by church leaders, bishops, and church members during sacrament meetings and in Sunday school classes. It is also repeated in the Proclamation on Marriage. Nelson goes on to address unmarried adult members of the church with a vague glimmer of hope based on the premise that God is just: "But what of the many mature members of the Church who are not married? Through no failing of their own, they deal with the trials of life alone. Be we all reminded that, in the Lord's own way and time, no blessings will be withheld from His faithful Saints. The Lord will judge and reward each individual according to heartfelt desire as well as deed" (94).

This hope is a relatively new development in the church, however, and its vague articulation hardly removes the central focus of LDS theology and culture on the need for marriage for life on Earth as well as in the kingdoms of heaven, where families can be reunited.

The promise of both temporal and spiritual happiness can engender great joy for those married with children. However, it can also engender great stress and anxiety for those who are not. Again, personal revelation narratives reflect the deep-seated fears and concerns engendered by LDS theology and culture while simultaneously providing hope in the face of those fears through the narration of success stories.

Finding a Spouse

Men and women receive revelation about marriage in approximately equal measure, though the scales tip in favor of women. Gender is not irrelevant, however. Women tend to be proactive about marriage, receiving revelation in response to sincere and humble prayer. Men, on the other hand, are more likely to receive revelation about their future spouse out of the blue, prompting them to action. This general pattern, along with the medium through which revelation is received, varies according to the type and nature of the revelation.

The most common type of revelation about marriage is descriptive, providing an image of the person one is destined to marry. Not surprisingly, these visions come in either dreams or visions, particularly when the future spouse is not someone currently known. A man dreams of a tall woman with long, dark hair. When he meets a woman fitting the description, he knows she is the woman for him (Nielson 1990, Wilson Archives). A man dreams of being on a roller coaster with a woman whose long hair is blown back to reveal a mole on her cheek. When he meets a woman with a mole on her cheek, he knows she is to be his future wife (Nielson 1990, Wilson Archives). A woman prays about the man she will marry and that night dreams about a man with spiky hair. Only in hindsight after marriage does she realize her new husband is the man from her dream (Johnson 2006 interview). In yet another story, a perplexing dream is ultimately resolved:

> When I was a recently returned missionary, I was sleeping one night and I had a dream. In that dream I saw a certain blonde-haired woman and she was wearing her hair in a certain way and she was wearing a striped shirt and bell-bottom pants because it was the style of the day. No words

were spoken. I just saw her. In the dream, I had the impression it was supposed to be my wife, and then in that same dream I found myself in a red VW Bug with a brunette lady in the passenger seat. A particular and familiar song was playing on the radio, and we were driving across the San Francisco Golden Gate Bridge. At that moment I had a distinct feeling she was to be my wife. That was the end of the dream.

I went on with my life, and only a few months later I found myself talking with this blonde-haired woman who was wearing those exact same clothes that I saw in my dream. It was the same lady which had appeared in my dream.

Soon after, we were married.

A few years went by, and my wife passed away due to cancer. I didn't feel much like dating or finding another wife, but I was set up on a blind date by some friends with a certain young lady. At the time I was living in the San Francisco Bay Area.

I went out with this lady, who happened to be a brunette, and coincidentally I had a red VW Bug at the time. I had pretty much forgotten about my dream. I took my date north of the Bay Area and as we were driving across the Golden Gate Bridge, that same particular song in the dream played on the radio, and it was at that moment that my dream was recalled to memory. Everything was the same as it appeared in my dream; the car, the song, the bridge, and the same girl. There I knew that she was to be my future bride.

We were later married and had six children. (Nielson 1990:3, Wilson Archives)

Distinguishing physical characteristics serve as the primary agents of revelation, guiding the person to identify their destined spouse. Hair tops the list, though other factors such as height, clothing, and physical marks such as moles are also helpful indicators. In one case, a man's future spouse is identified by the song she is singing (Fife and Fife 1956:218–9).

While dreams and visions dominate revelations about unknown future spouses, feelings and voices dominate revelations about people a person already knows. A man drives a woman to school and gets the strong impression that she is the person he is to marry (Parker 1971, Wilson Archives). A man hears a voice telling him that his close female friend is actually the woman he is to marry (Broderick 1982, Wilson Archives). A young missionary dreams of riding on a bus with his girlfriend back home. When the bus stops at a gas station he gets out, and the bus leaves without him. He frantically chases it down, climbs a mountain, then goes down a rope until he finally catches up to the bus, and more importantly, to his girlfriend. He interprets this as the trials he will face before they ultimately end up together, an interpretation borne out in time (Nielson 1990, Wilson Archives). In another account, a woman is dating one boy but writing to another. She prays about what to do and receives a revelatory dream:

> Carla was dating a return missionary her junior year in college at BYU. He was an awesome guy and the relationship was starting to get pretty serious. She was starting to feel that there was something off about the relationship and that maybe it wasn't the best thing to be involved with the guy that she was dating. She began to be prayerful about what direction she should go in the relationship and had the following dream.
>
> She dreamt that the missionary with whom she was writing came home from his mission, and she got married to him a few hours later. The guy that she was presently dating showed up at the reception. She realized that she had not told him about the missionary that she was dating or that they had never really broken up, except for the fact that he went on his mission. To complicate matters, she was now married, and he thought they were still dating. Carla was extremely embarrassed and felt horrible about the entire situation.
>
> She woke up and realized that she had to tell the guy that she was dating about a missionary that she was writing to, because he probably had different intentions with their relationship than she had. She told him about her boyfriend out on a mission, and they soon broke up, because they were at different stages in their life, and realized that things wouldn't work out between each other. (Lietz 2000:24, Wilson Archives)

Not only does this revelation reveal the person she is to marry, it reveals that it is *not* the person she is currently dating. In fact, this is a common revelation. A woman is dating a guy she likes but feels there is no chemistry between them. She prays about it and dreams that she is married to a man with blond hair, and they have three blond children. The boy she is dating has brown hair, so she breaks up with him. She is now married to a man with blond hair and assumes three kids are on their way (Brennan 1986a:7, Wilson Archives). A man dreams he is a shepherd on a mountain and meets a woman he understands to be his wife. The woman is not the person he was considering marrying, so he breaks it off with her. Soon after, he meets a woman on a mountain matching the one in his dream (Nielson 1990, Wilson Archives). A young woman is thinking about her fiancé in the celestial room in the temple when she receives "a distinct impression that she should not marry him." When she wonders who she *is* supposed to marry, the name of another young man comes into her mind (Schoemaker 1989:46). Just before heading out on his mission, a young man prays about whom he will marry and dreams about five women standing on pedestals:

> Right before I left on my mission I was dating a girl I really loved and hoped that she would wait for me to return. I had prayed about our

relationship and had a dream one night of five girls on a pedestal. Each one was a bit higher than the one before. I recognized the first two as old girlfriends and the third one was my present girlfriend.

I went on my mission, and she didn't wait.

I attended BYU right after I returned home. I began dating a girl.

One night I had the same dream I had a couple years previous. It was five girls on a pedestal. This time I could see more clearly the last two girls. One was the girl I was presently dating. The other one I could see clearly but I never met her.

I decided to take a self-defense class. I walked into the class and there sat the fifth girl in my dream. I was really scared to ask Jolene out. I attended the temple frequently.

One day I prayed in the temple that if the Lord wanted us together she would have to ask me out. I was too scared. Well, Jolene asked me to escort her to a dance. I pursued the relationship. I asked her to marry me twice before she said yes. Her parents weren't too pleased at first but we were able to work it out.

There must be opposition in all things. We were married a little short of two years after I met her. (Broderick 1982:9, Wilson Archives)

The corollary to receiving revelation that confirms you are dating the wrong person is revelation that confirms that you have chosen well. Most members pray for such confirmation before asking a person to marry them. The answers may be subtle if they are received at all, a general feeling that the choice they have made is right. Vague, subtle experiences rarely get narrated as examples of personal revelation, though they may be shared as part of a family's "origin myth" of how a couple met and married. Explicit revelations are more common in the narrative tradition. Tim Sampers prayed before proposing to his girlfriend and received a dream confirming his choice. "And so the next day I ran out and bought a ring, and just like that, bam [*claps his hands*], I don't need to think about it anymore.[17]

Another recurring type of revelation received about marriage is constructed around a single motif: instant recognition of one's future spouse. One of the legends of how Hugh Nibley met his wife involves immediate, revelatory recognition (see chapter 4 for complete narrative). It also appears as a motif in Mary's story about her brother Fred's revelation about the woman he would marry. The dream came to him soon after his first wife died:

He had a dream that he would marry someone who was tall with dark, long hair. His first wife was short and blonde. So it was rather peculiar. Not long after this dream, my brother and I were at a children's parade in Provo on the Fourth of July (1975), and a tall brunette woman (a Mary Tyler Moore type), approached him.

I'm not sure how the conversation started, whether they were introduced or they just happened to start up a conversation, but they talked for about five to ten minutes. After she left, he turned to me and said, "I think I'm going to marry that girl."

She could have thought that I was Fred's wife because I was pregnant at the time and it was just him and me standing together. The strange thing about it was someone from Bill's work had been trying to introduce him to someone and later came to find out that it was the same lady at the parade that he had met.

They ended up getting married.[18]

Along with specific guidance in choosing a spouse comes the comfort that there is a person out there for everyone—a message that comes as a particular relief to unmarried young women. In recording Carla's story about how painful and awkward it would be to marry someone she didn't know well, Heidi Lietz added relevant contextual data that illuminates both the cultural context of marriage for young LDS members and the social context for Carla specifically: "Carla was at the age and period in her life where many of her friends were married or getting married. She was dating a lot of different guys and thinking about what she wanted and didn't want in a relationship. She felt that this dream relayed the message to her that she shouldn't be too hasty and should take her time in finding the guy that she would someday marry."

The message is a particularly salient one for young LDS men and women. As Heidi Lietz explains: "It is common for LDS couples to date for short periods of time before they get married. They often believe that they know whom they should marry because of an answer to a prayer or a feeling instead of how well they actually know the person. There are certain advantages and disadvantages to short courtships and engagements. One of the dangers of short courtships includes not knowing your husband or wife as well as you would if you dated them for a long time" (2000:26). Revelations such as Carla's help to assure young women that they need not rush into marriage. The same is true for a legend Cheryl Moore shares from her Book of Mormon teacher:

Once a girl got really discouraged at the dating situation here at the Y,[19] so she examined her life to see what she was doing wrong, repented of her sins, and made a sort of deal with Heavenly Father. She prayed that she could at least have some sort of reassurance that she would get married, and if she could have this reassurance, she could wait forever for the guy if it was necessary.

That night she had a dream that she would marry her family home evening father, who had also been her home teacher the year before. What was so bad was that her ex-home teacher knew all her bad habits, and she felt really uncomfortable about it.

The next day, the guy caller her up and said that he had had the same dream about her, and was equally displeased. They prayed about it, then decided to date for a while to get to know each other on a romantic plane.

In three months they were married.

According to collector Ruth Riddle, Cheryl identifies closely with the girl in this narrative. In fact, Ruth argues that many of the young women at BYU can sympathize, including Ruth herself: "This story is one of Cheryl's favorites. The idea of a girl praying for a vision of her mate, the guy having the same vision, and their eventual marriage is an appealing theme to a BYU coed. Cheryl especially likes such stories because she doesn't have a boyfriend right now, and the idea of Heavenly Father playing matchmaker, if one is worthy, is a very appealing concept. Cheryl would like to believe in miracles and does believe that God reveals Himself in dreams, therefore, the idea of seeing a vision of one's future mate in a dream is very appealing to her, and, I might add, to this collector herself. Because of the precariousness of the dating situation here at BYU, such stories function to Cheryl, and to most of us, as a positive reinforcement: God hears our prayers and will help us find a mate if we are worthy" (Riddle 1976, Wilson Archives).

Anxiety about marriage is particularly high at BYU, where a constellation of factors including age, LDS theology, LDS culture, and collegiate culture—all contribute to a heightened, potentially overwhelming expectation to get married. That anxiety may lead to misinterpreted or manipulated revelation. There are stories of overeager young men who have cited their recent revelations as reasons why their girlfriends should accept their proposals of marriage (see chapter 2: Performance).

Within the personal revelation narratives of marriage, the missionary experience looms large. Many of the revelations about marriage come to young men either while in the missionary field or soon after their return, and to young women who are (or are not) waiting for boyfriends to return from their missions. Going on a mission is a rite of passage, spiritually, culturally, and socially. Missionaries leave as boys but return as men. The next stage in their progression through adulthood is marriage, and many returned missionaries embrace the search for a spouse with the same zeal they had for missionary work in the field.[20] This particularly fertile moment for marriage in young men's and women's lives is reinforced by the delay instituted for young women who want to go on a mission. Young men typically go on their mission at age nineteen; young women must wait until they are twenty-one. Officially, this delay is so that young women are better prepared to handle themselves in a world where females must be more careful than males of the dangers of knocking on the doors of strangers. However, there is a pervasive perception among church members that a mission is a backup alternative for young women who have not yet married. Going on a mission is not the death knell for a woman's marriage prospects, but it is an alternative rather than expected route, one that many see as running counter to an ideal path for building a family.[21]

Having Children

Once married, thoughts turn quickly to children. Couples ponder and pray about when they should begin trying to start a family and how many children they should have. The second question quickly eclipses the first, however, since it extends throughout the childbearing years. The types of revelations about children vary according to the interests of the person receiving them. They fall roughly into two camps. There are people anxious for children, praying to know when they will have them or when they should start trying. And there are people who either are not considering children or have decided not to have any more. Underlying the revelations for both is a consistent religious message stressing the importance of children in LDS theology and culture.

Eager for Children

The assumption of most church members is that all couples will have children at some point if they are physically able. This message comes through clearly and consistently from both institutional and informal cultural avenues. N. Eldon Tanner, who served as First Counselor in the First Presidency, wrote on the topic of celestial marriages and eternal families and outlined the significance of children: "Into this happy home and pleasant atmosphere will eventually come the children for which the marriage was consummated, and who will add immeasurably to the joy and fulfillment which God the Father intended when he instructed Adam and Eve to multiply and replenish the earth.

"When parents understand the purpose of their existence, that they are literally the spiritual offspring of their Father in Heaven and that they have a responsibility to provide mortal bodies for others, then they rejoice in the miracle of birth as they realize they are copartners with God in the creation of each child who comes into that home" (1980).

BYU student Heidi Lietz explains that "having children is a very large part of the Lord's plan while on this earth. The LDS religion believes that we grow closest to our Heavenly Father by becoming parents and experiencing what is involved in being parents, like our Father experiences. It is such a huge part of our Father's plan that one of the requirements to enter into the celestial kingdom is to be in a celestial marriage, which involves having children" (2000:14,

Wilson Archives). Heidi Lietz's interpretation reflects a common understanding about the importance of having children in order to attain the highest degree of celestial glory and become divine, but there is no specific theological rule that demands children in order to attain a celestial marriage. That said, a family without children makes little sense in an LDS worldview where the family is central to eternal life and progeny are a fulfillment of divine power.

Such an important decision is often prayed over. For Jen and her husband, that decision was particularly difficult, as each had a different idea of when they should start:

> Jen and I were engaged in February, winter semester 2000. Along with our engagement came decision making as far as our family was concerned. One area specifically was family planning—deciding whether or not we were going to start our family right after marriage or to use birth control and wait. And we both prayed about it, and she continued to feel like we should wait, and I continued to feel like we should start right away.
>
> After our feelings and the points of view that we had continued for a while, I decided that I needed to go fasting to the temple.
>
> I went to the Mount Timpanogos temple one night, and in the temple I had said a prayer. I can recall being somewhat tired, but I don't know exactly what happened, if I either was kind of sleepy or what, but I remember my eyes were closed and I was aware of this impression that I was having that I could see an image or an impression of light or shapeless objects proceeding from me, and I took it to mean that it was my posterity. I felt like that was an answer to my prayers.
>
> Shortly after, I attended the Provo temple alone and performed some other ordinances in the sealing room and there, as you look in the mirrors, you can see forever, and it kind of reminded me and symbolized that posterity and the eternal aspect of the families.
>
> Jen prayed about it some more, too, until finally we were on the same page.
>
> And two months after we were married, Jen got pregnant.
> (Vigil 2002:20, Wilson Archives)

Despite the joy that the expectation of children can bring, the line between eagerness and anxiety can be thin. Women in particular express anxiety about meeting this religious, cultural, and social expectation, especially if they do not get pregnant as quickly as they would like. Personal revelation can provide great comfort in the face of this stress. Heidi Lietz retold a story her roommate Sue shared with her about the revelation her mother received about her birth:

> Sue's mom and dad were trying to have children for the first five years of their marriage but simply couldn't get pregnant. They tried every possible fertility method and drug that was available, but nothing was working

After several tries and many years, they decided to try to adopt children. However, that was not looking hopeful either because Sue's mom had several health conditions which make it difficult to adopt kids. They were giving up hope and thought that they were never going to be able to have kids, until her mom received the following dream.

Sue's mom had a dream in which Sue appeared to her as a young woman in her teens and told her that she was going to have kids and had to be patient. It just wasn't the right time, but when it was, Sue was going to be part of their family.

Her mom had a very clear vision of what Sue looked like in the dream. She knew that Sue was going to be her child and that in the Lord's time she would be blessed with a beautiful daughter.

A few months later, Sue's mom was pregnant with Sue.

Sue had really bad eyes and teeth growing up, which her mom would always remind her daughter would pass in time because she knew what she would look like as a young lady from the dream that she had before she was born.

Sure enough, the description of the girl that appeared to her mom in the dream matched what Sue looked like later in life. Her mom was blessed with four healthy children after Sue. (2000:14, Wilson Archives)

Pat Franklin prayed about when she would become pregnant, particularly in the face of a new marriage and fulfilling career:

Pat had only been a member of the Church of Jesus Christ of Latter-day Saints for a little over a year before she was married. She had been working as a registered nurse and was excited about her career and wanted to pursue her occupation.

As she thought about becoming pregnant, she had a feeling come over her that told her to "Be still."

She was told to know that it was right, to not listen to the world and quit manipulating everything. Pat felt a comfort that she "would not be alone" and that it would be "the best thing that's going to happen" to her.

She conceived just a few months after marriage and her daughter, Clara, was born the next May.

Pat still feels very close to Clara. She knows she is special and that she was supposed to come to earth at the time she did.[22]

These stories encourage patience, a comfort in knowing that good things are in store. But not everyone is destined for large families or for any children at all. Some revelations are given to provide comfort in the face of news that more children are not on the way. Tim Sampers and his wife, Meredith, went to the temple to pray about when they should start having children, when he felt the spirits of two children pass through him. He had always thought they would have four children, but the feeling was very clear. He didn't know their gender, but he knew there would be only two. After their second child was born, it became dramatically clear that medically they could not have any more children. Jennifer Vigil's mother also received revelation preparing her for future problems in having children:

> I had had Jennifer in August of 1979 and we had always planned on having four children. Jennifer was quite a handful as a small child, as an infant and small child. And so we waited a while to have another one, have another child.
>
> When I was pregnant for Erin, along sometime during the time that I was pregnant for her, and I don't remember exactly when, on at least two occasions, but one I remember in particular, I was sitting in a chair in our house and I remember hearing a voice say, "Enjoy this pregnancy because it will be the last time you're pregnant."
>
> And on the occasions that it happened and including that one, I kind of brushed it aside. But as it turned out that I was pregnant again two years later and did not know that I was and it turned out to be a tubal pregnancy that ruptured. I almost bled to death from that experience and after that was afraid to attempt again to have more children.
>
> And so, it turned out that that pregnancy really was my last one.
> (2002:14, Wilson Archives)

For men and women excited about the prospects of a large family, such revelations can be initially devastating. Yet knowing that the size of their family has been sanctioned by God can ultimately be a comfort.

Unaware or Wary of More

Not all men and women are consciously or actively seeking more children, however. Revelations can catch people off guard. In these unsolicited revelations, God seems to prod people, encouraging them to remember the importance of children and the joy, both temporal and spiritual, that they bring. A bishop and his wife living in Germany already had children, but one night the bishop had a dream in which he saw "a lovely, blonde child who was made known to him to be one of his children." Not long after, he and his wife adopted a young girl whom he recognized as the girl in his dream (Palmer 1998, Wilson Archives). The bishop and his wife seem receptive to having more children, even if they are not actively seeking more. Such revelations may come unsolicited as one more piece of divine guidance from God.

Common in the narrative tradition, however, are spirit child revelations that come after a couple has decided they are through having children. In these cases, the idea of having more children is greeted tepidly at best. The expectations for large families soon after marriage can place a heavy strain on a family, particularly as more women aspire to careers outside the home. A young married couple at BYU wanted to finish their education before having children, but both received such strong and regular impressions to have children that they finally did, and everything they needed was given to them (Vigil 2002:15, Wilson Archives). After she and her husband decided not to have any more children, a woman had a recurring dream about a little boy wandering around her house. Eventually, she discussed the dream with her husband and they decided to have another child. Years later, she saw that her son looked just like the boy in her dream (Bedke 1999, Wilson Archives).

While many revelations involve promptings, feelings, and the knowledge that a couple should have more children, others include direct appeals from unborn children. Such experiences typically occur in dreams or in visions during which a child appears and begs to be born. "My husband was against having any sort of much of a family," explains one woman. "But I felt that I was to have this baby, and one night, I had a dream about the girl who was very anxious to come, and I could see her quite plainly." The woman goes on to describe finally becoming pregnant seven years later, and knowing when she looked into her daughter's eyes that she was the same little girl from her dream (Rollins 1977:77–8, Fife Archives).

Camille Brennan's grandmother told her about a dream she received about her two as yet unborn sons. A few years later, Camille got her grandfather to tell the story, with her grandmother and other relatives gathered around. Camille provides the context: "After having four children, the last one being Down Syndrome, my grandparents decided not to have any more children." The divine response she received suggested otherwise:

Mother bore this story in a testimony one day.[23]
    We wasn't going to have no more children because our family was big enough.
    Mother dreamed one night that she was in the spirit world and she was going down a long hall. Doors on both sides. Pretty much like a hospital, I suppose it was.[24]
    Anyway, she went by one door and there was a little boy playing on the floor. And he came and got her by the dress and got talking with mother and said he would like to come to earth, "But you won't let me come."
    And anyway, she went on down the line and saw this other little boy come out and said practically the same thing.
    So Ronnie and Billy were born. (1986b, Wilson Archives)

Like Camille Brennan's grandmother, Joyce Gant had decided not to have any more children. The response she received was immediate:

I've had four children, and the fourth one was exceedingly difficult. Physically, I was quite tired and it was just a difficult pregnancy.

I was standing at the sink one day peeling potatoes, I think it was, and looking out of the window. And I was saying within myself that this just had to be the last, because I just couldn't take any more of this. I was so exhausted and so tired. It had been so hard and so long.

And I felt a tug at the back of my skirt. It was really quite a strange sensation, and I turned around and looked, and there was a little blond-headed boy with great big blue eyes. And he said, "Oh, no, Momma, wait for me."

And it was gone just as quickly as it was there. In fact, I doubted, questioned myself afterwards as to whether it had really even happened. It was so completely out of touch with the rest of what I was doing.

And then it was four years later that we had a little boy that in some ways does resemble him, and yet with our last child, he's a dark-headed boy. He was quite difficult, too. In fact, we thought it was a tumor for a long time.

And my husband, after he had fasted and prayed about this and they had given me a blessing, he had a dream one night.

And he saw a little blond-headed boy playing in the garage of a new house. And he knew that it was his son.

And yet it is not any of the children that we now have.

Now, whether we are still to have another son, I don't know. But it was entirely real. But it is not any of the children we have now.

The collector, Kerril Sue Rollins, followed up with Joyce Gant: "I guess if it does come to pass and you have this little child, you'll think then that you can rest." Mrs. Hall replied, "Yes. Yes. We've finally got him" (Rollins 1977:68–9, Fife Archives).[25]

Tale Type: More Children Waiting

These stories of individuals and couples who either have not considered having more children or have actively decided against more, who then receive revelation suggesting otherwise, make up a recognizable tale type of spirit child narrative:[26]

1. *More Children Not Considered*: Parent or couple either is not thinking about having more children or has actively decided not to have more children.

2. *Revelation: Glimpse of Child*: Revelatory dream or vision reveals the image of an unborn child. The person "knows" that the child is meant to be his or her son or daughter.

3. *Optional Motif: Appeal to be Born*: In some cases, the spirit child appeals to parent or couple, asking to be born. The child typically approaches the adult appearing to already know the adult as his or her parent.

4. *Act to Have Another Child*: Parent or couple heeds the revelation and has another child.
5. *Optional Motif: Recognition*: Years later, parents recognize the face of their child as the face from their dream or vision.
6. *Optional Motif: Acknowledgment of Blessing*: Recognition that the child has been a blessing.

The narrative tradition of personal revelation favors stories that support church doctrine. In narrative performance, parents often mention explicitly how much of a blessing the child has been. Erika Layland's father-in-law shared with her the revelation his wife received about their son. With four children and no plans for any more, the couple visited the temple, and in prayer in the celestial room, she received an "overwhelming feeling" that she was to have another baby. After she and her husband discussed it, they decided she had indeed received personal revelation, and they had another child. Her father-in-law concluded his story: "As with all of our children, Pete has been an indispensable part of our family" (Layland 2001, Wilson Archives).

When these stories are shared *outside* the family, the typical context is the church—whether during church service or in one of the many church classes (see chapter 2). These contexts encourage faith-promoting narratives that support church teachings. This mandate is particularly strong in church magazines. In one particularly pointed story, a woman is prompted again and again to choose having more children over her career. The message is hardly subtle:

When I was a teenager, I decided that when I grew up I wanted to be the leader of a large corporation. I planned the rest of my education based on that decision. I took foreign language and advanced-placement classes in high school and majored in marketing and economics in college, all to strengthen my résumé and progress along the path toward corporate leadership.

I had my life mapped out. After my mission, I would graduate with a law degree and a master's degree in administration, work for several years, get married—not before age 30 at the earliest—and then, after a couple of years, I would *maybe* consider having a child.

Right in the middle of my graduate studies, the Spirit strongly told me I should marry the young man I was dating. Luckily, I listened—Brent was too good to pass up! He was worried about my attitude toward having children, but he followed the promptings he received to marry me anyway.

While waiting outside the Salt Lake Temple for Brent and me to come out, my sister asked my mother, "Do you think they'll have any kids?" My mother responded, "I think Shauna will have one, just to say she did it."

Shortly after we were married, Brent and I both felt strongly impressed that there was a child who needed to come to our family right away. I don't think I have ever seen Brent more surprised than he was when I told him, "I think Heavenly Father wants us to try to have a baby soon." His response was, "I felt the same way, but I was too afraid of your reaction to bring it up." Less than a year later, we welcomed our son Malachi into our family.

I still dreamed of being a corporate leader. My husband was supportive and helpful. We promised each other to live by the Spirit and follow those promptings. As we talked about our life plans with each other and with our Heavenly Father, it seemed to us that my goals were acceptable to the Lord.

Fast forward a couple of years. As I was finishing graduate school, I interviewed with a large international company for a position in their prestigious two-year training program. This program seemed to be the fast track to corporate leadership, my dream come true.

The compensation package was amazing—about four times as much as anything else I had been considering. The competition was fierce, so being offered a position would be extremely gratifying. The company had an even more enticing compensation and reward package to encourage graduates of the program to stay with them. If I were accepted, it seemed that once I completed the program I could design my own future. I envisioned someday wearing power suits to my penthouse office, dazzling my co-workers and employees with my expertise, and cashing paychecks that truly reflected my value.

After my third fly-back interview, I received a telephone call from corporate headquarters. They were offering me the position. There were so many reasons to accept this job. The money could be used to pay off my pending student loan debt. The recruiters' views of my university might be tainted by a refusal. And mostly, this position seemed to be everything I had trained and planned and worked for during the past 15 years.

I figured that after completing the program I could work part-time while our children were young and then return to full-time work when I was ready to more actively pursue my dream of corporate leadership. I could have it all!

But just as the elation and excitement at being offered the position began swelling within me, a different feeling emerged: the sinking feeling that this was not what Heavenly Father wanted me to do.

Brent was supportive. He prayed and counseled with me, and he promised to support me in whatever decision I reached through prayer and counsel with the Lord.

I prayed that night and told Heavenly Father the unbelievable benefits of this position. But still the Spirit let me know that I should refuse it. I called back and turned down the offer. It was one of the hardest things I have ever had to do. I felt I was giving up my chance to make something of my life—that I was giving up my well-earned reward for four grueling years of graduate study, giving up my chance to be fulfilled in this life, giving up my dreams. Even though I knew it was the right decision, it was really, really hard.

Brent and I prayed to know what to do next. A job fell into my lap, and I ended up working with a company I enjoyed, with flexible hours. It wasn't quite the high-powered career I had envisioned, but it paid the bills. Brent stayed home with Malachi and worked on his fledgling business on the side while I worked full time. While this decision may not be right for everyone, we had prayed about this new direction for our lives, and it was right for us. We promised the Lord we would try to stay close to the Spirit and always make prayerful decisions about our lives. As a result of these prayerful decisions, we welcomed our daughter Sophia into our family.

After four years with this company, I felt that I was not supposed to work outside the home anymore. After another long night of counseling with my husband and with the Lord, I told the company owner I would be leaving. This decision took a leap of faith because we still had bills to pay, including student loans, and we had recently welcomed another daughter, Aerie, to our family. But I had learned that I am happiest when I follow the Lord's plan for my life rather than my own personal plans.

Three years after this difficult decision to leave my job, our daughter Aerie asked me, "Mom, if someone said you could have ten thousand million diamonds or your Aerie, what would you choose?" I told her, "I would choose my Aerie." She went on, "If someone said you could have ten million hundred dollars or your Aerie, what would you choose?" Again I told her, "I would choose my Aerie." She jumped up and down, crying with glee, "I knew you would say that! I just knew you would say that!"

It hit me then that I *had* chosen my Aerie. Had I taken the position with the large international company, I probably would not have her in my life. And she is truly a joy, as are our four other children. (Dunn 2007:9–12)

The story is accompanied with a number of family photos, past and present, a testament to the joy Shauna Bird Dunn has found in her role as mother. Further, she concludes her narrative with a testimony of her knowledge of the blessings of being a mother, referencing a promise made to mothers by Elder Jeffrey R. Holland of the Quorum of the Twelve Apostles: "Yours is the work of salvation, and therefore you will be magnified, compensated, made more than you are and better than you have ever been" (13; citing "Because She Is a Mother," *Ensign*, May 1997:36).

Material published by the church is uniformly direct regarding the importance of motherhood over any other life goal for women.[27] This message is picked up by church members and can become part of oral tradition. A BYU student shares a story he read in a packet of information about marriage and family planning given out during a Gospel Principles class:

In the early days of the Church, there was this lady whose husband was not able to provide for her children. And so she had a difficult time raising the children by herself, and she decided not to have any more children.

One night she dreamed that she passed out of her body and looked down at herself on the bed. It became clear to her what the Lord approved of and what he did not. The only thing that was held against her was her rebellious attitude of having more children.

She realized that before she came to earth she had promised to be a mother to a certain number of children, and there were two or three that were still unborn. She knew the number she was supposed to have exactly, but after she came back, she couldn't remember for sure.

When she realized that she had failed to keep her promise to the Lord, she was really upset. And she knew that this feeling would never end. After a while, she saw a man coming toward her. And when he was talking to her, she told him that she didn't want any more children because they weren't cared for. He told her that was a trick of the devil.

And after she woke up, she realized that she didn't want to break her promise with the Lord, so she had two more children. (Brennan 1986a:15, Wilson Archives)

Performance contexts for these narratives, coupled with expectations about faith-promoting stories more generally, discourage extended commentary about whether or not a person or couple felt manipulated by the revelation. Nonetheless, the narrative texts suggest that instead of a blessing, having more children can feel like an obligation, a sacrifice made to one's religion. Many of these stories begin with a woman worrying about the hardships she will have to endure if she has more children.

That anxiety may derive partly from cultural and social pressures within the LDS community to begin having children immediately upon marriage and to continue having children until they have fostered large broods of faithful sons and daughters. In her study of spirit child narratives, Margaret Brady argues that women who have chosen not to have more children are defying church doctrine and feel terrible guilt about their choice. Spirit child revelations can actually alleviate this anxiety by providing a clear, divine counterpoint that makes the choice to have more children virtually irrefutable, thus drawing them back in line with religious, cultural, and social norms (1987:445–6). Such an interpretation is supported by stories such as the one John Wainwright retells from church pamphlets and dovetails comfortably with George Schoemaker's interpretation of marriage confirmation narratives that allow some fence-sitters to transfer the onus of making a decision from themselves to the divine (1989:40).

Such an interpretation has merit, but must be expanded and elaborated. First, a more accurate interpretation would recognize that any guilt women feel about not having more children is variable, rather than intense and inherent. Carl and Patty Miller, for example, have both received revelation that they have another child waiting to be born, but neither is rushing to action. "We keep getting promptings that we should have another one, but we keep being stubborn," admits Carl. "We're saying, 'Nope. Three is enough for us right now'" [*laughter*].

"We have another one out there," Patty adds, "but we're just not ready to have another kid, so we keep dragging our feet. We figure it's kind of, push us along, get the ball rolling, I don't know [*laughter*]. Maybe just to say, 'Hey, I'm still here. Don't forget about me' [*laughter*]. Because we've considered stopping. Probably keep reminding us it's still there."

Second, it is not clear from these narratives that all women initially see their choice to have no more children as a clear violation of church doctrine or cultural norms. Many believe that the size of their families is sufficient, personally, socially, culturally, and theologically. Revelation of a spirit child waiting to be born is often just that: a revelation, awareness of something previously unknown or unconsidered.

Third, these narratives are not confined to women. While women are twice as likely as men to receive revelation about children, they are only marginally more likely to receive unsolicited revelation that follows the tale type described above.[28]

An alternative interpretation can be found by paying attention to the larger context of personal revelation. Such an approach shifts the focus from revelation as either being coercive or alleviating guilt to revelation as personal blessing.

Social or cultural pressure from a bishop, ward members, or family to have more children can breed resentment, deriving as it does from the mortal rather than the divine. One size does not fit all. Revelation from God, however, carries a distinctly different message and promise. First, personal revelation is personal, not broadly doctrinal. Church doctrine argues generally for large families, as do cultural and social norms, but "large" is a vague term, and such broad doctrinal tenets are not universally applied. Not all families have lots of children; celestial marriages can be achieved with a single child. What may be a good idea for most Mormon families may not be good for individual ones. In fact, personal revelation is predicated on the idea that individuals will receive personal *and* *personalized* guidance from God (see chapter 1). Receiving a dream about *your* family, *your* child, is intensely powerful. A person's choice to have more children is not made in a vacuum but rather with a consideration of relevant factors.

A powerful experience such as a vision of one's child in heaven can quickly tip the balance. New factors, new decision.

Personal revelation provides a promise that to follow God's revealed path is to reap great blessings and benefits. The choice to act on revelation is not always an easy one. Revelations to take a new job that would uproot your family, go back home when you are already late for work, and skip your sister's wedding may run counter to logic as well as personal desires. Such revelations may be avoided, ignored, or dismissed as mundane. The result, however, is uniformly dismal. To ignore revelation is to forfeit God's blessings (see chapter 3). Personal revelation provides divine confirmation. A couple worried about raising more children may feel resentment toward peers who invoke cultural and scriptural dicta to have more children but be reassured if God has sanctioned, even encouraged, the choice through revelation. Follow God and blessings follow. As church members remind themselves of the larger picture, of the primary function and promise of personal revelations, promptings that seem to ask the impossible can be reinterpreted as not only feasible but desirable.

Raising Children

Decisions about when to have children and how many to have appear throughout the narrative tradition, though as particularly sacred experiences, they are shared with caution. Once the children are born, the stories shift to protection. As discussed earlier, children in peril dominate the narrative tradition. Yet experientially, parents regularly rely on personal revelation to help them in the mundane decisions that accompany raising a child. Such revelations are often subtle, small, and timely and rarely register as remarkable enough to narrate over and over again. Yet recent experiences and conversations with topical relevance can jog the memory, as it does with the Mullens. Struggling to find the right school for her daughter, Lee Mullen prayed and received guidance that a particular school she had been considering was the right one. Driving along and chatting about the joys and trials of parenting, Ken Mullen talks about bonding with his youngest son, Phil: "Talk about personal revelation. I felt inspired to take him fishing. I was just inspired to do it. And it's been great. It's something we share now." So much so, that when Phil was heading out to go fishing with his friends recently, he told his mother he wished his dad was coming too.

Finding a Home and Job

Finding a home is a concern deeply woven into the fabric of the Mormon experience. The early years of the church were heavily shaped by attempts to find a place to settle where Latter-day Saints would not be attacked by angry mobs, local politicians, or the federal government. Anti-Mormon senti-ment ultimately forced the Saints to leave Zion—where they were to gather once again in these latter days to await Christ's Second Coming—and resettle out west in Salt Lake City. Today, these concerns are far more humble and personal.

While a home for the church has been found, the search for a home for one's own family continues for every new couple and often throughout one's life. Contemplating a move out of state, Monty Jenkins prays for guid-ance. That night, he has a dream in which he sees the house they should buy. A month later, a realtor takes him to the house in his dream and they buy it (see chapter 3 for complete narrative). Wanting to move back to Utah, a woman prays with her husband and her aunt and receives a recurring dream of the place the Lord has chosen for her:

> When Jimmy and I were living down in California, and I sort of wanted to come back to Utah, I prayed a lot. We moved to a ranch then, and I thought I would be satisfied, but I just wasn't when Jimmy was. But I kept praying. I saw a big place in California then, and I wanted to buy it, thinking it would be good for raising a big family. I felt satisfied with this, then Jimmy's aunt talked with us about it. She said, "Let's pray." So we prayed. This aunt was not a Mormon, but it was a sincere, powerful prayer, and I felt like I would get an answer.
>
> That night I dreamed and felt like I was on a sort of magic carpet, and I kept saying, "I'm going to Utah." Then it seemed I was looking down from above some mountains on this lonely, desolate place. I said, "Surely, Lord, you don't want us to live there." But the penetrating voice said, "Well, see how peaceful it is there."
>
> Then I thought I was back in California, in that home again. I told Jimmy about this, during which telling I saw it in detail again. It seems I told it again, because I saw it for a third time. I had no doubts.
>
> In about a year, we moved to Greenville.
>
> I had a dream three times; I would be in a room where it was dark and cloudy. When I looked out the window, I saw a picture of this place, the place I saw in my first dream. But it seemed more beautiful in this dream, the last dream.
>
> Once when Jimmy and I were traveling from Milford after putting money down on this place, we were traveling in a snowstorm, and it was dark and snowy, and we got to the place and this picture was shown to me, the one that I had had in my dream. I saw the first dream again in detail and heard the voice of the Lord.
>
> "Well, surely, Lord, you don't want us to live there."
>
> And again this penetrating voice of the Lord said to me in answer: "But see how peaceful it is there."

And in this dream, which I saw as I looked at the picture of the place in the snowstorm, I saw again that all the trees around the house were dead; I could see the board fence, the old barn, the house, the very living picture of it. For sure enough, the place looked exactly like the dream. I had passed that place countless times, but it had never hit me until now, in the snowstorm, that it was the place in my dream.[29]

The conclusion of the story echoes the well-known phrase Brigham Young is said to have uttered upon seeing Salt Lake for the first time (see chapter 4). In a story collected by Susan Christensen and Doris Blackham, the parallel to Brigham Young's narrative is more explicit. While searching for a home, a woman's husband dreamed of travelling from Sterling to Manti and finally to Ephraim, where he saw a little home with trees and a corral. So he took his family to Ephraim to search for a home, and a fellow Mormon drove him straight out to the house from him dream. When they got to the house, her husband exclaimed, "Why, this is the place!" (1971, Wilson Archives; for complete narrative, see chapter 3).

Like finding a home, finding a job is as common and relevant a concern for contemporary Mormons as it is for any other adult. However, also like finding a home, revelations about finding a job are conveyed, received, and interpreted in ways specific to LDS culture.

Marriage, children, and careers are often intertwined. The revelations that Pat Franklin and Shauna Bird Dunn received to choose children over careers reflect a common theme in LDS revelation that places one's commitments, allegiances, and obligations to God and the church above temporal pursuits such as careers. However, in some cases, an initial act of faith and obedience is rewarded; people can have their cake and eat it, too. During seminary class, Blake Garrett heard John Anderson share his story of recommitting himself to the church after a powerful revelation. Blake recounts the story with a mixture of specific detail and general summary, including the context for John Anderson's original narration:

John Anderson joined the LDS church in 1956 and was attending college in 1958. While at college and while at home during summer vacations, he was quite inactive in the church. Although he did attend a few meetings, he many times felt that he could be spending his time much better if he stayed home and studied instead of attending sacrament meeting.

On April 3, 1958, when John was 29, he tells of a special dream he had in which he was standing before God. He was being judged, and as he stood here all by himself, he noticed that he was all alone. He expected that when this day came about, his family, friends, and relatives would also be there, but no, he was completely alone with God.

As God looked at him, all he could say for himself was, "I have this piece of paper," which was his college degree.

Again he said, "I have this piece of paper."

And as he looked up to God, John saw him just shaking his head. John was filled with torment and saw all of his years of college wasted.

In telling this story to a seminary class, he used this personal story to emphasize the point that spiritual goals *must* be achieved before temporal goals. He then went ahead and told the class that after he quit college, he became very active in the church and became ward clerk. He even found a better job and found that he did not need a degree to get this job. He is now a stake missionary in southern California. (Bice 1964, Wilson Archives)

The pattern of direct blessings is woven deeply into LDS culture and theology. It appears most often in stories of tithing. A typical story involves a family making a budget and realizing there is no way they can tithe and still pay their bills. They decide to tithe anyway and miraculously, they remain in the black each month.[30] The message is clear: pay money to the church as prescribed and receive financial blessings in return. The same logic applies with careers. Put the church ahead of your career and you will be blessed with a great career.

Such beautifully symmetrical blessings cannot be expected all the time, however. In many cases, decisions truly are either/or. Careers may remain on hold indefinitely, but people speak of the joy and happiness they have received following the path God laid out for them rather than the path they once thought so important. Serena Gammon prays for guidance about her own career path and is prompted to wait on graduate school and go back home first, where she meets her husband and starts a family. The decision did not come without trade-offs. "I secretly . . . my own personal desire was to achieve something big, you know? But instead, I felt peaceful about going to Utah," Serena explains.

"I went there, I lived with a friend, everything fell into place. She lent me her car. I stayed with a friend for cheap. Her and her husband, they had an extra room. I saw my sister all the time. I made some awesome friends and was in an awesome social environment, the best I'd ever had in Utah. And I took some courses and I substitute taught and I did just a whole bunch of other stuff that was not my great achievement thing that I wanted to do, it wasn't career oriented, but it was just . . . I was so happy, I was so happy," she laughs.

"So basically, those blessings did come. I was so happy, met Dave, we dated . . . ."

"I don't have a PhD. I don't have a master's degree. I didn't do any of the things I thought I would do," she concludes, but she is happier than she could have imagined possible. Follow God's counsel and you will be blessed.

Revelations where professional careers take a backseat to other priorities and paths appear far more often to women than to men. In fact, of the two stories in the narrative collection of a man sacrificing his career for the church after receiving revelation, one resulted in a successful career (cited earlier), the other suggests a similar happy ending is on the way—at least for the man. The story is shared by the man's wife, Colleen:

> Before I had Tammy, who is our first daughter, it was really important for me to finish my education and for my husband to finish his education and at the time we still had several years to finish our education.
>
> And I started having very strong impressions from the Spirit that we should get pregnant and have a baby. And then my husband did, too, quite strong. And sometimes that doesn't happen very often. And so both of us at the same time kept having these impressions.
>
> As time went on, I kept talking myself out of it. Anytime the thought came to mind or the impression came, then I would just talk myself out of it and convince myself that we didn't have money and education and just all the things you worry about before having a baby, that we couldn't do it.
>
> And so, the impressions just kept coming so strong that they were undeniable.
>
> And so we decided to go ahead and follow the Spirit, to have the baby instead of wait.
>
> And so, we were blessed with everything that we needed for a baby. We had things come out of the blue—the clothes and the stroller and anything for the baby that we couldn't have afforded.
>
> We had all kinds of things work out for his work and his school.
>
> The education thing is still working itself out, and has worked itself out.
>
> We just felt very prompted and that everything had worked out how the Lord had wanted it to for our family.[31]

While the husband's education and career remain on track, the wife's career is still a work in progress.

The bulk of the revelations about new homes and new jobs come to men.[32] However, decisions about children and careers affect the whole family; so, like Colleen and her husband, both members of a couple may receive revelation. The same was true for Ken and Lee Mullen when Ken was contemplating a new job in New York:

> Lee: When we were first married, I actually thought I had the whole revelation thing down. Because things came to me in a certain way. And so, when it came to me, like Ken was saying, you learn to trust that feeling. You can't explain it, you don't

know why it's happening, from where it comes or where it goes, but you learn to trust the feeling.

And we lived in Dearborn and we had just bought our first house and I loved that house, I just loved it. And he had a job that was OK, but it was paying more than we . . . you know, we had been students for a long time or whatever. And he . . . . Where were you Ken, when that happened?

Ken: I'm not sure what you're talking about yet.

Kenny: [*laugh*]

Lee: About when . . .

Ken: [*laughing*] Don't laugh.

Lee: The job . . . to New York . . . moving to New York.

Ken: Where was I when what happened?

Lee: And revelation.

Ken: Did we tell you that story?

Lee: I don't think we did.

Tom: No . . . You mentioned Dearborn and moving, but I don't know . . .

Ken: Well, do you want *me* to kind of tell it? [*to Lee*]

Lee: Yeah.

Ken: And you jump in. Interrupt me when you want.

Lee: Yeah, you tell it, only because, this changed a lot for me.

Ken: I'll tell it from my perspective, then I'll let Lee tell you what happened to her.

I was looking for a new job. And I had interviewed with General Motors right there in downtown Detroit and probably would have got that job, but other things happened.

Interviewed with some other companies, wasn't finding anything, and I said . . . .

And I was really at a crossroads in my career. I was kind of working in HR, human resources, *and* in accounting, and kind of going both ways and I didn't know where to go. And finally I started looking for a job as an accountant, a comptroller, that's what I thought I wanted to do and felt good about that.

But anyway, I start sending résumés out all over the country. I don't even know if she knew.

Did you . . . ? [*Lee shakes her head no.*] Yeah.

And so I get a call from New York. Want me in for an interview.

And so I come home; I'm sure I was very nervous, but it's been too long for me to remember now. And totally, I was going to New York for an interview.

OK? And I'm going to let her tell her side in just a minute.

Anyway, we were nerve-racked about this, both of us really were. After I actually set the interview date, I thought, "What am I doing?"

And I'm standing finally at the airport at Detroit Metro, crowded as all get out, it was just chaos in the airport, the security line was super long, checking your luggage, super long. It was awful. Now this was back in 1989, yeah, '89, and I felt just, "What am I doing, you idiot?"

And then all of a sudden, the wind comes.[33] And I mean it felt like somebody opened the top of my head up and poured the Spirit in. I'm standing there, complete peace. And I start tearing up. Here I am, in the airport, you know? And I'm looking down, kind of doing that. "We're going to move to New York. We're going to move to New York. I'm doing the right thing." I mean it was completely . . . . The fear and anxiety was gone, gone, in a moment.

And, went to my interview and everything went great.

Now you tell your side of that.

Lee: Now he told me, "I've sent these things out, I want to go to New York," or "They want me to come for an interview." So it had been a long time since he interviewed, so I was kind of like, "Well, just go on the interview; it'll help get your skills up," or whatever.

I was not going to New York. I mean, I thought Detroit was bad enough, I was not going to New York [*laughter*].

And so I thought, "Yeah, that'll be great."

And I remember I was laying in bed. And I always had a certain way where I was used to the Spirit, the feeling, that I would get, and I would know that that's what it was. And this particular night, I actually heard a voice that said, "You will move to New York."

And I thought, "No."

And it was so real. But . . . it wasn't a voice that I understood, but it wasn't a voice that frightened me.

Ken: Weren't you angry before that?

Lee: Yeah. I was mad.

Ken: Yeah, she was angry. I mean, that's important to note.

Lee: Yeah.

Ken: Laying there on the bed. I think you were even crying, weren't you? I can't remember. You told me you were very upset at me.

Lee: [*pause*] Probably [*laughter*].

Ken: That's what I remember.

Lee: I don't remember that part.

Ken: I thought women remembered everything [*laughter*].

Lee: Highly likely.

Anyway, but I heard the voice and I thought, "Move to New York? Are you kidding me?" So I thought, there's just no way. And then it was interesting because he came back and was telling me about, you know, "We're going to move . . ."

Now you've got to remember we had a mortgage on our house for two hundred and eighty dollars.

Ken: A month.

Lee: A month.

Tom: Oh, OK.

Lee: We lived in a nice neighborhood. We liked the ward we were in. We were close to family. I wasn't working; I didn't have to work. And he comes back and with the offer that they had given him, we would have to rent a house for almost two thousand a month . . .

Ken: Nine hundred a month.

Lee: Nine hundred?

Ken: Uh-huh.

Lee: Oh, OK. It was a significant difference to rent. I mean, there were just so many things that were just . . . . I would have to go to work and do all those things. And we'd move away from family, and we'd be in a place where we didn't know.

And we went to Poughkeepsie and I went up there and we're looking around and we can't find a place to rent. And all this is going on and I'm thinking, "What are we doing? This is crazy."

And we were in a phone booth trying to call somebody in the paper to find a place to stay and Ken said to me, I said, "Ken, this just doesn't make sense. We just need to go back home."

And he said, "Lee. Trust the feeling," is what he told me.

And then later on looking back on that, I'm pretty strong headed, and I don't humble myself well, I'll just say that. [*To Ken*] So you don't have to. [*pause*] Poker face.

Ken: I'm not going anywhere with that [*laugh*].

Lee: Yeah.

And I realized that the normal, good feeling probably would not have worked in that situation. And I had received revelation in a totally different way. And I've never received it that way since. But I would not have moved had that not occurred.

So that was really a learning experience for me. And I think it gave me the understanding that God knows us personally. And he knows our strengths and our weaknesses. And he knew there was no way Ken was going to budge me out of that house that I liked in Dearborn Heights, had I not had that other experience.

And Ken, I'm thinking, did I even know that you were serious about the job? Or that it was going to . . .

Ken: I don't remember; I don't know.

Lee: I'm thinking that it didn't even register to me.

Ken: But it led to here.

Lee: Yeah.

Ken: We were only there four years. And then I got a job here and I was promoted here. I mean, it's been a great ride.

Lee: And it allowed him to change his focus of his career.

But it was interesting, the different way that revelation sometimes occurs. And that you could . . .

And I don't think I've ever shared that, maybe once or twice. Because that's a real personal one for me. Because it was just so real.

And we made that leap of faith from that. Because we didn't . . . . Everything, everything was telling us this is crazy.

Ken: There was a cut in pay. My pay in real dollars went down thirty percent.

Tom: But you just knew.

Lee: We trusted in that feeling.

Ken: We weren't blindly going either. I mean, this was a position that was going to obviously give me some very good experience. So I mean it wasn't like any old position either. So, that was . . .

Tom: There was some logic behind it.

Ken: Absolutely. Absolutely. Study it out in your mind. Doctrine and Covenants Section Nine. Study it out in your mind. And then bring it to me in prayer, the Lord says. And that's what we did, in that case.

For Craig and Josette Bailey, the job was Craig's, but the revelation came only to Josette.

Josette: As far as family, the biggest one [revelation] I can think of is when we moved out here and Craig got the job offer . . . well, he didn't get the job offer.

And I knew, I had the vision in my head of us out here and everything. And I was upset. I was . . . I'm like, "No, that's not right. Not right."

I mean, he got the job offer, it just wasn't worth coming out. And I was so upset that he said no. I said, "No." I mean, I was all upset, in tears, everything.

Got over it.

But a couple of months later they called back with a better offer, and everything else and we came out.

So as far as family, I think that's my biggest one.

Craig: And it was my job and I didn't have any of that. I mean, I did a lot of praying and I was just like, looking back it makes more sense to me, but I didn't have any promptings that said I should go or I shouldn't go. It was just like, nothing.

And as I look back on that now, we had our reasons why we wanted to leave, but there was not any particular reason why we *had* to leave. So as I look back, the answer for me was that I didn't get an answer. So it was basically the Lord saying, "It's your choice. If you want to go, go. And if you don't want to go, then stay. But you don't have to," sort of thing.

And our lives have been much better since we've been here, in every facet. Our relationship's better, the income's better, the job potential and the future is a thousand times better. The opportunity that's been open to me is a thousand times better.

Josette: For me also.

Craig: But if we were still living in Utah, I mean, I don't think we'd be destitute and poor and sleeping in a cardboard box, so . . . [*laughter*]

So she gets this vision that she can picture North Carolina yet she's never been there, and I'm the one who's on my knees praying every day, "Do I take this job? Do I not take this job?" And there's like, no answer. So it's really kind of weird [*small laugh*].

Craig was the one praying for revelation, but Josette was the one who received it. Neither Craig nor Josette fully understand why, but they know that the decision was the right one for both them individually and as a family.

Church Work

As members of a lay church, Latter-day Saints are expected to actively participate in the work of the church, from the practical (such as cleaning the church and producing the Sunday morning program), to the social (directing church plays, hosting parties for baptisms and missionary departures and returns), to the organizational (such as setting the missionary split schedule and temple recommend interviews), to the educational (such as teaching in Primary, Sunday school, and seminary). These jobs can be time consuming, dominating many Saints' lives outside of work and the home. As a lay church, the LDS Church provides a religious identity that is expected to trump any other social identity, figuratively and literally.[34]

Revelations received for the specific job people are called to do in the church are often viewed as distinct from the revelations received to guide them in their personal lives. Revelations that set people apart from the rest of the membership and grant power and often specific keys to conduct their jobs are often viewed as institutional as much as personal (see chapter 1). However, there are some church jobs—mission work, teaching, genealogical work—that are expected of all members, whether called specifically or not. Many of the revelations experienced in these contexts are narrated as personal revelation, where the personal and religious overlap in service to the church. Of the 441 narratives of personal revelation analyzed, almost a quarter involve people engaged in work for the church, whether missionary work, teaching or speaking in church, or temple work (see chart 6 in the appendix).

Missionary Work

Missionary work is hardly confined to nineteen-year-old men in the church. The religious mandate to build up the kingdom of God in these latter days falls to all church members and can be performed anywhere, anytime, by any faithful member of the church. That said, the bulk of the stories of personal revelation dealing with missionary work are in fact experienced and narrated by young men serving a two-year mission for the church.[35]

Looming large in their stories is the recurring theme of danger. Like other righteous church members, missionaries receive personal revelations to help them avoid traffic accidents (Jara 2000:13–5, Wilson Archives) and natural disasters (Oliveros 2001:17, Wilson Archives), as well as more dramatic threats such as terrorist bombings (Cope 2003:26, Wilson Archives). The most common threat, however, comes from the people they are trying to save. The mission field is often likened to a battlefield, a paradoxical metaphor combining religion and war that is not uncommon in evangelical faiths where missionary work thrives.[36] The work to save souls places young men and women away from home, often in foreign lands and foreign cultures. Their job is to encourage faith in a church whose miracles are recent, whose prophets are living, whose theology can seem blasphemous to other Christian denominations, and whose religious culture is often saddled with stereotypes of fanatical polygamists.

Sitting one afternoon with Elder Spencer Bourgeous and Elder Adam Wicker, two missionaries to the Burlington First Ward, conversation turns to the importance of invoking and maintaining the Holy Ghost as a companion while teaching and tracting:

> There are times where I've had those promptings and I didn't listen. Like with Elder Staley.
> We were tracting. And I felt bad about this street. But Elder Staley just, you know, wanted to go to this street, whatever. I just had this horrible feeling.
> And this is where I got stabbed.[37]
> And so, there's this guy sitting on his porch. And I just saw him up there.

And, you know, as I look back on it, I've recognized the feelings I was having. But you know, when I was there, I didn't listen to anything. It was just like, "Yeah, we got to talk to everybody, we're missionaries."

So I said, "Hey, what's up?"

And he just goes like [*imitates waving*], waves his hand at me to come here and I was like, "Oh no, he's going to Bible bash."

But the whole time I had this thing that just told me, "Get away from this guy. Just leave."

I went up and started talking to him; it was a very friendly conversation. He was pretty simple minded. I think he had done a few drugs in his days. You know, he wasn't like he had mental setbacks, as far as mental retardation. His mind was just fried.

And so I was just, we were just kind of talking, not about religion, and I just had something inside of me just saying, "You need to leave."

And so I kept trying to . . . I'd look at Elder Staley and give him the head nod thing, you know? And Elder Staley was just like [*imitates wide-eyed, helpless look*]. We talked for a half hour and in that, Staley said maybe ten seconds of conversation. He was just like, shocked. And I think he felt that same Spirit too, but he didn't know how to handle it. I mean he was just frozen.

So finally at the end, even after he stabbed me, we were there five more minutes; Staley wouldn't leave. Like he was just mortified. And I, like my hand was bleeding, and I was like, "C'mon, man, we've got to go."

So there was those things telling me, "You need to go," but I didn't act on it, because I just thought it was my own fear.

Adam shares a few other stories of receiving personal revelation before the conversation returns more generally to the Holy Ghost. Elder Spencer Bourgeous picks back up on this thread:

> Spencer: I've also experienced things—that the Spirit would tell me to leave, like to leave a house, and come to find out later, you know, someone was stabbed and robbed five minutes after we left. And then, it was just like, "OK, well, that's good that we left." The importance of listening to the Spirit.
>
> Tom: Were you mentioning a hypothetical when you left and five or ten minutes later someone was robbed?
>
> Spencer: No, that was real [*laugh*]. That was when I was in Raleigh. Me and my companion were visiting a family that lived in, what do you call it?
>
> Adam: Boarding house type deal.
>
> Spencer: Boarding house.
>
> Adam: Half-way house kind of.
>
> Spencer: And we were visiting a family that lived in this little one . . . one . . . [*he's searching for "one-room" apartment*], a room about this big [*indicates the size of the small classroom we're*]

in, which was probably ten by ten], a family of four. And they were like the second door on the right, down the hallway. And as me and my companion walked in, you know, everyone there, you know, was having those struggles with drugs and alcohol. And they were under the influence of things that just weren't good.

And, so we walk in, and a couple of the guys there were acting, you know, buddy buddy at first with us. And then one of them, who we met on the streets a couple of weeks earlier so we knew who he was and he knew who we were, and he kept trying to get us to come to this room with him. And he was on something. And I told him, you know, we'll be there in a little bit, we're visiting this family, we'll come back.

Anyway, we went and visited the family, and I was standing in the hallway because, you know, we shouldn't go into the rooms of a single woman, that's what it was, so we're just kind of standing in the hallway, and he kept coming back out of his room into the hallway, and you know, saying, "I told you I wasn't finished with you yet. Get back in the room." And we kept telling him, "We'll be right there. We're visiting these people." He kept going in and out saying the same thing, like four or five times, and I kept giving him the same answer that we'll be right there.

And at that point, I just remember the . . . like the . . . you know, it's the . . . the Spirit, and it wasn't like an audible voice, but it was a voice that you feel, you know, telling you to leave, that you needed to get out of there right now.

And so I told my companion that we needed to leave. And as we were walking out, you know, I knew we had to walk by his door to get to the front door, so I was just praying, you know, for something to happen for us to be protected.

And as we walked up to the door, I peeked in and I saw him sitting right next to the door, but his eyes were closed. So we snuck out, and there was another man that was in there with him. His name was Shorty, that's what they called him. So there was two men, Mike and Shorty, and uh, as we were leaving, Mike was the one sitting by the door with his eyes closed.

And we got up to the front porch and then Shorty started yelling for us to pray with him. And I was just waiting for Mike to wake up, because Shorty was yelling to come out to try to get us again. But then, Mike never woke up.

And so, Shorty came out to the front porch, and we prayed with him again one more time, and then we left, because we were able to get another member of the church to come back and pick up this family to take them to dinner. So we were planning on coming back in five minutes and so we left, contacted the member, said a prayer, asked for protection as we . . . before we went back.

Went back, and we're not even gone five minutes, and when we got back, the Raleigh police department was all there. And we get out and the guy, Shorty, was standing on the porch and he was holding a napkin, he was bleeding, he was stabbed. And he was yelling that he robbed him.

And Mike, and his wife I guess, were there as well, and they took off.

And the police caught them and brought them back.

And we were like, "Yeah, that's them," and, "We know his name."

Tom: Oh, *Mike* robbed them.
Spencer: Yeah. Mike robbed him and stabbed Shorty.

And the member of the family that was in the room next door, she heard the shoving and the yelling so she locked her door and called the police on her cell phone. So.

I mean, that was just, you know, the Spirit was just like, "Don't go in that room," and "Get out of here." And so as we listened, and as we left, the Lord protected us on our way out and then, we were gone, and then it happened, and then everything was taken care of.

But it was one of those experiences that shakes you up a little bit, but makes you grateful for the Spirit and the importance of living your life to where you recognize those promptings and like I know I need to do this. And then you go and do it. The Lord has protected me, in that situation.

As a strategy to mitigate against the difficulties of finding people open and willing to listen to LDS gospel and the dangers posed by angry, anti-Mormon, anti-religious, or mentally unbalanced individuals (see Condie 1994:14, Wilson Archives and Cope 2003:13, Wilson Archives), missionaries may engage in spiritual tracting. Spiritual tracting is typically a proactive process, where missionaries actively set out to identify willing people to talk to. This can involve general prayer or more direct requests, such as praying over a map of their assigned area. Julia Condie remembers a story her fiancé told her about his experience with spiritual tracting:

When Mike was on his mission, he and his companion decided to start using the spiritual tracting method. They would pray in the morning that they would find willing investigators and would then look at a map and the Holy Ghost would give them a good feeling about some of the street names.

They did this one morning after a dry spell (no investigators), and that day, on the street they had prayed about, they gave four discussions and eventually baptized one of these people. (1994:13, Wilson Archives)

During fast and testimony meeting, one of the sister missionaries in the Burlington First Ward testified to how important this process is for her: "As a missionary, we pray all the time to know where to go. 'Where should I go today, where do you want me to be?' I've had hundreds of times where I've been in the right place at the right time. Hundreds of times."

Not all missionaries readily accept spiritual tracting as a viable method for their work, however—at least not until they see it work. Merrill Long wrote down the story of his experience as a missionary, a story he shared during his homecoming talks and that he plans to continue sharing, despite being ambiguous about how to interpret it. "This story means a lot to me," he explains. "I don't know if we were guided to this house because he prayed or not, and since there is no way to ever find out, I just like to think that his prayer was answered and that we were part of a big plan."

> I was in Australia on my mission, and I was on splits with a guy. He wanted to pray to find out which street we should tract, but I'm not a big believer in that sort of thing. But we prayed anyway, and he said he felt good about a certain street, and he pointed to it on the map.
>
> We walked to the street, and it was an industrial area with a bunch of warehouses and factories. As we walked down it, there was either one or two houses (I can't remember) tucked away behind some trees. If there was more than one house, only one person was home. His name was Gavin O'Reilly, and he invited us in.
>
> It was a dirty house, music blaring, nothing to sit on but a case of beer on the floor. We taught him the discussions and he came to church. He was very interested and very sincere.
>
> He eventually told us that two or three days before we came, he prayed and told God he wanted to change his life but did not know how. He believed that we were sent because of his prayer.
>
> And since he had very strong faith, and because we also prayed, I think it is a possibility. I don't know, but I do know that this is a true story because it happened to me. (1995:15, Wilson Archives)

While spiritual tracting is not uncommon, missionaries speak more often of simply keeping themselves spiritually prepared and open to the Spirit, attentive to any promptings they may receive while knocking on doors. Stories of these unsolicited prompts are the most common type of personal revelation narrative among missionaries and are recognizable as a distinct tale type with a common constellation of motifs.[38]

Tale Type: Guided to Investigators

1. *Tracting*: A pair of missionaries are out tracting.
2. *Reason Not to Stop*: Often, the missionaries are tired and dejected from a long day of having made no contacts. Other times they are wary of a particular street, home, or person.
3. *Revelation: Knock on This Door*: Just as they are about to call it a day or walk on past, one of the missionaries receives a prompting to approach a particular house or person.
4. *Resistance*: Either the missionary receiving the revelation, or his companion, resists. Typically, they end up resolving to follow the prompting.
5. *Investigator Found*: Following the Spirit, they find someone eager to hear the gospel.
6. *Conversion*: The story's climax and fulfillment come with the investigator's conversion to the church and ultimate baptism.
7. *Optional Motif: Superlative Ending*: Newly baptized member goes on to be a leader in the church, get sealed in the temple, and have a large family.

Ken Mullen was a greenhorn missionary,[39] only one week into his mission, when he received a prompting to talk to a rough-looking guy in Argentina. Ken squashed the feeling but ended up talking to him all the same, ultimately baptizing him and ten members of his family (for complete narrative, see chapter 4). In another story, a missionary is prompted on two separate occasions:

> One day, Carl and his companion were walking down the street and saw a barbershop. Craig hadn't planned on it, but he felt that they should go inside.
> They went in and got their hair cut from a lady named Fannie.
> A few days later, Carl had a feeling they should go visit her, and they fast became friends. She took the discussions, and she and her family of four, plus two others in her family, were baptized because of her. (Condie 1994:15, Wilson Archives)

The climax of conversion is praiseworthy not only for the person baptized but for the elders who succeeded in their mission. The stories that continue to be told all share this conversion moment, as well as many of the additional superlative ending motifs that signal an LDS "happily ever after" (see chapter 4). However, for missionaries currently in the field, their work is in progress; so, too, are their stories. One evening, missionaries from the Burlington First Ward and the Burlington Second Branch (the Spanish branch) had been tracting together and sat down to talk, along with church member Matt Larson, who had gone out on splits with them. Elder Aaron Chavez, from the Spanish branch, remarked that personal revelation is common to missionaries:

> Sometimes, while doing missionary work you have a lot of those experiences, and, like for example, me and my companion, a couple of days ago, weeks probably, we were knocking doors in this neighborhood, and I remember, I saw these trailers, saw these trailers.
>
> Since I was there, since the first day I got there, I just had this feeling I should just go knock those doors. But we never had time, or, "Ah, let's do it another day."
>
> But I remember that day, we had a little bit of extra time, and that knock came again, that feeling. So, my companion, he was saying, he was like, "Ah, let's go for lunch."
>
> I'm like, "Aw, c'mon. Let's go, just knock these doors" [*laughter*].
>
> So, "OK" [*laughter*].
>
> So, we go there and we find this person. We knock the first door, no one's home. We knock the second door, they're not really interested. OK. We knock the third door, and we find this lady, and she always had a question: "Why those Mormon missionaries never come talk to me?" So we was talking with her and she told us that. So I was like, "Wow."
>
> It's so important to just follow those promptings, those feelings that you have. You do them.
>
> Because she was from Chile. And since Chile, she always saw those missionaries but, she always wanted to talk to them but just missionaries never went to her house.
>
> So, we were happy that we found her and she's now . . . we're teaching her. She's learning more about the Mormon Church. And she really likes it. So.
>
> So I'm sure almost every day, well, probably not every day, but at least once a week, a missionary can experience those kind of . . . experiences.

While the narrative tradition is dominated by stories from young men's missions, one does not need to be young, male, or on a formal mission to have a "missionary moment" and receive guidance from the Holy Ghost to spread the gospel. The task of mission work falls to all active members of the church. Priesthood meetings in the Burlington First Ward often begin with a request for men to share any recent missionary moments. Many of those moments are small, mundane experiences that nonetheless encourage others to persevere in the work of the Lord. Occasionally, however, the experiences involve personal revelation. Craig Bailey recounts the time he was prompted to talk to his coworker about his faith (see chapter 2 for complete narrative). Keith Stanley recounts his experience of inexplicably changing his work route and returning to the warehouse, where he runs into a woman who had been taking discussions with one of the missionaries. She calls him outside and asks him a question about the church. When he suggests this may have been coincidence, Bishop Michael Doyle stands and reminds the brethren that there are no coincidences. And Steve Anderson offers an experience that was "small" but nonetheless important to him. He was playing a gig in South Carolina and was hungry afterwards.

"I had had some burgers," he says, "but they weren't satisfying."

He drove around, but the only place he could find that was open was a Chinese restaurant in a strip mall. Inside, it was deserted except for three Chinese men working. Steve noticed a small temple with a statue of Buddha set into the wall above the counter. Despite this symbol of religious identity, Steve felt a prompting to go get a pass-along card from the car.[40] "I rarely give these out," he says, noting that he prefers to talk to people directly, "but I felt the Holy Spirit prompting me to go get this. So I did."

Steve chatted with the men, first about Buddha and then about his own beliefs. He then gave them the card. "I feel like I was led there that night," he says, before wrapping up his story with a reminder to his fellow brethren to be on the lookout for chances to spread the word of God.

While church members expect to receive revelation if they are living righteously, nonmembers can also receive revelation during missionary work. In fact, this is the fervent hope of missionaries: that the people they meet will have been prepared for their arrival through the power of the Holy Ghost (as opposed to the *gift* of the Holy Ghost; see chapter 1).

One night a woman dreams she is sitting on her porch shelling peas when two young men approach with important information for her and her family. Less than a week later, the dream is fulfilled: the men are Mormon missionaries, the important information is the LDS gospel (see chapter 1 for the complete narrative). John Foss dreams of two men in dark suits: dark jackets and white shirts. He doesn't know who they are or what they want, but he knows he is supposed to follow them. Later that week, two Mormon missionaries arrive on his doorstep (see chapter 4 for the complete narrative). Elder Kenny Cox heard a similar story from some fellow missionaries:

> I heard one, just some story that someone was telling us in my last area in Raleigh, that, I don't know if it was to them or, you know, they heard, they heard, they heard, but . . .
>   This guy had a dream that two guys in suits would knock on his door and that they would give him a book that would have fifteen books in it and that this book would be the best book that he ever read, it would save his life.

The Book of Mormon has fifteen books in it.

It was years later and eventually these two guys in suits showed up and gave him this book, and they talked about it and how they knew it was true. And he asked them, like, "How many books are in it?"

And they're thinking, one, two, three . . . they said "Fifteen."

And he said, "All right." And he believed it right then.

Such stories reach back to the beginning of the church, before the missionary structure was formalized. Portia Pyle recounts the story of how her great-great-grandfather Isaac Newton Goodale came to the church.

When he (Isaac Newton Goodale) was fifteen years old, his folks moved to the Michigan wilderness near Lapier, Michigan. When twenty-four years of age, he had a marvelous experience which changed his life.

He had gone to bed and was awakened by a bright light, and two men walked toward him with an open book. He was so frightened that he pulled the bedclothes over his head until he regained his composure. When he uncovered his head, the room was dark again.

The next day as he was coming in from the field, one of his brothers met him and told him that two Mormon missionaries were in the house and to come hear the things they were telling them.

As Isaac came into the house, the missionaries arose and came toward him with an open book. Isaac recognized them as the men he had seen the night before.

His family was very much against his joining the Church, and connections were more or less broken from the time he did join.

He was called on several missions by the Prophet Joseph Smith and at one time lived with him for several months. There was never any doubt in his mind as to the truthfulness of the gospel and that Joseph Smith was a prophet of God.

He later assisted in the building of the Nauvoo Temple and was near Nauvoo when the Prophet and Hyrum Smith were killed. He arrived in the Salt Lake Valley in September, 1847, just two months after the first Saints had come to the Valley.[41]

Again, these experiences are so similar as to generate a body of narratives recognizable as a distinct tale type.[42] They serve as a natural corollary to the experiences of missionaries led to willing converts; the roles and perspectives are simply reversed.

Tale Type: Dream of Coming Missionaries

1. *Dream of Two Men in Black Pants, White Shirts*: A nonmember dreams of two men in black pants and white shirts who come bearing something important, valuable, or wonderful.

2. *Two Men Arrive*: Usually within the week, the dream is fulfilled. Two men arrive fitting the description of the men in the dream. The important information is news of the Mormon Church.

3. *Conversion*: The power of the revelation, coupled with the power of the gospel, helps convince the person to join the church.

Occasionally, God guides both the missionaries and the nonmembers at one and the same time, a divine convergence that seems destined to result in conversion. During sacrament meeting one Sunday, Robert Foster shared a powerful experience that occurred while he was a missionary in Paraguay, a story he shared again at home where he could elaborate in ways not possible with the time constraints of sacrament meeting:

I was a missionary there and I was actually right there in the center of Asunción, the city.[43]

And, we had, as missionaries, tried to get a lot of the . . .

Because the Paraguayan church is still very young, and ten years ago it was even younger. And when I say young, I mean the people there were actually very young as well. It's kind of hard to try and help people change their way of life when they've reached a certain point in age sometimes.

And, we had a single . . . every Monday night we would get together with a group from our ward. And most of them were single adults and we'd have a theme. You know, "This Monday, we're going to do faith." And everybody would bring a scripture or a story or something related to faith and share that.

And we decided to go along with this same group and get them to talk to their friends and neighbors about sharing the gospel.

And I just didn't feel comfortable. So we prayed about it, my companion and I. And we felt inspiration that a certain family, the Moreno family, we should talk to them about sharing the gospel.

So we went to their house the next night—we met Monday night, had our thing, the next night was a Tuesday night, and we went to their house. And we talked to them about sharing the gospel. And we prayed with them and it was kind of weird.

I'm going into a lot more detail than I did in the talk.[44] I hope that's OK.

It was kind of a weird, unsettling moment because we were thinking, you know, three months from now, four months from now, you guys are going to have somebody you want to share the gospel with, and we'll teach you the first discussion in your home. This was basically about God, Jesus Christ, and the Book of Mormon. And we just didn't feel right about that date, so we talked more, then we finally prayed about it. A family member, all of them actually, agreed that two weeks from that day they would have somebody ready. And that's a pretty big step, so [*claps hands*], "Well, we all feel right about it, so we're going to go ahead and do it."

A week had passed since that point and we went back to see them. "How's it going guys?"

And they were very nervous. "We're not ready, we don't even know who to talk to or what to talk about."

And I said, "Well, obviously, we all felt good about this one date. So we need our Heavenly Father's[45] help, we need God's help; we cannot do this by ourselves. And if he wants us to keep our commitment, then he's going to help us."

So we wrote down everybody's name that they knew, and we had a list in front of us and prayed. We prayed specifically that they would know who to talk to and that if these people were ready, that they'd be, you know, one last nail in the coffin, something to drive it home, that they're already ready to hear the gospel. "We need your help to make them especially ready for us to be able to share it with them. Because we're not that confident [*laugh*]. We need help."

And, we closed the prayer with a special blessing.

And then that following Sunday, one of the Moreno sisters came up and told us the story.

That her friend Sylvia was talking to her at work and had had a dream. And in the dream she saw two men wearing white shirts and dark pants, and they gave her a golden book. And she took the book and it made her feel very good inside. And she gave it to her husband and he read the book as well.

Some other stuff I didn't share in the talk, in her dream also . . .

She left the men in there, that had the shirts on, with the book, and started walking and saw her family on the side of the road. They were kind of walking down this dirt road. And her family started throwing rocks at her and her husband. And she took the book to shield her face from the rocks and she wasn't hit by any more of the rocks. And she kept walking along her way until eventually her family followed behind.

So we felt these were the people we need to talk to. So we invited them to talk to . . . or they invited them to talk to us about the Book of Mormon. We shared the first discussion with them and gave them the Book of Mormon.

By this time, Sylvia was just in tears. Had shared the dream with her husband and he was in complete awe and amazement at what had happened. And we decided to pray right then and there.

"Look, you've already had some kind of sign. And I'm not a big person on signs but you've had the sign. And we want to read a little bit with you."

So we read a little bit out of the Book of Mormon with them. And we read the last chapter in the Book of Mormon, or the second to last chapter, which, the last guy to write in it actually says, "These are true events.

This is true scripture. And if you want to know if it's true, just pray about it and you'll know."

And so we prayed about it.

And right then, she received a witness from Heavenly Father that was true.

So, prophecy.

Of course later on, I was transferred to another area and heard she was getting a lot of flak from her family. I hadn't ever, you know, I left the mission before I could find out if the rest—where her family followed behind—came to pass, but I feel confident that it did.

Inspiration, I guess that's the best way to summarize each one of those; we felt inspired to go and talk to this particular family and pray with them.

We received revelation that somebody was ready. They received revelation to be ready. And they received revelation in answer to their prayer.

Prophecy, the dream itself. I guess that's the best way for me to break those down.

A year later, in August 2007, people in wards across the country were sharing a story of an experience from the late 1800s that had been reprinted in the *New Testament Gospel Doctrine Teacher's Manual* used in Sunday school. Shawn Tucker heard the story twice, in two separate wards that month:

While living with the Heywood family in Salt Lake City during the late 1800s, John Morgan dreamed one night that he was traveling down a road in Georgia. He recognized the road because he had used it often as a soldier in the United States Civil War. He came to a fork in the road and saw Brigham Young standing there. Although the right fork led to the next town, President Young told him to take the left fork.

Mr. Morgan, who was not a member of the Church at the time, told Sister Heywood about his dream and asked what she thought of it. She told him she believed he would join the Church and serve a mission in the southern states, and that one day he would find himself on the road he had seen in his dream. When that happened, he should remember Brigham Young's counsel and take the left fork.

Many years later, after John Morgan had been baptized and called as a missionary to the southern states, he came to the fork in the road that he had seen in his dream. He remembered the counsel to take the left fork, so he did. An hour later, he found himself at the edge of Heywood Valley—a beautiful place with the same name as the family with whom he had been staying when he had the dream years earlier.

As he traveled throughout the valley preaching, he found that the people were well prepared to hear the gospel. After hearing him teach, several families mentioned that a stranger had come through the valley ten days before, asking permission to mark their Bibles. The stranger had told them that another messenger would come and explain the marked passages to them. John Morgan had explained these marked passages as he taught the gospel. During the following weeks, Elder Morgan taught and baptized all but three of the twenty-three families in the valley.[46]

Motif: Distinctive Appearances and the Color White

These revelations include a number of recurring motifs. One is the clothing of the missionaries. Like the hair and height of future spouses, some distinguishing trait is found in these visions and dreams so that people recognize fulfillment of their dream when it happens. For stories of coming missionaries, the universal LDS missionary uniform—white shirt and black pants—serves as that distinguishing trait. Clothing also helps identify the divine—whether God, angels, deceased prophets, or one of the Three Nephites. In these cases, white robes reveal their holy nature. The color white generally indicates good and the divine; black, evil and Satan (as noted earlier).

For deceased prophets, beards specific to their historical period may help determine their identity, as in the dream shared by Peter Zaine during a fast and testimony meeting in Florida in 2007, in which he saw a man dressed in white with a distinctive long beard, cut straight across at the end.[47] The man bore two books, saying, "These books are very good." Upon waking, Zaine believed the books to be the Bible and the Book of Mormon. He began reading the Old Testament, followed by the New Testament. He then read the Book of Mormon followed by the Doctrine and Covenants and the Pearl of Great Price. Still hungry for more, he looked on the shelves and found a book by Joseph Fielding Smith. The moment he saw Smith's portrait, he recognized the man from his dream. "This is when I knew it was time to get baptized," he said, ending his talk with a testimony about the power of revelation.

While most of these dreams involve two missionaries, some, like Peter Zaine's experience, involve past church presidents who appear to guide a person to the LDS Church. In another story, for example, an investigator in Guatemala prays about the truth of the church and finally receives a revelatory dream where he is faced with three paths. His story begins with the ardent attempts of two missionaries to talk to him, but he is always working in the field when they come to his home. Finally, he instructs his wife to have them come back at a time when he can see them:

The missionaries fixed a visit for the next day at seven p.m. at which time they presented Stephen and part of his family the first lesson.

Stephen enjoyed it very much, but the rest of his family had different feelings and didn't want the missionaries to return. But Stephen desired more information about this new church and invited the missionaries to come back.

After the fourth lesson Stephen began to pray about the truthfulness of the church, but he received no answer. He prayed again, but still received no response. It was not until after his fourth sincere prayer that he went to bed and received the following vision.

He saw himself walking along a road with beautiful surroundings. After a short walk, he came upon a crossroads that had three alternative routes. There was a man at each route. The first addressed Stephen by name and said, "Come with me." But a feeling within Stephen told him it wasn't right. A second man issued the same invitation, but a similar feeling was aroused and Stephen chose not to follow him.

In front of the third path stood a tall white haired man who issued the same invitation of "Come, follow me" to Stephen. The man introduced himself as David O. McKay, president of the Church of Jesus Christ. He told Stephen that he was a prophet and that the Lord was pleased with him for the study and dedication for learning about his church. They walked together and President McKay explained many wonderful things and assured Stephen that the Church was correct and that he was walking in the truth.

The next day, Stephen explained to the two missionaries about the vision he had had and related the name of the man who professed to be the president of the Church. This took the missionaries by surprise as they had not mentioned the name of President McKay to him.

One of the missionaries then took four pictures from his briefcase: one of President McKay and three of past presidents of the Church. He placed these pictures side by side on the table in front of Stephen and said, "Which is the man that appeared in your dream?"

Immediately Stephen pointed out President McKay saying, "This is the man. This is the prophet of God."[48]

Motif: Book of Mormon

The other dominant motif in these narratives is the Book of Mormon. Like the young men in white shirts and black pants or the old men in white robes, the Book of Mormon is described with traits that suggest, but do not dictate, its identity. The Book of Mormon may be described simply as a black book. In other cases, the exact number of books within the Book of Mormon is included, or the book is described as "golden," details ambiguous to the uninitiated but proof of its true identity once the missionaries arrive to explain that the Book of Mormon was transcribed from golden plates.

The Book of Mormon also appears in the more common experiences Latter-day Saints have of searching for an answer to a spiritual dilemma and being guided to a particular passage in scripture, whether the Book of Mormon or the Bible (see later in this chapter). It also serves as a protective talisman, protecting one man from a bullet in battle, a motif of its own that is common in folk narrative (see chapter 4).

Hope and Anxiety

Revelations predicting the arrival of missionaries and confirming the truth of the church help to soften the hearts of nonmembers in order to help them choose to join the LDS Church. Such revelations are clearly blessings to these families and their offspring, and the narratives of these conversion experiences serve as religious origin stories for families.

These experiences are also blessings to the missionaries in the field, whose arduous work is made a bit easier when God helps pave the way. Coupled with the revelations that missionaries themselves receive, these narratives provide comfort to the missionaries, providing hope that despite those long days tracting, facing unfamiliar and unfriendly faces, they will find people ready, willing, and prepared to hear and accept the gospel of the LDS Church.

There is, however, a psychological tension present in these stories of missionary work. Despite God's protection, the missionary field in the narrative tradition is typically depicted as a threatening, dangerous place. The non-Mormon public appear in one of three roles: (1) prepared and ready, (2) stubborn but malleable, or (3) angry and dangerous. The ideal person to encounter in the field is one who is open and willing to listen. Even better are people who have been prepared for the message, whether through a dream, a vision, or a visit by someone—human or divine. The worst are those people who are not merely closed to the message but take an aggressive stance against both the message and the messenger. The two poles—prepared versus dangerous—dominate the narrative tradition. While some stories focus on one or the other, many stories embody both types. The Morenos encounter a woman ready and willing but who dreams that her family stones her for her choice. Stephen Lister is invigorated by the church while his family stands opposed. In a fast and testimony meeting, an investigator of the church shared her story of being drawn to the church despite her mother's disapproval (see chapter 1). Such familial opposition is common in LDS conversion narratives.

Ideally, God will help missionaries distinguish between the three types of non-Mormons they might encounter, encouraging discussions with the prepared and the stubborn but malleable, and warning against the violent and close minded. That is the promise of personal revelation. But the fact remains that the very same narratives that confirm God's promise often contain images of darkness and violence. Further, if the number of conversions from tracting is any indication, the narrative tradition is decidedly optimistic.[49] Although church leaders and publications continue to encourage a focus on conversion, some members have pointed out during Sunday school and in informal conversation that the benefit of the missionary experience can be as much about the spiritual growth and confirmation of the missionary as it is about the conversion of new members.[50] The desire for faith-promoting stories belies the realities of the mission experience.

The result is that narrative performances have the power to both reduce and increase anxiety among missionaries. Stories of protection provide reassurance that God will protect. But stories that begin with the assumption that missionary work is hard and willing converts rare enough to warrant narration can tap into deep-seated, regularly confirmed anxieties. This paradoxical power is heightened by the most common audience for these narratives: fellow missionaries. Stories shared among church members may be interpreted as one more faith-promoting story, but stories shared among missionaries operate on a much more personal level, one rooted in their current daily lives. At the MTC, where such stories are shared widely, young men and women may worry that they have received personal revelation only rarely, and certainly not consistently enough to protect them on a daily basis. In the field, where these stories also thrive, many young men and women confirm this fear. While the narrative traditions suggest they will be guided every step of the way, they quickly realize that God encourages faith, not dependency, and that they must face trials in life as well as blessings.

Guidance in Speaking

The LDS Church calls its members to speak regularly—during sacrament meetings, fast and testimony meetings, Sunday school, priesthood and Relief Society meetings, and family home evenings. When speaking as leaders, people often view the revelations they receive as part of their calling. Yet when speaking as teachers and missionaries—who blur the lines between formal callings and regularly adopted roles in the church—or as faithful members, friends, or family, people typically consider the divine guidance they receive as *personal* revelation.

With such a high expectation for frequent public and semiprivate religious discourse, it is no wonder that the common fear of public speaking is reflected in the prayers people offer and the revelations they receive. This fear is not simply a personal concern about being on display in front of large groups. In fact, many speaking contexts are among groups as small as three, as when a pair of

missionaries meets with an investigator to discuss the church. Far more pervasive is the concern of knowing the right thing to say.

Many people share experiences where they temporarily received the Gift
of the Holy Ghost of Teaching, Wisdom, and Knowledge.[51] Church members
describe getting up in front of the congregation or a Sunday school class not
sure what they are going to say and then finding that the Holy Ghost takes over
and guides them. Jean Chandler teaches the seminary class to the Burlington
First Ward high school students. At the crack of dawn five days a week, she must
lead these young men and women in spiritual education and exploration. The
challenge is daunting:

> I teach seminary every day. So I'm up every morning, praying, "Oh please,
> oh please, oh please" [*laugh*]. It's probably one of the most rewarding call-
> ings that I've ever had. Difficult, yes. But extremely rewarding. Because
> I'm constantly praying for the Spirit. Constantly asking for direction.
> Constantly asking for personal revelation about that lesson. How should
> I teach it? How can I approach these teenagers with this particular view?
> How do I take something that happened in 1820 and make it important
> in their life now? How can I revolve and evolve that, you know, revelation
> from the Doctrine and Covenants, which is what we're studying this year,
> into today.
>
> There are mornings when I'm on my way to seminary after preparing
> that lesson for two hours the night before and thinking, "I don't know
> how I'm going to do that."
>
> And yet, we have a prayer, we have a song, and the lesson will start.
> How it happens? It happens. Things will just come out of my mouth.
> Things will start to just . . . happen.
>
> And it's not me. I didn't think that, I didn't read that. I'm able to relate
> it to the kids. They're suddenly awake and responding and it was totally
> not what I had prepared.
>
> And those are mornings when I sit back and go, "Whoa. Thanks."

During Gospel Principles class, Elder Ballantyne shared a story from the first
few weeks of his mission, before he had become comfortable leading discussions with people about the LDS Church. To his surprise, however, he found
himself speaking at great length about the church, unaware both of what he had
said and how long he had been speaking (see chapter 2 for complete narrative).
When Elder Ballantyne had finished, Paul Clayson spoke up. "This is meant as
no disrespect to your knowledge, but you probably didn't have the wisdom to
say those things. The Spirit allowed you to say the right things to him."

Like the paradox of missionary stories of spiritual tracting, such stories can
mislead members into believing they can rely on the Holy Ghost entirely, putting

forth no effort of their own. So leaders and fellow members remind each other that they must take the time to prepare their church talks, regularly quoting D&C 9:8: "But, behold, I say unto you, that you must study it out in your mind; then you must ask me if it be right, and if it is right I will cause that your bosom shall burn within you; therefore, you shall feel that it is right." The Holy Ghost is a guide, not a substitute for human thought, preparation, agency, and action.

Experiences where the Holy Ghost takes over, when the person is not cognizant of what they are saying or what they have said, are clear examples of the Gift of the Holy Ghost of Teaching, Wisdom, and Knowledge. Such stories require faith but no agency. As direct intervention, such experiences fall outside or are on the margins of vernacular definitions of personal revelation (see chapter 1). Instances when people are guided in their teaching or public speaking that include a prompt, however—whether to share a particular story, cite a particular scripture, or get up and speak in the first place—fit firmly within the narrative tradition of personal revelation.[52]

Struggling with a Primary class that rarely paid attention, Wayne Chandler was prompted to share a story about his son. The class immediately grew quiet, hanging on every word. When the story was over, the children asked questions that were both insightful and edifying. Dave Gammon was struggling with how to reach out to members in his ward. After frequent prayer, a particular scripture jumped out at him. Later, during an Institute class, Dave was inspired to share the passage with a fellow classmate. "And when I shared it to her, it was like this veil or this darkness over her mind or this mist suddenly cleared" (see chapter 2).

Elder Richard Rowe and Elder Joshua Hoffman were prompted simultaneously to respond to the concerns of an investigator with whom they were working:

> A couple of weeks ago I was with Elder Hoffman and we were doing a media referral. She had called into Salt Lake and ordered a "Joy to the World" DVD. So we went out there with a member to deliver it.
>
> And, we delivered it to her, we're talking to her for a minute and she made a couple of comments that were a little different. She said, like, she didn't think God loved her, that God had a plan for her.
>
> And you know, a great part of missionary work is listening to the people and figuring out what they need. And, you know, at that time, when she had made those comments, we were sitting on her couch talking with her and, without even talking to each other, Elder Hoffman or I, you know, we both reached in and grabbed the plan of salvation pamphlet, which you know talks about God's plan for each and every one of us, and kind of the meaning of life.

So, it was a kind of shared personal revelation I guess that as soon as we heard that, we were like, "Oh, we know exactly what she needs." I guess it wasn't even that we know, it was the Spirit knowing. But, you know, we shared that with her, and she was in tears halfway through. I know she enjoyed it. It was a really powerful experience.

People are prompted to say just the thing that the audience needs to hear. It may be a story or a kind word. It may also be a question. Kenny Mullen Jr. was explaining the importance of studying scripture when he was reminded of the following experience:

I learned a lot about why we do the daily study as missionaries. Because then, it's my firm belief that if we do that, we are worthy of the Lord's revelation during the teaching situation. We're worthy of receiving that. It's here, you've read it, you've studied it.

It happened with the last girl that was baptized before I left Panama. She felt . . . we asked her what she felt about baptism and she said, "I don't know." She said, "I haven't received my answer."

And I received . . . the thought came to my mind, the inspiration to ask her what kind of answer she was waiting on. And I looked at her and I said, "Well, what do you think you need to happen for you to know? What kind of answer are you looking for?" And then she said, she just looked at me with a blank look and was like, "I don't know."

And it occurred to me we never really taught that to her. Like, you will receive an answer, but a lot of times people need to know what that's like, what it can be like.

And so in Galatians chapter five, verses twenty-two and twenty-three, it talks about the fruits of the spirit. What happens when the spirit touches you.

Kenny discusses some of the feelings the Holy Spirit can inspire, moving back and forth between English and Spanish. His parents joke that he knows the scriptures better in Spanish than English:

But I remember . . . she started . . . I said, just to give you an idea what the Spirit's like. You're waiting on an answer from the Spirit. I said, "God's not going to take the roof off your house and look at you in the eyes and go, 'This is what you need to do.'" I mean, I said that probably—it *could* happen—but probably not.

And I remember she was reading that scripture out loud and then she stopped reading about halfway through it. And I looked at my companion and I just thought she was stumbling over it. And I kept looking at my scriptures, reading along, and I look over, and she was completely in tears. Completely in tears. And I just kind of look at my companion and like, "Is that bad? Or is that good?" [*Ken laughs.*] And then, she looked up and she was like, "I want to get baptized on Saturday. I just received my answer."

That's all she needed. She needed to know what the Spirit felt like. And she felt right there in that moment, she said, "I feel what this is saying and I feel all of them at the same time," and she got baptized that Saturday.

And so, I was prompted to just share scripture with her. I didn't think that was going to happen. I thought I was just going to give her an idea, and we were going to be like, "All right. Something to think about. Look for an answer this week and we'll be back later this week."

And little did I know.

And so . . . I thought I was going to leave. It was my last weekend there. I thought I was going to leave, and she would be baptized later or not at all, I don't know. That was one incident. Things like that happened to me a lot.

Knowing what to ask can be even more useful than knowing what to say, particularly in counseling others. In this way, a person need not feel their agency or stewardship has been stripped away. Offering advice can seem patronizing or worse, a violation of one's stewardship (see chapter 1). Offering a question that inspires self-reflection, on the other hand, can be empowering.

Knowing what to say to others is a benefit ultimately directed outward. Yet people often seek guidance from God for themselves. The Holy Ghost may provide answers by prompting a particular action that resolves their dilemma. The Holy Ghost may also provide answers somewhat more indirectly by directing a person to a particular passage in scripture. This experience is so common that people often slip it into conversation rather than narrating it as a full-fledged spiritual experience. An experience early in Paul Clayson's life, however, stands out to him as a particularly important moment for him:

Oftentimes our minds will be prompted: go to a certain scripture. Open up to it and see what that has to say for you.

When I was a very young man I was really troubled about some things and just didn't know what direction to follow. And I kept thinking about them. And one day I just sat down and I said, "I wonder if I can find the answer in the scripture."

And I opened up into the scriptures and I just kind of flipped open, not knowing where to go, and it opened up to section ten verse five of the Doctrine and Covenants. And it said, "Pray always, that you may come off conqueror; yea, that you may conquer Satan and the servants of Satan who uphold his work."

And it just hit me so powerfully. That was precisely what I needed to do more often. Instead of thinking I knew the answers, I needed to pray more often.

I mean these kinds of things happen.

The message derived from such revelation is clear: the answers are already at your fingertips. Regular reading of scriptures can be a constant source of guidance, comfort, and inspiration. Sometimes people just need to be reminded of how useful, not just how sacred, their scriptures are.

Temple Work and Genealogy

In the center of the narrative tradition of personal revelation is the Holy Ghost. As the messenger for God, the Holy Ghost is the most common conveyer of divine communication of many types, revelation included. However, angels may prompt people in ways typical of the Holy Ghost: warning them of danger, confirming their choice of a spouse, and providing comfort in times of stress, sadness, or fear.[53] BYU student Kerril Sue Rollins collected eighty-five narratives of experiences with the spirit world, three-quarters of which involve a deceased relative acting as a guardian angel returning to Earth to help his or her living relatives (1977, Fife Archives). These stories mirror stories involving the Holy Ghost, though the connection to the divine is far more personal.

One-quarter of the stories Rollins collected, however, involve requests by the dead for help from the living: typically to have their temple work done for them by providing proxy baptisms, which allow people to be baptized in the church even after they have died. Temple work done on behalf of the dead is specifically significant for deceased relatives, since they are the ones who will benefit most directly from such work.

Sue Patterson retells a memorate her young women's president shared while teaching a lesson on temple work. Sue noted that her teacher, Naomi, and all the young women present were sitting in a circle "and the Spirit was very strong."

> Naomi was planning on attending the Toronto temple to do family files with her husband.
>
> In order to get to the temple by the ten o'clock session, she had to leave her home in Michigan at five a.m. She had a really rough night the previous night, and when the alarm went off in the morning to go to the temple, she decided to turn it off and go back to bed because she was too tired.
>
> When she went back to bed, she had a dream that there was a group of men and women dressed in white that were in a building. They said to themselves, "Well, I guess nobody is coming to do our work," then proceeded to file out of the building with very sad looks on their face.
>
> Naomi immediately jumped out of bed and told about the dream that she had just had. She realized that her ancestors were waiting at the temple for her to do their work, so that they could receive the ordinances needed to enter into the kingdom with their Father. She and her husband got out of bed and went to the temple that day to do the names that they had on family file.

This dream made her realize how important it is to do temple work and how many ancestors who have passed on into the Spirit world rely on us to do the work necessary for them to enter into heaven. (Lietz 2000:12–3, Wilson Archives)

In many of these dreams, deceased ancestors appear but the Holy Ghost remains the messenger, inspiring the dream itself. In other revelations, the ancestor is the messenger. A woman dreams of ironing her temple garments while her deceased father looks on. He finally tells her she needs to go to the temple one more time. In her dream, she responds saying she's already been married twice, once civilly and a second time in the temple, so surely she does not need to go again. However, when she wakes, she reflects back on the dream and realizes he wasn't asking her to go to the temple to be married again, but to do his temple work, work she had planned to do but that circumstances had prevented (Rollins 1977:34–7, Fife Archives). A woman receives a similar request from her father in another story so personal and private she rarely shares it with others:

One early morning in January of 1970 I received a visitation from the spirit world.

I was lying in bed, probably more asleep than awake, yet I believe this experience. There at the foot of my bed was my father, who had been dead for over six years.

He didn't speak to me, but I heard him in some way communicate the message he had to tell me. He told me he was ready to have his temple work done for him, and he wanted me to do it for him.

He left as quickly as he had come, and I lay quietly in bed for a while thinking before I finally slept again. (Rollins 1977:38, Fife Archives)

As thanks for doing their work, the deceased may act as guardian angels for the living. This is particularly evident when help is needed while a person is in the temple performing sacred rites. A common narrative type involves a person in the process of performing temple work when they receive revelation to protect them and their family.

One day Natalie was in the temple doing endowments for the dead. She was feeling anxious for some reason unknown to her. Normally, she did two or three sessions at a sitting.

During the session, she heard her little boy calling out to her. She turned but he was nowhere to be found.

Natalie, feeling something to be amiss, left the session early and called home to the babysitter. The line was busy. She raced home to find the babysitter talking on the phone. She cried, "Where is the baby?"

Turning to the empty crib, the babysitter exclaimed, "He was in his crib a minute ago."

As if Natalie had seen it in her mind, she raced to the backyard where the gate to the pool lay open. She raced to the water to see her son in the bottom of the pool. She dove in and brought him to the edge. There, she was able to start him breathing again.

The doctor said, "If the infant would have been left in the water a minute longer, it would have been lucky to survive."[54]

In similar legends, the person bearing the warning is the person who is having temple work done on his or her behalf. A story collected by LaRae Parker describes "a lady who saved a boy from drowning. The lady had already died but the boy's parents were doing the same lady's temple work that day, and she saved their son" (1971, 4, 22, Wilson Archives; see also Toelken 1991:194–5).

None of this temple work would be possible without genealogical work to identify the people needing proxy baptisms. Some people go to the temple and conduct baptisms for people who have requested such work done on behalf of their ancestors, providing a service to their religious community. Others conduct work for their own ancestors. Maintaining connections to one's ancestors is mutually beneficial, both for the living and the dead. The dead stand to gain eternal life and salvation; the living stand to be reunited with their ancestors in the afterlife as well as to receive special protection in this life.

"I believe part of that is as our ancestors pass beyond, that we are still connected," explains Pauline Clayson. "That's why genealogy is so important that we stay connected to our forefathers, and those that learned and knew before us. And those that care about us deeper than the man next door.

"Like, as far as my children are concerned, I have no doubt that their grandparents watch over them very, very carefully, guiding them, directing them, prompting them. I don't know in what way, and they've not said, but I do believe that that's the intertwining of this life and the life beyond, that keeps it very wide, so that we can benefit and help one another."

Genealogical work is not always easy, however. Despite the massive databases that the church continues to update and develop, holes in family lineages can be difficult to fill. This recurring problem has spawned repeated revelations to overcome such obstacles. A particularly common type of revelatory experience is the discovery of genealogical information that allows people to continue their work in the temple. Here again, a typical structure for these narratives can be identified as a distinct tale type.[55]

Tale Type: Genealogical Assistance

1. *Genealogical Work*: A person, usually a woman, is in the process of completing the family genealogy.
2. *Dead End*: The person eventually hits a dead end, unable to continue without a particular ancestor's name.
3. *Revelation of Missing Ancestor*: Often through a dream, the person is guided to information needed to continue the genealogical work, whether directly or by going to a particular place or person. Often this information is the name of an unknown ancestor.
4. *Fulfillment*: The person heeds the revelation and confirms the missing ancestor.
5. *Optional Motif: Additional Success*: Often, the name does not resolve just one generation but opens up the genealogical record to trace far more distant ancestors.

A woman who has been working on her genealogy for years is stuck tracing her ancestors. After years of prayer, she sees a newspaper in the yard and "is impressed to look at it." It has birth, marriage, and death information for a woman with the same name as the ancestor she had been looking for (Skaggs 1975, Wilson Archives; for complete narrative, see chapter 4). The night before a woman goes to the Salt Lake archives, she has a dream of a house in Salt Lake City that presumably she needs to visit. The next day she drives to the house despite never having been there before and finds the new tenants about to burn an old box of records left in the attic. She looks at the records and they contain information about her ancestors. The information allows her to continue her genealogy work (Healy n.d., Wilson Archives). In her journal, Martha Morris Ford writes that she was prompted to ask her bishop one more time for records that he had already told her had burned. The bishop's wife answers the door and in the process of reiterating that the records had burned, she remembers that she recently found two of the old record sheets lying in the road. The pages are the exact documents the woman needs to continue her genealogy work (Moon 1970, Wilson Archives). A woman gets stuck doing her genealogy, prays for help, and receives a dream about four-leaf clovers. After a series of seemingly random occurrences, she discovers a Bible with four-leaf clovers pressed between its pages for sale in an antique shop. She buys it and discovers that it's her great-grandfather's Bible and includes her family's genealogy (Jeppson 1981, Wilson Archives). In a story shared during a fast and testimony meeting in Santa Ana, California, in 1968, a woman talked about the importance of genealogy by recounting an experience that happened to another LDS member, Sister Connor:

Genealogy and tracing and gathering family records is a very important thing in the Mormon church. The job is one of great seriousness,
because the ordinances must be done for the dead by the living in these
latter days.

Sister Connor realized the importance of this principle, and was working on her family line but with little success. She went to the library
regularly and used all the books that were of any relevance to her line but
could find no records of anyone past two generations back.

Sister Connor prayed and fasted for help in seeking out her family and
was instructed to return to the library. When she went back, she used the
same books, but this time she was directed and led to the right information. It was as if her eyes and understanding had been newly opened.

So great was the help that Sister Connor received, and so hard did
she work, that she has one line traced all of the way back to Adam.
And a while ago, she had given up all hope of even going back three
generations.[56]

In the majority of the stories, women rather than men are engaged in genealogical work. Of the stories specifically of this tale type, the only exceptions
I have found were two stories in the Wilson Archives collected by Gardener
Brown. In the first, a library worker has been paid to conduct genealogical work.
Not insignificantly, he was hired by a woman who was working on the genealogy of her husband's family. In the second, a man dreams he is handed a piece of
paper with a name on it that turns out to be one of his wife's old friends. While
the man does the initial research, the experience most affects his wife, who is
encouraged to devote "much of the last fifteen years of her life to genealogy
work."[57] While men certainly do genealogical work, it is often not until they are
retired, at which point they join their wives, who have already been hard at work
completing the family trees of both their husbands and themselves. Because of
this trend, conducting genealogy is typically perceived as women's work.

Thematic Variation

Within these broad themes and patterns lie individual expressions and perspectives. Not everyone shares the same hopes, dreams, and fears; nor are these
hopes, dreams, and fears static over the course of a person's lifetime or over the
course of the history of the church. One approach to understanding this variation is to identify the individual in tradition, focusing on the specific constellation of interests, beliefs, values, anxieties, and fears of individual church members. A performer-centered approach to narrative can be richly rewarding (see
Cashman, Mould, and Shukla *The Individual and Tradition* 2011). However,

with cultural norms that buck against the slightest hint of self-promotion, the sharing of sacred personal revelation narratives does not comfortably accommodate the cultivation and sustained analysis of individual "star" performers (see Mould "A Backdoor Into Performance" 2011).

Eschewing individual analysis does not mean thematic analysis ends at the macro level, however. A median path is possible, one that moves between the aggregate and the individual. Variation in region and historical era might explain or illuminate some patterns, while variation in age and gender might explain or illuminate others. The first pair is infinitely more difficult to address than the second.

Region and Era

There are no doubt correlations between theme and region and theme and historical period. The data, however, do not readily permit sustained exploration of either. In terms of region, the majority of the narratives recorded in Utah and the Intermountain West were collected by students from family or fellow students at BYU. Most of the narratives recorded from *outside* the Intermountain West were collected by me in the Burlington First Ward in North Carolina among adult members of the church and young men on their missions. In between are vast areas with little representation, both within the United States and outside it. As the archives grow and fieldwork is undertaken outside of Utah and its surrounds, such analysis will become more feasible (see the afterword for some discussion of these avenues for research).

In terms of historical analysis, the data does exist to address this intersection, but such a study would demand years of careful archival analysis outside the scope of this project. Thousands of diaries and journals have been archived, though few have been indexed in a way that would alleviate a complete and careful read of each diary. While LDS pioneer journals have been analyzed by theme, few have paid specific attention to personal revelation. One exception is Susan Swetnam's study of pioneer journals of Mormons in southeast Idaho between 1860 and 1930. What becomes clear in her study is not only the relevance and prevalence of personal revelation in the past but the continuity of many of the same themes that continue to appear in the narrative tradition today. Revelation is provided to protect the Saints from physical harm, both to themselves and their children. Adult members are guided in their search for a spouse, a home, and their ancestors as they compile their genealogies. They receive guidance from angels and deceased relatives as well as the Holy Ghost. There are also interesting differences. Present in the past but uncommon today are revelations that local church leaders and missionaries received to make prophecies about blessings for their fellow Mormons and curses for their anti-Mormon neighbors. Underlying these stories is confirmation of the power of prayer and the blessings given to the faithful and righteous.

Conversely, there are themes clearly evident today that Swetnam does not mention: no stories of missionary tracting, advice on career paths, or spirit children asking to be born. Conversion must have appeared in these journals, but Swetnam makes little mention of it.

Any conclusions that I might make between theme and historical period would be tentative at best. Of the 441 stories that I examined, almost two-thirds describe experiences that occurred after 1950. One-third occurred before 1950, but the range is fairly large, spread out over 120 years beginning in 1830. In terms of when these stories where shared, however, the range is much narrower. All but 15 of the 441 stories (97 percent) were still being shared after 1950, deflecting, if not fully eradicating, criticism about assuming an ethnographic present for much of this study (see chart 9 in the appendix).

Age and Gender

Revelation is nothing if not relevant. That relevance may not always be clear until fulfillment, and the assumption persists that the guidance provided is spot on, a divine blessing not to be ignored. Young men and women concerned about missions and marriage receive revelation about missions and marriage. Engaged and married couples wonder about starting a family and receive revelations about children. Older members nearing the end of their lives begin to think about death, and again, revelation provides comfort and insight.

Revelation can also sneak up on a person. An older couple who has decided not to have more children may be surprised to receive revelation that they have more children waiting to be born. Yet while personal desire and revelation may initially be at odds, life trajectory and revelation are fairly closely synced.

Children provide the one major exception. Primary teachers and parents work with the children in the church to help them identify the Holy Ghost in their own lives. Since many children born in the church choose to be baptized at age eight, one assumes that they have received spiritual revelation about the truth of the church and that at least with respect to this belief, have felt the Spirit. However, both the narrative tradition and ethnographic data suggest that until their teenage years, most young men and women have not received personal revelation that they can clearly identify and subsequently narrate. Many members spend a lifetime honing the ability to discern the Spirit; youth can hardly be expected to master it so quickly. Instead, parents are entrusted to receive revelation on their behalf.

In performance, one pattern that emerges among the youth is the predilection for legends. This should come as no surprise. The youth are still maturing in their spiritual and temporal knowledge. They do not yet have years of experience distinguishing between a fantastic, heartfelt experience and simply a fantastic one. If one's grandmother could have a dream about an avalanche that threatened her husband, what other supernatural events might be revealed?

Even more common than underdeveloped discernment is the youthful pleasure of sharing titillating stories. Such enjoyment wanes for adults, who see the potential harm in speaking too lightly of the sacred, but boundary testing is a fundamental part of growing up, and youth are far more willing to share stories they believe to be false, that are only loosely attributed, or both (see chapter 2).

As with age, some patterns apparent in personal revelation narratives are far more common for one gender than the other, reflecting social norms within LDS culture and in many cases, US society more broadly. Throughout personal revelation narratives, gender roles are fairly conservative. Men work outside the home, women within it. Men and women both work to protect their children, though women are more often the ones nearby to save a child from a domestic accident. When they are not, it is remarkable, as in the story of the man summoned home to save his son from drowning because his wife is inattentive (see chapter 4 for complete narrative).

Traditional gender roles for married couples extend into decisions about children and careers. While both men and women receive revelations about these topics, and many couples are prompted together, women are twice as likely to be prompted about having children. The mandate within LDS doctrine and culture to have large families, coupled with the traditional gender role of the man as the main breadwinner of the household, means many women put careers outside the home on hold indefinitely. New career paths often mean moving to new cities, decisions that husband and wife make together. Accordingly, both men and women receive revelation about careers, though the focus is typically on the husband's job.

Both men and women receive revelations beyond the veil that separates the temporal world from the spiritual world. However, women typically receive revelations about the premortal existence, where unborn children remain waiting to be born, while men more often receive revelations about the afterlife of the spirit world, where angels provide insight into both the temporal and spiritual.

Doing the work of the church also follows conservative gender roles reflected both in US society and in the structure of the LDS Church more specifically. Until the beginning of the twentieth century, single women were not called on missions for the church. And not until the 1970s did young women go on missions in any substantial number. The number of young women completing missions today is still relatively low.[58] The result is that the bulk of the narratives about receiving revelation while tracting are experienced and shared by men.

If missionary work has been perceived primarily as men's work, then genealogical work is perceived primarily as women's work, trends as true in real life as in the narrative tradition. Promptings for knowing just what to say also fall more heavily to men, partly because the context for these revelations is so often in the mission field or as leaders in the church. While women hold positions of leadership among other women, only men serve as leaders over entire wards and stakes.

The one major variation from traditional gender roles is the common US stereotype of women desperate to marry and men just as desperate to hold off as long as possible. The centrality of marriage in LDS theology, as well as the strict taboo against premarital sex, weighs heavily on men and women alike. There are differences, however. While women are often proactive about marriage— praying to know whether they will marry, when, and to whom—men more often receive unsolicited revelations, helping them to recognize their future wife when they see her. Such revelations do confirm the gendered norm of men proposing to women, but they highlight both a desire for marriage and an anxiety about finding a spouse that are not always explicit in US social norms generally.

Conclusion

Analyzing the themes that emerge most frequently in the narrative tradition of personal revelation suggests how the revelatory experience functions in the lives of Latter-day Saints. The Holy Ghost warns people of present and future dangers, protecting people from very tangible threats in the world. The Holy Ghost also guides people in the decisions they face daily and throughout their lives. Major life events—marriage, children, careers—dominate the narrative tradition, despite the regularity of subtle and small inspiration provided daily. Because the term "personal revelation" is typically used to refer to the daily guidance of the Holy Ghost, as opposed to "revelation" more generally that focuses on attaining spiritual knowledge and confirmation of religious principles, the majority of the stories are grounded in temporal affairs.

And yet, the two worlds of the spiritual and temporal cannot be fully separated. While guidance to avoid a car crash or find a job is clearly focused on the temporal world, and guidance to convert is focused on the spiritual world, many of the recurring themes of personal revelation make it clear that the two worlds are impossible to disentangle. Death marks the end of temporal life and the beginning of eternal life. Finding a spouse is immensely important and rewarding in the temporal life, but it is also integral for perfection in the afterlife. Guiding missionaries to a particular door is practical help in this world but fosters spiritual salvation for all eternity. While most conversion narratives are shared as testimonies, those that involve temporal predictions in addition to spiritual knowledge blur boundaries between revelation and personal revelation. Temple work, like missionary work, is also God's work—that is, spiritual work done in the temporal world—once again blurring the line between the spiritual and the temporal.

The primary focus of personal revelation is the individual. However, because God uses his faithful servants to fulfill his promises and achieve his will, personal revelation also functions to help others. Narratives of personal revelation therefore depict not only faithful members blessed by divine protection and guidance but generous, charitable people who go out of their way to help others. Lee Mullen was prompted to buy a dress for her babysitter (see chapter 1). Kara Breit's great-great-grandfather is prompted to take six hundred dollars to the stake president, the exact amount needed to pay for stained glass windows for the new temple (1999, Wilson Archives). A young man is prompted to return home from Germany to help his family financially (Condie 1994, Wilson Archives). A fellow ward member is prompted to visit Josette Bailey, who has temporarily dropped away from the church (see chapter 1). In all, over 20 percent of the narratives involve primary aid to someone else. And of that aid, the most common beneficiary is one's children.[59]

Sometimes these acts of help are completely selfless. Other times, the benefits of personal revelation are shared. A father's prompt to take his son fishing benefits both parties by strengthening their relationship. Warnings to avoid danger often protect whole families, not just the individual receiving the prompting. The same is true for major decisions about marriage, careers, and new homes. Revelation helps people fulfill their obligations to those in their stewardships, not just themselves. Couples often receive revelation about when to have children and how many children to have. The focus in many of these revelations is trained on the would-be parents, guiding them in their family planning. In some cases, however, the unborn child takes center stage, pleading to be allowed to be born. In these cases, the focus shifts to the child for the opportunity to come to Earth. Again, both parties benefit, but the primary focus differs.

Missionary work also suggests shared benefit. Missionaries receive promptings to knock on a particular door or approach a particular person. For young missionaries working hard to spread the gospel, finding a willing investigator feels very much like a personal reward. Yet the gift of guidance for the missionary pales in comparison to the gift of the gospel received by the person behind the door. Genealogical work operates in much the same way. Revelations are received and stories are told by the individuals struggling to piece together their family's past. The ultimate goal is to facilitate temple work and baptize dead ancestors. Again, the primary benefit is to the ancestor, who has been drawn into the fold and saved for all eternity. Yet the boon of finding a name feels like a personal success, and the benefit of an eternal reunion with one's ancestors is a major payoff indeed.

Help radiates outward from the personal to the communal. While the individual sits at the heart of personal revelation, family follows close behind, with a sizable gap before friends, ward members, and outright strangers. All can be drawn together in acts of charity, kindness, warning, and mutual aid, but family is the dominant arena for stewardship that extends beyond the self. The importance of family is clear in thematic analysis of the narrative tradition. It is also reflected in the messenger. While the Holy Ghost dominates the center of the narrative tradition of personal revelation, deceased relatives appearing as angels can also function to watch over the living and provide guidance from God. The temporal family is thereby drawn into communication with the eternal family, thus reinforcing a central tenet of LDS theology.

Yet despite the fact that personal revelation narratives are typically shared as faith-promoting stories, the narratives themselves belie easy virtue and a harmonious world. In fact, many of these stories reveal a tension between an ideal world of divine justice and the reality of an uncertain world. William A. Wilson is right to argue that LDS folklore helps persuade its audiences that the world is ordered and just (Wilson 1976a:133,138 and 1988:22), and that the main concerns of the church are also the main concerns of individual church members—living lives that make people worthy to enter the temple, sealing themselves to family, taking the message of the gospel to the world (Wilson 1988:21–2, 25). However, it is also true that these confirmations emerge out of a world where such divine justice is remarkable enough to narrate, surprising enough to instill awe. Stories of protection and guidance while tracting are shared among young men who know firsthand how difficult missionary work is. Stories of women blessed with beautiful children after deciding they would have no more are shared among women faced with the daily hardships of raising large families. While the moral is clear, hope strong, and doctrine confirmed, personal revelation narratives also reveal the fears, struggles, and tensions of living righteously as Latter-day Saints.

Synthesis: Pattern in Performance

Transmission and the Creation of Genre

This book has taken performance as the primary point of entry into analysis. This favors the text, context, and social interaction as the loci of meaning. Integral to the concept of performance is the concept of intertextuality. Intertextuality reminds us that every performance is embedded not only in the moment but also in past performances, providing a historical dimension to performance easily ignored or overlooked. That historical dimension is particularly important as narratives are picked up by audience members and shared as part of their own repertoire.

Though often overlooked, transmission plays a vital role both in the construction of meaning and the creation of genre. Personal experience narratives become second, third, and fourthhand narratives. In the case of the supernatural story, we see a shift not only in point of view but also in etic genre, as the memorate becomes the legend. This shift in generic type is testament to the importance of the narrator's position in stories where belief and truth are central to the experience and negotiated in performance. A similar watershed shift in genre can happen in the creation of prophecy. One person, voicing hope or fear and projecting it into the future, may consider his or her discourse conjecture, hypothetical posturing, or rational thought, but not prophecy. Heard by others, however, the predictions may take on greater significance. Among the Mississippi Choctaw, such discussion by elders has in more than one case led to the assumption of prophecy (Mould 2004:139–55), an assumption that is not necessarily wrong, since the powers of the divine and supernatural are broad and often hidden from human view. The same phenomenon can be found among Latter-day Saints who recognize the hand of God in the anecdotes of friends and family who see only the mundane (see chapter 4). At each point of transmission from one person to another, there is the opportunity for new interpretation that can transform meaning, importance, impact, genre, and even the fundamental nature of the experience itself.

Scholarly study of the transmission of folklore has paid little attention to its effect on genre. Instead, the bulk of the literature has focused on a few central issues—monogenesis versus polygenesis, normal forms and Ur-forms, the distribution of tale types, and the recognition of variants such as oikotypes—virtually all of which initially assumed that transmission resulted in deterioration. Of course, folklorists have been right to point out the "negative" effects of transmission. Oral transmission of folk narrative can mirror the children's game "telephone," where a person whispers a phrase into the ear of the person beside her, and so on around the circle until it reaches the person who initiated the phrase, who inevitably hears a completely altered phrase. In fact, for a brief moment, first in 1920 and then in the 1970s, folklorists attempted experiments that mirrored the telephone game in order to understand the effects of transmission (Bartlett 1920, Clements 1973, and Oring 1978). These experiments were typically faulted for not mirroring natural transmission patterns, and continued attempts to improve the experiments appear to have been abandoned. Their primary conclusions, however, endured, confirming just how corrosive an effect transmission has on a text.

Alan Dundes has rightly pointed out the folly of assuming such a negative connotation, arguing that "change is neutral; it is neither good nor bad. It may be either; it may be both" (1969:19). New narrators may improve on a joke or story; new potters may do the same with a particular form, finding a better balance between weight and sturdiness.

Saving the oft told tale from unfair dismissal as a pale imitation has been effective; folklorists have remedied the theories that guided them in the first half of the twentieth century that viewed change as corruption. However, the story is decidedly different for nonfiction genres, and again, rightly so. The concerns voiced over and over by Latter-day Saints of the fears of embellishment and distortion in stories shared fourth, third, even secondhand have resulted in a narrative tradition of revelation dominated by firsthand accounts. Yet just as stories picked up and retold by audience members can remain faithful to experience and pack a rhetorical punch even stronger than personal experiences (see chapter 4), so too can firsthand narratives be shaped by cultural factors, risking accusations of distortion, no matter how unintentional.

Experiential Source Theory versus Cultural Source Theory

Such fears return us to the debate between experiential source theory and cultural source theory raised briefly at the beginning of chapter 3. The two theories were developed by David Hufford in his book *The Terror that Comes in the Night*. In it, he explains the two approaches: cultural source theory assumes that personal experience and accounts of supernatural events "are either fictitious products of tradition, or imaginary subjective experiences shaped (or occasionally even caused) by tradition" (1982:14), while experiential source theory assumes they contain "elements of experience that are independent of culture" (15). Hufford recognizes that no experience shared orally can be entirely unaffected by cultural influence; rather, his theories raise the question of degree. Nonetheless, this tension between personal experience and cultural norms, between the concrete and the abstract, is foundational and is in many ways an articulation of the much broader nature versus nurture debate, where one side allies with a perspective grounded in the objective, universal, and biological, and the other is grounded in the socially constructed, situational, and cultural.[60] While we are learning more and more about the interplay between these two Forces—nature and nurture—a final resolution is hard to imagine ever emerging. At the risk of capitulating too soon, it seems fair to say the same is true for experiential source theory versus cultural source theory. That said, the progress made by Hufford and those who have followed (see Walker 1995) has made it clear that while it is impossible to completely separate the two, it is possible to identify experiences with the supernatural that "occur independently of a subject's prior beliefs, knowledge, or intention (psychological set)" (Hufford 1995:28). Both David Hufford and Christine Cartwright have recorded narratives of supernatural and spiritual experiences by people unfamiliar with or unaware of a shared pattern for such experiences or narratives: Hufford with the Old Hag, Cartwright with miraculous healings (1982). Their argument is simple: these experiences must have some degree of validity outside the confines of cultural construction.

Hufford has taken scholars to task for dismissing anomalous events as part of a common academic stance of disbelief, which has no doubt been true and likely remains true for many scholars today. I would suggest, however, that the continued interest of folklorists in how cultural contexts shape narratives of personal experience arises not from a position of disbelief in the supernatural and divine but rather one of broad acceptance. This has certainly been my own stance in exploring religious memorates. While I do not necessarily share the same beliefs as the people I am working with, I begin my analysis with the same assumption that people within the community do: that these experiences are empirically real. The question, then, is not, how has culture manufactured experience? but rather, how has culture helped to shape the interpretation of personal experience? Such an approach recognizes the power of culture as a resource for interpretation—one that can unearth the divine in the seemingly mundane, as in the case of the culturally accepted phenomenon of retroactive revelation among Latter-day Saints—but assumes the validity of the initial stimuli and events that prompted reflection in the first place.

A reasonable analytical path forward, therefore, would be to consider how cultural patterns can shape what we choose to highlight, see as significant, and ultimately incorporate as meaningful in our narratives. William Clements argues such a stance boldly: "First-person storytelling involves the imposition of patterns upon recollected experience. Such patterns manifest themselves in the chronological ordering of episodes in the experience, in the development of cause-effect relationships among those elements, in the establishment of a narrative point of view from a consistently delineated persona, and in the integration of characterization with theme, setting and plot. . . . No story captures the elusive reality of experience; instead story reconstitutes experience into patterns, one function of which is to provide experience with the semblance of communicability" (1982:105). Such a stance suggests wide-reaching and substantive effects of cultural patterns. An only slightly less ambitious position is suggested by Renato Rosaldo based on his work with the Ilingot people of the Philippines: "Their statements about the past were embodied in cultural forms that highlighted certain facts of life and remained silent about others through their patterned way of selecting, evaluating and ordering the world they attend to" (Rosaldo 1980:17).

Motifs in Personal Experience Narratives

I might suggest a somewhat more specific claim as well: that those cultural forms operate not only on the broad level of genre but also on the more specific level of motif. My contention is not that the use of motifs indicates fabrications of experience but rather that motifs may be regularly associated with a particular experience and therefore the narratives of that experience. The result is that when those motifs accurately reflect a person's experience, they are much more likely to be included as significant elements of the narrative.

The use and function of motifs may change, however, when stories shift from firsthand to second, third or fourth. In stories where experience has been heard rather than lived—that is, is secondary rather than personal—motifs can serve as the creative building blocks of generic performance, filling in gaps and adapting the story to generic expectations and norms.

In both cases, common motifs can derive from the specific culture or phenomenon—as with initially ignoring a prompting or superlative endings such as becoming a leader in the church with a large family—or from more widely shared cultural norms—such as the recurrence of the number three or "happily ever after" endings. With patterns repeated again and again in stories, it is unavoidable that those patterns are learned. When sharing one's own story, memory and personal experience help ensure one will be able to narrate faithfully. But when sharing someone else's story, motifs may be borrowed, whether for personal or narrative purposes.

That said, scholars and community members alike appear to assume fabrication in second, third and fourthhand narratives at a much greater rate than actually exists. While retellings of the Wilford Woodruff narrative clearly exhibit the application of recognizable motifs (see chapter 4), repeated motifs do not appear in legends at a significantly higher rate than in memorates. In fact, the opposite is as often true (see chart 7 in the appendix). This is significant. The deep-seated skepticism given to stories removed even just one or two tellings from the person who received the revelation may be far out of proportion to the actual danger of fabrication.

Such a conclusion provides one more piece of evidence in favor of a theory of interpretation that validates *both* personal experience *and* shared cultural patterns. It also helps to erode the deterioration theories that have guided folklore scholarship of the not too distant past and continue to color vernacular interpretations of oral storytelling. The presence in the United States of contemporary, or "urban," legends that are known to be false but are nonetheless told frequently and disseminated widely continues to remind us that a healthy dose of skepticism is important. However, here too we can be overly cautious. Consider Gary Alan Fine's research that uncovered forty-five cases of contaminated soft drinks in the United States from 1914 to 1976. Fine points out that this number does not include cases settled out of court, cases that were not appealed—since only appellate courts reported their decisions—or instances never brought to court in the first place (1979:479). When he considers this number in light of the statistics on the number of appeals out of the number of cases brought to the court and the number of claims brought against Coca-Cola that actually go to trial, Fine estimates as many as 180,000 cases of mice in soft drink bottles. With such estimates, legends about mice in Coke bottles are harder to dismiss as completely spurious, even when considering only the forty-five documented cases.

Just as some contemporary legends are borne out as true, we should be hesitant before assuming that narrative distance necessarily equates with greater embellishment and addition of culturally patterned motifs. Rather, we should be attentive to patterns specific to particular motifs. Quoting the Holy Ghost is more common in memorates than secondhand stories or legends, a finding that can be attributed primarily to the degree of intimacy with the sacred experience such quoting suggests, but may also be due in part to its nature as a stylistic rather than topical or thematic element of performance. The complete absence in legends of double revelation without concrete fulfillment hints at the personal nature of these experiences, and the personal motivations for sharing them (see chapter 4). Close attention to the use of motifs as stories are disseminated demands more than a cursory look, particularly one that assumes greater and greater corruption. Rather, these trends help reveal motivations for performance, vernacular modes of interpretation, aesthetic dimensions of narration, structural and social demands of performance, and processes for narrative construction.

Tale Types in Personal Experience Narratives

The same is true for tale types, which are shared plots that reflect a common constellation of motifs that regularly appear together. Like motifs, tale types have been examined almost entirely in fictional narratives. None of the many tale type indices include nonfiction narratives. Yet as narrative collections attest, there is a wealth of personal experience narratives that reflect common experiences and may be shared in such similar ways as to suggest a coherent tale type within a community. Studies of topical subgenres of personal narratives such as stories of victims of urban crime (Wachs 1988), Peace Corps volunteers (Polonijo-King 2004), hospice workers (Cole 1992), asylum seekers (Shuman and Bohmer 2004), flood survivors (K. T. Erickson 1976), and Mormon missionaries (Wilson 1981 and Rudy 2004) reveal how common tale types for nonfiction narratives are. While folklorists have identified common structures, plot elements, characters, and styles in these narratives, they have avoided analyzing these subgenres as tale types. Yet attending to broad, coherent, and repeated patterns in nonfiction narratives can reveal a great deal about shared experience and shared processes of interpretation of that experience, not just shared patterns of narration.

In the personal revelation narratives shared among Latter-day Saints, narratives that fit a particular tale type appear in firsthand memorates, secondhand stories, and legends, all. Unlike the pattern of distribution of motifs, the distribution of tale types more closely mirrors what we might expect to find, with at least a rough correlation between narrative distance and frequency of tale types. Recognizable tale types appear significantly more often in secondhand stories and legends than memorates: 14 percent of the time among memorates, 23 percent of the time in secondhand stories, and 20 percent of the time among legends (see chart 7 in the appendix). When we look more closely at specific tale types, however, this pattern varies: it holds for tale types of warnings to move, preparations for coming missionaries, and genealogical help, but not for more children waiting or being guided to missionaries. While the number of examples is small, making significant conclusions difficult to draw, the variation is suggestive. As Scott Mitchell (2004) and Margaret Brady (1987) have argued, stories of spirit children are intensely personal. Legends far removed from their source run counter to the added degree of respect and deference attributed to such personal, personal revelations. In many ways, the opposite is true of the revelations missionaries receive guiding them to possible investigators. These stories are shared widely. With so many missionaries, and so many prayers requesting help tracting, most Latter-day Saints do not have to reach far for a story of revelation in the mission field, whether from their own lives, or that of their family and friends. With a vibrant memorate tradition, legends may simply be unnecessary. In my study of the oral traditions of the Mississippi Band of Choctaw Indians, I found a similar pattern. Virtually everyone in the community had either encountered *bohpoli*—the little people—or knew a family member or close friend who had (see Mould 2004:96). Legends of *bohpoli* are accordingly rare, while memorates are shared widely.

The picture that emerges of the relationship between narrative distance and deterioration that would undermine believability is a complicated one. A simple continuum between two poles simply does not reflect living oral traditions. Further, perception and performance may be at odds with one another. Theorized ideals for performance may value narrative distance above all else, while performance patterns suggest a more complex negotiation of multiple factors that shifts according to the particular constellation of factors.

CHAPTER 6

A RECORD-KEEPING PEOPLE

Folklore has often defined itself in opposition to elite and popular traditions. For narrative, text-based genres of folklore, this has meant the elimination of written traditions. A legend told by an old woman by the fire is folklore; a legend published for mass consumption is not. One of the most succinct and pervasive definitions of folklore is Dan Ben-Amos's description of "artistic communication in small groups," a definition developed in part to help folklorists navigate the regular intersection of multiple media, in particular the oral and written (1971:14). Unfortunately, his solution was powerfully restrictive: "A song, a tale, or a riddle that is performed on television or appears in print ceases to be folklore because there is a change in its communicative context" (14). By defining folklore according to process and performance, Ben-Amos defined small groups as face-to-face interaction and echoed earlier folklorists such as Richard Dorson, who declared that "the literary document, fixed and unswerving, can never be folklore" (1964:497).

The field of folklore has come a long way since these initial repudiations of the written word. Xeroxlore, latrinalia, chain letters, and e-mails have all been usefully studied by folklorists. However, the origins of the field defied these restrictions from the start in the form of the broadside ballad. Study of the ballad was central to the development of folklore as an academic discipline in the United States. In its origins in the US, folklore had two branches: anthropological and literary. The anthropological was focused on the study of American Indian culture. The literary included tales and songs as well as their natural progeny, the ballad. Ballads dominated the scholarship of the early literary folklorists, thanks in no small part to Francis James Child and George Lyman Kittredge, two professors of English at Harvard University, who more than any other American scholars brought the ballad to scholarly attention. Ballads were sung, but they were also written, printed by the thousands, and disseminated as broadsides. Printed ballads fueled and fostered the oral tradition just as the oral tradition spawned written collections of ballads.

What was clear to the early folklorists, was clear to Ben-Amos and Dorson more than half a century later, and is also clear now, is that folk traditions have repeatedly moved back and forth between oral and written media, although what to call these traditions during their stopover in mass mediated forms has been debated. This intersection remains vibrant in ballad performance: "The Naomi Wise story has bounced in and out of the written record, popular culture, recorded and unrecorded song, oral story and legend, regional traditions, racial groups and geographies for 185 years," claims Gerald Milnes. "No doubt it will continue" (1995:388). Of course, the bouncing of folklore across media is hardly confined to ballads. In the verbal arts alone, folk tales, legends, jokes, proverbs, adages, and folk speech easily and regularly move back and forth between oral and written traditions, both feeding off and fueling the other (see Brunvand 2001, Dégh 1994). Oral performance gets written down just as written texts are pulled from the page, adopted by other artists, repeated in multiple versions, and altered to fit personal and cultural norms and beliefs. The variation, dynamism, and shared nature of these traditions make for comfortable additions to old definitions.

However, bias remains. It is a bias that is understandable. The field of folklore is centered on the idea of shared traditions of forms, functions, content, and styles recognizable among a group of people and reflecting, albeit not perfectly, shared values, ideas, and worldviews. By the very nature of the medium, written traditions favor the individual over the group, the original over the repeated.

While these biases are useful for orienting the discipline, they quickly fall apart when examining folklore in context. Just as distinctions between fine art and folk art are useful for disciplinary definitions in an attempt to open the canon to a broader vision of art, they are problematic in analysis and downright destructive in evaluating merit. Further, old distinctions between oral and written cultures simply do not apply to contemporary cultures where both exist vibrantly side by side. For Latter-day Saints, writing and record keeping have been central elements to religious and cultural life, as has the sharing of oral testimonies. These two traditions, written and oral, have derived from the same wellspring of spiritual experience. Further, they regularly intersect, overlap, and feed each other. In such a community, any meaningful analysis of the oral tradition demands attention to its parallel written tradition.

The Written Tradition in Mormon Folklore

Record Keeping: A Scriptural Foundation

The written tradition has played an extensive and integral role in the religious and cultural life of Latter-day Saints. From the beginning of the church, Mormons have been inveterate record keepers. On the day the Latter-day Saints were formally organized as a church, Joseph Smith received a commandment from God: "Behold, there shall be a record kept among you" (D&C 21:1). That commandment to keep records has been followed in many ways, interpreted and expanded upon with related scriptures from the Book of Mormon and subsequent revelations in the Doctrine and Covenants.

One of the most basic records kept is a list of church members. Considering the importance of genealogical research in order to perform baptisms for the dead, such records are vitally important, both practically and theologically. In a press release published on the LDS Church website, church statistician Glen Buckner links his work of maintaining accurate records of church members with scripture: "We believe we have a scriptural mandate to keep records in the Church, particularly (those) of our members, and we go to great lengths to try to ensure their accuracy." The press release goes on to explain: "That scriptural mandate comes in part from the Book of Mormon: 'And after they had been received unto baptism . . . their names were taken, that they might be remembered and nourished by the good word of God' (Moroni 6:4)" (2007 "Salt Lake Church Statistics Reflect Steady Growth"). The Doctrine and Covenants provides a further mandate in the context of conducting baptisms for the dead: "When any of you are baptized for your dead, let there be a recorder, and let him be eye-witness of your baptisms; let him hear with his ears, that he may testify of a truth, saith the Lord; That in all your recordings it may be recorded in heaven; whatsoever you bind on earth, may be bound in heaven; whatsoever you loose on earth, may be loosed in heaven. . . . And again, let all the records be had in order, that they may be put in the archives of my holy temple, to be held in remembrance from generation to generation, saith the Lord of Hosts" (D&C 127:6–9).

In addition to names, record keeping has included maintaining a history of the church. Early church leaders recorded both the mundane—minutes of meetings, information about priesthood membership, business and financial policies—as well as the spiritual—patriarchal blessings and revelations to church leaders, most notably Joseph Smith's revelations, which were eventually organized as scripture in the Doctrine and Covenants.

Most relevant to this study, however, is the mandate to keep personal records. Church manuals such as *The Latter-day Saint Woman: Basic Manual for*

Women have noted that "from the beginning, keeping and using sacred records have been important to the people of God. In Adam's time, God commanded men to keep a 'book of remembrance' (see Moses 6:4–6). Moses also kept a record (see Moses 1:40–41). The prophets since the time of Adam have kept records as commanded by God." The passage comes as part of a lesson on the importance of and process for recording family and personal histories (lesson 19, part B, 152). This mandate also dates back to the beginning of the church. Evidence of how earnestly church members embraced this dictum can be seen in the vast collection of pioneer journals and diaries archived at the BYU library, the Utah Humanities Research Foundation, and the church archives in Salt Lake City.

The benefits of keeping journals and producing family histories are broad and varied, directed both inward toward writers and outward toward readers. In both cases, written and oral traditions intersect and overlap, both within the family and outside it, thanks to the mass media. In particular, personal stories submitted to LDS Church magazines are published and shared among Saints around the world, first in writing, and then in many cases orally, as compelling stories are retold during church services, meetings, and among more informal settings with friends and family. The result is yet another move that combines the centrifugal with the centripetal. Family stories draw relatives closer together, binding them in story just as sacred temple rites such as sealings and baptisms of the dead bind them in eternity. Stories in the mass media, on the other hand, spin outward, projecting the personal into the public sphere for mass edification.

The Written Tradition for Personal Discovery

Personal record keeping serves as an important tool in the perfection of the Saints. Reflecting on one's temporal and spiritual life in writing transforms transitory experience into a tangible product that can be returned to again and again for spiritual contemplation, confirmation, and growth. Rich Tenney regularly writes down his dreams, inspired thoughts, and revelations. "I know that in the church when you do feel the Spirit, a way to confirm that feeling is to write it down. It's almost like a second witness to yourself that, 'Yeah. I felt the first witness, and I'm going to witness again and write it down.' As well as to say to the Spirit 'I value what you just gave me.'"

Rich worries that regular revelation can lead to taking the Spirit for granted if one is not careful. "The Spirit speaks to you," he explains, and you are initially edified. "'Oh, that's a great idea, that's wonderful.'

"And then I walk out the door.

"How much was that revelation really weighted for you? How important was it?

"But then to say I receive that revelation, I know that's important, and then to write it down, to confirm it and to make it . . . there. And how the Lord would say, 'Great job.' You know, 'You really have . . . you've taken my advice and counsel and made it important.' You've made it real, to where you can call upon it again."

By taking revelation to heart, pondering it, valuing it, heeding it, a person draws closer to God, moving toward more constant and consistent revelation. Recently returned missionary Justin Clayson points out that the prophets have said repeatedly that writing begets revelation. "So if you get a prompting, you know, a thought comes into your mind about something, you write it down, and then you can receive more on that subject after you do."

Writing can confirm revelation for the self in the same way that narrating can confirm revelation through mutual edification. Writing can also encourage future revelation by showing respect to the Spirit and drawing one closer to God by heeding his counsel. In this way, writing can be added to the model for the magnification of the spirit, where "Narrate Experience" can be understood as both oral and written narration (see figure 2-2).[1]

While writing can provide a valuable alternative to narration for particularly sacred revelations that should not be shared with others, more often, it *encourages* oral performance by providing people with the confidence that their experience was divine and worthy of sharing among their religious peers. Written records can also serve as memory enhancers, clarifying details and ensuring accuracy, both of which can instill confidence in narration. Finally, the act of writing can clarify the past as people search for connections to build a coherent, linear narrative. In this way, writing can function like oral storytelling, since both demand narrative coherence (see chapter 3 for a discussion of the interpretive demands of narrative construction).

Any personal journal can function this way, but one of the most widespread types of journal to do so is the missionary journal. While all Saints are encouraged to keep a journal, it is an expectation for missionaries. The reasons are varied. First, there are benefits to the missionaries, helping them work through their trials, recognizing God's hand in their lives, and charting their spiritual progress. On a more temporal level, these journals record a moment in the young missionary's life that is often marked by immersion in a foreign culture and maturity into adulthood. The mission is a rite of passage, and missionary journals can chart that passage in significant and personal ways.

There are also benefits to the people the missionary teaches. Both the trials and the epiphanies of missionary life can provide useful examples for people investigating the church. Ward mission leader Steve Anderson points out that sharing personal revelations is an important part of the teaching model espoused by the church, and journals are a way to remember those experiences for later use.

"What you study as missionaries is . . . probably about forty percent is how to teach," he explains. "You're constantly evaluating your life for when these kinds of things might have happened.

"And so you teach your principle, and then at the end, it [the missionary manual] gives you a little prompt: share an experience" [*laugh*].

However, Steve points out, "It's hard to remember them all. I guess that's why we keep journals."

Because missionaries are so deeply immersed in the gospel, missionary journals are often bursting with faith-promoting stories, and personal revelation specifically. However, unlike many of the journals kept by Latter-day Saints as adults, most missionary journals are intensely personal and are rarely given over directly for family histories. Instead, missionary journals become resources for the authors themselves, serving as mnemonics that can prompt the sharing of personal experiences as part of the oral tradition both in and outside the mission field.

Robert Foster once tried to type up his journal so that he could search it more easily, but the computer crashed and he lost all of his work. After twelve years, he hasn't been able to face the prospect of trying again. In the meantime, however, Robert refers to his journal the old-fashioned way: by thumbing through it, either haphazardly for inspiration or more concertedly when looking to clarify a particular memory of an experience. Twice in the course of one of our many conversations, Robert read directly from his missionary journal when sharing a revelation he had received (see chapter 3). Robert is wary not only of the legends people share all too easily but also of his own stories, knowing that the passage of time can encourage the embellishment of some elements, the eroding of others.

In this way, the missionary journal can serve as a parallel record to the oral tradition that can serve to strengthen memory and support oral performance when appropriate. These stories can help guide missionaries in the field to make useful connections between life and scripture that will help investigators see the continuity and truth of their religion. For returned missionaries, the journals may serve as more practical memory prompts, reminding them not only of the specifics of their experiences but of the dilemmas, interpretations, and epiphanies that accompanied them.

There is a tension that writers face, however, between using the journal solely as a place for personal confirmation and contemplation, and constructing a document of one's life for future generations. The two audiences—self and family—are rarely perfectly compatible. The writer who writes in the act of self-discovery embraces her failings as much as her successes. No secrets are kept, no manufactured personas invoked. The writer who writes for posterity, however, projects the self outward into a social realm of family, some of whom are known but most only imagined. In this realm, keeping secrets may be as altruistic as it is self-serving. The image of the self is more likely to be idealized: an image of who one wants to be and how one wants to be remembered.

The two audiences are virtually impossible to reconcile in a single document. In LDS culture, posterity almost always wins out. Rich Tenney explains that while he is writing, he contemplates whether a particular story would be beneficial to his children. His compromise is to edit as he writes, committing himself first and foremost to his obligation to the future. Others do not attempt compromise at all and throw themselves fully into the future, writing directly to their descendents. In all of these cases, however, the records they leave behind serve as a treasure trove for future oral performance.

The Written Tradition in Family Records

Family Stories

Despite the obvious benefit to the individual record keeper, the main thrust of record keeping in the LDS Church is directed to one's family, particularly one's descendents. The importance of family and the related need for accurate genealogies make personal histories deeply important to future generations. The benefit is practical, personal, and spiritual. Elder Theodore M. Burton of the First Quorum of Seventy explains the importance of keeping family records by describing the impact his own family journal has had upon him:

> What Grandfather Burton did for me was to write a sacred family record, the small plates of Burton, or, if you will, an inspirational family record. Much of what we now regard as scripture was not anything more or less than men writing of their own spiritual experiences for the benefit of their posterity. These scriptures are family records. Therefore, as a people we ought to write of our own lives and our own experiences to form a sacred record for our descendants. We must provide for them the same uplifting, faith-promoting strength that the ancient scriptures now give us. (1977:22)

Family records can serve as personalized scripture—faith-promoting stories compiled by one's family, for one's family, of one's family. Such family histories are not a substitute for LDS scriptures and are expected to encourage rather than reduce the reading of religious scriptures. Elder Marlin K. Jensen, member of the Seventy and current church historian, argues: "The relationship between Church and family history is also worth considering. Usually a study of one will lead to a study of the other. Many of the Church's greatest stories are contained in personal and family histories, and these are a part of our individual and family heritages" (Jensen 2007:26–31). Comparing the lives of one's ancestors to the lives of one's prophets humanizes religion and its leaders and erases artificial walls between past and present, making religion more relevant to one's daily life as well as eternal life. These family records become fodder for oral performance, shared among other family members, friends, and at church for the edification of all.

Unlike journals for personal ends, family histories introduce new narratives to the contemporary oral tradition by resurrecting past experiences and providing a life for them beyond the life of the individuals writing their histories. As successive generations write their own stories and compile those of their ancestors, family histories become rich narratives, drawing into dialogue voices that span time and space. The pattern is one of both accumulation and addition. For some, the gathering of the stories of the past is a verbal enterprise, listening to and retelling the stories of their parents and grandparents. For others, it means inscribing those stories on the written page. Yet even in recording the stories in writing, the oral tradition thrives. Writing is not a replacement for storytelling but rather a safeguard against memory loss.

Eric Eliason speaks of a "'family novel' passed down orally with help from a much-photocopied, four-page account written by my great-uncle Ivar" (1999:141). A similar document serves as the source for a story about a revelatory dream shared by Elder Staley, a story written down by an ancestor from so long ago he has lost track of the "greats" that precede her title:

> I think it's my great-great-great-great grandma, something like that,
> she . . . her maiden name is Neilson I think. And she grew up in one of
> the Danish countries or something like that, or Sweden or something like
> that. And she and her family, I think they were members of the Lutheran
> church. And then they saw missionaries. And then they started talking
> with them, then they became converted.
> And, anyway, this is kind of background information.
> So. They moved from there to England, and they sent the father to
> start out in Wyoming. And that's not too far away from Salt Lake City

where all the members of the church were gathering at that time. And so they were saving money to get them to come. And, he met a guy named . . . I can't remember his first name but Christensen was his last name. So he helped pay for everyone else to come. And he ended up marrying his daughter, my great-great, whatever grandma, I'm just going to say "great" and call it good.

Anyway, she was one who had visions. And a lot of it came true.

And one such instance I can think of for, you know, like prophecy, personal revelation, was she was dreaming one time that she saw an avalanche come. And she saw this man, she couldn't see the face, just the backside. And that the avalanche just went over him and killed him.

And she woke up, she was scared. So she warned her husband, she said, "I think someone's going to die. Don't go outside." And he had a mining contract that he needed to go to do. And he's like, "Um, I need to do this. It's important." She said, "No, please stay." And he wouldn't listen.

Just as men are, you know, they just go do their thing [*smile*].

So he went, did his thing. Sure enough, the avalanche came. But he came back. And she said, "Oh. You didn't get caught in the avalanche?" And he's like, "No." She said, "Well then, who's dead." Like, "I don't know." And they went and looked and they found someone dead in the avalanche.

And so, often times, Heavenly Father speaks to us through visions.

The story is particularly useful to Elder Staley, who as a young missionary has not yet amassed enough experiences of his own to apply to all the questions an investigator of the church might ask. So when an investigator asked for help deciding whether her dream was divine or not, Elder Staley shared a story about a divine dream that his ancestor had, a story written down that he read when he was still at home, a copy of which he wishes he had now, "so I could read over it." The story allows him to provide guidance to the woman: "Sometimes we don't know, and we just have to exercise our faith to find out."

Further, as a young man in a specific family—a Staley among a history of Staleys and Nielsons and Christensens—the story is useful in introducing Elder Staley to his ancestors and helping him maintain them as a living, recognizable force in his own life. His knowledge of his ancestors is not as strong as he would like, as attested to by his halting introduction, but his effort to contextualize the teller within the tale is common to family stories and highlights the power of such stories—whether of personal revelation or not—to encode family history.

Recording, compiling, and learning this family history is not a pedantic exercise.

"It offers strength to us as well as an understanding and connection," explains Rich Tenney. "I get to love my grandfather. So if I were to go to the

Temple and do his work, if his work were done, I know him. I have this rela-tionship. Instead of just becoming a grandfather, he becomes a person to me. I know him.

"So this family is so important in the gospel, extended and future, and that's what the gospel is based on, this family unit. And these records," he says, quoting scripture, "help turn the hearts of the children to the fathers and the fathers to the children.[2] It just all comes hand in hand."

Rich highlights the power of family stories, their connection to scripture, and their role in drawing families closer together, both here on Earth and in all eternity. The temple work he mentions will help ensure that his ancestors will join him in the afterlife, ancestors that he can know now, on Earth, through family stories as well as through sacred temple rites.

For some families, the written record is sparse and scattered: a photo-copied page here, a journal there. There is work to be done to gather the genealogy and the family stories together more concertedly. For others, a good deal of that work has been done. Families self-publish books of family stories and hand them out during family reunions and at holidays. Steve Anderson's family has done some of this work with records drawn from early pioneering ancestors.

"The church has always really emphasized being . . . record keeping, you know, keeping a journal," explains Steve. "That's another way that a lot of these stories are recorded.

"And we have some in my family. I can think of an author, her name is Mrs. David Smelly, a most unfortunate last name [*laugh*]. But she wrote a book about my first ancestor to come across the plains, and he wrote about, or he told about his father and his experience.

"So I think that's how some of it is passed down. Some of it's passed down through the records. I think those are good stories to share."

Dave Gammon's family also believes these are good stories to share. His family has compiled several histories of distant ancestors, including one from a great-great aunt who was orphaned when the American Indian tribe to which she belonged was massacred. About three-quarters of the family histories that he has are thanks to the work of his mother. To keep them for posterity and facilitate sharing, Dave typed some and scanned others into the computer.

Josette Bailey's family began a bit closer to home, recording the stories of living grandparents. "This past summer we went up camping with my family and it was my grandfather and his brothers and sisters. And we were able to sit down, we had them up in front of us and sat back here as a family and we just shot questions at them about how they grew up and how it was with our great-grandparents and that kind of stuff. A lot of the church was brought into that in stories and what not of them growing up and what they went through.

"So it was very fun. Nice feedback. I mean, there was like four or five generations there," Josette recalls. "I believe my uncle has it on tape."

What began as a storytelling session was recorded for future dissemination, with the hope that the stories will once again be shared orally. In the meantime, her grandparents took it upon themselves to compile their most valued stories in writing to share with their children and grandchildren. "My grandparents just this last past Christmas gave us all, all of us married and their children, all a family history book, kind of. It was their life stories and our great-grandparents and so on and so forth. All of us have a copy of that now. And it's pieces of their journals and how the family got to where it's at."

Life histories given as Christmas presents by aging relatives are a tradition common among Mormon families and repeated in the Tenney family on a regular basis. "My grandmother, every Christmas, she would give us packets, little excerpts of letters or journal entries, and so I have a book of remembrances of my own that has all this stuff." However, like Theodore Burton, Steve Anderson, and Josette Bailey, Rich Tenney's family also has a more permanent compilation. "In my family, stories are important, important," Rich explains. "We've got a whole book called the Breadbasket of Family Stories."

The book is an invaluable resource not only to the Tenney family but to those seeking to understand the LDS narrative tradition. The stories were recorded on audiotape and appear in print as near verbatim texts.[3] The book establishes the family lineage with a single patriarch and matriarch: Nathan Orson Tenney and Myrtle Mary Wear. Nathan Orson Tenney had died by the time the book was conceived, so his contributions come from his journal, letters he wrote to his children, minutes from sacrament meetings he attended, and blessings he received. His wife, Myrtle, however, was a driving force in getting this book compiled, and she introduces the book in addition to being interviewed for it. The rest of the book comprises interviews with Nathan and Myrtle's ten children. In each of their sections, they share stories of their parents' lives as well as their own, followed by a "Memories" section of the memories their children had of their grandparents Nathan and Myrtle Tenney. The book also includes family charts and genealogies. Because the book focuses on a single nuclear family, the same experiences are narrated in multiple versions, providing a fascinating glimpse into communal memory.[4]

The book is broad in scope, covering secular but personally and historically meaningful experiences such as going to school, receiving presents as children, horse wrangling, getting through hard times, moving around, working, dealing with the Depression, and courting and marrying (especially among the female narrators), as well as spiritual experiences such as miraculous healings, answered prayers, and prophecies and personal revelations through visions, dreams, and promptings. The result is a book that serves as a resource for faith-promoting stories as well as family histories.

These stories are pulled back into oral circulation by subsequent generations. Rich Tenney mentions a story about a box of apples and forgiveness that his father shares whenever sibling offenses risk damaging family harmony. The story has mundane rather than divine origins, but spiritual stories can operate similarly.

Just as personal revelation is personalized scripture, family stories of revelation serve as family scripture. "It's important to have these books," Rich Tenney explains. "It's vital. We know that record keeping is. In the same way the Book of Mormon is vital. We learn from other people's experiences.

"Though the Book of Mormon is revelation through prophets, there's also life experiences. You see Nephi, there are those that have sinned and they've repented and they've shown the blessings of their repentance. They've had these life experiences that we often can draw on and say, 'I see that he's gone through a challenging time and he relied upon the atonement of Christ. He's been blessed.'

"The same that I can look back at my grandfather's or my grandmother's experiences and say, 'Wow. That was a tough time in their life. But I know it worked out better for them and I can have faith in my experience with my Father in heaven and I know that things will work out as I continue. Not that it's going to be easy or everything's going to be hunky-dory or I'm going to miraculously recover from an illness or anything, but it's there.'"

Concurrent Living Traditions

Steve Anderson's family records depict pioneers of the past. So do Elder Staley's copied pages. Many of the narrators in *The Tenney Breadbasket* have either passed away or are well into their eighties, though it is clear both from the book's origins from audio recordings and the testimonials of children and grandchildren that the written tradition reflects a vibrant contemporary oral tradition. Eric Eliason's family novel also records the stories of ancestors now deceased but exists primarily as an oral tradition, with a scant four pages to maintain memory. The assumption is that the written record will always outlive the original teller but that it will continue to remind and inspire the oral tradition. In the cases above, this is clearly so. Written documents support, and eventually help create and re-create, the oral tradition.

Yet unlike the journals and family histories of ancestors now dead, contemporary journal writing provides a picture of a written record that coexists with its author and therefore with its parallel oral tradition. Josette Bailey is able to listen to her grandparents tell the stories that they recorded in their journals. Dave and Serena Gammon have a similar luxury. Both come from families where narrator and writer are one and the same, living and active contributors of their own stories in multiple media.

In comparing concurrent written and oral traditions, the oral tradition consistently trumps the written in importance and transmission. Further, in comparing the two traditions, it is clear that neither simply reflects the other. Rather, as with different genres, different media are capable of different work.

Despite extensive record keeping, Serena Gammon assesses her family traditions and concludes, "We have more of an oral tradition." Her mother has compiled a scrapbook with genealogies and photos. Her father has written an autobiography. But Serena is partial to the stories she has heard from her parents while growing up. Many of these family stories are secular: of living in England during World War II, and of the time a mouse dropped into the cake batter and they buried the bowl and threw away the mouse instead of the reverse. But there are faith-promoting stories, too.

"The ones that were faith promoting, that have been told over and over again, are my parent's conversion stories. Those have been told over and over again. And also, the way they met, and how that was inspired, that's told over and over and over again.

"And new details have come out as I've gotten older and they've been willing to share more [*laugh*].

"And those are faith promoting because by that time they were both from the church, and they look back on it and see how the Lord led my dad to my mom and led my mom to my dad. And those are very interesting."

Gordon Griffin, Serena's father, records some of these stories in his autobiography, a self-published book that begins with his birth in 1930 and ends in 2005 as he finalized his manuscript for publication in 2007. He wrote the book for others, evidenced by regular asides to the reader explaining his motivations for including a particular event or summing up a period in his life, as well as by his introduction: "This then, is my personal story of how I got to where I am today. I hope you enjoy my history . . ." (ellipses his; 2). Dominating the book are two interwoven narratives: one of his career path, the other of his relationships with his wives, in particular his first wife, Beryl, and third wife, Dionis. Both narratives are remarkable for their highs and lows, consistent fluctuations from joy to turbulence and back again.

Some of the events covered in the autobiography are not part of Serena's family's oral tradition, and some of the stories that are part of her oral tradition are missing from the book. This is not surprising. Many of Serena's stories record experiences she participated in, while her father's book is focused on his own life. One story that appears in both oral tradition and print, however, is the story of how Serena's parents met and married. Serena's husband, Dave, knows the story so well they narrate it together:

> Serena: My dad often says that when he looks back now, he can see how everything led up to where he is right now. Everything. Even all the hard times. You know, if he hadn't, oh, if he hadn't . . . what's one example?
> Dave: If he hadn't have had a failed business trip.
> Serena: That's right. If the business trip hadn't been . . .
> Dave: Failed timing.
> Serena: If this particular business hadn't . . . that he was invested in, or sort of he had been their advisor, and had sort of been let go . . .
> Dave: Oh, this was something else. OK. That's right.
> Serena: He advised them to move to Texas but instead they moved to Connecticut, and he said, "That's a horrible move. Don't move to Connecticut," but they did anyway. And then when it failed . . .
> Dave: They got stuck in Connecticut.
> Serena: Well, then when it failed, they asked him to come back and help them piece it back together, and so he arrives in Connecticut and he thinks this is horrible, this is horrible. But he went to church and was asked by some women in the singles ward to drive them to a singles activity. And on the way there, one of the women felt inspired to tell him, "You should really meet Dionis."
> Dave: That's her mom.
> Serena: Now my mom was in upper state New York at the time, and of course, my dad, a bachelor, he'd been divorced before, you know, by now all his fears about women were gone. He was like, "Well, I'll call her up." Just, "If you tell her I'll call her, I'll call her." He phoned my mom up and said, "Can I come visit you in New York?" [*laughter*]
> Dave: He was completely fearless.
> Tom: "Who are you?" [*laughter*]
> Dave: Yeah, that was what she wondered exactly.
> Serena: Yeah [*laughter*]. He's like, "I'd like to come meet you."
> Dave: And she was adventurous, too. She was like, "Sure. Why not? What could it hurt?"
> Serena: She was running an inn at the time, so she had an extra room.
> Dave: And they were both older, too. She was in her thirties and he was in his forties at the time.

> Serena: And she asked everybody she knew, everybody she knew
> to come stay with her so it wouldn't just be her and this *man*,
> you know? [*laugh*] But no one could come and stay,
> except my dad. And he says when he first heard her play
> Chopin's "Nocturne in E Flat" . . .
>
> Dave: It was Chopin, yeah.
>
> Serena: . . . that he fell in love. He knew this was the woman for him.

Her father's published version is much longer and more detailed. But there are other more interesting differences. His story appears chronologically under the header "1979," following a description of his business dealings. He begins fairly abruptly:

> I had been going regularly to church every Sunday, and enjoyed meeting some nice people. There was a lady who coordinated activities for the singles in the wards who happened to mention that there was a stake singles weekend coming up in May, she could not go but would I like to go? I attended a meeting at the area church center and met some of the organizers. I agreed to take four of the girls in my car; they were all in their early twenties! So, on the appointed Friday, I drove to Hartford, Connecticut and I picked up the girls. At my age of 49, they must have thought me a safe elderly man! The conference was very good, with good speakers. There were not girls that I could have been interested in seriously. Nor had I been particularly looking. I was being guided, and I knew it, but only in a general sort of way.
>
> As I have said, I took four girls, one of which was a girl named Dottie Reed, who suddenly said on the return journey, to her friend on the back seat, that she did not like to be a matchmaker, but that for the second time, she had had the very strong impression that Gordon should meet Dionis. Naturally I was intrigued. Who was this person who lived elsewhere, that Dottie knew! Dottie was a very nice person, recently divorced and not particularly looking for another relationship just then, although I thought she was cute. After being told of the various attributes of this Dionis Spitzer, I said that this Dionis sounded to me like a very nice person, but perhaps she was already seeing another boy. What to do to find out? Returning to Hartford with Dottie and her friend, I managed to get Dottie to call Dionis on my phone card to make sure that I might be welcome and that she did not have any regular boyfriend at that time. Apparently she did not, so I then phoned her myself later, the road having been smoothed out for me!
>
> Dionis Spitzer lived about 100 miles away in Ghent, New York (Upstate New York). The following weekend, it being the first week in June, I drove to Decar Hill Inn where Dionis was managing an Inn, called Cedar Hill Inn. Dionis had apparently given up on any special relationships. I remember distinctly getting out of my car at the inn and seeing

this radiantly beautiful person coming down to meet me, I had found my perfect love! There was something very special about her, that I could see right away, so much so, that I had a very strong feeling that she was so perfect that I would probably not be able to get her to marry me, this feeling gave me a very sad feeling.[5] She was so superior, in so many areas, yet I too, had my strengths. So, hope reigned eternal, I determined that I would persevere! I found out later, that when she came down the pathway, she thought, "This person is a little old, but I will give him a pleasant weekend for him to remember and go back with." There was zero feeling that "This person, (THAT IS, ME) was going to be my husband!"

I had arranged with her that I would take her out to dinner, to the best restaurant available. So I thought that it would probably be some fancy restaurant. When I asked her where the restaurant was, she said that there was a little one in Chatham, not far away, and would I like to go square dancing afterwards. Well, I had hardly ever been to a square dance, but of course I said yes. We went to Chatham for an early dinner where there was a kind of hole in the wall shop. Some restaurant that sold Greek things. They had three tables, one facing out onto the street. No one was eating. We ordered our Greek meals, both different, and proceeded in part to share each other's plates! It was a beautiful evening; the late day sun was shining. I remember that I was a little glassy eyed, but could not say anything, in case I spoiled the occasion. Later we went to the square dance, a different type than I had gone to in Tasmania. Going round and round made me a little giddy, as it usually does.

The next Saturday, I woke up in an upper room of the Inn just above the piano, which was in the lounge, to the strains of a melody that sounded so beautiful to my ears; I thought for a moment that surely I was in heaven! It was of course Dionis playing one of Chopin's Nocturnes! It was a truly beautiful piece that I had never heard before. That day, we walked all over the twenty acres of her land that was part of the Inn, with one of her cats that wanted to keep us company! That evening, Dionis had made a reservation to go to a theater in the round. We saw *South Pacific*! Dionis had not apparently realized the significance of the story. Older man meets younger woman, etc.! Halfway through, I held her hand, to which I think that she was surprised! On the Sunday we went to her local church and I was introduced to everyone, given smiles, and generally sized up, I think. There did not seem any disapproval, thank goodness. The Branch President, who eventually married us, was particularly friendly. He had recently got re-married himself, after his wife had died of cancer. There is so much that happened over the next two months that it would fill several pages, it was like a whirlwind. However I will try to recount a few of them.

Gordon Griffin goes on to describe a visit to Vermont with Dionis to see her family, including asides about the people he met and his strategies for trying to convince her parents that he would be a suitable husband to their daughter:

> Later the following weekend, Dionis and I had gone for a walk and were discussing something where I had left the conversation needing a response.
> I said, "Perhaps I had better not ask."
> But she said, "I insist that you ask me the question!"
> So I said, "Dionis will you marry me?"
> Her instant reply was, "That is not the question I expected!"
> We had been on another subject! However she said she would have to wait, perhaps up to six months, before she could respond with an answer.
> I said, "What will you do in all that time?"
> She said, "Oh, perhaps meet or date other boys."
> I said, "If that is possible for you, then I suppose that I will also have that option too."
> With tears in her eyes, she said, "NO you do not."
> So I said I could wait and that I had hopes that in due time it might be possible to get a positive reply.
> The following Sunday, we went to church together again; she had been rather quiet, so I wondered if in some way I might have said something to displease her, however on the way back to her Cedar Hill Inn, she suddenly said, "I have been thinking Gordon, about your question, and I have decided to accept!" Well! I slammed on the brake and pulled into the side of the road to steady myself, it was so unexpected! So this was what my guidance had been all about! It felt very good. (2007:94–7)

Comparing Serena's story with her father's published version makes it clear that she is drawing upon an oral rather than written tradition, and likely, an oral version of the story from her mother rather than her father. She includes information about her mother's attempts to find a chaperone for Gordon's initial visit to the inn, something missing from her father's published version. She focuses on the revelation that her mother's friend Dottie received and makes no mention of the revelation that Gordon received in going on the singles weekend in the first place, a revelation that he uses to bookend his narrative.

The variations between the two versions support conclusions drawn in chapter 2 about the shift from personal story to secondhand narrative. Serena shares a faith-promoting story that doubles as family history; Gordon shares a much more complete story about the courtship of his wife. While the written tradition can handle extensive detail, numerous asides, and regular self-reflection (though even Gordon Griffin points out he must edit his story for length), those asides may quickly detract from the story and distract an audience in oral performance. Oral storytelling has a temporal dimension more pressing than reading. The reader can skim, pause, or skip past long passages. The listener is captive, a point the attentive storyteller must consider. Good oral storytelling, therefore, may be colorful, descriptive, and lengthy, but it can rarely accommodate more than a single dominant narrative trajectory at a time.

While Serena has read her father's book, she nonetheless grants primacy to the oral tradition in her own narration. For her husband, Dave, the favoring of the oral tradition over the written is a more conscious choice. Like *The Tenney Breadbasket*, many of the family histories in Dave's family cover the same event. However, Dave has noticed that these written versions do not always match the stories he has heard. Dave explains:

> Most of what I have read is intended to be faith promoting. As a scientist, I kind of read some of the stuff, I'm like, "I don't know if I believe it happened that way" [*laugh*].
>
> I had a great-grandfather who decided to live the law of polygamy after it had been abolished. It's like a couple of decades after it had been abolished. And so, he was on a mission and he left his wife and kids to go on and serve this mission in Australia, and then he went out and found his second wife there. And then she moved back. And he told his first wife, 'This is my second wife.'
>
> He ended up getting excommunicated. And he was separated from one of his wives, his second one I believe. And then he stayed with the first one, but it was like a decade and a half before he was reinstated as a member of the church.
>
> It's interesting to read two or three different accounts of it because some of them try to gloss over it and say he hadn't really . . . you know, "He had trials, *like we all do*" [*laughter*], but, you know, I mean, "He succumbed to temptation, *at times*" [*laughter*]. And I'm like, "He was . . . . What the heck?" You know, it was common knowledge, twenty years, what's he thinking?
>
> But most of it is pretty faith promoting.

Spinning the past in a positive light for future generations is a natural impulse, one Dave sees in his father's writings as well. He explains: "My parents have always been big into history and writing down your history, journal writing and things like that. And so my dad has been fairly self-conscious about that, writing down experiences that he feels are faith promoting from his life, of revelations that he received or experiences that he had that built his faith in some way."

However, Dave points out that "sometimes the memories of our own discussions are a lot more interesting than whatever he's written down. And sometimes what he's written down he intends, he wants to put a positive light on everything he's done, I guess. And we would prefer to talk about the way we think of it." Dave laughs, clearly sympathizing with his father. "My dad's a great guy, don't get me wrong."

Dave is certainly aware of the tendency to edit oneself in oral performance but sees the impulse as all the stronger when writing for posterity. Considering that the oral tradition is regularly accused of encouraging embellishment and distortion, the fact that it can trump the written word as a more honest depiction of the past is a refreshing reminder that written documents are also subjective texts that reflect individual perspectives and attention to audience. In oral performance, a narrator must negotiate the social context one performance at a time. In writing, the author must negotiate all possible audiences at once, a complex task even if that audience is reduced to simply "one's family." Because of the permanence of writing, people are more likely to err on the conservative, idealistic, heavily didactic side.

Yet another reason that the oral tradition trumps the written one when author and narrator are both alive is that storytelling occurs in social contexts. Sharing even the most serious, spiritual experiences is typically an enjoyable experience. Reading, on the other hand, is a solitary enterprise, and reading through family histories can seem like work. Dave Gammon admits that despite all the efforts in his family to record the stories of his ancestors, and his own efforts to preserve them digitally, he rarely looks at them. He laughs when I ask him how often he reads them, answering with a question: "Do you read your journal very often?"

Journals and histories dominate the written tradition of personal revelation within families, but letters and e-mail among family members are also used to share stories. Nowhere is this more common than between missionaries and their parents. While missionaries are restricted to two phone calls home a year—Christmas and Mother's Day—there are no restrictions on letters and e-mail. While some of this correspondence consists of shared reports of the mundane, these letters are also filled with discussions of the spiritual, whether in query, report, or reflection. Many missionaries report receiving letters filled with spiritual experiences of their parents intended as inspiration and encouragement for their own work (see, for example, Morrison 1997:18, Wilson Archives). Elder Richard Rowe received a packet of faith-promoting stories from his mother while he was still at the Missionary Training Center. The stories provided Elder Rowe with inspiration for himself and fodder for his discussions with investigators, just as Elder Staley's family stories have done (noted earlier in this chapter).

Even more often, however, it is the letters *from* the mission field that are packed with accounts of spiritual experiences, among them personal revelation.

These letters serve as ways to share stories among people who would normally share them orally but cannot because of distance and church restrictions. Letters from missionaries tend to operate as a temporary stopgap until face-to-face interaction can resume. Returned missionaries are expected to speak before the ward upon their return and regularly share stories from their mission. Except for the most personal experiences, many of the stories inscribed in letters are later shared with their home wards.

The Written Tradition in Publication

As LDS Church historian and record keeper Marlin K. Jensen has pointed out, church history includes more than just the stories of major church leaders. "There are other great stories in our history that deserve to be known and taught at church and at home. The lessons of Kirtland, the trials of Missouri, the triumphs and eventual expulsion of the Saints from Nauvoo, and the westward trek of the pioneers are stories that inspire Latter-day Saints in every land and language. But there are equally moving stories about the rise and progress of the Church and the impact of the gospel in the lives of ordinary members in every nation touched by the restored gospel. These need recording and preserving as well" (2007:26–31). The history of the church is reflected not only in the lives of the great leaders but in the humble lives of the Saints. In fact, many members point out that the Book of Mormon itself is a personal history of the church. Lehi, Nephi, Moroni—all of these men recorded their own personal experiences of temporal life and spiritual growth. Today, their stories are studied as both personal stories of striving to live close to God as well as scripture. Today, the same pattern applies. "I keep a journal that I write down my life experiences and my stories and my feeling and my emotions and my understanding of the gospel," explains Rich Tenney. "In fact, that's what the Book of Mormon is. It's a history of a people and their interactions with the gospel."

In terms of religious importance, there are significant differences between lay members and prophets, whether past or present, particularly in terms of scope and relevance. In terms of the fundamental nature of the enterprise, however, the personal records of today's Saints are no different from those of the Saints in scripture. Personal stories therefore can serve as shared history, modern examples of the same trials and failures, strengths, and successes that Latter-day Saints' scriptural ancestors faced. One's own stories are best. So are the stories of Lehi, Nephi, Moroni, and the other men and women of LDS scripture. But the stories of other Saints, particularly when sanctioned by the church, can also resonate deeply and be shared widely. While many of the stories from fellow

Saints will come from family and peers, others will come from much farther away: specifically, official church magazines.

Church Magazines: From Oral to Written and Back Again

One of the largest sources for published stories of personal revelation are the four monthly magazines produced by the church: the *Ensign* for adults, *New Era* for teens, *The Friend* for children, and *Liahona* for members outside the United States. The magazines serve as modern-day records that can be read as a contemporary sidebar to scripture. Not surprisingly, the content of the magazines is dominated by articles written by leaders in the church. Many of these articles are written directly for the magazines, but as often, the magazine publishes talks previously given by the General Authorities. The May and November issues of the *Ensign* and *Liahona*, for example, are devoted to the previous month's general conference talks, all of which are delivered by leaders in the church. However, these magazines also provide regular opportunities for lay members to share personal experiences, including personal revelation, for all the church to read. For the individuals who publish their experiences, the stories are typically part of an existing oral tradition among their own families and friends. Once published, however, they become fodder for oral traditions across the globe. Since all the magazines are available online and easily searchable through the church website, they provide an easy and useful resource for members asked to give talks in church. It is a rare Sunday that a reference to something read in one of these magazines is not made. Occasionally, these references involve the full narration of stories of personal revelation.

To appreciate the role these published stories play in the oral tradition of personal revelation, it is necessary to examine both the content of the magazines and the ethnographic data relevant to the access, use, and performance of these published stories.

Content Analysis

A brief word on methodology is useful here. For the content analysis of the magazines, I chose a single year of the *Ensign* magazine to examine. The *Ensign* is designed for adult members of the church in the United States, the demographic that this book has focused on. Further, more than any other church magazine, it was the *Ensign* that was referenced most often by the church members with whom I worked. I chose 2007, since it was the most recent complete year of publication before I began the major writing of this book. I initially coded articles according to four major categories—reference to revelation generally, reference to personal revelation specifically, articles devoted to personal revelation, and narratives of nonscriptural revelation (see figure 6-1). The first three categories represent articles. Revelation may have been referenced once or twenty times, but I counted the article only once. For the narratives, however, I recorded each revelatory experience shared. I further coded the narratives according to whether they were exclusively spiritual or both temporal and spiritual. Exclusively spiritual stories are narrated most often within the emic genre of testimonies. They are no less personal, no less revelatory, but they are not within the scope of this study (see chapter 1). This category of narrative was almost exclusively composed of stories of conversion, a common type of narrative in these magazines and in LDS religious culture. I did not code the stories of revelation in scripture that were referenced or retold, as such revelation pushes at the boundaries of a folk tradition and deserves a study of its own.

Every month, the *Ensign* delivers articles about spiritual and temporal issues facing the church and its members. The centrality of revelation is clearly manifest within the magazine's pages. Editors pray over stories to help guide them in choosing topics that their members most need to hear, using revelation as a standard mode of operation.[6] The content itself reflects the focus on revelation. Sixty-five percent of the articles referenced revelation and 49 percent referenced *personal* revelation. Five percent of the articles were devoted to the concept of personal revelation, often providing guidance on how to seek, recognize, interpret, and follow the whisperings of the Spirit. There were a total of 112 narratives of nonscriptural revelation, 84 of which guided people in their temporal as well as spiritual lives and fall within the scope of personal revelation as defined within the oral tradition. This is an average of seven narratives

Figure 6-1. Revelation in the 2007 Issues of the *Ensign* Magazine

Month of Issue	Total # of articles	Articles with reference to revelation	Articles with reference to personal revelation	Articles primarily *about revelation*	Stories of Non-Scriptural Revelation	
					Spiritual Only (Testimonies)	Temporal & Spiritual (Personal Revelation)
January	20	16	13	1	3	6
February	20	15	12	1	3	8
March	18	14	11	2	2	7
April	21	10	9	0	4	6
May	42*	34	22	1	2	13
June	24	18	15	1	5	9
July	20	10	8	1	0	7
August	18	11	9	1	2	6
September	19	8	6	0	0	4
October	21	9	7	1	3	6
November	45*	34	25	5	4	9
December	17	6	3	0	0	3
Total	285	185 (65%)	140 (49%)	14 (5%)	28	84

*The May and November magazines are devoted to publishing the talks from the most recent biannual general conference. They are typically double the size of the other monthly issues. The total number of articles listed here excludes business reports, which would have no expectation for addressing revelation.

of personal revelation per issue. To understand how these published narratives impact the oral tradition, I coded the stories according to whose voices were expressed and what those voices were saying. The most relevant factors were the following:

- *Gender*: of the person who received personal revelation as well as the narrator (if different)
- *Role*: General Authorities, editor of magazine or expert, or lay member
- *Connection to the experience*: memorate, secondhand, thirdhand, attributed or unattributed legend
- *Language*: use of explicit terms, scriptural language, quoting of the Holy Ghost
- *Medium*: how revelation came (e.g., thought, feeling, whisper, voice, vision, etc.)
- *Theme*: the content of the revelation (as discussed in chapter 5)

Authors

At first glance, the *Ensign* seems to be dominated by articles by the General Authorities (see figure 6-2). However, the May and November issues publish the talks from general conference, talks given only by high-ranking leaders in the church. Further, these issues are on average twice as long as any other month. The ratio of articles written by leader, editor or expert, and lay member shifts dramatically when omitting those two months, placing lay members at the top of the list of contributors, responsible for seventy-five articles, compared to seventy by editors, and forty-two by church leaders.[7]

The articles written by each group vary consistently in approach. Church leaders typically write articles that clarify doctrine and provide scriptural interpretation. Articles compiled or written by editors at the magazine also address points of doctrine but more circumspectly, often compiling a series of quotes from church leaders as a means of illuminating a particular topic. Articles

Figure 6-2. Role and Gender of Authors of Articles in 2007 Issues of the *Ensign*

	Leaders				Lay Members				Editors & Experts			
	Male	Female	Both/?	Total	Male	Female	Both/?	Total	Male	Female	Both/?	Total
All 12 Issues	126	12	0	138	16	39	20	75	41	9	22	72
10 Issues (Excludes General Conference)	40	2	0	42	16	39	20	75	39	9	22	70

submitted by lay members tend to have more humble aspirations: to support church doctrine with evidence from their own lives. These aspirations are not entirely self-imposed. In an article describing the process of writing, editing, and publishing the *Ensign* magazine, editors note: "Members often wonder how they can contribute to the Church magazines." The editors' response reinforces the divide between church authorities and lay membership: "You can send us manuscripts on almost any topic, but you will probably notice that articles teaching the meaning of doctrine or the meaning of scriptures are usually written by General Authorities.

"Your best opportunity to contribute to the magazines will be to write about your own spiritual insights or experiences. When you write about what you know and have experienced, your writing carries the weight of truth and authenticity. Please remember that what you write needs to be applicable in principle to readers in many nations and cultures" ("Making Church Magazines," 2008:69). While church authorities are valued as experts in doctrine and scripture and often use stories to explain a particular principle, lay members are valued as "experts" in day-to-day living, suffering the trials of life and being rewarded with the blessings of God through faith and righteous living.

In their formal guidelines for submission published online, magazine editors are even more explicit about what lay members should submit for publication. In addition to specific topics on marriage, parenthood, and single life, editors encourage members to consider submitting stories about spiritual experiences and testimonies, either for a section called "Latter-day Voices," or for a general-interest article published alongside articles from leaders and editors:

> *Latter-day Saint Voices*: We publish short first-person articles focusing on an individual spiritual experience and insight that teaches a gospel principle. These brief narratives might be like a journal entry. Manuscript length: no more than 750 words
>
> *Gospel-in-Action Stories*: We publish articles in which members share testimony and describe blessings that come from obedience to gospel principles and covenants. Some may be dramatic stories of action and physical crisis while others may deal with challenges overcome in the quiet chambers of the heart and mind—conversion, reactivation, resolution of lifestyle problems—but all illustrate the power of the gospel of Jesus Christ in changing and blessing lives. Manuscript length: 1,000–1,600 words.[8]

The bulk of the articles written by lay members come in response to these two prompts.

The result is that virtually all of the stories of personal revelation shared by lay members are memorates: firsthand, personal accounts. The few that are not are never more distant than the experience of a close family member such as a sibling or parent.

Church leaders are less restricted in their submissions. While they rely most heavily on memorates, they also find great benefit in sharing stories of lay members within their stewardship. Leaders often quote letters they have received from lay members in wards or stakes in which they have served or visited. Leaders share the only unattributed legends describing personal revelatory experiences, an indication of the high degree of esteem and authority they command. Editors and experts rely almost exclusively on the stories of others, working most often to compile rather than create.

Of all the stories of personal revelation shared in the magazine, lay members tell the most. While church leaders were responsible for 138 of the articles, they shared only 29 stories of personal revelation (an average of 21 percent of the time and 34 percent of the total stories of personal revelation told). Editors shared even fewer; responsible for 72 articles, they published only 10 stories of personal revelation (an average of 14 percent of the time and 12 percent of the total stories of personal revelation told). Lay members were responsible for 75 articles but shared 45 stories of personal revelation (an average of 60 percent of the time and 54 percent of the total stories of personal revelation told). In other words, lay members were almost three times as likely to share personal revelation as church leaders and four times as likely as the editors of the magazine (see figure 6-3).

In terms of gender, female lay members dominate the magazine. Lay women are responsible for almost three times as many articles as their male counterparts (see figure 6-2). In articles with multiple submissions, such as "Latter-day Voices" and "Q&A," it is a somewhat mixed bag. Men are represented slightly more often than women in "Latter-day Voices" (20 compared to 16), though women tell more personal revelation narratives. In the "Q&A" section, however, women's "answers" are published five times

Figure 6-3. Role and Gender of Narrators of Personal Revelation Experiences in 2007 Issues of the *Ensign*

	Leaders			Lay Members				Editors & Experts
	Male	Female	Total	Male	Female	?	Total	Total
Memorate	15	3	18	12	25	0	37	7
Report	8	3	11	4	4	0	8	3
Frequency within Group	18% (23/126)	50% (6/12)	21% (29/138)	100% (16/16)	74% (29/39)	0% (0/20)	60% (45/75)	14% (10/72)
Percentage of Total Personal Revelation	27%	7%	34%	19%	35%	0%	54%	12%

as often as men's (15 compared to 3). Assuming no bias among the editors, this would suggest a higher instance of responses for women. In other words, female lay members appear to engage with the magazine by writing articles and responding to questions far more often than their male counterparts. However, when men write articles, they consistently share personal revelation, more so than any other group. Because a single article could include multiple narratives, a ratio of 100 percent does not mean that every article included a narrative of personal revelation. Yet the 16 stories submitted by men included 16 stories of personal revelation. In other words, men are even more likely than women to share stories of personal revelation when they share at all (see figure 6-3).

While lay women surpass any other group in terms of representation in articles in the magazine, the gender imbalance reverses dramatically when it comes to the church leadership. This should come as no surprise. The LDS Church is a patriarchy where only men can hold the priesthood. The men selected to speak at general conference and write articles for church magazines are drawn from a religious authority held by a group of eighty-five men: three members of the First Presidency (the president of the church along with his two counselors), the Quorum of the Twelve Apostles, and the First Quorum of the Seventy. The structure mirrors the organization of the church during Jesus's lifetime according to LDS gospel principles drawn from Hebrews 1:1–2, Mark 3:14–19, and Luke 10:1. There are also regional groups that form the Area Seventy who are also occasionally asked to speak.[9] The women who speak at general conference and write for the *Ensign* are drawn from a separate system of church leadership. The highest leadership positions women can hold in the church are in the Relief Society, Young Women, and Primary. Women holding leadership positions in these organizations are asked to speak at general conference; men in parallel positions are not, a sign that the church has made an active effort to include women in general conference.[10] Their presence is slight in the regular proceedings, however, restricted primarily to separate Relief Society and Young Women's sessions held Sunday evening after the close of the conference.[11]

The result is that there are substantially more male leaders in the church, giving talks at general conference, publishing articles in the *Ensign*, and sharing stories of personal revelation. Yet when one accounts for the underrepresentation of women generally, the number of personal revelation narratives women shared is remarkable. Male leaders were responsible for 126 of the articles and shared 23 stories of personal revelation (18 percent; see figure 6-3). Female leaders were responsible for only 12 articles, but they shared 6 stories of personal revelation (50 percent). This suggests that female leaders are almost three times as likely to share a story of personal revelation as male leaders.

Themes

Even more than the oral tradition, the published articles in the *Ensign* consist primarily of memorates. The themes, however, are far more heavily focused on service than in the oral tradition. Further, even the most temporal of revelations is typically framed or glossed for its spiritual content. Both spirituality and service are well represented in the most common themes appearing in the personal revelation narratives published in the magazine. Religious conversion, often through missionary work, dominates the narratives (see figure 6-4). These narratives, which most often get narrated as part of a person's testimony, are the most spiritual revelations a person can receive. The majority of the twenty-eight exclusively spiritual revelations published in the magazine (see figure 6-1) centered around conversion experiences. However, many conversion experiences include temporal promptings as well, reflected in the personal revelation narratives examined here. Female lay members tended to share stories about conversion that included both temporal and spiritual elements more often than men, though male leaders also shared these stories. Surprisingly, however, women also narrated substantially more stories of mission work than men, many of which described their own experiences as missionaries. There are at least three explanations for why church magazines have outstripped the oral tradition in female missionary stories. One is that like the inclusion of female leaders in general conference, the magazine may be actively working to include female voices in areas where they have been fairly silent. A second is that the increase of young women in the mission field has been fairly recent

Figure 6-4. Themes in 2007 Issues of the *Ensign*

Theme	Total	Male Leaders		Female Leaders		Male Lay Members		Female Lay Members		Editors & Experts
		Experienced	Shared	Experienced	Shared	Experienced	Shared	Experienced	Shared	Shared
Conversion	22	3	5	0	1	4	3	15	10	3
Missionary Work	20	3	3	1	1	6	5	10	9	2
Calling	16	11	11	1	1	3	2	1	0	2
Coping / Comfort	15	3	2	1	2	6	5	5	6	0
Help Others	13	4	5	1	1	3	1	3	4	2
What to say	12	7	7	0	0	3	2	0	3	1
Raising Children	5	0	0	2	2	0	0	3	3	0
Temple work	5	0	0	0	0	1	0	3	2	2
Career / Move	4	2	2	0	0	1	1	1	1	0
Danger	4	1	1	0	0	2	2	0	1	0
Genealogy	3	0	0	0	0	1	0	2	0	3
Forgiveness	3	0	0	0	0	1	1	2	2	0
Marriage / Divorce	3	0	0	0	0	1	1	2	2	0
Child in Need/Peril	3	0	0	0	0	0	0	3	3	0

The total number of stories does not add up to 84, since more than one theme may be present in a single story.

(see chapter 5). Church magazines draw heavily on recent experiences, while the oral tradition reflects a lifetime of experiences. And third, I did not interview any sister missionaries as none were assigned to the Burlington First Ward while I was doing the bulk of my interviewing. (In 2009 I did hear a sister missionary speak during a fast and testimony meeting.) However, since my fieldwork comprises only a quarter of the 441 narratives analyzed, this is only a partial explanation.

Closely tied to missionary efforts are the callings that adult members receive in the service of their church. While revelations received concerning one's calling often sit on the peripheries of the oral tradition of personal revelation, they are fairly common among church leaders, who are disproportionately represented in church magazines. For the same reason, revelations about receiving guidance on what to say are regularly narrated by church leaders, as well as by adults in the general membership. In the magazine, men typically *receive* these revelations, though women may *narrate* them.

The one major deviation from the focus on service in the most dominant themes in the stories of personal revelation published in the magazine is the revelations people receive to comfort them in the trials of life. Such revelations are focused primarily inward rather than outward. These revelations remind people that God loves them and hears their prayers and that the Holy Ghost can bring great peace and comfort in the face of even the most dire of circumstances.

The second tier of most common themes reflects a combination of spiritual service and personal life. Temple and genealogy work are more common for women, as in the oral tradition, and reflect service to the church as well as to one's family. Conducting temple rites for one's ancestors can also reflect the most personal of endeavors, as people work to unite their families for all eternity. Marriage, raising children, and striving to grant and accept forgiveness are all firmly focused on one's personal life, though they also have important spiritual dimensions. In these narratives, only women receive and share revelations about raising children, reflecting conservative gender roles also seen in the oral tradition. In the case of marriage, one story involves a man unsure if he is ready to commit. The other two deal with divorce. One of these stories involves a woman's revelation that she should not go forward with her planned divorce but work through the problems in her marriage. She does and feels blessed, reifying the sanctity of marriage. The other narrative, however, takes a slightly more modern view of divorce. A woman receives revelation in order to help her cope with the divorce of her parents, in particular helping her to avoid feelings of anger and blame. In the case of divorce, the magazine is again ahead of the oral tradition in keeping pace with modern life. This may not be as forward thinking as one might hope, however. One divorced woman gave me a photo-copy of an article published in the September 2006 issue of the *Ensign* noting that the church was finally addressing the needs of single parents in the church. She was not the only person to have noticed this long overdue recognition of divorce and single parenting. Many members of the church, including her own sister, gave her a copy of the article, thrilled to see something that spoke to the issue and that might be of help to a person they valued and loved.

One of the most remarkable divergences between the narratives published in the *Ensign* and the oral tradition is the lack of stories in which the Holy Ghost prompts a person to avoid harm. This theme dominates the oral tradition. In the published record, however, such revelations are rare. One possible explanation for this trend is the favoring of stories that describe solicited revelation. Many of the published stories do not indicate whether a revelation was solicited or not, but those that do heavily favor experiences that begin with prayer. This process mirrors the prototypical way revelation is sought and received, a process strongly encouraged in church doctrine, by church leaders, and in church magazines. Most revelations that protect people from harm and warn of danger appear out of the blue. Such unsolicited revelations are more serendipitous. Living righteously will help ensure the more constant companionship of the Holy Ghost, but such a broad, general prescription is more vague and daunting than the specific regimen of humble prayer about a particular concern. Another possible explanation emerges when considering the magazine's preference for less dramatic stories than the oral tradition.

Medium and Style

Revelations that come out of the blue are often more dramatic than those that come as a response to prayer. While the oral tradition relies on the remarkable for a compelling oral performance, the *Ensign* magazine editors recognize that some experiences will be dramatic, while others will exist in "the quiet chambers of the heart and mind" ("How to Contribute to the *Ensign*"). While the oral tradition often excludes such stories as not remarkable enough or explicit enough to convince audiences of their divine provenance, church magazines embrace such experiences. God is found everywhere, even in the seemingly mundane. Subtle feelings of peace and comfort can nonetheless alert faithful Latter-day Saints that they are in the presence of the Holy Ghost. In a story in the May issue, a woman and her family were facing difficult trials, so they gathered together to pray for guidance and "almost immediately we realized we were surrounded by goodness" (Parkin 2007:34). As in the oral tradition, however, revelation often emerges upon reflection. In a story in the June issue, a young man who was not yet a member of the church looked to a friend who *was* a member for help. The friend offered little help, but he did offer what turned out to be a profound suggestion.

"'Sometimes when I don't know what to do,' he said, 'I talk to my bishop.'

"'Your bishop? Who is he?' I asked.

"'He is the head of my ward,' my friend replied.

"I now recognize my next question to be a distinct prompting from the Spirit, but at the time it was the most out-of-character question I could imagine coming from my 17-year-old mouth. 'Do you think he'd meet with me?' I asked" (Staples 2007:56).

The overarching message is that God is everywhere. His blessings are there to see for the observant. People must be diligent in reflection, making sure to count their blessings and never dismissing as coincidence or luck the work of the Lord.

While the range of experience extends deep into the realm of the quiet chambers of the heart and mind, it does not extend equally in the other direction. The magazine warns against submissions that are too personal or too sensitive: "We are not interested in book-length manuscripts, fiction, plays, self-promotion, travelogues, near-death experiences, or exceptionally personal or sensitive material" ("How to Contribute to the *Ensign*"). As a magazine produced by the church, stories included must follow church norms. Church leaders have warned against freely sharing dramatic stories involving the supernatural (see chapter 2). The *Ensign* naturally adheres to this mandate. The result is a search for middle ground.

James W. Ritchie shares a story of facing a water shortage in Ghana while training at the MTC there. The villagers' tap ran dry while the taps at the MTC continued to run. Word got out and people showed up with buckets. Ritchie helped convince the custodian to allow the villagers to use their taps. The water should have run out almost immediately, but the tap never stopped. The story echoes the biblical story of the loaves and fishes that multiply, yet the writer refers to this experience not as a miracle but more modestly as "a wonderful thing" (Ritchie 2007:71). Conversely, Anne Grenzebach writes about trying to turn the hearts of her family to the church. While she has a number of impressive personal revelations, it is the seemingly mundane experience of having her non-Mormon mother watch general conference and enjoy it so much she bought the video that she refers to as a miracle (2007:62). Subtle experiences are embraced rather than ignored, while dramatic experiences are tempered and downplayed if they are included at all.

Both written and oral traditions edit by exclusion and revision. Magazine editors warn that stories that are overly dramatic or sensational are inappropriate for publication. Some stories may be edited, whether by the magazine or the writer, to downplay sensational elements. In the oral tradition, the most dramatic and personal of spiritual experiences are also rarely shared, but the same is true of stories that lack clear evidence of the Holy Ghost. Revising the chart from chapter 1 that charted the oral tradition suggests a more dramatic tradition in oral narratives and a less dramatic tradition for church magazines (see figure 6-5 and figure 6-6; for a numeric comparison between the published tradition in the *Ensign* and the oral tradition, compare figure 6-6 with chart 2 in the appendix).

One reason the written tradition can sustain narratives where the divine is implicit or ambiguous is the power of church authority. The *Ensign* is published by the church and undergoes multiple stages of review by church leaders. Proposed content for the magazine is reviewed by the General Authorities. Once the content is set and approved, the magazine is edited. The edited articles are then reviewed by members of the Seventy. Once these articles are approved, the magazine is laid out. The final designed pages go through one final review by members of the Seventy and one or more members of the Quorum of the Twelve Apostles ("Making Church Magazines," *Ensign*, Jul 2008, 64–9). If a story appears in the *Ensign*, a reader can be assured it has received approval by leaders in some of the highest offices of the church. The power and truth of these experiences and their divine provenance are above reproach.

The downplaying of the supernatural and more dramatic aspects of personal revelation appears not only in the selection of the articles and narratives. The people in published stories of personal revelation in the *Ensign* rarely quote the voice they hear and never hesitate in following the prompting of the Spirit. In the 83 narratives of personal revelation, revelation is quoted directly only six times, once by an editor, twice by lay members, and three times by church leaders, an average of 7 percent of the time. That average in the oral tradition is more than double, at 15 percent of the time. Further, while no one might expect the General Authorities to hesitate before listening to the Spirit—after all, an accepted assumption is that General Authorities have risen to their positions

Figure 6-5. Medium of Personal Revelation: Comparison between Oral Tradition and the *Ensign* Magazine

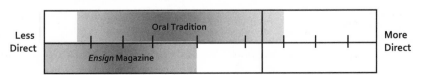

Figure 6-6. Medium of Personal Revelation in the *Ensign*

Medium	Total	Male Leaders		Female Leaders		Male Lay Members		Female Lay Members		Editors & Experts
		Experienced	Shared	Experienced	Shared	Experienced	Shared	Experienced	Shared	Shared
Internal	86	21	23	3	6	23	16	39	31	10
• Feeling	25	3	4	0	1	6	6	16	12	2
• Thought†	31	10	12	0	1	10	7	11	10	1
• Voice	9	0	0	2	3	2	0	5	4	2
• Prompt†	20	8	7	1	1	5	3	6	5	4
• Dream	1	0	0	0	0	0	0	1	0	1
• Vision	0	0	0	0	0	0	0	0	0	0
External	0	0	0	0	0	0	0	0	0	0
• Voice	0	0	0	0	0	0	0	0	0	0
• Vision	0	0	0	0	0	0	0	0	0	0
• Visitation	0	0	0	0	0	0	0	0	0	0
Total	86‡	21	23	3	6	23	16	39	31	10

*People use many terms to describe their experiences in addition to those listed in the chart. Others include "impression," "inspiration," and "knowledge." All three correspond most closely with "thought," which is where I have counted them.

†"Prompt" is an umbrella term used to describe experiences that people clearly see as internal, but not dreams or visions. With no clearer articulation, I have used "prompt" to indicate those ambiguous revelations.

‡Two of the stories (both told by female lay members) include two distinct revelatory experiences, so the total adds up to 86 rather than 84.

by leading exemplary lives committed to God and the church, by now have mastered the ability to hear the whispering of the Spirit, and would understand the importance of following it unquestionably—lay members writing in the *Ensign* would be held to no such expectation. Yet their narratives, too, display a uniformity of skill in hearing and obeying the Spirit. There is not a single mention of hesitation or delay in responding to the Spirit in the narratives in any of the twelve issues published in 2007. A possible explanation for this pattern can again be found in the explicit instructions to lay members by the editors in the online document "How to Contribute to the *Ensign*": "We publish articles in which members share testimony and describe blessings that come from *obedience to gospel principles and covenants*" (italics added).

A more comprehensive explanation for the pattern of downplaying the revelatory experience is found in the primary focus of both the magazine and the church more generally on gospel principles. For the Latter-day Voices section of the magazine, submissions must focus "on an individual spiritual experience and insight that teaches a gospel principle." For Gospel-in-Action stories, a name that leaves little to doubt, articles must "illustrate the power of the gospel of Jesus Christ in changing and blessing lives." Personal experiences are relevant to a national and international audience insofar as they can illustrate a fundamental principle of LDS doctrine. Stories humanize the gospel, making doctrine concrete and understandable. Yet despite how attractive and effective the vehicle is, it is the message, not the medium, that church leaders and magazine editors want to ensure takes center stage. To facilitate this goal, editors use subheadings throughout their articles that often highlight the gospel principles exemplified in the stories. In Anne Grenzebach's story about joining the LDS Church, subtitles highlight the gospel principles at the heart of her experience—Serving Families, Blessings through the Temple, Continuing in Hope (2007:60–2). Editors may also add quotes from scripture before or after an article to frame the story submitted. Magazine editor Adam C. Olson draws together a series of stories from young adults in Germany as a testament to the presence and power of Jesus Christ. In doing so, he frames the article, as well as each of the young people's stories, with a relevant passage from scripture (2007:16–20). Editors may also reference scripture within a person's story. In a letter submitted asking for anonymity, a young woman recalls a comforting experience that may or may not have been revelation but was nonetheless a divine act: "A visit from an angel would not have been sweeter. I still felt the pain, but I no longer felt I carried it alone. That simple yet divine act gave me insight into what it means to mourn with those who mourn and comfort those who stand in need of comfort (see Mosiah 18:9)" ("The Letter I Didn't Receive" 2007:54–5). Editors recognized the parallel with scripture and cited it accordingly. Even more frequently, editors employ past talks from the General Authorities to serve as the coda for an article. After an article about being prompted to choose motherhood over a career outside the home, editors added a quote from Elder Jeffrey R. Holland of the Quorum of the Twelve Apostles about the powerful blessings that come to the dedicated mother (Dunn 2007:9–13).

In writing, lay members themselves also help to clarify the connection between experience and the gospel—both explicitly by quoting scripture, and implicitly by echoing the language of scripture. Without the temporal constraints of oral performance that demand the construction of narrative in real time, writers have the luxury of contemplation, multiple revisions, and the use of reference books—most notably LDS scripture. Where editors frame narratives with scripture, lay members embed it into the body of their narratives. In a story about his missionary work in Argentina, for example, Sergio Adrián López testifies to the power of the Holy Ghost in guiding both himself and the investigators he was working with by quoting both scripture and the president of the church (2007:70–1):

> Over the next few weeks my testimony was strengthened as the Holy Ghost witnessed to the Balva family of the gospel's truthfulness and enlightened their understanding in Spanish. Heavenly Father knew the desire of their hearts and recognized the sincerity of their prayers to find truth. Together, the Balva family, Elder Allred, and I experienced the joy described in D&C 50:22: "Wherefore, he that preacheth and he

that receiveth, understand one another, and both are edified and rejoice together"—not because we spoke the same language but because of the universal language of the Spirit.

The Balva family introduced us to another Russian family, whom we were also privileged to teach. Both families made covenants with Heavenly Father by entering the waters of baptism not long after we met them. I am a witness that the words of President Ezra Taft Benson (1899–1994) are true: "The influence of the Spirit is the most important element in this work. If you will allow the Spirit to magnify your callings, you will be able to work miracles for the Lord" (new mission presidents' seminar, June 25, 1986).

When writing, lay members may also borrow the *language* of scripture, echoing past prophets. The only time in my fieldwork that a person echoed biblical language was when Robert Foster was reading from his missionary journal as he narrated his revelatory dream, employing the phrase "said unto me." In his story of surviving a night alone in the arctic, published in the *Ensign*, Todd Crosland not only borrows the language of scripture but employs a range of strategies and styles to link his experience to those in scripture.

Lost on the Tundra

By Todd Crosland

Alone on the unforgiving Alaskan tundra, I gained strength during the night from the scriptures written in my memory and in my heart.

This was to be an adventure of a lifetime. Exploring the Alaskan tundra had been something my friends and I had talked about for years. Finally, our dream had become a reality. We were on our way to the ruggedly beautiful land of Alaska.

We began our journey in mid-April, a time when the Alaskan wilderness was still blanketed with snow. We arrived in the late evening in Talkeetna, a town near the Denali National Forest. We met with our guide, who had arranged for snowmobiles and a place for us to stay. Our plan was to wake up at dawn and begin exploring.

Lost and Alone

The weather was unseasonably warm for Alaska, so the snow was soft and slushy. Cutting through the heavy, wet snow was difficult on a snowmobile, and each of us had trouble and kept getting stuck.

At one point in our adventure, I became separated from the rest of the group. My snowmobile kept sinking into the slushy snow, and I kept lifting it out, only to travel a few feet and then become stuck again. Eventually, my snowmobile got stuck and sank four feet into the snow. I tried to pull it out of the slush, but that was like trying to drag the machine out of wet cement. I spent the afternoon and all my strength trying to pry my snowmobile loose from the strong hold of that slushy bog. I kept praying that my guide and friends would return to help me. Hour after hour went by, but there was no sign of anyone.

When it began to get dark, I really started to worry. Although I had dressed warmly, my clothing was completely drenched with perspiration underneath my parka from my efforts to pull the snowmobile free. As the sun began to set, I felt the intensity of the harsh Alaskan climate. I shivered uncontrollably as the temperature dropped below freezing.

"They've got to come back to me soon," I thought. "Certainly, they'll find me in a matter of minutes." Minutes soon turned to hours. I was alone in the wilderness—hungry, cold, and afraid. I had to accept the reality that I was going to spend the night by myself in the middle of the unforgiving Alaskan tundra.

Strength in the Scriptures

I tried lighting a fire to stay warm, but there was little firewood to be had in the tundra. What wood I found was so wet that I couldn't keep a fire going. I had a little bit of food and water, but I knew it would last only a short while.

From my years of Scout training, I knew I shouldn't fall asleep. With my wet clothes and the unbearably cold temperature, I was afraid that if I fell asleep, I might never wake up.

Sitting in the dark, I could hear the sound of wolves howling. This didn't frighten me nearly as much as the sound of avalanches crashing down in the bitter night. My fear was that my friends might have been caught in an avalanche. I prayed for their safety also.

Time seemed to stand still. I spent the night thinking of my wife and four children, all of them tucked warmly in their beds and unaware of the danger I was in. I tried to pass the time singing hymns and reciting scriptures to myself. I tried not to look at my watch too often. When I thought an hour had passed, I'd look down at my watch and see that only 20 minutes had passed. I asked myself if this night was ever going to end. "Am I going to get out of here safely?"

Strength in Prayer

When it began to snow, a feeling of dread sank in my stomach. "I've got to get out of here right now," I thought. "The snow will cover my tracks. No one will ever be able to find me, and I will never be able to find my own way out. I've got to leave now or die in the wilderness."

Once again my thoughts turned to the scriptures. I thought of some of the strong and brave men in the Book of Mormon—Nephi, Helaman, Mormon, and Moroni.

"Father in Heaven," I prayed, "please give me the strength of these great men. I haven't the strength to pull my snowmobile out of the sludge on my own. Please, Father, if it be Thy will, give me the strength of 10 men."

After finishing my prayer, I walked over to the snowmobile in a very weakened state. I was cold and hungry, but even though my body was weak, my faith was strong. I knew by the comforting Spirit I felt when I prayed that my Father in Heaven was watching over me. He would help me in this desperate time of need.

I gripped the handles of the embedded snowmobile. Amazingly, I pulled the machine out on the first try. I had indeed been blessed with the needed strength. I started the snowmobile. Since the cold had hardened the snow, I could drive without sinking, so I began to follow the tracks back to camp.

I looked eastward and noticed the sun was just beginning to peer over the horizon. I also noticed the silhouette of men on snowmobiles. As the men drew near, I realized that they were my friends. I discovered that they had also been lost and had not known where to look for me.

Strength in the Savior

Many of us can relate to the feeling of being alone in the wilderness. Each of us will have times in our lives when we will struggle with adversity, personal problems, or trials of our faith. Like a bog of wet, heavy slush, life's circumstances may leave us feeling trapped and alone, unable to muster the strength to make it on our own. At these times of difficulty, there is One who will never forsake us. There is One who will bless us with the strength to pull ourselves out of our problems and press forward. We have a loving Savior, ready and willing to bless us in our individual needs.

In the Doctrine and Covenants, we read: "Draw near unto me and I will draw near unto you; seek me diligently and ye shall find me; ask, and ye shall receive; knock, and it shall be opened unto you. Whatsoever ye ask the Father in my name it shall be given unto you, that is expedient for you" (D&C 88:63–64).

I bear testimony that this scripture is true. As I called out to the Lord in prayer, He inspired me to know what I needed to do; He blessed me with what was "expedient" for me. I am grateful to Him and for the scriptures in which I found comfort that night.

Answers in the Scriptures

"Scripture study deepens understanding. The years have taught me that if we will energetically pursue this worthy personal goal in a determined and conscientious manner, we shall indeed find answers to our problems and peace in our hearts." President Spencer W. Kimball (1895–1985), *The Teachings of Spencer W. Kimball,* ed. Edward L. Kimball (1982), 135.

The coda from Spencer W. Kimball is an addition from the editors, as are the subtitles and quote at the beginning, but the author himself actively ties his experience to scripture by employing phrases such as "the spirit bore witness," "we invited the Holy Ghost into our home," and "I knew by the comforting Spirit I felt when I prayed that my Father in Heaven was watching over me."

He also prays in the language of scripture: "Please, Father, if it be Thy will, give me the strength of 10 men."

Apart from explicit religious language, the literary aspects of written narratives are understandably more conscientiously developed, particularly in parallelism, metaphor, simile, and description. In the narrative above, Todd Crosland writes that "even though my body was weak, my faith was strong," and "like a bog of wet, heavy slush, life's circumstances may leave us feeling trapped and alone, unable to muster the strength to make it on our own." The shift in medium allows more careful construction and editing, with specific words worried over and redundancies and false starts excised.

The published narratives are not, however, more artful in local color, colloquialisms, idioms, or regional dialect, areas where the oral tradition dominates (see chapter 4). Such verbal artistry appreciated among people in one region may be alienating to people in another. Magazine editors struggle to make each magazine appropriate to their intended audience, explaining: "Editors understand that this is also happening as teenage readers mature. Those who produce articles for adults try to keep in mind that readers differ in ages, stages of life, and marital status. Add to this the complexity of addressing the needs of readers all over the world, and the task can seem daunting" ("Making Church Magazines" *Ensign* 2008:66).

Ethnographic Analysis

Content analysis of the narratives published in the *Ensign* magazine provides a basic understanding of the type and nature of the narratives people are exposed to in one of the primary vehicles of the written tradition. Such an understanding provides a point of comparison when exploring the question of how church members view and use these published stories in their own lives and in their oral traditions.

The reasons Latter-day Saints read church magazines vary. Many use them to teach. Having been vetted by church authorities and framed to convey a particular gospel principle, stories published in church magazines provide valuable and regular fodder for Sunday talks. For the same reasons, many people turn to church magazines for spiritual and personal edification and are comforted in knowing that there are others out there struggling with the same problems they themselves are facing. Pauline Clayson describes the power and authority church magazines can wield: "As teachers or leaders, we are encouraged not to use secular . . . you know, 'I read this in *Time* magazine,' but to draw upon the scriptures and the *Ensign* and *The Friend* and church publications, the *Church News*.

"Because the articles that you read in there have passed the desk of the First Presidency and have been designed to enlighten our minds. So, those are the things we are asked to draw our knowledge and strength from—as well as our own experiences—but to draw our knowledge from because they are correct principles."

There are also more quotidian reasons for reading church magazines. They serve as wholesome entertainment, an enjoyable diversion from the worries and cares of earthly life. Parents often bring *The Friend* magazine to church as a suitable distraction for their children during sacrament meetings and general conferences, where talks may be geared for a more adult audience.

Having stories in written form makes them particularly transportable. It can also make them particularly effective for reflection and edification. Where an oral performance is ephemeral and depends on immediate edification, written stories can be read and reread. Further, they can be read when a person has prepared oneself for the Spirit, and not at the whim of a narrator. "They're just as powerful written," says Josette Bailey, discussing narratives of personal revelation. "Sometimes, sometimes almost even more so because you can keep going back to it. Things kind of jump out at you I think sometimes when they're written, at least for me.

"Sometimes I can get more out of reading an article than I can out of a talk at church, but that could be because my kids are over here [*she points to her two children seated on the sofa*] and I can sit down quietly and read. I guess it just depends, and it also depends on the Spirit because it's going to jump out at you when it needs to, when you need it."

Reading the stories in the *Ensign* can operate in much the same way as reading the stories in the Bible and the Book of Mormon. Both the *Ensign* and the scriptures are rich with spiritual experiences that can edify and produce new revelations into the truth of the church. "The prophets will say that one of the most prolific ways you'll receive revelation is by reading scriptures or reading other experiences or reading the *Ensign* or things like that," explains Paul Clayson. "The Lord will work through the *written* word. I can kneel down, and I can pray and say I need wisdom, I need revelation, I need to understand what I need to do in my life. And I may not know what to do, but then I'll be reading something, and it will stand out, and that's when the revelation comes and says, 'Focus, pay attention to this, because here's your answer.' It absolutely works that way."

Many people pray for guidance and receive promptings to turn to a particular passage in scripture for the answer (see chapter 5). Such revelation accustoms people to searching for help in the words of prophets past and present.

The *Ensign* gives voice to both, as well as to readers' peers who have been blessed by the Holy Ghost. People recall times they faced a particular problem in their lives and found solace or advice in an article or story in the *Ensign*. One woman describes how a story in the *Ensign* about a mother with depression helped her with her own postpartum depression.

Recognizing that one's own trials are shared by others has less obvious, more lasting benefits as well. As Richard Rowe, Aaron Chavez, and Matt Larson all point out in a discussion one evening, not only does the publication of shared experiences help people see that they are not alone, it helps to unify members around the globe. "If you're reading through it and you do find something in there that you're going through, you know, and you can kind of find out how they got through it, and you're like, 'All right, well maybe I could try that,'" says Elder Rowe. "Definitely talking person to person about it is a little more meaningful, but it still does have its meaning in there."

"I would agree with that," concurs Matt Larson. "The church is the same everywhere. Everyone has very similar experiences." For spiritual experiences that may seem unbelievable, seeing similar stories in church magazines can validate the experience. "Sometimes they may not believe it because they don't see it somewhere else. But if they read about it, and realize they're having the same experiences . . . .

"Because it's not one church on this block and it's not a different church on the other block, it's the same. It's the Church of Jesus Christ. It's the same church."

Yet for all the benefits of the written tradition, published stories may not be as immediate, relevant, or sincere for a listener as a story shared orally. "For me, too, it's got to be real," explains Dave Gammon. "Sometimes, if it's too fluffy around the edges, I have a hard time connecting with it, myself." Dave clarifies. "If it's too perfect. You know, like somebody that just, [*said in a slight falsetto*] 'Ahhhhhh,' that everything is going to work out perfectly, and they knew it would, and the world is a rosy place.

"And I'm like, 'No, the world is *often* a rosy place, but not *always.*'"

Shawn Tucker agrees, believing that some of the life of the story will be lost in the process of cleaning it up for publication. "There's going to be several things that are done. One, obviously a lot of specifics are going to be gone. Also, specifics like, if it's a story about . . . let's say that you had gone out carousing and you felt a prompting saying, 'Don't go there, don't go do this thing.' It's going to say you'd gone out carousing, or you've gone with some friends and you've become involved in some inappropriate activities or behaviors. I mean, that is going to be watered down. It's not like, 'After my fifth Bud, which I don't like as much as Michelob, by the way. . . .'"

In contrast to the oral tradition, where ambiguity, confusion, moral weakness, and hesitation are not just present but often highlighted, the stories published in the *Ensign* are clear, faith-promoting stories that depict inspired and inspiring actions of people ever ready to follow the Spirit. Such idealized behavior can risk alienating readers as providing too rosy and perfect a picture of religious life. Positive role models are only effective as long as they appear attainable.

For the most part, however, people seem to believe the *Ensign* has struck this balance. Even for those who perceive the magazine as portraying life too neatly point out that many stories nonetheless inspire and edify them. One reason is that the magazine has begun to tackle thorny social issues. Content analysis suggested that the magazine is fairly proactive compared to the oral tradition in addressing issues such as divorce and female missionaries, a conclusion drawn by many readers as well. Dave and Serena Gammon, for example, have been pleased with this development:

> Serena: The *Ensign* has recently tried to deal with real issues, not so much the fluffy stuff. There will almost always be at least one *Ensign* article that's by Anonymous. And it's usually about something like a drug addiction, like a child who . . .
>
> Dave: Or homosexuality or something.
>
> Serena: Homosexuality. Or a child who, one of them was about a woman who had a child who had been date-raped and remembered it, and dealing with the aftermath, the psychological aftermath of that, how her daughter felt like she was worthless in the sight of God for a while. And she left the church and suddenly made this big turnaround from being a beautiful, really, really on-the-straight-and-narrow girl to feeling, like, lesser, a victim . . .
>
> Dave: She was dirty.
>
> Serena: And joining the wrong group of friends. But that her mother . . . and her mother didn't even know what happened. But eventually when the child was a junior or something and was in a health class and the subject of date rape came up, it sort of it all came tumbling out. And how eventually through faith and lots of struggle, then she was able to heal and eventually get married in the temple. So the story turns out well [*laugh*].[12]

Performing Published Stories

As in the oral tradition, narratives of other people's experiences are intended primarily to inspire rather than to be repeated whole. Norms against sharing the sacred and the expectation that everyone should seek his or her own revelation contribute to the reluctance to tell other people's stories (see chapter 2). There are, however, important and widespread exceptions.

In the oral tradition, regular repetition of family narratives is not only acceptable, it is encouraged. The nature of the familiar and familial relationship erases social and cultural prohibitions against sharing other people's stories. In the written tradition of church magazines, exceptions are either time sensitive or thematic. Recently read stories may be shared as a point of common ground, a resource logged in the short-term memory and shared in conversation. Older stories may be resurrected thanks to online searching when members are pressed to give a talk in sacrament meeting.

The changes that occur in translating a personal story to a secondhand one in the oral tradition are compounded when further translating from one medium to another, as when Suzy Carter retells a story submitted by Geri Walton and published in the September 1986 issue of the *Ensign*. Geri's story was published as follows:

> One morning, early, my husband, Dennis, and I awoke to find that we had both experienced the same profoundly revealing dream.
>
> We seemed to be together in a hospital delivery room, and I was involved in the intense stages of labor. Dennis was comforting me, and although the setting was familiar the circumstances were very different. Our previous four children had been born by cesarean section; this time we seemed to feel that the baby wasn't going to be delivered in a surgical unit. As the dream continued, a baby girl was born to us, smaller than any of our first children.
>
> Then the dream ended abruptly for both Dennis and me, and we awakened simultaneously. We began to discuss the new baby as naturally as if I had just truly given birth to her. I recall being concerned about her tiny size, but we both were impressed with what a pretty and sweet baby she was.
>
> Why had this happened to us? Was this a spiritual experience to prepare us for the opportunity to share together the natural birth of an infant? Or was there more to the dream than we recognized?
>
> We continued in the glow of the moment until some of our "little people" began to invade our space. The pace of the day picked up rather rapidly, and routine soon pushed any more thought about the dream to the back of our minds.
>
> On a Saturday morning about nine days after the dream, I was doing my breakfast dishes when the phone rang. Dennis was in the backyard with the children, mowing the lawn and tidying the yard.
>
> After introducing herself, the caller said, "I'm calling on behalf of the Social Services Department. I know that it's rather unusual to bother our

foster families on a weekend, but we have an emergency situation and need some help." She spoke guardedly.

"Can you tell me more specifically what we are being asked to do?" was my only response.

"Well, we have a baby that has to be moved from a hospital nursery this morning. She's rather ill, quite small, and as a matter of fact she's been under observation for the last week or so. However, she's no longer considered to be at intense risk. I should mention, though, that I've been informed she cries a lot and isn't thriving. Basically, we require a home that can observe her for a week or so before we place her for adoption," she replied.

At this point I asked, "How old is this baby?"

"Oh, I'm sorry, I haven't noticed. Let's see. . . . She's about nine days old."

My heart leapt within me and tears swelled in my eyes. Trying to stay calm, I replied, "What time would you like to drop the baby off?" After I hung up, I ran to the back door and got Dennis's attention. Still crying, I told him about the baby.

A young woman brought the baby to the door after lunch and reaffirmed that they'd take her off our hands in a week or so when they found the right adoptive home for her. I found myself listening to her words and playing the usual role, all the while waiting for them to hand her to me and knowing there had to be more to our future together than a few days. The baby's name was Stacey, and she was exactly as I'd remembered her in the dream.

I could, but won't, explain in detail how we discovered her health problems—heroin drug addiction, double hernias, a heart murmur, brain seizures, milk allergy, and even the doctor's presentiment that she could be retarded due to the combination of her health problems. Needless to say, as time and information revealed these tidbits, her adoptability level decreased and she stayed with us longer and longer.

Attending education week at BYU a year later was a boost to our spirits, because one of the faculty members took time to bear testimony to us about his family's special problems in adoption and how they'd been overcome. We took heed and began to move toward adopting Stacey, prayerfully overcoming every obstacle put in our way. She was about 2 1/2 years old when her final adoption papers were signed in our living room, and shortly thereafter we went to the Alberta Temple for the sealing ceremony.

She's now six years old, and believe me, she's not retarded. She's bright and inquisitive and a delightful test to our patience. We always felt she was meant for our family, and our Heavenly Father blessed us abundantly in bringing our dream to fulfillment.

Two months later, Suzy Carter retold the story to her friend Camille Brennan while shopping. Brennan was a BYU student at the time and was required to collect stories for her folklore class. She asked Suzy to write the story down for her:

This one couple awoke one night after having the same dream. They had dreamed that they were together in a delivery room where the wife was in labor. They seemed to have the feeling that the delivery was not the usual kind of delivery from where their other children had been born. They also noticed that the baby was much smaller than their other children.

Not knowing the meaning of this spiritual dream, they got back into their everyday routine. Nine days later, they received a phone call from the Social Services Department. They explained of an emergency situation where a little girl needed a home immediately. The girl had been born addicted to drugs and her life had been endangered. Since she was out of immediate danger, she needed a home.

The social worker also said the girl had been born very small.

The wife asked how old the baby was, and she was told it was nine days old. The couple knew this was the little girl they had dreamed of.

They adopted the baby and now have a healthy little girl.

Camille Brennan contextualized the story with the following information: "Suzy and I discussed several stories one day while we were shopping. I asked her to write them down and send them to me. The following is how she wrote it. Suzy believes this story. She read [it] in the *Ensign* several months ago. This story reassured Suzy that children are meant to come to earth. She realized that parents are very close to their children, even before they are born. She said this story made her believe that adopted children belong to their adoptive parents. Suzy likes to hear these stories because they remind her that she needs to be close to the Lord" (Brennan 1986a:14, Wilson Archives).

Although Suzy's version was written down, she initially narrated it. While her written version does not capture the orality of performance, it nonetheless reveals some of the revisions made as narratives move from the published page into social contexts. Suzy's retelling is shorter than the original, and her choices of what to include and exclude are telling. Suzy's version focuses on the supernatural part of the experience. She includes the fact that both husband and wife had the dream, that the delivery was different from the deliveries of their current children, and that the baby was smaller than the others. Suzy even remarkably remembers the exact number of days between the dream (and birth), and the phone call. Suzy also recounts how the couple went about their daily lives until the phone call, when fulfillment of the dream occurs. She includes all the details that convinced Geri, and would presumably convince an audience, that the dream was divine and prophetic. She ends the story with a single sentence: "They adopted the baby and now have a healthy little girl."

The original story, however, includes far more information about the decision to actually adopt the child, not just accept her temporarily. In other words, there is much more information about the mundane elements of the experience, not just the supernatural, a move in keeping with the magazine's stated desire to avoid focusing on the sensational. However, the audience for the *Ensign* is not an audience of Geri's friends and family, and Geri (or magazine editors) had already edited her narrative to exclude much of this story about the trials and struggles of the first months with baby Stacey: "I could, but won't, explain in detail how we discovered her health problems," she writes. One might safely assume that when Geri Walton narrates this story to friends and family, she includes far more of this information, since this narrative is more than a faith-promoting story; it is a rich, emotionally tinged account of a major life experience. Geri adapts her story to a public audience, just as Pauline Clayson adapted her story about her mother to accommodate a public audience during sacrament meeting by removing personal details relevant to her but not to the spiritual experience (see chapter 2). When a woman who does not know Geri, her husband, or their children picks up that story from a magazine and narrates it to a friend, it becomes even easier to omit personal details irrelevant to the divine revelation.

The *major* revisions to the narrative content can be explained, therefore, by shifts in perspective and audience. The shifts in medium—from written to oral and then to written again—also contribute to revisions in the narrative, revisions that reflect the process of committing experience to the page in reverse. The formal language of scripture—"revealing dream" and "we took heed"—disappears. So, too, does the descriptive language and emotional resonance: "My heart leapt within me and tears swelled in my eyes," and "the glow of the moment." And specific references to the divine—"our Heavenly Father blessed us abundantly in bringing our dream to fulfillment"—disappear.

The same shifts can be seen in Serena Gammon's retelling of a story she read in the *Ensign* two months earlier.[13] Serena shares the story in brief summary:

> I was talking about when you have trials. Well, a lot of the *Ensign* articles have to do with people going through . . . having a test of faith.
>
> So one of the stories is about a woman whose patriarchal blessing included the words, "You will have and give birth to children." Well, she couldn't have . . . she wasn't able to have children, so they adopted like eight kids. But it started really grating on her, the feeling that . . . "It says I'm going to give birth."
>
> So when she was finally able to get past that, "You know what? I still believe in the church. Even if this never happens. Even if I never give birth myself."
>
> And after she got through that, then she had two kids through natural birth.
>
> So, you know. You sort of remember that.

While Serena dispenses with the bulk of the context, detail, and emotional resonance, the kernel of the narrative remains intact, as does its message about the power of faith. In this way, the story fulfills its primary goal: to lead people to a clearer understanding of gospel principles. Further, while the original author never quoted the patriarchal blessing directly, Serena Gammon does, a narrative strategy common in oration but fairly rare in written narratives.

In retelling other people's stories from the *Ensign*, Suzy Carter and Serena Gammon strip the basic content of the story from the context of a church magazine and embed it in a new performance context, tailoring the story to fit their needs. In this way, stories can come to life for new narrators and new audiences. In some cases, that new life surpasses the life the story had while confined to the page.

"The head and the feet have been cut off of it," Shawn Tucker says, describing stories published in church magazines. "I mean, it's had to be sort of made generic.

"I think that stories have a lot more to do with the context in which they're given. So a story in *The Friend*, anybody has to be able to read it; it's just a generic story. So, you know, this level of formulaic, just this level of . . . you know.

"And it's not to say it isn't great, because you may read a story, and the value of those is, 'OK I read through this. It either connects with my experience in a meaningful way,' which is great, or I say, 'Oh, this would be great for a lesson I'm giving.' Because I can use this part of the story, and then I can elaborate it. I can put the head and the feet back on it by connecting it with my experience or this thing that we're doing or this person and stuff like that. I can sort of revitalize it by placing it back in a context."

The performance contexts for stories drawn from the pages of church magazines can include any of the same contexts as narratives from the oral tradition, though the most common are in casual conversations with friends to provide support and guidance, during family home evenings as a resource of discussion, and above all else, in sacrament meeting talks where topics are given, not chosen. Church magazines and online resources are treasure troves of information for any topic a person might be asked to speak about, including personal revelation. "Most of the *Ensign* articles that I've heard shared have been in church," explains Dave Gammon. "Because members are asked to prepare lessons, to prepare talks, and so they're often looking for source material. So they'll search online and a magazine article will come up. Or they will have read something in the past month that they say, 'Oh wow, that's a great article, I'll include that.'"[14]

In these contexts, old stories can serve as well as recent ones and do not rely on memory to be used. Yet neither are they likely to become permanent fixtures in a person's repertoire. Like stories remembered because of being recently read rather than because they made a deep personal impression, stories culled for a particular talk tend to be associated more with the topic than with personal interest and may be forgotten quickly.

Of course, published stories *can* strike a particularly resonant chord and become embedded in a person's repertoire.[15] Eventually, these stories may lose their attribution and enter the world of the legend, where ties to specific people become tenuous, ignored, or unknown. This is the case with a story told by Sandy Johnson about a woman prompted to pull her car into another lane of the road moments before a truck comes careening around a curve and crosses into the lane she had been in (for the complete narrative, see chapter 5). Sandy does not remember where she heard it but thought she may have read it in the *Ensign*.

Conclusion

The written tradition is pervasive, powerful, and varied within the LDS Church. Family records that log the stories of generations past serve as history books, genealogical documentation, and personal scripture. They may also serve as a wellspring for oral narrative, maintaining the experiences, and the people, of the past as relevant for the present and inspirational for the future. Yet despite this power, the oral tradition clearly dominates, both in frequency and in authority. In concurrent traditions, the living story trumps the written one. The visceral, experiential, personal perspective—even of events shared secondhand—can sidestep claims of bias in a social context where the written text has no defense. As record keepers themselves, contemporary audiences are all too aware of the subtle siren song encouraging writers to gild the past when writing for posterity.

While family stories are expected to be adopted by contemporary generations, stories published in church magazines typically live much briefer lives. A particular story resonates with a problem a friend is facing and the story is shared. A person receives the call to give a sacrament meeting talk or has a more consistent calling in the church and searches church magazines for stories to help illustrate a particular theological point. Stories from church magazines get quoted, retold, and read verbatim as a regular part of religious life. Occasionally people read a story that resonates so strongly in their own lives that they share it again and again, incorporating the story into their repertoire of spiritual narratives for the rest of their lives. More often, the wealth of available published stories in constant supply alleviates the need or desire to hold on to someone else's story for long.

Stories published in church magazines also contribute indirectly to the centrality of revelation in contemporary life by reinforcing the power and utility of sharing stories with other faithful members of the church and providing a model for how people can and should share their own stories. The care speakers take in church to tie their stories to gospel principles clearly derives from informal enculturation processes of watching other speakers do the same, but the written tradition explicitly and repeatedly stresses this point to a degree that cannot be ignored. Further, the inclusion of stories depicting subtle and implicit experiences with the divine encourages members to reconsider their own lives for times when God blessed, protected, or guided them. Such reflections give rise to retroactive revelation, where people realize the divinity of their experience only in hindsight (see chapter 4).

Both oral and written traditions provide ample support for the existence of God's love and guidance. Yet the two are unequal in nature and impact. The written tradition in family records, with its face to the future and an audience of posterity, is often heavily didactic and assumed well polished. The written tradition in church magazines is similarly didactic, with its insistence on direct ties to gospel principles. Both serve as a practical and spiritual resource, whether as prompt or for inspiration. But when the hours are logged, it is the oral tradition rather than the written one that dominates. Dave Gammon's critique rings all too true: "Do you read your journal very often?" Less likely yet, "Do you read your ancestor's journal very often?" But ask how often church members share stories about their lives and the answer is given in times per day or week, not per month or year.

Synthesis: Oral and Written Traditions

The Dilemma of Written Traditions

Folklorists have had an uneasy relationship with written traditions over the past two centuries, and while many of the artificial obstacles have been removed, the field continues to struggle with how and to what extent written and other mass mediated traditions can and should be drawn into the folklorist's frame.

Initially, entire cultures were cast as either literate or oral, suggesting that this divide was fundamental and all-encompassing. Oral cultures operated one way, written cultures another. While it is certainly true that there were and continue to be some small groups that remain preliterate, scholars began to recognize that most cultures employed both oral and written means for communication, and that no matter how dominant the written tradition, oral traditions inevitably coexisted in widespread, powerful ways. That coexistence was assumed to be uneasy, even antagonistic. Written traditions were viewed as the antithesis of oral traditions and the antithesis of folklore. While folklore was assumed to be dynamic, created collectively, and authentic in capturing the democratic voice of the "folk," written traditions were assumed to be fixed, created by individuals, and reflective of the views of the elite in power. Such a view grew partially out of the well-meaning but misguided political impulse to empower the folk and reveal their inherent worth to the nation-state. The result, however, was restrictive and distorting, forcing "the folk" into a wardrobe that simply did not fit. In order to be authentic, their traditions had to be untouched by the taint of the literary world, a presumption that unfairly cast the folk as illiterate and the literate as hegemons. It further reified folk and elite as categories clearly demarcated and mutually distinguishable, a divide repeated again and again through folklore studies with binaries such as fine art versus folk art, and the individual versus the collective.

Despite the critique of monolithic cultures and the ideological assumptions bound into both oral and written traditions, two critical issues continue to drive the unease folklorists have with written traditions and mass mediated traditions more generally: dynamism and shared voice. Both folklore as product—riddle, story, pot, dance—and folklore as process—artistic communication in small groups—demand dynamism, that ability for people to shape performance to fit their specific situational and cultural contexts. Dynamism makes shared voice possible. Forms and experiences are adapted to reflect—whether directly or indirectly through various forms of critique or distortion—the views and voice of the performer situated within a particular culture. In the field of folklore, concerted attention to the individual in the act of performance and not merely the collective has emerged only in the last few decades of the twentieth century. The field continues to be dominated by analyses that approach folklore as traditional, steeped in past precedent, and most productive when trying to understand a culture rather than an individual, an enterprise that makes sense within the social sciences though somewhat less within the humanities.

As a result of these two driving principles, written traditions pose problems in that they are assumed static by virtue of being codified in print, and individualistic by virtue of being traceable to specific authors. When that writing is disseminated widely, it also comes under criticism for being unable to be traced to self-identified, bounded culture groups, representing instead popular culture, market forces, and transitory interests. While all of these critiques have been deconstructed as inef-fective criteria for division—the boundaries of culture are permeable and operate on multiple scales; folk artists, for example, are also subject to market forces, and traditional culture is dynamic and therefore also reflects transitory interests—they remain useful heuristically to define the field and to focus analysis on particular aspects of expressive culture that might otherwise be ignored.

Operating according to these general assumptions and orientations, writ-ten traditions are often ignored, sidelined, or given only cursory attention. That said, folklorists have nonetheless found useful ways to engage written traditions, both by identifying folklore forms in literature and mass media—such as folk-tales in television ads, proverbs in Shakespeare, and oral structures in American Indian literature—and by recognizing the dynamic and expressive nature of some written or published genres—such as chain letters and e-mails, memorial poems, latrinalia, recipes, and Xeroxlore. With the shift from thinking about folklore primarily as product to folkloristics as a way of examining expressive culture, written and mass mediated modes have been opened up to folklore analysis, helping to smash artificial boundaries according to media and form. Where the field continues to struggle, however, is in attending to the regular interplay between oral and written traditions, particularly for genres that do not simply thrive in one medium while fostering a pale cognate in another, but thrive in both.

The Cycles between Oral and Written

The question of moving between media has been explored most consistently and extensively in the study of fairy tales and ballads. For fairy tales, scholars have been particularly consumed with questions of origins: Did fairy tales begin in the oral tradition and get co-opted by literary figures, or the reverse? Scholars argued the former until the 1960s, when compounding evidence suggested the latter. More recently, a third, compromise position has been posited, suggest-ing a cultural history of multiple sources (Apo 2007:21). With the destruc-tion of "the myth of orality," fairy tale scholarship has paid greater attention to the movement back and forth between written and oral fairy tale traditions, whether through popular chapbooks (see Apo 2007, Bottigheimer 2002 and 2003, and Kaliambou 2007) or public performance such as British pantomimes (see Schacker 2007).

Ballads have garnered a similar degree of attention with the question both of initial creation—with ballads divided according to those that emerged from a "pure oral tradition" and those broadside or "street" ballads that emerged from the pen for commercial gain—and of the regular intersection of the two media.

In her book *Oral Poetry*, Ruth Finnegan traces this movement back and forth between oral and written forms as she deconstructs the utility of maintaining the assumption of an oral/written divide (1992:160–9). She points out that ballad printers often sent their writers "into the country" to record ballads from the oral tradition to use for their printed broadsides. Further, one of the strategies for selling street ballads was to sing them in public, much the way a newsboy would shout the headlines from that day's paper to encourage a sale. In turn, particularly popular broadsides were adopted by people throughout both cities and countryside, so that whether ballads began primarily in an oral tradition or a written one, they moved regularly between the two media. The addition of new media has expanded this cycle. In his study of the folk song of the murder of Naomi (Omie) Wise, Gerald Milnes tracks the song as it moves among oral performance, recorded song, pamphlet, published news account, and folk collection, recognizing this process as a regular part of the transmission and distribution of folk songs, rather than as an aberration or hiccup in an otherwise "pure" oral tradition (1995).

Folklore studies that have fully acknowledged both oral and written traditions as fundamental aspects of the same tradition exist outside the scholarship of ballads and fairy tales, though they have been relatively few (see, for example, Stahl 1979, Dégh 1994:110–52). One of the most vibrant areas for such exploration has been the study of contemporary, or "urban," legends, since such legends are fueled in great part by both oral performance and written dissemination. A story published in a newspaper may spawn a vibrant oral tradition, just as that oral tradition may spawn newspaper articles, ultimately fueling continued narration.[16]

The study and recording of oral traditions has added another dimension to this interchange, where collections of stories and songs become sourcebooks for continued oral performance. Such benefits do not come without a tradeoff. Since at least the very beginnings of the nineteenth century, narrators and singers have worried that translating the oral into print would strip the traditions of their vitality, their significance, and their meaning. In 1801, James Hogg entertained Sir Walter Scott, author of, among other things, *The Minstrelsy of the Scottish Border*, in his home while his mother sang ballads for him. She then criticized Scott: "It is an auld story! But mair nor that, excepting George Warton an' James Stewart, there were never ane o' my sangs prentit till ye prentit them yoursel', an' ye hae spoilt them awthegither. They were made for singing an' no for reading; but ye hae broke the charm now, an' they'll never be sung mair. An' the worst thing of a', they're nouther right spell'd nor right setten down" ([1834] 1882: 3–4). Hogg writes that his mother's dire prediction came true: "My mother has been too true a prophetess, for from that day to this, these songs, which were the amusement of every winter evening, have never been sung more" (4).

Yup'ik Eskimo scholar and elder Elsie Mather echoes many indigenous storytellers when she worries that fixing oral traditions to the page replaces the fluid with the static, closes them off to variation, opens them up to analysis that removes their mystery and ability to encourage multiple interpretations, and separates teller and audience, undermining the social cohesion storytelling fosters (1995). There is also fear that writing will confer an undue degree of authority to a particular version of a story or song, so that to narrate or sing other versions, or to alter the text, whether consciously or unconsciously, is to perform it wrong.[17]

Voiced by storytellers and singers, these concerns are grounded in specific contexts and traditions, rather than theorized abstractly. Ethnographic analysis provides an avenue for exploring these issues as they exist in situ, grounded in the specific. The wealth of possible relationships between oral and written traditions extrapolated through cross-cultural analysis can be made sense of by returning to the case study. In the study of personal revelation narratives among Latter-day Saints, for example, it is clear that oral and written traditions not only coexist but feed each other in a symbiotic relationship of mutual benefit. Published sources rely on a regular supply of stories from lay members and leaders in the church, and lay members rely on published stories to construct their church talks and lessons. Further, a deep tradition of personal record keeping has ensured that written traditions exist not only in mass publication but also in more humble dissemination among families. Ethnographic study of how these two traditions are actively created and drawn together in performance reveals the factors that help determine this use and relationship, including: authority and familiarity of the source; relative permanence of the medium; individual orientation toward secondhand stories and legends; vibrancy of either tradition within one's family; exposure to published literature; and function, including instruction, edification, and family cohesion. Most importantly, such study reveals that the shift in audience so often accompanying a shift from oral to written may be as important as the shift in mode itself.

The Importance of Audience

When scholars have examined the process of oral traditions becoming written, or written traditions becoming oral, they have tended to look for formal and stylistic changes made in order to accommodate the new mode of communication, assuming that each mode has distinct and identifiable characteristics and demands. The work of Axel Olrik in the first decades of the twentieth century to uncover the "epic laws" of oral performance ([1922] 1992) laid the foundation for future studies that tackled oral and written traditions together. Some of the most enduring of those studies have been conducted by Walter Ong. In *Interfaces of the Word*, Ong maps many of the textual characteristics of oral narratives that distinguish them from their written counterparts, including: standardization of themes, focus on action, minimal description, simple syntactic structures, limited vocabulary, heavy use of formulas including clichés, stock characters, symbolic rather than analytic engagement with the past, verbosity, and repetition (1967:17–87 and 1977:102–17).

A number of other scholars followed suit, primarily in the field of linguistics (for example, Chafe and Tannen 1987, Goody 1987, Murray 1988, and Tannen 1982a and 1982b). In folklore, Sandra Dolby Stahl asked similar questions about the personal experience narratives Larry Scheiber shared orally among his family and friends, and in writing in a column in his local newspaper. She gathered her results into a chart that contrasts parallel stylistic features for oral and written narratives: interaction between storyteller and audience in oral narratives versus paragraphing in written ones; common frame of reference versus popular allusions; paralinguistic features versus punctuation; repetition versus variety and innovation; context-sensitive language versus language directed toward the anticipated sensibility of the reading audience; forward movement versus movement back and forth; and variable text versus fixed text (Stahl 1979:48–9). My own content analysis of personal revelation narratives in the official LDS Church–published *Ensign* magazine confirms many of these claims, while adding conclusions specific to religious narratives, LDS culture, and the *Ensign* in particular (see earlier in this chapter).

Without downplaying the significance of this shift in mode, the shift in audience is often at the heart of this shift, suggesting that movement from the oral to the written and back again may not be as great a watershed moment as we have assumed. Or rather, the importance we have placed on the shift in mode owes a great deal to the shift in audience that typically accompanies it. It is not coincidence that when Gary Schmidt and Donald Hettinga brainstormed the questions plaguing teachers and writers in the fields of children's literature, American literature, and medieval literature, they coupled mode and audience: "What happens to a tale when it goes from an oral telling and an adult audience to a print version and an audience of children?" (1992:xi–xii). Nor is it surprising that when Denise Murray compared conversation with e-mail among coworkers, she found the specific situational context more relevant than whether the discourse was oral or written (1988:370). When Latter-day Saints sit down to record their spiritual experiences for future generations, they imagine an audience that shapes what they choose to include, exclude, and highlight. The audience may be imagined as vast, or relatively small, but in all cases, it is imagined. The dimension of the unknown encourages a degree of idealization less inherently pervasive in oral performance.

This negotiation of audience is ultimately inseparable from mode, however. Idealization that occurs because of an unseen audience is certainly also attributable to the assumed permanence of writing. Further, each medium has a set of expectations for what an audience expects to encounter. The pregnant pauses; "ums," "ahs," and "you knows"; false starts; and repetition rarely even noticed in oral performance are anathema to most written traditions, not because writing cannot accommodate them (this sentence clearly proves otherwise) but because of assumed audience expectation. In this way, audience is a common denominator for oral and written performances alike. We are reminded, therefore, that the process of creation for oral and written media can be similar in substantial ways, even if the product is substantially different, and that shifts in audience can powerfully affect form, style, and meaning, as much as can shifts in medium.

Just as those of us folklorists studying narrative have been aware of the impact of audience but continue to produce studies that focus primarily on text and performer, so too have we been aware of the vibrant intersection of multiple media but continue to produce studies that focus primarily on oral transmission. I am not convinced that these priorities and foci are out of balance. The world is a complex place. In order to make sense of it, academic disciplines have carved up the study of the world into manageable chunks. Folklorists will continue to focus on oral traditions as the bread and butter of their enterprise, while literary scholars will continue to focus on written ones. Yet as we see with generic systems of narrative, categories blur. The growth in academic programs has been a move toward interdisciplinary studies, with an explosion of programs such as Environmental Studies, Ethnic Studies, American Studies, and Communication and Culture, all of which cross departmental boundaries in order to examine phenomena that refuse to be corralled by a single discipline.

A reasonable path forward should include becoming increasingly informed by these realizations, so that medium does not always determine the boundaries of study. In some cases, it will remain dominant, as is clearly the case for the Scottish ballad singer and the Yup'ik elder Elsie Mather. But we should be open to the possibility that in many cultures, native epistemologies and semantic systems order their expressive culture according to other criteria that may draw oral, written, visual, and material evidence together as part of a coherent phenomenon. This book is hardly a model for such analysis, easily faulted for focusing almost entirely on the oral tradition and tackling the written tradition in a separate chapter rather than as an embedded part of a holistic system. It is, however, a step in what I believe to be the right direction, providing a foothold for the next study of personal revelation, one that draws the experiential, narrative, and written traditions even more tightly together.

Afterword

Personal revelation is a fundamental and integral element of LDS religion and culture. Its power and influence pervades scripture; its promise is repeated in church, at home, and while tracting; and its impact is felt directly and personally by virtually every member of the church. The idealized role of personal revelation in the lives of the Saints is one of constant companionship. Through prayer and righteous living, Latter-days Saints invite the divine into their lives and listen carefully for the whispering of the Holy Ghost. In conversations and talks during church lessons, people often cite scripture to remind themselves that while the Holy Ghost can become a constant companion for those who live in close accordance with the covenants they have made with God, they remain mortals with agency to choose and an obligation to study it out in their minds before turning a hopeful eye to God.

In practice, however, the role of personal revelation varies among members according to personal values, views, and ideologies. Some Latter-day Saints view personal revelation as a rare but powerful gift. They accept the possibility of subtle thoughts and feelings but are wary of their fellow ward members who regularly hear voices, see visions, or receive prophetic dreams. Others take to heart the regular exhortations of LDS scripture and the teachings of the early prophets in the church and open themselves up to a wide range of revelation, believing firmly in the constant and democratic nature of the Holy Ghost. So while no active LDS member would deny personal revelation, some are more open to it than others. The result is that personal revelation as part of human experience is heavily dependent on the ability and tendency to perceive the divine. When those experiences are shared, the personal and social dimensions of personal revelation are drawn into ever greater relief.

It is the social dimension of personal revelation, brought to life in the act of sharing stories of revelatory experiences, that has claimed the focus of this book. Experience and narrative are drawn together in a complex relationship guided by the abilities of the human mind to comprehend the divine; the communicative abilities to express the ambiguous, the visceral, and the spiritual; and the cultural norms and expectations for narrative, performance, and the construction of social identity.

The narratives people share about their experiences receiving personal revelation are interpreted, constructed, and narrated within this web of social and cultural norms. Meaning is shaped dialogically: experience informs expectation, expectation informs experience. In the broadest theological dimension, narratives of personal revelation provide the pervasive message that God is watchful, attentive, and loving. Such stories provide hope in a world structured as a test of faith, where temptation lurks and Satan lives.

Even in this temporal world where Earth is a threatening place and a reunion with God is far from assured, God has not abandoned his children. He has a number of weapons in his arsenal to combat Satan, including a restored church, holy scriptures, living prophets, and perhaps most powerful of all, his messenger the Holy Ghost. Personal revelation through the Holy Ghost comes as much needed, much valued protection against the dangers and corruption of a mortal existence.

There is a paradox posed by narratives of personal revelation, however. Their most explicit message confirms God's love and protection, providing hope and comfort for the listener. However, the landscape of these narratives is the world described in the plan of salvation, a world of danger and confusion, with peril at every turn. Stories of personal revelation are often referred to as faith-promoting stories and are typically shared as such. But for the Latter-day Saint who struggles to find a path through life when prayers may be answered neither immediately nor in ways immediately understandable, stories of personal revelation can be subtle reminders of just how much of a trial mortal life can be. Again, personal values, views, and ideologies shape how personal revelation is interpreted.

Yet this book has focused on individual performances as part of a collective tradition rather than as the aesthetic, competent performances of individual people with distinct histories and personalities. The rationale derives from two embedded cultural norms within the LDS religious community: the obligation for humility and the focus on the spiritual rather than the artistic in expressions of personal sacred experience. Sacred stories of personal revelation should direct glory—whether spiritual or artistic—to God, not to human narrators. Analysis that places too great an emphasis on the communicative competence or the spirituality and authority of the individual can be distracting, misleading, and misguided.

The tradeoff, however, is that more subtle variations among Latter-day Saints remain underexplored. This is only one of a number of underexplored areas of the book. One of the most ripe for analysis is the area of spiritual revelation. While all revelation is inherently spiritual, LDS revelation is provided either in the guidance of daily life and temporal affairs, or in the understanding and confirmation of religious truths. This book has focused on the former for a number of reasons. I came to this study through an interest in predictive prophecy and prophetic narrative. Temporal revelation is typically both predictive and shared in clear narrative form. Spiritual revelation, on the other hand, is eternal rather than future-oriented and is shared in testimonies that make up a recognizable verbal genre but are rarely narrative in structure. Further, the content of spiritual revelation was more daunting for cultural analysis. Temporal revelations take as their primary fodder the mundane aspects of daily life, activities widely recognizable—traveling, choosing a spouse, finding a job, raising children—though culturally informed. Spiritual revelations, on the other hand, deal with religious doctrine specific to the LDS Church, doctrine that continues to be shaped through contemporary revelation. As a non-Mormon, I cannot access certain elements of the LDS Church, such as temple rites and ordinances. Even within the church, members have varying access to spiritual understanding. As one builds a testimony, greater and greater truths are revealed. People regularly speak of not yet having a firm testimony on one doctrinal tenet or another. Others mention encounters with members of the church leadership who reference knowledge they have gained as part of their church calling. Accordingly, spiritual knowledge and the spiritual revelations that help build it pose theological challenges that demand a theological background for which neither my training nor my own religious affiliation have sufficiently prepared me.

Yet hardly should the study of spiritual revelation be abandoned, either by Mormon or non-Mormon scholars. A firm background in religious studies coupled with an equally firm background in cultural studies, anthropology, or folklore should prove sufficient to tackle this topic. Further, with spiritual revelation as arguably the most vital link between LDS theology and religious practice, analysis of spiritual revelation as a distinct verbal genre is long overdue.[1] As Ken Mullen points out, it is spiritual revelation, not temporal revelation, that provides the focus for our mortal and immortal lives: "The thing that I have learned in the last few years, as a spiritual principle, is the Lord sees the end from the beginning, as he talks about in the scriptures. And that these experiences . . . his work and his glory is to bring to pass the immortality of eternal life of man. Not to give Ken a career."

A focus on spiritual revelation over temporal revelation has the additional benefit of recentering Mormon folklore studies on the spiritual and sacred, but not necessarily supernatural, dimension of LDS life. The first study of LDS folklore was published in 1892 by the Reverend David R. Utter and was titled "Mormon Superstitions." In this brief initial foray into the study of Mormon folklore, Utter describes the widespread belief in the Three Nephites, the three apostles from the Book of Mormon who chose to remain on Earth until the time of Jesus's return. Since then, the Three Nephites have dominated narrative folklore scholarship in LDS studies. Virtually every major scholar of LDS folklore in the twentieth century has written about the Three Nephites and their appearance on Earth as encoded in a vibrant legend tradition—Wayland Hand in 1938, Austin M. Fife in 1940, Hector Lee in 1942 and 1949, and Richard M. Dorson in 1959 and 1964. William A. Wilson also began his folklore career with a study of the Three Nephites, responding to the prediction that Three Nephite legends were disappearing from the Mormon cultural landscape (they weren't). Wilson has repeatedly examined Three Nephite legends in articles published in 1969, 1975, 1976, 1988, and 1995. However, he has come to realize that the study of Three Nephite legends has perpetuated an assumption that Mormon folklore and culture more generally are consumed with the numinous and, worse, the specious.

Wilson recognizes that divine experiences are a fundamental part of LDS culture; but so, too, are the mundane experiences that reveal "the quiet lives of committed service" (1989:109). Narrative, however, poses a distinct, though not insurmountable, problem in uncovering this quiet tradition. Narratives typically demand some degree of the unusual or extraordinary in order to be regularly shared and successfully received. For the same reasons that narratives describing daily answered prayers may be eschewed for stories of unique experiences with more dramatic tension, stories of "the quiet lives of committed service" may also fail to earn regular narration. Wilson's call to arms, therefore, may be somewhat more difficult to achieve in the study of narrative, particularly in a community where humility is so highly valued and touting one's own service can be problematic (see chapter 2).

More difficult, but hardly impossible. Stories may be intensely dramatic and contain no mention whatsoever of the divine. These may not be the "quiet" stories Wilson calls for, but they may nonetheless describe a daily life of service while still meeting the formal and generic demands so common to narrative. Further, not all narratives depend on the unusual or extraordinary. As John Robinson points out, narratives may also be viable for repeated performance based on their function and on particular resonance within the conversational context (1981). The emotional dimension that a person draws forth from an experience or creates through performance can heighten its repeatability. These stories may be quiet but pack an emotional or contemplative punch that warrants repeated narration.

One evening, for example, chatting with the current ward missionaries and Brother Matt Larson, who had joined the missionaries for splits that evening, conversation turned to missionary work. Elder Aaron Chavez shared a story of being guided to talk to a woman who had been waiting for the missionaries to knock on her door. The experience is a common but powerful one. There was a pause, and then Matt Larson picked up the conversation:

> Sometimes it's hard, because sometimes you have really wonderful, wonderful experiences. And sometimes there are experiences that are extremely difficult. [Matt describes being sick off and on for nine months of his mission in Colombia.] There were many hard times during those months; but there were also many wonderful moments.
>
> So those types of experiences I'll always cherish for the rest of my life. Those stories are wonderful. I'll always keep them. Will I always share them? Probably not. The good experience ones, absolutely. Always. People do love for me to talk about my mission and I love, I love to talk about it. It's wonderful. But sometimes you want to focus on the better side of it.
>
> I mean, I've been back for twelve years now, and I still remember it very well. Just because it can be very painful at times.
>
> But, you also remember the stories, the people who you taught, the lives that you've touched. For instance . . .
>
> Just a couple of years Ago—I was here in North Carolina, I'm originally from Arizona, and my wife and I moved out here—and a couple years ago, I got a call from a gentleman in Salt Lake, who I don't know who he is, and he said his son was currently serving a mission in Colombia and that he met one of the ladies I had taught and I had baptized her–and the elder had asked, "What do you want for an Easter present?" And she had just said, "I just want you to tell Elder Larson that I am still active, I'm going to the temple, and just to tell him that she's doing great [*teary*]."
>
> And so . . . that's just a wonderful experience.
>
> So he called me just to tell me that. And so it feels good. Those stories are wonderful. That's one story I will definitely tell my children. When I have some [*laughter*].

One need not move outside the realm of personal revelation for productive areas for future research. Throughout this book, areas for further study have emerged that are impossible to fully address within a single monograph. Revelations granted as part of one's church calling and revelations conveyed by loved ones who have passed into the spirit world deserve particular attention. Parallels among different types of faith-promoting stories can also provide fruitful areas for analysis, linking experiences according to other emic categories such as answered prayer and miracles that blur divisions between divine promptings and divine intervention, especially now that individual genre studies have been undertaken. Studies of umbrella genres such as supernatural stories, faith-promoting stories, and missionary narratives excited the interest of early scholars in LDS narrative from the 1930s to the 1960s. Such broad strokes were useful for inaugural studies but were restricted in their analysis since case studies had not yet been undertaken. Recognizing the need for individual genre studies, the second wave of folklorists studying LDS narrative from the 1970s to the1990s focused more heavily on the genres and subgenres within these large groups—women's visionary narratives of unborn children, conversion narratives, premonitions, and stories of near-death experiences. The study of personal revelation narratives fits firmly within genre studies but cuts across many subgenres and parallels many umbrella categories. With a range of studies addressing multiple levels of the narrative tradition, it would seem to be a good time to revisit larger categories that suggest coherence among experiences common to LDS culture, particularly according to emic criteria recognized within the community. The concept of performance provides a particularly useful strategy to reexamine semantic categories constructed by narrators by encouraging analysis of story-telling sessions, where one story leads to the next.

I have already mentioned the problem of ignoring regional variation when examining LDS culture and noted how my fieldwork has supported assumptions of regional and cultural diversity not only in how personal revelations are shared but in how they are received (see chapter 1). These assumptions about Mormons in other regions and other countries are typically made by returned missionaries, basing their conclusions on personal experience. Such exoteric constructions of the identity of other Mormons are worthy in their own right but tell us far more about the people doing the describing than the people described. Studies of missionaries in other countries have continued this focus on US Mormons in other countries (see Knowlton 1994, Rudy 2004). However, studies that shift the focus from this primarily white, US Mormon population to examine how Mormonism is interpreted and enacted in social, cultural, and religious contexts around the world would begin to provide a more accurate picture of Mormonism as a global religion.

There is a nascent body of scholarship attempting this analysis. Much of the work focuses on religious history, explaining how Mormonism took hold in particular countries (see, for example, Britsch 1986 and 1988, and Browning 1997). However, there are also studies that examine cultural variation and expression, such as F. LaMond Tullis's book *Mormons in Mexico*, Grant Underwood's work in New Zealand with the Maori (2000), Eric Eliason and Gary Browning's work in Russia (2002), and a growing number of articles in the journal *Dialogue: A Journal of Mormon Thought*, including

Jennifer Huss Basquiat's work in Haiti (2004). In 2008, the *British Journal of Mormon Studies* was launched, describing itself as "a British based internationally focused, peer-reviewed online and printed scholarly journal." By the second issue, the journal had changed its name to the *International Journal of Mormon Studies*. The revision appears to be hopeful rather than reflective, as the articles in the two issues published so far focus almost entirely on Europe and the United States.

Ethnic variation in Mormon culture and religious thought and behavior is also beginning to be explored in diasporic communities in the United States. Scandinavian immigrants have been a popular subject (see Christensen 1971, Johnson 1973, Wilson 1979). But increasingly, non-Anglo groups are also being studied, such as Hispanics (Embry 1997, Iber 2000) and Asians (Embry 1999). Studies of expressive culture and folklore, however, remain rare. Although John Sorenson claimed in 1973 that "at least at this time there is no significant evidence that the values and doctrine of Tongan Saints, for example, differ markedly from those of American Mormons in their roles as Latter-day Saints." He did follow up by saying, "Research on this topic would, of course, be welcome" (25).

Finally, cross-cultural analysis that considers personal revelation in other cultural and religious traditions would prove invaluable in terms of a humanistic approach to religious practice and belief. The Holy Ghost and the still small voice for Latter-day Saints can be usefully compared to the Holy Spirit among many other Christian faiths, particularly Pentecostal. It would also be useful to consider promptings of the Spirit outside of religious contexts, comparing them to phenomena described variously as intuition or women's intuition, sixth sense, premonition, hunch, and inspiration, among others. An experience-centered approach, as employed by David J. Hufford in his work on numinous experiences that intersect with medical ailments (1982, 1995), would be particularly useful in such cross-cultural analysis.

Cross-cultural connections are already being made among Latter-day Saints. Some narrators, BYU students in particular, have referred to revelations received by their family or friends as premonitions (see Allen 1996 and Orden 1971). Other Latter-day Saints have recognized revelation in the stories shared by their non-Mormon friends. Julia Condie's younger sister Missy had a high school friend Laura, who was not a member of the church, but who shared her experience of being prompted to leave a party where a few minutes later, people were shot and killed. Julia and her sister both see the Holy Ghost at work: "When Missy told me this story, she said that she was sure that the Holy Ghost had prompted Laura to leave. Beth said that even though Laura isn't

Mormon, she, too, believes that divine intervention prodded her to leave in time" (1994:8).

Camille Brennan grew up with mostly non-Mormon friends, including her friend who told her about a dream she had:

> After I broke up with Mark, I was like really upset. You know, I just didn't know where my life was going. And I felt so . . . well . . . alone.
>
> Anyway, I had this dream.
>
> You're going to think I'm losing it, but I had this dream. And it was like, so weird.
>
> I was like, in church, but it wasn't my church, it was like a totally different church. And I was sitting there, and I was like the only one in the chapel. And all of a sudden they called me up, this priest did. And he had this baby he was going to baptize. And I was like really surprised because this baby was mine. And they named him Kevin.
>
> And, Camille, I really believe this baby is mine. (1986a:17, Wilson Archives)

Camille Brennan adds in her notes: "I also believe this story is true." She also believes it to be revelation from God, a God who provides guidance to all of his children, regardless of their religion. "The research I have collected has led me to believe that having premonitions about children is fairly common, not only in the Mormon Church, but also with nonmembers" (3).

Revelation, inspiration, premonition—the phenomena of receiving visions of the future and prompts to action are widespread in both religious and nonreligious realms. Such experiences provide plans of action, food for thought, and grist for narrative. While narrative provides only one entry point for analysis, it is a particularly powerful one. Sitting at the intersection of interpretation—transforming the abstract into the concrete, experience into meaning, thought into words—narrative provides both an effective vantage point for study and a vivid medium that highlights the creative dimension of human experience. To ignore this complex, multilayered dimension of experience is to ignore not only the aesthetic but the interdependence between the impulse to understand and the need to create.

Appendix

In order to facilitate the study of such a large number of stories, I coded each narrative according to the thirty-two criteria (with forty-eight separate columns for specific themes and motifs, the most significant of which appear in chart 5), listed below. However, because the data were incomplete for many stories, not all of these criteria could be usefully employed in analysis. The charts that follow provide a numeric breakdown for the categories that were most complete and most useful in my analysis. These charts are referenced in the text of the book.

Summary
Personal—Legend
Setting
Narrator
Relationship between
    narrator and receiver
    of revelation
Relationship between
    narrator and collector
Collector
Gender of narrator
Gender of collector
Verbatim/Notes

Year told/recorded
Year of event
City occurred in
City told in
Medium of revelation
Terms used to
    categorize experience
Origin of revelation
Prescriptive/Descriptive
Solicited/Unsolicited
Positive/Negative
Tractable/Intractable
Action suggested

Action taken
Fulfilled/Unfulfilled
Themes
Motifs
Direct quote of Holy
    Ghost
Hesitate before acting
Double confirmation
Function
Stewardship
Stated belief

Chart 1. Narrators and Types of Stories Told

	Narrators	Stories Told	Revelatory Experiences	Stories By Type				Legend	
				PEN	Family	Acquaintance	Unknown	FOAF	Unattributed
Male	144	211	260	108	42	36	0	10	15
Female	162	214	171	77	67	37	7	11	15
Unknown	16	16	10	4	5	2	0	2	3
Total	322	441	441	189	114	75	7	23	33

FOAF stands for Friend of a Friend, a common acronym used to describe contemporary legends, where specific attribution is difficult to pin down.

Chart 2. Medium

Medium	Total*	Female		Male		Both	Unknown
		Experienced	Shared	Experienced	Shared	Experienced	Shared
Internal	418	154	191	252	212	12	15
• Feeling	121	42	55	71	60	8	6
• Thought†	67	24	34	42	31	1	2
• Voice	59	16	21	43	36	0	2
• Prompt‡	24	9	8	14	16	1	0
• Dream	129	60	67	68	58	1	4
• Vision	18	3	6	14	11	1	1
External	40	19	29	20	10	1	1
• Voice	8	5	6	2	2	1	0
• Vision	4	3	4	1	0	0	0
• Visitation	4	2	3	2	1	0	0
Unknown	24	9	16	15	7	0	1

*Some of the stories include multiple experiences. In other charts, those are marked by the "Double" category, since the choices are between two options: descriptive or prescriptive, solicited or unsolicited. Here, however, there are multiple options. In order to accurately indicate the media through which revelation is received, I have counted each experience, meaning that the totals add up to more than 441.

†People use many terms to describe their experiences in addition to those listed in the chart (see chart 3 that follows here in the appendix). Others include "impression," "inspiration," and "knowledge." All three correspond most closely with "thought," which is where I have counted them.

‡"Prompt" is an umbrella term used to describe experiences that people clearly see as internal, but not dreams or visions. With no clearer articulation, I have used "prompt" to indicate those ambiguous revelations.

Chart 3. Terms Used to Describe Experience

Term	Total*
Explicitly Religious Term	20
• Burning of the Bosom	1
• Miracle	2
• Revelation	10
• Still Small Voice	
Ambiguous Term	438
• Came to Mind	12
• Dream	123
• Experience	4
• Feeling	117
• Knowledge	21
• Impression	44
• Inspiration	21
• Prompting	43
• Thought	20
• Told	13
• Vision	21
• Voice	64
Modifier	47
• Distinct (impression/feeling)	12
• Good (feeling)	3
• Peaceful (feeling)	8
• Strong (impression/feeling)	24

*The total number of terms is more than 441 since some people use multiple terms in their stories. Also, I have not included ambiguous terms used fewer than three times.

Chart 4. Solicited versus Unsolicited

Solicited vs. Unsolicited	Total	Female		Male		Both	Unknown
		Experienced	Shared	Experienced	Shared	Experienced	Shared
Solicited	90	33	43	55	46	2	1
• Directly*	67	23	30	43	36	1	1
• Indirectly†	23	10	13	12	10	1	0
Unsolicited	332	129	160	195	157	8	15
Double‡	7	4	4	3	3	0	0
Unknown	12	5	7	7	5	0	0

*Solicited directly: personal revelation received in response to a specific prayer.
†Solicited indirectly: personal revelation received after a person prayed, but the prayer was not directly related to the revelation that followed.
‡Double: a single narrative that includes two revelations, one solicited, one unsolicited.

Chart 5. Prescriptive versus Descriptive

Prescriptive vs. Descriptive	Total	Female		Male		Both	Unknown
		Experienced	Shared	Experienced	Shared	Experienced	Shared
Prescriptive	205	77	92	124	108	4	5
Descriptive	173	77	98	92	67	4	8
• Primarily Descriptive	130	60	74	67	50	3	6
• Heavily Prescriptive	43	17	24	25	17	1	2
Both	29	7	8	21	20	1	1
Double	8	2	5	5	2	1	1
Unknown	20	6	8	14	11	0	1

*The high number of descriptive revelations corresponds to the high rate of revelatory dreams in the narrative tradition: 103 of the 173 descriptive revelations came as dreams. Only 6 prescriptive revelations came as dreams.

†Primarily descriptive: personal revelation confined primarily to a vision or understanding of what is, will be, could be, or should be

‡Heavily prescriptive: personal revelation with a prescribed action inherent in the vision or understanding provided

**Both: personal revelation that explicitly includes both a vision or understanding and a prescribed action

††Double: a single narrative that includes two revelations, one descriptive, one prescriptive.

Chart 6. Themes, Tale Types, and Motifs According to Gender

Themes, Tale Types & Motifs	Total	Female		Male		Both	Unknown
		Experienced	Shared	Experienced	Shared	Experienced	Shared
Danger	172	68	93	99	73	5	6
• Away from home	132	39	61	90	67	3	4
• Home	38	29	32	7	5	2	1
• Children	61	33	49	23	11	5	1
• Move	44	11	18	33	25	0	1
Death	76	34	41	42	31	0	4
• Possible	11	5	5	6	5	0	1
• Own	6	2	3	4	2	0	1
• Near	12	0	3	12	9	0	0
• Prepare	47	27	30	20	15	0	2
Spirit World	15	0	5	15	10	0	0
Finding a Spouse	30	14	17	16	12	0	1
Getting Married	32	16	18	16	13	0	1
Having Children	34	21	23	10	10	3	1
• More Waiting	11	6	5	4	6	1	0
Finding a Home	5	1	2	4	3	0	0
Finding a Job	17	6	7	10	10	1	0
Missionary Work	71	10	18	60	50	1	3
• Tracting	23	4	18	19	19	0	0
• Youth	58	6	6	52	52	0	0
• Guided to Investigators	13	0	0	13	13	0	0
• Dream of Missionaries	8	1	3	7	4	0	1
• Conversion	48	13	18	35	28	0	2
• Baptism	30	8	10	22	19	0	1
Guidance Speaking	8	0	0	8	8	0	0
Temple Work	18	10	11	7	7	1	0
Genealogy	11	7	8	4	3	0	0
• Assistance	6	4	4	2	2	0	0
Help Others	98	41	58	53	36	4	4
Quoting the Spirit	66	20	29	44	35	2	2
Hesitate	123	48	58	71	62	4	3
Number 3	31	13	17	17	13	1	1
Additional Confirmation	69	23	32	39	31	7	6
Double Confirmation	14	4	8	8	6	2	0
Superlative Endings	12	3	5	9	6	0	1

Chart 7. Motifs According to Narrative Distance

	Total Stories Told	Quote Holy Ghost		Hesitate		Number 3		Additional Confirmation		Double Revelation		Superlative Ending	
		# Told	% of Total	# Told	% of Total	# Told	% of Total	# Told	% of Total	# Told	% of Total	# Told	% of Total
Memorate	189	36	19%	59	31%	15	8%	29	15%	8	4%	5	3%
Secondhand	189	23	12%	48	25%	10	5%	28	15%	6	3%	5	3%
Legend	56	5	9%	16	29%	4	7%	12	22%	0	0	2	4%
Unknown	7	0	0	0	0	2	29%	0	0	0	0	0	0
Total	441	64	15%	123	28%	31	7%	69	16%	14	3%	12	3%

Chart 8. Tale Types According to Narrative Distance

	Total Stories Told		Total Tale Types Told		Warning to Move		More Children Waiting		Guided to Investigators		Coming Missionaries		Genealogical Assistance	
	# Told	% of Total	# Told	% of Total	# Told	% of Total	# Told	% of Total	# Told	% of Total	# Told	% of Total	# Told	% of Total
Memorate	189	42.9%	27	14%	13	7%	5	3%	7	4%	1	1%	1	1%
Secondhand	189	42.9%	44	23%	24	13%	5	3%	5	3%	6	3%	4	2%
Legend	56	12.7%	11	20%	7	13%	1	2%	1	2%	1	2%	1	2%
Unknown	7	1.5%	0	0	0	0	0	0	0	0	0	0	0	0
Total	441	100%	82	19%	44	10%	11	2%	13	3%	8	2%	6	1%

Chart 9. Historical Time Period

Time Period	Experience Occurred*	Narrative Shared†
1830-1849	10	0
1850-1869	12	0
1870-1889	20	0
1890-1909	18	0
1910-1929	20	0
1930-1949	44	15
1950-1969	79	82
1970-1989	98	113
1990-Present	125	231
Unknown	15	0

*Experience occurred: while many of the stories do not have specific dates for when a particular revelation occurred, contextual data locates all of them in one of these periods or another except for fifteen for which a specific era could not be established.

†Narrative shared: while not all of the stories had specific dates for when they were recorded, contextual data from the story and from archival notes makes it possible to roughly sort the stories into twenty-year increments.

Notes

Introduction

1. The religious landscape of New England at the turn of the nineteenth century has been explored in depth by a number of works (e.g., Carroll 1997, Gaustad 1974, Hughes and Allen 1988, Marsden 1970, Pointer 1988, Sandeen 1970, Schlesinger 1967). Within this historical context, often termed the Second Great Awakening, the "primitive gospel" movement most clearly articulated the need for a more personal connection to God, one that the individual could attain without the intercession of trained clergy. Mormonism fits within this larger religious context in its demand for a restoration of the gospel, the reliance on a lay church, and its belief in a personal relationship with God available to all people.

2. A number of scholars have argued that these gaps have resulted in only the broadest outlines of a coherent Mormon theology. In his comparative study of doctrine developed at the local level and doctrine espoused by church presidents, Richley Crapo argues, "The church has not formalized an officially sanctioned theology beyond a surprisingly small number of central beliefs, most of which were set forth by the church's founder, Joseph Smith, Jr.," citing substantial scholarship that supports this view (1987:467).

3. A keyword search for "personal revelation" in the gospel library database on the church's website, for example, returns literally thousands of articles. The exact number of hits was 3,802 when I typed it in on December 1, 2008, and had increased to 3,947 by August 29, 2009. However, a number of sources were repeated in the returned list.

4. One of the most well known and heavily used series of books is the *Faith Promoting Series* developed by the Juvenile Instructor Office of the church. The stated goal of the series is to serve "as a means of promoting a home-produced alternative to popular novels." The series includes seventeen volumes. Some are devoted to church leaders: volume 1 describes George Q. Cannon's missionary work, and volume 3 draws pages from Wilford Woodruff's journal. Others are compilations of stories from pioneer men and women that provide testaments to the righteousness, fortitude, and courage of church members who otherwise would be lost to history outside their family records. Today, stories from the series are regularly used in Sunday school instruction and in church talks.

5. The Fife Folklore Archives at USU, for example, has copies of BYU student papers from 1968 to 1978, while the BYU archives has copies of USU student papers from 1978 to 1984. For a discussion of the origins of these archives, see "College and University Folklore Archives" in Stanley 2004:262–7.

6. For readers not familiar with the tale, see Louise and Yuan-His Kuo's book *Chinese Folk Tales* (1976:83–5). The story dates back to the Han Dynasty (202 BC–220 AD), though there are early versions in India and Africa as well. Today, the story is spread widely across the globe.

7. The reason for this shift is not particularly interesting, though I will provide an explanation for those contemplating their own analysis. I found ATLAS.ti cumbersome in adding my own thoughts and comments as I coded. The same was true for identifying correlations between codes. This is not meant as an indictment of ATLAS.ti, as I am sure with more patience I could have learned to manage these issues more efficiently. However, by

creating a basic but extensive Excel spreadsheet (it ultimately included seventy columns), I was able to constantly sort my data in an easy-to-view format that facilitated my analysis considerably.

Chapter 1

1. Divisions between formal religions and folk religions are archaic. At least since Jack Santino's article on Catholic folklore (1982), scholars have recognized the fallacy of assuming some religions have no formal institutional structures and others have no folklore. Leonard Primiano goes further, arguing against the division between official and unofficial church structures within a particular religion as commonly applied by scholars, a division that suggests church leaders practice religion in an official way while folk practice it in an unofficial way. He acknowledges, however, that people *within* a religion may in fact distinguish an official church, a designation useful for scholars to address (1995:45). This is clearly the case with Mormon religion, despite the fact that it is a lay church.

2. Chapter 134 is a declaration of belief by church leaders in 1835. Chapter 135 is an eyewitness account by Elder John Taylor of the martyrdom of Joseph Smith and his brother Hyrum Smith. Neither of these chapters is an example of revelation. Chapter 136 follows the rest of the D&C with a revelation by President Brigham Young on January 14, 1847, guiding him and his followers west to settle the church. Chapter 138 records a revelation by President Joseph F. Smith on October 3, 1918, about Jesus Christ's visit to the spirits of the dead. (Chapter 137 is another revelation by Joseph Smith.)

3. The Mullen's oldest daughter, Nicole, was on a mission in Argentina at the time.

4. An even more ambiguous case that makes it difficult to discern official church revelations from spurious ones is the case of the White Horse Prophecy. Mormons have lined up on both sides, some declaring the prophecy ridiculous fabrication, others asserting its truth. When General Authorities have specifically named the prophecy, they have soundly denounced it. Yet church leaders at both national and local levels have referred to individual elements of the prophecy, speaking out in favor of their truth. The result is continued confusion among many in the general membership today. The debate over the truth of the prophecy seems to be waged primarily in nonscholarly media by men and women who argue their cases with clear prejudice, both in favor of and against the prophecy (e.g., Cobabe 2004, Crowther 1962:301–22). I have been unable to find a statement clarifying whether the church takes an official stance on this prophecy today.

5. In his article "The Legend of the Three Nephites among the Mormons," Austin Fife describes the Three Nephites as "ancient apostles of the Christ on the American continent, appointed as His special emissaries to live upon this continent until His second coming, and to go among all peoples as special witnesses of the truthfulness of Christ's church" (1940:1). For other folklore studies of this legend tradition, see Dorson 1964, Fife and Fife 1956, Hand 1938, H. Lee 1949, Utter 1892, and Wilson 1988.

6. The Fifes wrote: "According to Mormon belief, the powers enjoyed by one holding the higher priesthood are so great that they make him an extended arm of the Divine Being. He may officiate in all the ordinances of the restored gospel and in every phase of the spiritual life of the church. He enjoys the gift of prophecy, the capacity to talk in tongues and to interpret them. He enjoys divinely inspired dreams, visions, and visitations" (1956:183).

7. The University of Utah Folklore Archive, located in the Marriott Library, also follows this system of cataloguing thanks to collaborative work between Wilson and Marriott Library archivist Ann Reichman. For an explanation of Wilson's system, see Wilson 1993:535–38.

8. The archives at BYU recently added an index cataloging personal experience narratives separately from the legend materials.

9. In the United States, for example, communication between lay members and the divine shared in oral narrative is particularly common among evangelical Christian faiths, Pentecostals, charismatics, Neopagans, and in many religious and spiritual traditions that can be categorized under the umbrella of New Age religions (Pike 2004:vii, Lewis and Melton 1992:x–xii). For folkloric studies of spiritual memorates in religious contexts, see, for example, Clements 1980, Hinson 2000, Lawless 1984 and 1988, Mullen 1983, Orsi 1996, Titon and George 1978, and Titon 1988. See also the discussion of religious memorates at the end of chapter 3.

10. See, for example, B. McConkie 1981; Oaks 1999.

11. In fact, dictionary definitions in general are popular starting points for sacrament meeting talks, biblical or secular. High Councilman Eddie Blount, from the stake presidency in North Carolina, gave a talk on the importance of integrity and, after quoting the D&C, quoted the online Webster's dictionary for "integrity" (February 27, 2007). Just over a year later, Katrina Smith was asked to speak on the topic of integrity, and she too quoted Webster's dictionary (March 9, 2008).

12. When I asked Ken Mullen whether there are differences between the revelations he receives as Second Counselor in the stake presidency and other revelations he receives, he explained: "Yeah. I don't think I talk to Lee [his wife] much about things that are of my calling. You know, we'll talk about things that are happening, but not about decisions that we're pondering and impressions we're receiving about those decisions. [*Turning to Lee*] I don't know that I ever talk to you about those. I just don't. There's a place for that and it's in the stake president's office when we're sitting there. So yeah, there are differences." This norm changes when stories move from personal experiences to legends. As Todd Coleman noted during a meeting of the Elder's Quorum, there are lots of stories about church authorities naming someone that they've never met to be stake president (January 6, 2008). Stories severed from specific names avoid the taboo of keeping private matters private. For a more complete discussion of the difference between personal experiences and legends, see chapter 2.

13. Thomas S. Monson delivered the talk on Saturday evening, September 30, 2006. A transcript of the talk can be found on the church's website at http://www.lds.org by following the links to Gospel Library, then General Conference. It can also be found in the November 2006 *Ensign* magazine (general conference talks are traditionally published in the following month's *Ensign* magazine). In 2008, when Gordon B. Hinckley died, Thomas S. Monson became the president of the church.

14. L. Tom Perry of the Quorum of the Twelve Apostles articulates this idea in much the same way church members do today: "There is order in the way the Lord reveals His will to mankind. We all have the right to petition the Lord and receive inspiration through His Spirit within the realm of our own stewardship. Parents can receive revelation for their own family, a bishop for his assigned congregation, and on up to the First Presidency for the entire Church. However, we cannot receive revelation for someone else's stewardship. The Prophet Joseph Smith declared: 'It is contrary to the economy of God for any member of the Church, or any one, to receive instruction for those in authority, higher than themselves'" (2003:83–8; the quote from Joseph Smith comes from *Teachings of the Prophet Joseph Smith* (J. Smith 1976:21).

15. The name of Serena's friend is a pseudonym.

16. "Here" is North Carolina.

17. Explicit naming of the Holy Ghost or Spirit appears in almost a quarter of the narratives. Conversations surrounding the narrative performance make it clear in many more that the narrators credit the Holy Ghost as the source of their revelation. One reason explicit naming is not more prevalent relates to the issue of humility in performance, a topic discussed in chapter 2. Also, Latter-day Saints do not believe in a Holy Trinity where God,

Jesus, and the Holy Ghost are all one. Rather, they are three separate entities, referred to as the Godhead. God and Jesus have corporeal bodies, the Holy Ghost does not. As a spirit, the Holy Ghost serves as the messenger for God. For a discussion of the Holy Ghost in Mormon theology and religious practice, see Davies 2009.

18.   For church teachings about the plan of salvation, see units 1, 2, and 10 in the *Gospel Principles*, lessons 19 and 20 in the *Doctrine and Covenants and Church History: Gospel Doctrine Teacher's Manual*, and chapter 37 in *Teachings of Presidents of the Church: Brigham Young*, all of which are available online at http://www.lds.org. Mormon doctrine posits that all people, not just Latter-day Saints, arrive in the spirit world after their mortal deaths.

19.   For examples from the Wilson Archives, see Gibb 1999, Jensen 1997, Miles 1980, Jara 2000, Asay 1992, and from the Fife Archives, Rollins 1977.

20.   For a discussion of "spirit children" narratives, see Brady 1987 and Mitchell 2004, as well as chapter 5 here. For examples of these narratives in the Wilson Archives, see Layland 2001 and Vigil 2002. For a discussion of angels in the LDS faith, see Eliason 2002, in which he explains: "To Latter-day Saints, angels are not a different class of beings, but are persons at a different point along a path of progression. Angels can be spirits from the pre-earth life, or people who have died but have not yet been resurrected, or people like Moroni who have received their resurrection." See also M. H. Cannon 1945.

21.   This distinction between the power and the gift of the Holy Ghost is laid out clearly in the LDS Bible Dictionary entry for "Holy Ghost": "The Holy Ghost is manifested to men on the earth both as the *power* of the Holy Ghost and as the *gift* of the Holy Ghost. The power can come upon one before baptism, and is the convincing witness that the gospel is true. It gives one a testimony of Jesus Christ and of his work and the work of his servants upon the earth. The gift can come only after proper and authorized baptism, and is conferred by the laying on of hands, as in Acts 8:12–25 and Moroni 2:1–3. The gift of the Holy Ghost is the right to have, whenever one is worthy, the companionship of the Holy Ghost. . . . When a person speaks by the power of the Holy Ghost that same power carries a conviction of the truth into the heart of the hearer (2 Nephi 33:1). The Holy Ghost knows all things (D&C 35:19) and can lead one to know of future events (2 Peter 1:21)" (1991:704). Joseph Smith taught this distinction: "There is a difference between the Holy Ghost and the gift of the Holy Ghost. Cornelius received the Holy Ghost before he was baptized, which was the convincing power of God unto him of the truth of the Gospel, but he could not receive the gift of the Holy Ghost until after he was baptized. Had he not taken this sign or ordinance upon him, the Holy Ghost which convinced him of the truth of God, would have left him (see Acts 10:1–48)" ("Baptism and the Gift of the Holy Ghost," chapter 7 in *Teachings of Presidents of the Church: Joseph Smith,* 2007:88–100). The gift of personal revelation brought by the Holy Ghost is only one of the many gifts of the Holy Ghost. For a complete list, see D&C 46:9–33. This passage is also cited regularly to clarify the connection between the power of the Holy Ghost and the Light of Christ. The two are often described as fulfilling the same function of bringing the Spirit of God to all men and women, particularly in the act of conversion. Spencer J. Condie of the Seventy, for example, also cites the story of Cornelius and Joseph Smith's interpretation in his article "Living by the Light of Christ" under the subheading "Enlightenment on the Light of Christ" (2008:56–8). However, Joseph B. Wirthlin of the Quorum of the Twelve Apostles writes: "The Light of Christ should not be confused with the personage of the Holy Ghost, for the Light of Christ is not a personage at all. Its influence is preliminary to and preparatory to one's receiving the Holy Ghost. The Light of Christ will lead the honest soul to 'hearkeneth to the voice' to find the true gospel and the true Church and thereby receive the Holy Ghost" (2003).

22.   Past President Spencer W. Kimball calls continuous revelation "the very lifeblood of the gospel of the living Lord and Savior" (Lund 2007:15, citing E. Kimball 1982:443).

23. Fellow ward member Lee Mullen also made this connection on February 25, 2008, as did
     the president of the Elder's Quorum on May 11, 2008. A picture of a radio dial is the cover
     of Gerald N. Lund's book on personal revelation (2007). The metaphor is regularly used
     by church leaders (see Faust 2004:67) and in teacher's manuals for the church ("I Will Tell
     You in Your Mind and in Your Heart, by the Holy Ghost," lesson 6 in the *Doctrine and
     Covenants and Church History: Gospel Doctrine Teacher's Manual* [1999:29] and "Joseph
     Smith Translates the Gold Plates," lesson 7 in *Primary 5: Doctrine and Covenants: Church
     History* [1997:31]). The metaphor is used by church members internationally (see Chilean
     member Maria Espinoza Aveal's write-in response to the question "Sometimes speakers in
     church will say, 'The Spirit is so strong here today'—but I haven't felt a thing. Are they
     just imagining things, or is something wrong with me?" (1995). The first instance of the
     metaphor that I have found comes from Harold B. Lee, who tells a story of counseling a
     man who has not been keeping his covenants with God. His metaphor does not exploit
     the parallel of dialing in, however: "In my home I have a beautiful instrument called a
     radio. When everything is functioning properly we can dial it to a certain station and
     hear the voice of a speaker on the other side of the world, but after we have used it for a
     long time the radio tubes begin to wear out. The radio may sit there looking just like it
     did before, but because of what has happened on the inside, we can hear nothing. Now,
     you and I have within our souls something like what might be said to be a counterpart of
     those radio tubes. We might have what we call a 'go-to-sacrament-meeting' tube, a 'keep-
     the-Word-of-Wisdom' tube, a 'pay-your-tithing' tube, a 'have-your-family-prayers' tube, a
     'read-the-scriptures' tube, and, as one of the most important—one that might be said to
     be the master tube of our whole soul—we have what we might call the 'keep-yourselves-
     morally-clean' tube. If one of these becomes worn out by disuse or inactivity—if we fail to
     keep the commandments of God—it has the same effect upon our spiritual selves that a
     worn-out tube has in a radio" (1980:38).

24. See chapter 2 for a discussion of fast and testimony meetings as a distinct performance
     venue. These meetings should be viewed as separate from the concept of the testimony
     itself, since many people use fast and testimony meetings to talk about a range of topics
     and issues, some of which are only marginally related to their testimony in the truth of the
     principles of the Mormon Church.

25. For analysis and examples of verbatim LDS testimonies, see Gilkey 1979 and Lawless 1984.

26. "Laurels" refers to the young women in the church between the ages of sixteen and seven-
     teen. At eighteen, they become eligible to join the Relief Society. The other subcategories
     of the Young Women are: beehive for ages twelve to thirteen, and mia maid for ages four-
     teen to fifteen. Boys have a parallel structure: deacons (ages twelve to thirteen), teachers
     (ages fourteen to fifteen), and priests (ages sixteen to seventeen).

27. The story does not end with her own conversion but continues to explain how her hus-
     band's heart was also finally turned to the LDS Church. In the course of his conversion,
     Cora experienced at least one miracle, probably two, which make this story particularly
     compelling when shared among others (Williams 1976). Compare this story to the
     subgenre of stories of people being prepared to accept the LDS gospel, discussed in
     chapter 5.

28. The issue of "proof" of the divine nature of a person's experience is addressed in chapter 3.

29. In an example of polygenesis, both Gerald N. Lund and I have charted the modes of
     personal revelation along a continuum. My first articulation of such a chart was in 2006.
     A year later, I picked up Lund's book and found a similar chart (2007:126). I had not
     included the Light of Christ and had separated thoughts and feelings from the still small
     voice. I did not include intervention, while Lund did. I have used Lund's concept of
     direct and indirect to revise my model but believe my model reflects the oral tradition—as
     opposed to theology or experience as Lund has devised—accurately. However, I have been
     more explicit in distinguishing between internal and external media.

30. Quorum of the Twelve apostle Boyd K. Packer describes the still small voice by citing numerous relevant scriptures: "The voice of the Spirit is described in the scripture as being neither 'loud' nor 'harsh.' It is 'not a voice of thunder, neither . . . voice of a great tumultuous noise.' But rather, 'a still voice of perfect mildness, as if it had been a whisper,' and it can 'pierce even to the very soul' and 'cause [the heart] to burn.' (3 Nephi 11:3; Helaman 5:30; D&C 85:6–7.) Remember, Elijah found the voice of the Lord was not in the wind, nor in the earthquake, nor in the fire, but was a 'still small voice.' (1 Kings 19:12) The Spirit does not get our attention by shouting or shaking us with a heavy hand. Rather it whispers. It caresses so gently that if we are preoccupied we may not feel it at all. (No wonder that the Word of Wisdom was revealed to us, for how could the drunkard or the addict feel such a voice?) Occasionally it will press just firmly enough for us to pay heed. But most of the time, if we do not heed the gentle feeling, the Spirit will withdraw and wait until we come seeking and listening and say in our manner and expression, like Samuel of ancient times, 'Speak [Lord], for thy servant heareth' (1 Samuel 3:10)" (1983).

31. Dramatic revelations are assumed to be reserved for church leaders and those who are particularly righteous, the second being a criterion for the first, since leaders are viewed as men and women who are called to higher duty because of their strong faith and obedience to God. These assumptions are reinforced by the recognition of the most famous LDS visitation: that of God and Jesus to Joseph Smith in the woods of Palmyra, New York. Joseph Smith received numerous revelations afterwards by the Holy Spirit and "heavenly messengers" (e.g., D&C 27); many of these visions, visitations, and more humble revelations are recorded as scripture in the Doctrine and Covenants. The rest of LDS scriptures are filled with such dramatic encounters. Rather than lessen the importance of dramatic revelations, such frequency in scripture more firmly binds these divine experiences to the Saints' most sacred texts. There are nonscriptural records of visions and visitations, but they tend to be cast as legends rather than personal experience narratives, or supernatural experiences rather than revelation.

32. See chapter 2 for a more thorough discussion of these norms.

33. The divergence between personal revelation as experienced and personal revelation as narrated is explored further in chapter 3. See also chart 2 in the appendix for a detail of the medium for the 441 narratives that form the core of this analysis.

34. "Matt Larson" is a pseudonym.

35. The demographic statistics come from the Pew Forum on Religious Diversity. Between May 8 and August 13, 2007, the Pew Forum conducted a nationwide survey of more than 35,000 adults in the United States. They published their results online on June 23, 2008 (religions.pewforum.org). The other ethnic groups identified are as follows: 7 percent Hispanic, 3 percent Black, 1 percent Asian, and 3 percent Other/Mixed.

36. These stories have alternatively been called "belief legends" or "belief stories." Despite Gillian Bennett's attempt to retain the latter term (1989), it has been critiqued out of existence by numerous scholars, including Linda Dégh, who initially helped propagate it (1996), and Marilyn Motz, who argues for a concept of belief "as a process of knowing," a practice rather than an entity, "a verb rather than a noun" (Motz 1998:340, 349).

Chapter 2

1. Keith Stanley argued this point emotionally and succinctly in his entreaty to the youth of the ward while bearing his testimony during fast and testimony meeting on September 3, 2006: "I encourage them [the youth] to bear their testimonies so that they may strengthen them." As discussed in chapter 1, testimonies are built upon spiritual revelation.

2. The power that narrating sacred experiences can confer upon spiritual growth is not confined to Latter-day Saints. Speaking specifically of conversion narratives, Peter Stromberg points out, "It is through the use of language in the conversion narrative that the processes of increased commitment and self-transformation take place" (1993:xi).

3. Institute is a class of religious instruction geared primarily toward single adults in college, but it can include some young married adults.

4. These statistics come from the Baylor Religion Survey, conducted in 2005 as part of a grant from the John M. Templeton Foundation. The Gallup Organization collected the data from 1,721 adults in the United States.

5. For surveys of anti-Mormon sentiment in America, see Bunker and Bitton 1983, Fife and Fife 1956:109–25, Lythgoe 1968, Mauss 1984:447, Nelson 1977, Stathis and Lythgoe 1977 and Stathis 1981. For more contemporary polls that suggest continued negative perceptions of Mormons (as well as some positive ones), see two surveys conducted in 2007, one by the Pew Forum on Religion and Public Life (cited in Keeter and Smith 2007) and one by the Gallup Poll, reported and cited by the Pew Forum (cited in Ruby 2007).

6. Carl is referring to the experience of hearing the voice of his unborn child saying "Hi," an experience he has had with each of his three children, as well as with a fourth (see the endnotes of chapter 5 for elaboration). Also, Carl and Patty Miller are pseudonyms, and while the syntax is otherwise verbatim, I have changed some of the specific activities and titles in this story to protect their identity.

7. Apostle Merrill's experience occurred in 1855. He narrated the story for publication in the October 15, 1892, *Juvenile Instructor*. The story is reported in full in the *Latter-Day Saint Biographical Encyclopedia* (Jenson 1901, vol.1:157–8).

8. Martha M. Hancock was the third wife of Mosiah Lyman Hancock, son of Levi Hancock, who was one of the first seven presidents of the Seventy. Mosiah's journal has been a regular source for LDS scholars, particularly in helping to trace the origins of plural marriage, and it has been published and referenced in multiple LDS sources (for published version, see *Chronicles of Courage* [1995]; for digital version, see the Book of Abraham Project sponsored by BYU: http://www.boap.org; for archival journal, see Hancock 1956, Wilson Archives).

9. Ken Jarvis has helped me change some of the details he initially mentioned, to avoid sharing sensitive information. "Casting pearls before swine" is commonly quoted when speaking of the sacred. The biblical passage comes from Matthew 7:6: "Give not that which is holy unto the dogs, neither cast ye your pearls before swine, lest they trample them under their feet, and turn again and rend you." Carolyn Flatley Gilkey discusses the concern over preserving the sacred in her study of testimony meetings. Some of the church members she interviewed "felt that some personal matters would 'not be appreciated' or could be misinterpreted and should not be discussed in Testimony Meeting" (1979:53). She quotes one member as saying: "And it is very, very difficult because there are things inside you want to share, you want to speak, but you can't. They are *so* sacred" (54; italics in original).

10. D. Todd Christofferson's 2004 fireside address is available online at http://www.lds.org/broadcast in the Archives. An abridged version was published in *New Era* magazine, June 2006:28–31.

11. In an article published in the *Ensign* magazine titled "Why Symbols?" editors pose the question: "Why do people say the temple ceremony is sacred, not secret?" (2007). The explanation given highlights the connection between the sacred and public sharing by quoting a number of church authorities. From Hugh Nibley: "The important thing is that *I* do not reveal these things; they must remain sacred to *me*. I must preserve a zone of sanctity which cannot be violated. . . . For my covenants are all between me and my Heavenly Father" (1992:61, 64). From Boyd K. Packer: "We do not discuss the temple ordinances outside the temples. But it was never intended that knowledge of these temple ceremonies would be limited to a select few who would be obliged to ensure that others never learn of them. It is quite the opposite, in fact. With great effort we urge every soul

to qualify and prepare for the temple experience. . . . The ordinances and ceremonies of the temple are simple. They are beautiful. They are sacred. They are kept confidential lest they be given to those who are unprepared. Curiosity is not a preparation. Deep interest itself is not a preparation. Preparation for the ordinances includes preliminary steps: faith, repentance, baptism, confirmation, worthiness, a maturity and dignity worthy of one who comes invited as a guest into the house of the Lord" (1992:32; also republished in the February 1995 issue of the *Ensign*).

12. See chapter 3 for the complete narrative.

13. While none of these terms carries the weight of revelation, some appear regularly in LDS doctrine and have been subjected to religious and scholarly study. Apostle James E. Talmage distinguished between revelation and inspiration in his *The Articles of Faith* ([1899] 1924:296), a book current apostle L. Tom Perry quotes in an attempt to clarify terms that continue to blur together: "*Revelation* signifies the making known of divine truth by communication from the heavens. . . . The word *inspiration* is sometimes invested with a [significance] almost identical with that of *revelation,* though by origin and early usage it possessed a distinctive meaning. To inspire is literally to animate with the spirit; a man is inspired when under the influence of a power other than his own. Divine inspiration may be regarded as a lower or less directly intensive operation of spiritual influence upon man than is . . . revelation. The difference therefore is rather one of degree than of kind." (2003:85). BYU student Reid Bankhead's master's thesis, titled "A Study of the Meaning of the Terms Inspiration and Revelation as Used in the Church of Jesus Christ of Latter-day Saints," examined references through the LDS scriptures to "revelation" and "inspiration" and identified key differences between the two (1949). Even when terms are used in scriptures, however, esoteric definitions may not be widely known and shared in the community. Both in the past and today, members of the general membership and the General Authorities regularly use inspiration as a synonym for revelation (for historical use by the General Authorities, see, for example, President Wilford Woodruff [Compton 1991:34, citing an article on counter hierarchical revelation in the October 9, 1892, edition of the *Deseret Weekly* 45:545]; for contemporary use, see Second Counselor in the First Presidency James E. Faust [2002]).

14. The one exception Ken and Lee could think of was in 1978, when the president of the church issued a proclamation extending the priesthood to all worthy male members, regardless of race. This declaration is codified as scripture in the Doctrine and Covenants as Official Declaration 2.

15. The transcript and video for Thomas S. Monson's talk can be found on the official LDS website at http://www.lds.org. The scriptural references are part of that transcript. In Monson's spoken address, the scriptural quotes are not voiced, though in other parts of his speech, they appear as text on the screen. Also, the transcript does not reflect Monson's exact words, as speakers often deviate slightly from the written text of their speech. In the passage above, I have edited the text to reflect his speech. The alterations are minor but can be compared to the transcript online for the few points of variation. Also, when Monson gave this talk, he was not yet president of the church but rather the First Counselor in the First Presidency.

16. As teachers and leaders, the General Authorities are expected to be role models, encouraging their flock to seek revelation and recognize it as such. General conference, when church leaders speak to members throughout the world, is intended to be both inspirational and educational. In such teaching contexts, leaders recognize the importance of explicitly acknowledging the role and power of personal revelation in their lives. However, even in these contexts, less explicit synonyms for revelation dominate.

17. I recorded this exchange as it happened with handwritten notes and transcribed the event an hour later when I returned home.

18. From the cadence of her speech, it is clear Serena is quoting scripture. Later, Dave provided the scriptural references: Psalms 46:10 and Doctrine and Covenants 101:16.

19. Serena Gammon's narrative describes a series of small revelations that she received after being stranded in Washington, DC. These revelations guided her on decisions about her career and where she should live.

20. "Susan" is a pseudonym.

21. William "Bert" Wilson shared this story in written communication on October 11, 2010. In LDS theology, "sons of perdition" include those people who have "denied the Holy Spirit after having received it" and will not attain any of the three kingdoms of glory but be exiled with Satan for all eternity (see D&C 76:25–38). The term also appears in the Bible in John 17:12 and Thessalonians 2:3. Also, it is worth nothing that stories like the one recorded by Cheryl Nielson abound in the Wilson Archives with respect to plural marriages. Many first wives have demanded revelation of their own to match that of their husbands, who proclaim a divine prompting to marry again (see Schoemaker 1989 and Wilson 1996:155; see also chapter 5 for continued discussion of coercive revelations on marriage and having children).

22. Both of these stories are from handwritten notes taken during Sunday school and transcribed immediately afterwards. Also, while the teacher felt comfortable sharing the names of the men in the stories, both of whom were from far outside North Carolina, I have provided pseudonyms, since this book has the potential to reach a wider audience.

23. A. Roger Merrill pulls the story from Gene R. Cook's book *Teaching by the Spirit* (2000:140). Cook quotes Kimball from a Church Educational System meeting, June 30, 1989 (Merrill 2007). For a discussion of the formal qualities of bearing one's testimony, and of fast and testimony meetings in general, see LDS member and anthropologist David Knowlton, who argues: "When we hear a "good" talk or testimony we feel moved and fed. Generally, though, we grumble about the tediousness and poor quality of most talks and testimonies. We see them as hackneyed, repetitive, and ordinary" (1991:24).

24. Referring to spiritual narratives, Jeff Todd Titon and Ken George have noted that "in leisurely conversation these narratives will expand and fill with detail; at a church testimonial meeting when others are waiting to take their turn the story will be shorter but the essential elements will be there" (1978: 69). See the case studies that follow as examples of this tendency.

25. As Henry Glassie found in his analysis of folk houses in Middle Virginia, a small set of rules can account for a wide range of house styles. Here too, a small set of rules can go far in explaining a wide range of performance styles in various settings.

26. A survey conducted in 2000 by the Glenmary Research Center for the Religious Congregations and Membership book confirms these numbers: 88 percent of the population in the Provo-Orem area is LDS, but that number jumps to 98 percent when factoring out those adults who are not religious adherents (the survey can be accessed online at the Association of Religion Data Archives at http:// www.thearda.com).

27. One of the prominent buttons on the first page of the official church website is "Prepare a Talk." The link provides a list of hundreds of topics. For each, there are summaries of main points, previous talks from church leaders, church magazine articles, scriptural references, and additional online resources such as the *Encyclopedia of Mormonism*. In many of the talks and magazine articles are anecdotes and memorates, including personal revelation.

28. Rarely is everything said during a fast and testimony meeting strictly part of a person's testimony about their knowledge of the truth of the church, its doctrine, and its leaders. Paul Clayson remembers a recent general conference that stressed that fast and testimony meetings should be composed of true testimonies of the church, rather than becoming "a travel-mony, thank-imony or fan-imony" (Carolyn Gilkey found similar emic categories of testimony talks in her study of testimony meetings, 1979). When Paul was a missionary, his mission leader was very strict about the "keep it brief and gospel centered" mandate, giving them each two minutes to bear their testimony. In practice, testimony meetings are far more open.

29. Tears are often assumed to be visible signs of the presence of the Holy Ghost. This assumption is so widespread that *The Friend* magazine, published by the church for children, adapted and published the story of a young girl who thought tears were *the* sign of the Holy Ghost because of her experience sitting through fast and testimony meetings. Associating tears only with sadness, the girl was surprised to find that the Holy Ghost brought joy (Schetselaar 2006). In terms of gender, Elaine Lawless argues that tears are specific to women's testimonies (1984:90–4), a point my fieldwork clearly contradicts. Tears are more acceptable for women than men, but they are hardly uncommon for men.

30. My fieldwork in the Burlington First Ward suggests that fast and testimony meetings typically involve elements of both. Some people's testimonies are self-contained, while others are inspired by the testimonies that preceded them. This is borne out by Carolyn Flatley Gilkey's fieldwork in Eugene, Oregon, as well (1979).

31. This story was recorded by Natalie Shiozawa from her sister (1997, Wilson Archives). It is unclear whether this narrative is verbatim. The addition of the moral at the end without a discursive introduction (such as "The moral is . . .") suggests it may not be. What is clear is that the moral is part of the text, not a contextual note added by the collector. Also, the story's having been heard in so many church settings suggests it was published at some point in a church-sponsored magazine. A search of the church magazine archives reveals a story titled "Billy's Second Chance" in *The Friend* magazine (R. Erickson 1972). The parallels between the two stories are striking: both involve a young boy named Billy, his glasses, and a pop fly. However, the story in *Friend* does not involve a prompting, and the "moral" centers on team play that demands the boy keep his glasses on (rather than taking them off).

32. At least one BYU student has attempted to explain this phenomenon, suggesting that because men are in positions of leadership, they are regularly warned about spreading rumors and spurious legends and are therefore more wary of doing so (see Mower 1975, Wilson Archives).

33. There are seventeen permanent Missionary Training Centers around the world. The MTC in Provo is the oldest and largest.

34. Richard Bauman writes: "One especially productive line of investigation examines the varying ways in which and degrees to which particular genres in a speech community may be formatively adapted to their immediate contexts of use. . . . Analysis of this kind requires close attention to the formal means and device by which discourse may be anchored to its context of use. . . . Likewise, it requires close attention to forces that work in the opposing direction, that is, to how different kinds of generic regimentation may render an utterance or a text relatively impervious to and detachable from the situation in which it is used, such that form or meaning remains relatively constant from one context to another. It is illuminating in this regard to track the use of what is considered to be the same genre across different kinds of situational context, recalling, as we must, that notwithstanding conceptions that define genres in terms of specific situational contexts, it is in the very nature of genre to be recognizable outside those conventional settings. Empirical investigation reveals clearly that certain genres in any given community's repertoire may be adapted to multiple contexts" (2006:755).

35. The "too" refers to me. Craig, Josette, and I had been talking about our religious beliefs and backgrounds when I shared my own background of growing up Catholic.

Chapter 3

1. Richard Bauman's definition of genre is particularly useful and informative and represents well the past few decades of the application of performance theory in the study of folklore: genre is "one order of speech style, a constellation of systematically related, co-occurrent

formal features and structures that serves as a conventionalized orienting framework for the production and reception of discourse" (Bauman 2004:3).

2. Genres of performance are often labeled folklore because of the process of enculturation through informal face-to-face interaction rather than through formal instruction. This process of enculturation into the narrative genres common to LDS religious experience is noted by many in the church, particularly in conversation about youth who bear their testimony in church. Many members are embarrassed by what they regard as a parroting of adult testimonies without the understanding of what a testimony is and what it truly means to "know," for example, the church is true. Elaine J. Lawless recorded a woman's testimony from a service in Boise, Idaho, in the 1980s; the woman is struck by how quickly children are enculturated into verbal genres in the church: "My children were playing and they had a toy and decided it looked like a microphone. And they were playing around with it and John took it and started bearing his testimony. I was amazed. He's so wiggly I thought nothing at church ever sank in. And he was saying all the things he hears especially, uh, young people say when they bear their testimony. And I was very pleased. Well, something is getting through" (1984:84). In fact, Lawless argues, children are an effective barometer for formulaic elements of testimony: "Testimonies of children are, in any religious context, a clue to the formulaic quality of testimonies. The first lines the children recognize and deliver are the formularized lines they have heard repeatedly in testimony service" (85–6).

3. The inspiration for the cow example comes from Marvin Harris's well-known, regularly cited studies on the sacred cows of India, beginning with his 1966 article "The Cultural Ecology of India's Sacred Cattle" (51–9), followed by comments and replies by other scholars (60–6). Cow-tipping is a prank typically perpetrated by rural teens in the United States, who sneak up on sleeping cows, then throw their weight into the cow to tip it over, presumably befuddling the cow. The example of the falling statue describes an experience I had with Harold Comby, the police officer mentioned (see Mould 2003:79).

4. The story was recorded by a BYU graduate student in 1976 from fellow *New Era* magazine staff members who were sharing humorous stories about the General Authorities one afternoon in the office (Peggy 1976, Fife Archives). Bruce R. McConkie was a prolific writer and well-known figure in the church. He was serving as church apostle under President Joseph Fielding Smith at the time the story was told in 1976. He was a member of the First Council of the Seventy at the time the story was said to have taken place. The initials "G. A." are an abbreviation for General Authorities.

5. The "silent train" phenomenon explains one of the benefits of being an outsider to the culture one studies, a topic of great interest to folklorists and anthropologists. The danger of being an insider is that aspects of the culture may be so normalized they are ignored. This is not, of course, to dismiss the numerous challenges of being an outsider. For academic studies of how supernatural experiences can be heavily shaped by and interpreted through psychological, physical, cultural, social, and generic factors, see Honko 1964:16–7, Neitz and Spickard 1990:25, and Wuthnow 1992:13.

6. David Hufford's argument is based on his research into supernatural phenomena that appear globally, seemingly irrespective of culture (see, for example, his study of the Old Hag, 1982, 1995). He argues that these "core spiritual experiences" are stable and derive from a rational process of analysis. While one could make the argument that revelation is a global phenomenon with widely shared characteristics and thus merits inclusion as a "core spiritual experience," my claim is less ambitious, settling for an emic analysis that validates the beliefs of the people encountering the supernatural.

7. Hufford himself acknowledges this: "Stating that these experiences refer 'intuitively' is *not* a naïve claim that such experiences are unmediated, but rather that, like many ordinary perceptual experiences, *they are not necessarily mediated by the concepts to which they give rise*"

(italics in original; 1995:28–9). He follows with an example about perceiving a hummingbird. Whether one has seen a hummingbird before or not, she will perceive a small flying object with fast-beating wings. The specifics will vary from culture to culture and meaning will vary, but initial perception may be global. The same is true for core spiritual experiences. The perception will share similarities, even if meaning diverges. See chapter 7 for a more detailed discussion of this tension between personal experience and cultural pattern.

8. Prayer for "all things" is not clear cut. There is some disagreement among LDS members whether some concerns are too small to bother God with. Serena Gammon jokes that she used to pray fervently that God would help her get off at the right bus stop every morning for school. Her husband, Dave, assures her that there is nothing wrong with that. The idea of a God too busy to help, whose "to do" list is too long, is a foreign one for most.

9. This quote is from Brunvand 1970:55. George Romney is Republican politician Mitt Romney's father.

10. George and Sandy Johnson are pseudonyms. The name of their daughter and the city where this happened have been changed to provide them some degree of anonymity.

11. This revelation received by Joseph Smith and recorded in the Doctrine and Covenants was directed to Oliver Cowdery, who had expressed discontent with acting as merely a scribe rather than a translator of the Book of Mormon. According to the concordance in the Book of Mormon, the burning in the bosom references Luke 24:32: "And they said one to another, Did not our heart burn within us, while he talked with us by the way, and while he opened to us the scriptures?" Mormon scholars, theologians, and church leaders also cite Acts 2:37, which describes being "pricked in the heart." Both biblical passages describe the apostles' reactions to the resurrection of Jesus.

12. This process of affirmation continues as the new callings are brought before the ward as a whole. With each new position, church leaders stand before the congregation and ask whether each member can sustain the person being called with the sign of an upraised right hand. Such affirmation at this level is not expected to be confirmed through revelation, but it can be. More often, it is viewed as a rote act. No one I spoke to remembered someone raising a hand in response to *not* being able sustain someone to a position, though they may have questioned the choice. A J. Golden Kimball story pokes fun at how this ritual process may not receive the attention it deserves. The story goes that Kimball was reading a particularly long list of recent church callings, when church members began to doze off. Droning on in the same tone, Kimball added: "It has been proposed that Mount Nebo be moved from its present site in Juab County and be placed on the Utah-Idaho border. All in favor make it manifest by raising the right hand; opposed, by the same sign." The few still awake laughed and woke the others out of their stupor in order to finish (Fife and Fife 1956:305).

13. Ken Mullen is referring to the keys of the priesthood that give him the power to affirm revelation. It is within the power and rights afforded men in the priesthood to seek revelation to confirm revelation within their stewardship. Although women do not have these keys (not being members of the priesthood), many couples take an equitable approach to decision making, both seeking divine counsel through prayer and making decisions collaboratively.

14. The USU Fife Folklore Archives has archived such stories as "Supernatural Religious Legends," often under the subcategory "Unknown Beings Protect or Aid," with the numeric prefix 1.1.3.2.

15. The Word of Wisdom came as revelation to Joseph Smith on February 27, 1833, after he pondered and prayed about the use of tobacco during their meetings (D&C 89). The exact parameters of the Word of Wisdom have been debated in the church since the beginning and have shifted through time, particularly the interpretation of the mandates against eating meat but sparingly and against "hot drinks" (today uniformly interpreted as coffee and tea but leaving the "caffeinated beverages" question ambiguous). For a discussion of the Word of Wisdom, see Bush 1981, Ford 1998.

16. In the "Questions and Answers" section of the March 2007 *Ensign* magazine, the question posed is: "I have difficulty distinguishing between promptings of the Spirit and my own personal feelings. How can I tell the difference?" (58–61). The magazine reprinted twelve of the responses written in by church members and included a reference to an earlier, virtually identical question posed in the same section of the magazine (then called "I have a Question") from the June 1983 edition: "How can I distinguish the difference between the promptings of the Holy Ghost and merely my own thoughts, preferences, or hunches?" (27). The response was written by Dallin H. Oaks, who had earlier been president of BYU and would be called to be a member of the Quorum of the Twelve Apostles just under a year after writing this response. As for Shawn Tucker's joke about the burrito, Stephen R. Gibson notes that some of the anti-Mormon public poke fun at the idea of revelation and a burning in the bosom, having "even likened it to indigestion from too much pizza" (1995:59). Shawn makes a similar joke, but one intended to highlight the struggle to interpret the Holy Ghost rather than demean their religion. This may be an example of reclaiming the language, but such descriptions are likely less fraught with the politics of culture and simply express the sense of humor members often exhibit about esoteric elements of their religion.

17. In an article in the *Ensign* magazine, Boyd K. Packer, then a member of the Quorum of the Twelve Apostles, tells a story of a conversation he had with an atheist where he attempts to explain how he *knows* there is a God. He compares knowing what salt tastes like to knowing there is a God, that in comparing present experience with past experiences, one can come to know something otherwise difficult to explain (1983:51–6).

18. According to the Bible Dictionary, "The light of Christ is just what the words imply: enlightenment, knowledge, and an uplifting, ennobling, persevering influence that comes upon mankind because of Jesus Christ. . . . Its influence is preliminary to and preparatory to one's receiving the Holy Ghost" (725).

19. Dallin H. Oaks, former president of Brigham Young University, describes the strategies for determining the Holy Ghost and highlights in particular the fact that the content of revelation should support, not counter, church doctrine (1983:25). This strategy dominates the talks and writings of church leaders (see Lund 2007:222–59).

20. The quote comes from page 97 of the manual. The relevant scriptural quotes are Moroni 7:13, 16–17.

21. It is worth noting the degree to which members rationally work to distinguish the Holy Ghost from other sources, both mundane and supernatural. Patrick Mullen points out that even scholars who accept supernatural experiences as valid often describe folk belief as intuitive rather than rational. Yet as Mullen argues, people regularly interpret their experiences using rational thought (2000:133). This is certainly true of LDS members.

22. They are also made clear by the General Authorities. In a general conference talk given in October 1994 as a member of the Quorum of the Twelve Apostles, Boyd K. Packer warns, "The voice of the spirit speaks gently, prompting you what to do or what to say, or it may caution or warn you. Ignore or disobey these promptings, and the Spirit will leave you. It is your choice—your agency" (1997). More recently, in a stake conference talk to the Durham North Carolina Stake on Sunday, February 17, 2008, newly appointed Second Counselor to the First Presidency Dieter F. Uchtdorf added a more specific mandate to Packer's practical counsel: "We are all prompted by the Spirit; it is our responsibility to follow."

23. In his study of Zionist dreams and revelations in South Africa, J. P. Kiernan has also recognized the importance of the interpretive questions that arise with ambiguous revelation, which he terms "indirect revelation": "The Spirit does not assume a standardized form. Its manifestations tend to be disembodied, and it reveals itself in its messages. These tend to be of two kinds: direct, and indirect or symbolic. The latter requires some interpretation. When a prophet announces, 'I see hail,' or 'I see a coffin,' or 'I see a car crash,' it is

reasonably clear that his vision is related to danger, death or injury. But which of these is it, and has the event taken place or is it anticipated? Is the occurrence conditional, i.e. can it still be prevented by prayer? At whom is the misfortune directed? Most if not all of these questions have to be resolved before the vision can have any meaning" (1985:308).

24. The only context provided for this narrative is that this is "a story from my Mom, Linda, as told to me" (5.2.0.3.1, Wilson Archives).

25. The Massacre at Haun's Mill, as it has come to be memorialized in Mormon historical narrative and contemporary memory, occurred on October 30, 1838, after a series of increasingly violent encounters between Mormon settlers and the local Missouri government. During the massacre, Missouri militiamen attacked a Mormon settlement, killing at least eighteen people, including at least one young boy, and assaulting many of the women. For historical narratives of the event, see Blair 1972. The specific story referenced here was recorded by Diane Campbell in May 1971 from a friend who told this story about his great-grandfather (Campbell 1971, Wilson Archives). Compare this man's dream to President Wilford Woodruff's dream of a room full of snakes that turn black, swell up, and die at his presence. The dream prepared him to face an apostate Saint and an angry mob, many of whom died in exactly this way (Woodruff 1881a:13–15).

26. The story was collected by Maren McDaniel from his mother, who had collected it from her uncle, who had put in his "personal history." The protagonist in the story is the uncle's father (McDaniel 1972, Wilson Archives). See also President Heber C. Kimball's dream of fields of wheat turned to smut or trampled by a bull. Upon waking, he interpreted the fields of wheat as religious faith, first in England and then in their own area of Rochester. The smut was the vacancy of true religion in England, the bull an anti-Mormon clergyman of the Church of England (H. Kimball 1882:41–3).

27. Cheryl Nielson recorded this story from a fellow BYU student, who is the girlfriend mentioned in the story. It was her husband who received the revelation that they should marry (1990:8, Wilson Archives). For other metaphorical dreams serving particularly as omens, see Fife and Fife 1956:218.

28. Roger L. Judd collected this story from a Polish man he met while on his mission in Scotland between 1962 and 1964 (1966, Wilson Archives).

29. The story was collected by Jay Healy from the woman who was driving the woman in the story to Salt Lake City. While she did not receive the revelation herself, she was present during the fulfillment of the dream (1.7.0.9.1, Wilson Archives).

30. This story was collected in 1977 by Melvin Jeppson while on his mission in Cherokee, North Carolina, from adult missionaries in the church who had known the woman in the story (1981, Wilson Archives).

31. See, for example, the numerous scriptures listed under "God, Presence of," and "Face" in the index to the Book of Mormon, Doctrine and Covenants, and Pearl of Great Price; and "God, Presence of," "Face," "God, Manifestations of," and "God, Privilege of Seeing" in the topical guide to all of the LDS scripture, including the Old and New Testament. See also the scriptures quoted in the discussion of the ambiguity of divine communication at the end of this chapter.

32. Brennan adds the following contextual information: "Judy Barnes is fifty-three years old. She has lived in Springville for the last eight years. She was raised in Grand Junction, Colorado. She is the mother of eight children. She is a returned missionary and an active member of the Church of Jesus Christ of Latter-day Saints. She is my aunt. Judy told this story one afternoon when several members of my family were gathered at my grandparents' home. I taped the conversation, so this story is in her own words. This story also appeared in the *Ensign* (a magazine of the Church of Jesus Christ of Latter-day Saints). My great-great-great-grandmother joined the Church because of her experience. The story has been handed down for generations. Everyone in my family believes this story to be true. It is

said that because of my ancestor, my family lives in the western part of the states" (1986b, Wilson Archives).

33. This story was told by Mrs. John Patterson, "an elderly widow," to Susan Christensen and Doris Blackham in Ephraim, Utah (1971, Wilson Archives). This theme of finding a home is a common one, and the specific language of "this is the place" has been codified in Mormon history as the declaration that Brigham Young made upon seeing the Salt Lake valley for the first time (see chapter 4).

34. Monty Jenkins is a pseudonym, as are the names of his wife, daughter, and realtor. "Gertie" is Monty and Nancy's oldest daughter. I have also changed specific location and names in the story to provide some degree of anonymity.

35. Normally, Monty's revelation of who the person was would have come later in the narrative, but I caught on to the story because Monty had actually told me about Brother Heller previously, and I let on that I realized he must have been the realtor in the dream.

36. Frank Nielson is a pseudonym. Before sharing these stories, "Frank" asked me to turn the tape recorder off; these experiences were too emotional, too sacred, too personal to share widely. A year or two later, he shared the stories again, this time on tape but asked that I reference them only generally. Stories of receiving revelation as preparation for the death of a relative are not uncommon in the narrative tradition (see, for example, Hall 1969, Wilson Archives, "Woman's premonition of son's death helps prepare her for it").

37. The exceptions are rare but rhetorically and aesthetically revealing and will be explored in chapter 4.

38. One might imagine an exception to this in cases where the prompting was deemed to originate with Satan. Such an experience could be usefully shared with others to highlight the dangers of not seeking confirmation. Such an experience would also provide a particularly compelling narrative from a performance perspective. However, I have recorded no such narratives in my own fieldwork nor uncovered any in the Fife Folklore Archives at USU or the William A. Wilson Folklore Archives at BYU.

39. A BYU professor narrates a remarkably similar story about a couple she knew in Wisconsin. The couple "had a very strong premonition that it was going to be a boy." However, the baby turned out to be a girl. The professor notes: "Now, they didn't drop out of the church or anything because the baby was the other gender, but it didn't draw them together either. They eventually split up and were divorced, and so it wasn't a happy ending, 'Oh, we'll try again.' And I don't know how they actually worked through the issues of faith of being so sure it was a boy then it wasn't" (Mitchell 2004:76). Unlike Shawn and Nicole Tucker, this couple was unclear about whether they interpreted the experience in a way that would make the continued narration of this story relevant within LDS contexts.

40. The passage Shawn paraphrases is D&C 124:49. The introduction in the Doctrine and Covenants explains that Joseph Smith received this revelation on January 19, 1841, in the midst of being forced to move: "Because of increasing persecutions and illegal procedures against them by public officers, the saints had been compelled to leave Missouri." In other words, the revelation comes in the specific context of having to abandon Nauvoo, another place the prophet had predicted would be home to the Saints. In a recent general conference talk, in October 2008, D. Todd Christofferson of the Quorum of the Twelve Apostles suggests the failure was on the part of the Saints, not their persecutors, an explanation repeated in church publications such as *Teachings of Presidents of the Church: Joseph Smith* (2007:182–91) and the *Doctrine and Covenants Institute Student Manual* (2001:248–9).

41. Camille Brennan recorded this story from fellow BYU classmate Marcia Nesbitt, noting: "Marcia related this story to me and my roommates one evening when we [were] discussing personal revelation. It was a very casual discussion, but the atmosphere in the room was very strong. Marcia was hesitant to share this story with us because it never happened. However, she believes that her sister did have the children she dreamt of through her

miscarriages. Marcia feels sure the dream was meant to give her sister comfort in the years to come, because she had the dreams before her miscarriages. Marcia believes that the miscarried babies are sealed forever to Susan. She mentioned that Susan has always been very spiritual and able to tune into messages. The story is presented in Marcia's words as I taped the conversation" (Brennan 1986a:19, Wilson Archives).

42. The extent to which generic expectations for personal revelation can reveal the divine in the seemingly mundane becomes clear in the process of retroactive revelation discussed in chapter 4.

43. See, for example, the Zulu (Kiernan 1985), Irish (Bander 1979; Cross 1942: 98–9, 111–5; Glassie 1982:324; O'Hanlon 1870:308–12; O'Kearney 1856), Scottish (MacRae 1908: 190–200), Europe generally (von Döllinger 1872; Thomas 1971:389–432), Polynesia (Luomala 1949; Underwood 2000:142–5), and the vast prophetic traditions among indigenous peoples throughout North and South America, such as the Cheyenne (Grinnell 1908:281, 319–20), Choctaw (Mould 2003, 2004), Hopi (Geertz 1994), Interior Salish Nlha7kápmx nation (Hanna and Henry 1995:123), Jicarilla (Opler 1938:95–111), Kalapuya (Jacobs 1945:67), Lenape (Bierhorst 1995:99–107), Maya (Craine and Reindorp 1979; Edmonson 1982, 1986; Sullivan 1989), Micmac (Rand 1894:225–6), Nomlaki (Goldschmidt 1951:311), Ojibwe (Kohl 1860:244–7), Taos (Miller 1898), Wishram (Sapir and Curtain 1909:229–31), Wailaki (Murphey and Young 1941), Yaqui (K. C. Erickson 2003), and Zuni (Quam 1972:3).

44. LDS scriptures regularly refer to writings that were sealed up until God deemed mankind ready and faithful enough to receive them. See, for example, Isaiah 29:11 in the Old Testament; Revelation 5:1 in the New Testament; Luke 3:8 in the Joseph Smith Translation of the New Testament; 2 Nephi 27:8–10 and Ether 3:27–4:5 in the Book of Mormon; and Doctrine and Covenants 77:6.

Chapter 4

1. For an early discussion of this process in personal experience narratives, see Sandra Dolby Stahl 1989, where she argues: "The personal narrative always involves some manipulation of the truth of the experience. Such manipulation involves a degree of falsification, but generally only so much as to produce appropriate story material. This relatively minor degree of falsification occurs at three levels: (1) in the teller's perception of the experience, (2) in the initial telling of the personal narrative, and (3) in the readaptations of the story to the varying contexts of retelling" (18).

2. In the field of folklore, the motif is most often discussed in cross-cultural analysis. Folklorists, among other lay and academic scholars, realized that the elements of one story may appear in other stories with very different plots. A lost slipper used as a means of identification (AT motif H36.1) may show up in a story told two thousand years ago in Greece of an eagle that dropped a stolen sandal beside a pharaoh (Sierra 1992) as well as in a version of "Cinderella" told in Germany at the turn of the nineteenth century (Grimm 1963; for a more complete list of stories with this motif, see page 374 in Thompson's *Motif-Index of Folk Literature*, 1966). Such borrowing is not confined to motifs; whole scenes may be ripped from one story and employed in another. The recognition of the existence of motifs helped open the door to understanding storytelling as a process, not merely a product. Narrators skillfully construct rather than simply repeat stories. This shift from product to process facilitated the development of important theories used in the analysis of oral narrative today, including the oral formulaic theory initially developed by Albert B. Lord and Milman Parry in their study of Homer's epic poetry (Lord 1960). For a discussion of motifs as defined and employed in folklore studies, see Baughman 1966, Ben-Amos 1980,

Daemmrich 1985, Dorson 1972, and Aarne and Thompson 1961. In my use of the term, I have omitted the idea of motif as the smallest recognizable unit of a folktale, since motifs are far more often constellations of ideas, characteristics, and themes than irreducible elements, a point Dan Ben-Amos makes clear in his survey, cited above, of the development of the motif as a concept in folklore studies.

3. See chart 7 in the appendix for how often these motifs appear.

4. Shawn's age changes because the story spans many months; he was sixteen when he was in Hawaii, turned seventeen in November, and his friend died the following March.

5. All of these quotes are pulled directly from recorded narratives, either from my own fieldwork or from the archives at BYU and USU.

6. This story was collected by USU student Elise Alder from her "adopted Grandma," a woman who served in this role for many of the neighborhood children. Elise prefaced the story by noting: "While I listened to this story, I could feel the deep faith that Opal has carried throughout her life. She stresses to me through this story the importance of being in tune with the spirit, especially when someone else is depending on you. As you read this story, you will also recognize testimony" (1984:12–3, Wilson Archives). The other stories mentioned are from my own fieldwork.

7. Camille Allen recorded this story from a fellow BYU student, who heard it from her Merrie Miss teacher, the woman in the story. After telling the story, the student added that she believes people do receive promptings, even though she has not received one: "I like stories like that even though I've never had one because it makes me believe that I could have one" (Allen 1996, Wilson Archives).

8. Wilford Woodruff published the story in the *Millennial Star* newspaper twice (first on December 12, 1881, and again on October 12, 1891), in the *Deseret Weekly* (September 5, 1891), and in his journal, parts of which were published by the Juvenile Instructor Office as *Leaves from My Journal* (1881a:89). He also told the story during a general conference in 1898 (*Conference Reports* 1898:30–1). Since then, other leaders have retold the story, resulting in its republication in church magazines (see, for example, G. Hinckley 1982) and church newspapers (see "Withstanding Life's Storms" in *Church News* [Hyde 2001]). Church teaching manuals have also picked up the story for use in their Primary lesson books ("The Holy Ghost Helps Me," lesson 7 in *Primary 1: I Am a Child of God*, 1994:19–21) and in the *Teachings of Presidents of the Church* series, a kind of greatest hits of past church presidents, one volume of which is devoted to Wilford Woodruff (2004:46–7). Finally, the story has been reprinted in faith-promoting books such as Preston Nibley's *Faith Promoting Stories* (1943:24), the Daughters of the Utah Pioneers' book *Heart Throbs of the West*, Vol. 3 (1941:339–40), church histories such as *The Discourses of Wilford Woodruff* (Durham 1946:295–6), and church-sponsored books such as General Authority Gerald N. Lund's *Hearing the Voice of the Lord* (2007:108–9), as well as scholarly works such as Austin and Alta Fife's *Saints of Sage and Saddle* (1956:211–2) and Austin Fife's "Popular Legends of the Mormons" (1942:111–2).

9. Brother Williams was a local member of the church. Orson Hyde was a member of the Quorum of the Twelve.

10. Sandy Johnson told this story on August 6, 2006, just days after having read the Wilford Woodruff story in the August *Friend* magazine with her children. See chapter 5 for additional discussion of the Wilford Woodruff story as a specific tale type.

11. There is an extensive body of Christian literature on biblical numerology written primarily by clergy or religious lay persons (see, for example, Bullinger [1894] 1967, Connor 2007, and Vallowe 1995). Such religious exegeses make for interesting but not scholarly reading. If one wanted to simply identify the numerous examples of the number three in Christian scripture, however, these books would certainly provide a useful guide.

12. The passage is as follows: "And he said, Go forth, and stand upon the mount before the Lord. And, behold, the Lord passed by, and a great and strong wind rent the mountains,

and brake in pieces the rocks before the Lord; *but* the Lord *was* not in the wind. And after the wind an earthquake; *but* the Lord *was* not in the earthquake. And after the earthquake a fire; *but* the Lord *was* not in the fire. And after the fire a still, small voice" (1 Kings 19:11–12). It is worth noting that God comes after three false alarms, suggesting importance for the fourth rather than the third. However, the church member interpreted the passage to confirm the significance of the number three.

13. This story was submitted to the Wilson Archives and accessioned under the number 1.7.1.26.1. The collector, storyteller, and date are unknown.

14. Mosiah Lyman Hancock was born in 1834 and died in 1907. The event he describes took place in 1862. His diary was deposited in the Wilson Archives in 1956 but can be found online at http://www.boap.org/LDS/Early-Saints/MHancock.html.

15. The story was written down by BYU student Melissa Chalk in 1999. She originally heard it in 1997 at a stake conference but heard "about twenty different versions of the story" repeated over the next three years during Young Women activities, at girls' camp, and at parties within the ward (note: there are two archival documents numbered 1.7.0.39.1 in the Wilson Archives; this version is the second one with this number).

16. This is true of other types of stories as well. Significance is found only in hindsight. Sharing a story of how God blesses those who tithe in the *Ensign* magazine, Elwin C. Robinson writes, "This would have remained just a fond memory if it hadn't been for our conversation three months later" (2007:69). When he finds out that the car he gave to a fellow ward member came at the exact moment the man was filling out his tithing check, his "fond memory" became a sacred experience shared orally among his own family, friends, and ward members, and in written form to hundreds of thousands of LDS readers.

17. The story was shared by a man identified only by his initials, H. G. B., in *Gems for the Young Folks*, Faith-Promoting Series, vol. 4 (1881:22–4). The abbreviated story cited here was republished by Duane S. Crowther in his book *Gifts of the Spirit* (1983:35–6).

18. The story was recorded by Alta and Austin Fife from Mrs. Marion King on May 23, 1945, in Manti, Utah. Mrs. King is James C. Snow's granddaughter. The Fifes quote this story in their book *Saints of Sage and Saddle* (1956:148–9), though the full narrative can be found in the Fife Folklore Archives at USU (King 1945).

19. Marianne Reamey interpreted the story by arguing: "This story not only reflects the concern which many students feel over this matter but also helps to alleviate this concern by encouraging us to put our trust in the Lord and providing a specific instance of the Lord's fulfillment of this trust" (Reamey 1972, Wilson Archives).

20. The story was collected by Shirley Richins. Although no contextual data is included, a parenthetical addition suggests that this is a family story, the man a nephew of her grandmother's (Richins, n.d., Wilson Archives).

21. For other stories with superlative endings, see Brennan 1986b (see chapter 3 for complete narrative), Campbell 1971, Giles n.d., and Pyle n.d., among others, all in the Wilson Archives. Such endings are not confined to stories of revelation. Sitting around a campfire, Zeke Johnson told "a faith-promoting story" to the Mormon Boy Scouts surrounding him about two friends, headed to California. One was converted and stayed in Salt Lake. The other continued on. They both ended up dying within a week of each other. The Mormon, progenitor to over a hundred descendents, was loved by many and had a packed funeral. The other man died penniless and unknown (Fife and Fife 1956:194–5).

22. This story was recorded by Sherami Jara on November 5, 2000, from a friend and coworker at the Missionary Training Center (Jara 2000:25, Wilson Archives). The narrator was not sure the story was true but finds it both amazing and comforting. The feeling the senior companion received is understood by both the narrator and the collector as revelation. Also, it is worth noting that the man got his gun at the *third* knock (see discussion of the number three as a motif earlier in this chapter).

23. For similar narratives, see two memorates recorded by Julia Condie from two returned missionaries (pages 10 and 11, respectively, in the Wilson Archives, one of which is reprinted in chapter 5), a memorate recorded by Karen Williams from her grandmother (see chapter 1 for complete narrative), and the story of John Morgan disseminated widely in Bryant Hinckley's book *The Faith of Our Pioneer Fathers* (1956:242–4) and in Sunday school lesson plans (see chapter 5 for complete narrative).

24. This version is substantially longer than the story Jackie Foss told during Sunday school. As discussed in chapter 2, without the time constraints of church, people elaborate upon the narratives by adding far more detail and personalizing the story with asides and deeper contextual information. Jackie told the story in Sunday school on July 30, 2006. I recorded this story on September 30, 2006, in her home sitting at her kitchen table.

25. See chapter 2 for a discussion of the reasons people do or do not share personal revelation stories.

26. Boyd Tenney is the son of Nathan Orson Tenney and Myrtle Mary Wear. He is one of ten children, many of whom narrate the other versions of the story that follow. The brothers and sisters are: Naydene, N. S., Delbert, Opal, Nina, Lyman, Eudora, Edythe, and Pearl. *The Tenney Breadbasket* has many authors and editors. Marsha Romney and Clifford J. Stratton seem to have done the bulk of the compiling (Marsha is Pearl's daughter). Pat and Linda Hendrix served as publisher, getting all the materials in shape for publication (Pat is Edythe's son). Georgia Hatch then edited the final document. For citation purposes, I have used Pat and Linda Hendrix's name, since they introduce the book. See chapter 6 for more information on *The Tenney Breadbasket*.

27. Most of Pearl's remembrances have been intentionally removed from the book, however, and no account of the fire exists in the part that remains.

28. See the story quoted earlier in this chapter. For other versions, see BYU 4.14.1.2.2–.5, all collected by BYU student Sandra Baliff in 1972, the same year Marianne Reamey heard the story from a classmate at BYU. Not one of the other four versions suggests that his decision was immediate or divinely inspired. This lends credence to the idea that personal revelation can often function as a motif, particularly in legends shared widely and far from their original sources.

29. See chapter 2 for a discussion of the distrust some members have when they hear the same people tell one fantastic revelation after another.

30. I have adapted the term "retroactive revelation" from Jarold Ramsey's concept of retroactive prophecy in his book *Reading the Fire* (1999:194–207). My use of the concept, however, differs significantly. Ramsey argues that much of American Indian prophecy is retroactive. Just as myth projects the past into the present, the present can be projected into the past, creating prophecies that foretell the events currently unfolding. Ramsey argues this is a conscious act of invention to make sense of events that appear foreign, alienating, and unsettling. While the occasional LDS member may invent revelation for social ends, I argue that the tradition of retroactive revelation among Latter-day Saints is one of interpretation, not invention.

31. Sherene Asay recorded this story from her mother, who told her that "she doesn't know if she even has this written in her journal, but she thinks it is a story that should be passed down" (Asay 1992:9, Wilson Archives). I have not changed the name of the sister, since Sherene received and granted permission to use the names in her work.

32. He is referring to his wife's prompting.

33. A person may hear an owl hoot outside his home ten, twenty times in his life. But the time an owl hoots the day before a relative dies is remembered. For many, this phenomenon undermines the validity of omens and other supernatural means of foresight. For most LDS members, however, reflecting on the past and seeing the hand of God is a positive process, not a negative one.

34. The refrain "there are no coincidences" is often heard in response to stories shared by people hesitant to call their experiences divine. Bishop Michael Doyle says this in response to Keith Stanley's story about taking a different route to work (see chapter 2). Paul Clayson avers, "There are no coincidences in life. That said, I believe that our Heavenly Father will guide us in every aspect of our lives." See also Lund 2007:101, 105.

35. Janece Hoopes wrote out two of her own stories as part of her BYU class project titled "The Three Nephites and Other Spiritual Visitors" (1987, Wilson Archives). The first story she categorized as a story of "Attending Spirits," titling it "Traffic Stood Still" (5). The second story she categorized as a story of "Unseen Whisperers," titling it "Removed from a Car" (1). The "box" Janece mentions seems to refer to the trailer her brother was living in. Her family was living in two trailers at the time while their house was being built.

36. Writing in the *Ensign* magazine, LaRene Halling Petersen notes: "Some of my choicest experiences have been these spur-of-the-moment visits, when people knocked on my door unannounced and simply said, 'I've been thinking about you and just felt I should come.' I don't suppose these people know how much their visits helped, but I do know the Lord sent them in answer to my prayers" (2007:65).

37. This narrative was collected by BYU student Mike Morrison from his mother, Mary Morrison. Mary Morrison is *not* a pseudonym, unlike the rest of the narrators cited from archival documents, since the forms indicate "no restrictions" on the material. Mike notes: "This experience is one that my mother was strongly affected by because she witnessed it first-hand. She feels that it was a blessing to witness this event. This narrative is also significant because it strengthened her belief that the general authorities are true men of God and are inspired" (Morrison 1997:18–21, Wilson Archives).

38. The use of the word "inspired" is equivalent to revelation, as discussed in chapter 2. Further, the collector, the daughter of the narrator, categorized this story as "Promptings by the Spirit" (Miles 1980:8, Wilson Archives).

39. Hardy provides evidence of numerous dissenting voices, including Apostle Marriner W. Merrill, who wrote in his journal, "I do Not believe the Manifesto was a revelation from God but was formulated by Prest. Woodruff and endorsed by His Councilors and the Twelve Apostles for expediency to meet the present situation of affairs in the Nation or those against the Church" (August 20, 1891; cited in Hardy 1992:150).

40. This quote appears on page 96 of the Fifes' *Saints of Sage and Saddle*. The Fifes are likely referring to the Deer Creek dam and reservoir in Wasatch County, which was begun in 1938 and completed in 1941.

41. For a discussion of how forward thinking by respected community members can be interpreted as prophecy by subsequent generations, see Mould 2003:139–55.

42. William A. Wilson and Jesse Embry survey the scholarly literature on the subject as well as contemporary Mormons about their understanding of key events in Mormon history (1998: 84–5). That literature includes: Esplin 1981, Harper 1996, Jorgensen 1996–97, and Quinn 1976. See also Fife and Fife 1956:91.

43. The phrase has become iconic. Publicly, it provides the name for the This is the Place Monument, located in This is the Place Heritage Park in Salt Lake City and commemorating the historical trek. Commercially, it has been used for businesses (This is the Place Bookstore in Maryland touts itself as "Your one stop for LDS Products"), books (*This is the Place* by Carolyn Howard-Johnson, a novel about the religious conflict of a Mormon youth, and *Utah, The Right Place: The Official Centennial History* by Thomas G. Alexander), and songs (including "This is the Place" sung by Ed McCurdy on the *Mormon Pioneers* record; "This is the Place" in *Easy Duets for Latter-day Saints* by Penny Gardner; and even the Utah state song, which was changed in 2003 from "Utah, We Love Thee" to "Utah, This is the Place").

44. According to the footnotes to President Hinckley's talk printed in the May 1997 *Ensign* magazine, Hinckley is quoting B. H. Roberts, *A Comprehensive History of the Church,*

volume 3 (1965:224). Roberts, however, is in turn quoting Wilford Woodruff from *The Utah Pioneers* (1880:23). Woodruff's account is the first written record of Brigham Young's quote. Brigham Young's own account does not include the phrase but does describe revelation: "July 23rd: I ascended and crossed over the Big Mountain, when on its summit I directed Elder Woodruff, who kindly tendered me the use of his carriage, to turn the same half way round, so that I could have a view of a portion of Salt Lake valley. The Spirit of Light rested upon me, and hovered over the valley, and I felt that there the saints would find protection and safety. We descended and encamped at the foot of the Little Mountain" (from the *Manuscript History of Brigham Young* [Watson 1971], cited in B. H. Roberts 1965:224, volume 3). Whether that "Spirit of Light" simply confirmed the place, affirmed they would be safe there, or actually revealed the Saints' home for the first time is open for debate.

45. For a discussion of the story of the gulls and crickets and various historical exegeses, see Bitton and Wilcox 1978, Hartley 1970, Madsen and Madsen 1995, and Wilson and Embry 1998:93–4.

46. The Defense of Marriage Act (DOMA) was passed in the US Congress and signed into law by Bill Clinton on September 21, 1996. DOMA allows states to refuse to recognize or allow marriage between members of the same gender. The LDS Church issued this proclamation during these debates. Resurgence of the issue in US politics and culture as states have attempted to legalize gay marriage has many LDS members returning to the proclamation as prophetic revelation, both divine and predictive.

47. Member of the Stake High Council Hollan Pickard spoke to the Burlington First Ward on October 28, 2007. The scripture he is referencing is likely Luke 6:44–45: "For every tree is known by his own fruit. For of thorns men do not gather figs, nor of a bramble bush gather they grapes. A good man out of the good treasure of his heart bringeth forth that which is good; and an evil man out of the evil treasure of his heart bringeth forth that which is evil."

48. The LDS Church formally encourages caution in sharing other people's stories. In the church publication *Teaching, No Greater Call: A Resource Guide for Gospel Teaching*, members are encouraged to "make sure you tell the stories accurately. Do not share stories about others that may not be true or that may have elements that are not true. Before sharing a story, go to the source to confirm that what you say is factual" (1999:158).

49. BYU student Reynol Bowman recorded this story from memory; he originally heard the story at a high school football game in 1966 (Bowman 1972, Wilson Archives).

Chapter 5

1. Other tale type indices have been developed to extend to other geographical areas as well. See, for example, indices that cover Aboriginal Australia (Waterman 1987), the Arab world (El-Shamy 2004), North America and England (Baughman 1966), northern East Africa (Arewa 1967), and central Africa (Lambrecht 1967).

2. See Dundes 1982, 1989, and 1996, and Edmunds and Dundes 1983.

3. Examining all 441 narratives, 224, or 51 percent, involve danger or death, (see chart 6 in the appendix). Note that many, but not all, of those involving death also involve danger.

4. Of the stories involving danger, 78 percent describe danger faced away from home, and 22 percent describe death faced at or near home (such as in the fields on one's farm). Of stories involving the threat of death, 67 percent describe death faced away from home, 16 percent at home, and 17 percent were indeterminable (see chart 6 in the appendix).

5. Margaret Jo Virden wrote this story after hearing it from her mother in May 1970; the story was submitted for class in 1975. The contextual information included explains that this is part of their "family lore": "The incident related happened to my parents and grandmother

as they were driving from Cedar City, where I was attending college, to their home in Price" (Virden 1975, Wilson Archives). The expression of doubt about the source of the voice is not uncommon, even in stories generally believed to involve the divine (see chapter 2).

6. The narrative was written from memory on May 4, 1971, in Provo, Utah, by T. Kathleen Sant. She writes: "My mother told me this story about my grandfather (my father's father), which happened about thirty-five years ago" (Sant 1971, Wilson Archives). She titled the story twice: "Pull Over" and "Miraculously Saved." I made one change to her narrative; in the second sentence, she wrote "left" for both the mountain and the sharp dropoff. I have changed one of these to "right."

7. The Council of Fifty was established by Joseph Smith as a theocratic government in preparation for the Second Coming. It was formed in 1844, defunct by 1884, and officially eliminated in 1945 with the death of its last remaining member, President Heber J. Grant (see Quinn 1980).

8. A dugway is a trail cut into the side of a mountain, dug down below the surface. It is typically very steep.

9. Johnson's autobiography can be found online at http://www.boap.org/LDS/Early-Saints/BFJohnson.html. The online version does not have page numbers, but it does contain Johnson's chapter divisions. This blessing occurs in chapter 3 of the autobiography.

10. In folklore studies, such prototypes are often referred to as Ur-types, referring to the ancient civilization of Ur from which all other civilizations were purported to derive. The expectation and search for such prototypes have generally been discounted as impossible to determine and rarely productive (for an early critique of the Ur-form and the Finnish historical-geographical method more generally, see Dorson 1972:7–12). However, in some cases, prototypes are not only identifiable, they are referenced implicitly or explicitly within a culture. In these cases, the process of performance can be usefully explored and explained. Eric Eliason, for example, suggests that Joseph Smith's vision and conversion stands as an Ur-type for Mormon conversion stories (1999:142).

11. Of the 61 stories involving children in danger, 28 occurred in the home, 33 outside it, or 46 percent and 54 percent of these types of experiences, respectively. Danger remains highest outside the home, but the percentages contrast strikingly with the averages for all stories involving danger: 22 percent in the home and 78 percent away from it, numbers that include the stories of children in danger (see chart 6 in the appendix).

12. The other three stories involve revelation received by both parents.

13. The two stories are remarkably similar, particularly with the shared motif of being tracked by a mountain lion that provides comfort to the child while suggesting increased danger to adults.

14. There are exceptions. Elder Wicker received a warning that his girlfriend back home was going to break up with him. A Mormon couple received revelation that they would have only two children, fewer than they had hoped. These revelations provide comfort by preparing people for the emotional blow. However, such exceptions are rare.

15. Seventy-six, or 17 percent of all the narratives analyzed, involve death in some way. Of those narratives, 47 of them (or 62 percent of all narratives about death) involve preparing someone for the death of a loved one (see chart 6 in the appendix).

16. See, for example, stories collected by Kerril Sue Rollins (1977, Fife Archives), Celia Frank (1961, Wilson Archives), and Austin and Alta Fife in their book *Saints of Sage and Saddle* (1956:218). I have also recorded a number of these stories in my own fieldwork, though people have asked to keep those stories confidential.

17. "Tim Sampers" is a pseudonym. See also George H. Schoemaker's article on marriage confirmation stories (1989). He argues that many Mormons seek out divine confirmation for their choice of spouse for a variety of reasons, including wanting to escape from feeling the entire weight of the decision on their own shoulders (40).

18. As contextual information, Nielson adds: "Fred's wife had died, leaving him with five children. Shortly after, he had a dream which he thought was a revelation showing him who he would marry. Mary said that she didn't feel this was coincidental, but that this was inspired" (1990:6, Wilson Archives). See also Schoemaker 1989:43 for a discussion of the phrase "you will know your wife when you see her" and an example of such a story of personal revelation. The idea of knowing one's spouse at first sight also appears in other types of narratives—for example, the story Darlene Farnes's father tells about his patriarchal blessing (1970:67, Wilson Archives).

19. "Y" is a slang term recognized throughout Utah and among most Mormons in the United States; it is short for BYU, which is short for Brigham Young University.

20. LDS member and BYU college student Heidi Lietz explains: "In the LDS religion, dating return missionaries is usually serious because they are usually looking to get married. It is LDS culture that if you are seriously dating a return missionary, you are both looking towards marriage. If one party knows that they don't feel it is right, you should probably not pursue the relationship. Usually LDS couples are prayerful about the relationships that they are in because the bonds of marriage are one of the most serious covenants that we make here on this earth. It is one of the most important decisions that a young adult can make and should be done with a lot of thought and prayer (Lietz 2000:24, Wilson Archives).

21. Initially shared in 2004, but repeated as a coda to a story submitted by a sister missionary in the *New Era* church magazine in 2007, President Gordon Hinckley explained: "With reference to young sister missionaries, there has been some misunderstanding of earlier counsel regarding single sisters serving as missionaries. We need some young women. They perform a remarkable work. They can get in homes where the elders cannot. But it should be kept in mind that young sisters are not under obligation to go on missions. They should not feel that they have a duty comparable to that of young men, but some will wish to go. If so, they should counsel with their bishop as well as their parents" (G. B. Hinckley 2004: 27).

22. Jennifer Vigil took notes as her aunt Pat told her the story over the phone. Despite how close the two women are, Jennifer sensed that Pat seemed reluctant to share the story with her, something not uncommon for stories held to be deeply personal and sacred (Vigil 2002:17, Wilson Archives).

23. "Mother" refers to his wife. The *Oxford English Dictionary* notes that in regional and colloquial usage, a man may call his wife "mother," referring to her role as the mother of their children.

24. The use of "spirit world" is confusing here. This term is typically used for the world between the temporal world (Earth) and the celestial kingdom after resurrection. Here, it is being used to describe the premortal existence.

25. In her study of these types of narratives, Margaret Brady suggests that "when the new baby is not the vision-child, it is immediately clear to the mother that there is still another child waiting to be born, and that another pregnancy is imminent (1987:464).

26. Margaret Brady suggests a similar subtype of narrative in her study (1987). Scott Mitchell also identifies this tale type in his analysis of spirit child narratives, finding that fully 25 percent of the narratives about unborn children adhere roughly to this structure (or 10 out of 40) (2004:43). In my own analysis of 441 narratives, 34 stories (8 percent) describe people receiving personal revelation about having more children, 11 of which (32 percent of the stories about children) follow this tale type structure (see chart 6 in the appendix).

27. See, for example, the argument made by church leader Melvin J. Ballard in 1949 and quoted by First Counselor in the First Presidency N. Eldon Tanner in 1980 in the *Ensign* magazine: "There is a passage in our scriptures which the Latter-day Saints accept as divine: 'This is the glory of God—to bring to pass the immortality and eternal life of man' [see Moses 1:39]. Likewise we could say that this is the glory of men and women—to bring

to pass the *mortality* of the sons and daughters of God, to give earth-life to the waiting children of our Father. . . . The greatest mission of woman is to give life, earth-life, through honorable marriage, to the waiting spirits, our Father's spirit children who anxiously desire to come to dwell here in this mortal state. All the honor and glory that can come to men or women by the development of their talents, the homage and the praise they may receive from an applauding world, worshipping at their shrine of genius, is but a dim thing whose luster shall fade in comparison to the high honor, the eternal glory, the ever-enduring happiness that shall come to the woman who fulfils the first great duty and mission that devolves upon her to become the mother of the sons and daughters of God" (*Sermons and Missionary Services,* Salt Lake City: Deseret Book, 1949, pp. 203–4, italics added; Tanner 1980:17). See also the stake conference talk given by Susan W. Tanner, general president of the Young Women, on February 17, 2008, in which she quotes President Spencer Kimball as saying the righteous woman helps her husband. She argues that Satan is working right now to confuse women about their roles and what they should be doing, convincing some that they don't need to have kids right now, or get married. She goes on to quote President Gordon B. Hinckley and his talks to the Relief Society echoing similar sentiments. She also references "The Family: A Proclamation to the World," informally known as the proclamation on the family, which has become like scripture to many LDS members and stresses the importance of marriage between a man and a woman and of having children.

28. Of the thirty-four stories of personal revelation about having children, twenty-one were experienced by women, ten by men, and three by couples where both husband and wife received the same revelation. Of the eleven stories that followed this tale type, six were experienced by women, four by men, and one by both husband and wife (see chart 6 in the appendix). Mitchell and Brady both found a preponderance of stories from women, but such a result was inevitable; both specifically targeted female consultants (see Brady 1987:461–2 and Mitchell 2004:21).

29. Taking handwritten notes, BYU student Kerril Sue Rollins recorded this story from a close family friend in 1970 (1977:79–80, Fife Archives). Rollins points out that such dreams are common in Mormon folklore, referencing two other stories she recorded as well as stories recorded by Austin and Alta Fife (1956:218–9).

30. I heard stories of this type of experience shared twice in the Burlington First Ward, once by Jackie Foss during Sunday school, the other by Craig Bailey during priesthood meeting.

31. Jennifer Vigil recorded this story over the telephone from Colleen, a female friend, the daughter of the man who baptized her husband. She got the impression that her friend did not share this story often, likely only to family and close friends in a private setting (2002:15, Wilson Archives).

32. Men are twice as likely to receive revelation about a new home or new job as women (see chart 6 in the appendix).

33. Ken is referencing a discussion earlier that evening of how the Spirit often comes to him as a wind.

34. In their study of the role of missionary work in the LDS Church, Gordon and Gary Shepherd argue: "The lay religious organization aims to assign a 'master status' to one's membership in the church, that is, to establish church membership as the single most important status for defining one's social identity, so the church can assume priority claim on its members' commitment and personal resources. (In Mormonism, this priority claim is symbolically articulated in a temple endowment ceremony as the Law of Consecration, which devoted members covenant to obey for the rest of their lives)" (2001:168).

35. Of the 71 stories of personal revelation involving missionaries (16 percent of the total number of personal revelation narratives), 52 (74 percent) involve young men on their 2-year missions, 6 (9 percent) involve young women on their 18-month missions, and 13 (18 percent) involve adult members conducting the daily work of proselytizing.

36. Gordon and Gary Shepherd not only identify the common military analogies used to describe missionary religions, they articulate specific areas of overlap with LDS missionary work. They note of course that the analogy goes only so far and that missionary work depends on "persuasion and conversion rather than force" (2001:163–4).

37. Adam Wicker had already told me about his stabbing and references this in his narrative. Normally, he would save this information as a dramatic climax for those not familiar with this event, as he did when he first told it to me and as I heard him do in oral performances with other members in the hallways after church.

38. Of the 71 stories that involve missionaries, 23 (32 percent) involve the active process of tracting. Of those 23 stories, 13 (57 percent) involve a missionary being prompted to talk to a particular person, following the broad outlines of the tale type described (see chart 6 in the appendix).

39. A greenhorn, or "greenie" for short, is the slang term for new missionaries in the field.

40. Pass-along cards are like business cards for the church. They typically provide some brief information about the church along with contact information for receiving additional free information about the church. Pass-along cards were introduced in 1998. The church printed its 150 millionth pass-along card in 2005 (Cooley 2005).

41. This brief account of conversion is accompanied by a similarly brief life history composed not of information focusing on Isaac Newton Goodale but of important moments in the history of the church. In many ways, these additions function like the superlative endings discussed in chapter 4; here, the new convert does not just join the church but becomes a confidante of the prophet Joseph Smith, is nearby at his death, and is part of the great migration out West to Salt Lake (Pyle n.d., Wilson Archives). I have not used pseudonyms, as these are historical figures. A similar example of an early experience in the church is shared in a letter by "Furious" Murius McFadden about the great-grandfather of his sister-in-law (McFadden 1981, Wilson Archives).

42. The majority of the stories involving missionaries are told from the perspective of the missionaries themselves. In these stories, however, the perspective shifts to the soon-to-be-convert. Of the 15 stories from this perspective, 8 (53 percent) are of this tale type (see charts 6 and 8 in the appendix).

43. "Robert Foster" is a pseudonym; I have changed the name of the country where he fulfilled his mission and the names of the families with whom he worked.

44. Robert Foster is referring to his talk the previous Sunday during church. Also, he explicitly points out that he is providing a much fuller account of the experience than he did during the church service.

45. "Heavenly Father" is the most common term LDS members use to refer to God, although "God" and "Lord" are also used ("God" is also used repeatedly throughout Robert Foster's narrative, for example).

46. The story was originally printed in Bryant S. Hinckley's *The Faith of Our Pioneer Fathers*, 1956:242–4. It was edited and summarized in the *New Testament Gospel Doctrine Teacher's Manual* as part of lesson 31: "And So Were the Churches Established in the Faith," 129. The original version, printed by Hinckley from an account written by John Morgan's son, Nicholas G. Morgan Sr., includes much more detail, particularly of the interchange between Morgan and Sister Heywood and his travels in Georgia.

47. Peter Zaine is a pseudonym.

48. A BYU graduate student shared this story, which he heard while he was serving a mission in Central America. "Stephen Lister" visited the BYU twenty-fifth ward during the Christmas holidays, a visit that would presumably lend credence to the experience in the mind of the collector, Geraldine Avant (1968, Wilson Archives).

49. The May issue of the *Ensign* magazine publishes general statistics about the church, including the number of converts baptized and the number of missionaries in the field. By dividing the baptisms by the number of missionaries, one can roughly estimate the number of baptisms for each missionary. Over the past five years, this average has hovered around five

baptisms per missionary per year. However, since not all conversions can be attributed to missionary work, this ratio may be artificially high, particularly in light of conversations with missionaries, who often quote a number of between two and five for *both* years in the mission field, with the majority of those from referrals rather than tracting.

50. See any of a number of talks given during general conference on the topic of missionary work. In particular, see the LDS missionary manual *Preach My Gospel*, which clearly describes the missionaries' primary goal and measurement of success: "Your success as a missionary is measured primarily by your commitment to find, teach, baptize, and confirm people and to help them become faithful members of the Church who enjoy the presence of the Holy Ghost"(2004:10). Although personal righteousness is required for and expected from missionaries, nowhere in the manual are missionaries encouraged to consider their own growth as part of a successful mission.

51. The Gift of Teaching, Wisdom, and Knowledge is articulated in Moroni 10:9–10 and is one of the many gifts of the Holy Ghost. For a brief discussion of these various gifts, see *Gospel Principles* 1997 [1978]:141–9. This LDS Church publication is often used to teach new investigators.

52. The result of this overlap between direct intervention and revelation demanding agency is that while the theme of receiving help in speaking is widespread in the culture and narrative tradition broadly, stories that fall within the more narrow parameters of personal revelation are misleading. Of the 441 stories analyzed, only 8 (2 percent) describe clear revelations where members make conscious choices about what to say. Further, all 8 stories were experienced and shared by men. However, as the example from Jean Chandler makes clear, women are certainly being guided to speak as well, thanks to the gift of the Holy Ghost.

53. For stories of dead relatives visiting the living to provide help and guidance, see student folklore collections in the Wilson Archives—Gibb 1999, Jensen 1997, Miles 1980, Jara 2000, Asay 1992—and in the Fife Archives—Rollins 1977.

54. This story was recorded by Scott Lowe from a female BYU student who heard it in a temple preparation class (1985, Wilson Archives).

55. As with being guided to speak, many of the stories about temple and genealogical work sit on the margins of the personal revelation narrative tradition—in this case, because angels rather than the Holy Ghost serve as common messengers. Nonetheless, the topic deserves attention because many people do not clearly distinguish between angels and the Holy Ghost in terms of their experiences. To ignore these experiences would be to ignore a major theme in a narrative tradition with large and blurry boundaries. However, my more focused analysis led to the underrepresentation of these stories. There are 18 stories out of 441 (4 percent) that involve temple work and 11 (3 percent) that involve genealogical work. Of the 11 stories of genealogical work, 6 (55 percent) are of this tale type (see chart 8 in the appendix).

56. The story was recorded in 1970 in Provo, Utah; the collector's name is unknown, but the story is accessioned under number 1.3.3.5.1 in the Wilson Archives. Also, member of the First Quorum of the Seventy and former BYU professor Spencer J. Condie included an account of this type of story in his talk about living righteously: "Sister Wendy Lelo is a faithful, persistent, competent area family history adviser in New Zealand. After making considerable progress on a family line, she suddenly ran into a brick wall. In exasperation, she laid aside her pedigree charts, certificates, and other records and began reading the scriptures. Like Lehi, as she read she was soon "filled with the Spirit of the Lord" (1 Nephi 1:12). The Spirit whispered impressions regarding some previously unexplored areas of research. After following those impressions she was able to link 10 additional generations to the family line she had been pursuing. If we live worthily, we too can know the truthfulness of the Lord's declaration that 'the power of my Spirit quickeneth all things' (D&C 33:16)" (Condie 2008: 56–8).

57. This quote is on page 8 of Gardener Brown's collection; the two stories can be found on pages 6–8 (Brown 1990, Wilson Archives). Of the eleven stories of genealogical work told, seven were experienced by women, four by men. Of these, eight were shared by women,

three by men. In other words, women were almost twice as likely as men to receive revelation about genealogical work and more than twice as likely to share stories about it. Of the specific tale type of receiving revelation to help complete genealogical work, four out of six were experienced and shared by women; the two stories experienced by men collected by Gardener Brown and described in the text of this book support, rather than undermine, the conclusion that genealogical work is done primarily by women.

58. Gordon and Gary Shepherd cite statistics from 1992 from personal correspondence with the LDS Church Missionary Department that 20 percent of the missionaries were young women (2001:170). When I called the LDS Church Missionary Department for current statistics, I was initially told that such statistics are not given out. After follow-up phone calls, I was later told they do not keep these statistics (December 11, 2009).

59. Of the 441 stories, 98 involve helping others (22 percent; see chart 6 in the appendix). Of those 98 stories, just under half involve helping one's children (42 stories, or 43 percent).

60. I am not the first to recognize the parallels to the nature versus nurture debate in understanding the formation of folk belief and its subsequent relevance for understanding memorates. David Hufford made the same connection in 1995 in his chapter on experience-centered theory in the book *Out of the Ordinary: Folklore and the Supernatural*, edited by Barbara Walker, now Barbara Lloyd (21).

Chapter 6

1. The following question appeared in the Question and Answer section of the March 2007 *Ensign* magazine: "I have difficulty distinguishing between promptings of the Spirit and my own personal feelings. How can I tell the difference?" LDS member Donna K. Maxwell wrote a response that lauds the merits of writing to discern revelation: "One way I have learned to recognize promptings is by keeping a daily journal and recording spiritual thoughts. I identify the specific feeling or thought and write down what I think it means and what I should do about it. If it is an answer to a specific question I have asked, I record that and the fact that I feel it is the answer. Then I act upon it when the opportunity is presented. It can be moments, days, or years later when I see the outcome. I record that spiritual verification also" (60).

2. Rich Tenney is quoting scripture here. The quote originally comes from the Old Testament, Malachi 4:5: "And he shall turn the heart of the fathers to the children, and the heart of the children to their fathers." However, the phrase is repeated five times by Joseph Smith in the Doctrine and Covenants (2:2; 27:9; 110:15; 128:17; and 138:47) and is often repeated when discussing the importance of the family, the nature of relationships expected between parents and children, and the power of the gospel to draw families together.

3. Janyce Lane Miller, daughter of Naydene Tenney, compiled her mother's section of the book and ends with a footnote: "This story [referring to the story of her life] was transcribed from interviews with Mother on various occasions. I have left some of her words with her colloquial manner of speaking as nearly as possible because I think it adds charm and flavor to her story. Until I started transcribing these tapes, I didn't realize how much of her early Southern Arizona country girl manner of speaking she had retained all her life. I have put my editorial comments in (brackets like this)" (Hendrix and Hendrix 1994:83). Other family compilers end with similar if briefer notes, such as "Recorded on tape when Boyd was 70 years old. Typed by Linda Tenney, 1986" (288).

4. For a brief analysis of these different variants of a single experience, see chapter 4.

5. Despite the language that perfectly echoes personal revelation, this feeling may be secular rather than divine.

6. In the July 2008 issue of the *Ensign* magazine, the editors published an article titled "Making Church Magazines" that describes how church magazines are put together (64–9). In it, the editors explain that planning begins with the *Liahona*, the magazine directed at members worldwide: "In planning monthly issues of the *Liahona*, editors prayerfully try to judge which articles are most needed by members worldwide. The choices of articles are reviewed by the General Authorities who are advisers to the Curriculum Department." Those same articles prayed over for inclusion in the *Liahona* make their way to the *Ensign*: "Church leaders have asked that as nearly as possible the content used in the *Liahona* match the content that is printed in the Church's English-only magazines: the *Ensign, New Era,* and *Friend*" (65).

7. I have grouped editors and experts such as professors at BYU, medical doctors, and psychologists. One reason for this is that clear distinctions between staff editors, regular contributors, and guest writers are not always made. Another is that articles from these various writers are similar both in nature and authority, although that authority may draw from more temporal sources in the case of professors and medical doctors. For the purposes of this study, this rough and loose grouping seems sufficient; for analysis focused less heavily on lay members and oral traditions, distinctions among these groups may be more appropriate.

8. These guidelines can be found online at http://www.lds.org on the *Ensign* home page, where there is a link "Do you have a story to tell?" Also relevant on this page are the general guidelines that note the following: "*For adults:* Stories that show the gospel of Jesus Christ at work in the lives of Latter-day Saints, especially personal experiences tied to gospel insights. Watch for the 'Call for Articles' on specific subjects. We are also looking for how-to articles and practical ideas on topics of interest to members, such as teaching, serving, strengthening marriages and families, and overcoming challenges. Articles about the Church and its members in various parts of the world and about specific individuals and families who are making a difference in their communities are also of interest."

9. For a history of the organization and repeated reorganization of the Seventies, see Tingey 2009. Area Seventies were organized in 1997 by Gordon B. Hinckley following a history of regional authoritative bodies often organized as Seventies.

10. The positions held by female leaders represented in the *Ensign* include: First Counselor in the Relief Society General Presidency, Second Counselor in the Relief Society General Presidency, Relief Society General Board, Recently Released Relief Society General President, Young Women General President, First Counselor in the Young Women General Presidency, Second Counselor in the Young Women General Presidency, and Second Counselor in the Primary General Presidency.

11. General conference lasts two days. It begins Saturday morning with an address to the entire membership. The conference continues that afternoon and Sunday morning for the entire membership. On Saturday evening there is a session for members of the priesthood only. The president gives formal closing remarks at the end of the Sunday afternoon session. The Young Women's meeting follows general conferences held in April; the Relief Society meeting follows general conferences held in October.

12. It is worth noting how Serena ends her summary narration of the story with the classic happily-ever-after ending discussed in chapter 4, an ending, it is equally important to note, that is faithful to the published story (see "A Hole in Her Soul" in the July 2006 *Ensign*).

13. The story Serena shares was submitted by Lorraine Jeffery and published with the testimonies of two other women in the April 2008 issue of the *Ensign* under the title "The Joy of Nurturing Children." Lorraine's story appears on pages 38–39. Editors introduced the article by noting: "Following are the testimonies of three women who show that the spiritual rewards of motherhood are for everyone" (35).

14. Ethnographic fieldwork bears this out. Stories from the *Ensign* were shared regularly in sacrament meetings. I did not systematically record this information throughout my three years of fieldwork in the Burlington First Ward, but between April and August 2007,

I noted in my field notes at least four times that men and women giving sacrament meeting talks shared stories from the *Ensign*.

15. Like much of verbal folklore, the jokes and stories we share are winnowed by memory. We assume that the jokes and stories we remember are the ones most significant to us, though my own experience with jokes suggests that occasion for narration is dramatically important. The jokes I remember today are the same jokes I told in the sixth grade, a particularly fertile time for sharing jokes. I remember those jokes not because they were great or particularly meaningful to me but because I repeated them often enough in a short enough span of time to cement them into my long-term memory. Of course, my joke repertoire is not shaped entirely by the capricious circumstances of my golden age of joke telling in the sixth grade. Jokes depending on racism, sexism, or other isms that violate my own politics and values have been winnowed upon hearing and with maturity, as have those whose humor is too juvenile to entertain adult audiences. I mention this not because we cannot read repertoire for personal and cultural meaning but because the various explanations for why we remember one story but not another are far more complicated than because it resonated with us.

16. See any of a number of Jan Harold Brunvand's books on urban legends, including *The Vanishing Hitchhiker*, *The Choking Doberman*, *The Mexican Pet*, and *Curses! Broiled Again!* as well as his article on folklore in the news and on the internet (2001).

17. A recent debate on the Publore Listserv, which is subscribed to primarily by folklorists working in the public sector, discussed the use and impact of the songbook *Rise Up Singing*. Sentiment was split; while some bemoaned the dependency on the book, far more defended the book, pointing out parallels with the broadside ballad tradition and arguing that moving between oral and written traditions is part of the folk process of transmission. In terms of the risk of codifying certain versions as "the right way to sing it," at least one writer noted that "traditional singers" nonetheless might bring out a book to prove how the song should be sung (December, 2008).

Afterword

1. Carolyn Flatley Gilkey wrote a dissertation on testimony meetings while a doctoral student at the University of Pennsylvania under the guidance of folklorist Dan Ben-Amos (1994). Gilkey published a preliminary article on her research in *Western Folklore* that focused on testimony meetings as a particular performance event (1979). Focused work on spiritual revelation, however, remains to be conducted.

Works Cited

Note: much of the archival material referenced in this book is shared in both the William A. Wilson Folklore Archives at Brigham Young University and the Fife Folklore Archives at Utah State University. I have cited these sources according to where I accessed them, since the call numbers for these documents are slightly different in each archive, even when they follow a similar numbering system. Unfortunately, this means that work done by BYU students may be cited below in the USU archives and vice versa.

William A. Wilson Folklore Archives
L. Tom Perry Special Collections
Harold B. Lee Library
Brigham Young University, Provo, Utah

1970. FA2 Box 32 1.3.3.5.1.
Alder, Elise. 1984. Spiritual Memorates and Folklore of Opal T. Jeffries: A Gem in More Than Name [Pseudonym]. FA1 1104.
Allen, Camilla. 1996. Premonitions and Promptings. FA1 1344.
Asay, Sherene. 1992. Religious Supernatural Experiences Associated with Death. FA1 1041.
Avant, Geraldine. 1968. 1.7.3.13.1.
Beckstead, Carol. 1961. 5.3.1.1.
Bedke, Julia. 1999. 1.1.4.3.3.
Bice, Russell. 1964. 1.7.3.10.1.
Bonnett, David. 1980. 3.2.5.0.6.1.
Bowman, Reynol E. 1972. Soldier Miracle: "Saved by a Book of Mormon." FA2 1.7.2.7.1.
Breit, Kara. 1999. 8.1.4.1.
Brennan, Camille. 1986a. Visions of Spirit Children. FA1 745.
———. 1986b. 1.7.0.38.1 and 1.7.3.19.1.
Broderick, Lynn Ann. 1982. FA1 484.
Brown, Gardener. 1990. Faith Promoting Family Stories. FA1 932.
Call, Ruby. 1966. 1.7.1.18.1.
Campbell, Diane. 1971. Haun's Mill. 1.7.2.10.1.
Carlisle, Colleen. 1984. 1.2.1.44.1.
Chalk, Melissa. 1999. Sister Jones and the Chocolate Pie. FA2 1.7.0.39.1.
Christensen, Susan, and Doris Blackham. 1971. 1.7.0.25.1.
Condie, Julia. 1994. Holy Ghost Stories. FA1 1155.
Cope, Jacob. 2003. FA1 2602.
Crowther, Joan. n.d. From the Journal of Brother William Tolman. 1.3.4.2.1.
Embry, Susan. 1962. 1.2.1.38.1 and 1.7.2.13.1.

Farnes, Darlene. 1970. Ways of Predicting the Future. FA1 230.

Fischio, Joye. 1970. Lost in the Mountains. 1.3.2.14.1.

Fletcher, Barbara. 1972. 1.3.1.20.1.

Frank, Celia. 1961. 1.2.1.34.1 and 1.7.1.19.1.

Gibb, Joanna. 1999. Spiritual Experiences: Large and Small. FA1 2018.

Giles, Verl L. n.d. A Conversion through a Dream. 1.7.3.5.1.

Hall, Vicki. 1969. 1.7.1.16.1.

Hancock, Mosiah Lyman. 1956. The Life Story of Mosiah Lyman Hancock. BX M270.1 H191.

Healy, Jay. Genealogy. FA2 Box 41 1.7.0.9.1 and 1.7.1.2.1.

Holt, Merlene. 1963. 1.7.0.9.1.

Hoopes, Janece. 1987. The Three Nephites and Other Spiritual Visitors. FA1 920.

Ice, Carole Lou. n.d. 1.3.4.66.1, 1.7.0.21.1, and 1.7.2.16.1.

Jara, Sherami. 2000. Angels to Bear Us Up. FA1 2524.

Jensen, Trish. 1997. 3.2.5.2.1.3.

Jeppson, Melvin. 1981. Four Leaf Clover Led Convert to Genealogy. FA2 Box 32 1.3.3.3.1.

Judd, Roger L. 1966. FA1 1104.

Kandare, Joanne. 1985. 1.7.0.2.11.

Layland, Erika. 2001. Family Spiritual Experiences: A Closer Look. FA1 2145 and 1.3.2.31.1.

Leavitt, Katrina. 1995. Revelations: The Calls for Women to Serve. FA1 1266.

LeBaron, Gail. 1965. 1.2.1.24.1.

Lietz, Heidi. 2000. LDS Dream Folklore. FA1 2141.

Long, Merrill Heber. 1995. Prayer Stories of the Latter-day Saints. FA1 1253.

Louder, Tamra. 1969. 1.2.1.16.1, 1.2.1.20.1, and 1.7.1.13.1.

Lowe, Scott. 1985. FA2 Box 28 1.2.1.40.1.

McDaniel, Maren. 1972. Dream of Death. FA2 Box 34 1.3.4.24.1.

McFadden, Tim. 1981. Faith Promoting Family Stories: "William Rowe." 1.7.3.17.1.

Miles, Kristy. 1980. Faith-Promoting Stories of the Franklin W. Miles and George P. Stock Families. FA1 72.

Mohler, Doris. 1980. Miracles. FA1 586.

Moon, Colleen. 1970. Help in Genealogy. FA2 Box 33 1.3.3.7.1.

Morris, Deborah. 1984. 1.3.2.18.1 and 1.3.2.24.1.

Morrison, Mike. 1997. Blind Woman. FA1 1444.

Mower, Mary LaVee. 1975. The Importance of the Miraculous and the Supernatural to Mormons. FA1 321.

Newell, David. 2002. The Icicle Incident. 3.2.5.3.1.1.

Nielson, Cheryl. 1990. Signs and Superstitions in Determining a Future Spouse. FA1 1104.

Noland, Sharlene. 1961. FA2 Box 44 1.7.2.4.1.

Oliveros, James. 2001. FA1 2618.

Paakanen, Ronald. 1966. 1.2.1.30.1.

Page, Kathy. 1982. 1.2.1.17.1.

Palmer, E. Paia. 1998. Stephanie Is Our Daughter. FA2 1.7.0.39.1.

Parker, LaRue. 1971. FA1 339.

Peterson, Mary. 1974. 1.7.0.22.1.

Pyle, Portia. n.d. 1.7.3.4.1 and 1.7.3.15.1.

Reamey, Marianne. 1972. Hugh Nibley's Courtship. 4.14.1.2.1.

Richins, Shirley. n.d. 1.3.6.10.1.

Riddle, Ruth. 1976. FA 2 Box 31 1.3.2.3.1.

Root, Michael. 1971. FA1 1104.

Sant, T. Kathleen. 1971. Miraculously Saved. 1.2.1.27.1.

Shiozawa, Natalie. 1997. FA2 1.7.2.19.1.

Skaggs, Virginia. 1975. 1.3.3.2.1.

Snow, Renee. 1971. FA2 Box 35 1.3.4.63.1 and 1.7.0.26.1.

Sollis, Cynthia. 1997. FA2 Box 32 1.3.2.34.1.

Steed, Leesa. 1984. FA2 Box 31 1.3.2.19.1.

Strong, Mary. 1930. 1.2.1.36.1 and 1.2.2.5.1.

Tuft, Gregory K. 1988. 1.7.3.18.1.

Vigil, Jennifer. 2002. Joy in Our Posterity: Personal Revelation about Having Children. FA1 2369.

Virden, Jo. 1975. 1.2.1.25.1.

White, Don L. n.d. FA2 Box 45 1.7.3.6.1.

Williams, Karen. 1976. 1.2.2.1.1.

Young, Kent M. 1984. The Saving Voice. 1.2.1.43.1.

Fife Folklore Archives
Special Collections and Archives
Merrill-Cazier Library
Utah State University, Logan, Utah

King, Marion. 1945. Fife Mormon Collection I: 121.

McClellan, Zitelle. 1931. An Account of Mother's Remarkable Healing. Fife Mormon Collection II: 2–11.

Peggy. 1976. Folklore Collection 8a Group 7 Box 15 Folder 27 L.4.M.2.3.1.

President McKay's Vision. 1976. USU Folk Collections 8a Group 7 Box 15 Folder 27.

Rollins, Kerril Sue. 1977. A Look at Mormons through Their Spirit World Memorates. Folklore Collection 7 Box 23 BYU 238.

Smurthwaite, Donald. 1977. The Peripatetic Prophet and Other Wandering Food Storage Stories. Folklore Collection 7 Box 24 BYU 255.

Sue. 1.7.2.3.2.

Turley, Wayne. 1970. Mormon Folklore Concerning the Last Days. Folklore Collection 7 Box 27 BYU 287.

Van Orden, Marilyn. 1971. Premonitions among Mormons. Folklore Collection 7, Box 27, BYU 288.

Published Works

Aarne, Antti, and Stith Thompson. 1961. *The Types of the Folktale: A Classification and Bibliography*. 2d revised ed. Helsinki: Academia Scientarum Fennica.

Aaron, David H. 2002. *Biblical Ambiguities: Metaphor, Semantics, and Divine Imagery*. Boston: Brill Academic Publishers.

Adamson, J. H. 1959. Tales of the Supernatural. *Western Folklore* 18(2):79–87.

Alexander, Thomas G. 1995. *Utah, the Right Place: The Official Centennial History*. Salt Lake City: Gibbs Smith.

Apo, Satu. 2007. The Relationship between Oral and Literary Tradition as a Challenge in Fairy-Tale Research: The Case of Finnish Folktales. *Marvels & Tales* 21(1):19–33.

Arewa, Erastus Ojo. 1967. A Classification of the Folktales of the Northern East African Cattle Area by Types. Ph.D. diss., University of California, Berkeley.

Arora, Shirley L. 1987. Memorate and Metaphor: Some Mexican Treasure Tales and Their Narratives. In *Perspectives on Contemporary Legend*, eds. Gillian Bennett, Paul Smith, and J. D. A. Widdowson pp. 79–92. Sheffield, England: Sheffield Academic Press.

Arrington, Leonard J. 1966. *Great Basin Kingdom*. Lincoln: University of Nebraska Press.

Arrington, Leonard J., and Davis Bitton. 1980. *The Mormon Experience: A History of the Latter-day Saints*. New York: Vintage Books.

Aveal, Maria Espinoza. 1995. Questions and Answers. *Liahona* 25(11):21–3.

Bailey, Wilfrid C. 1951. Folklore Aspects in Mormon Culture. *Western Folklore* 10(3):217–25.

Bander, Peter. 1979. *The Prophecies of St. Malachy and St. Columbkille*. Buckinghamshire: Colin Smythe.

Banfield, Jill Todd. 1983. *Draw Near Unto Me*. Salt Lake City: Bookcraft.

Bankhead, Reid E. 1949. A Study of the Meaning of the Terms Inspiration and Revelation as Used in the Church of Jesus Christ of Latter-day Saints. M.A. thesis, Brigham Young University, Provo, UT.

Bartlett, F. C. 1920. Some Experiments in the Reproduction of Folk Stories. *Folk-Lore* 31:30–47.

Basquiat, Jennifer Huss. 2004. Embodied Mormonism: Performance, Vodou and the LDS Faith in Haiti. *Dialogue* 37(4):1–34.

Baughman, Ernest Warren. 1966. *Type and Motif-Index of the Folktales of England and North America*. The Hague: Mouton.

Bauman, Richard. 1977. *Verbal Art as Performance*. Long Grove: Waveland Press, Inc.

———. 2004. *A World of Others' Words: Cross-Cultural Perspectives on Intertextuality*. Malden, MA: Blackwell Publishers.

———. 2006. Speech Genres in Cultural Practice. In *Encyclopedia of Language and Linguistics*, ed. K. Brown, pp. 745–58. Boston: Elsevier.

Bauman, Richard, and Pamela Ritch. 1994. Informing Performance: Producing the Coloquio in Tierra Blanca. *Oral Tradition* 9(2):255–80.

Ben-Amos, Dan. 1971. Toward a Definition of Folklore in Context. *Journal of American Folklore* 84(331):3–15 .

———. 1980. The Concept of Motif in Folklore. In *Folklore Studies in the Twentieth Century: Proceedings of the Centenary Conference of the Folklore Society*, ed. V. Newall, pp. 17–36. Ipswitch, UK: Boydell & Brewer.

Benedict, Ruth. 1935. *Zuni Mythology*. New York: Columbia University Press.

Bennett, Gillian. 1989. "Belief Stories": The Forgotten Genre. *Western Folklore* 48(4):289-311.

The Bible Dictionary. 1991. In *The Holy Scriptures, Inspired Version: Containing the Old and New Testaments, an Inspired Revision of the Authorized Version*. Independence, MO: Herald Publishing House.

Bierhorst, John, ed. 1995. *The White Deer and Other Stories Told by the Lenape*. New York: William Morrow.

Bitton, Davis, and Linda P. Wilcox. 1978. Pestiferous Ironclads: The Grasshopper Problem in Pioneer Utah. *Utah Historical Quarterly* 46(4):336–55.

Blair, Alma R. 1972. The Haun's Mill Massacre. *BYU Studies* 13(1):62–7.

Bottigheimer, Ruth B. 2002. Misperceived Perceptions: Perrault's Fairy Tales and English Children's Literature. *Children's Literature* 30:1–18.

———. 2003. The Ultimate Fairy Tale: Oral Transmission in a Literate World. In *A Companion to the Fairy Tale*, ed. Hilda Ellis Davidson and Anna Chaudhri, pp. 57–70. Cambridge, UK: D. S. Brewer.

Brady, Margaret K. 1987. Transformations of Power: Women's Visionary Narratives. *Journal of American Folklore* 100(398):461–8.

Brereton, Virginia L. 1991. *From Sin to Salvation: Stories of Women's Conversions, 1800 to Present*. Bloomington: Indiana University Press.

Britsch, Lanier R. 1986. *Unto the Islands of the Sea: A History of the Latter-day Saints in the Pacific*. Salt Lake City: Deseret Book.

————. 1998. *From the East: The History of the Latter-day Saints in Asia, 1851–1996*. Salt Lake City: Deseret Book.

Browne, Janet. 1983. *The Secular Ark: Studies in the History of Biogeography*. New Haven, CT: Yale University Press.

Browning, Gary. 1997. *Russia and the Restored Gospel*. Salt Lake City: Deseret Book.

Brunvand, Jan Harold. 1970. As the Saints Go Marching By: Modern Jokelore Concerning Mormons. *Journal of American Folklore* 83(327):53–60.

————. 1981. *The Vanishing Hitchhiker: American Urban Legends and Their Meanings*. New York: Norton.

————. 1984. *The Choking Doberman and Other "New" Urban Legends*. New York: Norton.

————. 1986. *The Mexican Pet: More "New" Urban Legends and Some Old Favorites*. New York: Norton.

————. 1989. *Curses! Broiled Again!: The Hottest Urban Legends Going*. New York: Norton.

————. 2001. Folklore in the News (and, incidentally, on the Net). *Western Folklore* 60(1): 47–66.

Buerger, David John. 1982. Speaking with Authority: The Theological Influence of Elder Bruce R. McConkie. *Sunstone* 10:8–13.

Bullinger, E. W. [1894] 1967. *Number in Scripture: Its Supernatural Design and Spiritual Significance*. Grand Rapids, MI: Kregel Publications.

Bunker, Gary L., and Davis Bitton. 1983. *The Mormon Graphic Image, 1834-1914: Cartoons, Caricatures, and Illustrations*. Salt Lake City: University of Utah Press.

Burton, Theodore M. 1977. The Inspiration of a Family Record. *Ensign* 7(1):13–23.

Bush, Lester E., Jr. 1981. The Word of Wisdom in Early Nineteenth-Century Perspective. *Dialogue* 14 (Autumn):47–65.

Canning, Ray R. 1965. Mormon Return-from-the-Dead Stories, Fact or Folklore? *Proceedings: Utah Academy of Science, Arts, and Letters* 42:29–37.

Cannon, George Q. 1882. *My First Mission: Designed for the Instruction and Encouragement of Young Latter-day Saints*. 2d ed. Salt Lake City: Juvenile Instructor Office.

Cannon, M. Hamlin. 1945. Angels and Spirits in Mormon Doctrine. *California Folklore Quarterly* 4(4):343-50.

Carroll, Bret E. 1997. *Spiritualism in Antebellum America*. Bloomington: Indiana University Press.

Cartwright, Christine A. 1982. "To the Saints Which Are at Ephesus": A Case Study in the Analysis of Religious Memorates. *New York Folklore Quarterly* 8(3–4):57–70.

Cashman, Ray, Tom Mould, and Pravina Shukla. 2011. *The Individual and Tradition*. Bloomington: Indiana University Press.

Chafe, Wallace, and Deborah Tannen. 1987. The Relation between Written and Spoken Language. *Annual Review of Anthropology* 16:383–407.

Christensen, James Boyd. 1971. Function and Fun in Utah-Danish Nicknames. *Utah Historical Quarterly* 39 (Winter):23–9.

Christofferson, D. Todd. 2004. A Sense of the Sacred. http://www.lds.org/broadcast.

Chronicles of Courage. 1995. Vol. 6. Salt Lake City: Daughters of Utah Pioneers.

Clements, William. 1973. Unintentional Substitution in Folklore Transmission: A Devolutionary Instance. *New York Folklore Quarterly* 29:243–53.

————. 1976. Conversion and Communitas. *Western Folklore* 35(1):35-45.

————. 1980. Public Testimony as Oral Performance: A Study in the Ethnography of Religious Speaking. *Linguistica Biblica* 47:21–32.

————. 1982. "I Once Was Lost": Oral Narratives of Born-Again Christians. *International Folklore Review: Folklore Studies from Overseas* 2(6):105–111.

Cobabe, George. 2004. The White Horse Prophecy. *FAIR: The Foundation for Apologetic Information and Research* December:1–11.

Cole, Phyllis. 1992. The Construction of Hospice and the Hospice Patient through Storytelling. *Folklore Forum* 25(1):29-40.

Compton, Todd. 1991. Counter-Hierarchical Revelation. *Sunstone* June:34–41.

Conference Report. [1898] 2001. Salt Lake City: Deseret Book Company.

Condie, Spencer J. 2008. Living by the Light of Christ. *Ensign* 38(12):56–8.

Connor, Kevin J. 2007. *Interpreting the Symbols and Types.* Portland, OR: City Christian Publishing.

Cook, Gene R. 2000. *Teaching by the Spirit.* Salt Lake City: Deseret Book.

Cooley, Walter. 2005. Pass-Along Cards Invite the World to Hear the Gospel. *Liahona* 29(12):N3–4.

Craine, Eugene R., and Reginald Carl Reindorp. 1979. *The Codex Pérez and the Book of Chilam Balam of Maní.* Norman: University of Oklahoma Press.

Crapo, Richley H. 1987. Grass-Roots Deviance from Official Doctrine: A Study of Latter-day Saint (Mormon) Folk Belief. *Journal for the Scientific Study of Religion* 26(4):465–85.

Cronin, Gloria. 1984. Who Shapes Oral Narrative: A Functionalist and Psychosocial Examination of the Lore of Two Mormon Female Tale-Tellers. *Mormon Letters Annual*:12-21.

Crosland, Todd. 2007. Lost on the Tundra. *Ensign* 37(1):30–2.

Cross, Eric. 1942. *The Tailor and Ansty.* New York: The Devin-Adair Company.

Crowther, Duane S. 1962. *Prophecy: Key to the Future.* Salt Lake City: Bookcraft.

———. 1983. *Gifts of the Spirit.* Bountiful, UT: Horizon Publishers.

Daemmrich, Horst S. 1985. Themes and Motifs in Literature: Approaches, Trends, Definition. *The German Quarterly* 58(4):566–75.

Davies, Douglas J. 2009. The Holy Spirit in Mormonism. *International Journal of Mormon Studies* 2(1):23–41.

Dégh, Linda. 1994. *Folklore and the Mass Media.* Bloomington: Indiana University Press.

———. 1996. What Is a Belief Legend? *Folklore* 107:33–46.

Dégh, Linda, and Andrew Vázsonyi. 1974. The Memorate and the Proto-Memorate. *Journal of American Folklore* 87(345):225–39.

Deonna, Waldemar. 1954. Trois Superlatif Absolu. *L'Antiquité Classique* 23:403–28.

Doctrine and Covenants and Church History: Gospel Doctrine Teacher's Manual. 1999. Salt Lake City: The Church of Jesus Christ of Latter-day Saints.

Doctrine and Covenants Institute Student Manual. 2001. Salt Lake City: The Church of Jesus Christ of Latter-day Saints.

Dorson, Richard M. 1959. *American Folklore.* Chicago: University of Chicago Press.

———. 1964. *Buying the Wind: Regional Folklore in the United States.* Chicago: University of Chicago Press.

———. 1972. *Folklore and Folklife: An Introduction.* Chicago: University of Chicago Press.

DuBois, Thomas A. 2006. *Lyric, Meaning, and Audience in the Oral Tradition of Northern Europe.* Notre Dame, IN: Notre Dame University Press.

Dumézil, Georges. 1958. *L'idéologie Tripartite Des Indo-Européens.* Brussels: Collection Latomus.

Dundes, Alan. 1964. *The Morphology of North American Indian Folktales.* Helsinki: Suomalainen Tiedeakatemia [sold by Akateeminen Kirjakauppa].

———. 1968. The Number Three in American Culture. In *Every Man His Way: Readings in Cultural Anthropology*, ed. A. Dundes, pp. 401–24. Englewood Cliffs, NJ: Prentice-Hall.

———. 1969. The Devolutionary Premise in Folklore Theory. *Journal of the Folklore Institute* 6(1):5–19.

———. 1982. *Cinderella: A Folklore Casebook.* New York: Garland.

———. 1989. *Little Red Riding Hood: A Casebook.* Madison: University of Wisconsin Press.

———. 1994. *The Cockfight: A Casebook.* Madison: University of Wisconsin Press.

———. 1996. *The Walled-up Wife: A Casebook.* Madison: University of Wisconsin Press.

———. 1998. *The Vampire: A Casebook*. Madison: University of Wisconsin Press.

Dunn, Shauna Bird. 2007. Mother Come Home. *Ensign* 37(4):9–13.

Durham, G. Homer, ed. 1946. *The Discourses of Wilford Woodruff*. Salt Lake City: Bookcraft.

Edmonson, Munro S. 1982. *The Ancient Future of the Itza: The Book of Chilam Balam of Tizimin*. Austin: University of Texas Press.

———. 1986. *Heaven Born Merida and Its Destiny: The Book of Chilam Balam of Chumayel*. Austin: University of Texas Press.

Edmunds, Lowell, and Alan Dundes. 1983. *Oedipus, a Folklore Casebook*. New York: Garland.

Edwards, Carol L. 1984. "Stop Me If You've Heard This One": Narrative Disclaimers as Breakthrough into Performance. *Fabula* 25(3-4):214–28.

El-Shamy, Hasan M. 2004. *Types of the Folktale in the Arab World: A Demographically Oriented Tale-Type Index*. Bloomington: Indiana University Press.

Eliason, Eric A. 1999. Toward the Folkloristic Study of Latter-day Saint Conversion Narratives. *BYU Studies* 38(1):137–50.

———. 2002. Angels among the Mormons. In *The Big Book of Angels*, ed. Beliefnet, pp. 96–104. New York: Rodale Books.

Eliason, Eric A., and Gary Browning. 2002. Crypto-Mormons or Pseudo-Mormons?: Latter-day Saints and Russia's Indigenous New Religious Movements. *Western Folklore* 61(2):173–207.

Eliason, Eric A., and Tom Mould. Forthcoming. *Latter-day Lore: A Mormon Folklore Reader*. Logan, UT: Utah State University Press.

Embry, Jessie L. 1997. *"In His Own Language": Mormon Spanish Speaking Congregations in the United States*. Provo, UT: Charles Redd Center for Western Studies.

———. 1999. *Asian American Mormons: Bridging Cultures*. Provo, UT: Charles Redd Center for Western Studies.

Erickson, Kai T. 1976. *Everything in Its Path*. New York: Simon & Schuster.

Erickson, Kirstin C. 2003. "They Will Come from the Other Side of the Sea": Prophecy, Ethnogenesis, and Agency in Yaqui Narrative. *Journal of American Folklore* 116(462):465–82.

Erickson, R. E. 1972. Billy's Second Chance. *The Friend* 2(6):16–9.

Esplin, Ronald K. 1981. Joseph, Brigham and the Twelve. *BYU Studies* 21(3):301–41.

Faith Promoting Series. 1879–1915. Edited by. G. C. Lambert. Salt Lake City: Juvenile Instructor Office.

Faust, James E. 2002. Communion with the Holy Spirit. *Ensign* 32(3):3–7.

———. 2004. Did You Get the Right Message? *Ensign* 34(5):61–8.

———. 2006. Spiritual Nutrients. *Ensign* 36(11):53–5.

Feintuch, Burt, ed. 2003. *Eight Words for the Study of Expressive Culture*. Chicago: University of Illinois Press.

Fife, Austin E. 1940. The Legend of the Three Nephites among the Mormons. *Journal of American Folklore* 53(207):1–49.

———. 1942. Popular Legends of the Mormons. *California Folklore Quarterly* 1(2):105–25.

———. 1948. Folk Belief and Mormon Cultural Autonomy. *Journal of American Folklore* 61(239):19–30.

Fife, Austin E., and Alta Stephens Fife. 1956. *Saints of Sage and Saddle: Folklore among the Mormons*. Bloomington: Indiana University Press.

Fine, Elizabeth C. 1984. *The Folklore Text: From Performance to Print*. Bloomington: Indiana University Press.

Fine, Gary Alan. 1979. Cokelore and Coke Law: Urban Belief Tales and the Problem of Multiple Origins. *Journal of American Folklore* 92(366):477–82.

Finnegan, Ruth H. 1992. *Oral Poetry: Its Nature, Significance, and Social Context*. Bloomington: Indiana University Press.

Fisher, Walter R. 1984. Narration as a Human Communication Paradigm: The Case of Public Moral Argument. *Communication Monographs* 51(1):1–22.

Ford, Clyde. 1998. The Origin of the Word of Wisdom. *Journal of Mormon History* 24(2):129–54.

Freeman, Robert C., and Dennis A. Wright. 2001. *Saints at War: Experiences of Latter-day Saints in World War II*. American Fork, UT: Covenant Communications.

———. 2003. *Saints at War: Korea and Vietnam*. American Fork, UT: Covenant Communications.

Freytag, Gustav. [1863] 1968. *Technique of the Drama: An Exposition of Dramatic Composition and Art*. Johnson Reprint Corp.

Friedrich, Paul. 1997. The Prophet Isaiah in Pushkin's "Prophet." In *Poetry and Prophecy: The Anthropology of Inspiration*, ed. John Leavitt, pp. 169–99. Ann Arbor: University of Michigan Press.

Front Matter. 2008. *British Journal of Mormon Studies* 1(1):i-iv.

Gardner, Penny. 2002. *Easy Duets for Latter-day Saints*. N.p.: the author, n.d..

Gaustad, Edwin Scott. 1974. *Rise of Adventism: A Commentary on the Social and Religious Ferment of Mid-Nineteenth Century America*. New York: Harper & Row.

Geertz, Armin W. 1994. *The Invention of Prophecy: Continuity and Meaning in Hopi Indian Religion*. Berkeley: University of California Press.

Gems for the Young Folks. 1881. Faith-Promoting Series, edited by G. C. Lambert, vol. 4. Salt Lake City: Juvenile Instructor Office

Gems of Reminiscence. 1915. Faith Promoting Series, ed. G. C. Lambert, vol. 17. Salt Lake City: Juvenile Instructor Office.

Gibson, Stephen R. 1995. *One-Minute Answers to Anti-Mormon Questions*. Bountiful, UT: Horizon Publishers & Distributors.

Gilkey, Carolyn Flatley. 1979. Mormon Testimony Meeting: Some Aspects of a Narrating Event. *Southwest Folklore* 3(4):45–59.

———. 1994. Verbal Performance in Mormon Worship Services. Ph.D. diss., University of Pennsylvania, Philadelphia.

Glassie, Henry H. 1982. *Passing the Time in Ballymenone: Culture and History of an Ulster Community*. Philadelphia: University of Pennsylvania Press.

———. 2006. *The Stars of Ballymenone*. Bloomington: Indiana University Press.

Göbel, Fritz. 1935. *Formen Und Formeln Der Epischen Dreiheit in Der Griechischen Dichtung*. Stuttgart: W. Kohlhammer.

Goffman, Erving. 1959. *The Presentation of Self in Everyday Life*. New York: Anchor Books.

———. 1974. *Frame Analysis: An Essay on the Organization of Experience*. Cambridge, MA: Harvard University Press.

Goldschmidt, Walter. 1951. Nomlaki Ethnography. *University of California Publications in American Archaeology and Ethnology* 42(4):303–443.

Goldstein, Diane E. 1989. The Smallest Group: Intensely Personal Experience Narratives. *Arv: Nordic Yearbook of Folklore* 45:43–9.

———. 1995. The Secularization of Religious Ethnography and Narrative Competence in a Discourse of Faith. *Western Folklore* 54(1):23–36.

Goody, Jack. 1987. *The Interface between the Written and the Oral*. Cambridge: Cambridge University Press.

Gospel Principles. [1978] 1996. Salt Lake City: Church of Jesus Christ of Latter-day Saints.

Goudy, Henry. 1910. *Trichotomy in Roman Law*. Oxford: Clarendon Press.

Grenzebach, Anne. 2007. Never Alone. *Ensign* 37(2):60–2.

Griffin, Charles J. G. 1990. The Rhetoric of Form in Conversion Narratives. *Quarterly Journal of Speech* 76(2):152–63.

Griffin, Gordon Douglas. 2007. *The Autobiography of Gordon Douglas Griffin, 1930–2005*. Savannah, GA: Image is Everything.

Grimm, Jacob. [1886] 1963. *Household Stories, from the Collection of the Brothers Grimm*, trans. L. Crane. New York: Dover.

Grinnell, George Bird. 1908. Some Early Cheyenne Tales II. *Journal of American Folklore* 21(82):269–320.

Hamilton, JoAnn Hibbert. 1998. *Personal Revelation: How to Recognize the Promptings of the Spirit*. American Fork, UT: Covenant Communications.

Hand, Wayland D. 1938. The Three Nephites in Popular Tradition. *Southern Folklore Quarterly* 2: 123–9.

Hanna, Darwin, and Mamie Henry, eds. 1995. *Our Tellings: Interior Salish Stories of the Nlha7kápmx People*. Vancouver: University of British Columbia Press.

Hardy, B. Carmon. 1992. *Solemn Covenant: The Mormon Polygamous Passage*. Chicago: University of Illinois Press.

Harper, Reid L. 1996. The Mantle of Joseph: Creation of a Mormon Miracle. *Journal of Mormon History* 22(1):35–71.

Harris, Marvin. 1966. The Cultural Ecology of India's Sacred Cattle. *Current Anthropology* 7(1):51–66.

Hartley, William. 1970. Mormons, Crickets, and Gulls: A New Look at an Old Story. *Utah Historical Quarterly* 38(3):224–39.

Heart Throbs of the West. 1941. Vol. 3. Salt Lake City: Daughters of the Utah Pioneers.

Hendrix, Pat, and Linda Hendrix. 1994. *The Tenney Breadbasket: History and Genealogy and Stories of Nathan Orson Tenney and Myrtle Mary Wear*. Denver: Anaconda Printing.

Hill, Reinhold R. 1996. Chapels, Baptismal Fonts, and the Curses of Cain: An Examination of the Obstacles to Conversion in Louisiana Mormon Conversion Narratives. *Louisiana Folklore Miscellany* 11:53–66.

Hinckley, Bryant S. 1956. *The Faith of Our Pioneer Fathers*. Salt Lake City: Deseret Book.

Hinckley, Gordon B. 1982. The Priesthood of Aaron. *Ensign* 12(11):44–7.

———. 1997. True to Faith. *Ensign* 27(5):65–7.

Hinson, Glenn. 2000. *Fire in My Bones: Transcendence and the Holy Spirit in African American Gospel*. Philadelphia: University of Pennsylvania Press.

Hogg, James. [1834] 1882. *Domestic Manners and Private Life of Sir Walter Scott*. Edinburgh, UK: William Brown.

"A Hole in Her Soul." 2006. *Ensign*, 36(7):16–9.

Honko, Lauri. 1964. Memorates and the Study of Folk Beliefs. *Journal of the Folklore Institute* 1:5–19.

Houghton, Carl. 1987. What Am I Doing Wrong? *New Era* 17(9):12–3.

How to Contribute to the Ensign. 2008. [cited 2008]. Available from ensign.lds.org.

Howard-Johnson, Carolyn. 2001. *This Is the Place*. Baltimore, MD: America House Book Publishers.

Hufford, David. 1982. *The Terror That Comes in the Night: An Experience-Centered Study of Supernatural Assault Traditions*. Publications of the American Folklore Society. Philadelphia: University of Pennsylvania Press.

———. 1995. Beings without Bodies: An Experience-Centered Theory of the Belief in Spirits. In *Out of the Ordinary: Folklore and the Supernatural*, ed. Barbara Walker, pp. 11–45. Logan: Utah State University Press.

Hughes, Richard T., and C. Leonard Allen. 1988. *Illusions of Innocence: Protestant Primitivism in America, 1630–1875*. Chicago: University of Chicago Press.

Hyde, Orson. 2001. Withstanding Life's Storms. *Church News*, July 14.

Hymes, Dell. 1974. *Foundations in Sociolinguistics: An Ethnographic Approach*. Philadelphia: University of Pennsylvania Press.

Iber, Jorge. 2000. *Hispanics in the Mormon Zion*. College Station: Texas A&M University Press.

Jacobs, Melville. 1945. *Kalapuya Texts*. Seattle: University of Washington.

Jensen, Marlin K. 2007. There Shall Be a Record Kept among You. *Liahona* 31(12):26–31.

Jenson, Andrew. 1901. *Latter-day Saint Biographical Encyclopedia: A Compilation of Biographical Sketches of Prominent Men and Women in the Church of Jesus Christ of Latter-day Saints*. 4 vols. Salt Lake City: Andrew Jenson History.

Johnson, Grace. 1973. *Brodders and Sisters: Being the Early Life and Times of the Mormon Town of Ephraim, Sanpete County, Utah*. Manti, UT: Messenger Enterprise Printing.

Jorgensen, Lynne Watkins. 1996–97. The Mantle of the Prophet Joseph Passes to Brother Brigham: A Collective Spiritual Witness. *BYU Studies* 36(4):125–204.

Journal of Discourses. 1854–1886. edited by G. D. Watt, vol. 3. Liverpool and London.

The Joy of Nurturing Children. 2008. *Ensign* 38(4):34–9.

Kaliambou, Maria. 2007. The Transformation of Folktales and Fairy Tales into Popular Booklets. *Marvels and Tales* 21(1):50–64.

Keeter, Scott, and Gregory Smith. 2007. How the Public Perceives Romney, Mormons. http://www.pewforum.org/Politics-and-Elections/How-the-Public-Perceives-Romney-Mormons.aspx, accessed November 30, 2010.

Kiernan, James P. 1985. The Social Stuff of Revelation: Pattern and Purpose in Zionist Dreams and Visions. *Africa: Journal of the International African Institute* 55(3):304–18.

Kimball, Edward L., ed. 1982. *The Teachings of Spencer W. Kimball*. Salt Lake City: Bookcraft.

Kimball, Heber C. 1840. *Journal of Heber C. Kimball*. Ed. R. B. Thompson. Nauvoo, IL: Robinson and Smith.

———. 1882. *President Heber C. Kimball's Journal*. Faith Promoting Series, vol. 7, ed. G. C. Lambert, Salt Lake City: Juvenile Instructor Office.

Kimball, Spencer W. 1977. First Presidency Message: The Things of Eternity—Stand We in Jeopardy? *Ensign* 7(1):3–7.

———. 1980. President Kimball Speaks out on Personal Journals. *New Era* 10(11):26–31.

Knowlton, David. 1991. Belief, Metaphor, and Rhetoric: The Mormon Practice of Testimony Bearing. *Sunstone* 15(1):20-27.

———. 1994. "Gringo Jeringo": Anglo Mormon Missionary Culture in Bolivia. In *Contemporary Mormonism: Social Science Perspectives*, ed. Marie Cornwall, Tim B. Heaton, and Lawrence A. Young, pp. 218–36. Chicago: University of Illinois Press.

Kohl, Johann Georg. 1860. *Kitchi-Gami: Wanderings Round Lake Superior*. London: Chapman and Hall.

Korom, Frank J. 2002. Caste Politics, Ritual Performance, and Local Religion in a Bengali Village: A Reassessment of Liminality and Communitas. *Acta Ethnographica Hungarica* 47(3-4):397-449.

Kuo, Louise, and Yuan-Hsi Kuo. 1976. *Chinese Folk Tales*. Millbrae, CA: Celestial Arts.

Labov, William, and Joshua Waletzky. 1961. Narrative Analysis: Oral Versions of Personal Experience. In *Essays on the Verbal and Visual Arts*, ed. J. Helm, pp. 12–44. Seattle: American Ethnological Society.

Lambrecht, Winifred. 1967. A Tale Type Index for Central Africa. Ph.D. diss., University of California, Davis.

The Latter-day Saint Woman: Basic Manual for Women. 2000. Salt Lake City: The Church of Jesus Christ of Latter-day Saints.

Lawless, Elaine J. 1983. Shouting for the Lord: The Power of Women's Speech in the Pentecostal Religious Service. *Journal of American Folklore* 96(382):434–59.

———. 1984. "I Know If I Don't Bear My Testimony, I'll Lose It": Why Mormon Women Bother to Speak at All. *Kentucky Folklore Record* 30:79–96.

———. 1988. "The Night I Got the Holy Ghost . . .": Holy Ghost Narratives and the Pentecostal Conversion Process. *Western Folklore* 47(1):1–20.

Lease, Emory B. 1919. The Number Three: Mysterious, Mystic, Magic. *Classical Philology* 14:56–73.

Lee, Harold B. 1980. Revelation and You. *Liahona* 4(2):38.

Lee, Hector. 1942. The Three Nephites: A Disappearing Legend. *American Notes and Queries* 2(3):35–38.

———. 1949. *The Three Nephites*. Albuquerque: University of New Mexico Press.

Lehmann, Alfred. 1914. *Dreiheit Und Dreifache Wiederholung Im Deutschen Volksmärchen*. Leipzig: Buchdruckerei Robert Noske.

The Letter I Didn't Receive. 2007. *Ensign* 37(4):54–5.

Lewis, James R., and J. Gordon Melton, eds. 1992. *Perspectives on the New Age*. Albany: State University of New York Press.

López, Sergio Adrián. 2007. Speaking the Language of the Spirit. *Ensign* 37(3):70–1.

Lord, Albert B. 1960. *The Singer of Tales*. Cambridge, MA: Harvard University Press.

Lund, Gerald N. 2007. *Hearing the Voice of the Lord: Principles and Patterns of Personal Revelation*. Salt Lake City: Deseret Book.

Lundahl, Craig R. 1979. Mormon Near-Death Experiences. In *A Collection of Near-Death Research Readings*, ed. C. R. Lundahl, pp. 165–79. Chicago: Nelson Hall Publishers.

Luomala, Katherine. 1949. Maui-of-a-Thousand-Tricks: His Oceanic and European Biographers. *Bernice Pauahi Bishop Museum Bulletin* 198.

Lythgoe, D. L. 1968. The Changing Image of Mormonism. *Dialogue* 3(4):45-58.

MacRae, Norman. 1908. *Highland Second Sight*. Dingwall, UK: George Souter.

Madsen, David B., and Brigham D. Madsen. 1995. One Man's Meat Is Another Man's Poison: A Revisionist View of the Seagull "Miracle." In *A World We Thought We Knew: Readings in Utah History*, ed. J. S. McCormick and J. R. Sillito, pp. 52–67. Salt Lake City: University of Utah Press.

Making Church Magazines. 2008. *Ensign* 38(7):64–9.

Marsden, George. 1970. *The Evangelical Mind and the New School Presbyterian Experience: A Case Study of Thought and Theology in Nineteenth-Century America*. New Haven, CT: Yale University Press.

Marsh, W. Jeffrey. 2000. *The Light Within: What the Prophet Joseph Smith Taught Us About Personal Revelation*. Salt Lake City: Deseret Book.

Mather, Elsie. 1995. With a Vision Beyond Our Immediate Needs: Oral Traditions in an Age of Literacy. In *When Our Words Return: Writing, Hearing, and Remembering Oral Traditions of Alaska and the Yukon*, ed. P. Morrow and W. Schneider, pp. 13–26. Logan: Utah State University Press.

Mauss, Armand L. 1984. Sociological Perspectives on the Mormon Subculture. *Annual Review of Sociology* 10:437-60.

Maxwell, Donna K. 2007. Questions and Answers. *Ensign* 37(3):60.

Maxwell, Neal A. 1986. God Will yet Reveal. *Ensign* 16(11):52–8.

McConkie, Bruce R. 1981. How to Get Personal Revelation. *Liahona (formerly Tambuli)* 5(4):4.

McConkie, Joseph Fielding. 1988. *Prophets and Prophecy*. Salt Lake City: Bookcraft.

McCurdy, Ed. 1965. Brigham Young the Western Pioneer. *This Is the Place*. Columbia Legacy LS 1024, LP.

McKim, Robert. 2001. *Religious Ambiguity and Religious Diversity*. New York: Oxford University Press.

McMurrin, Sterling M. 1974. *The Theological Foundations of the Mormon Religion*. Salt Lake City: University of Utah Press.

Merrill, A. Roger. 2007. To Be Edified and Rejoice Together. *Ensign* 37(1):64–9.

Miller, Merton Leland. 1898. *A Preliminary Study of the Pueblo of Taos, New Mexico*. Chicago: University of Chicago Press.

Milnes, Gerald. 1995. West Virginia's Omie Wise: The Folk Process Unveiled. *Appalachian Journal* 22 (Summer):376–89.

Mitchell, Scott. 2004. "You Have No Right to Do Such a Thing": An Insider Study of Entitlement of Spirit Child Narratives in Mormon Communities. M.A. thesis, University of Missouri, Columbia.

Monson, Thomas S. 1997. They Showed the Way. *Ensign* 27(5):50–2.

———. 2006. True to Our Priesthood Trust. *Ensign* 36(11):56–9.

Morgan, Mildred Pearce, and Vilate Oakley Pearce. 1941. Warnings. In *Heart Throbs of the West*, p. 340. Salt Lake City: Daughters of the Utah Pioneers.

Morse, Melvin. 1983. A Near-Death Experience in a Seven-Year-Old (Mormon) Child. *American Journal of Diseases of Children* 137(10):959–61.

Motz, Marliyn. 1998. The Practice of Belief. *Journal of American Folklore* 111:339–55.

Mould, Tom. 2002. Prophetic Riddling: A Dialogue of Genres in Choctaw Performance. *The Journal of American Folklore* 115(457-458):395–421.

———. 2003. *Choctaw Prophecy: A Legacy of the Future*. Contemporary American Indian Studies. Tuscaloosa: University of Alabama Press.

———. 2004. *Choctaw Tales*. Jackson: University Press of Mississippi.

———. 2011. A Backdoor into Performance. In *The Individual and Tradition*, eds. Ray Cashman, Tom Mould, and Pravina Shukla. Bloomington: Indiana University Press.

Mullen, Patrick B. 1983. Ritual and Sacred Narratives in the Blue Ridge Mountains. *Papers in Comparative Studies* 2:17–38.

———. 2000. Belief and the American Folk. *Journal of American Folklore* 113(448):119–43.

Müller, Raimund. 1903. Die Zahl 3 in Sage, Dichtung Und Kunst. In *XXX Jahresbericht Der K. K. Staats-Overrealschule in Teschen Am Schlusse Des Schuljahres 1902–1903*, pp. 1–23. Teschen: K. und K. Hofbuchdruckerei Karl Prochaska.

Murphey, Edith V. A., and Lucy Young. 1941. Out of the Past: A True Indian Story Told by Lucy Young, of Round Valley Indian Reservation. *California Historical Society Quarterly* 20(4):349–64.

Murray, Denise E. 1988. The Context of Oral and Written Language: A Framework for Mode and Medium Switching. *Language in Society* 17(3):351–73.

Neitz, Mary Jo, and James V. Spickard. 1990. Steps toward a Sociology of Religious Experience. *Sociological Analysis* 51:15–33.

Nelson, R. A. 1977. From Antagonism to Acceptance: Mormons and the Silver Screen. *Dialogue* 10(3):59-69.

Nelson, Russell M. 2008. Celestial Marriage. *Ensign* 38(11):92–5.

New Testament Gospel Doctrine Teacher's Manual. 2002. Salt Lake City, UT: The Church of Jesus Christ of Latter-day Saints.

Nibley, Hugh. 1992. Return to the Temple. In *Temple and Cosmos: The Collected Works of Hugh Nibley, Vol. 12 Ancient History*, ed. D. E. Norton. Salt Lake City: Deseret Book.

Nibley, Preston S. 1943. *Faith Promoting Stories*. Independence, MO: Zion's Printing and Publishing.

O'Hanlon, John. 1870. *Irish Folk Lore: Traditions and Superstitions of the Country with Humorous Tales*. Glasgow: Cameron & Ferguson.

O'Kearney, Nicholas. 1856. *The Prophecies of Ss. Columbkille, Maeltamlacht, Ultan, Seadhna, Coireall, Bearcan, &C*. Dublin: John O'Daly.

Oaks, Dallin H. 1983. I Have a Question. *Ensign* 13(6):25.

———. 1999. Teaching and Learning by the Spirit. *Liahona* 23(5):15.

Office of the First Presidency. 2008. False Statement, February 25. Issued to General Authorities; Area Seventies; Stake, Mission, District, and Temple Presidents; Bishops and Branch Presidents.

Olrik, Axel. [1922] 1992. *Principles for Oral Narrative Research*. Bloomington: Indiana University Press.

Olson, Adam C. 2007. All Things Bear Record of Him, *Ensign* 37(1):16–20.

Ong, Walter J. 1967. *The Presence of the Word: Some Prolegomena for Cultural and Religious History*. New Haven: Yale University Press.

———. 1977. *Interfaces of the Word: Studies in the Evolution of Consciousness and Culture*. Ithaca, NY: Cornell University Press.

Opler, Morris Edward. 1938. *Myths and Tales of the Jicarilla Apache Indians*. New York: G. E. Stechert.

Oring, Elliott. 1978. Transmission and Degeneration. *Fabula* 19:193–210.

———. 2008. Legendry and the Rhetoric of Truth. *Journal of American Folklore* 121(480): 127–66.

Orsi, Robert A. 1996. *Thank You, St. Jude: Women's Devotion to the Patron Saint of Hopeless Causes*. New Haven, CT: Yale University Press.

Packer, Boyd K. 1983. The Candle of the Lord. *Ensign* 13(1):51–6.

———. 1992. The Holy Temple. *Ensign* 35(2):32–7.

———. 1997. Personal Revelation: The Gift, the Test, and the Promise. *Liahona* 21(6):8–14.

Paredes, Américo, and Richard Bauman. 1972. *Toward New Perspectives in Folklore*. Austin: University of Texas Press.

Parezo, Nancy J. 1983. *Navajo Sandpainting: From Religious Act to Commercial Art*. Tucson: University of Arizona Press.

Parkin, Bonnie D. 2007. Gratitude: A Path to Happiness. *Ensign* 37(5):34–6.

Perry, L. Tom. 2003. We Believe All That God Has Revealed. *Ensign* 33(11):85–8.

Petersen, LaRene Halling. 2007. Reaching Out to Those Who Mourn. *Ensign* 37(2):64–6.

Peterson, Susan. 1976. The Great and Dreadful Day: Mormon Folklore of the Apocalypse. *Utah Historical Quarterly* 44:365–78.

Pierce, Norman C. 1963. *The 3 1/2 Years*. Salt Lake City: Pierce.

Pike, Sarah M. 2004. *New Age and Neopagan Relgions in America*. New York: Columbia University Press.

Pointer, Richard W. 1988. *Protestant Pluralism and the New York Experience: A Study of Eighteenth-Century Religious Diversity*. Bloomington: Indiana University Press.

Polonijo-King, Ivana. 2004. In Whose Words? Narrative Analysis of International Volunteer Stories from an Anthropological Perspective. *Folks Art: Croatian Journal of Ethnology and Folklore Research* 5(1):103–24.

Poulsen, Richard C. 1977. "This Is the Place": Myth and Mormondom. *Western Folklore* 36(3):246–52.

Pratt, Parley P. 1837. *A Voice of Warning*. New York: W. Sanford.

———. 1840. *Late Persecution of the Church of Jesus Christ of Latter Day Saints, with a Sketch of Their Rise, Progress and Doctrine*. New York: J. W. Harrison.

Preach My Gospel: A Guide to Missionary Service. 2004. Salt Lake City: Church of Jesus Christ of Latter-day Saints.

Primary 1: I Am a Child of God. 1994. Salt Lake City: Church of Jesus Christ of Latter-day Saints.

Primary 5: Doctrine and Covenants: Church History. 1997. Salt Lake City: Church of Jesus Christ of Latter-day Saints.

Primiano, Leonard Norman. 1995. Vernacular Religion and the Search for Method in Religious Folklife. *Western Folklore* 54(1):37–56.

Quam, Alvina. 1972. *The Zunis*. Albuquerque: University of New Mexico Press.

Questions and Answers. 2007. *Ensign* 37(3):58-61.

Quinn, D. Michael. 1976. The Mormon Succession Crisis of 1844. *BYU Studies* 16(2): 187–233.

————. 1980. The Council of Fifty and Its Members, 1844 to 1945. *BYU Studies* 20(2): 163-98.

————. 1998. *Early Mormonism and the Magic World View*. Salt Lake City: Signature Books.

Ramsey, Jarold. 1999. *Reading the Fire: The Traditional Indian Literatures of America*. Seattle: University of Washington Press.

Rand, Silas. 1894. *Legends of the Micmacs*. New York: Longmans, Green.

Ritchie, James W. 2007. One Person, One Bucket. *Ensign* 37(2):70–1.

Roberts, B. H. 1965. *A Comprehensive History of the Church of Jesus Christ of Latter-day Saints*. 6 vols. Provo, UT: Brigham Young University Press.

Roberts, Warren E. 1988. *Viewpoints on Folklife: Looking at the Overlooked*. Ann Arbor, MI: UMI Research Press.

Robinson, Elwin C. 2007. The Orange Car. *Ensign* 37(6):68–9.

Robinson, John A. 1981. Personal Narratives Reconsidered. *Journal of American Folklore* 94(371):58–85.

Rosaldo, Renato. 1980. *Ilongot Headhunting, 1883–1974*. Stanford: Stanford University Press.

Ruby, Robert. 2007. Public Views of Presidential Politics and Mormon Faith. http://www.pewforum.org/Politics-and-Elections/Public-Views-of-Presidential-Politics-and-Mormon-Faith.aspx, accessed November 30, 2010.

Rudy, Jill Terry. 2004. "Of Course, in Guatemala, Bananas Are Better": Exotic and Familiar Eating Experiences of Mormon Missionaries. In *Culinary Tourism*, ed. L. M. Long, pp. 131–56. Lexington: University Press of Kentucky.

Ryan, Marie-Laure. 1981. On the Why, What, and How of Generic Taxonomy. *Poetics* 10:109–26.

Sandeen, Ernest R. 1970. *The Roots of Fundamentalism: British and American Millenarianism 1800–1930*. Chicago: University of Chicago Press.

Santino, Jack. 1982. Catholic Folklore and Folk Catholicism. *New York Folklore* 8(3-4):93–106.

Sapir, Edward, and Jeremiah Curtin. 1909. *Wishram Texts*. Leyden: Late E. J. Brill.

Schacker, Jennifer. 2007. Unruly Tales: Ideology, Anxiety and the Regulation of Genre. *Journal of American Folklore* 120(478):381–400.

Schetselaar, Britney. 2006. Then Sings My Soul. *The Friend* 36(8):30–2.

Schlesinger, Arthur Meier. 1967. *A Critical Period in American Religion, 1875–1900*. Philadelphia: Fortress Press.

Schmidt, Gary D., and Donald R. Hettinga, eds. 1992. *Sitting at the Feet of the Past*. Westport, CT: Greenwood Press.

Schoemaker, George H. 1989. Made in Heaven: Marriage Confirmation Narratives among Mormons. *Northwest Folklore* 7 (Spring):38–53.

Shepherd, Gordon, and Gary Shepherd. 2001. Sustaining a Lay Religion in Modern Society: The Mormon Missionary Experience. In *Contemporary Mormonism: Social Science Perspectives*, ed. Marie Cornwall, Tim B. Heaton and Lawrence A. Young, pp. 162-81. Chicago: University of Illinois Press.

Shipps, Jan. 1985. *Mormonism: The Story of a New Religious Tradition*. Chicago: University of Illinois Press.

Shuman, Amy, and Carol Bohmer. 2004. Representing Trauma: Political Asylum Narrative. *Journal of American Folklore* 117(466):394–414.

Sierra, Judy. 1992. *The Oryx Multicultural Folktale Series: Cinderella*. Phoenix: Oryx Press.

Smith, Joseph Fielding, ed. 1976. *Teachings of the Prophet Joseph Smith*. Salt Lake City: Deseret Book.

Smith, Paul Thomas. 1996. *Prophetic Destiny: The Saints in the Rocky Mountains*. Salt Lake City: Bookcraft.

Sophocles. 1966. *The Theban Saga*, ed. J. Charles Alexander Robinson. New York: Franklin Watts.

Sorenson, John L. 1973. Mormon World View and American Culture. *Dialogue* 8(2):17–29.

Stahl, Sandra K. Dolby. 1979. Style in Oral and Written Narratives. *Southern Folklore Quarterly* 43(1–2):39–62.

———. 1989. *Literary Folkloristics and the Personal Narrative*. Bloomington: Indiana University Press.

Stanley, David. 2004. *Folklore in Utah: A History and Guide to Resources*. Logan, UT: Utah State University Press.

Staples, Joseph. 2007. Supporting Your Bishop. *Ensign* 37(6):56–60.

Stathis, Stephen W. 1981. Mormonism and the Periodical Press: A Change Is Underway. *Dialogue* 14(1):48–73.

Stathis, Stephen W., and Dennis L. Lythgoe. 1977. Mormonism in the Nineteen-Seventies: The Popular Perception. *Dialogue* 10(3):95–113.

Strand, Thea Amanda. 1958. *Tri-Ism: The Theory of the Trinity in Nature, Man and His Works*. New York: Exposition Press.

Stromberg, Peter G. 1993. *Language and Self-Transformation: A Study of the Christian Conversion Narrative*. New York: Cambridge University Press.

Sullivan, Paul R. 1989. *Unfinished Conversations: Mayas and Foreigners between Two Wars*. New York: Knopf.

Sutton, Brett. 1977. In the Good Old Way: Primitive Baptist Traditions. *Southern Exposure* 5(2-3):97-104.

Swetnam, Susan Hendricks. 1991. *Lives of the Saints in Southeast Idaho: An Introduction to Mormon Pioneer Life Story Writing*. Moscow: University of Idaho Press.

Talmage, James E. [1899] 1924. *The Articles of Faith: A Series of Lectures on the Principal Doctrines of the Church of Jesus Christ of Latter-day Saints*. Salt Lake City: Deseret News.

Tannen, Deborah. 1982a. Oral and Literate Strategies in Spoken and Written Narratives. *Language* 58(1):1–21.

———. 1982b. The Oral/Literate Continuum in Discourse. In *Spoken and Written Language*, ed. D. Tannen, pp. 1–21. Norwood, NJ: Ablex.

Tanner, N. Eldon. 1980. Celestial Marriages and Eternal Families. *Ensign* 10(5):15–8.

Tavenner, Eugene. 1916. Three as a Magic Number in Latin Literature. *Transactions of the American Philological Association* 47:117–43.

Teaching, No Greater Call: A Resource Guide for Gospel Teaching. 1999. Salt Lake City: Church of Jesus Christ of Latter-day Saints.

Teachings of Presidents of the Church: Brigham Young. 1997. Salt Lake City: The Church of Jesus Christ of Latter-day Saints.

Teachings of Presidents of the Church: Joseph Smith. 2007. Salt Lake City: Church of Jesus Christ of Latter-day Saints.

Teachings of Presidents of the Church: Wilford Woodruff. 2004. Salt Lake City: Church of Jesus Christ of Latter-day Saints.

Thomas, Keith. 1971. *Religion and the Decline of Magic*. New York: Charles Scribner's Sons.

Thompson, Stith. 1966. *Motif-Index of Folk Literature*. 2nd ed. 6 vols. Bloomington: Indiana University Press.

Tingey, Earl C. 2009. The Saga of Revelation: The Unfolding Role of the Seventy. *Ensign* 39(9):54-60.

Titon, Jeff Todd. 1988. *Powerhouse for God: Speech, Chant and Song in an Appalachian Baptist Church*. Austin: University of Texas Press.

Titon, Jeff Todd, and Ken George. 1978. Testimonies. *Alcheringa: Ethnopoetics* 4(1):69–83.

Toelken, Barre. 1991. Traditional Water Narratives in Utah. *Western Folklore* 50(2):191–200.

———. 1996. *The Dynamics of Folklore*. Logan: Utah State University Press.

Tullis, F. LaMond. 1987. *Mormons in Mexico: The Dynamics of Faith and Culture*. Logan: Utah State University Press.

Turner, Victor. 1969. *The Ritual Process: Structure and Anti-Structure.* Chicago: Aldine Publishing Company.

Underwood, Grant. 2000. Mormonism, the Maori and Cultural Authenticity. *The Journal of Pacific History* 35(2):133–46.

U.S. Religious Landscape Survey. 2008. Pew Forum on Religion and Public Life. http://religions. pewforum.org, accessed June 20, 2009.

Usener, Hermann. 1903. Dreiheit. *Rheinisches Museum für Philologie* 58:1–47, 161–208, 321–62.

The Utah Pioneers. 1880. Seattle: Shorey Book Store.

Utter, David. 1892. Mormon Superstitions. *The Folk-Lorist* 1:76.

Vallowe, Ed F. 1995. *Biblical Mathematics: Keys to Scripture Numerics.* West Bloomfield, MI: Olive Press.

von Döllinger, Johann Joseph Ignaz. 1872. The Prophetic Spirit and the Prophecies of the Christian Era. In *Dr. J. J .I. Von Döllinger's Fables Respecting the Peoples in the Middle Ages,* ed. H. B. Smith, pp. 273–426. New York: Dodd & Mead.

Wachs, Eleanor F. 1988. *Crime-Victim Stories: New York City's Urban Folklore.* Bloomington: Indiana University Press.

Waterman, Patricia Panyity. 1987. *A Tale-Type Index of Australian Aboriginal Oral Narratives, (FF Communications).* Helsinki: Academia Scientiarum Fennica.

Watson, Eldon J., ed. 1971. *Manuscript History of Brigham Young, 1846–1847.* Salt Lake City: Eldon J. Watson.

Why Symbols? 2007. *Ensign* 37 (2):12–7.

Wilson, William A. 1969. Mormon Legends of the Three Nephites Collected at Indiana University. *Indiana Folklore* 2(1):3–35.

———. 1975. "The Vanishing Hitchhiker" Among the Mormons. *Indiana Folklore* 7:79–97.

———. 1976a. The Paradox of Mormon Folklore. In *Essays on the American West, 1974–1975,* ed. T. G. Alexander, pp. 127–47. Provo, UT: Brigham Young University Press.

———. 1976b. The Study of Mormon Folklore. *Utah Historical Quarterly* 44:317–28.

———. 1979. Folklore of Utah's Little Scandinavia. *Utah Historical Quarterly* 47:148–66.

———. 1981. *On Being Human: The Folklore of Mormon Missionaries.* Logan: Utah State University.

———. 1983. Mormon Folklore. In *Handbook of American Folklore,* ed. R. M. Dorson, pp. 155–61. Bloomington: Indiana University Press.

———. 1988. Freeways, Parking Lots and Ice Cream Stands: The Three Nephites in Contemporary Society. *Dialogue* 21:13–26.

———. 1989. The Study of Mormon Folklore: An Uncertain Mirror for Truth. *Dialogue* 22:95–110.

———. 1993. Mormon Folklore: Cut from the Marrow of Everyday Experience. *BYU Studies* 33(3):521–40.

———. 1995a. Mormon Folklore: Faith or Folly? *Brigham Young Magazine* 49(2):46–54.

———. 1995b. Folklore, a Mirror for What? Reflections of a Mormon Folklorist. *Western Folklore* 54 (1):13–21.

———. 1995c. Mormon Narratives: The Lore of Faith. *Western Folklore* 54(4):303–26.

———. 1996. The Lore of Polygamy: Twentieth-Century Perceptions of Nineteenth-Century Plural Marriage. *Weber Studies* 13:152–61.

———. 2010. Written correspondence, October 11.

Wilson, William A., and Jessie L. Embry. 1998. Folk Ideas of Mormon Pioneers. *Dialogue* 31(3):81–99.

Wirthlin, Joseph B. 2003. The Unspeakable Gift. *Liahona* 27(5):26–9.

Wisdom of the Prophets: Personal Revelation. 2005. Sandy, UT: Leatherwood Press.

Wittgenstein, Ludwig. 1958. *Philosophical Investigations.* Oxford: Basil Blackwell.

Woodruff, Wilford. 1881a. *Leaves from My Journal.* Faith Promoting Series, vol. 3. Salt Lake City: Juvenile Instructor Office.

———. 1881b. *Millennial Star,* December 12, 790–1.

Woodward, Kenneth L. 2000. *The Book of Miracles: The Meaning of the Miracle Stories in Christianity, Judaism, Buddhism, Hinduism, Islam.* New York, NY: Simon & Schuster.

Wuthnow, Robert. 1992. *Rediscovering the Sacred.* Grand Rapids, MI: Eerdmans Publishing.

Young, Davis A. 1995. *The Biblical Flood: A Case Study of the Church's Response to Extrabiblical Evidence.* Grand Rapids, MI: Eerdmans Publishing.

Index